Yoshitomo Nara

Yeewan Koon

Introduction

In the corner of Yoshitomo Nara's studio is a scrap of paper scrawled with the words "Even if it isn't love or affection, I have a single strong power that will never be defeated." These are lyrics, translated by Nara into English, by the punk band the Blue Hearts. They are also words that encapsulate Nara's creative journey.

For over thirty years, Nara has been at the forefront of contemporary Japanese art with his iconic images of big-headed girls. It was in the early 1990s when Nara, as a graduate student in Germany, laid the foundations of his paintings. The Nara "girl" is a contrary figure: her childlike expressions resonate with adult emotions, her embodiment of *kawaii* (cuteness) carries a dark humor, and any explicit cultural references are intertwined with personal memories. Although these depictions are highly stylized, there is always something very familiar and intimate about them. Probing deeper, they convey Nara's conviction that art needs to find emotional connection and generate empathy.

But how are these qualities achieved? This monograph takes on the task of answering this question by returning to the basics of art history and the critical evaluation of style. This may seem at odds with the field's preference for more theory-driven arguments, but it is a method that champions close readings of artworks, and, as a path less taken, it provides new perspectives for looking at Nara's art. Forming the backbone of this book, these close readings map his stylistic traits and quirks, how his relationships with different artists and audiences impact his career, and why being an artist from northern Japan matters.

Nara is from Hirosaki, a small castle town over 400 miles from Tokyo. Growing up as a postwar child on the geographical margins of Honshū, the main island of Japan, shaped his sense of self: he is stoically independent, he connects to those who are from or have been displaced to border regions, and he is always slightly out of step with the conventions of his peers. Hirosaki lies close to a US Air Force base, and so Nara has always been acutely aware of his country's complicated history with war and nuclear weaponry and power. He shares this experience with many artists of his generation, including Takashi Murakami, whose Superflat concept, introduced in the late 1990s, theorizes the impact of World War II on a generation of artists influenced by the subcultures of manga and anime. Murakami's theory, bolstered by a series of traveling exhibitions, provided a cultural explanation of contemporary Japanese art to audiences in America and Europe. Murakami, Aya Takano, and the design team groovisions were all part of a new group of exciting artists who received international attention, and *Superflat* readily became a byword for their success. Although Nara is seen as one of its key proponents, as this book will show, he was never wholly committed to its theory, and his idiosyncratic relationship to Japanese subcultures suggests that there are alternative ways of looking at the contemporary Japanese art scene that emerged in the late 1990s and early 2000s.

Although Nara's paintings of big-headed girls have come to define his art, his oeuvre is substantially larger and more complex. Among his recent explorations are works that explore antiwar themes and have taken him to sites and communities in northern Japan. In part, these are responses to the aftermath of the 2011 Fukushima disaster, adding his voice to a growing political outcry against nuclear power. But they are also experimentations from an artist conscious of the legacy he will leave behind.

As with any monograph of a living artist, Nara's story does not end with this book. As the first major work of this kind, and as with any "first," the aim is not to be comprehensive but to provide a substantial foundation that can mobilize future research. It sets out to tell a story of an artist whose creativity is driven neither by passion nor ambitions for fame. Making art is simply what Nara does. He walks into his studio, turns on his music, and works through the night. It is this intuitiveness—this single, strong power—that has shaped his iconic style. His art, like the music he loves so much, remains fresh, urgent, and fluid. It will continue to seek new ways of moving forward.

It Started with Music

Some art students at the local national university said to me: "Nara, you're good at painting, why don't you go to art school?" But I found that I could not wrap my head around the thought that one could apply to such a specialized university. Art existed in a world so far from my daily life that going to such a place to study didn't seem within the realm of reality at all.[1]

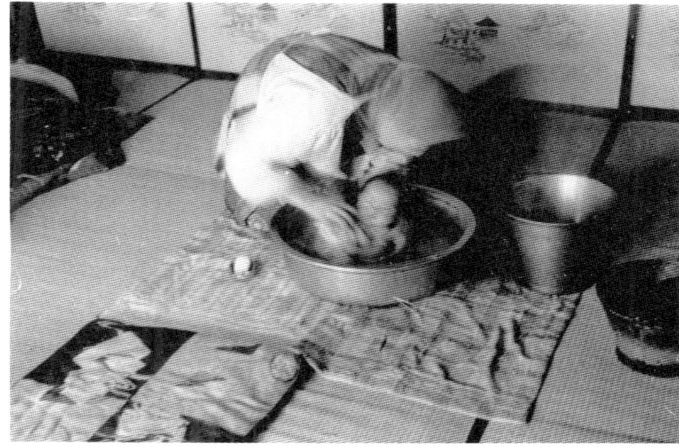

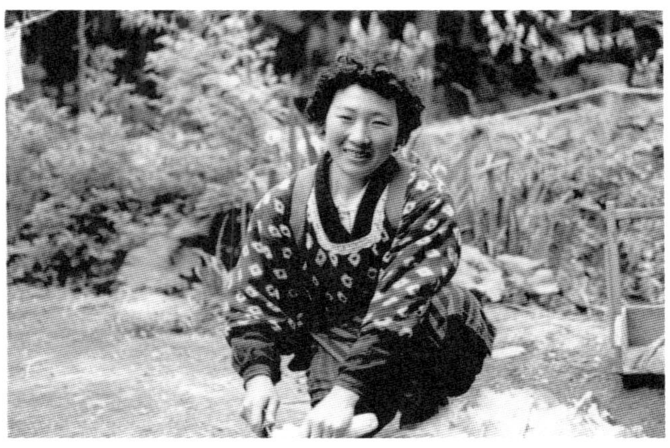

Yoshitomo Nara was born in 1959 in the small traditional castle town of Hirosaki in Aomori prefecture, the youngest child of three, with two brothers seven and nine years older. Like other families in Japan, the Naras had to adapt to a postwar milieu in which rapid socioeconomic changes had begun to redefine traditional roles and consolidate the unit of the modern nuclear family. For Nara, these changes were most vividly felt when, with both parents at work, he was increasingly left by himself, and his family home, which once stood alone on a hill, became surrounded by more and more neighbors.

Hirosaki in the 1960s was slowly expanding into a modern town, with a local university founded in 1949 as part of postwar educational reform and the widespread commercialization of regional apple farming.[2] Nonetheless, it maintained much of its gentle pace of life as a semirural town where horses and dogs wandered the unpaved streets. Its serenity also comes from its topographical position, nestled in the shadows of Mount Iwaki, an inactive volcano site steeped in tales of *oni* (demons) and *kami* (deities) of the Shinto world, stories that can be traced back to the medieval period.[3] Shinto, which does not have a founder or dogma, is deeply integrated into the lives of its believers. Although it is often described as an indigenous religion, it is more a way of life, with rituals and practices that celebrate transformative moments, such as weddings, births, and the all-important rite of passage Shichi-Go-San (Seven-Five-Three).[4] Eastern religious practices and gods can be absorbed within Shinto without any doctrinal conflicts, and it is not uncommon for shrines to incorporate the imagery of other religious deities and practices. Mount Iwaki, in particular, is known for its sacred powers for children, and temples and shrines often incorporate the popular bodhisattva Jizō, a protector of children and the unborn.[5] Contemporary statues frequently depict Jizō with childlike features, and worshippers often dress them in red cloaks, bibs, or hats in a ritual that asks for protection, good karma, and the remembrance of lost children.

Fig. 1
Nara and his mother shortly after his birth, Hirosaki, 1959

Fig 2
Nara's mother, 1955

The local Shinto shrines were important elements of the Hirosaki community, especially for Nara: his grandfather was a Shinto priest, and his father had briefly followed the same path, though he later gave up his priesthood for a salaried government job. Because of this connection, Nara's family was well-to-do and much respected within the community. His father, however, was largely absent, working or carousing with friends, and, by the time of Nara's birth, he was unwilling to devote time to a young son. His mother, by contrast, came from a more humble farming family. She had a strong work ethic, taking on employment herself after Nara was born when additional income was needed. Even when she was at home, she was constantly doing housework, often with Nara at her side silently watching her carry out her duties. He grew up with a sense of responsibility and admiration for his mother and a distrust of patriarchal structures.

From at least the age of five, Nara spent a good deal of time in the mountains behind the shrine where his father and grandfather had once worked. His sure-footed scrambles through the dense forest demonstrate a childhood without much adult supervision. He had enormous freedom, and, although at times this brought him loneliness, he was rarely unhappy. Precocious and watchful, he invented his own games and found companionship with his neighbor's cat. When he was six, together with a friend, he jumped on a train just to see where the tracks ended. But he was rarely reckless and seldom in trouble.

This freedom allowed Nara to escape the confines of his daily life, as did his love of music. At the age of eight, he built his own radio, which became a treasured companion and helped him understand that he belonged to a larger world. One night, half asleep, he woke up to unexpected music streaming through the family radio, and while it was in a language he did not understand, he was captivated by the melody and rhythm of the songs. Nara had unwittingly stumbled upon the music station of the nearby US Air Force base in Misawa. Thereafter, he would furtively tune in late at night, escaping into the thrills of American rock and country music.

Nara purchased his first single, by the popular Japanese band Takeshi Terauchi and the Bunnys, when he was only eight years old, an impressive feat given the remoteness of Hirosaki and the difficulties in gaining access to the latest music.[6] Hirosaki was approximately an hour away from the nearest city, Aomori, which is nearly 435 miles from Tokyo. Moreover, until 1979, the two cities were only connected

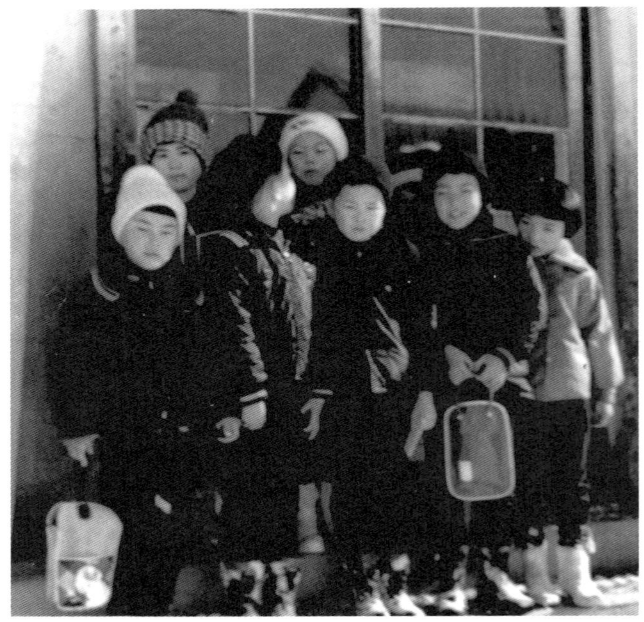

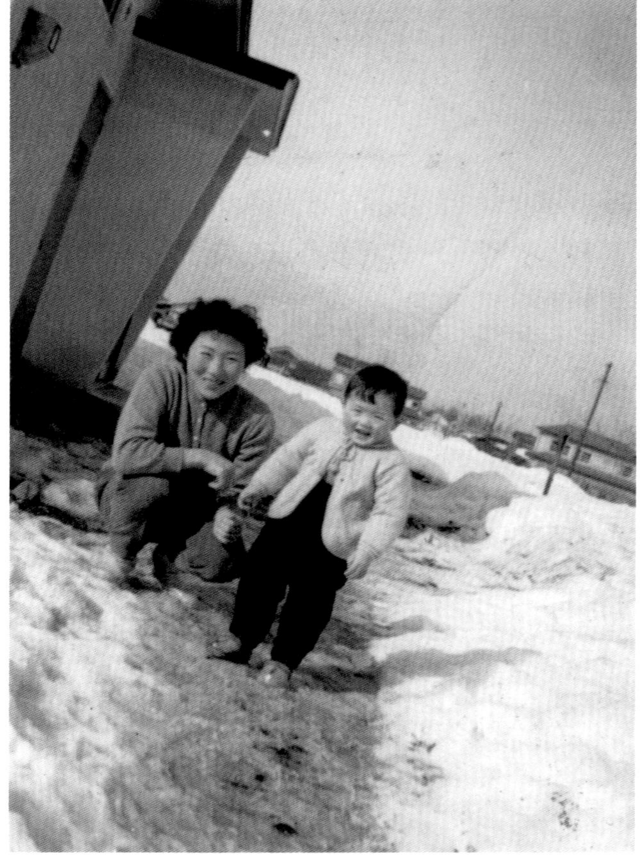

Fig. 3
Nara (first row, center) with classmates from Bunkyō Elementary School, Hirosaki, 1966

Fig. 4
Nara with his mother, Hirosaki, 1964

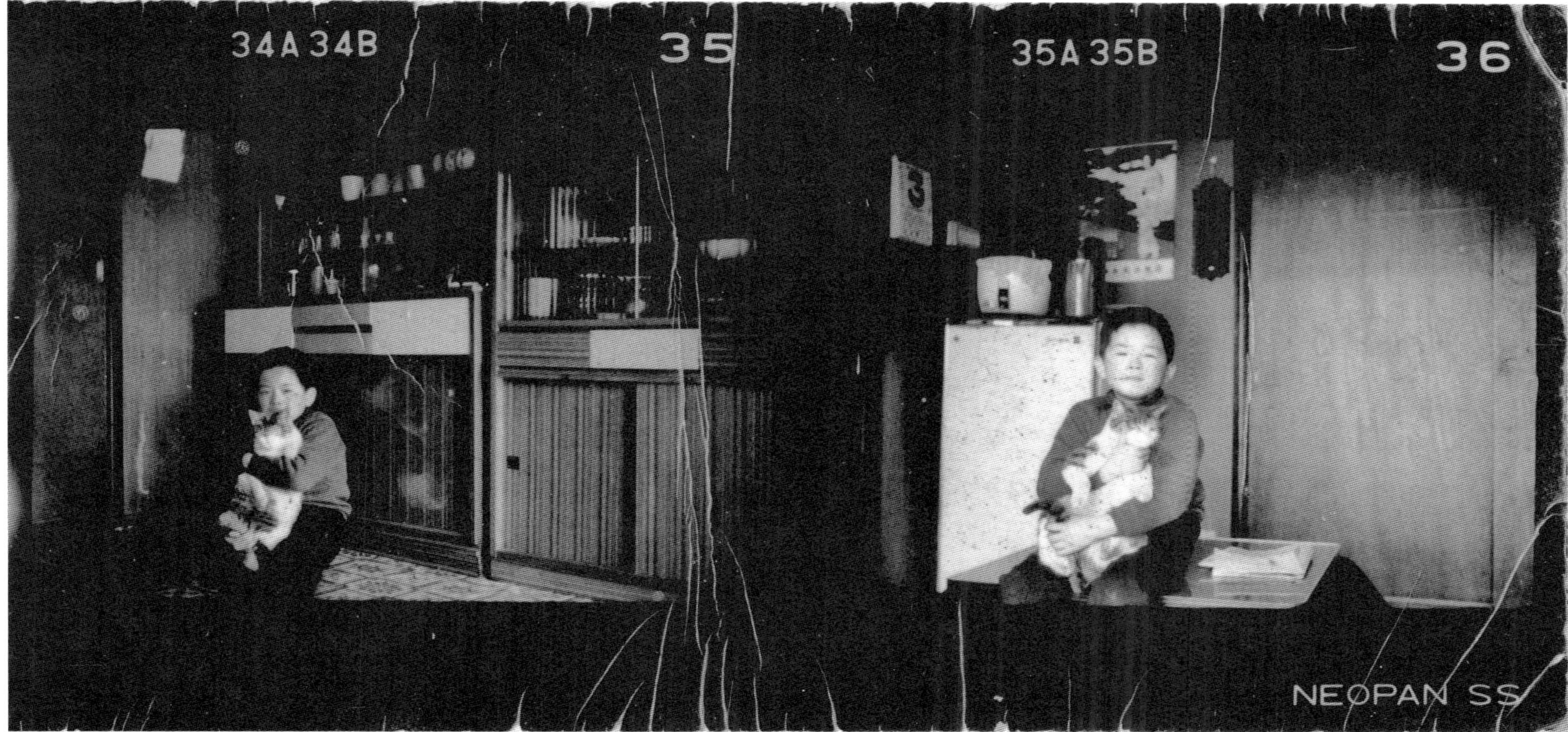

by highways and small roads, which resulted in a time lag in the arrival of the latest fashions and trends. This only cemented the perception of the north as the remote, unsophisticated counterpart to Japan's cosmopolitan heartland. For Nara, finding a newly released or hard-to-find recording was part of the excitement of transgressing such geographical boundaries. This was the first time he had purchased anything with his own money, and when he opened the door of the record store, he felt as if he were venturing into an illicit world of pleasures, terrifying and thrilling at the same time.

Nara consumed as much contemporary music as he could, from Terauchi to Janis Joplin, the Beatles, and Johnny Cash. He frequented the local university's café to listen to new music, spent hours browsing through music catalogues, made drawings of album covers he purchased, and doodled away to his favorite tunes. The visual energy of the albums' sleeves—the colors, the graphics, and the exoticism of foreign bands—provided great inspiration (Fig. 6). It was these albums that took him into the world of contemporary visual and sonic arts, which, for Nara, went hand in hand.[7] He credits music as the entry point to the exciting world of art, and the following chapters will show how they came together, through his work with musicians, the ways

Fig. 5
Nara with his cat, Chako,
Hirosaki, 1966

Fig. 6 (following spread)
Nara's record collection
Installation view: *for better or worse: Works 1987–2017*, Toyota Municipal Museum of Art, Japan, 2017

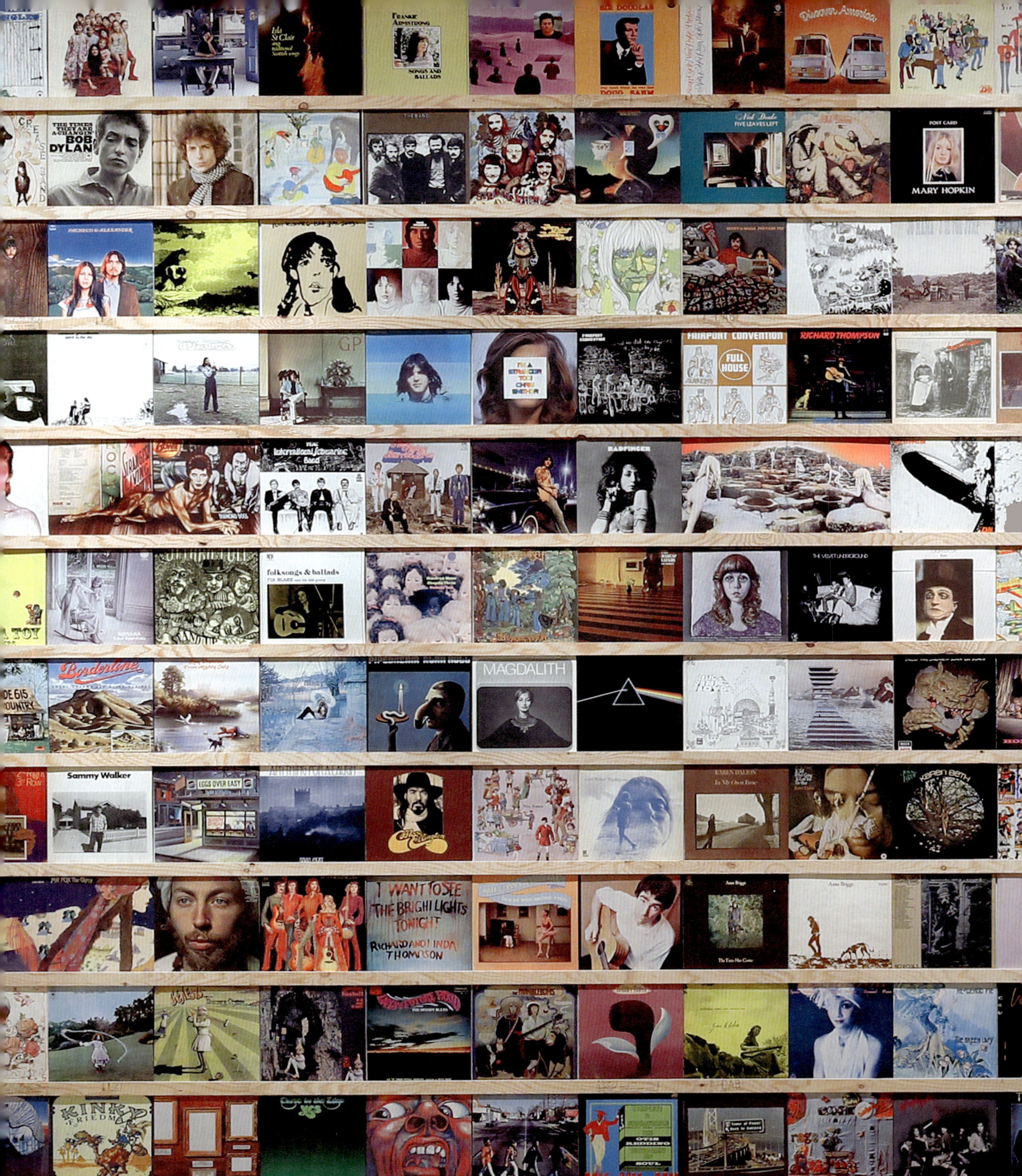

Frankie Armstrong
Songs and Ballads
Discover America
The Times They Are A-Changin'
Bob Dylan
Nick Drake
Five Leaves Left
Post Card
Mary Hopkin
Pacheco & Alexander
Fairport Convention
Full House
Richard Thompson
Badfinger
folksongs & ballads
The Velvet Underground
Borderline
Magdalith
Sammy Walker
Eggs Over Easy
Karen Dalton
In My Own Time
Karen Beth
I Want to See the Bright Lights Tonight
Richard and Linda Thompson
Otis Redding

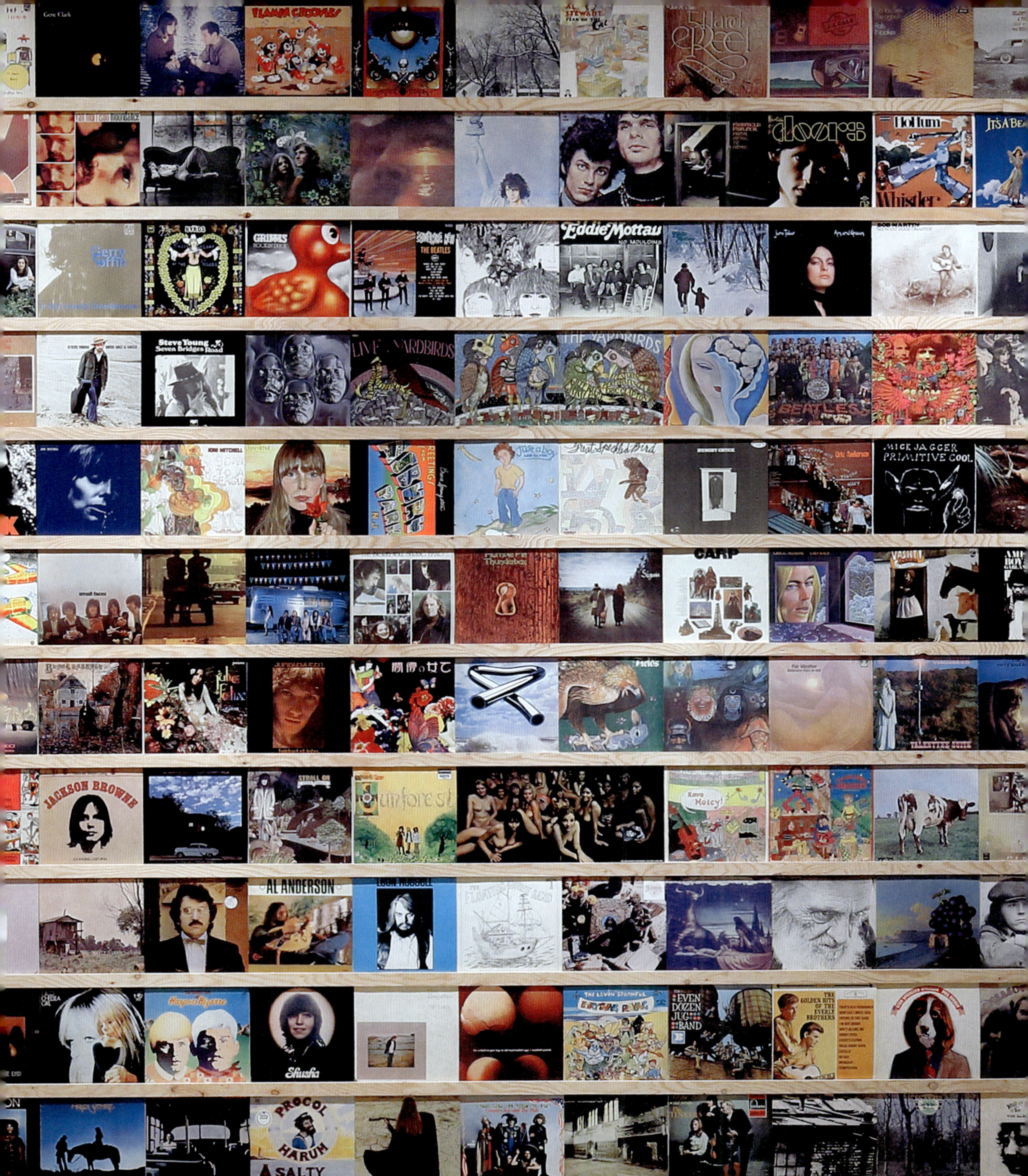

Gene Clark
FLAMIN' GROOVIES
AL STEWART
the doors
Whistler
Eddie Mottau
NO MOULDING
THE BEATLES
BOB MARTIN
Steve Young
Seven Bridges Road
THE YARDBIRDS
BEATLES
JONI MITCHELL
MICK JAGGER
PRIMITIVE COOL
CARP
small faces
Julie Felix
JACKSON BROWNE
Sunforest
AL ANDERSON
LEON RUSSELL
Harpers Bizarre
Shusha
THE LOVIN' SPOONFUL
EVEN DOZEN JUG BAND
THE GOLDEN HITS OF THE EVERLY BROTHERS
PROCOL HARUM
SALTY

in which he incorporated song titles and lyrics into his work, and his ability to capture the moods and feelings that his favorite music inspires. Music is now so deeply ingrained into his psyche that it readily leads him to visual spaces, to dreams, and to his creativity. To this day, when working, Nara blasts his music loud into the night, shut off from the world outside.

In the early 1970s, music became increasingly important to Nara, since it connected him to those redefining the spirit of a new generation. The period between the late 1960s and early 1970s is often seen as a zeitgeist moment in American counterculture, with mass protests against wars and rallies for civil rights, all buoyed by the rebellious, youthful energy of rock music, jazz, Beat poetry, and leftist heroes. Student radicalism was intense on the other side of the Pacific as well. In mid-1960s Japan, New Left organizations strengthened their campus bases in preparation for the 1970 renewal of the US-Japan Security Treaty. These groups brought together students, opposition parties, labor unions, and civil-society organizations. From the late 1960s onward, there were numerous large-scale antiestablishment protests on university campuses during which angry clashes erupted between students and police.

The New Left that was being consolidated in Japan at this time was heavily influenced by the communist organization Zengakuren, a league of students formed in 1948 that espoused a forceful anti-American sentiment. This contributed to the formation of a distinctly Japanese leftist movement, the cultural practices of which differed from those associated with a more commonly held Anglocentric view of 1960s counterculture. For example, while the rebellious nature of certain types of folk and rock music is often thought of as synonymous with radical movements of the time, in Japan, such music was associated with Western consumerism and as such was seen as hedonistic rather than revolutionary. Indeed, rock musicians were sometimes referred to as *futen* (slackers but closer in meaning to hippies)[8] by die-hard activists, who believed they lacked the conviction to be true counterculture radicals—playing a guitar on campus was considered frivolous rather than engaged intellectualism.[9] Although these attitudes would later change when younger members began to embrace American folk music and manga, these cultural differences are reminders of the historical complexities and local experiences of global phenomena.[10]

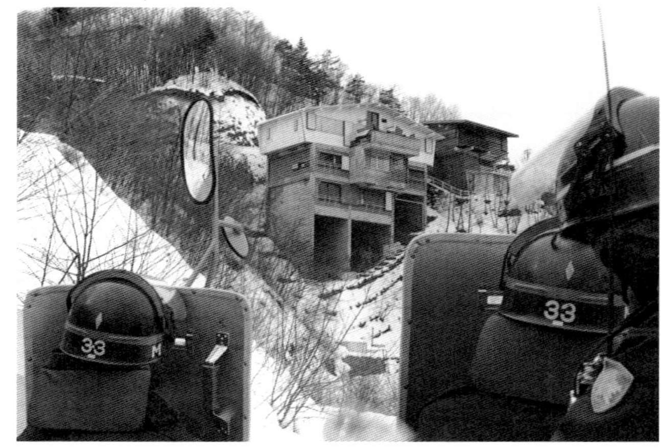

Fig. 7
Asama-Sansō incident, 1972

As student rallies grew in strength, so too did the violence between protesters and police. Three significant events mark this escalation. The first was a rally held at Haneda Airport on October 8, 1967, during which an eighteen-year-old student protester died, becoming a symbolic martyr for the New Left. The second major protest, which took place at the University of Tokyo, started as a sit-in of forty students before it escalated into an all-school strike and student occupation of campus, with school furniture turned into barricades against riot police. The police retaliated with water cannons laced with tear gas as students threw rocks, bricks, and Molotov cocktails. The standoff ended with 630 arrested and indicted.[11]

The last and most shocking began on February 19, 1972, when five heavily armed members of a small splintered leftist group, United Red Army (Rengō Sekigun), which included members from the extremist group Revolutionary Left Faction (Kakumei Saha), took cover from police in a tourist lodge at the base of Mount Asama and held a woman hostage in a siege that lasted ten days, during which two policemen and a bystander were killed (Fig. 7). On the final day, the police brought in a wrecking ball to destroy the facade of the building. This last part of the siege was broadcast live on television with an estimated viewing audience of almost 90 percent of households in the country. During the subsequent police interrogation, it was revealed that there had been a shocking internal purge in which fourteen of the twenty-nine members of the splintered group were violently killed. The live broadcast and the subsequent investigation shifted public sympathies. The tragic Asama-Sansō incident sounded the death knell of student radicalism.[12]

Nara was twelve when he watched the event unfold on television. He had been very aware of student protest movements—his second brother, who was at university at the time, was heavily involved in rallies decrying the mercury poisoning of Minamata Bay—but the Asama-Sansō incident was different, and for many who witnessed it, including Nara, it signaled a wariness towards collective radical mobilization. This may explain, in part, why Nara, who has always resisted social conformity and conventional authority, treads cautiously around divisive politics, preferring the *futen* attitude of nonparty political ideology, individuality, freedom, and healing.

Nara embraced this *futen* attitude early in life, and by high school he had assembled a motley group of friends, many of whom were older than him and who, in addition to sharing his love of rock music,

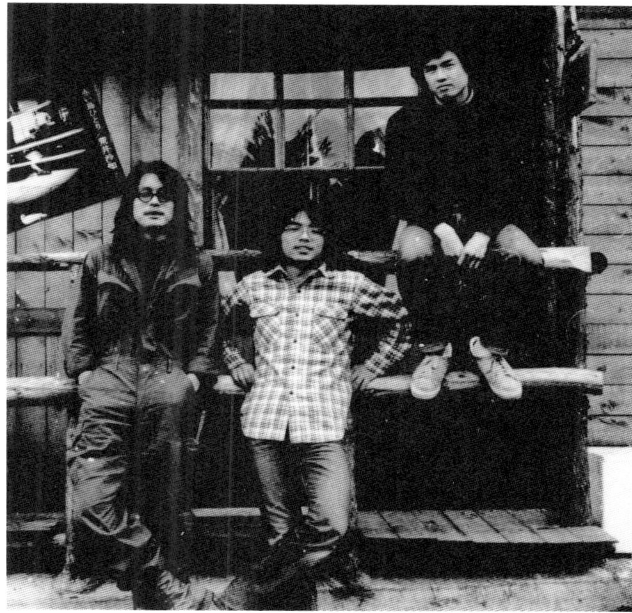

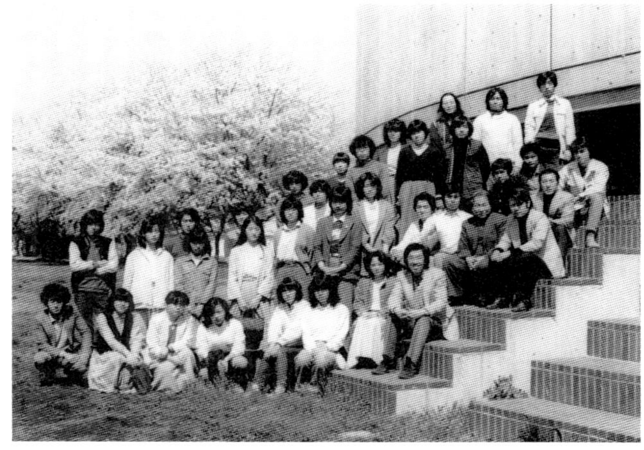

Fig. 8
Nara (right) with friends in front of 33 ⅓ rock café, Hirosaki, 1976

Fig. 9
Class picture at Musashino Art University, Kodaira, 1979, with Saburō Asō (sitting, second row from bottom, second from right) and Nara (third row from bottom, second from right)

encouraged him to take art more seriously. Nara had been drawing since childhood—illustrated flip-books, sketches inspired by his favorite album sleeves, book covers, and magazines—but they were casual undertakings rather than serious endeavors, and they reflect the easygoing nature of a young boy who was often lost in his own imagination. A major turning point for Nara in his path to becoming an artist came during high school when a friend decided to open a rock café, called 33 ⅓, and recruited Nara to help run it with him. Nara built, cleaned, and deejayed at the café, and it was also the site of his first large-scale artwork: a drawing of an American flag inspired by the Ramones' band logo on the window shutters and, on the back wall of the café, a large mural of a pair of cats playing guitars.

Nara's friends may have recognized a talent that he had yet to register himself. It was not until a few years later that an encounter with a stranger led him to his first formal training in art. One summer, when Nara was in Tokyo to take a course for university preparation, a young man approached him selling tickets for life-drawing classes. For Nara, this sounded more fun than the usual crop of summer courses, and he readily accepted.[13] His naive ideas about the frivolity of art classes were quickly dispelled as he began to learn the hard discipline of drawing and art in general. More importantly, it was here that the seeds of applying to an art university were sown. Thereafter, during high school semester breaks, he traveled to Tokyo to take art classes, expanding his repertoire to oil paintings and charcoal drawings.

In 1979 Nara enrolled at Musashino Art University in Tokyo, where he studied with Saburō Asō (1913–2010) and, through him, met Chōzaburō Inoue (1906–1995), both established painters known for their surrealist style and interest in the figural.[14] They belonged to a cadre of artists who had made self-reflective paintings during wartime Japan. While in the 1980s this style of art, and its association with Japan's past, was unfashionable, Nara's interest in their work was precisely because of this history and their penetrating ability to capture the human dimensions of war.[15] Nara was particularly drawn to the rawness and immediacy of Asō's works. In a 1937 self-portrait (Fig. 10), for example, Asō displays his ability to depict a haunting sense of pain and uncertainty, captured by an ambivalent sideways glance and enhanced with a saturated palette of burnished reds and blackened hues.

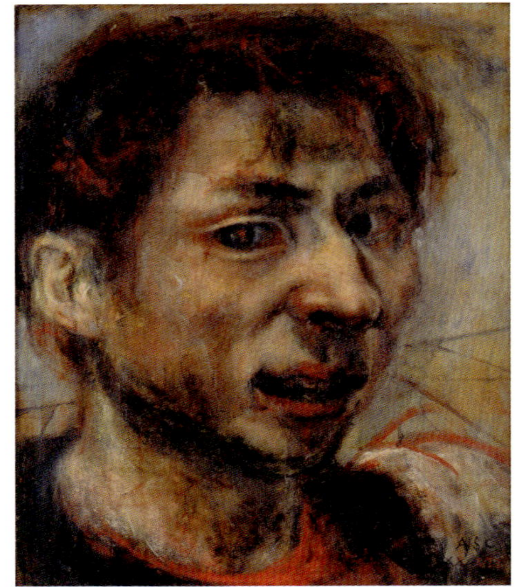

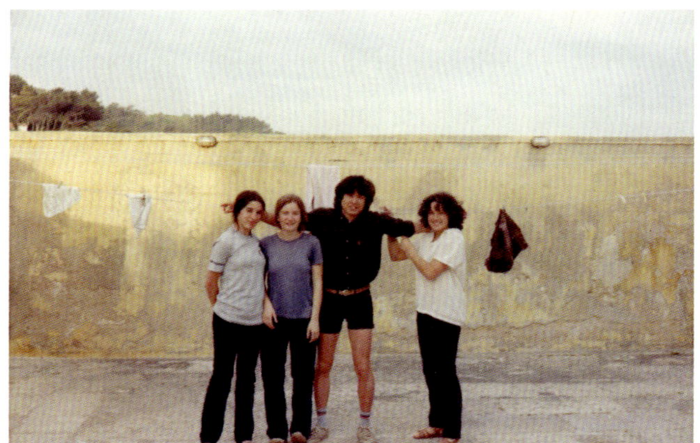

Fig. 10
Saburō Asō, *Self-Portrait*, 1937, Oil on canvas, 17 ⅞ × 15 in. (45.5 × 38 cm)

Fig. 11
Nara at a youth hostel on his first trip to Europe, Cascais, Portugal, 1980

Nara was not just interested in the art of these elders; he was also captivated by their stories of wartime Japan and their mundane or idiosyncratic acts of daily survival. Of the many stories that Inoue shared with Nara about life during the 1940s and 1950s, one in particular stayed with him. It was the story of how Inoue once placed a half-eaten bowl of udon in his coat pocket as he rushed for a train and then continued eating the noodles from his coat during his journey home. The story was intriguing partly because it depicted a time when wasting food was not an option but also because it illustrated the eccentric behavior of an artist who sought to live his life differently. Inoue and his fellow artists' irreverent, nonconformist ways and simple lifestyles made more sense to Nara than a postwar Tokyo that embraced and pursued a future of the synthetic, the fabricated, and the technological.

These stories may also have triggered Nara's desire to find his own set of new experiences. In February 1980, he used his tuition money to embark on a three-month summer trip to Europe, taking the long route via Pakistan. It was a daring adventure—backpacking was still a relatively unusual activity among his peers—but it was one that would have direct, though unexpected, consequences. In Europe, Nara saw many of the great masterpieces revered in art history books. The more he saw, however, the more detached he felt. He came to realize that technical mastery of form, which he had up until then held in the highest esteem, was less important than the ability to depict something that communicated an emotional world. For a young artist who had stumbled into art and harbored doubts about his own abilities, this was revelatory. It was during this trip that he developed an appreciation of modern and contemporary European art, and he reveled in the emotional power of works by artists such as Modigliani, Matisse, and Chagall.

Having exhausted his funds during his trip to Europe, Nara was no longer able to afford tuition at Musashino, and shortly after returning to Japan in spring 1981, he transferred to Aichi Prefectural University of Fine Arts and Music, a public institution in Nagakute, near the city of Nagoya. During his time there, he grew into a more confident artist and became less guarded, even audacious, about his passion. At Aichi, he made art, studied its history, and engaged in intellectual conversations with friends and the students he had as a part-time art teacher. But his time there fostered more than stimulating ideas.

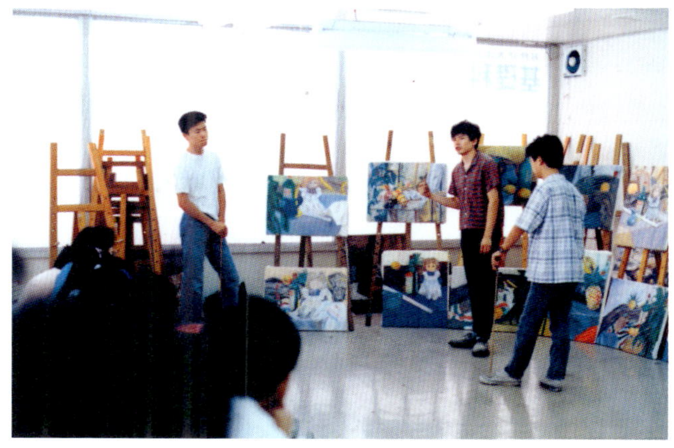

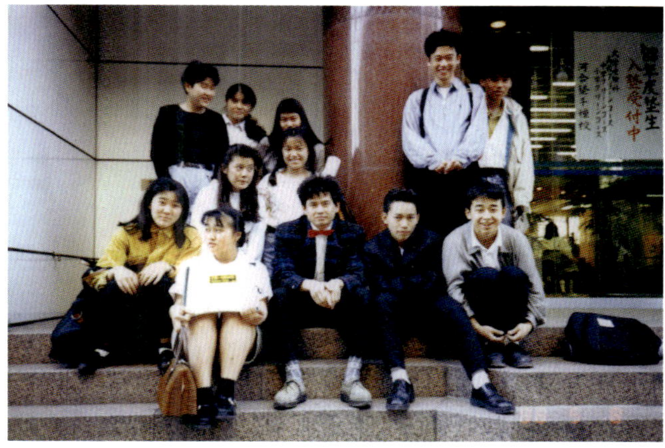

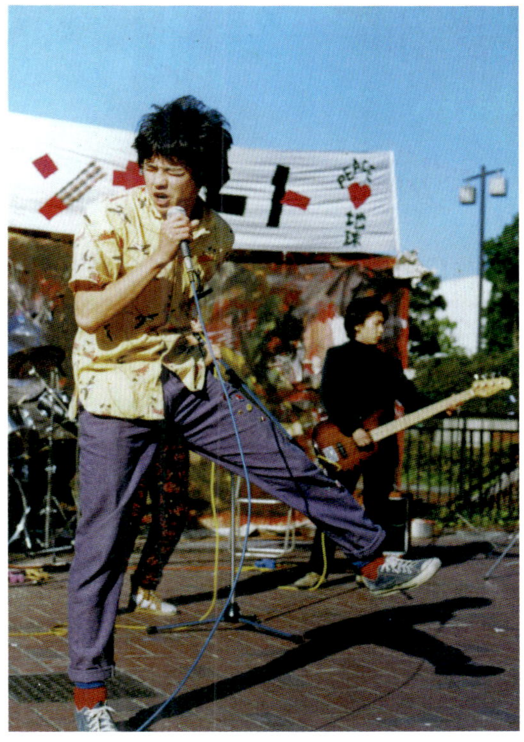

Figs. 12 and 13
Nara with his students from Kawai Juku prep school in Nagoya, 1985–87

Fig. 14
Nara singing in Hisaya Ōdori Park, Nagoya, 1984

It was a period when Nara's natural charisma found its full expression, and he attracted many friends with his fun-loving, gregarious, and adventurous spirit. To this day, the art school environment, in which everyone works and plays together, remains one of his favorite types of spaces and one to which he often returns.

The Europe trip had piqued Nara's interest in modern art, and it encouraged him to look more closely at Japan's own modernists, of whom he had already gained some knowledge through his former teacher Asō. He began to study more closely the work of some of Asō's peers, including Tetsugorō Yorozu (1885–1927) (Fig. 15), Kanda Nisshō (1937–1970), and Shunsuke Matsumoto (1912–1948). These wartime artists were instrumental in making claims for the autonomy of artistic subjectivity at a time when the state was heavily involved in using art as a form of modern nation building.[16] Nara often returned to paintings by Matsumoto, in part because he was drawn to the biography of the older artist, who had grown up in Iwate prefecture in northern Japan, not far from Hirosaki, blighted by a childhood illness that left him deaf.

Matsumoto was an unusual artist, one of only a few who spoke out against the government's wartime propaganda art program. In particular, he publicly countered the 1941 publication of the transcript of a military-sponsored symposium, "The National Defense State and the Fine Arts: What Should Artists Do?," which appeared in *Mizue*, a leading art journal. The text criticized current art practices, praised the use of art by the Nazi Party, and proposed that the fulfillment of the individual was through identification with family and the state and that art should serve the Japanese race. Matsumoto submitted a response by writing in a later edition of the same publication an article entitled "Ikiteiru gaka" (The Living Artist) that defended the rights of the individual and artistic subjectivity. His was the only voice of dissent against the state, and he urged his peers to do the same: "It is wise to keep silent, but I do not believe keeping silent today is necessarily the correct thing to do."[17] There were no other responses, and he was labeled a deviant. In his paintings, Matsumoto captured the ambivalence of being an artist during this period with urban landscapes painted with the darkened silhouettes of buildings that evoke industrial despair (Fig. 16).

Of the wartime artists Nara admired, perhaps the most influential was the illustrator Takeshi Motai (1908–1956) (Figs. 18 and 19), in particular,

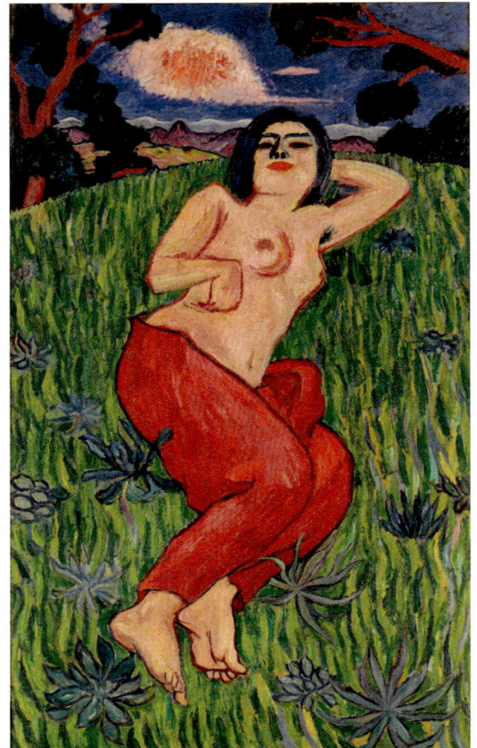

Fig. 15
Tetsugorō Yorozu, *Nude Beauty*, 1912, Oil on canvas, 63 ¾ × 38 ¼ in. (162 × 97 cm)

Fig. 16
Shunsuke Matsumoto, *Backside of Tokyo Station*, 1942, Oil on canvas, 19 ¾ × 23 ⅞ in. (50 × 60.6 cm)

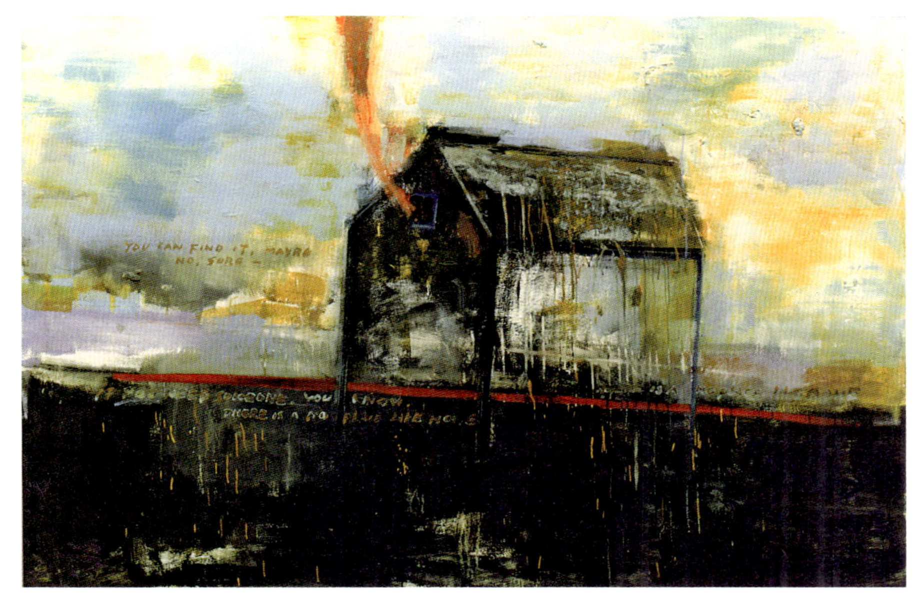

Fig. 17
Is There No Place Like Home?,
1984, Acrylic on canvas,
51 $\frac{3}{16}$ × 76 $\frac{3}{8}$ in. (130 × 194 cm)

his illustrations for the stories of Kenji Miyazawa (1896–1933).[18] Miyazawa's works were only recognized posthumously, but since the 1950s, they have been republished, translated, and adapted many times. He was an unusual figure: a poet, writer, Western classical music enthusiast, Esperanto student, and agriculture science teacher from Iwate prefecture. These different interests inform his stories—his religious beliefs lay at the foundation of his adventures, and his interest in agriculture is evident in fables that feature talking animals and display the awesome power of nature.[19] Miyazawa's dark humor also signaled to young readers the joys of breaching boundaries, while older readers were drawn to the nostalgic appeal of simpler times before the realities of a contemporary materialistic world had taken hold.[20] Motai's lively watercolors, which can be dark or full of glee, capture the spirit of these stories. He sometimes depicted the protagonists with blond hair, which was never a reflection on race but was meant instead to signal the inhabitants of faraway places waiting to be explored.

Nara's interest in these wartime artists and writers lay in his fascination with their histories, their spirits of independence, and the ways in which they channeled their experiences through art. Although the influence of music and his northern roots would become increasingly evident in his art as he matured, it was through the works of these artists that the young Nara first developed his stylistic vocabulary. In his early paintings, the way in which he thematized narratives of his childhood memories was in part the result of his tendency to view his past through the eyes of those who influenced him.

> **Even though fourteen years had passed since the end of war, things were still way behind out in the country. It was probably similar to what it had been like in Tokyo five years after the war. . . . There were remnants of the war all over the place. I had a physical sensation that the entire area was filled with debris and ghosts.**[21]

At the heart of Nara's work is the subject/object of the child, which, over the next forty years, he would explore in many and various ways. In the beginning, his works centered on his childhood memories, as seen in *Is There No Place Like Home?* (1984) (Fig. 17), one of the earliest works in his oeuvre and which only survives in photographs. It depicts

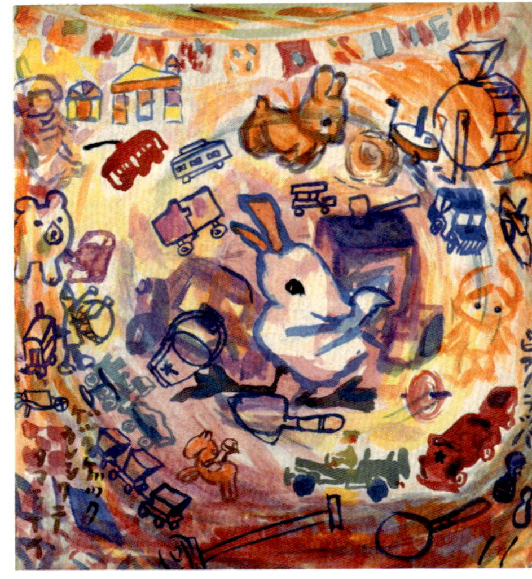

Fig. 18
Takeshi Motai, *A Piano and a Trumpet—Quack, Quack, I'm So Happy!*, 1947, Watercolor on paper, 10 ⅝ × 9 ½ in. (27 × 24 cm)

a lone, dark house standing on a hill, its silhouetted form showing his debt to Matsumoto's painting style. Nara's house takes on an eerie, humanlike presence, its darkness seeping out into the blue sky as a plume of fire shoots out of a window. The house is a reference to Nara's childhood home, which once stood alone on a hill, and the fire a symbol of growing up in an agricultural town where he saw it as both fearful—its blazing power that could destroy their wood-framed home—and comforting—the warmth it brought to the hearth. Nara drips paints and scrawls lines over his black house and imbues the scene with an ominous foreboding, even while reflecting on a nostalgic past. The line "You can find it. Maybe. No. Sure," written in black with deliberate punctuation, speaks to a sense of elusiveness.

Nara's approach was to use his childhood memories as a visual starting point, but they are not the thematic subjects of his paintings. Instead, he cites certain motifs that allude to his childhood and repeats them time and again, creating a sort of pictorial code that becomes a shorthand reference to that period in his life. These motifs are embedded within landscapes and alongside objects, animals, and young children that do not belong together but which, when assembled, exploit their disassociations to create ambiguity and a hint of threat. He never repeats motifs in the same way, varying them to explore the different intensities of pictorial effects and to capture a range of personal emotions. The house in *Is There No Place Like Home?*, for example, takes on a ghostly form in *Futaba House, Waiting for Rain Drops* (1984) (Fig. 22), is reduced down to its skeleton in *Lost Memory* (1984) (Fig. 20), and is rendered as a collage in *Untitled* (1984) (Fig. 21). Taken together, these various formal approaches convey an overwhelming sense of the instability of the house/home.

Connected to the house is the fire, a reference to life in Hirosaki, and the other recurring emblem is a *futaba* (double-leafed sprout), which represents both a child and the idealized promise of the future. *Futaba* is also a term used to describe a typical two-story house and, thus, can be seen as another reference to Nara's home. While fire and the *futaba* would continue as motifs throughout Nara's career, from around 2001, the lone house fades from his repertoire.[22]

Nara has often spoken about the importance of memories and the act of reflection in his work. If nostalgia, as described by Svetlana Boym, is "a mourning for the impossibility of mythical return, for the loss of an enchanted world with clear borders and values," then Nara

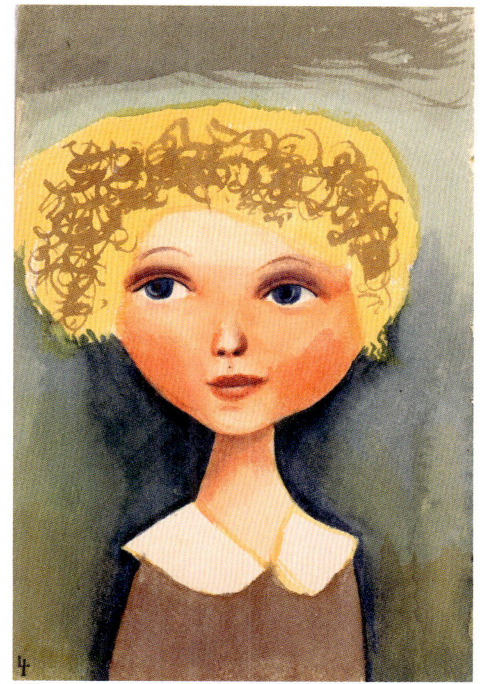

Fig. 19
Takeshi Motai, from the sketchbook *La Croix Blanche*, 1931–35, Watercolor on paper, 7 ⅜ × 4 ⅞ in. (18.6 × 12.5 cm)

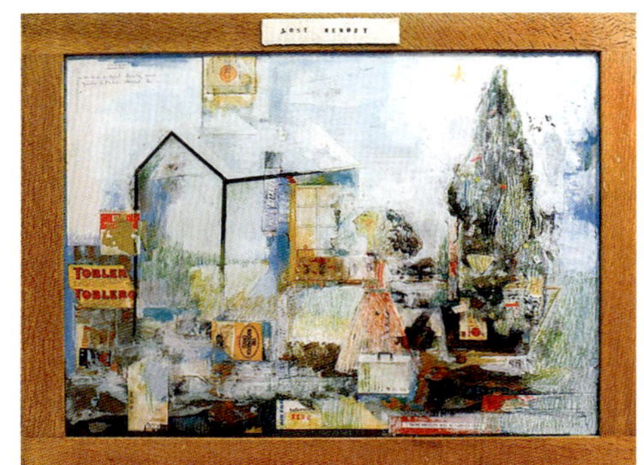

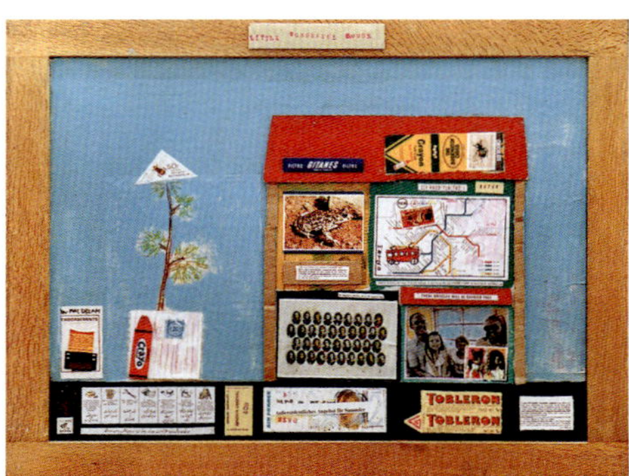

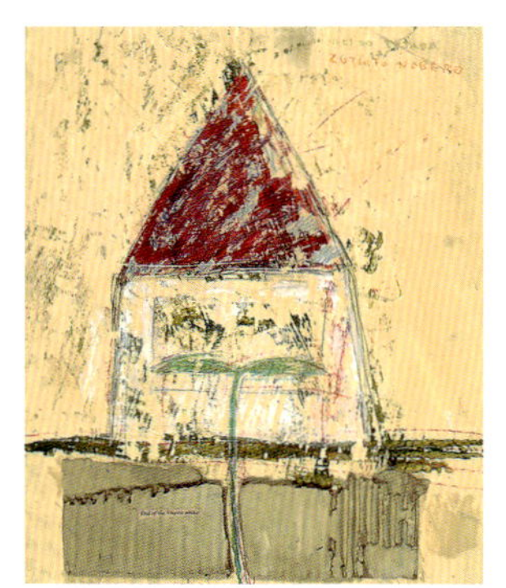

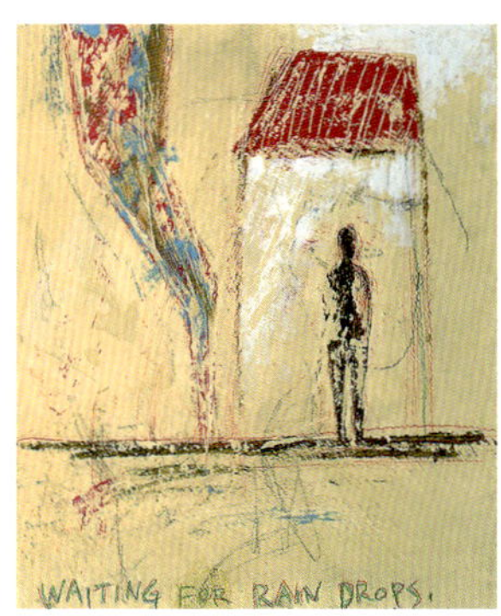

is making that impossible return by mythologizing a childhood that cannot have been truly experienced or remembered.[23] In other words, his paintings are not of the past itself, nor do they depict a yearning for it. Rather, they use nostalgia to create alternative worlds where the whimsical and childlike exist alongside the fantastic and dangerous, creating a tension that threatens their stability.

In the final year of his studies, Nara achieved a more coherent body of work. There is a greater stability of composition, and his subjects begin to suggest a narrative, albeit one with an elusive meaning. It is this storytelling potential that marks the influence of Motai and Miyazawa, who likewise transported readers into alternative worlds. An example of this is Nara's graduation painting, *Innocent Being* (1986) (Fig. 23), a work that recalls his elementary and high schools in Hirosaki, which were originally army barracks and which as a child he imagined were full of ghosts and wartime debris. But how he processes those memories in the painting embodies the uneasiness of recall itself. In *Innocent Being*, the young blond boy balances precariously on a bare foot in front of the tail of a warplane protruding from the ground. A red fox stands on its head, and the *futaba* house takes on a ghostly presence in the background. With the exception of the buried plane, every component appears unstable or insubstantial and on the verge of collapse, teetering at the edge of meaning. None of these motifs belongs with any another, but joined together, they take on an allegorical presence suggestive of meanings that are too slippery to grasp.

This early period also sees Nara take on a gothic playfulness, with Christian iconography, such as crosses, fallen angels, and serpents, appearing in his work. His early references to these symbols may have been a subtle act of rebellion against his father's Shinto roots, or they may suggest how the young artist found the exoticism of

Fig. 20 (left)
Lost Memory, 1984, Acrylic and colored pencil on paper mounted on board, Size unknown

Fig. 21 (center)
Untitled, 1984, Acrylic and collage on paper mounted on board, Size unknown

Figs. 22a–b (right)
Futaba House, Waiting for Rain Drops, 1984, Acrylic and colored pencil on wood board, each 17 11/16 × 14 3/16 in. (45 × 36 cm)

Fig. 23 (opposite)
Innocent Being, 1986, Acrylic and colored pencil on canvas, 76 3/8 × 51 5/16 in. (194 × 130.3 cm)

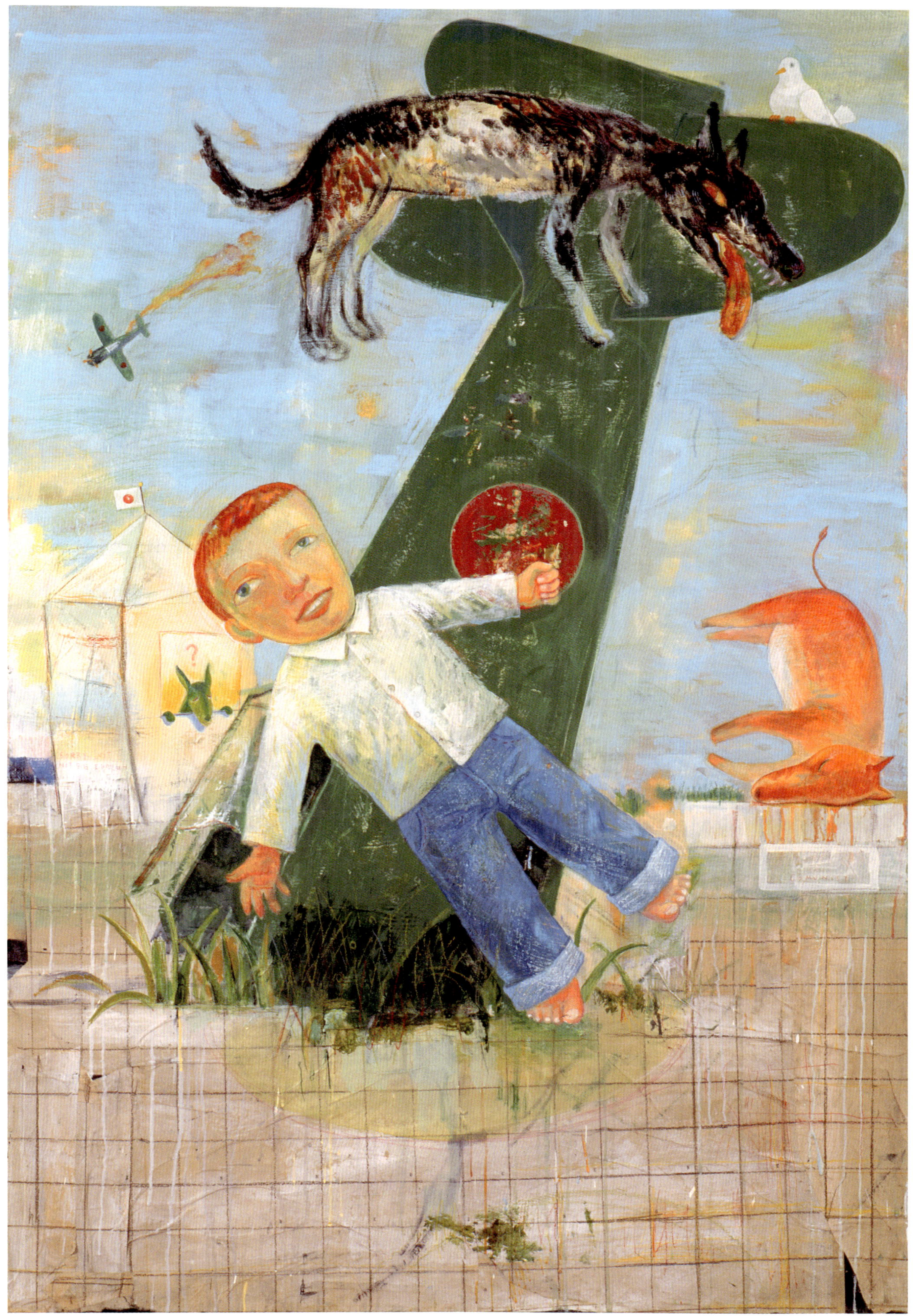

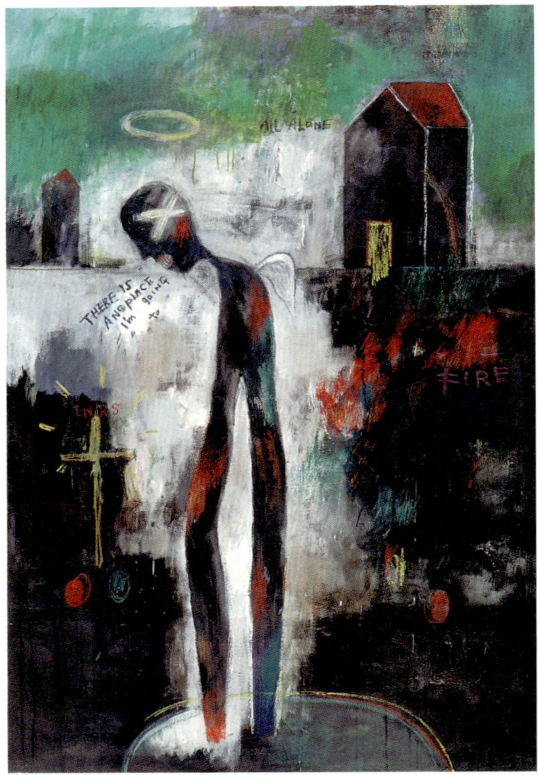

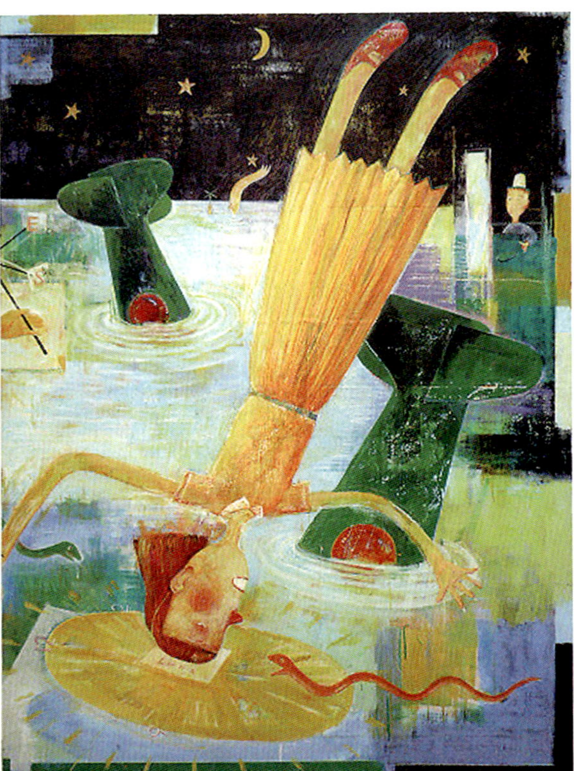

Christianity and its history a means of escape. In *All Alone* (1986) (Fig. 24), a winged figure carries the heavy black pigment like a cape, while a white cross resembling a bandage appears on his head, evoking the idea of a wounded soul.[24] In *Untitled* (1986) (Fig. 25), the moonlit sky and broken horizon line evoke a dreamscape in which logic cedes to the cluttering of nonsensical forms, with heads appearing out of puddles, broken warplanes submerged in water, and a young girl falling as a snake glides toward her.[25]

These enigmatic early paintings show how Nara grappled with imagination, memory, and his painterly craft. At times, his treatment of the fantastic and mythical appears too forced and literal, a symptom of a young artist who was not always comfortable with his own voice. But it was the search for this voice that fueled his endless experimentations and generated new meanings and techniques in his work. For example, in *Untitled* (1988) (Fig. 26), the cross shifts from a motif to a compositional grid device, and Nara stretches his subject across the canvas's axial points while still utilizing the form's powerful symbolism of biblical sacrifice to call into question whether the figure is asleep or injured. This cross-shape composition later breaks apart, as in Nara's Master's graduation painting, *Merry-Go-Round* (1987) (Fig. 27), which

Fig. 24
All Alone, 1986, Acrylic and colored pencil on canvas, 76 × 51 5/16 in. (193 × 130.3 cm)

Fig. 25
Untitled, 1986, Acrylic on canvas, h. 63 ¾ in. (162 cm) [left side broken and lost]

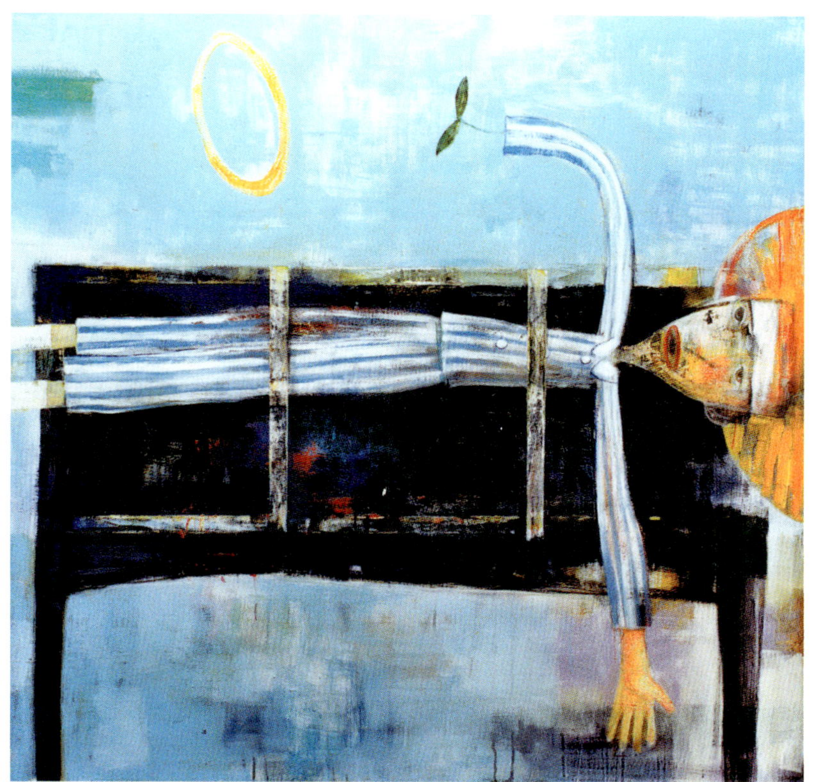

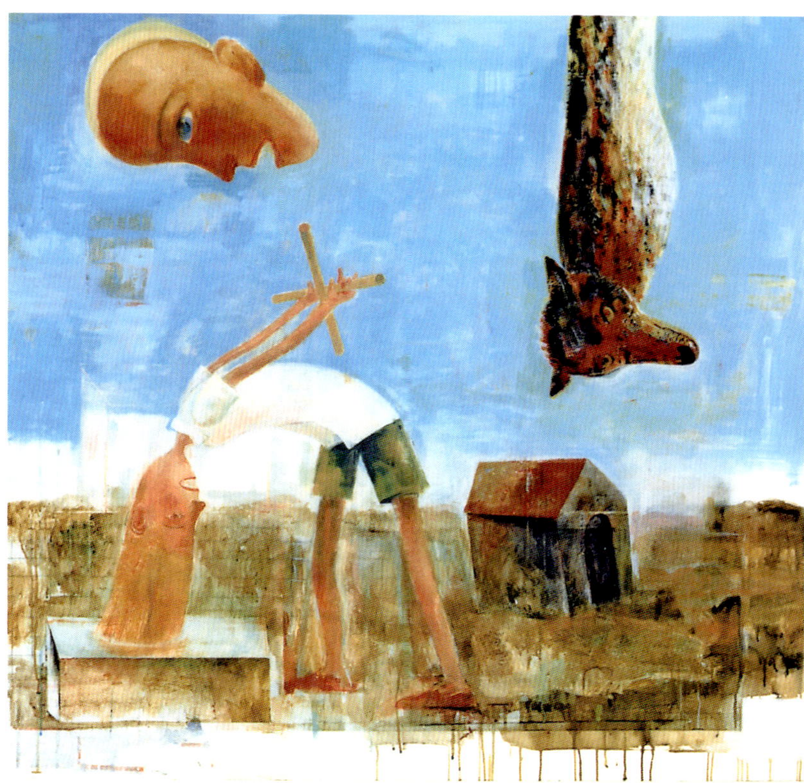

shows the key figures now occupying their own individual quadrants—the falling fox looking perplexed on the right and a child bent over with his hair in a trough on the left. The absurdity of the scene is heightened by the cross-like composition that holds them together, balancing the vertical with the horizontal, movement with stability.

Nara's works during the period from 1986 to 1990 contain touches of humor, reflecting an important side of his character that finds pleasure in the playful moments in life. This is in stark contrast to the more commonly held view of Nara as a melancholic and rebellious loner. As Nobuya Hitsuda, his mentor at Aichi, recounts, Nara used to drop by his home, "looking through art books, or eating and drinking. He never went to class but was always hanging around the school. You know, in order to do some mischief. He'd take over the vocals for the last stage performance at the school festival; he was always taking the good parts. That's why he stood out. He'd get everyone together to have a huge party, but then slip out by himself, saying, 'I'm so lonely!' He is like a dog, a little shy, but trying to get close, and other times he's proud like a cat. Light and shadow live together in him."[26]

These two sides of Nara's personality—his charismatic energy and generosity in contrast with his introspection and loneliness—feed

Fig. 26
Untitled, 1988, Acrylic on canvas, Size unknown

Fig. 27
Merry-Go-Round, 1987, Acrylic on canvas, 51 5/16 × 51 5/16 in. (130.3 × 130.3 cm)

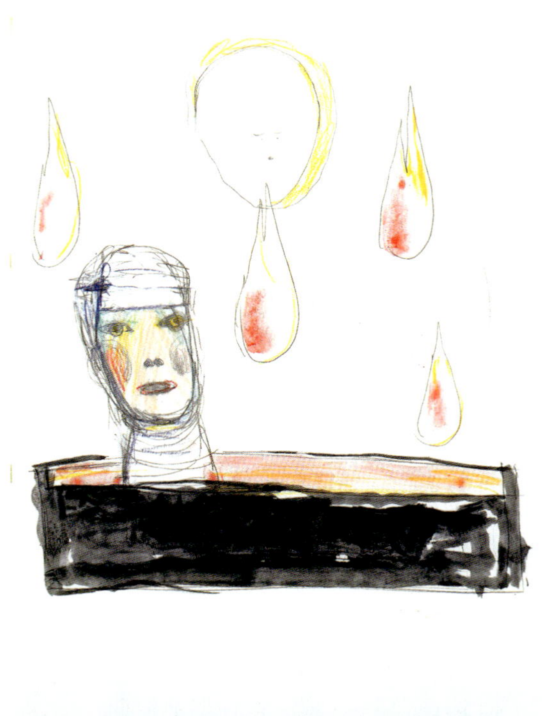

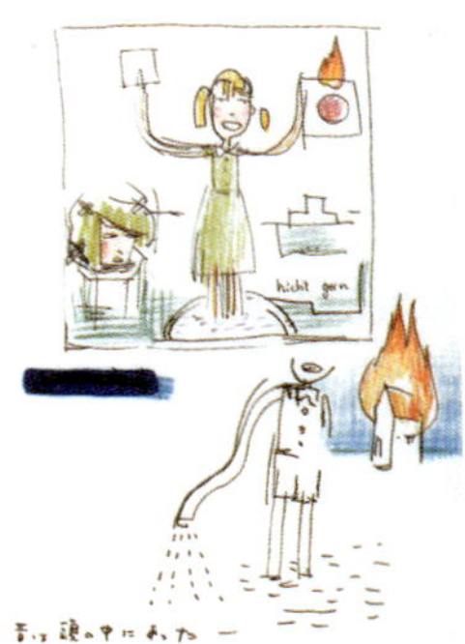

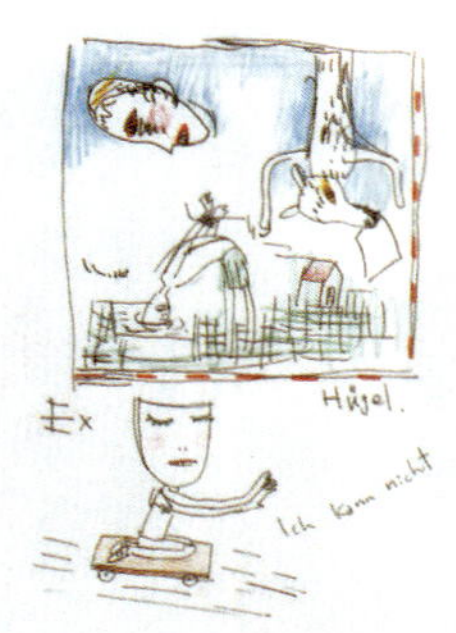

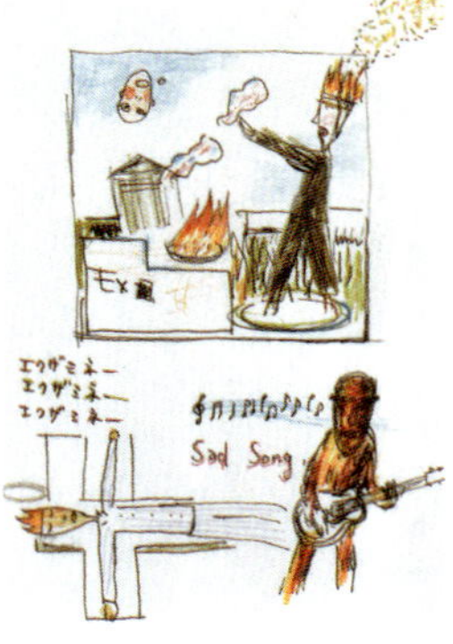

into his practice and struggle with one another at times. In his paintings, particularly in his early works, conscious of how they would be judged at school, he is more guarded about displaying these different aspects of his personality, using narratives of his childhood to obscure the reality of his present self. In his drawings, however, his sly humor, explosive energy, and more contemplative side are readily seen. The drawings are his private musings, and they take him back to the certainty of his roots, to that instinctive young man in the rock café when his life was more carefree. They are sometimes made on torn envelopes and paper scraps and suggest impulsive doodling. The range of themes and subjects is broad, from working out compositions to scribbling lines from a song, but most are random and fun, from mummy-like figures rising from coffins to guitar-playing rockers (Figs. 28 and 29). He often includes writing, song titles, or spontaneous thoughts that sometimes spill over onto the drawings themselves. It is also in his drawings that one finds more direct commentary on darker political themes. *Somewhere Somewhere* (1986) (Fig. 30), for example, portrays a nuclear mushroom cloud with a strangely humanlike presence, penetrated by a nail. In front of it lies a crucified man singing a tune, while above, in Japanese, are the words, "There may be death more noble than life, (just) maybe." The nuclear

Fig. 28
Untitled, 1988, Acrylic, colored pencil, and pencil on paper, 11 ⅝ × 8 ¼ in. (29.5 × 21 cm)

Figs. 29a–c
Untitled, 1988, Colored pencil and pen on paper, overall 14 $\frac{9}{16}$ × 10 $\frac{13}{16}$ in. (37 × 27.5 cm)

Fig. 30 (opposite)
Somewhere Somewhere, 1986, Pen on paper, 7 $\frac{3}{16}$ × 5 $\frac{1}{16}$ in. (18.2 × 12.8 cm)

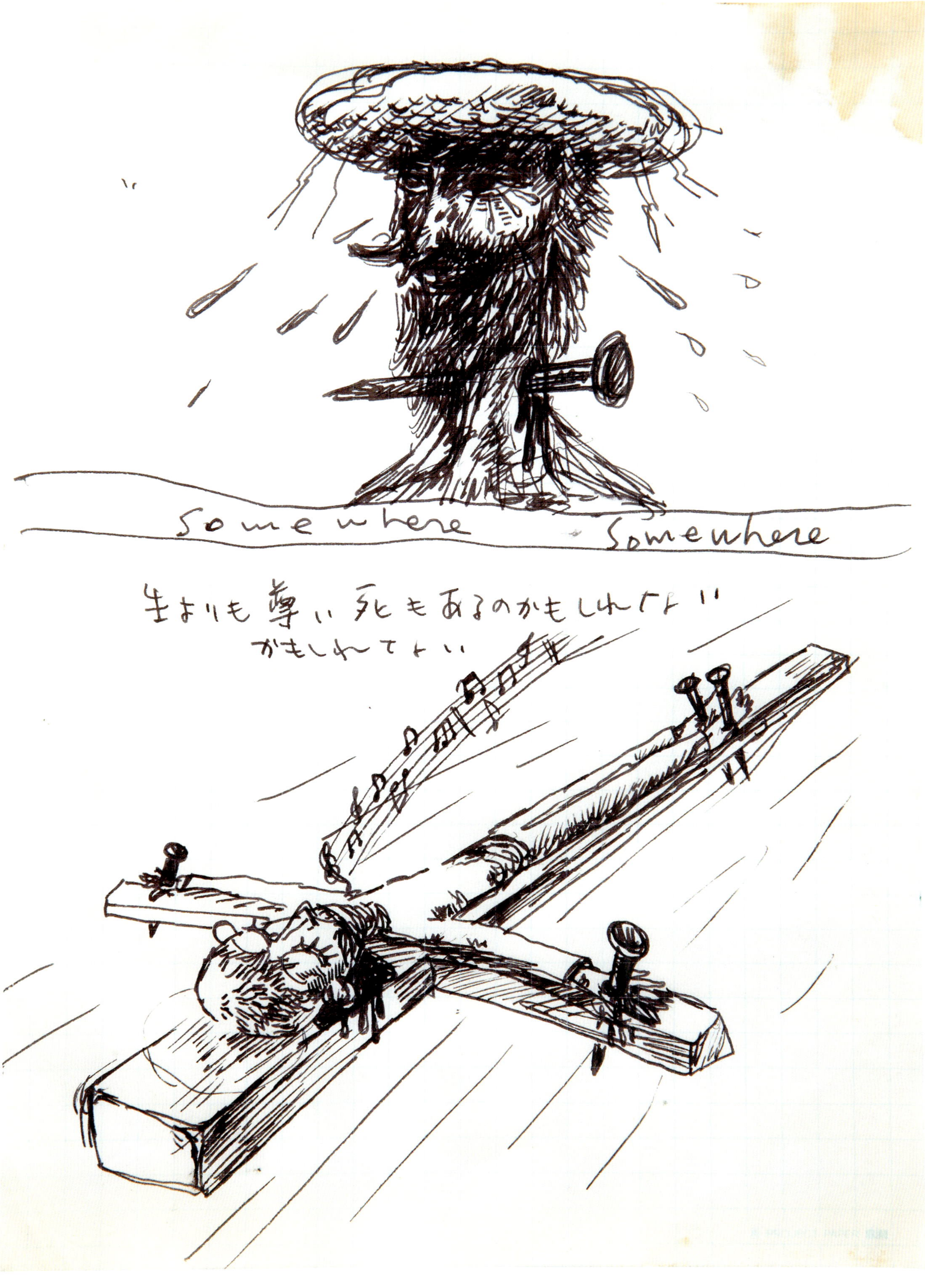

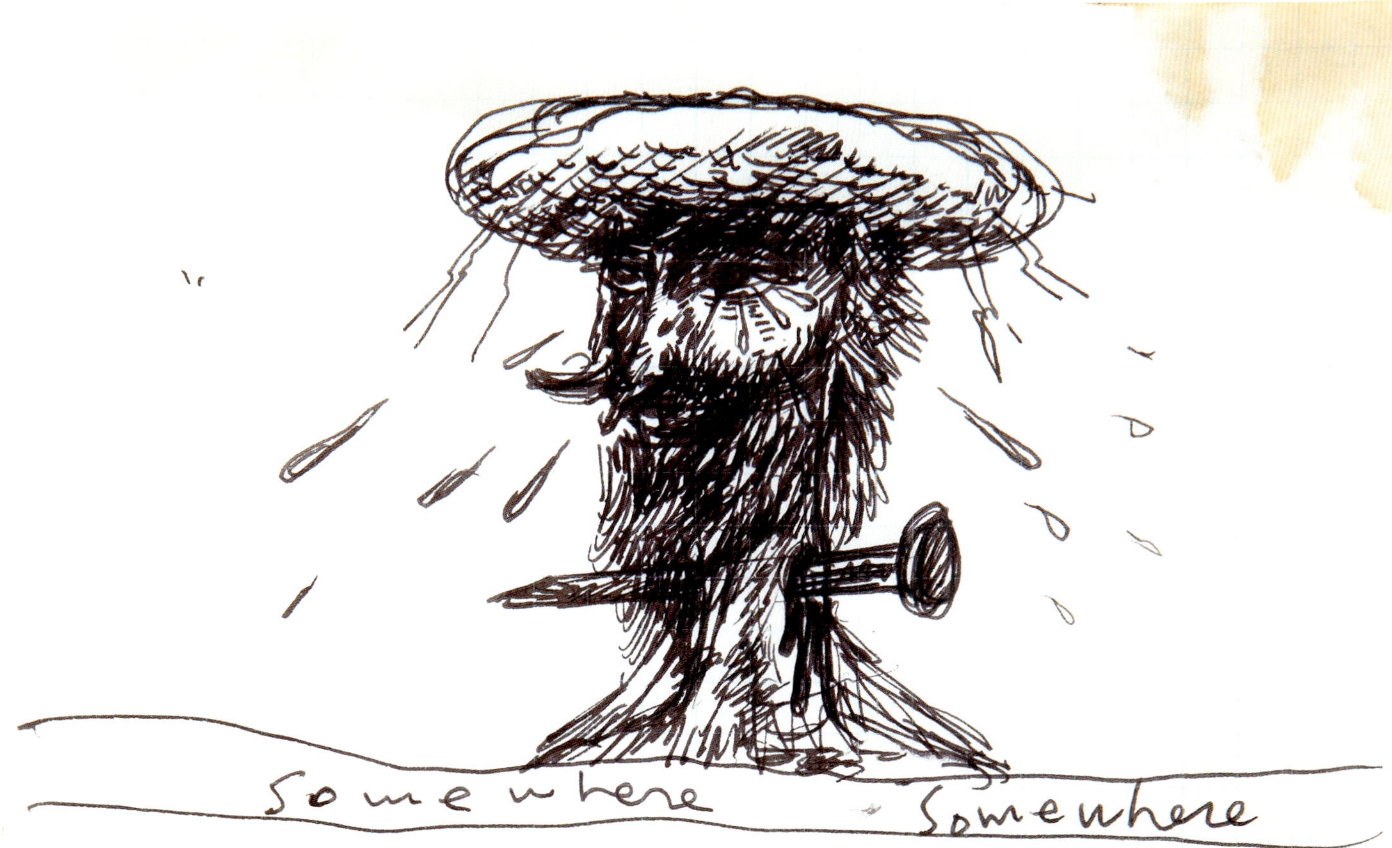

生よりも尊い死もあるのかもしれない
かもしれない

mushroom cloud seems to perspire—or bleed—in the presence of defiant death.

What these examples show is that Nara, in his private life, worked hard and often used his drawings as ways of developing ideas. Sometimes they are fully evolved images akin to his paintings, but many more of them are sketch-like and appear unfinished. Ultimately, they act as records of his personal anecdotes, impressions, and stories, and, because he makes them for himself, they are unmoored from the obligation he often feels to explain his work. They also demonstrate his compulsive need to draw, to scribble on any surface, and, like diary entries, they capture the many sides of his personality.

> **For me, the center of the world was still the student life around the university, and I continued with the art discussions and rowdy parties, though slightly more evolved. . . . I started to think pretty highly of myself, and I think I spouted a lot of idealized philosophies at my students. I was a slacker throughout my student days and I talked a big game, but now, as a teacher, I started to feel like I was lying to my wide-eyed students. I began to think that I needed to go back to school, be like my students who are always eager to learn, and study everything all over again.**[27]

In Nagoya, Nara was becoming recognized for his art and had his first solo show shortly after his graduation in 1984. Four years later, his work was shown in an exhibition, *Innocent Being*, at the Galerie Humanité in Nagoya and Tokyo, and he was given his first overseas show at the Goethe-Institut Düsseldorf. The early 1980s saw the expansion of a commercial art market in Japan that was crucial to the survival of young emerging artists—it was not until the 1990s that the government played a significant role in supporting the arts in Japan. The Japanese art world in the 1990s also saw a shift away from earlier conceptual practices and a return to painting and an interest in materiality.[28] In this way, artists could speak about the present in modes that resonated with contemporary art practices in Europe and the United States. Artists like Yoshiro Negishi (b. 1951), for example, were experimenting with colors with an obsessiveness that undercut the intellectualized world of avant-garde art (Fig. 31).

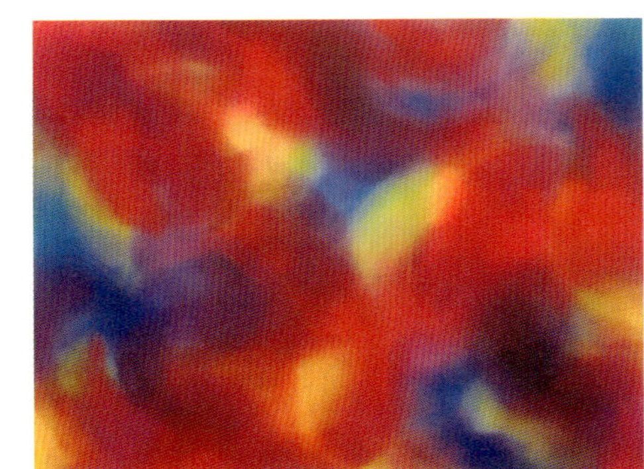

Fig. 31
Yoshiro Negishi, *88-8-21*, 1988, Acrylic on canvas, 70 ⅞ × 91 ⅜ in. (180 × 232 cm)

The return to painting and its emotional power represent a point of commonality between Nara and these artists, but Nara's creation of childlike worlds and his fascination with postwar Japanese artists marked a striking difference from his peers. It is perhaps unsurprising, then, that Nara was beginning to feel out of step with the art world, even becoming increasingly uncomfortable with the label of *artist*. Part of this ambivalence was driven by his guilt about being called *sensei* (teacher) by his students when he felt he had not achieved that distinction. Believing that he had much more work to do to deserve either title, and wishing to continue making art that was distinctive from that of his peers, he decided to go back to school.

In 1988 Nara moved to Germany to undertake further studies at the Kunstakademie Düsseldorf, where he studied with A. R. Penck (1939–2017) (Fig. 32). Originally, he had hoped to study with Fritz Schwegler (1935–2014), but when his class was full, Schwegler advised Nara to find a teacher who would encourage him to explore new things or, as Nara recalls, "go a little crazy." Penck, an artist with a bold personality, largely left his students to develop work on their own. Although he was often absent due to his hectic schedule, he generously provided his students with large independent studio spaces. And he gave Nara a simple piece of advice that would have a long-term impact: to combine his drawing with his painting.[29]

The explosive energy in Penck's art is often seen as a response to the trauma of World War II, including the destruction of his hometown of Dresden. Once again, Nara found direction and inspiration from an artist who had been deeply affected by the war, although Penck approached the past differently than Nara's mentors in Japan did, preferring iconoclastic expressions made with a lexicon of markings that utilize fake alphabets and stick figures. Their graffiti-like presence was, in part, a response to street art, but they were also responses to prewar German Expressionism, in particular the works of Ernst Ludwig Kirchner (1880–1938). As with Kirchner's work, Penck's paintings are critical reflections on society. His symbols of wartime aggression on canvases overloaded with signs are powerful expressions that capture the tension between figuration and abstraction and between fabrication and imagination, characteristics that would indirectly impact Nara's own work.

In an unusual set of drawings in acrylic paint, Nara produced a series of figures with guns and barbed-wire fences, their faces flooded

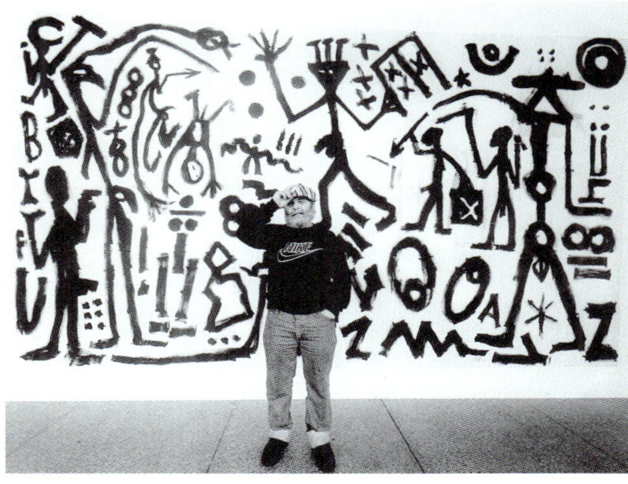

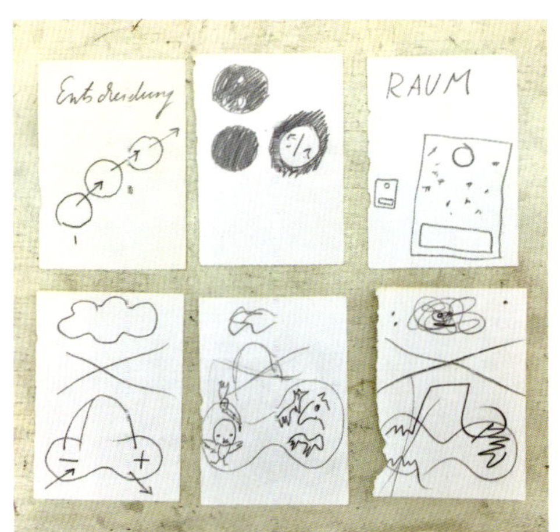

Fig. 32
A. R. Penck, 1988

Fig. 33
Sketches by A. R. Penck given to Nara

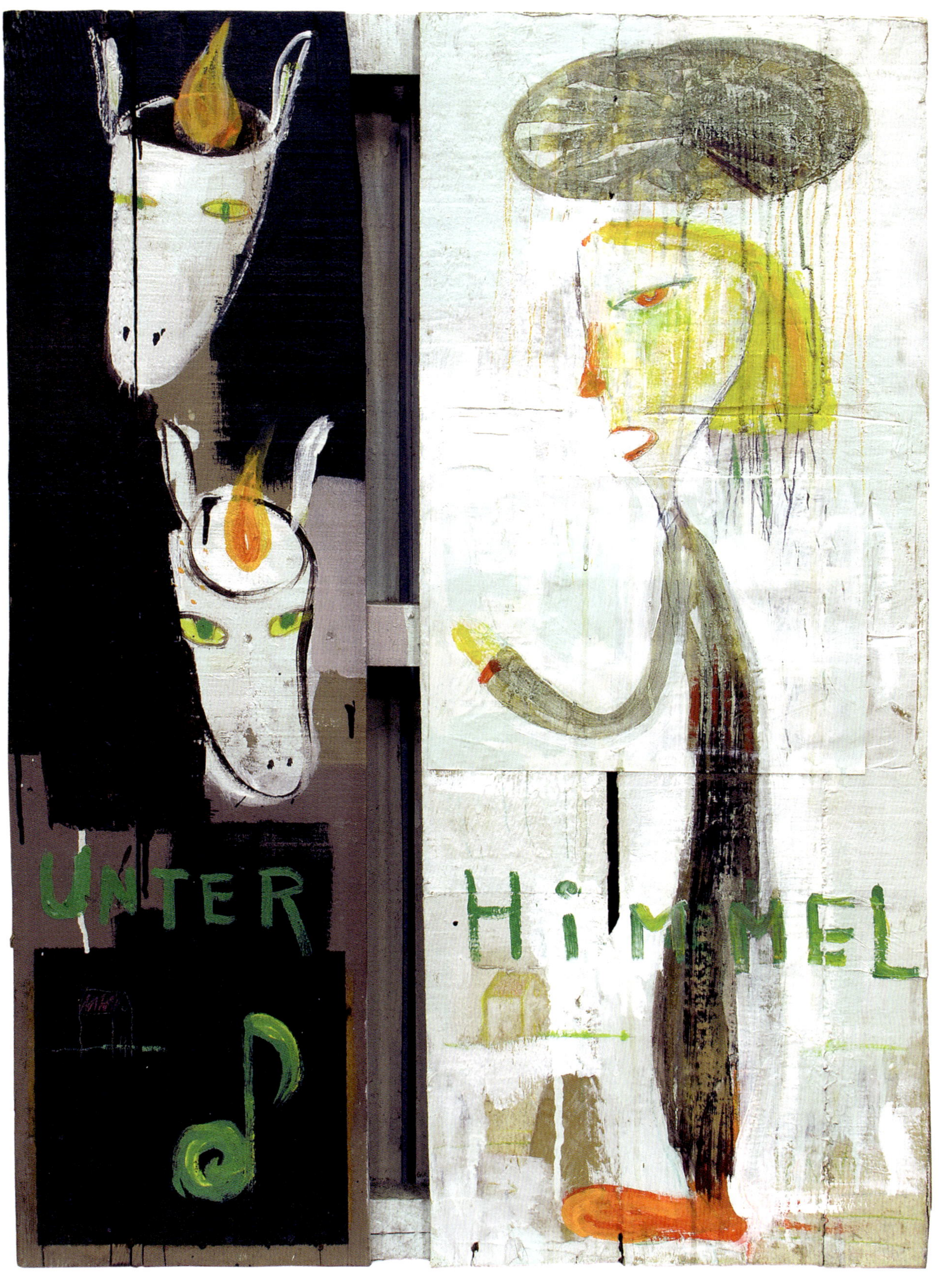

Fig. 34
Untitled [after overpainting], 1987–97, Acrylic on paper and wood, 35 1⁄16 × 24 13⁄16 × 3 3⁄8 in. (89 × 63 × 8.5 cm)

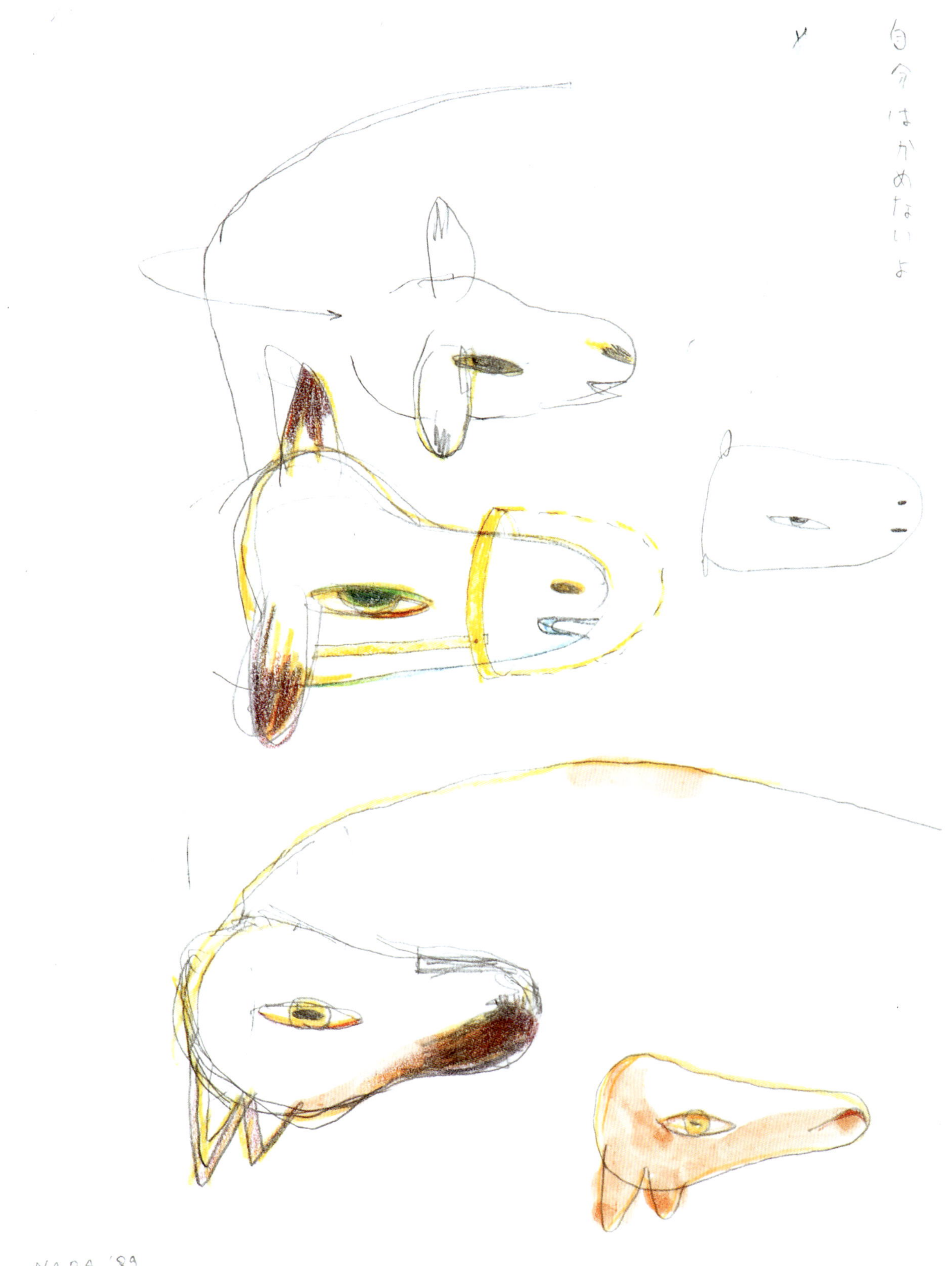

Fig. 35
I Can't Bite., 1989, Watercolor, colored pencil, and pencil on paper, 8 1⁄16 × 5 11⁄16 in. (20.5 × 14.5 cm)

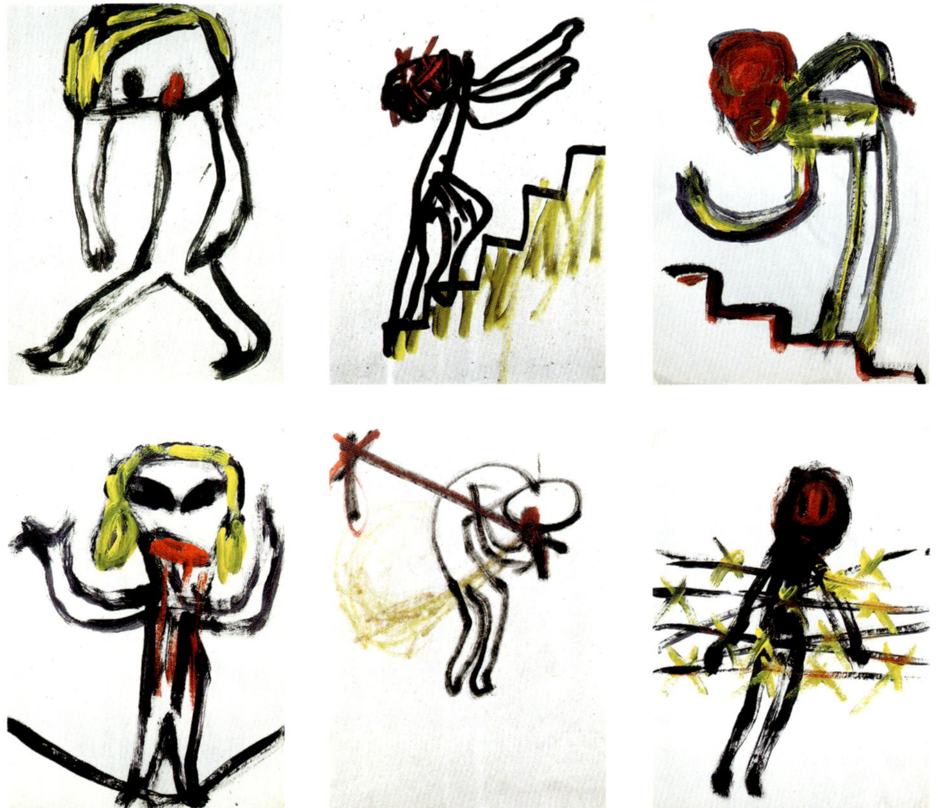

with paint that blurs or exaggerates their features (Figs. 36–41). These are similar to Penck's works in their violent rawness, but whereas Penck's drawings lead to abstraction and patterning, Nara's never lose their figuration. The repetition of bold black lines, painted yellows, and streaks of red cut across the body creates an integrated language that allows for accidents of the drawn line and its violent imperfections.

It was by paring down his enigmatic stories to simpler and bolder forms that Nara successfully connected his two practices of drawing and painting. He continued to explore the effect of bold outlines in *Irrlichter* (1989) (Fig. 42), adapted from one of his drawings but painted against broad streaks of layered yellows. In *Hannya Neko (Hannya Cat)* (1989) (Fig. 43), a human/cat face with yellow teeth, fleshy tones of pinks and creams, and a long writhing red tongue evokes a threatening unease. These works indicate a significant shift for Nara, moving away from a grid composition of composite parts to a unified and relatively flat background against which motifs gain greater presence and are pushed further into the foreground, as we shall see with his portraits of big-headed girls. One immediate effect of this shift in compositional structure is a greater confidence with

Fig. 36 (top left)
Untitled, 1989, Acrylic on paper, 19 ½ × 13 ¹¹⁄₁₆ in. (49.5 × 34.7 cm)

Fig. 37 (top center)
Untitled, 1989, Acrylic on paper, 13 ⅜ × 9 ⁷⁄₁₆ in. (34 × 24 cm)

Fig. 38 (top right)
Untitled, 1989, Acrylic on paper, 19 ½ × 13 ⁹⁄₁₆ in. (49.5 × 34.5 cm)

Fig. 39 (bottom left)
Untitled, 1989, Acrylic on paper, 19 ½ × 13 ⁹⁄₁₆ in. (49.5 × 34.5 cm)

Fig. 40 (bottom center)
Untitled, 1989, Acrylic on paper, 13 ⅜ × 9 ⁷⁄₁₆ in. (34 × 24 cm)

Fig. 41 (bottom right)
Untitled, 1989, Acrylic on paper, 19 ½ × 13 ⁹⁄₁₆ in. (49.5 × 34.5 cm)

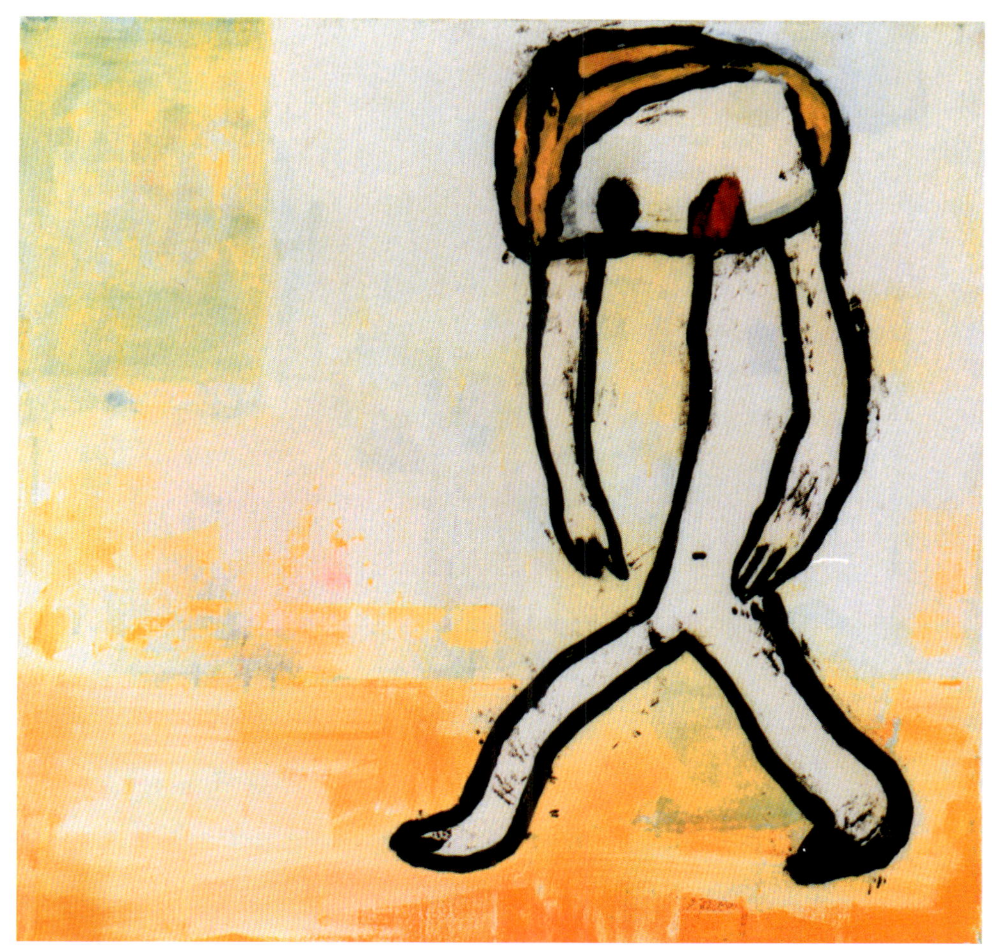

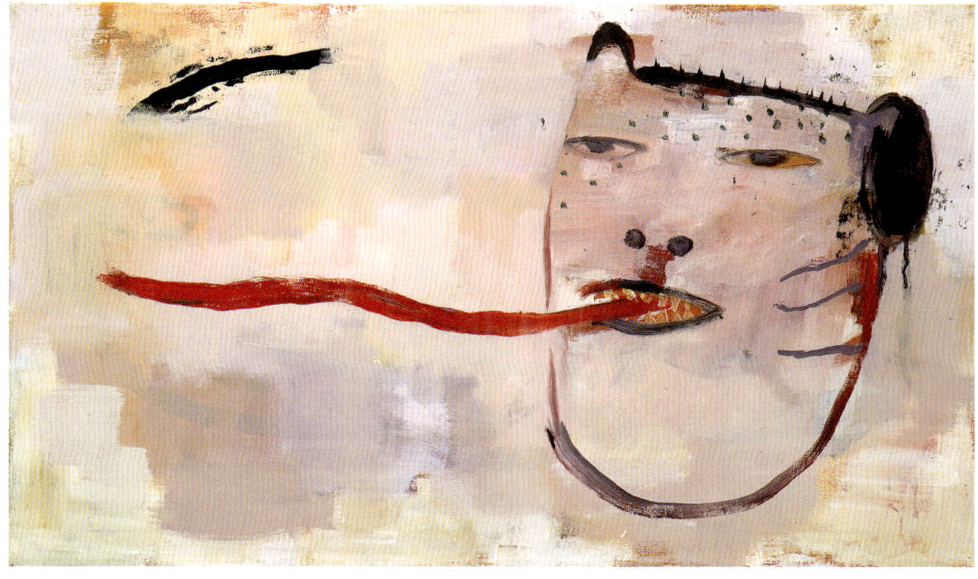

Fig. 42
Irrlichter, 1989, Acrylic on canvas, 25 9⁄16 × 25 9⁄16 in. (65 × 65 cm)

Fig. 43
Hannya Neko (Hannya Cat), 1989, Acrylic on canvas, 23 5⁄8 × 39 3⁄8 in. (60 × 100 cm)

color—whereas he used to smudge, erase, and at times overwork surfaces, now there is almost a sense of release as he plays with strong hues across expanses of canvas.

Another noteworthy stylistic development made at this time, which comes from Nara's earlier interest in gravity (things falling), is the exploration of the experience of lightness and weight through varying levels of density and transparency. In other words, he wanted to create a sense that forms were emerging from, or retreating into, the canvas rather than moving vertically or horizontally across its surface. As a technique, this achieves several effects, including a sense of corporeal tactility, making it applicable to themes that blur the borders between bodily experience and ethereal imagination. *Give You the Flower* (1990) (Fig. 47) depicts an encounter between two lovers, not quite human, who share an intimate moment as they face each other, one holding a knife, the other a rose. These otherworldly lovers, with their earthly passions of violence and romance, are at the same time fleshed out and erased by different qualities of white acrylic paint applied in thin layers on the canvas. The opacity of the paint gives the figures a material presence that underscores the potential for pain from the knife (and from their romance). In this work, Nara incorporates relatable adult exchanges into his imagined childlike world.

Less successful is *People on the Cloud* (1989) (Fig. 49), which also explores the substance of things through textures of paint but the overall diffused composition of which is still reliant on his earlier style of bringing together an array of disconnected figures: angels, an astronaut in a spaceship, a beheaded girl, and doglike creatures. What is striking about this work is how Nara draws his figures primarily onto a canvas of blues and yellows, creating an overall airy quality with little differentiation between planes and grounds and a very flat surface that appears closer to a drawing. The only exceptions to this flatness are two pockets of thicker white paint that capture the girl's floating head and the figure of an angel, both outlined in black. Here, in somewhat contradiction to what is depicted, the contrast of tones gives the figures a greater physical presence, allowing these small patches of canvas to escape the more submerged world around them.

Another important work from this period, and one that successfully blends Nara's drawing and painting practices, is *Make the Road, Follow the Road* (1990) (Fig. 48). Here, he uses the bold black line

Fig. 44
Drawings, 1988, Acrylic, colored pencil, and pencil on paper, each 8 ¼ × 5 ¹¹⁄₁₆ in. (21 × 14.5 cm)

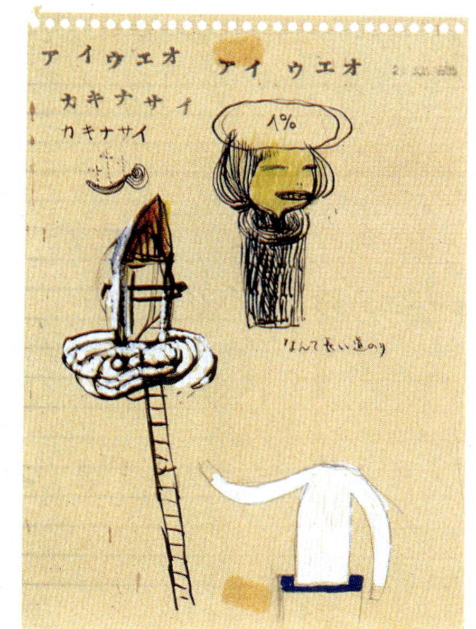
アイウエオ アイウエオ
カキナサイ
カキナサイ
1%
なんて長い道のり

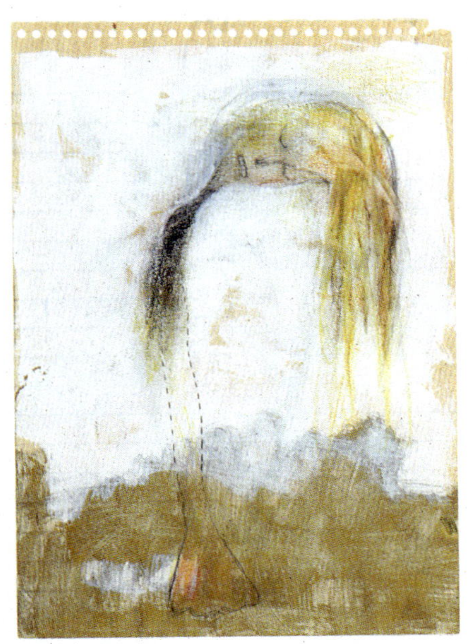

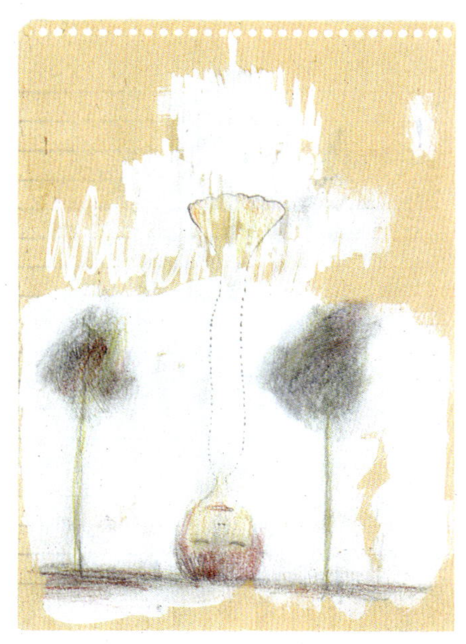

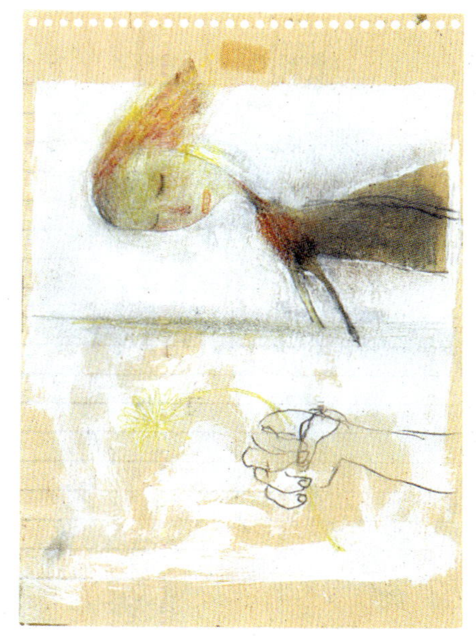

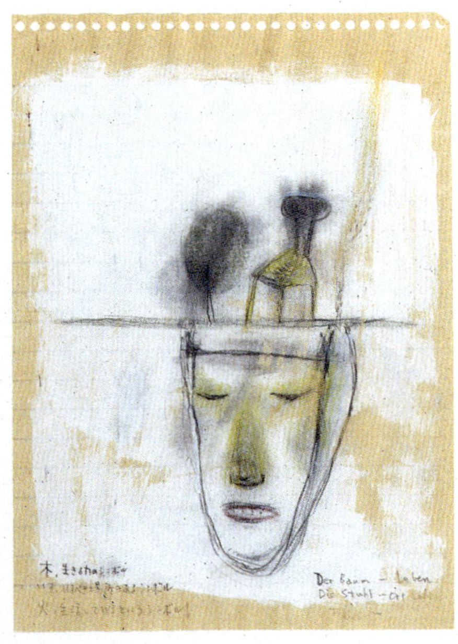
Der Baum – Leben

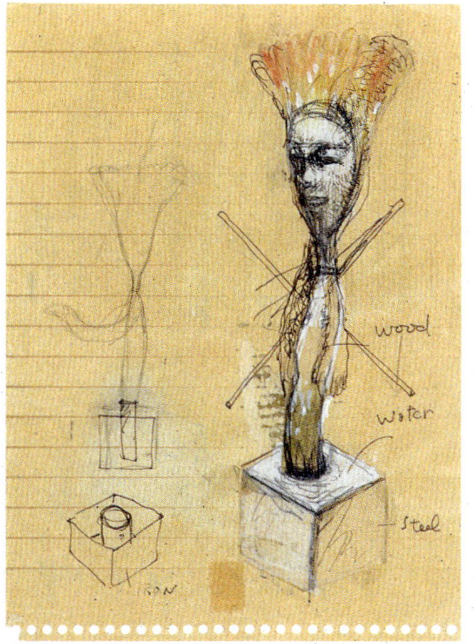
wood
water
steel
IRON

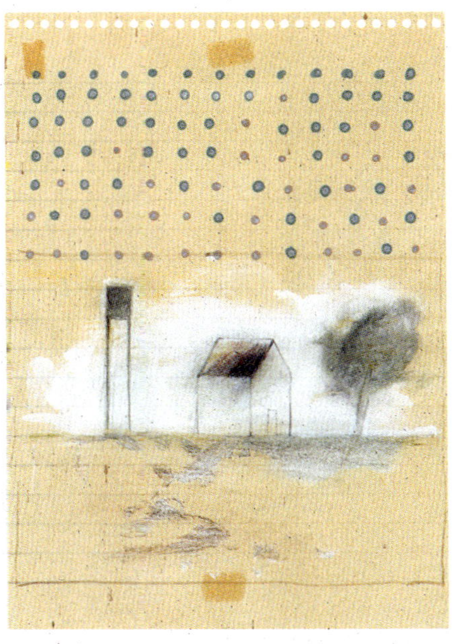

sparingly in a work that is thematically closer to *Give You the Flower*. A young girl presents a knife to a standing cat, although it is unclear whether it is a gift-giving gesture or a threat of aggression. In her other hand is a small fire from which a trail of bold red streaks across the surface like a bloody cut, in contrast to the more insubstantial treatment of the body that retreats into the canvas. Deeper in the background is the faint outline of a lone house, overpainted with a blanket of radiant yellow. These layers create a shallow depth and are at variance with the spatial dimension of the figures. Once again, the potential for physical pain suffuses this imagined childlike world with adult fears.

Nara also explored this tension of otherworldly presence and the corporeal body in his three-dimensional works, for which he began utilizing found materials, such as pieces of leftover wood, to create masks (Fig. 46) and figural forms. There are clear crossovers here with his drawings and paintings, with many of his figural sculptures balancing a house, a fire, or a cross on their heads (Fig. 45). Most, as in *Flaming Head I* (1989) (Fig. 50), are formed from a single block, emerging from the wood in an architectonic column of tubular forms, cubes, and half globes. Overall, these early shamanic masks and totem figures embody a ritualistic, almost primitive presence, in which the deliberately crude carving on raw wood contrasts with the serene faces of children rendered in bright pigments. The playful, relic-like presence of a child, who appears as if born from the wood itself, finds more explicit expression in later sculptural works such as *Pray* (1991) (Fig. 51), built up with papier-mâché and canvas scraps, depicting a child in a cat-eared shroud with hands clasped in prayer. In this early rendition of the child dressed as animal, a figure that he would continue to develop into the 1990s, Nara uses the tactility of the material and the precariousness of the figure's tilted posture to capture a sense of vulnerability. At the same time, the work carries a whisper of Shinto influence in its resemblance to the figure of Jizō.

Nara's paintings gain further strength around this time through the size of his figures, increased sometimes to the extent that they overpower their surroundings. The giant scale of the girls in *Sorry, Just Not Big Enough* (1988) (Fig. 53) and *Romantic Catastrophe* (1988) (Fig. 52), for example, recall Alice's unexpected growth in Wonderland or Gulliver in Lilliput. With awkward charm, they hold up their hands, offering either a sprout or a light, perhaps as symbols of hope.

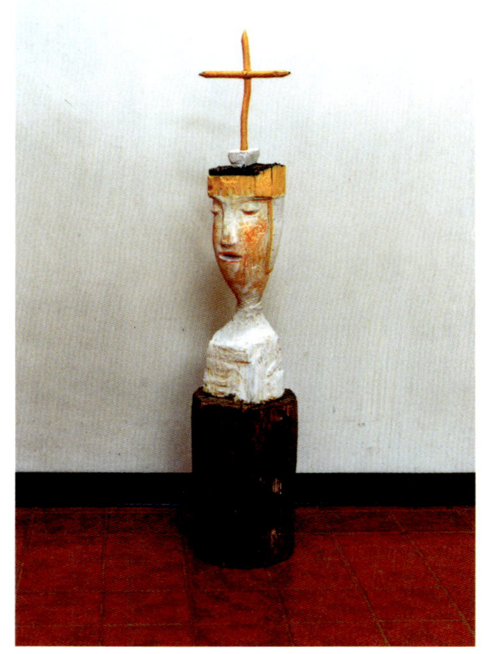

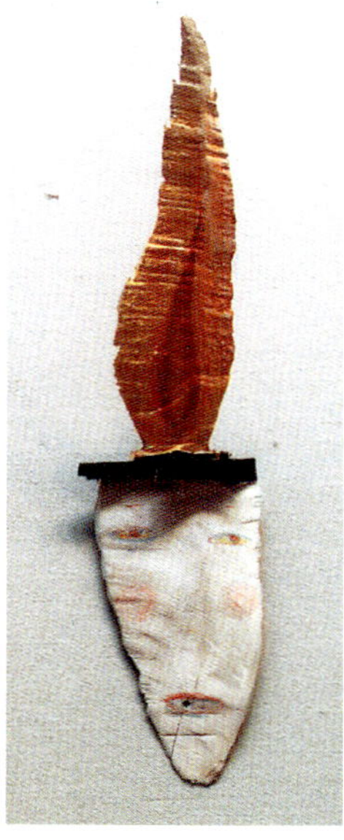

Fig. 45
Untitled, 1988, Acrylic and colored pencil on carved wood, h. 38 3/16 in. (97 cm)

Fig. 46
Untitled, 1986, Acrylic and colored pencil on carved wood, Size unknown

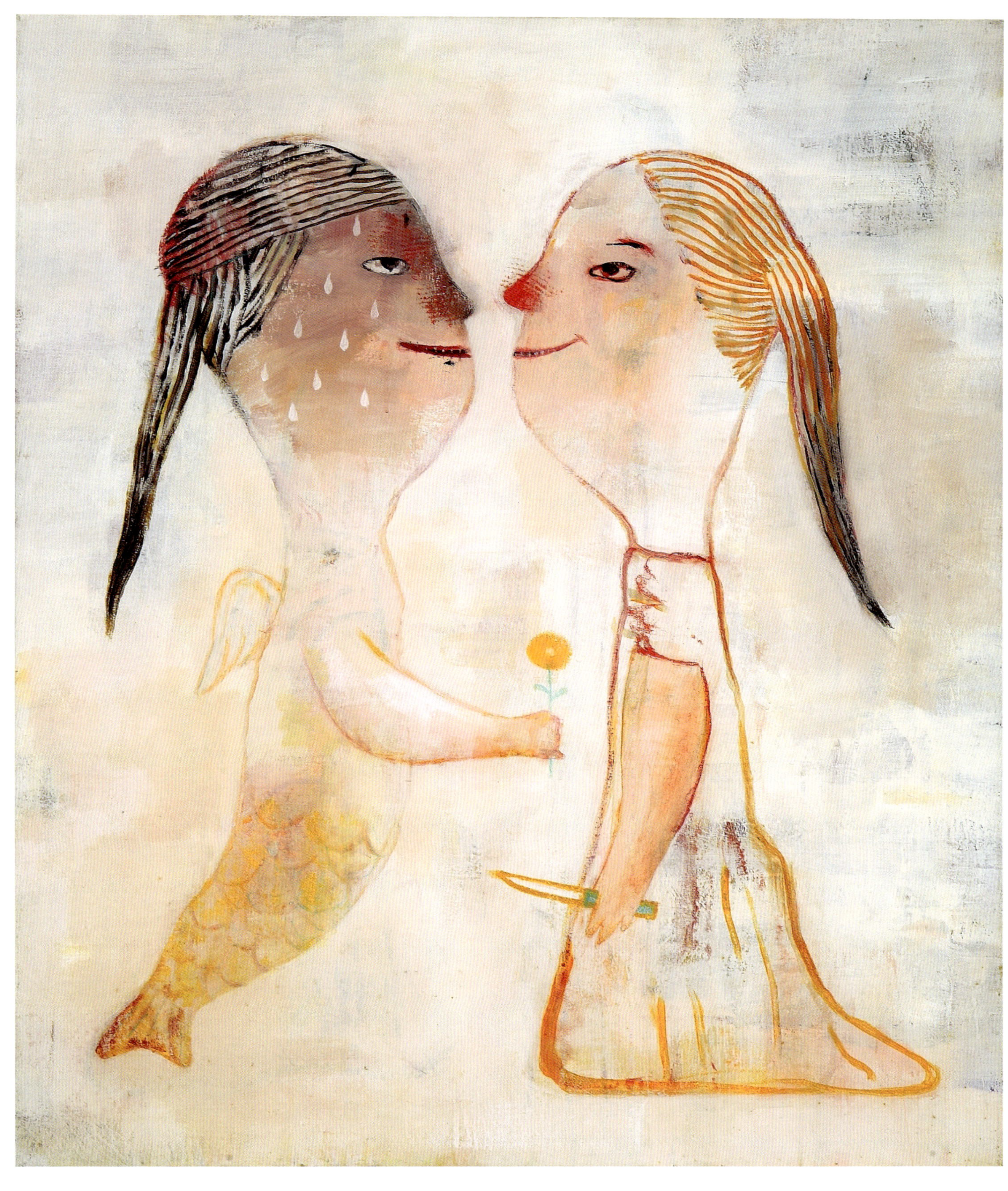

Fig. 47
Give You the Flower,
1990, Acrylic on canvas,
43 11⁄16 × 36 3⁄16 in. (111 × 92 cm)

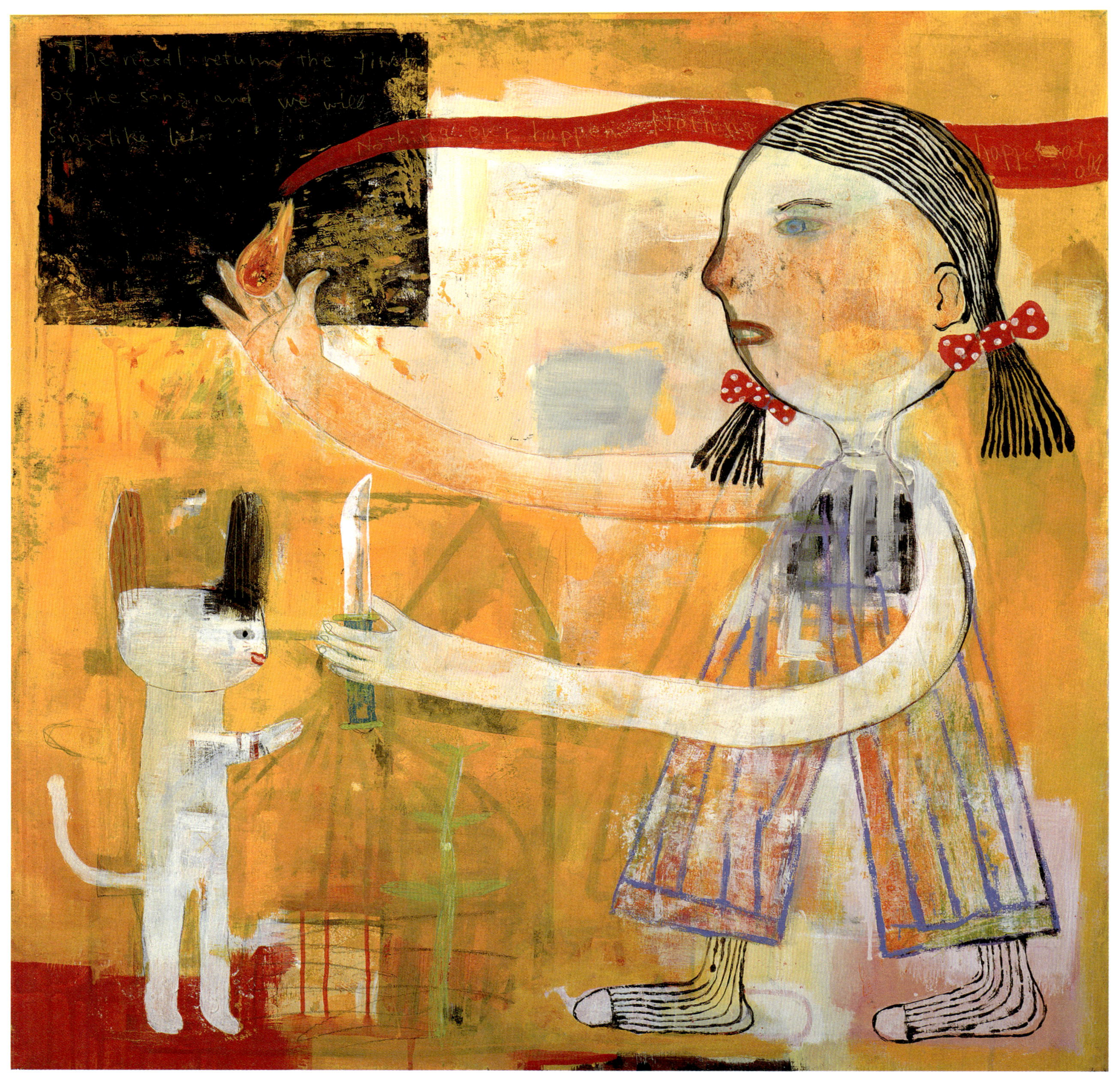

Fig. 48
Make the Road, Follow the Road, 1990, Acrylic on canvas, 39 ⅜ × 39 ⅜ in. (100 × 100 cm)

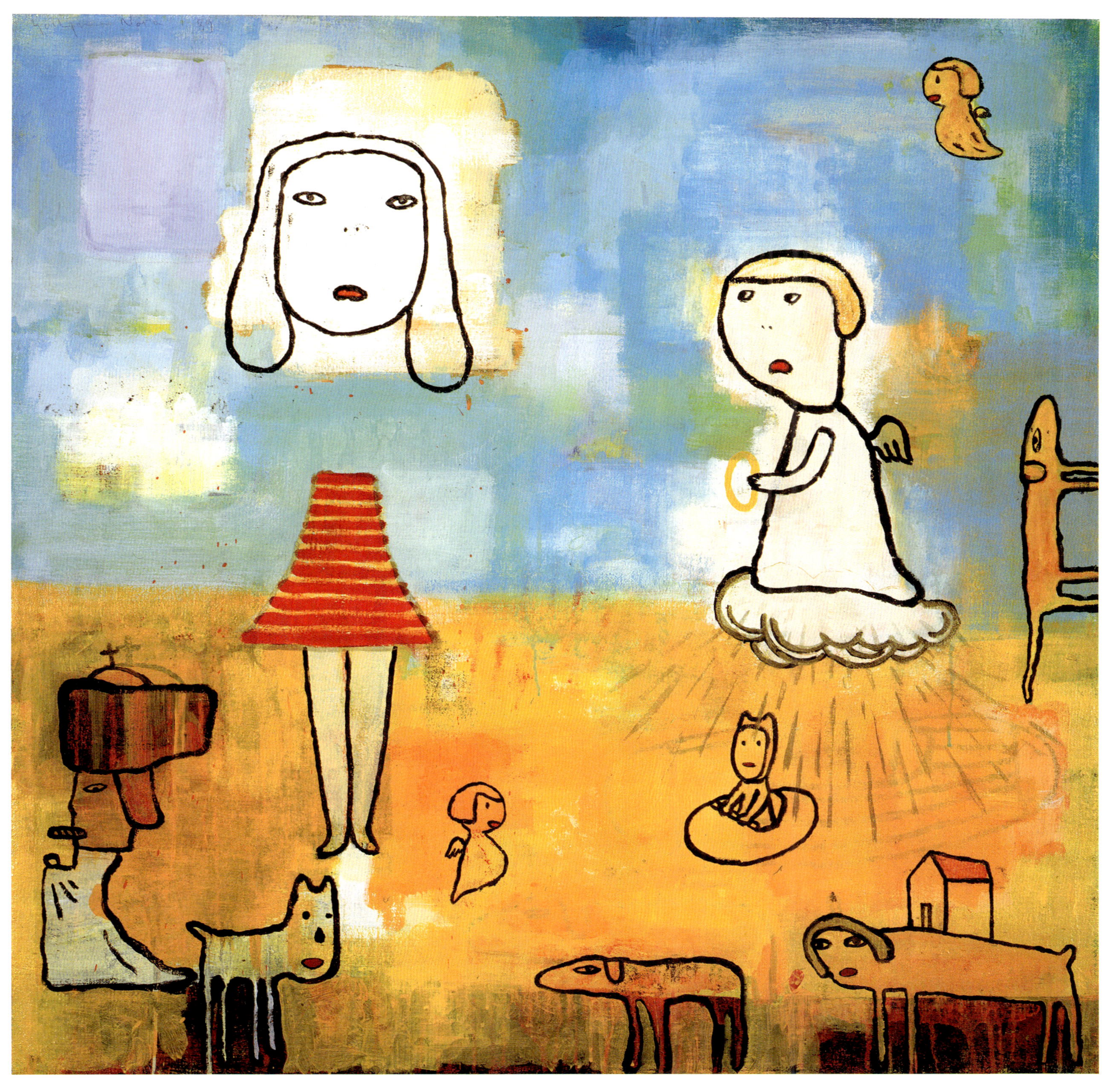

Fig. 49
People on the Cloud, 1989,
Acrylic on canvas,
39 ⅜ × 39 ⅜ in. (100 × 100 cm)

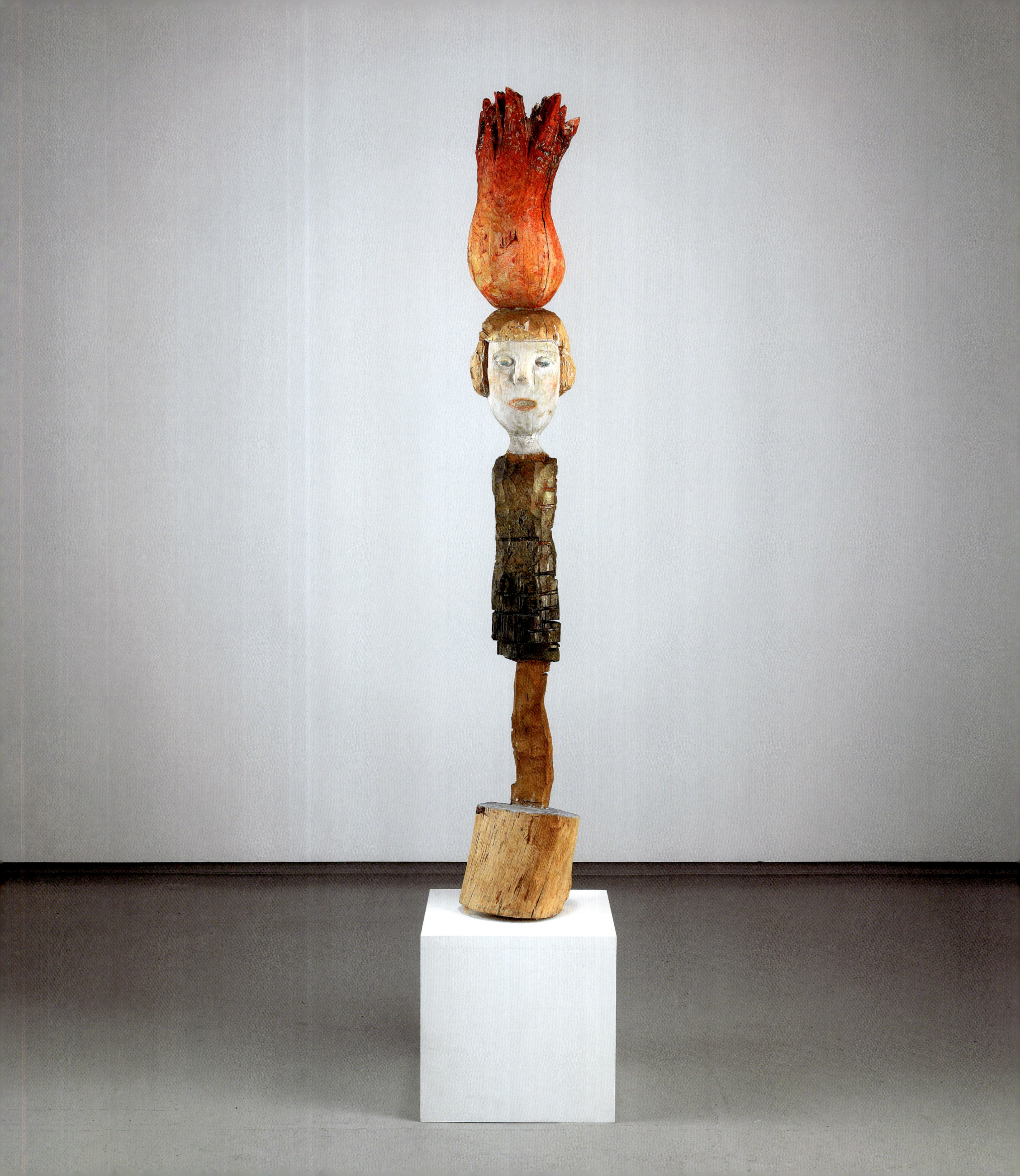

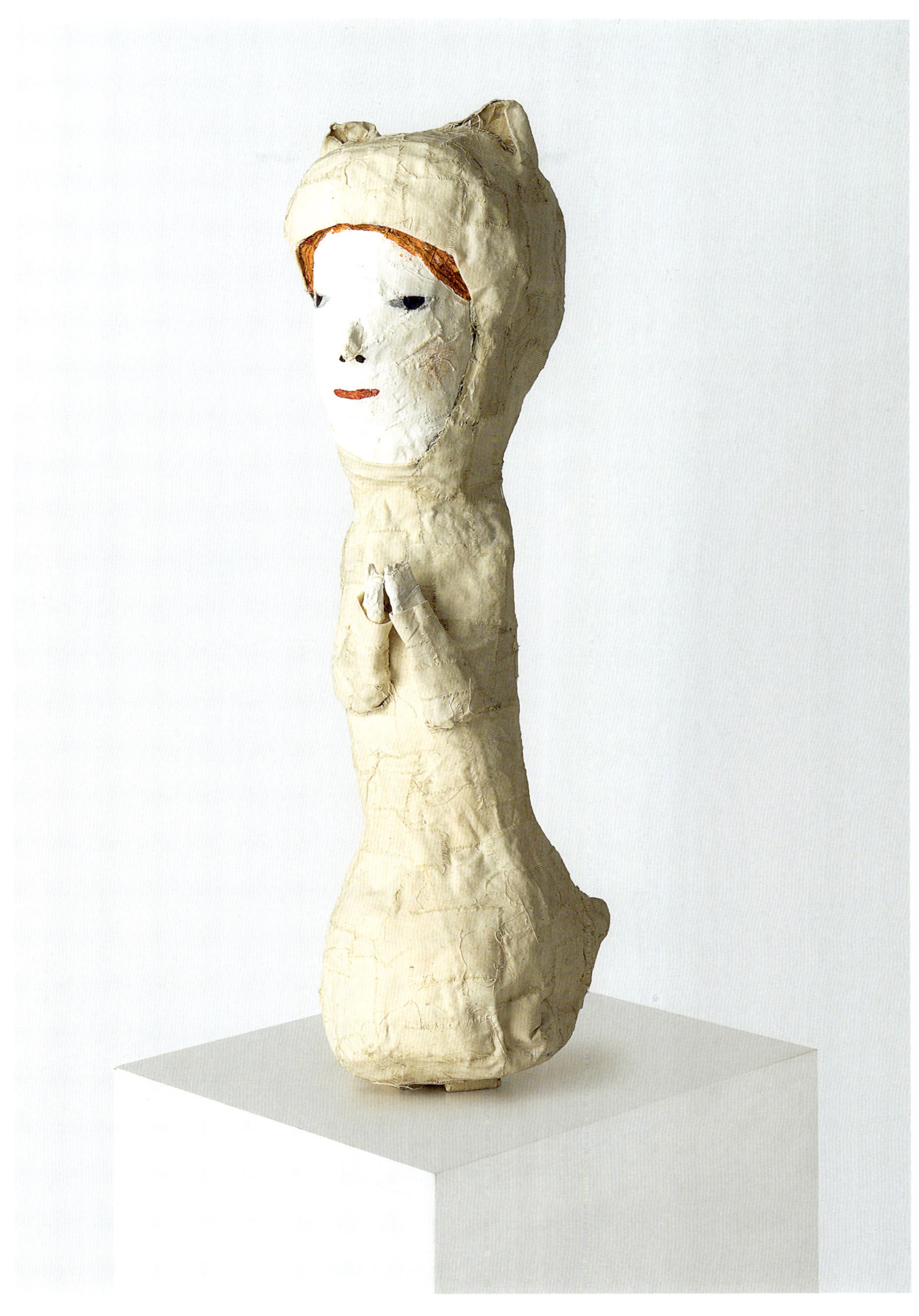

Fig. 50 (opposite)
Flaming Head I, 1989, Acrylic on wood, 60 ⅞ × 9 ⅛ × 10 13⁄16 in. (154.7 × 23.2 × 27.5 cm)

Fig. 51
Pray, 1991, Acrylic on papier-mâché and canvas collage, h. 26 ¾ in. (68 cm)

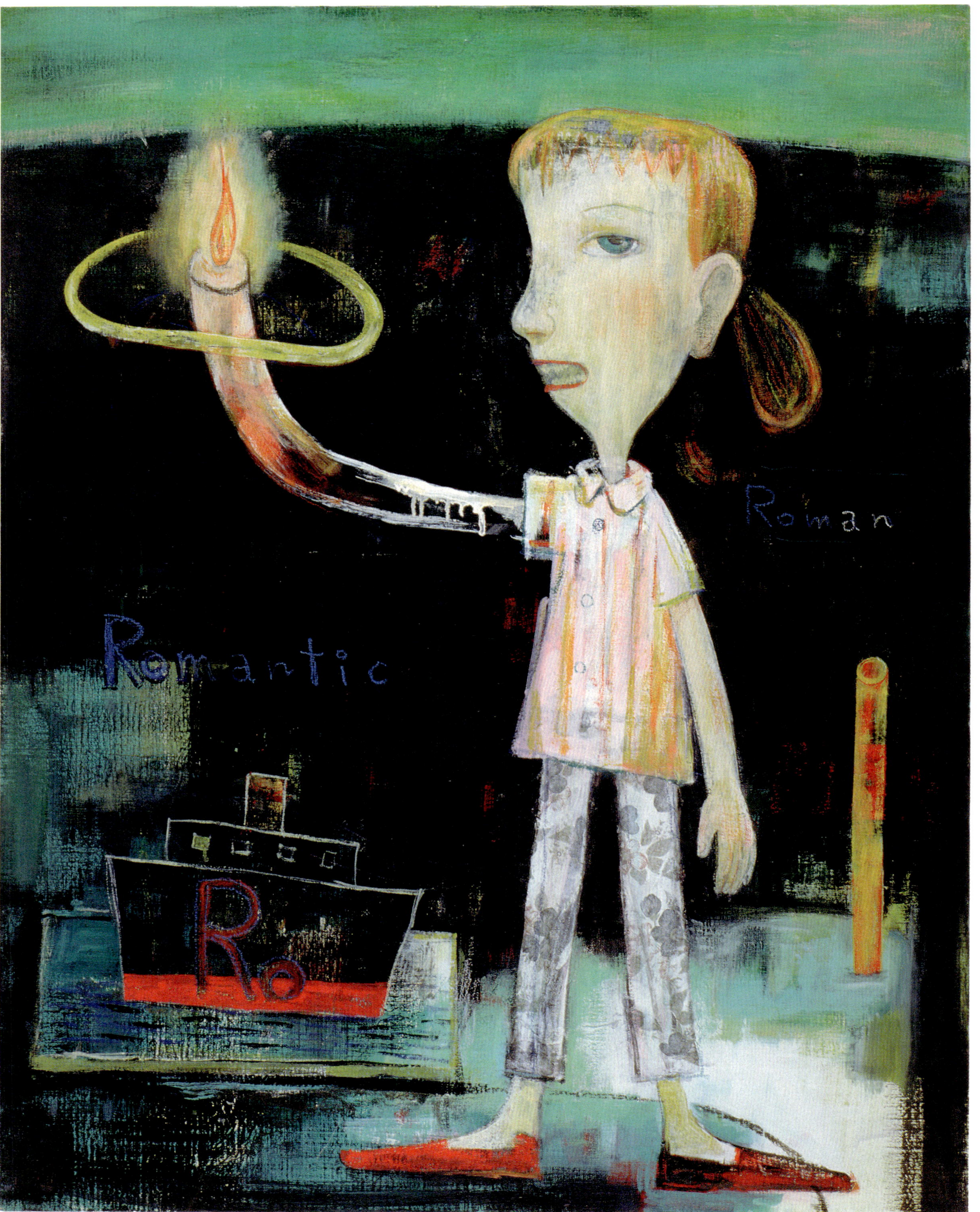
Roman
Romantic
Ro

Romantic Catastrophe, one of Nara's strongest paintings from this period, with its vivid treatment of greens and blacks, shows traces of German Neo-Expressionism. The ponytailed girl stands bold, tall, and poised above a ship while what appears to be a submarine's periscope emerges from the sea. Her steadfastness and haloed flame make her appear like a statuesque lighthouse in the choppy seas. But her wary eye staring out toward the viewer and her opened mouth suggest that she is crying in pain or roaring to be heard in the dark night. In these later works, Nara moves away from the ambiguity of a narrative theme and begins to concentrate on central figures who embody greater emotional depth, setting the foundation for his signature paintings of big-headed girls.

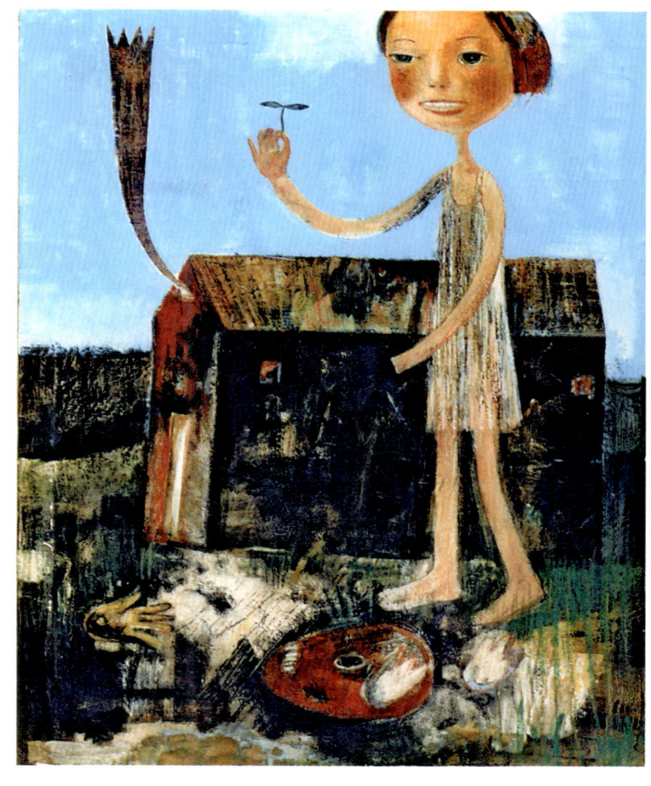

Fig. 52 (opposite)
Romantic Catastrophe, 1988, Acrylic and colored pencil on canvas, 45 15/16 × 35 13/16 in. (116.7 × 90.9 cm)

Fig. 53
Sorry, Just Not Big Enough, 1988, Acrylic and tempera on board, 35 13/16 × 28 5/8 in. (90.9 × 72.7 cm)

Those Big-Headed Girls

> **It is as if I'm confirming my own sense of self—as if I am speaking to myself (and sometimes I am) as I paint the face . . . but at some point it starts to develop its own personality, like something I can't control. And it asks of me to finish it quickly. That's something I'm conscious of. I'm not painting for someone else. I'm painting for myself, or, more accurately, I'm painting for what is being painted. Because midway through that process of painting, there emerges a sense of responsibility to give it form.**[1]

In 1991 Nara painted *The Girl with the Knife in Her Hand* (Fig. 56), a seminal work that marked the beginning of his paintings of big-headed girls. On a canvas of sumptuous purples stands a little girl in a ruby-red dress staring up at her audience: us, the adults who loom over her. We take in the exaggerated roundness of her face, her wide bean-shaped eyes, and the lock of hair grazing her forehead. And then we notice the knife in her hand. In that moment, any assumptions we may have had about her innocence are overturned. Outlined in thick black lines, *The Girl with the Knife in Her Hand* stands in a space between the flattened surface of drawing, the world of illustrations and comics, and the material textures of painting. We see elements of Nara's earlier works and influences, such as the use of bold outlines, which can be traced to his 1989 *Irrlichter* (Fig. 42), and the motif of the girl with a knife from *Make the Road, Follow the Road* (1990) (Fig. 48), but in its pared-down simplicity, the persona of the child has become emboldened. She exerts a personality that is recognizable, perhaps even identifiable: we all know that person who struggles against the restraints of having to be good.

This chapter focuses on Nara's iconic images of big-headed girls and their formal development over the course of the 1990s and early 2000s. The aim is to show how he moved from his earlier enigmatic and narrative-driven worlds of childhood imagination to figurative images that thematize the internal conflicts of child/adult subjectivities. Of particular importance is how he constructed a pictorial language that explores qualities associated with childlikeness and how, in the 1990s, his work responded to Japanese subcultures. The chapter is divided into two key periods, 1991–95 and 1995–2001, and is bookended by key exhibitions that propelled Nara's career, including a series of international exhibitions curated by Takashi Murakami under the theme of Superflat.

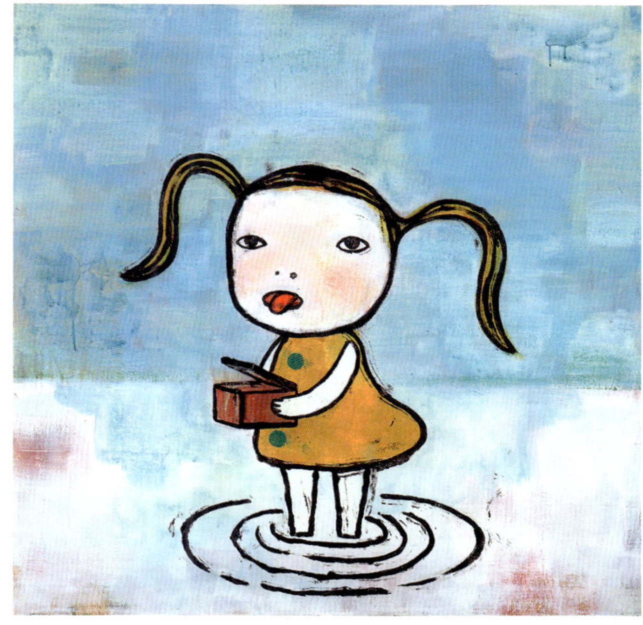

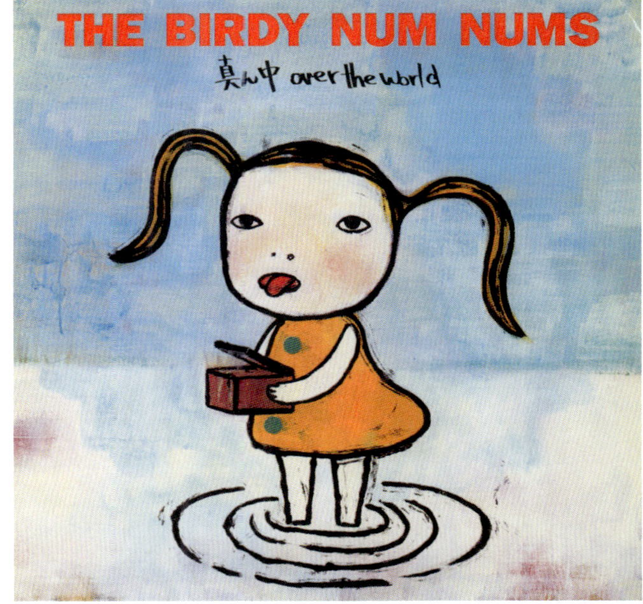

Fig. 54
Pandora's Box, 1990, Acrylic on canvas, 35 7/16 × 35 7/13 in. (90 × 90 cm)

Fig. 55
The Birdy Num Nums, *Mannaka over the World*, King Size Records, Germany, 1991

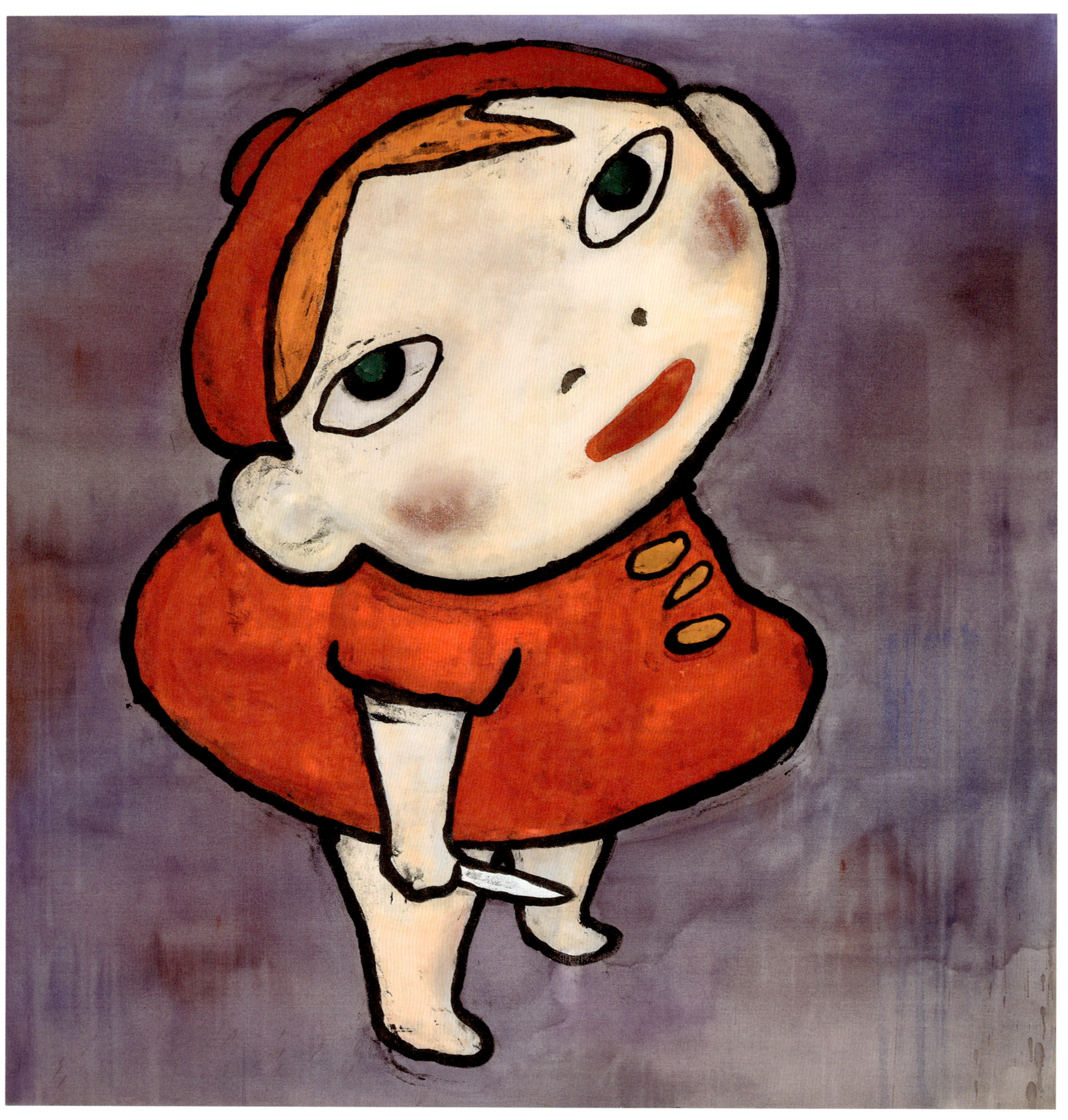

Fig. 56
The Girl with the Knife in Her Hand, 1991, Acrylic on canvas, 59 ¼ × 55 ⅛ in. (150.5 × 140 cm)

This chapter also integrates a visual analysis of Nara's works with broader discussions, including the concept of *kawaii*, the importance of subculture versus the mainstream, and the relevance and limitations of the Superflat manifesto in relation to Nara's works. Providing a coalition of voices and perspectives, it speaks to the atmosphere of productive creativity in the 1990s art world, when artists contributed to cultural landscapes that went beyond their disciplinary and territorial borders. The chapter concludes with some of the artistic directions Nara took after 2001, as he set the stage for his big-headed girls to "grow up," moving away from that 1991 knife-wielding child in a red dress to a quieter, older one who just wants to be left alone.

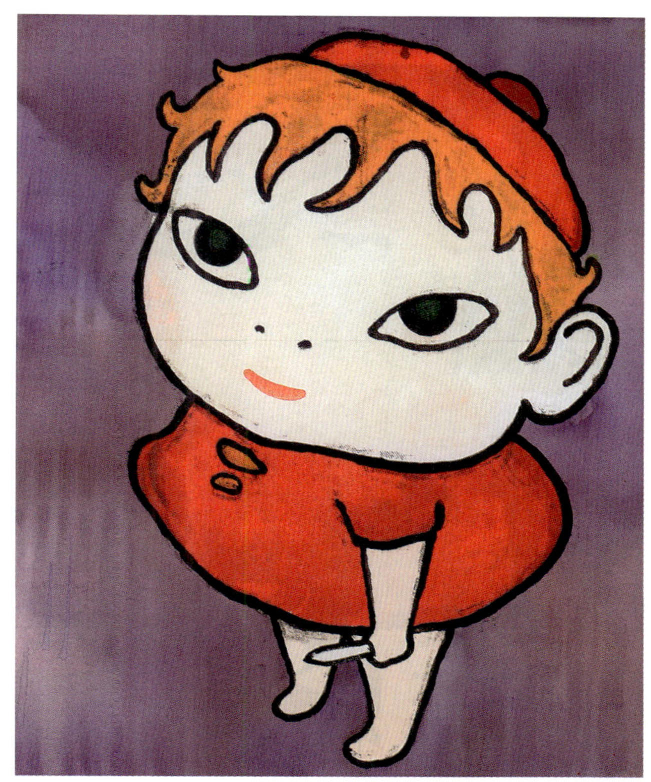

Fig. 57
The Girl with the Knife II,
1993, Acrylic on canvas,
39 ⅜ × 31 ½ in. (100 × 80 cm)

Early Beginnings

The Girl with the Knife in Her Hand was first shown at the Kunstakademie Düsseldorf's annual student show in 1992. This was a much-anticipated event at the school: at a time before the dominance of fairs and high-profile art-world events, the graduation show provided important exposure for emerging artists. Nara, unlike many Japanese students studying abroad, did not receive a government grant or scholarship to attend art school, supporting himself instead with various part-time jobs, including as a dishwasher in a Japanese restaurant. He had already gained some recognition before his graduation: in 1990 he started working with the Amsterdam-based Galerie d'Eendt, and in 1991, a local indie band, The Birdy Num Nums, used Nara's painting *Pandora's Box* on the cover of their album *Mannaka over the World* (Figs. 54 and 55). That same year, Nara received his first review in *Bijutsu techō*, then the leading art journal in Japan. Nevertheless, for an artist living abroad with little money to his name, there was much at stake.

In the early 1990s, American artists dominated the contemporary art scene in Germany, and only a small number of Japanese artists were well known in Europe, almost exclusively those who had already gained international recognition in the late 1960s and 1970s, such as Yayoi Kusama, Yoko Ono, Shusaku Arakawa, and On Kawara. Nara's paintings were, therefore, not initially seen through the lens of Japanese contemporary art and even less as part of Japanese popular culture. Indeed, when Jörg Johnen, a Cologne-based gallerist, first saw Nara's

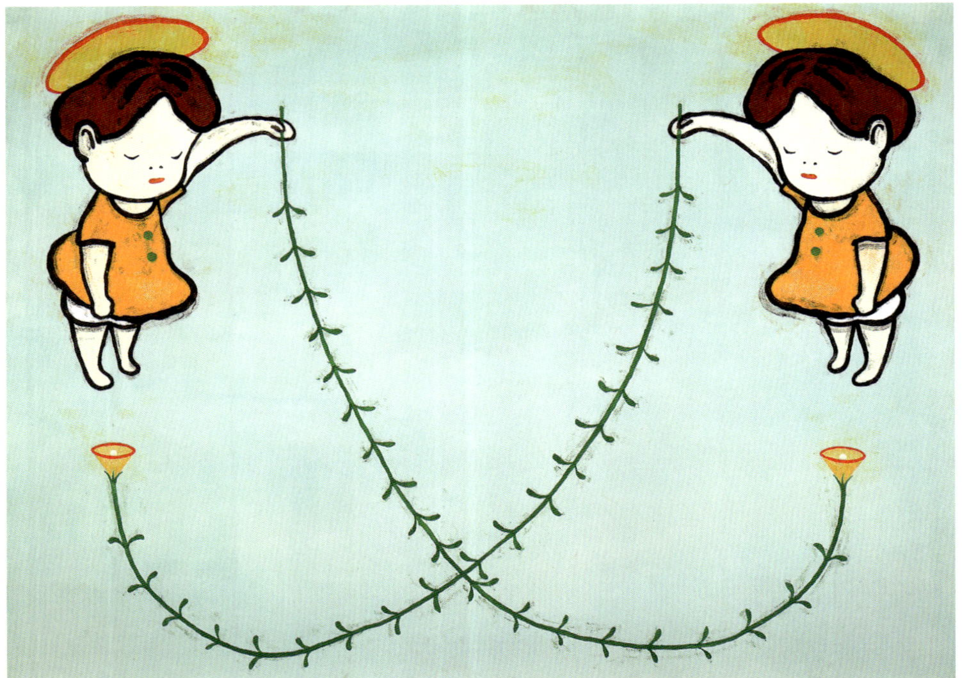

work at the Kunstakademie graduation show, he was surprised to learn that the artist was Japanese. What had drawn Johnen's attention was that Nara differed significantly from his peers through oddly humorous and menacing works that, while containing Pop and comic elements, exuded a genuine painterly quality.[2]

Johnen quickly took Nara on as an artist, adding him to an impressive roster of established names that included Thomas Ruff, Dan Graham, and Katharina Fritsch. Subsequently, Nara, with the help of Johnen, moved to Cologne and into a bare-bones studio in an abandoned factory. The following year, Johnen selected *The Girl with the Knife in Her Hand* for a show at his gallery, Johnen + Schöttle. It was an exhilarating time to be in Germany. The fall of the Berlin Wall had reignited the cultural vitality of the country, and many artists from different backgrounds lived and worked in close quarters in the old Gothic city. For Nara, it was an enriching and productive time, but also a simple one: "I would ride my bike around Cologne, checking out the gallery district, enjoying a cup of coffee in a café, and then start painting in the evening. I spent every day like this, and I wanted for nothing in my life in Germany."[3]

The popularity of *The Girl with the Knife in Her Hand* encouraged Nara to continue exploring this new aesthetic direction. The most significant change from his earlier work was removing the patchwork

Fig. 58
Lampflowers, 1993, Acrylic on canvas, 59 1/16 × 78 3/4 in. (150 × 200 cm)

scenes of mismatched motifs in favor of a bare monochrome background. The seeming simplicity of Nara's big-headed-girl compositions—a foregrounded image of a girl against an empty background—belies the formal difficulties he encountered in playing with this new structure to generate a corpus of meaningful work, and some of his experiments within this scheme were more successful than others. Nara rarely plans the thematic direction of a work in advance, although the germination of a painting may start from a sketch or a drawing. Instead his focus lies in the formal construction of the figure, which can change based on instinct as he paints. He is unconcerned with what sort of character, whether rebellious, lonely, sweet, pathetic, or cheeky, will emerge, trusting that in the act of creating, it will develop its own personality organically.

Nara's tendency in his earlier works to repeat motifs extended now to reiterating stylistic features: a type of line, a compositional arrangement, or a color palette. This allowed him to shift from depicting motifs drawn from his memories to creating a personal style that enhanced or tested what can be seen as universal markers of a childlike sensibility. Three early paintings from 1993, *The Girl with the Knife II* (Fig. 57), *Lampflowers* (Fig. 58), and *Untitled* (Fig. 60), are examples of this method of creative repetition. They also show how Nara, in the early evolution of the big-headed girl, experimented within this pictorial schema until he either achieved a breakthrough or exhausted the possibilities of its revisions.

In *Lampflowers*, Nara portrays the mirrored image of a girl. Painted in yellows and baby blues, she is seen with her head down, holding a long thorny stem attached to a light bulb / flower. The painting was made for a small exhibition, *Harvest*, held in 1993 at the studio of his friend and fellow artist, the sculptor Shiro Matsui (Fig. 59). When displayed, its curved stems echoed the metal arcs of Matsui's sculptures and played against the wooden beams of the space. While as a stand-alone work, *Lampflowers* may carry less emotive range than *The Girl with the Knife in Her Hand*, its key feature—the long sinuous stem that moves across the surface—transforms more successfully into a skipping rope in *Untitled* (Fig. 60) and a giant lily pad in *Walk On I* (1993) (Fig. 61), a notable work that also exemplifies the asymmetrical compositions Nara was fond of during this period. While the lily flower, recalling a specific type found in northern Japan, references Nara's upbringing, it plays an important compositional role as well, its fragile coiling pulling the viewer back toward the center of the canvas.

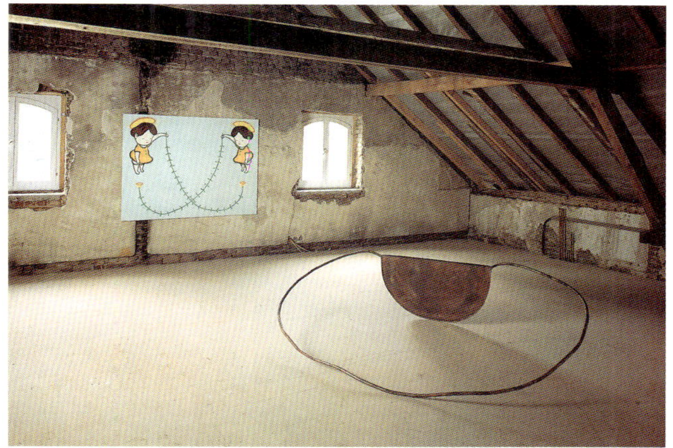

Fig. 59
Exhibition view: *Harvest '93*, Haus Bockdorf, Kempen, Germany, 1993

The connective themes among Nara's paintings in this period extend to his works in other media, particularly his assemblages of readymades. These installations may seem anomalous for an artist better known for his figurative paintings and works on paper, but they have in fact always been part of his practice and are often shown alongside his paintings in exhibitions. Nara's early readymades also offer insight into the humorous side of his personality and reflect his obsessive collecting, whether of albums, books, small toys, or other tchotchkes, all of which sit in his studio space and form a crucial part of his work environment (Fig. 62).

Nara arranged these early readymade installations in ways that reenacted human situations in order to emphasize the objects' artificiality—a deviation from his paintings of the time, which, through their highly stylized treatments, foregrounded their subjects' emotions. Nonetheless, these two different approaches exist on the same spectrum of a creative practice in which Nara teases out aspects of human nature through the tension between subject and object, the real and the fictional. In *Monkey Brothers* (1994) (Fig. 63), two windup musical toys are displayed on pedestals, while in the space between them a hinged picture frame displays their portraits like a family keepsake, announcing their identities as brothers. *Telepathy* (1994) (Fig. 65) is composed of two small doll figures tilted with their heads touching, the absurdity of their so-called telepathy amplified by their cheap plastic material and the scene's saccharine sweetness. In *Don't Cry, No Tears, Love Me* (1994) (Fig. 64), three tambourines backlit with fairy lights are edged with small plastic heads like girls in a chorus line. The title of the work, inspired by a Neil Young song, is broken up among the three tambourines to capture the pauses in the line when it is sung.

Nara's most daring readymade installation was his 1994 *Hula Hula Garden* (Figs. 66 and 67), first shown in a solo show at Galerie d'Eendt in Amsterdam and later adapted to different sites. For this work Nara placed lifelike dolls face down, spread out on a carpet of artificial grass and flowers or on a wooden floor among books and fallen toys. For some of these installations, Nara mounted masklike heads on the walls, watching silently and adding a sense of menace (Fig. 66). In others, particularly the earliest renditions on artificial grass, the still, faceless dolls evoke mass deaths as much as sleeping children (Fig. 67). Nara's staging, as with his paintings, adds a shadow of threat and dark humor to an otherwise innocent childlike world.

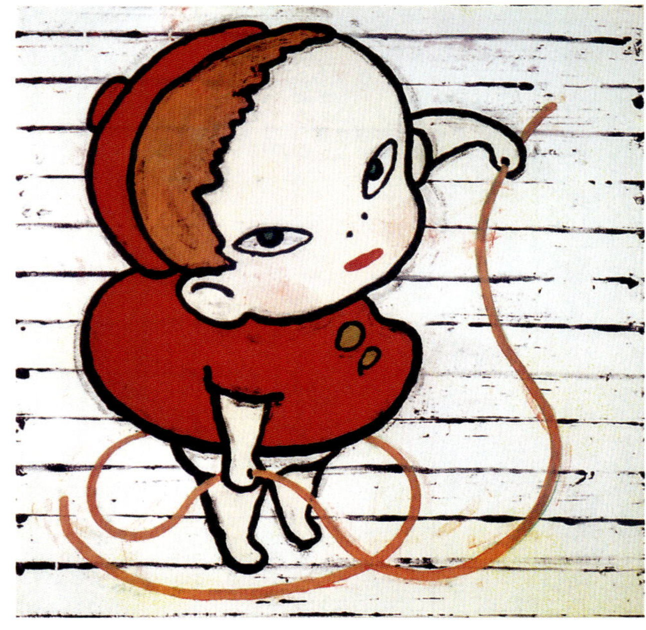

Fig. 60
Untitled, 1993, Acrylic on canvas, 34 ⅝ × 34 ⅝ in. (88 × 88 cm)

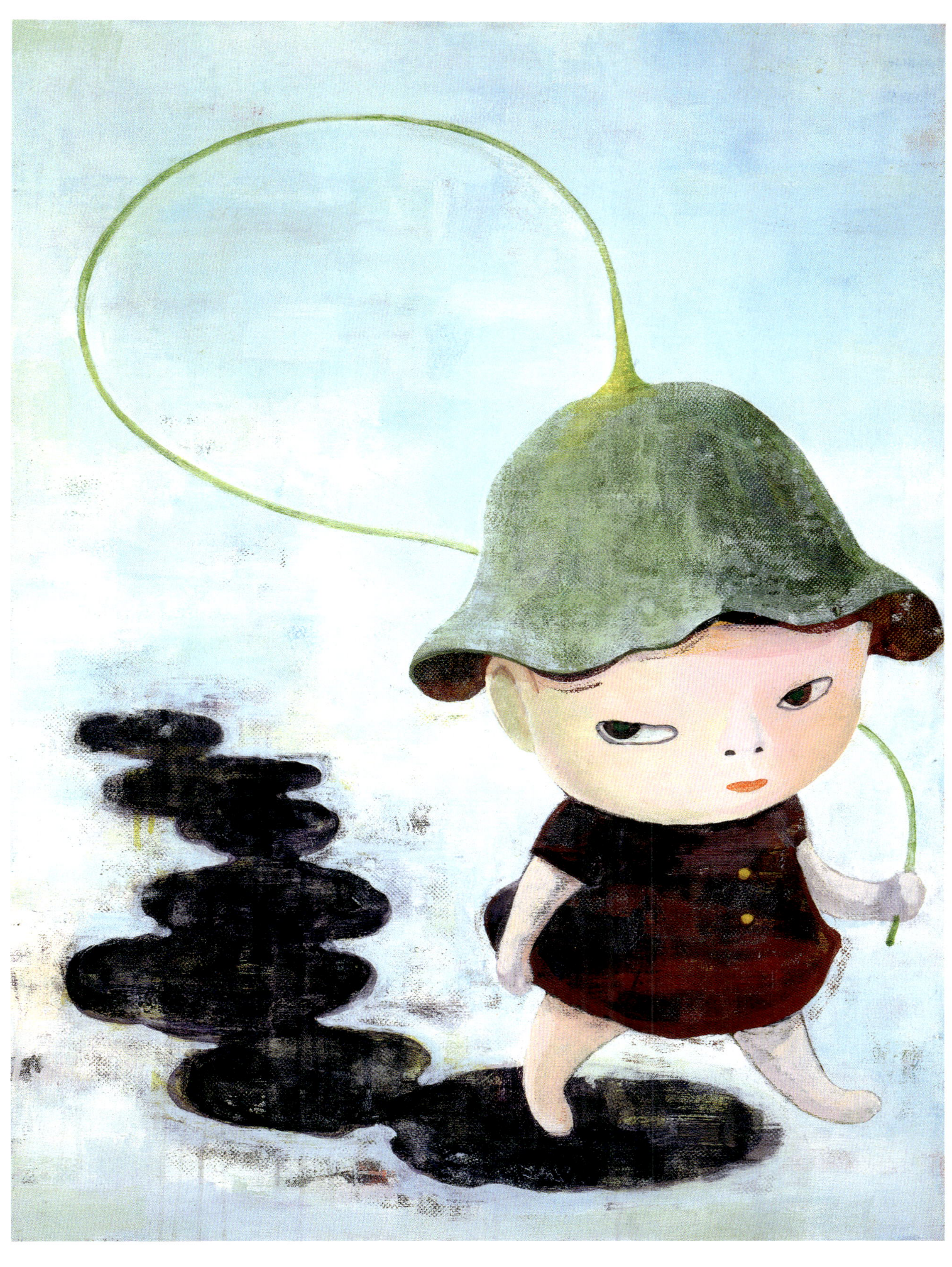

Fig. 61
Walk On I, 1993, Acrylic on canvas, 39 ⅜ × 29 ½ in. (100 × 75 cm)

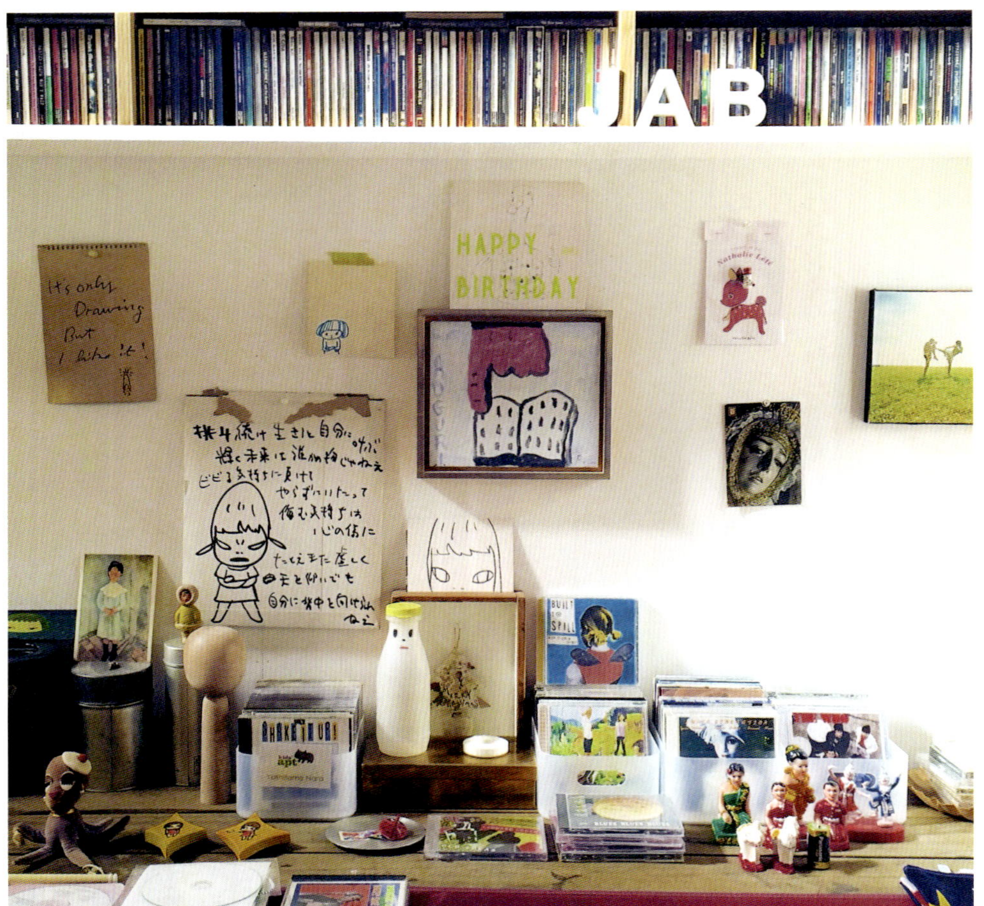

Fig. 62
Nara's studio, 2014

The Aesthetics and Agency of *Kawaii*

> ***Kawai-i*** **(adjective): 1. Looks miserable and raises sympathy. Pitiable. Pathetic. Piteous. 2. Attractive. Cannot be neglected. Cherished. Beloved. 3. Has a sweet nature. Lovely. (a) (of faces and figures of young women and children) adorable. Attractive. (b) (like children) innocent. Obedient. Touching. 4. (of things and shapes) attractively small. Small and beautiful. 5. Trivial. Pitiful (used with slight disdain).**[4]

Within a few years of his 1991 painting, Nara had turned his focus almost exclusively to the singular figure of the child. Perhaps subconsciously, he was developing his own visual language that emphasized the cuteness of children, depicting them in bold colors with large heads, rounded contours, and bean-shaped eyes and situating them in imaginary spaces that can be interpreted as sites of childhood fantasy.

The term *kawaii* began to be used in association with Nara's work in the mid-1990s as he started to attract a larger audience in Japan and abroad. By 2001 it had entered into a global mainstream art lexicon, having been appropriated by the artist Takashi Murakami in his influential Superflat manifesto.[5] An examination of the key meanings of *kawaii* can help establish a foundation upon which to investigate the changes in Nara's pictorial strategies, his engagement with Japanese subcultures, and the term's relevance and limitations within the Superflat discourse.

According to the aforementioned definition, *kawaii* has a wide semantic range, from being sweet and lovely to pitiful and pathetic. What is important to note is that these meanings are descriptions of a mode of response. In 1943 the Nobel Prize–winning ethnologist Konrad Lorenz proposed the idea of *Kindchenschema* (baby schema) as an analytical model that identifies certain traits recognized as being cute—a big head, round face, and large eyes—to determine how cuteness can serve an evolutionary function, triggering protective behavior that increases the likelihood of offspring survival.[6] His work has long been the cornerstone of research on cuteness, but more recent studies have pushed his universalist theory to consider how cuteness, or what can be called the "Aww" factor, can lead to more complex social behaviors, including companionship, cooperative action and play, and communication through emotional reciprocity.[7] Although this generalized "Aww" factor does not take into account cultural differences in social behaviors, it nonetheless stresses how cuteness has agency, which is, at its most primal, an agency of social survival.

Nara's work translates this notion of *kawaii* into a process of aesthetics and affect in which the works he creates can cultivate responses that summon emotions and imaginations that feel familiar and can prompt empathetic connections. There are a number of ways in which he achieves this: first, his paintings utilize colors associated with children, charming figurative forms, and simple compositional structures that facilitate connection with the viewer. Second, the lack of any background scenery limits the potential for narrative context, leaving the image open to multiple responses and interpretations. Third, Nara not only opens up the range of potential meanings but also combines different attributes of *kawaii*, such as being both pitiful and innocent or sympathetic and trivial, into a single work, which further

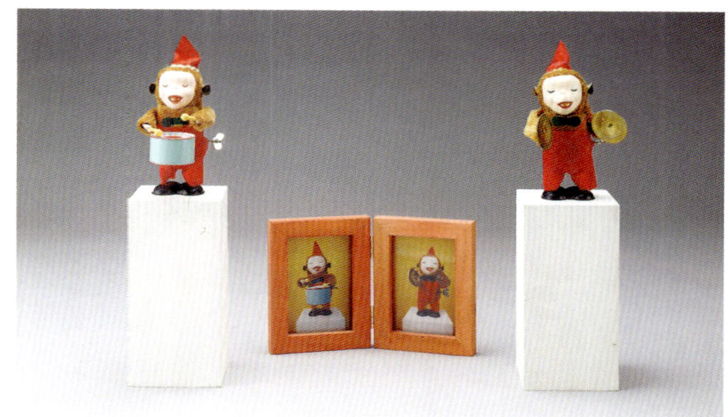

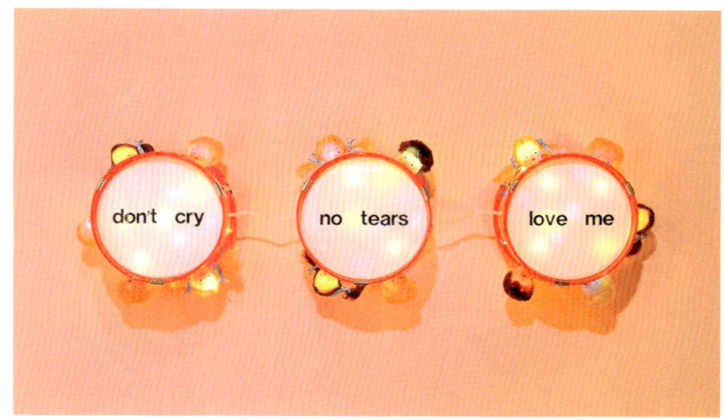

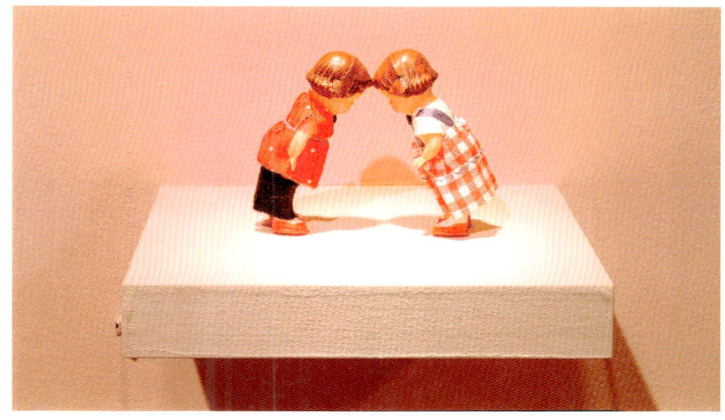

Fig. 63
Monkey Brothers, 1994, Mixed media, Dimensions variable

Fig. 64
Don't Cry, No Tears, Love Me, 1994, Mixed media, 9 1⁄16 × 27 15⁄16 × 5 1⁄2 in. (23 × 71 × 14 cm)

Fig. 65
Telepathy, 1994, Mixed media, 5 1⁄4 × 5 11⁄16 × 4 5⁄16 in. (13.3 × 14.5 × 11 cm)

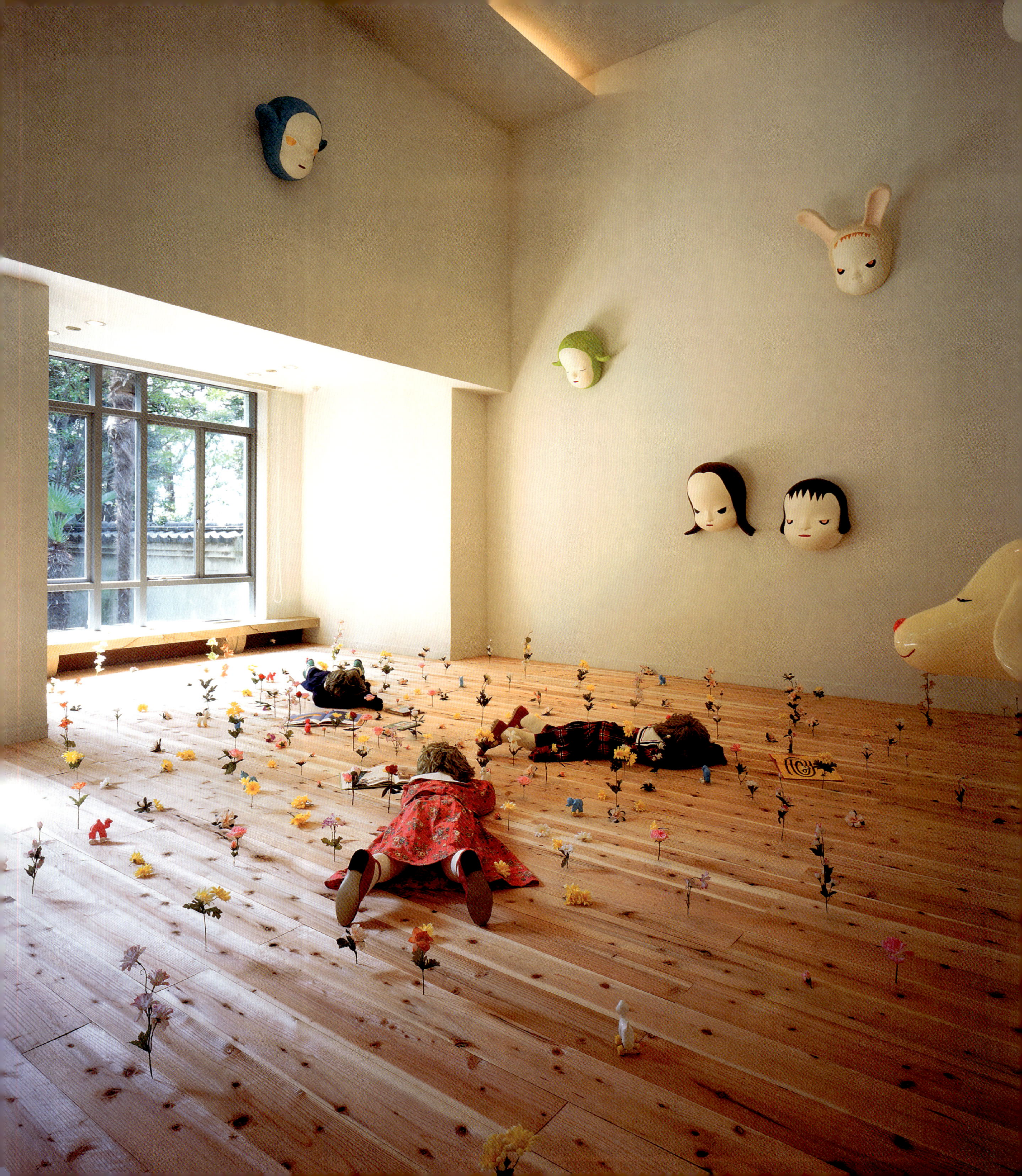

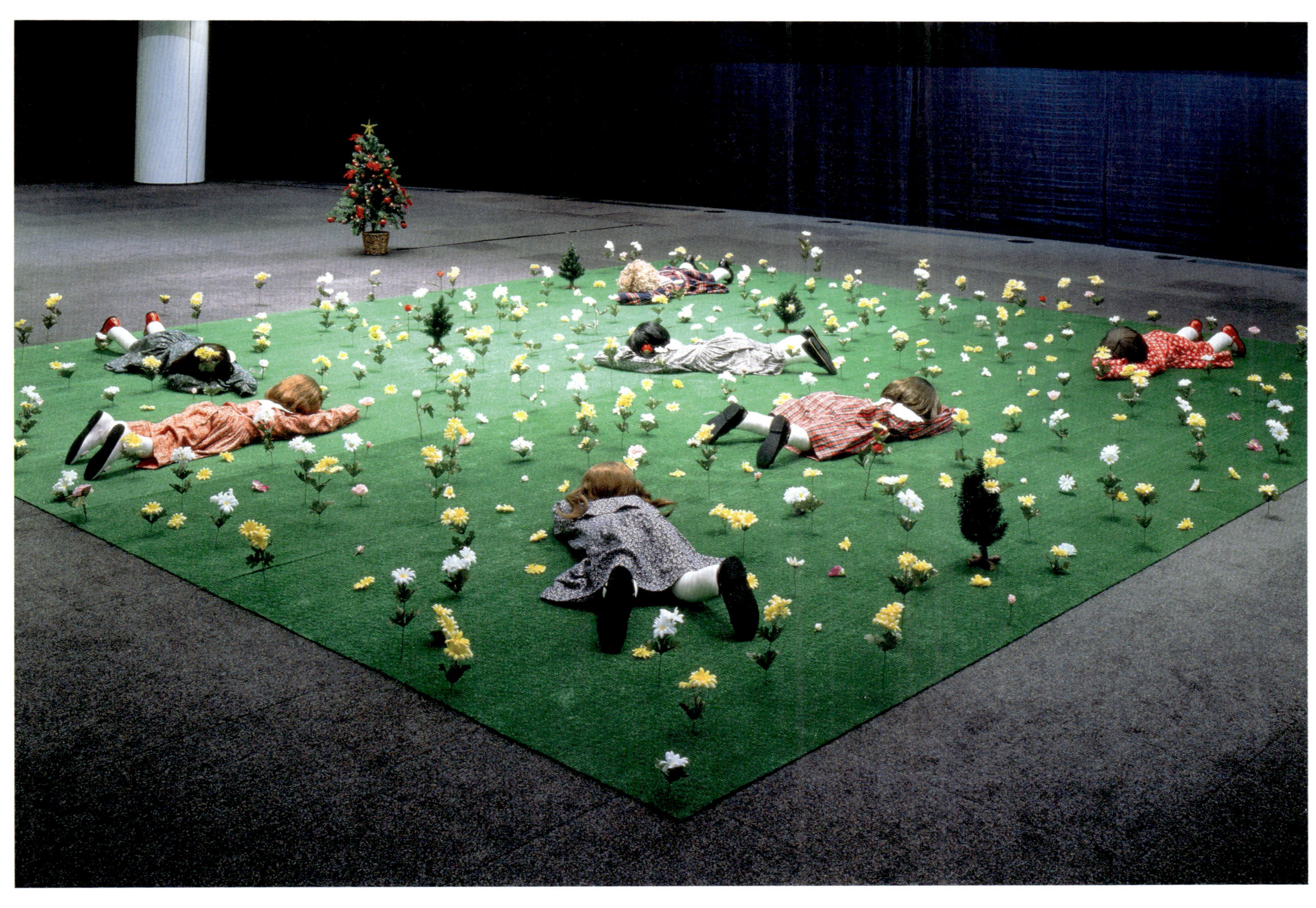

Fig. 66 (opposite)
Hula Hula Garden, 1994, Mixed media, Dimensions variable
Installation view: *Yoshitomo Nara: From the Depth of My Drawer*, Hara Museum of Contemporary Art, Tokyo, 2004

Fig. 67
Hula Hula Garden, 1994, Mixed media, Dimensions variable
Installation view: *Christmas for Sleeping Children*, Itoki Crystal Hall, Osaka, Japan, 1994

undermines the concept as a monolithic construction. Lastly, he is able to entice viewers into his world and invites them to acknowledge the fundamental human behavior of empathy. Nara holds a deep-seated belief that art needs to have the affective capacity to generate empathy and affinities between people who share a delight in the complexities of its expression. The challenge he sets for himself is how to reach that potential, and doing so requires him to transcend his own ego so that his child figures can independently create connections with their viewers.

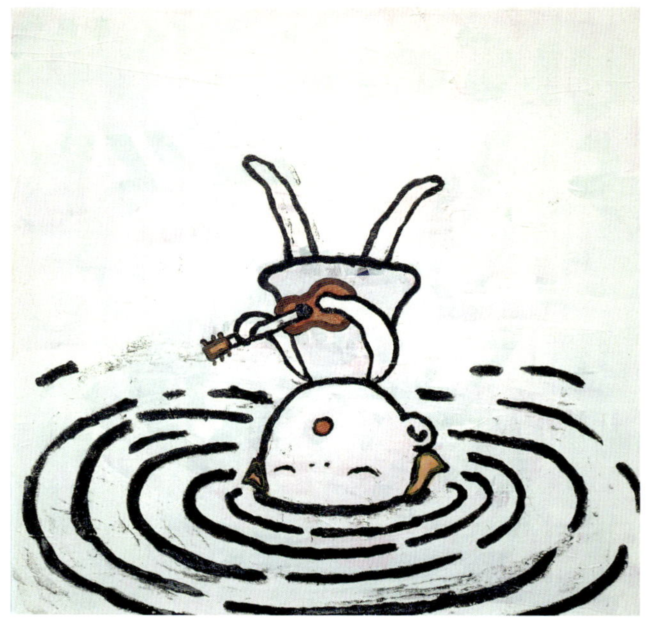

Fig. 68
Rock'n Roll Suicide, 1992,
Acrylic on canvas,
35 7/16 × 35 7/16 in. (90 × 90 cm)

Paintings: 1995–2001

A major turning point in Nara's career came in 1995 when his show *In the Deepest Puddle* opened at SCAI THE BATHHOUSE, one of the leading galleries in Tokyo. In the works that populated this former bathhouse, visitors encountered a cast of children, all exuding brazen confidence and a rebellious obstinacy. Containing some of Nara's strongest works, many of which are now considered touchstones in his oeuvre, the exhibition revealed an artist who had come into his own. What marks the success of these works is Nara's ability, through the dichotomy between the cuteness and vulnerability of children on the one hand and the anger, anxiety, and pain often associated with adult experiences on the other, to transport viewers into the internal world of the child.

A close reading of three paintings shown in this exhibition provides insight into how Nara achieves this imaginative reconstruction of his subjects' internal emotional states through a stripped-down aesthetic. The first painting, *In the Deepest Puddle II* (1995) (Fig. 69), is a continuation of the motifs seen in many earlier renditions of bandaged heads and kids caught in puddles, such as *Rock'n Roll Suicide* (1992) (Fig. 68) and *All Alone* (1986) (Fig. 24). As with *The Girl with the Knife in Her Hand*, Nara, in this work, succeeds in quickly activating the relationship between subject and viewer: here, a little girl with a bandaged head is submerged in a puddle, seeming to walk away while glaring back and rejecting any offers of help. We immediately become both the subject and object of her entangled feelings before we regain our position as viewer. As we return our eyes to the painterly surface of the work, we follow the arc of its asymmetrical composition, landing on the small

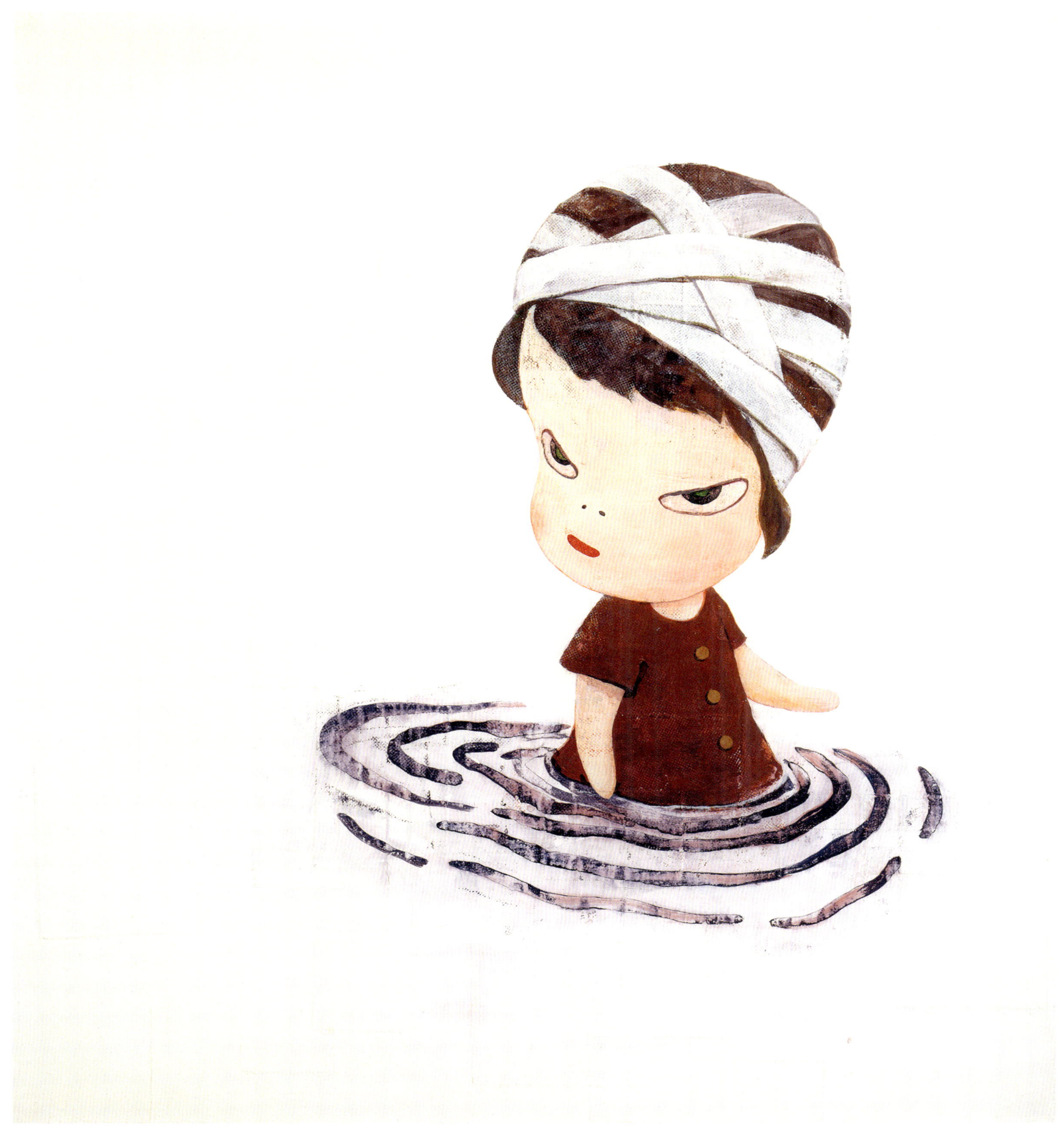

Fig. 69
In the Deepest Puddle II, 1995,
Acrylic on cotton mounted
on canvas, 47 ¼ × 43 5⁄16 in.
(120 × 110 cm)

gap of white space between us and the girl: a place of shallow depth, a space to breathe.

The Longest Night (1995) (Fig. 71) picks up the same color palette as *The Girl with the Knife in Her Hand*, with its striking combination of bold reds and purples that helps lead us into the imaginary world of a child. Here, our big-headed girl walks fearlessly on tall stilts, carrying a Japanese lantern. The absurdity of the image is undercut by the determination of her bold stride—we dare not laugh at the earnestness of her action. The painting is also a reference to a theme made popular in the eighteenth-century *ukiyo-e* prints by artists such as Suzuki Harunobu (1725–1770) (Fig. 70). *Ukiyo* is a term that denotes the leisure districts of Japan in the Edo period (1615–1868), made up of the colorful delights of Kabuki theaters, sumo wrestling, teahouses, and brothels.[8] It was a seductive world of hedonistic pleasures, made all the more appealing by the print industry that idealized the lifestyle of those who inhabited or visited it. Harunobu, one of the leading artists of *ukiyo-e*, was known for his colorful prints of willowy young beauties and *mitate-e* (parody images), which blended puns and allusions from classical literature with contemporary images of courtesans and actors. His aim was to create unexpected juxtapositions of opposites, such as the literary and the profane or the austere and the flamboyant, which, for those able to decode the works, provided a layer of wry humor. Here, Nara's citation of Harunobu carries elements of this *mitate-e* tradition as he turns the Edo motif of a traditional beauty, yielding in posture, into a defiant young girl. Although this reference may not be immediately recognizable to every viewer, it reflects Nara's interest in the art of the Edo period, which he would later pursue more directly.

Another character in Nara's growing portfolio of portrait types is the child dressed in an animal costume, a theme that has roots in his drawings and the sculpture *Pray* (1991) (Fig. 51) and that he developed more fully in two paintings, *Harmless Kitty* (1994) (Fig. 72) and *Abandoned Puppy* (1995) (Fig. 73). The combination of animals and children, a doubling of *kawaii*, pushes the tropes of cute things to touch on themes of solitude, anger, and vulnerability—all complex, contradictory states that he mediates with bold artificial colors associated with make-believe. *Abandoned Puppy*, painted on patched-up cotton canvas, plays with the texture of bandages, a motif represented pictorially in *In the Deepest Puddle II*. The child sits in a box wearing the cap of a Zero pilot,[9] which both evokes a puppy's ears and harks back to one of

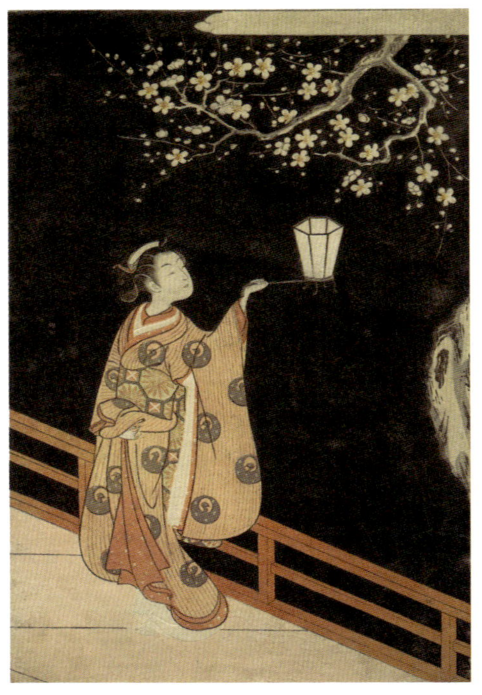

Fig. 70
Suzuki Harunobu, *Woman Admiring Plum Blossoms at Night*, Edo period, Polychrome woodblock print with embossing (*karazuri*); ink and color on paper, 12 ¾ × 8 ¼ in. (32.4 × 21 cm)

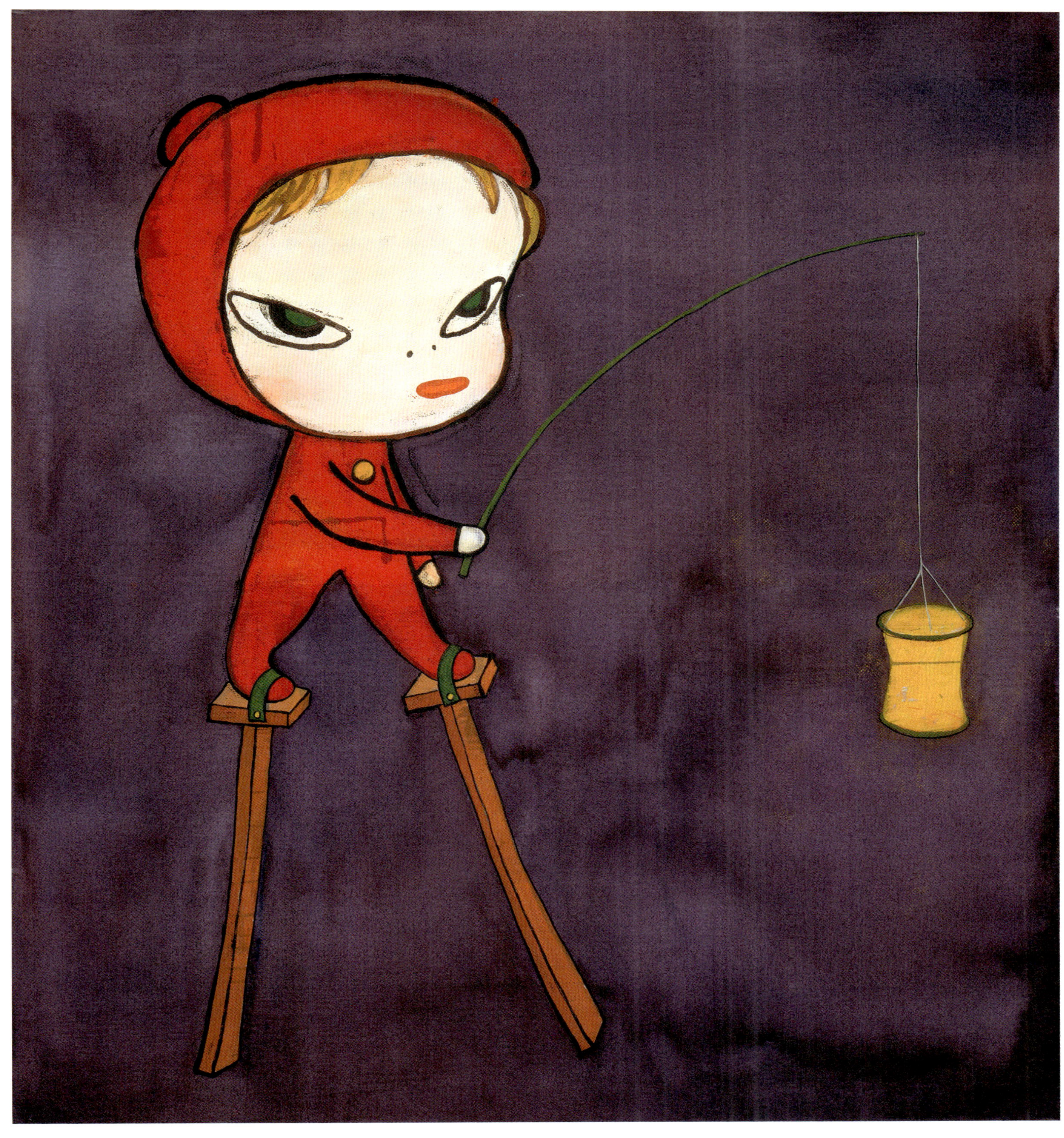

Fig. 71
The Longest Night, 1995,
Acrylic on canvas,
47 ¼ × 43 5/16 in. (120 × 110 cm)

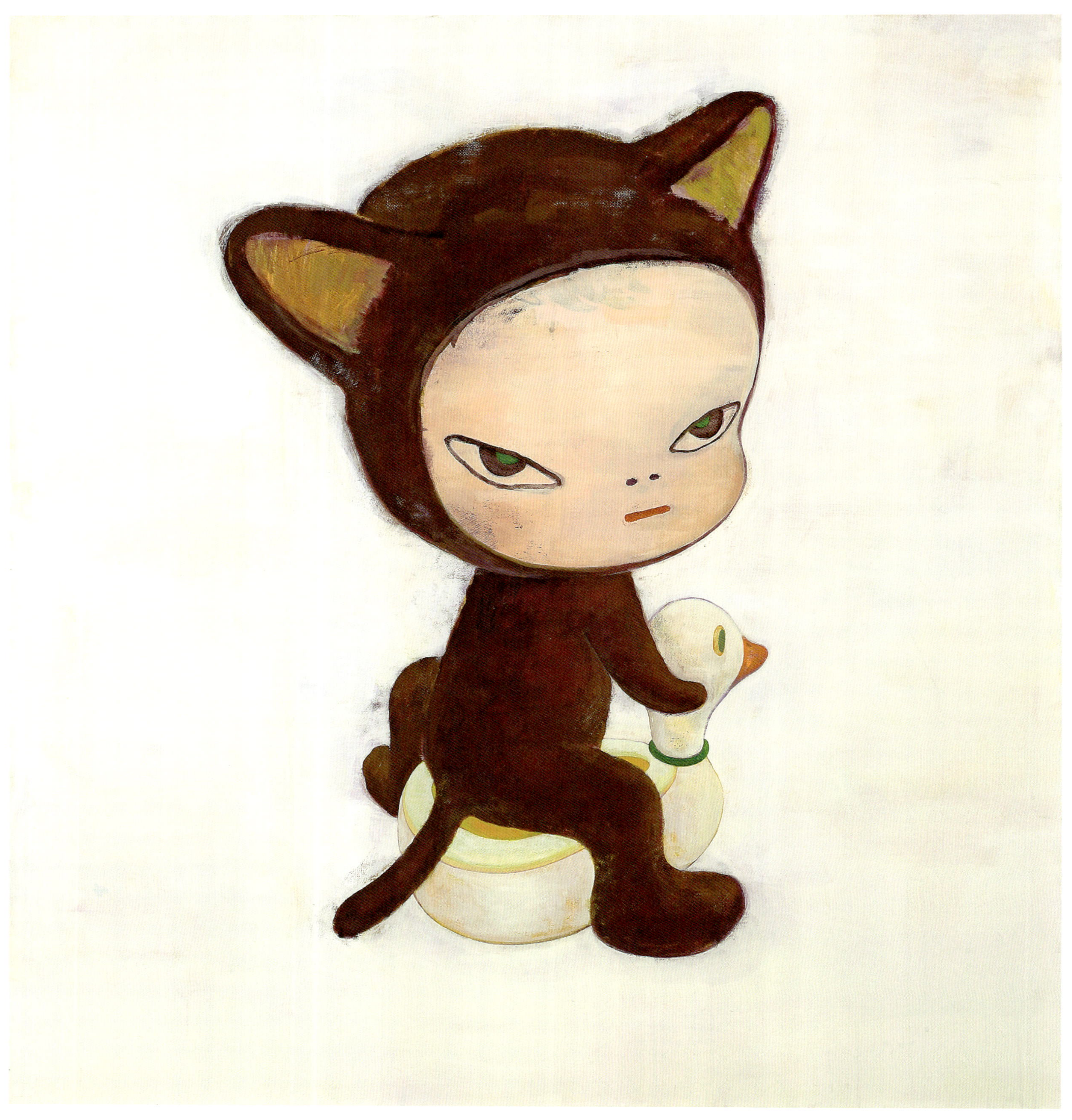

Fig. 72
Harmless Kitty, 1994, Acrylic on canvas, 59 1/16 × 55 1/8 in. (150 × 140 cm)

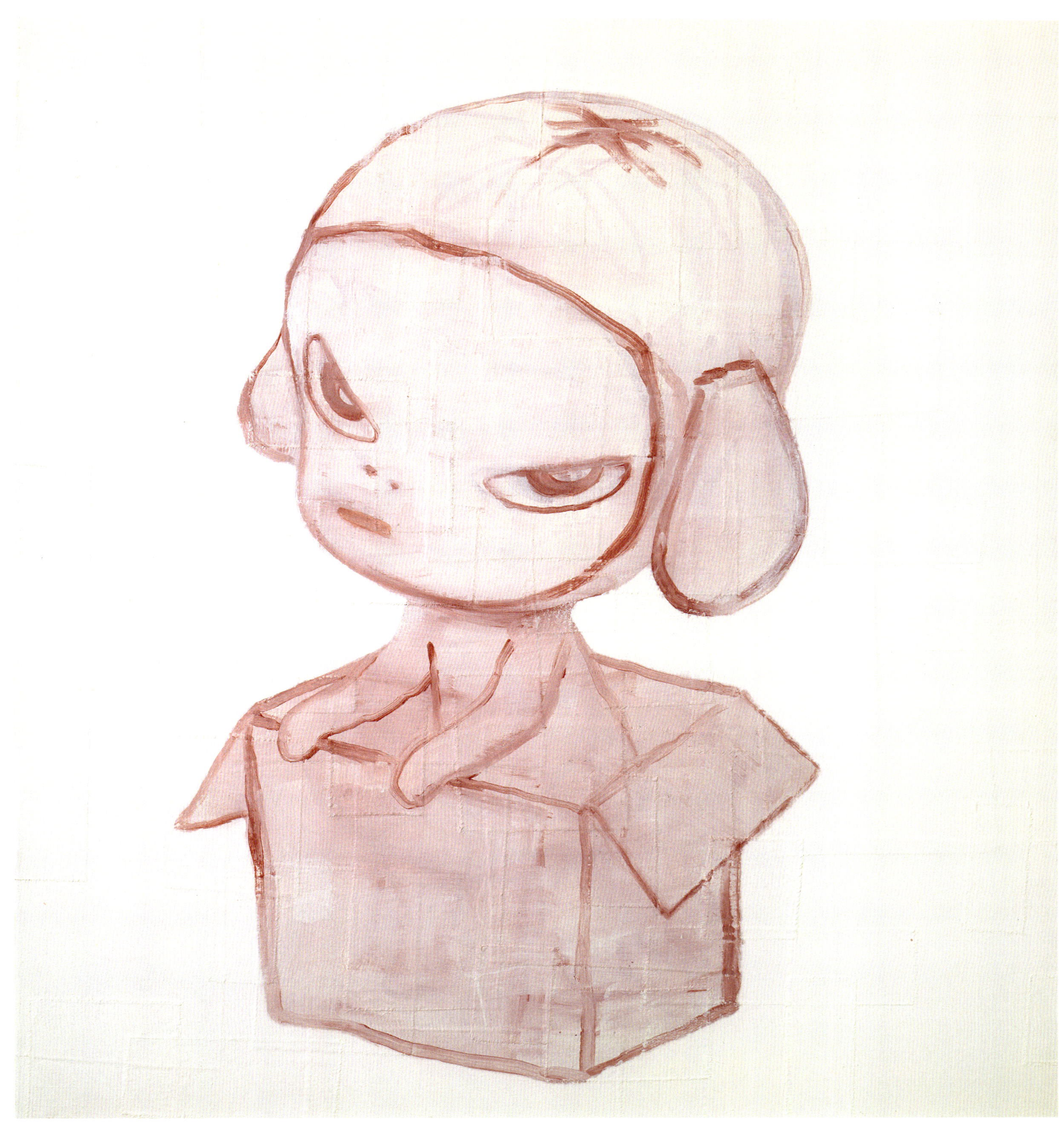

Fig. 73
Abandoned Puppy, 1995,
Acrylic on cotton mounted
on canvas, 47 ¼ × 43 5⁄16 in.
(120 × 110 cm)

Nara's favorite childhood activities of playing with boxed sets of plastic aircraft models. On a formal level, this work, despite its limited palette, shows a sophisticated use of paint and color. Nara employs thin layers of red acrylic paint that merge with the white background to create a softly defined figure, set against the bandaged surface like a glowing wound. Unlike the graphic black lines in *The Girl with the Knife in Her Hand*, which detach the figure from the background, here they are blended into and grounded within the canvas.

Abandoned Puppy captures some of the key formal approaches undertaken by Nara at this time. He complicates the *kawaii* aesthetic through the subject's indignant stubbornness and by introducing formal elements such as painterly lines and the absence of colors, which belong outside conventional expressions of *kawaii*. Taken together, these three paintings show that by the mid-1990s, Nara had developed a coherent painting practice in which children fully occupy the frame and claim the empty background as active spaces of their own. Borrowing from his childhood memories and referencing his own body of past works, he created a band of big-headed figures who behave in ways that deviate from conventional ideals of cuteness with their aggression, irreverence, and wit. Overall, these paintings show how Nara mines and transforms different stylistic properties from one work to another and across media and time. This is less a serial approach—the works do not necessarily follow one another chronologically—than it is an association between characters that form something similar to a kinship network.[10] This explains why Nara's figures, with their distinctive individual presence, are familiar and, arguably, familial, in that in any one work there is the lingering presence of other members of the gang, constructing a collective and mythological childhood world.

The success of the SCAI THE BATHHOUSE exhibition drew the attention of Timothy Blum, of the Santa Monica gallery Blum & Poe, who in 1995 organized Nara's first show in the United States, entitled *Pacific Babies*. The show included several important works, such as *There Is No Place Like Home* (1995) (Fig. 75)—a smaller variation of *Hula Hula Garden* accompanied by a small painting of the same name—and *Dog in Boy* (1995) (Fig. 74), one of the earliest paintings of the white dog that would become a staple in Nara's oeuvre. In the United States, Nara found an audience that more readily accepted the ways in which his works blurred the lines between the domains of fine art and the

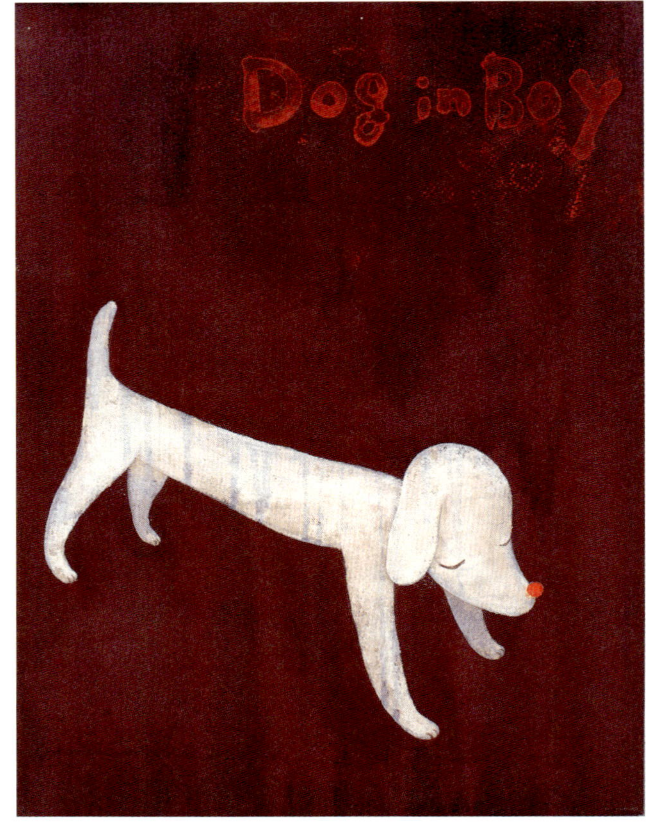

Fig. 74
Dog in Boy, 1995, Acrylic on canvas, 25 × 19 in. (63.5 × 48.3 cm)

subcultures of *kawaii* and nonmainstream music. This reception may be connected to the West Coast's own vibrant subcultures and its relatively young history of established art institutions, which held a more receptive attitude toward contemporary art. Moreover, Nara's works contrasted with the typically conservative and overwhelmingly white art world at a time when issues of identity politics were becoming prevalent in discourses of American art establishments.[11]

After 1995 Nara's fame steadily grew both in Japan and overseas, and around this time, he returned to his studio in Cologne, where he began expanding his portfolio to include other approaches to his now-familiar child figure. One was the introduction of a softer palette and a more painterly surface that departed from the vibrant tones and thicker outlines of his earlier works. In *Sleepless Night (Sitting)* (1997) (Fig. 73), the child figure in a cat suit is now outlined in a thin red line whose blurry edges shimmer against a dark background, capturing the aura of nighttime. Despite the softness of the colors, there is an air of lingering tension: a watchful figure silently waiting for the night to end. Nara applies a similar sinister effect to *Night Cat* (1999) (Fig. 77), one of his rare images of an adult, although her vampiric teeth suggest that we may not have left the fantastical world of childhood imagination.

At the other end of the color scale is Nara's use of creamier pastel shades. Here, unlike in the nighttime paintings, he reduces the tonal saturation, especially in the background, which he now renders monochromatic to produce a flatter effect. He also expands the size of his canvas, as in *Princess of Snooze* (2001) (Fig. 79), one of his largest paintings, which depicts a girl in deep sleep—or the pretense of being asleep—snoring away with her mouth agape as she stretches across the middle of a flat, empty space. The scale of the figure is now smaller in relation to the canvas, and the monochromatic background strips the scene of any sense of space. The background generates a feeling of suspension, creating a nonspatial world like a self-contained laboratory where nothing else exists. In other works, Nara extends the monochromatic background to a new format: a large, shallow dish, sometimes covered in small strips of canvas. He expands the color range to include baby blues, jade greens, and burnt browns, emphasizing the artificiality of the spaces his figures inhabit. The dishes' concave sides further trap the children inside a suspended, fictional world (Figs. 80, 81, and 84).

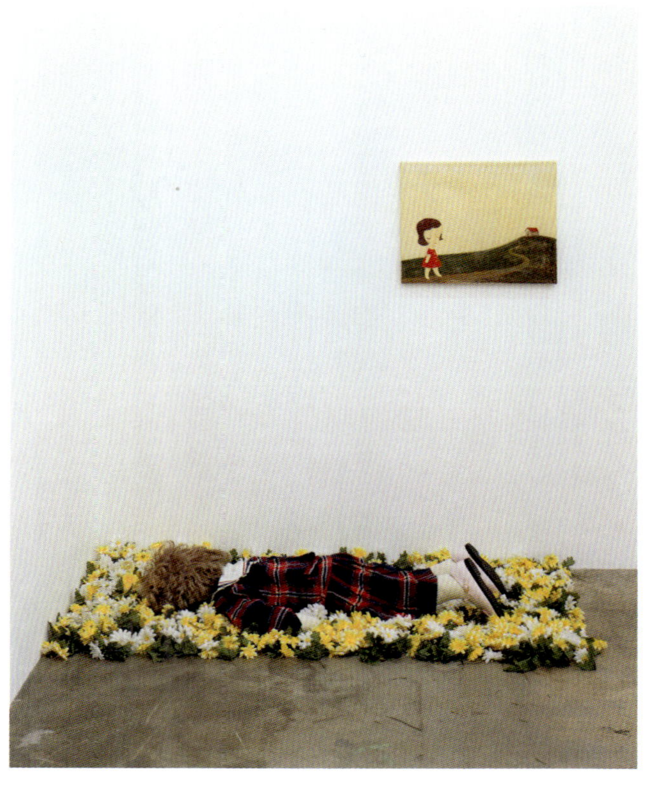

Fig. 75
There Is No Place Like Home,
1995, Painting: Acrylic on canvas,
16 ¼ × 19 ¾ in. (41.3 × 50.2 cm),
Sculpture: Mixed media 9 ⅞ ×
47 ¼ × 15 ¾ in. (25.1 × 120 × 40 cm)
Installation view: *Pacific Babies*,
Blum & Poe, Santa Monica, CA, 1995

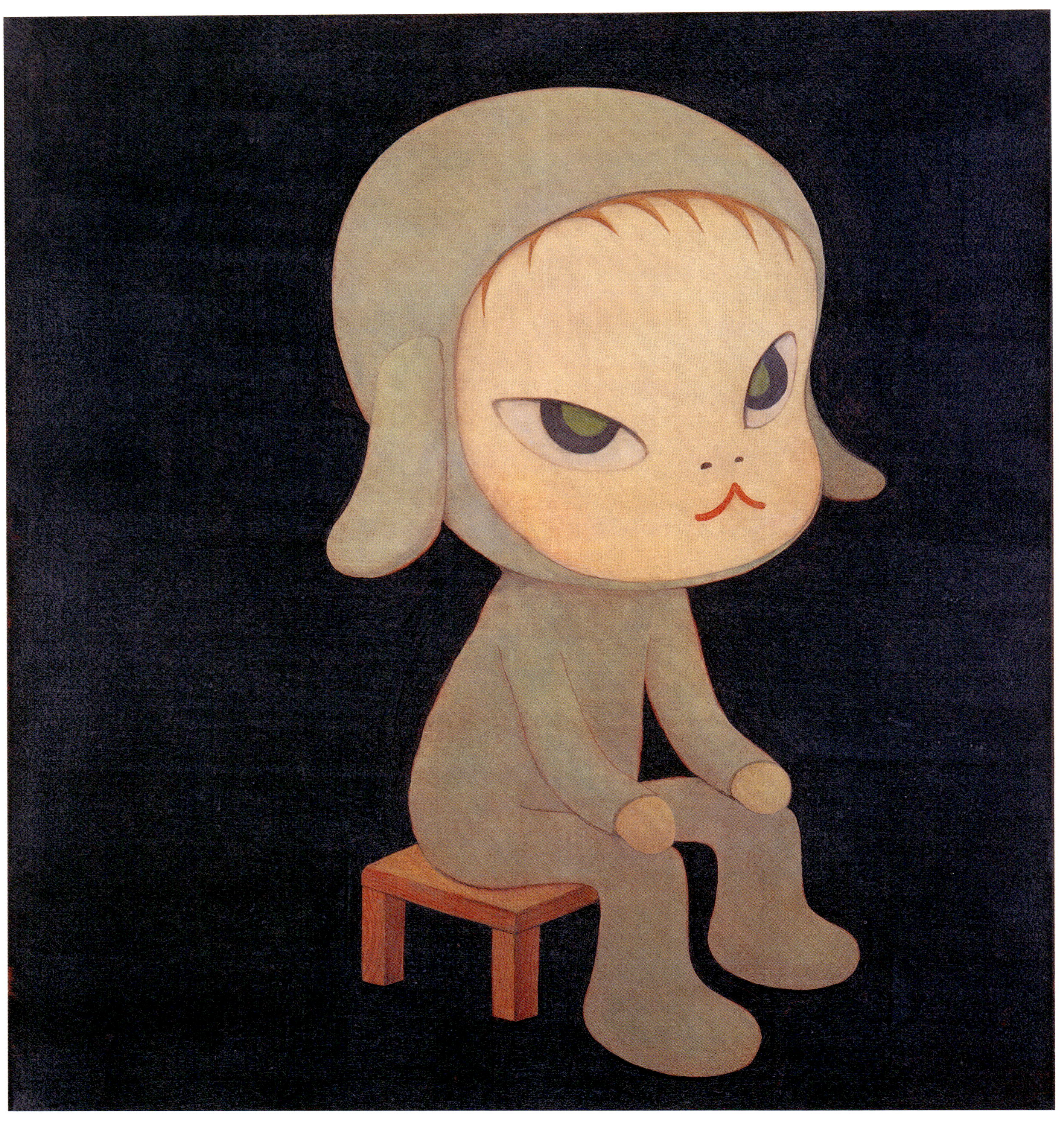

Fig. 76
Sleeplessness Night (Sitting),
1997, Acrylic on canvas,
47 ¼ × 43 ⁵⁄₁₆ in. (120 × 110 cm)

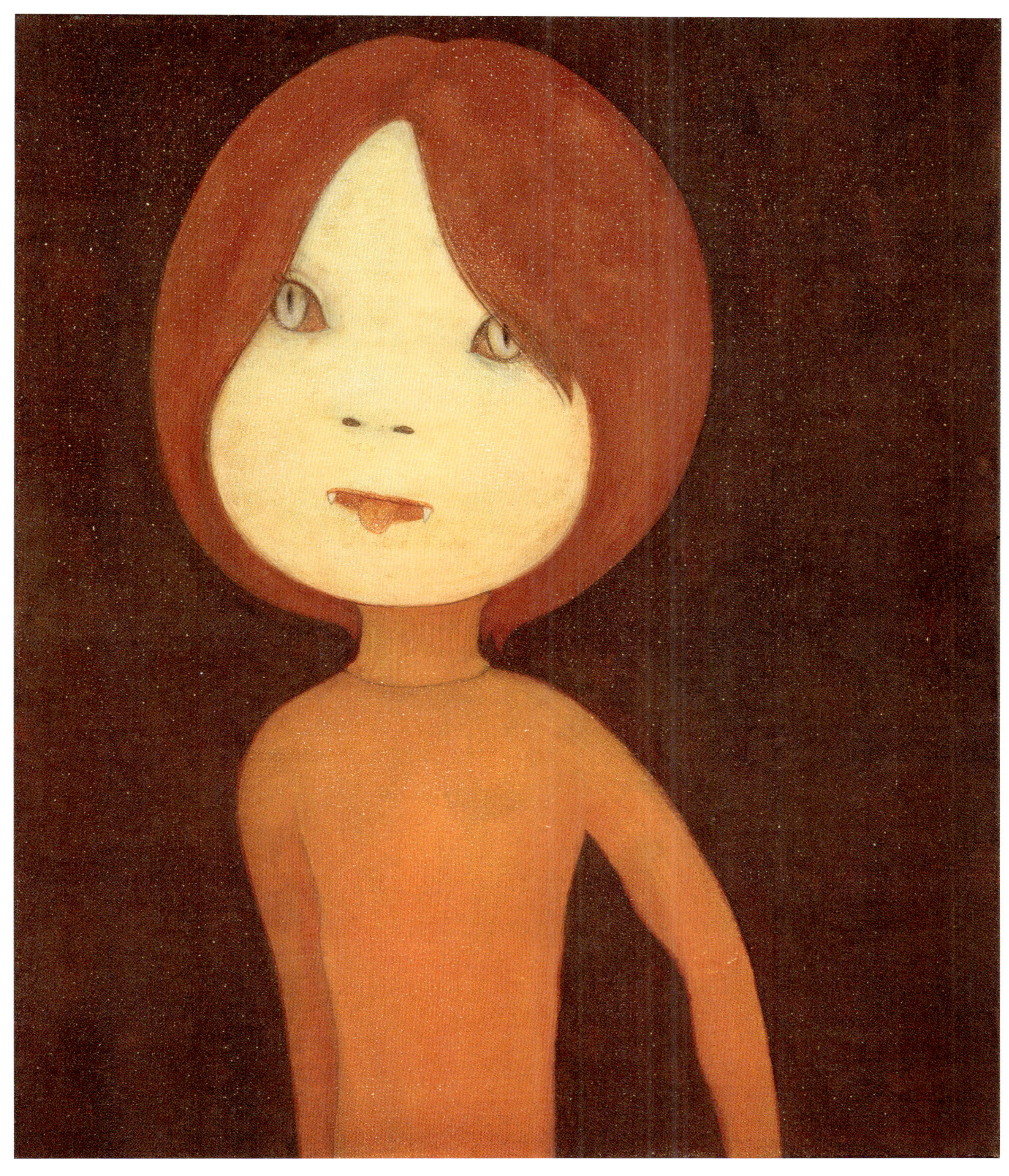

Fig. 77
Night Cat, 1999, Acrylic on canvas, 23 7⁄16 × 19 11⁄16 in. (59.5 × 50 cm)

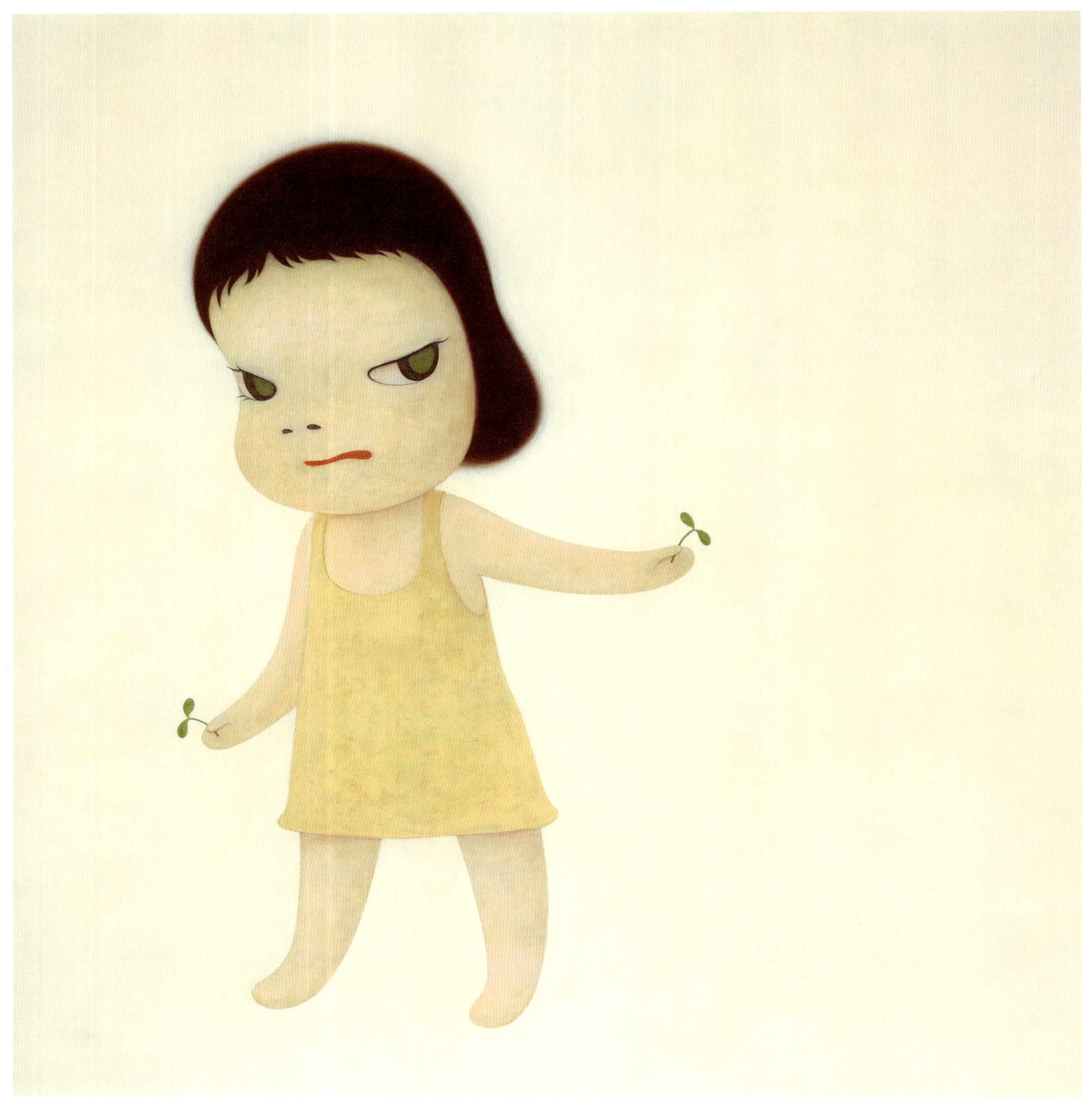

Fig. 78
Sprout the Ambassador, 2001,
Acrylic on canvas, 82 × 78 in.
(208.3 × 198.1 cm)

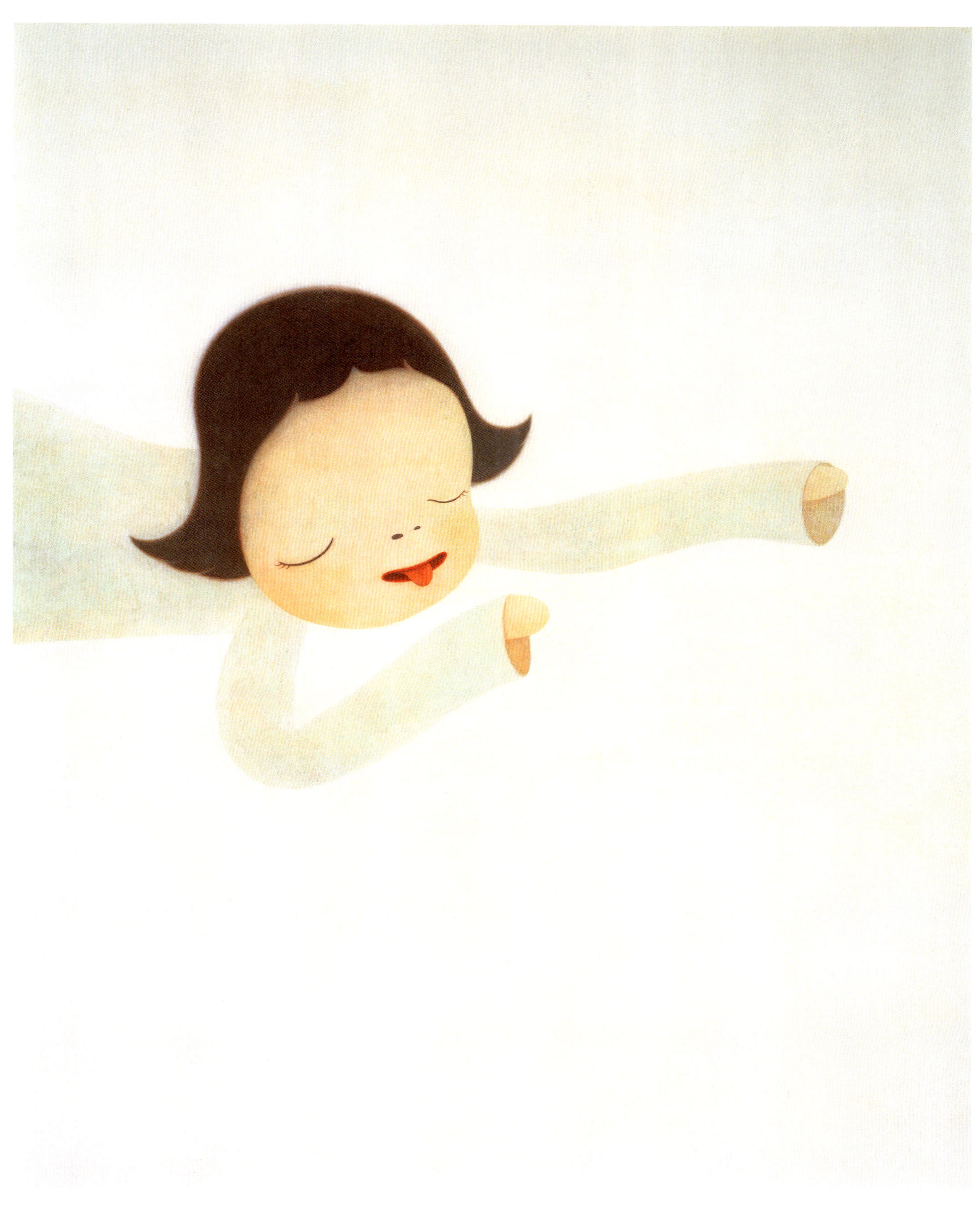

Fig. 79
Princess of Snooze, 2001,
Acrylic on canvas, 113 ⅜ × 71 9/16 in.
(288 × 181.8 cm)

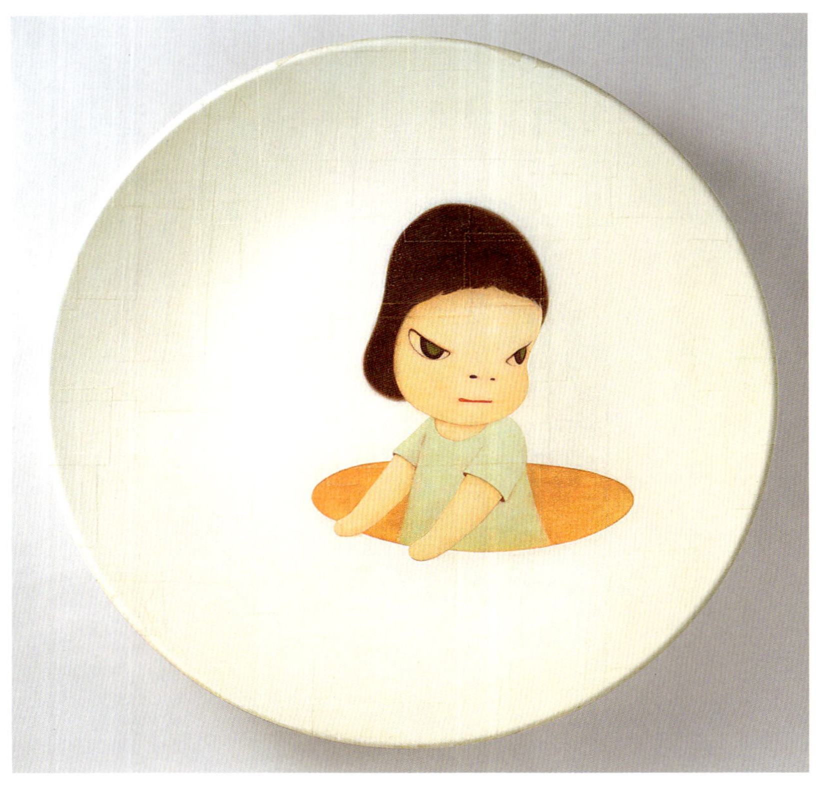

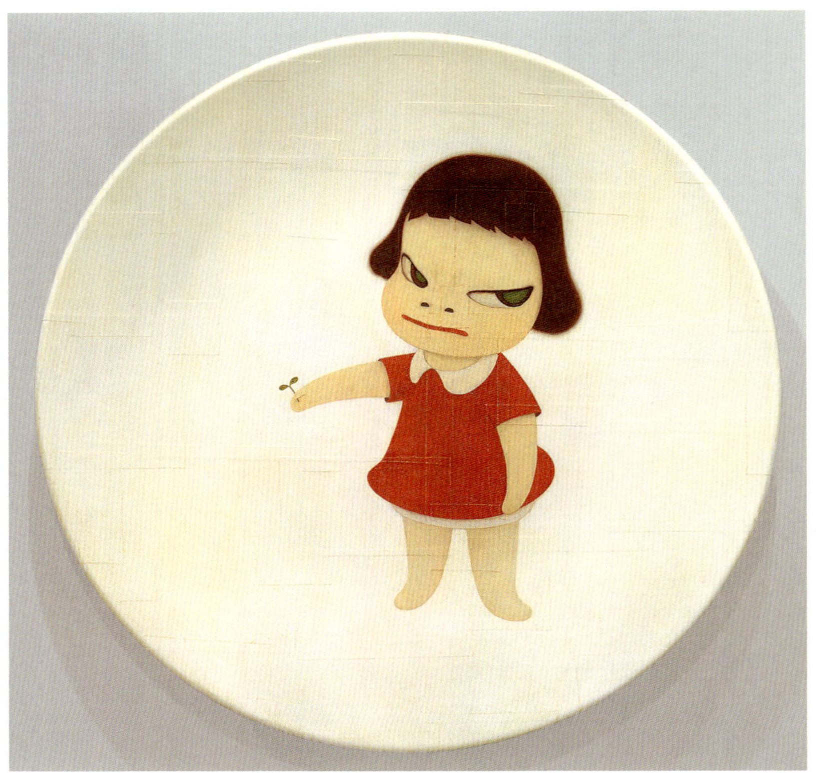

Another direction that Nara briefly explored in this period took the figurative into a different planar territory. In both *Pee "Dead of Night"* (2001) (Fig. 82) and *Thinker* (2001) (Fig. 87), the protagonists appear like tall stick figures with their heads tilted forward, parallel to the bottom of the canvas. Unlike his more familiar portrait types that seem to seek human connection, these images turn their viewers into voyeurs. The paintings borrow from modernist aesthetics in their use of circles, triangles, and blocks of color, but they nevertheless retain a comic contemporaneity. Nara pursued this style only for a short time, but not before he combined its graphic quality with his portrait style of big-headed girls in *Keep Your Chin Up* (2001) (Fig. 88).

In the second half of the 1990s, Nara began making fiberglass sculptures of white dogs, works that engaged more actively with audiences through their various scales and arrangements in installations. Fiberglass was a relatively new material in the art world, popularized in the early 1990s by artists such as Anish Kapoor, who altered the material through varied surface treatments to create tactile sensations through color and light; Duane Hanson, who used its malleability to create hyperreal casts of real figures; and Jeff Koons, who with its shiny materiality captured the kitsch world of postindustrial

Fig. 80
Ready to Scout, 2001,
Acrylic on cotton mounted on fiber-reinforced plastics, diam. 70 × d. 10 in. (177.8 × 25.4 cm)

Fig. 81
Sprout the Ambassador, 2001,
Acrylic on cotton mounted on fiber-reinforced plastics, diam. 70 ⅞ × d. 10 ¼ in. (180 × 26 cm)

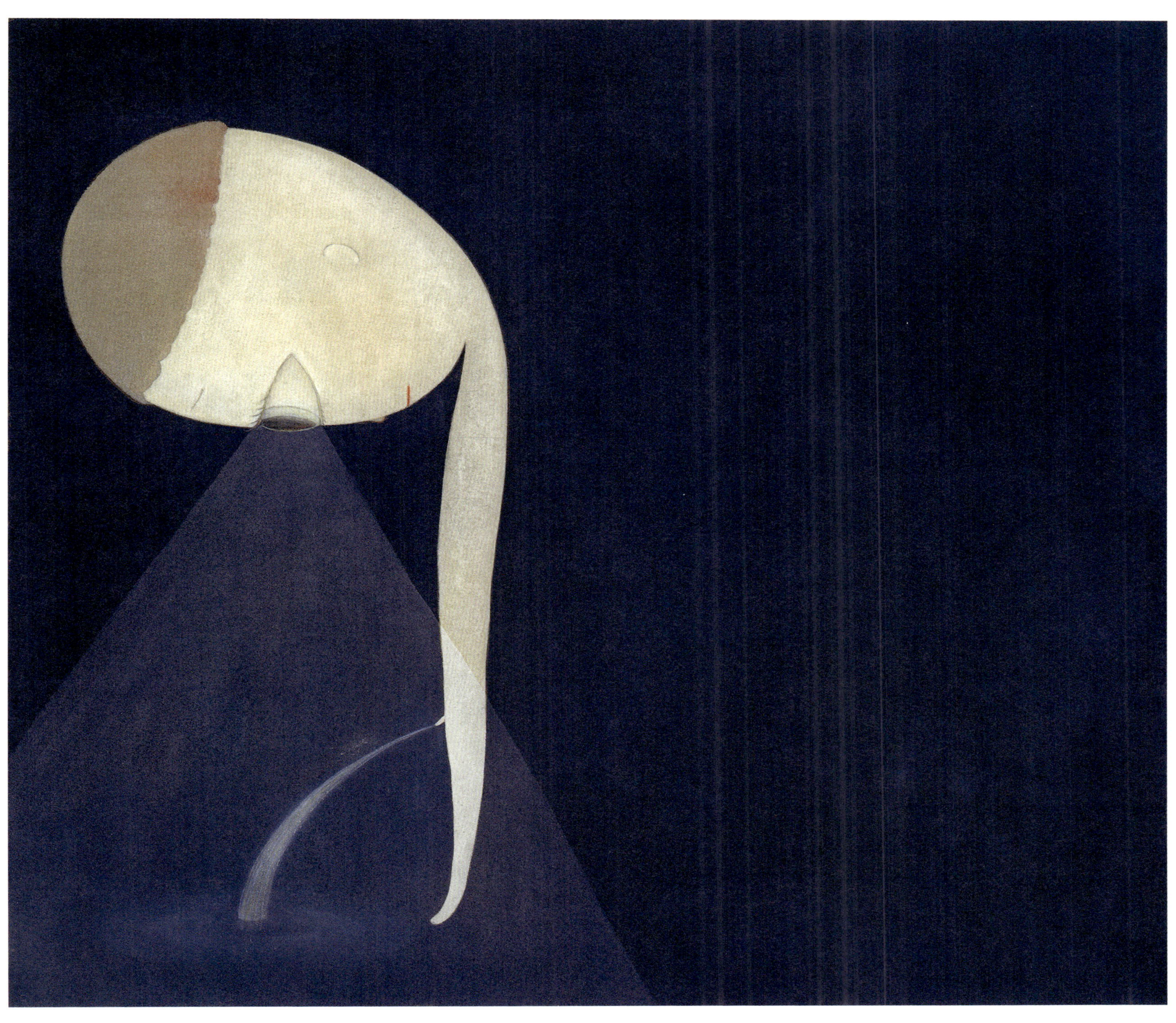

Fig. 82
Pee "Dead of Night," 2001,
Acrylic on canvas, 31 11⁄16 × 35 7⁄8 in.
(80.5 × 91.2 cm)

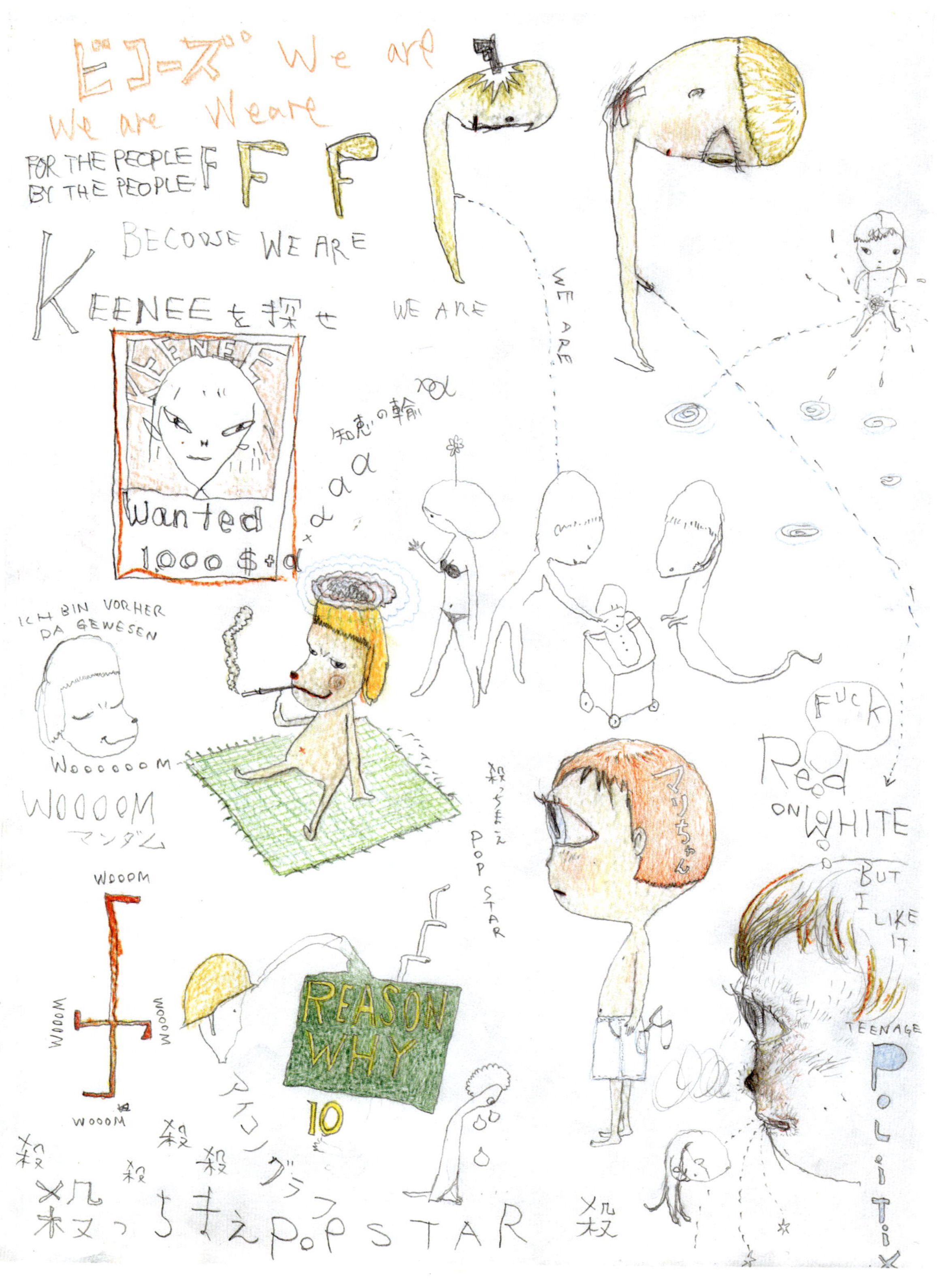

Fig. 83
For the People, 1992–2000,
Pencil and colored pencil
on paper, 11 ¾ × 8 ¼ in.
(29.8 × 21 cm)

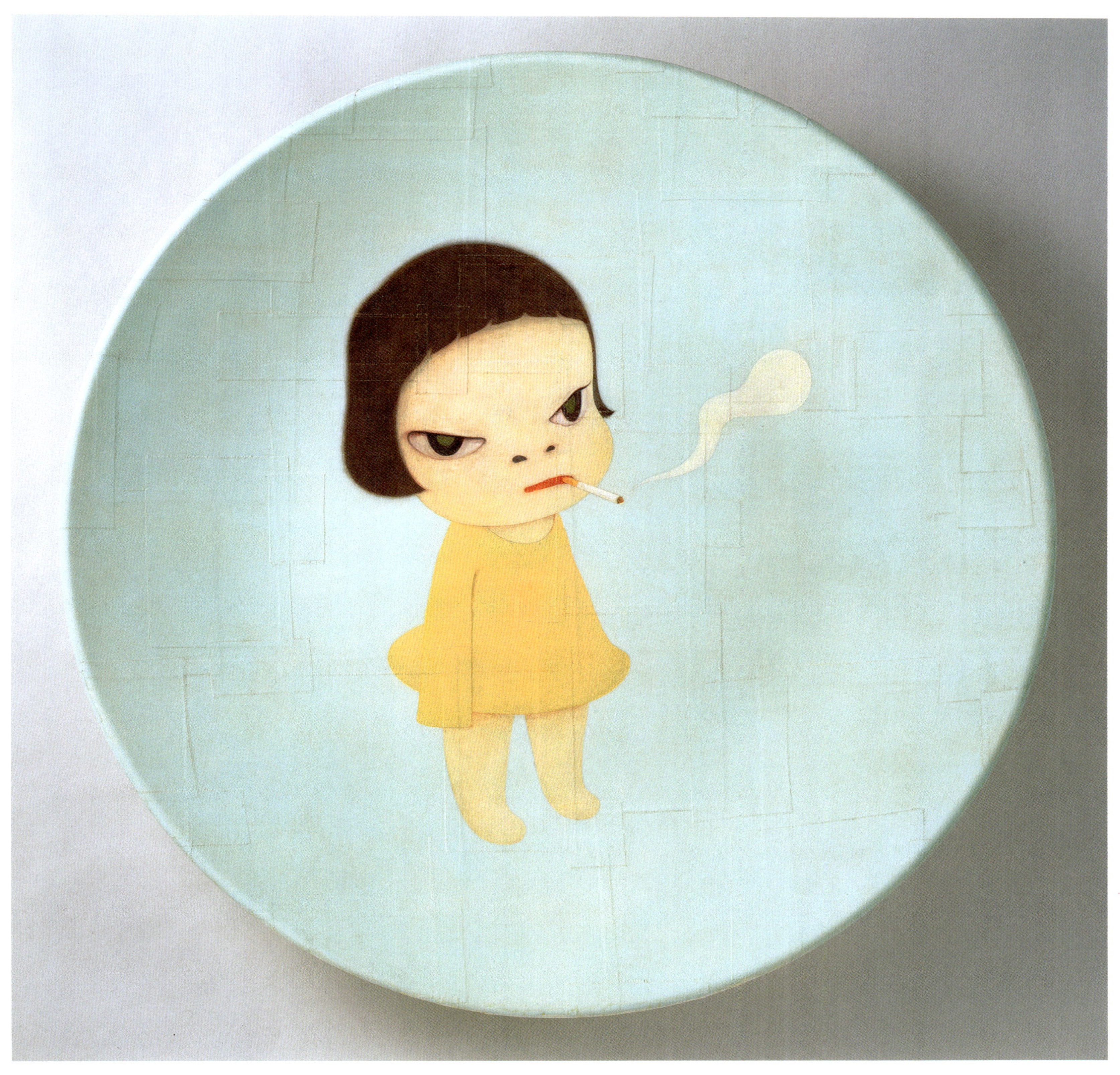

Fig. 84
Too Young to Die, 2001,
Acrylic on cotton mounted on
fiber-reinforced plastics, diam.
70 × d. 10 in. (177.8 × 25.4 cm)

America. Nara's interest in the much-loved character of the dog began in the late 1980s and early '90s, as seen in early drawings (Fig. 86) and his painting *Hundeberg als Trugbild* (Fig. 85), whose sharp, straight canine legs are translated into three dimensions in Nara's earliest dog sculpture, *One Way Dog* (1994) (Fig. 90), rendered in fiberglass. To make these sculptures, Nara first sculpted forms out of Styrofoam to use as molds (Fig. 91), a process that also steered him towards making more curved and rounded sculptures.

By the mid-1990s, the white dog had taken the form of an endearing creature with floppy ears and a goofy grin, as seen in the painting *Dog in Boy* (Fig. 74). Nara used a monochromatic palette for his sculptures, usually limited to white or black with occasional touches of red, preferring to play with scale instead, to create unexpected elements of aggression and pathos in his characters. The monumental size of *Aomori-ken (Aomori Dog)* (2005) (Fig. 92), permanently installed at the Aomori Museum of Art, arouses both fear and wonder in the viewer, but also, as in Koons's own giant dog sculpture, *Puppy* (1992), an exuberance that celebrates life. Nara also scaled down and multiplied his dogs—as a pack placed on stilts (Fig. 93) or gathered around puddles (Fig. 94)—and presented one as the main character in his first authored storybook, *The Lonesome Puppy*, originally published in 1999 (Fig. 89).

Working in white fiberglass, whose reflective surface can distort and invert the viewer's sense of space, Nara was faced with new compositional challenges, such as how to construct compelling flows in three-dimensional space while responding to the material's tactility and reflectiveness. One form that proved particularly difficult was the head of his child figure, which he first sculpted as an orb with an almost sheeplike face. While the form without a body felt complete in itself, it proved difficult to assemble multiple heads together to create a sculpture that was compositionally sound. In 1999 Nara made a version with a totem pole of heads rising up from a giant spinning teacup, reminiscent of old-fashioned fairground rides (Fig. 97). In other renditions, he arranged sets of individual totem cups inside a given space, but he was never completely satisfied with these presentations, feeling that they were not able to capture interesting spatial dynamics. It was not until 2001, with *Fountain of Life* (Figs. 95 and 96), that he finally reached the outcome he desired. Half-submerged heads peek up from the surface of the water in the cup, recalling his shallow puddles of 1995 (Fig. 69), while the addition of a motor spins the heads around

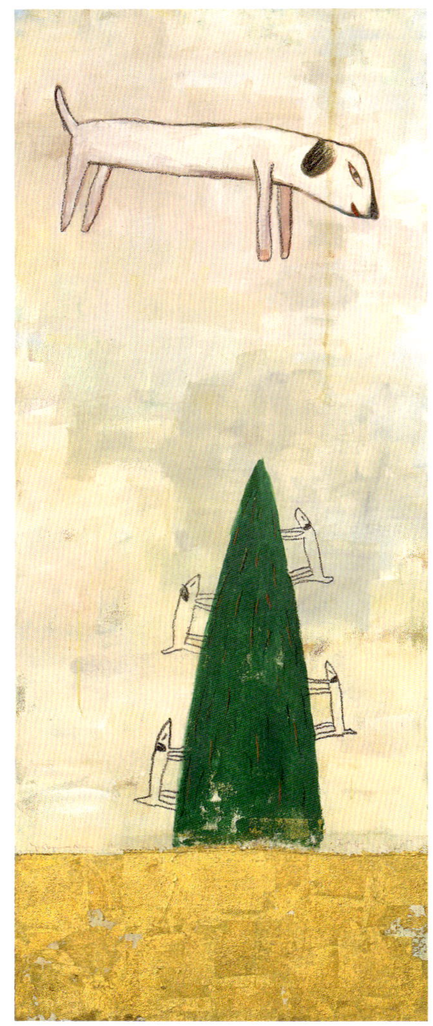

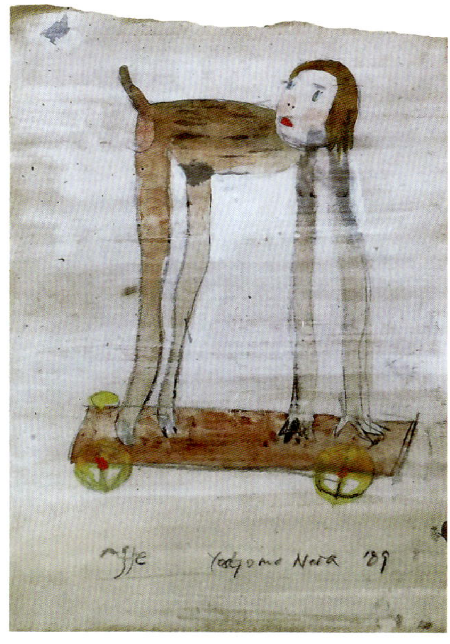

Fig. 85
Hundeberg als Trugbild, 1991, Acrylic on canvas, 64 × 25 ⅜ in. (162.5 × 64.5 cm)

Fig. 86
Untitled, 1989, Acrylic and colored pencil on paper, 14 ⅛ × 9 ⅜ in. (35.8 × 23.8 cm)

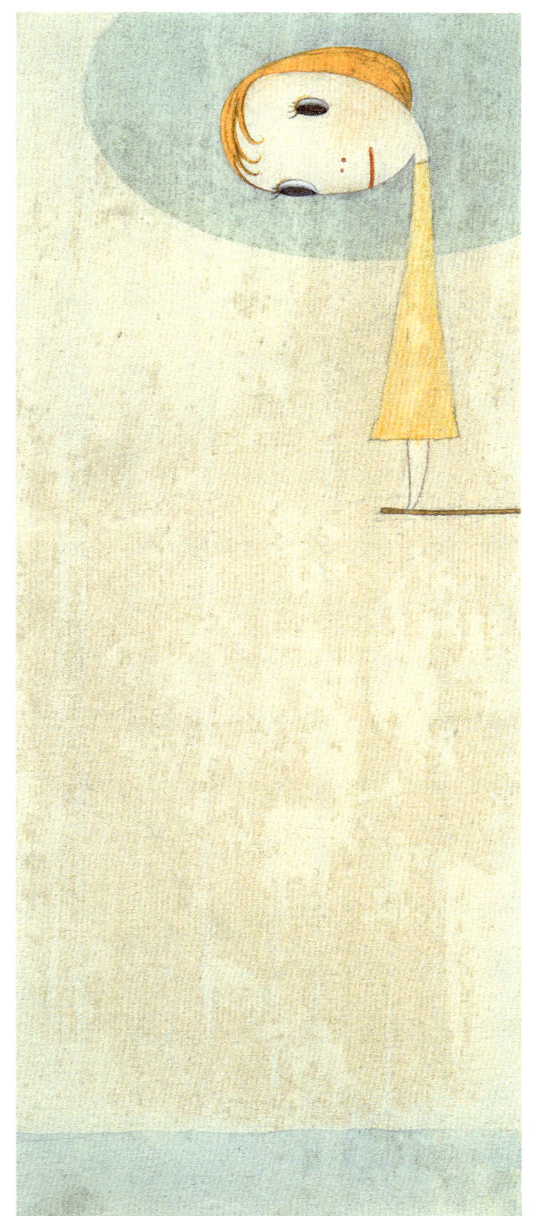

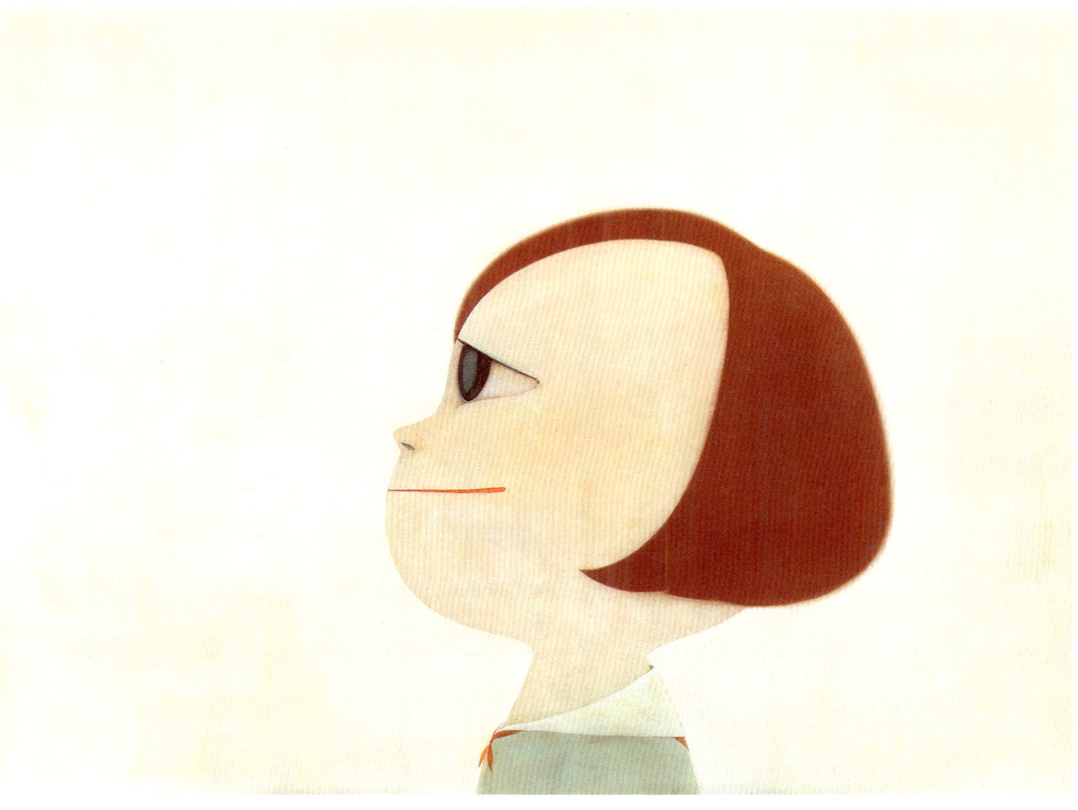

Fig. 87
Thinker, 2001, Acrylic on cotton mounted on plywood, 14 1/16 × 5 13/16 in. (35.7 × 14.7 cm)

Fig. 88
Keep Your Chin Up, 2001, Acrylic on canvas, 76 3/8 × 102 1/16 in. (194 × 259.3 cm)

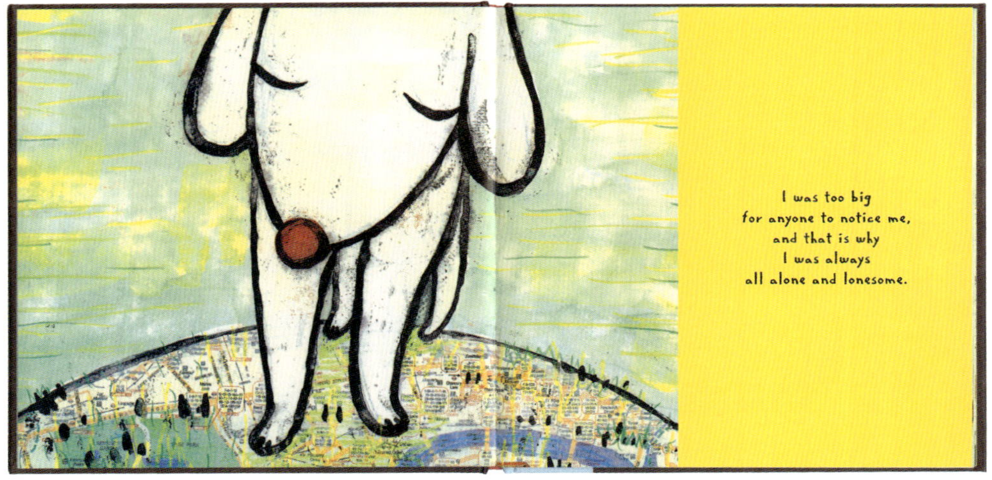

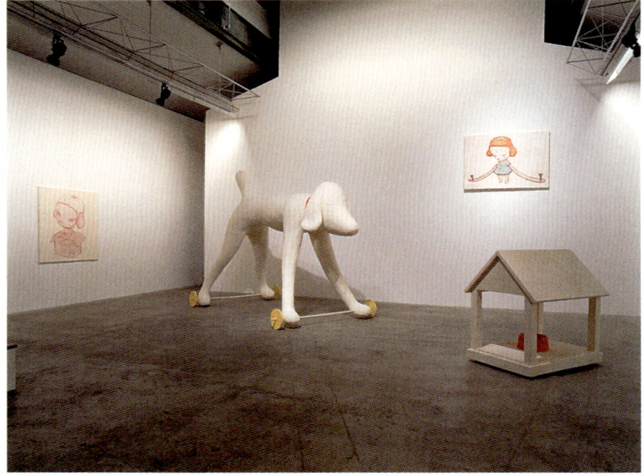

as tears stream down their faces. Through these innovations, as well as by stacking the heads in an asymmetrical zigzag so that their faces turned in multiple directions, Nara created a work of dynamic movement that invites viewing from any angle.

Nara and Japanese Subcultures, 1995–2001

> **I'm not good at explaining with words, and when I start explaining, I often get confused about what I'm saying. That's why I make paintings and sculptures. . . . There are people who will never understand [your work] no matter how many words you use, and there are also those who don't want to understand, and others who want to reject it. But if there are people who want to understand even a little, and they see my paintings in person, they'll understand me. At the same time, those people who look at my paintings in that way also rediscover their own selves. I'd like it if I could create that kind of relationship.**[12]

One of the earliest attempts to examine Nara's work critically was in 1995, when the prestigious art journal *Bijutsu techō* chose Nara's *Yellow in Blue* (1994) (Fig. 98) to adorn the cover of its July issue, entitled "Kairaku Kaiga" (Pictures That Bring Pleasure). Although this demonstrated that the art world was attuned to the relevance of Nara's work, his coverage in the journal placed him on the margins of the art establishment, presenting his *kawaii*-inspired work as a foil to the more academically focused art of his peers who were also included in the issue.

Fig. 89
Spread from *The Lonesome Puppy* (US edition), published by Chronicle Books, San Francisco, 2008

Fig. 90
One Way Dog, 1994, Mixed media, Dog: 90 ½ × 129 ⅞ × 66 ⅞ in. (230 × 330 × 170 cm), Home: 41 × 31 ½ × 39 ⅜ in. (104 × 80 × 100 cm)
Installation view: *In the Deepest Puddle*, SCAI THE BATHHOUSE, Tokyo, 1995

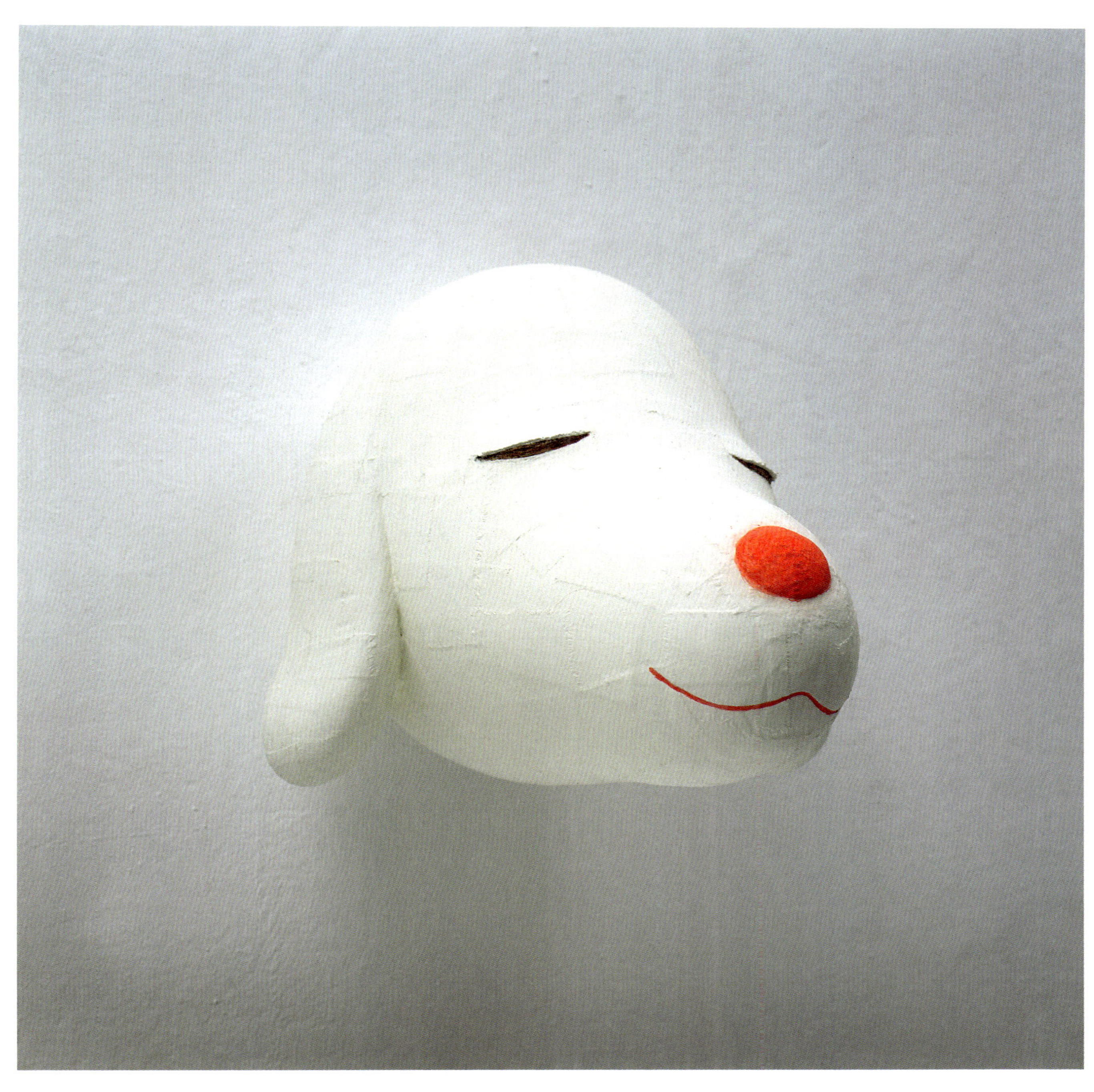

Fig. 91
Dog from Your Childhood (prototype), 1997, Acrylic and cotton on Styrofoam, 16 ⅛ × 16 ⁹⁄₁₆ × 18 ⅞ in. (41 × 42 × 43 cm)

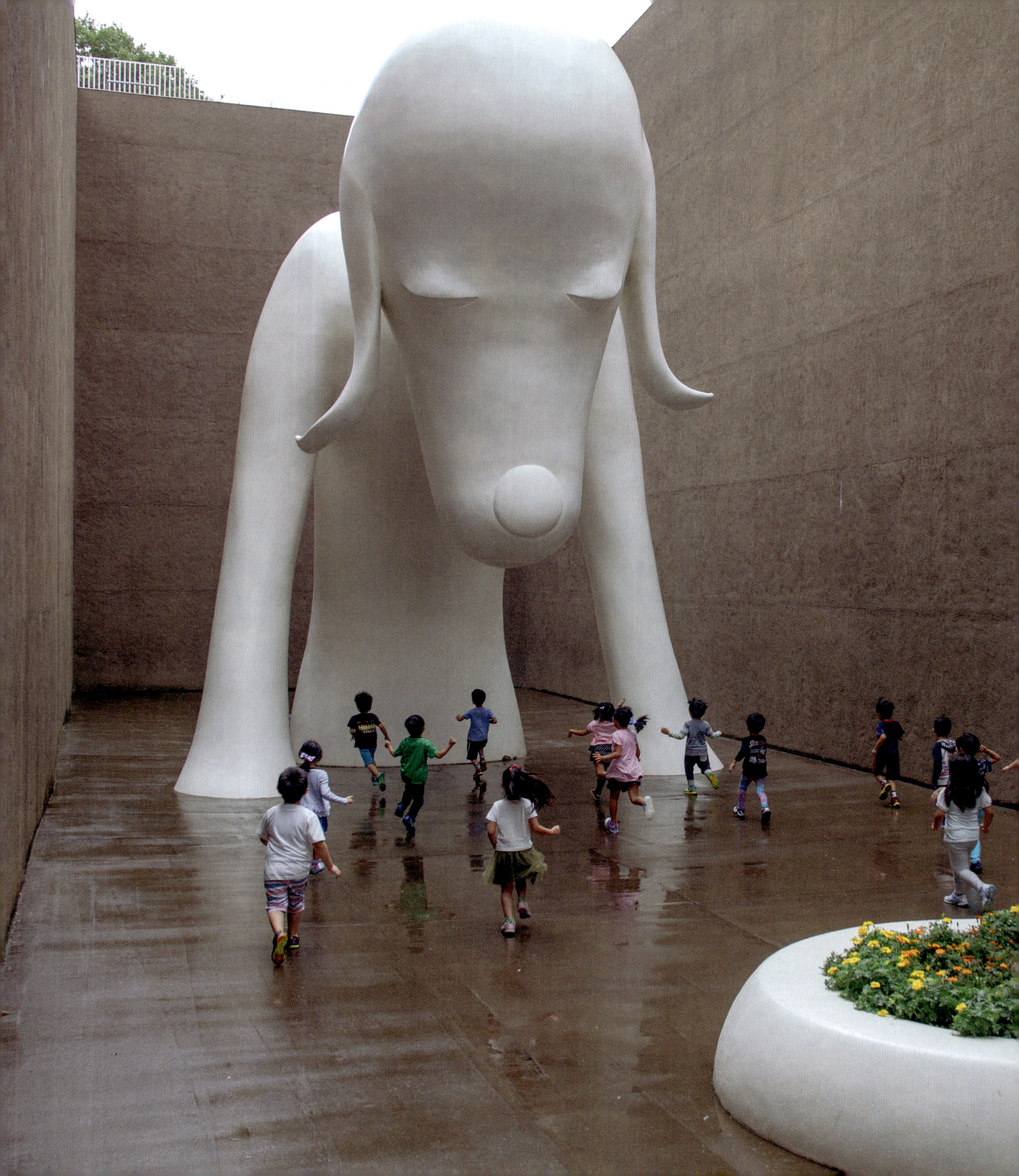

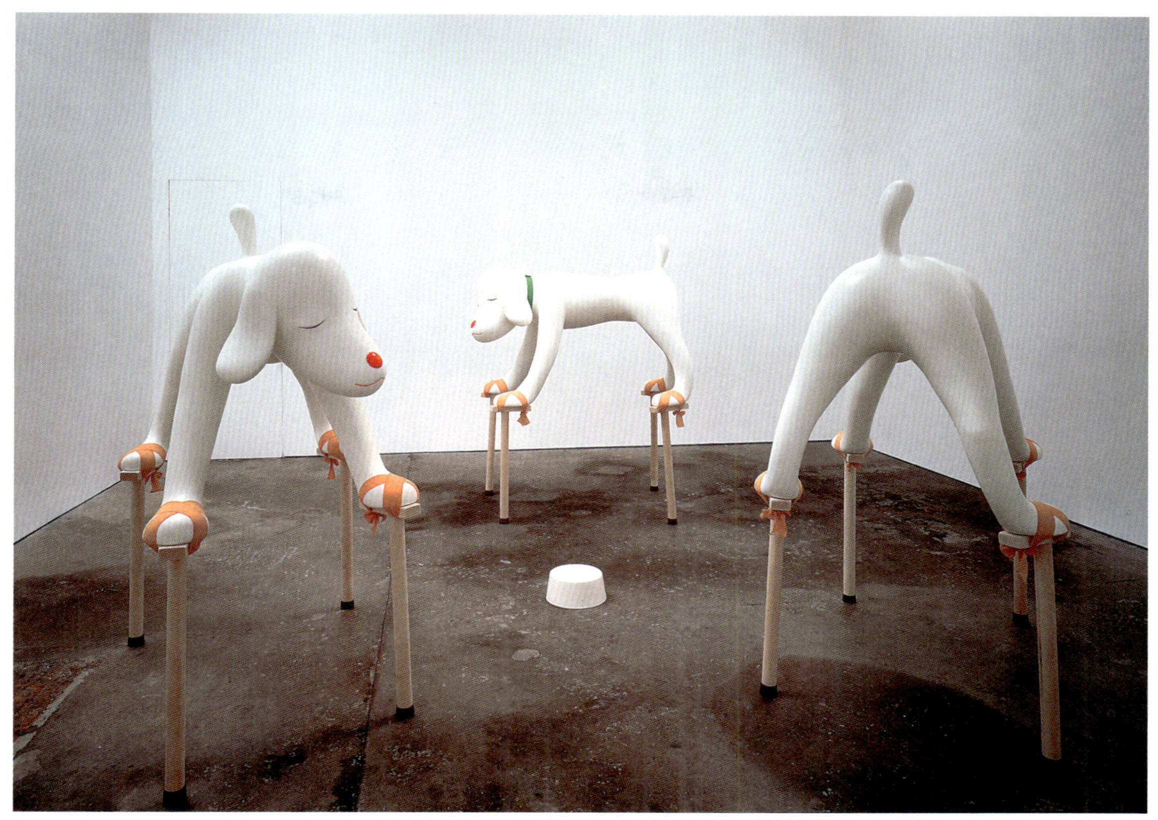

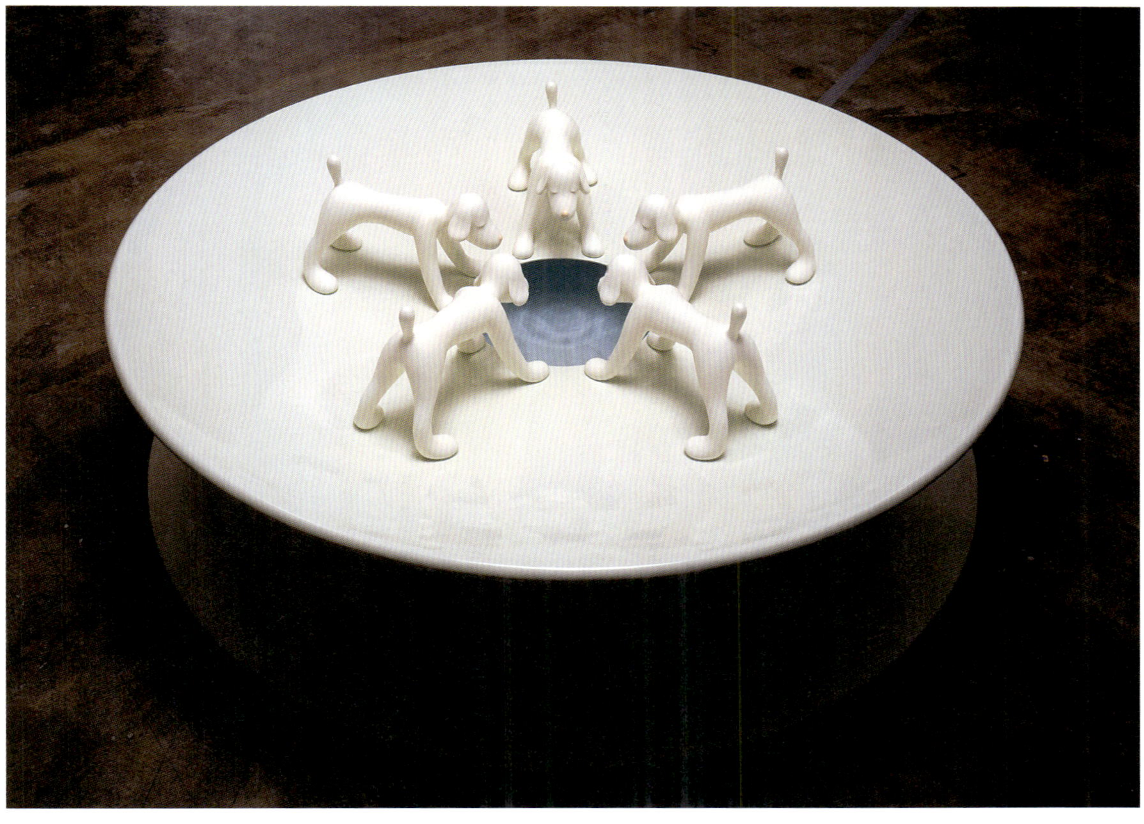

Fig. 92 (opposite)
Aomori-ken (Aomori Dog), 2005, Reinforced concrete, 334 ⅝ × 263 ¾ × 354 ⅜ in. (850 × 670 × 900 cm)

Fig. 93
Dogs from Your Childhood, 1999, Acrylic, lacquer, and urethane on fiber-reinforced plastics, wood, each 59 ¹³⁄₁₆ × 36 ¼ × 39 ¾ in. (152 × 92 × 101 cm)

Fig. 94
Fountain of Sorrow, 2001, Lacquer and urethane on fiber-reinforced plastics, motor, and water, h. 26 ⅜ × diam. 70 ⅞ in. (67 × 180 cm)

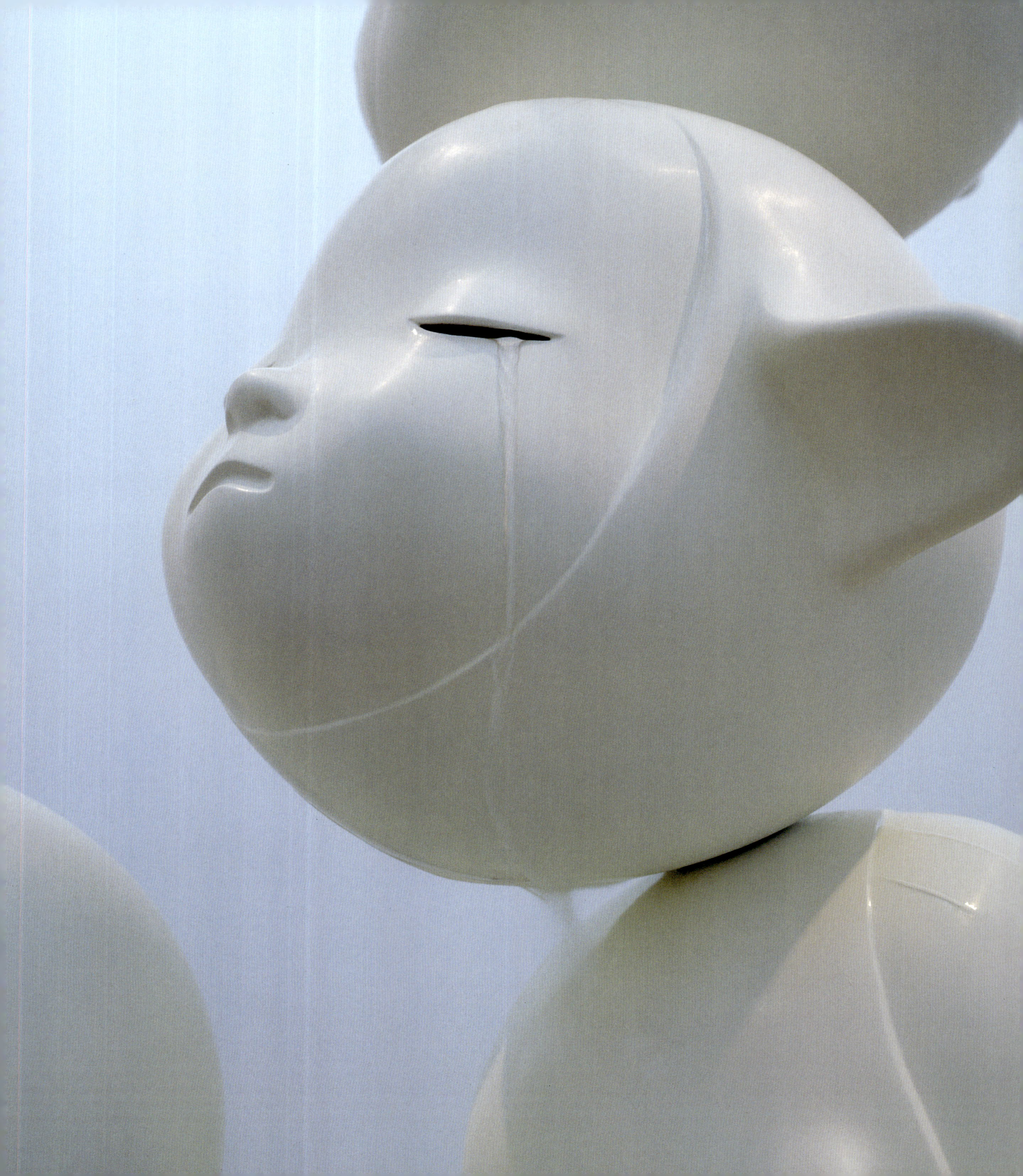

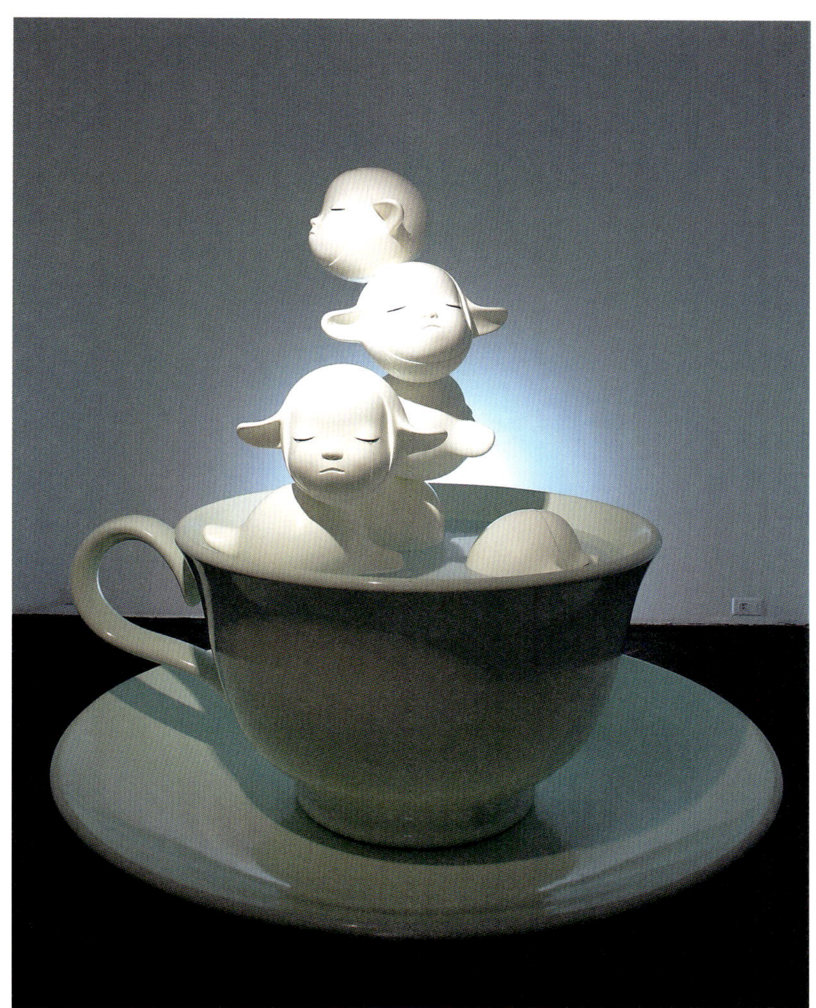

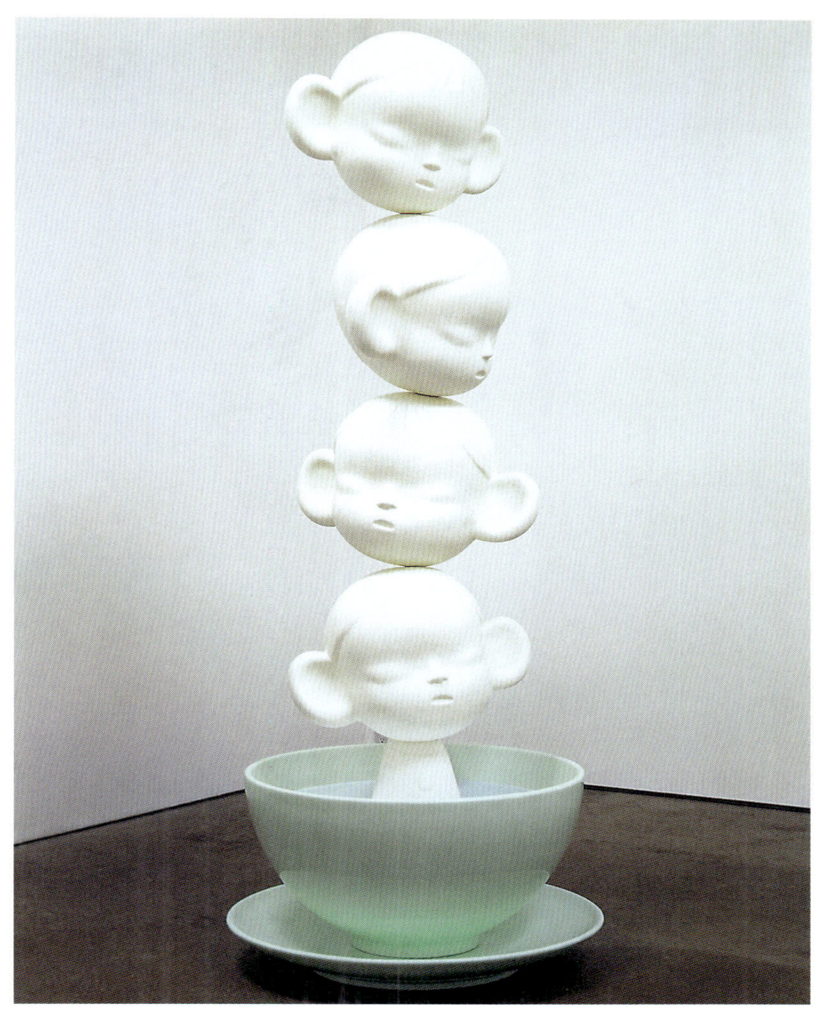

Fig. 95 (opposite)
Fountain of Life (detail), 2001

Fig. 96
Fountain of Life, 2001,
Lacquer and urethane on fiber-reinforced plastics, motor, and water, h. 68 ⅞ × diam. 70 ⅞ in.
(175 × 180 cm)

Fig. 97
Quiet, Quiet, 1999, Lacquer on fiber-reinforced plastics, h. 78 ¾ × diam. 35 13/16 in.
(200 × 91 cm)

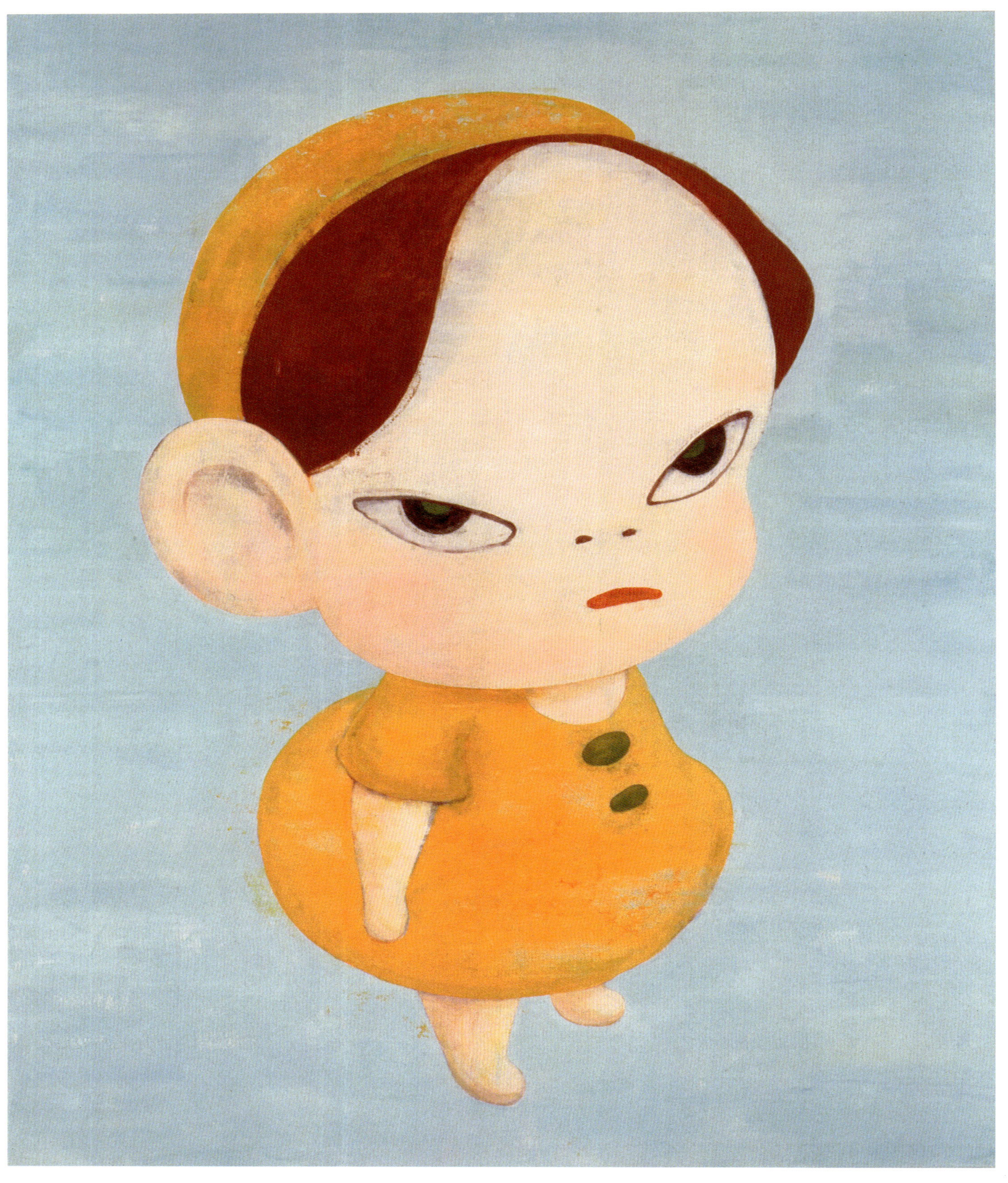

Fig. 98
Yellow in Blue, 1994, Acrylic on canvas, 70 ⅞ × 59 ¹⁄₁₆ in. (180 × 150 cm)

Nara was typically seen by curators and writers as part of the postmodern narrative of Japanese/Tokyo Pop, which was gaining critical traction at the time.[13] The narrative, which would gain even more prominence by the end of the 1990s, emphasized how artists appropriated imagery and products from various Japanese subcultures —namely, anime, manga, and gaming—into their fine-art practices as a way of emphasizing a self-reflexive, even ironic, awareness of their artistic and cultural identities within a new capitalist regime. Nara's work, however, never fit easily within this narrative and its related discussions of Neo-Pop and Micropop, not least because he seldom appropriated images from the contemporary manga and anime worlds.

There have also been exhibitions that view Nara's artwork through the lens of punk rock or indie folk music, constant inspirations for his creative process, largely by presenting images directly related to the theme of music (Fig. 99).[14] However, it is also possible to ask whether there is a link between the aesthetics of music and the formal properties of some of his works. Perhaps one can connect the stripped-down aesthetics of punk, for example, with its raw energy and irreverent lyrics, to the frenetic scribbles of Nara's *Somewhere Somewhere* (1986) (Fig. 30) or the aggression of *The Girl with the Knife in Her Hand*; or the melodic simplicity of indie folk, with its whimsical individuality and harmony, to *Princess of Snooze* (Fig. 79). This certainly fits in with the idea that Nara, rather than appropriating from existing subcultures, was producing new visual forms and cultivating an idiosyncratic style, which, to some viewers, came to represent a subculture of its own.

It is important to note that in Japan, the subcultural and the mainstream were not seen as two entirely different spheres of cultural production. Unlike their counterparts in Europe and the United States, Japanese subcultures were not always concerned with transgressing authority or resisting mass culture, and in fact, the distinction between the two was often blurred. There was one area where there had rarely been any overlap—the world of high culture—but even those divisions were beginning to break down. In 1990 the National Museum of Modern Art in Tokyo presented a retrospective exhibition of the cartoonist Osamu Tezuka (1928–1989) (Fig. 100), the first time a national art museum had showcased the work of a manga artist. Tezuka's contributions to Japanese culture include the much-loved character Astro Boy, a figure he created in 1951.[15] Astro Boy, a reluctant superhero, fights against the misuse of technology and attempts to protect a dystopian world in which

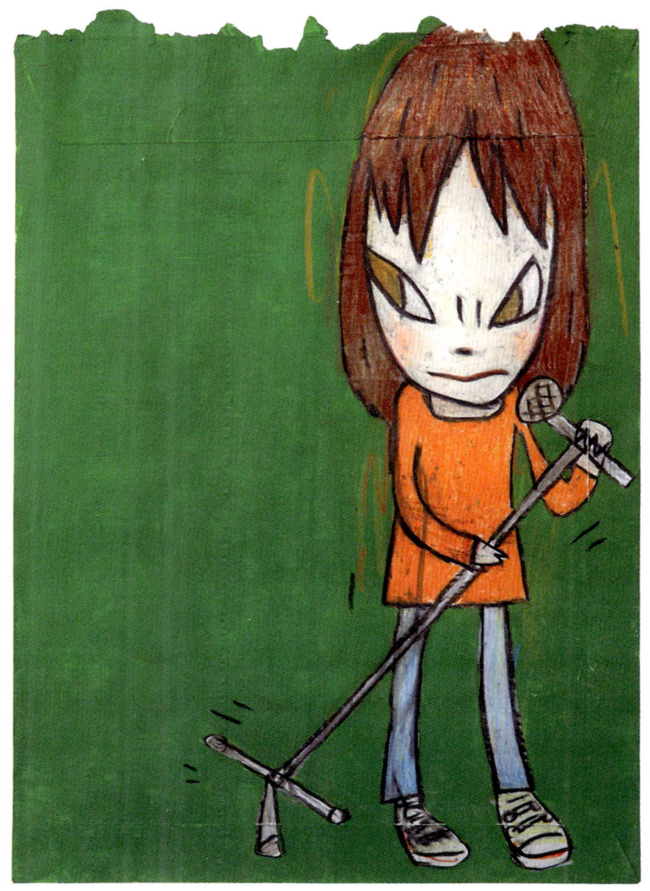

Fig. 99
Untitled, 2008, Colored pencil and acrylic on paper, 13 × 9 in. (33 × 22.9 cm)

science has destroyed nature and threatened humankind. The 1990 exhibition framed Astro Boy as a populist response to postwar Japan, a creation by a serious artist whose countless drawings and sketches of the animated figure were adapted from the comic book to the television screen.

In a sense, by showcasing manga through an art-historical lens, the exhibition presented a narrative that kept the potential unruliness of subculture at a distance. However cautious the scope of the exhibition may have been, it was significant that a high-profile art institution embraced popular visual culture at this time in a way that would attract a more inclusive viewing public. Unsurprisingly, many intellectuals voiced concern about the trend of popularizing the establishments of the so-called high arts. In a particularly extreme example, the critic Akira Asada, writing a critique of Nara and other artists like him who incorporated manga aesthetics into their work, cautioned against the sort of national image that was being presented when institutions showcased works he saw as infantilizing Japan. He wrote, "The West, rooted in its history of human-centric subjects, projects a sense of excitement about this 'fool's paradise' of Japan, with its infantile, animal-like non-human imagery in art."[16]

Despite the resistance he encountered, Nara was making strides in a changing global art world, navigating traditional institutions as well as more experimental, cutting-edge art spaces and projects. In 1998 he was invited to be a visiting artist at the University of California, Los Angeles, and the same year, he held his first solo museum exhibition in the United States at the Institute of Visual Arts at the University of Wisconsin, Milwaukee, quickly followed by shows at the Museum of Contemporary Art in Chicago and Santa Monica Museum of Art (both in 2000). In Japan, Nara took part in numerous gallery and museum group shows, but developments in the Japanese art world allowed him to take on more noncommercial projects as well. The 1990s, despite being a period of economic decline in Japan, saw the growth of independent art spaces, socially engaged art, and privately funded and government-supported large-scale public works projects.[17] Part of this growth was a response to the recession, which raised questions about sustainability and government and public social responsibility. For artists, these debates, which led to more active participation in civic and social fields, were important because until then, it had been in large part commercial galleries that provided financial support.

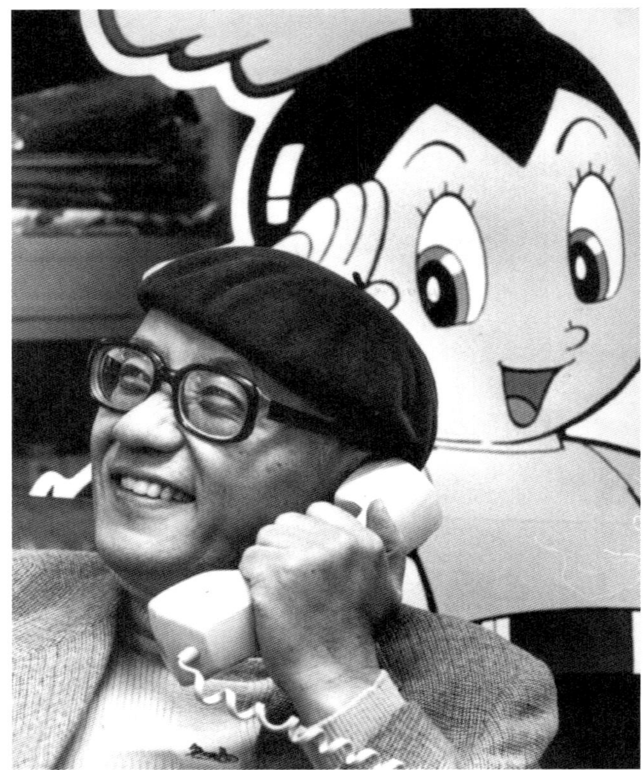

Fig. 100
Osamu Tezuka and Astro Boy, 1984

These changes gave Nara the chance to pursue more unusual curatorial projects. In 1997 he curated a nonselling art show entitled *World Peace Café*, which ran in parallel with a gallery presentation at the gallery Hakutosha in Nagoya. For the show, Nara filled the walls of a café with artworks from his own collection along with tear sheets from manga magazines and books that he liked. All of the proceeds from ticket sales were donated to UNICEF. This was a small project, one that challenged his usual practice of working with galleries, and it represents a strategy to which he would return when seeking alternative modes of engaging with audiences outside of traditional exhibition modes.

Nara also worked closely with curators who were presenting alternative voices to mainstream contemporary art discourse, including Takashi Azumaya for his exhibition *ART/DOMESTIC: Temperature of the Time* at Setagaya Art Museum, Tokyo, in 1999. Underscoring the concept of this group show was Azumaya's assessment that the Japanese art scene had become a muted version of Western conceptualism and was beginning to perpetuate a Eurocentric view of global history. Azumaya's response was to select artists whose works drew on more local and domestic interests that could redefine a Japanese identity beyond manga and anime, including Takashi Nemoto (Fig. 101), Yuichi Higashionna, and Shinro Ohtake. He subverted the authority of the white cube, also seen as a symptom of Western cultural hegemony in the arts, by presenting the artworks in a more ad hoc fashion, using pins or tape to "hang" them, displaying them cluttered and unframed, and placing them under various types of lighting. Nara's *The Little Pilgrims (Night Walking)* (1999) were clustered in a deep alcove, presenting a sinister collection of sleepwalking children trapped in a confined space, while a few others were scattered throughout the show, for now still free to escape (Fig. 102).

Perhaps what distinguished Nara the most from his peers at this time was the support he gained from a large community of admirers outside the art world itself. It is difficult to pinpoint the precise reasons why his work resonated so much with certain segments of the general public, but it is worth noting that one of the consequences of the 1990s economic depression was a spike in unemployment rates for young adults in particular, which fostered a general anxiety and distrust of the establishment among Japanese youth. Nara's art captured the tensions that existed in this generation between conformity and deviance,

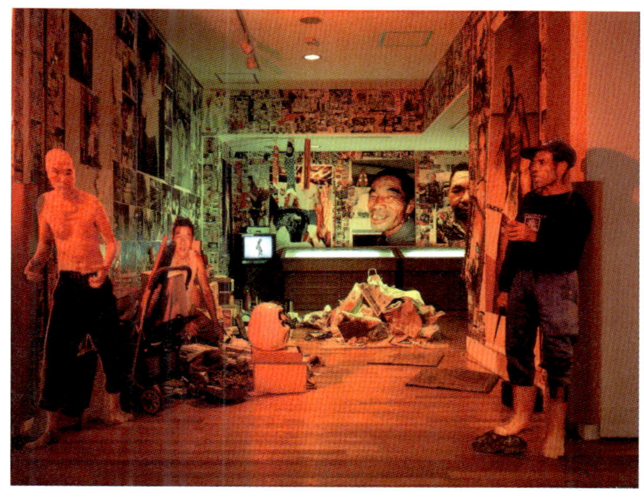

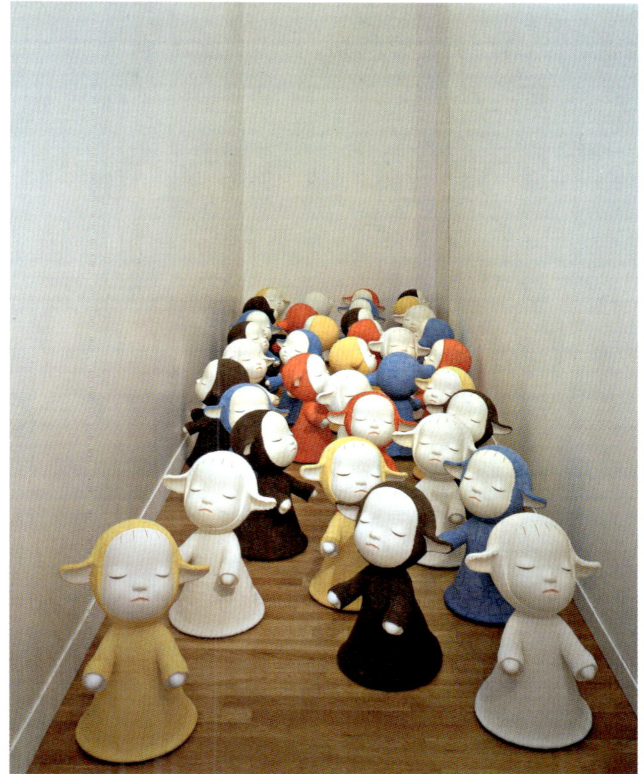

Figs. 101 and 102
Exhibition views: *ART/DOMESTIC: Temperature of the Time*, Setagaya Art Museum, Tokyo, 1999

appealing to the frustrations of those who felt disenfranchised by the invisible hand of an erratic market economy.

By the end of the decade, Nara had amassed a sizable community of fans who wore T-shirts emblazoned with his art, read his books, and collected his interviews from magazines. Many of these fans gained access to Nara's world through his illustration projects with Banana Yoshimoto, including the very successful *Hinagiku no jinsei* (The Life of Hinagiku), published in 2000, as well as his own illustrated tale *To the Earth*, commissioned for *Bijutsu techō* the same year. Furthermore, as Nara began to have more shows, exhibition catalogues and related items, especially those of limited runs or accompanying important shows, also became highly collectible among fans, including the books *In the Deepest Puddle* (1997) and *Slash with a Knife* (1998).[18]

Even more significant was the online community that mobilized around him. In 1999 admirers of Nara set up the online fan club HAPPY HOUR, named after the 1998 album by punk-pop group Shonen Knife whose cover Nara illustrated (Fig. 205), where contributors and readers could post responses and opinions and engage in discussions about Nara and his work. Still based in Germany, Nara found that this online community allowed him to maintain a meaningful connection with Japan. For a short period of time, he even shared his diary entries on the website for his fans to read. Although today it is almost impossible to think of a world without internet or social media, it was not until 1995, when the Windows 95 software was released, that online communication became widespread and the word *internet* became commonplace in Japan. Nara's utilization of this new medium of communication early on brought him to the forefront of digital social engagement and was instrumental in raising his profile. As Nara himself acknowledges, in an interview in *Bijutsu techō*: "I was made famous by the public, not the approval of critics."[19]

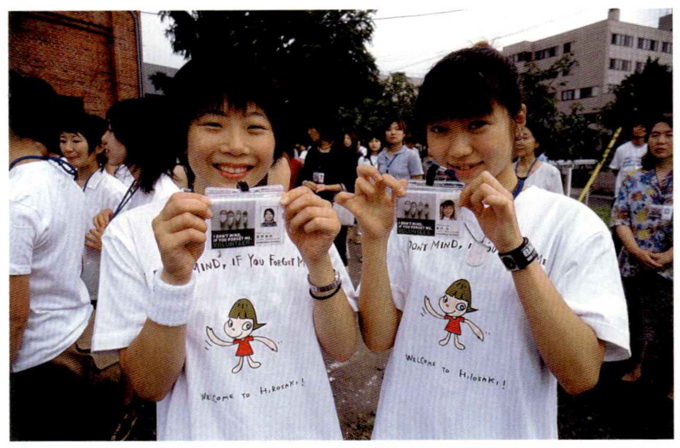

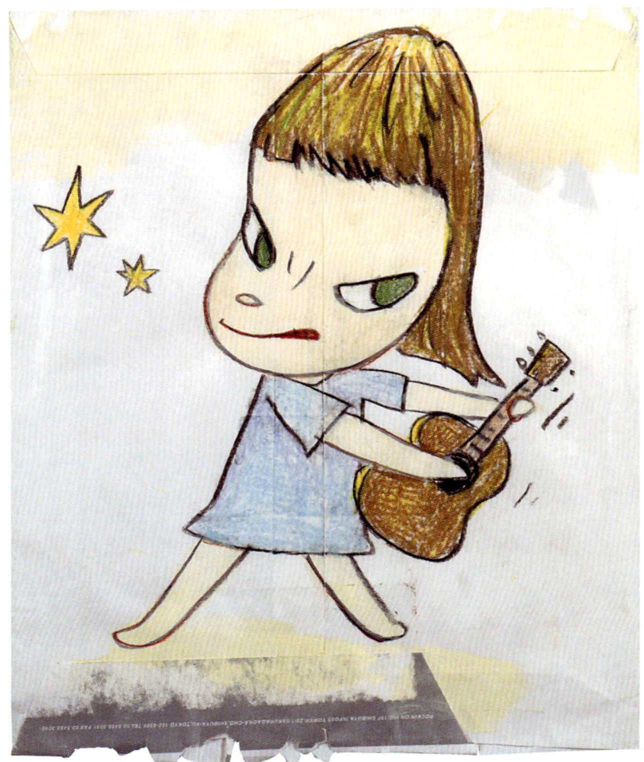

Turning Point, 2001

> **Finding a studio in suburban Tokyo was easy. . . . I was able to rent a two-story prefab warehouse. I could see the American landing strip at Yokota Air Base from a second-floor window. The toilets, which were outside, were shared with the factory next door. Of course there was no bath, so I created a shower room next to the sink. The prefab**

Fig. 103
Volunteers at the exhibition *Yoshitomo Nara: From the Depth of My Drawer*, Yoshii Brick Brew House, Hirosaki, 2004

Fig. 104
Time of My Life 2001, 1998–2001, Pen and colored pencil on paper, 10 ½ × 9 ⅜ in. (26.7 × 23.9 cm)

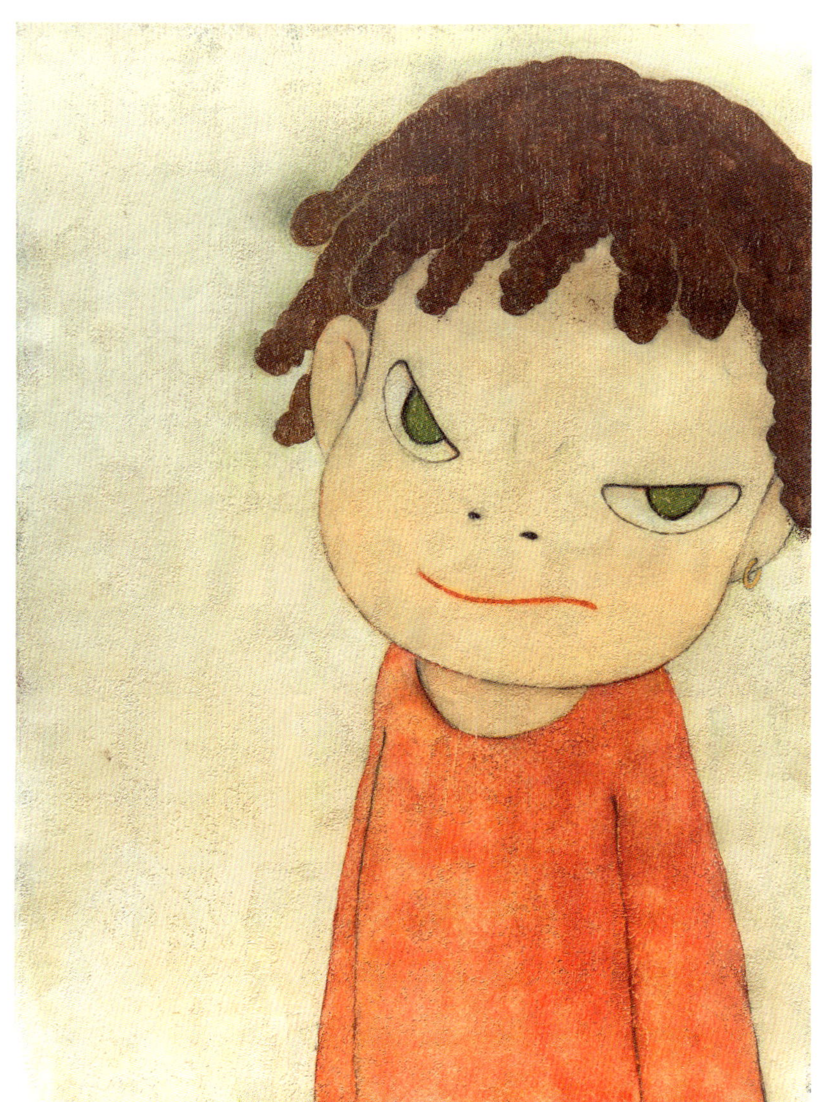

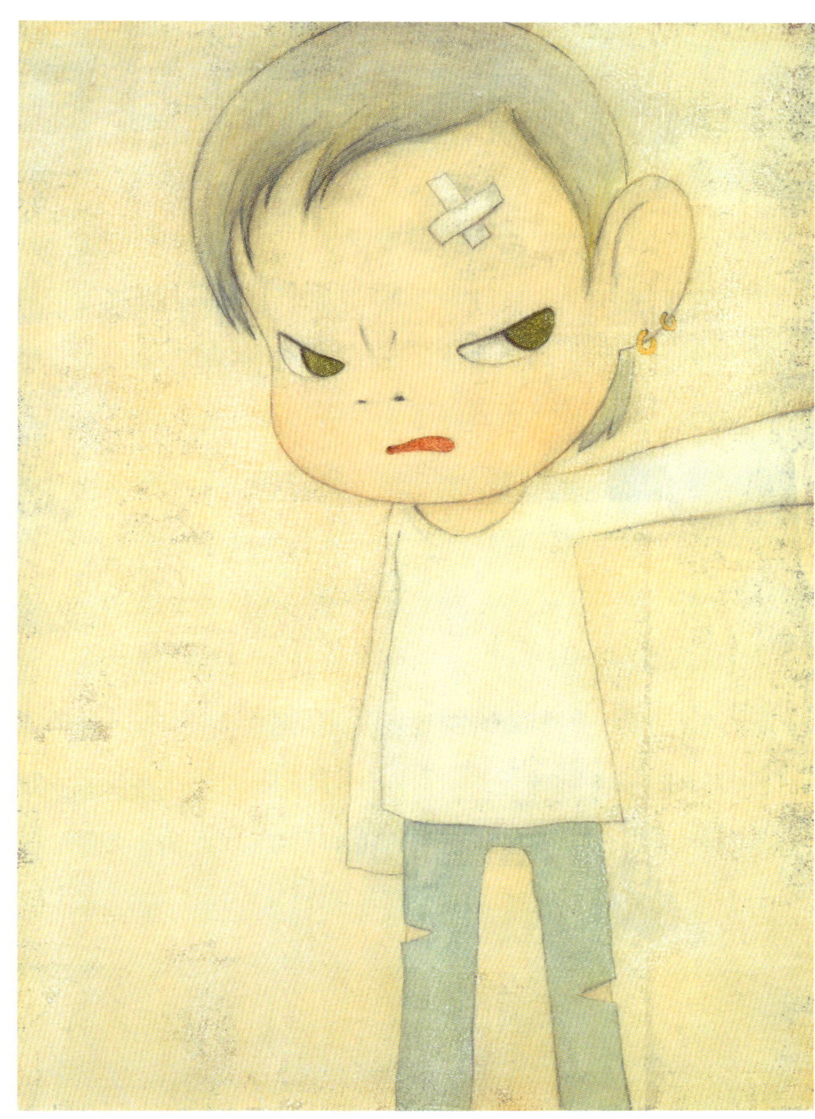

Fig. 105
Spin • Kids / Pi-ta, 2001,
Acrylic and colored pencil
on paper, 19 5⁄16 × 13 5⁄8 in.
(49 × 34.6 cm)

Fig. 106
Spin • Kids / Houka, 2001,
Acrylic and colored pencil
on paper, 19 5⁄16 × 13 5⁄8 in.
(49 × 34.6 cm)

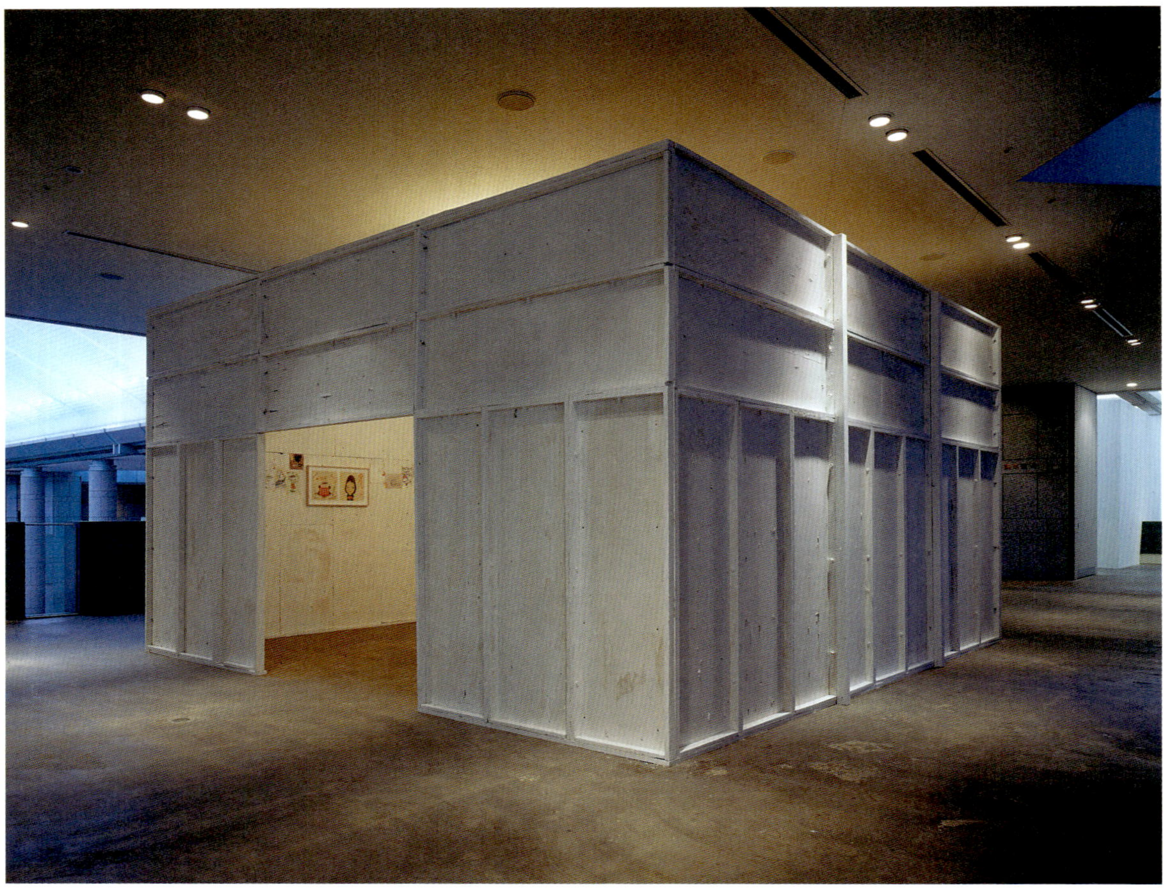

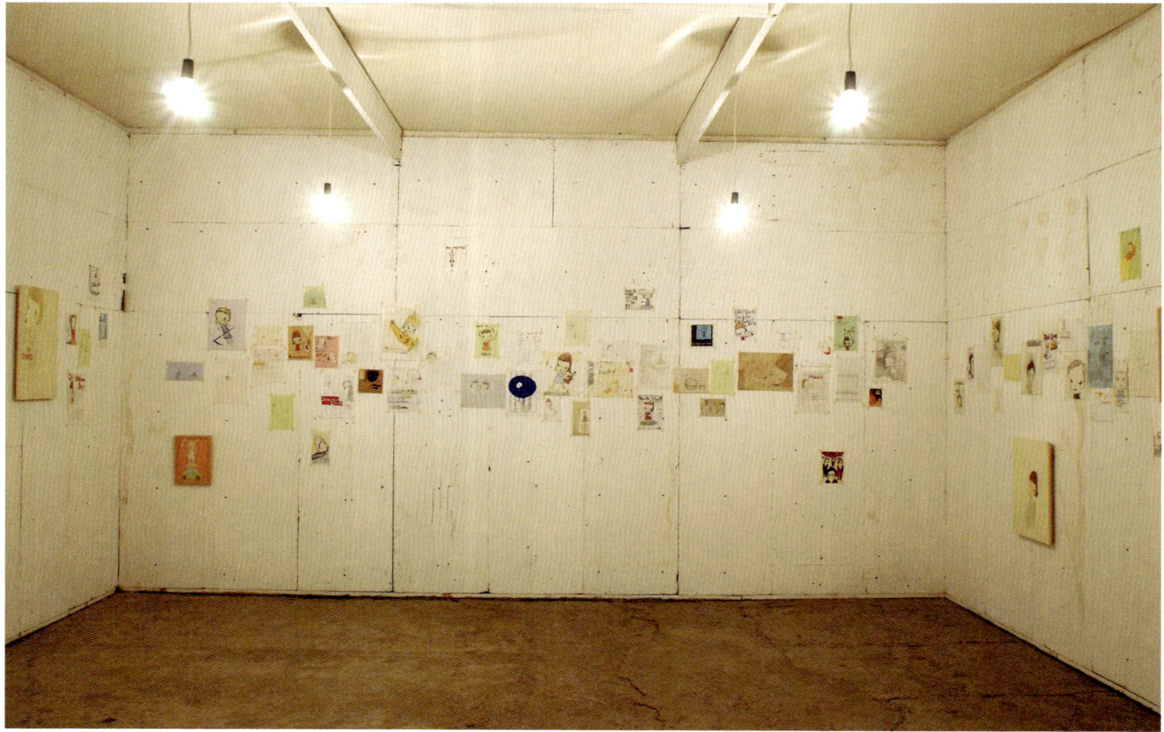

Figs. 107 and 108
Time of My Life, 2001, 93 drawings, plywood, water paint, and light bulbs, 118 ¾ × 217 ¾ × 212 ⅝ in. (301.5 × 553 × 540 cm)
Installation view: *Yoshitomo Nara: I DON'T MIND, IF YOU FORGET ME.*, Yokohama Museum of Art, Japan, 2001

walls were thin: summers were hot like a sauna, and winters were so cold the pipes would burst many times. The noise of jets taking off and landing at the American air base was terrible, but I fought back by turning up the volume on my stereo. At night when the factory was quiet and my lights burned bright, I worked accompanied only by my loud rock music blasting through the night.[20]

In 2000 Nara decided to move back to Japan after twelve years in Germany, partly because his Cologne studio was scheduled to be torn down and partly in anticipation of his upcoming show at the Yokohama Museum of Art. *I DON'T MIND, IF YOU FORGET ME.*, which opened in August 2001 and toured through 2002 to four other Japanese venues, was his largest and most comprehensive exhibition yet, spreading over five rooms and presenting dozens of works, most made after 1995, including *Fountain of Life*, *Princess Snooze*, *Pee "Dead of Night," Too Young to Die*, *Keep Your Chin Up*, and variations of *Dog from Your Childhood*.

One of the most significant aspects of this exhibition was how, working with the curator, Nara presented different ways for audiences to experience his works. For example, for his dog sculptures, he played with freestanding display walls, which seemed to be penetrated by a kennel, at various scales, with the dog's head protruding from one side and its tail from the other (Figs. 109 and 110). There was also a room built into the gallery space constructed with broken wood panels, which he dedicated to his drawings (Figs. 107 and 108). In keeping with the ad hoc nature of these works, some were taped on the walls and others framed. Colored pencil drawings of hipster boys (Figs. 105 and 106) and parts of a diary series, *Time of My Life 2001* (1998–2001) (Fig. 104), which range from scribbles on envelopes to detailed colored works on paper, together provided an intimate look into his everyday practice.

Perhaps the most innovative aspect of this show was the way in which Nara engaged directly with visitors in the titular work that formed the centerpiece (Figs. 111–113). For this piece, he asked volunteers to make dolls by hand based on designs that he shared through HAPPY HOUR and then send them to the museum. Some of these dolls were stuffed inside clear acrylic containers that spelled out the statement I DON'T MIND, IF YOU FORGET ME. From afar, the squished forms of the dolls create a jumble of patterns that make the title almost illegible. Crushed within the clear acrylic letters, they become the subject of this odd

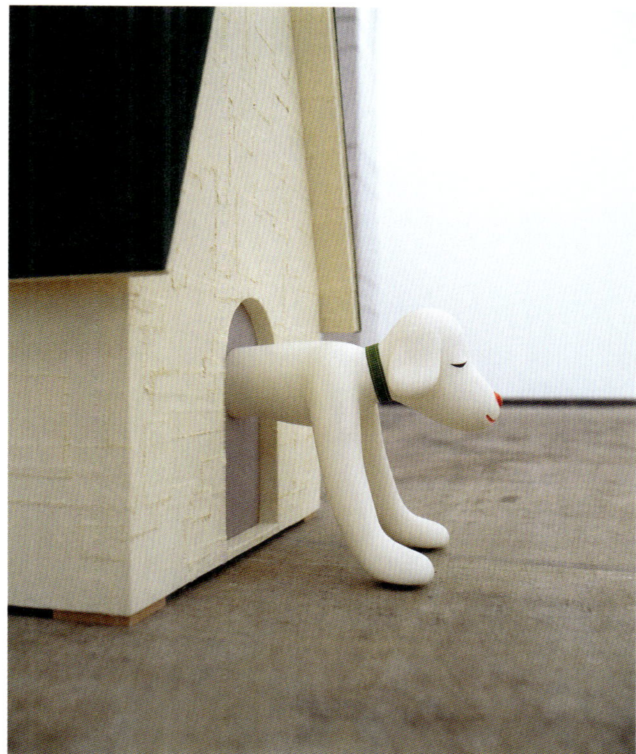

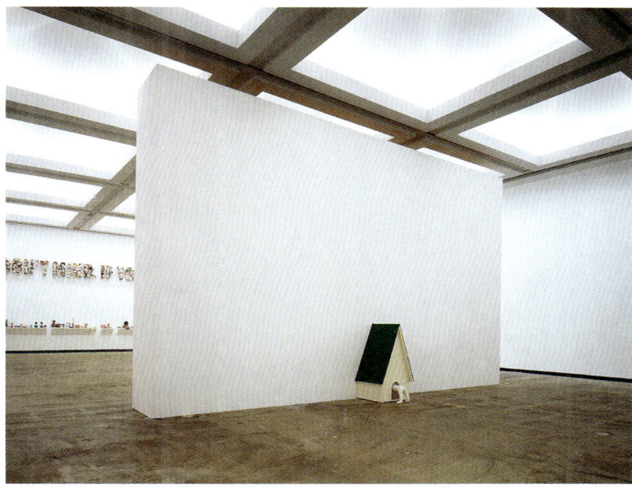

Figs. 109 and 110
Dog from Your Childhood, 2000, Fiber-reinforced plastics, plywood, cotton, and acrylic, 63 3/16 × 23 1/8 × 97 5/8 in. (106.5 × 58.8 × 248 cm)
Installation view: *Yoshitomo Nara: I DON'T MIND, IF YOU FORGET ME.*, Yokohama Museum of Art, Japan, 2001

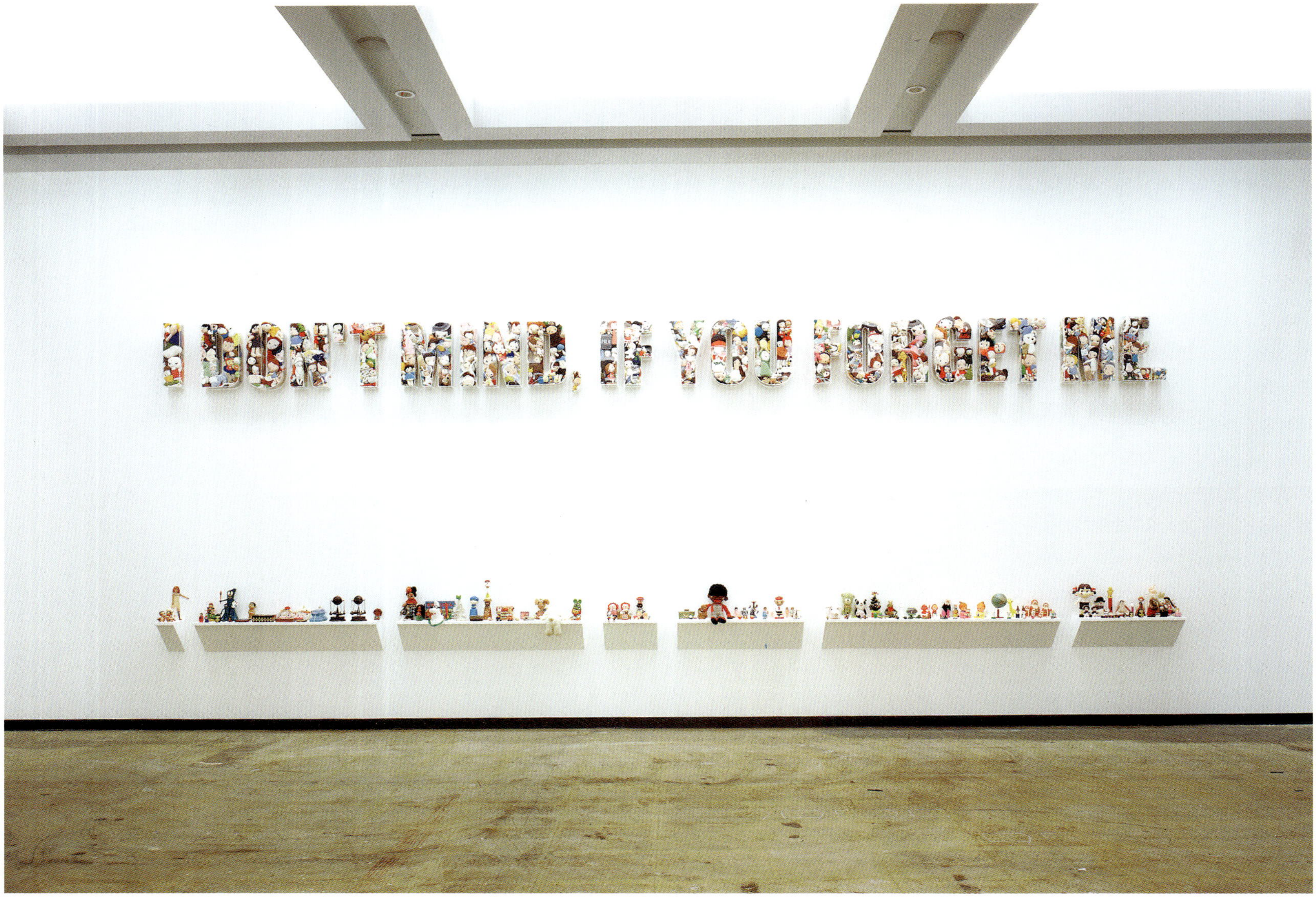

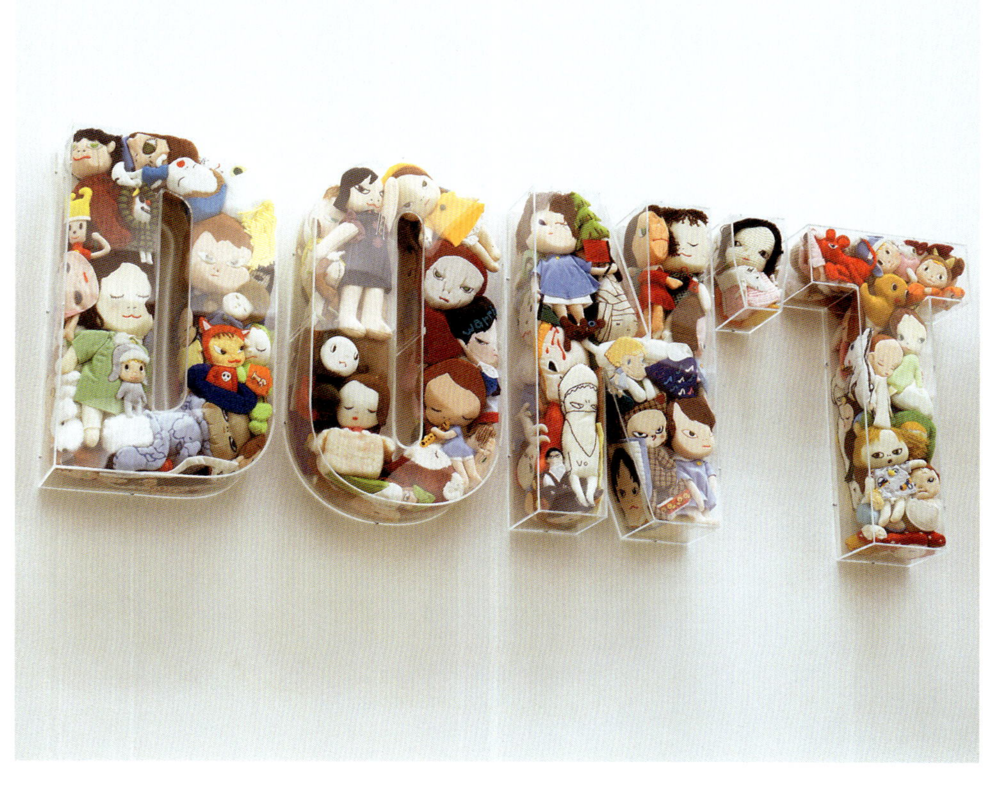
DON'T

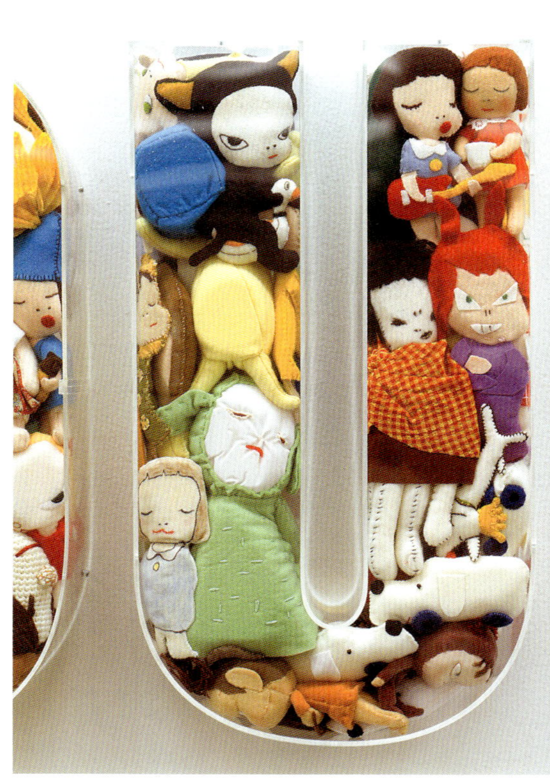

sentence—the I who is in fear of being forgotten—adding yet another layer to the concept of the show and highlighting the importance of childhood memories in Nara's art.[21] The open call generated an overwhelming response—more than 1,500 dolls were submitted—and those that did not fit into the letters were piled along a wall in another room, against a mirror imprinted with the words YOUR CHILDHOOD (Fig. 114).[22] The work can be seen as a grassroots intervention into an elitist space, where amateur fans become producers of fine art. But it also speaks to a different form of relationship between an artist and his audience that recalls the practice of gift giving, a social ritual that carries great significance and respect in Japan, as well as the religious practice of offering figurines to Jizō, protector of children, mothers, and the unborn child.

As part of the exhibition, the museum invited fans who had submitted dolls to write messages about their participation, which were shared with visitors. One volunteer, named Nanao, writes,

> First off, I was deeply impressed by how the exhibit was put together. . . . Seeing so many brothers and sisters, filled with loving care, I was so happy I could hardly stand it. No matter how many there were and even though there were so many of them, I thought they were all works familiar to me in their innocence. (I had a weird [*fushigi na*] feeling when I saw myself reflected in the mirror.) I thought it was really wonderful that I could participate. When I found my child [*ko*] in the exhibition hall, I thought, "It really did arrive in good order!" and I started to cry a little.[23]

Nanao's message evidences the strikingly intimate relationships people had with the project and the strong emotions it elicited. It also reveals the not-uncommon tendency of Nara's fans to address each other as brother and sister, which here extended to referring to the dolls as children. These fictive family ties challenge traditional concepts of the auteur and the aura of the originality in works of art. Seen in this context, Nara's installation becomes not a singular product of an artist's practice but a manifestation of a kinship network. This populist gesture shows that in the late 1990s and early 2000s, he was already experimenting with how to challenge the commercialization of art, a phenomenon that, ironically, he would increasingly be placed under scrutiny for in the years that followed.

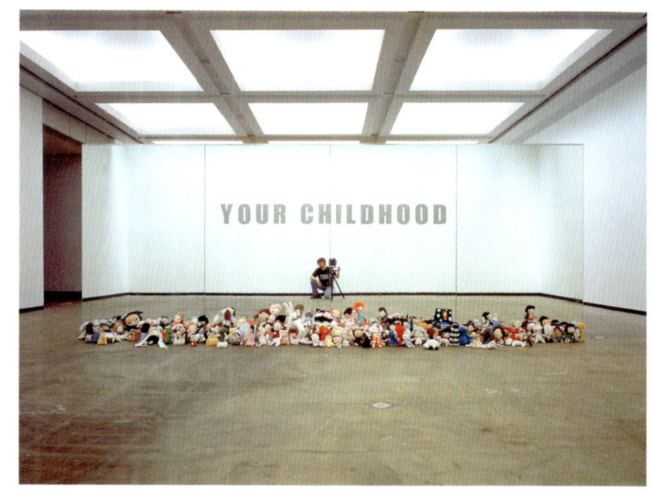

Figs. 111–113 (opposite)
I DON'T MIND, IF YOU FORGET ME., 2001, Plexiglass, stuffed animals and figurines, plywood, and various playthings, Top: 22 ½ × 293 ¼ × 4 in. (57 × 745 × 10 cm), Bottom: 21 ¼ × 293 ¼ × 13 ¼ in. (54 × 745 × 33.5 cm)
Installation view: *Yoshitomo Nara: I DON'T MIND, IF YOU FORGET ME.*, Yokohama Museum of Art, Japan, 2001

Fig. 114
YOUR CHILDHOOD, 2001, Plywood, water paint, fiber-reinforced plastics, acrylic on cotton mounted on plywood, vinyl sheets, mirrors, stuffed animals, and figurines, Plywood walls: 94 ½ × 236 ¼ × 31 ½ in. (240 × 600 × 80 cm), Dog (not pictured): 43 ⅞ × 39 ⅛ × 29 ½ in. (111.5 × 99.5 × 75 cm), Letters: 21 ⅝ × 233 ½ in. (55 × 593 cm)
Installation view: *Yoshitomo Nara: I DON'T MIND, IF YOU FORGET ME.*, Yokohama Museum of Art, Japan, 2001

Nara and the Superflat

Nara's meteoric rise at the beginning of the twenty-first century was also fueled by his involvement with the artist Takashi Murakami. Nara first met Murakami in 1998, when they were both visiting professors at the University of California, Los Angeles, and two years later, Murakami curated the first of a series of three exhibitions that opened over the course of five years: *Superflat* at the Parco Galleries in Tokyo and Nagoya (2000),[24] *Coloriage* at the Fondation Cartier pour l'art contemporain in Paris (2002), and *Little Boy: The Arts of Japan's Exploding Subculture* at Japan Society in New York (2005).[25] The exhibitions brought together an array of artworks that embodied Murakami's groundbreaking Superflat manifesto, which quickly became accepted as a theory and method for looking at Japanese contemporary art, especially for an international audience.[26]

In broad strokes, Superflat is the visual and conceptual manifestation of a postmodern collapse of hierarchies and the fragmentation of the modern subject in Japan.[27] On a visual level, it is an aesthetic that embraces surfaces rather than depth, the spectacle rather than the cerebral, and the flattening of the distinction between high and low culture. This visual world of flatness is rooted in two different but connected worlds: the realm of *kawaii* and its relationship to consumer culture, and the subculture of *otaku*, a Japanese word with no direct English equivalent, but which roughly translates to *geek* or *nerd*.

The *kawaii* world is an important component of Murakami's theory of Superflat, and he frames it within a broader discourse of mainstream commodification. He interprets the large-scale consumption of *kawaii* products, such as plush Hello Kitty dolls or Doraemon tchotchkes, as part of a refusal to grow up—to leave the comforts of a capitalist economy that provides this indulgence—a disposition that can only give way to a sense of impotence.[28] At the same time, he participates with enthusiasm at this juncture of art and market, following in the footsteps of Andy Warhol and Jeff Koons and corroborating the common perception of a hyperconsumerist postmodern Japan.[29] These three interrelated elements—massive levels of consumption of *kawaii* goods, the blurring of art and commodity, and the defining of a Japanese cultural identity—inform Murakami's argument that Superflat is about the collapse of hierarchies between high art and commercial culture. Stripped of these categories, cultural motifs are

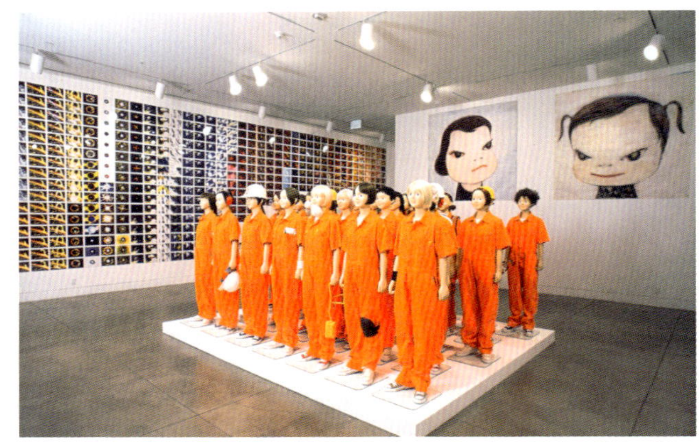

Fig. 115
Exhibition view: *Superflat*, MOCA Pacific Design Center, Los Angeles, 2001

Fig. 116 (opposite)
Only Faces Appear in My Mind, 2000, Acrylic and colored pencil on paper, 79 5/16 × 80 1/8 in. (201.5 × 203.5 cm)

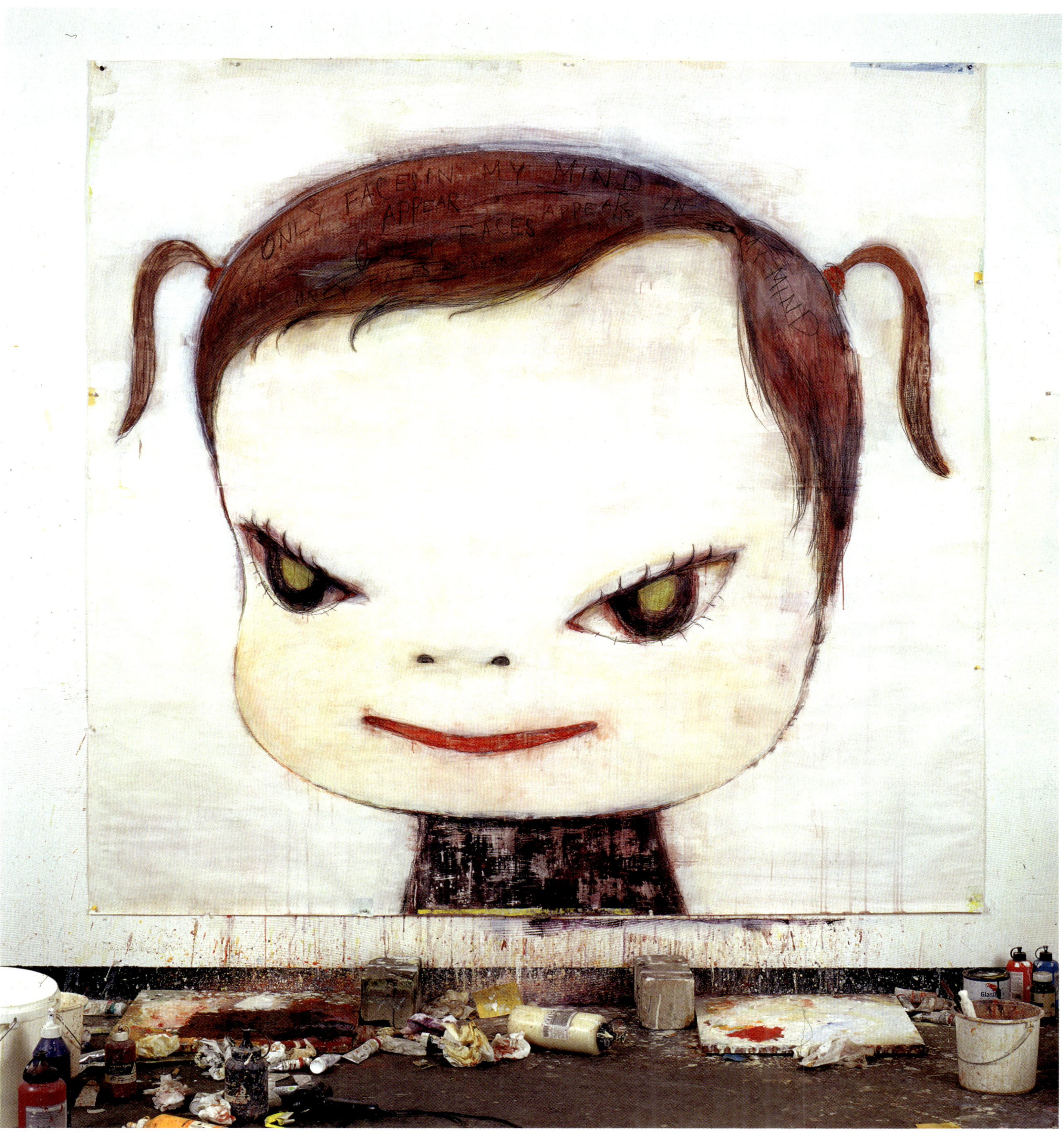
ONLY FACES IN MY MIND
APPEAR
IN
ONLY FACES APPEAR
MIND

all rendered the same and thus have no inherent value. They are, in other words, conceptually depthless: super flat. Murakami's response to this idea is to depict *kawaii*-inspired motifs within formats that recall traditional Japanese screens or on large-scale canvases in order to establish an association with the world of high art. Murakami then paints their surfaces with reflective or synthetic colors, creating flattened, glossy surfaces that eradicate the illusion of depth. Of his many *kawaii*-inspired motifs, perhaps the best known is Mr. DOB (Fig. 117), a Mickey Mouse–inspired character with sharp teeth whose name derives from the Japanese slang term *dobojite?* (why?)—a rhetorical shrugging of the shoulders that captures the assertion of meaninglessness, of being Superflat.[30]

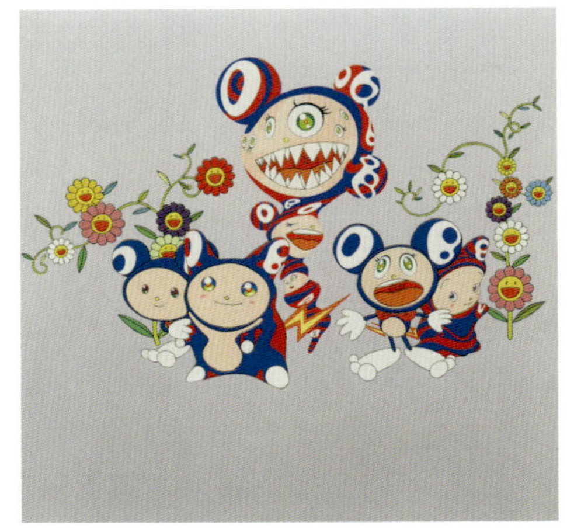

Fig. 117
Takashi Murakami, *Mr. DOB All Stars (Oh My the Mr. DOB)*, 1998, Acrylic on canvas mounted on board, 15 ¾ × 15 ¾ × 1 ¾ in. (40 × 40 × 4.5 cm)

There is extensive literature on the *otaku* yet little consensus regarding who or what it represents.[31] A common definition regards the *otaku* as a type of person—usually male, who indulges in video games and comic books—but it is perhaps more accurate to define it as a mode of social being. The term is typically used to describe those who indulge in deviant behaviors by reveling in the excessive and the extreme, intensely obsessed with fan merchandise, and overly absorbed in a world of virtual sociality. Furthermore, the *otaku*'s obsessive behavior leads to sexual and violent fantasies, captured by the popular manga genre *lolicon* (a reference to Vladimir Nabokov's *Lolita*), which features young heroines with big eyes and childlike speech patterns and dressed in outfits that emphasize their long legs and prepubescent bodies.[32]

The theme of deviant behavior linked to the *otaku*, along with the idea that cultural meaning disappears in late consumer capitalism, is supported in the Superflat manifesto by two more ambitious ideas aimed at defining postmodern Japan. The first is that the *otaku* is indicative of a contemporary Japan still reeling from the trauma of defeat in the Pacific War. Japan's denial of its own history of nuclear destruction, in Murakami's formulation, induces a psychic state that has kept it perpetually infantilized, producing a society in which the incessant pursuit of a "childlike culture" cannot be separated from the memory of the atomic bomb. The indulgence of childish things, for Murakami, can be seen as a mode of "flatness," in that the linear narrative of history has been halted in its tracks, leaving Japan in a permanent suspended state of being beyond which nothing can exist.

The notion of the bleak destruction and stunted growth of a nation that underscores the Superflat theory is provocatively captured in the title of the last of Murakami's three exhibitions: *Little Boy*, the code name given to the nuclear bomb that decimated Hiroshima in 1945.[33] The subsequent nuclear fallout, Murakami suggests, gave rise to apocalyptic tales in anime and manga, such as Godzilla and Astro Boy, that became popular in the subsequent decades, in which monsters, violence, sexuality, and youthful sweetness form a dystopian future. Murakami's *My Lonesome Cowboy* (1998) (Fig. 118), a fiberglass sculpture of a beatific young boy with futuristic hair who turns his ejaculated sperm into a lasso, brings together these strands of Superflat by conflating the innocence, violence, and heightened sexuality that express the sentiments of the manga dystopia so beloved by the *otaku*.

Murakami's second postulation is that Superflat is an inherently Japanese cultural phenomenon whose history can be traced back to the Edo period when woodblock prints favored flat aesthetic qualities and belonged to the consumerist world of Edo's pleasure quarters. Murakami posits Edo as a repository of traditions that form an authentic Japanese past, a precursor to Japan's consumerist present. His position follows in the footsteps of other scholars who also trace the history of manga to earlier traditions in Japanese art, in some instances going as far back as the twelfth century to the *emaki* scrolls of the Heian period.[34] For Murakami, this history strengthens his argument for a specifically Japanese modernity that does not follow a Western model, although at times it downplays the impact of American culture on postwar Japan.

What differentiates the Superflat theory and its related exhibitions from other postmodern Japanese narratives that were being espoused around the same time is that Murakami brings together all the various components—*otaku* and *kawaii* subcultures, Japan's recent history of violence, a genealogy of Japanese art history—under one single term and presents material evidence through his exhibitions of how his theory takes visual form.[35] Together, these qualities create a neatly packaged framework for understanding contemporary Japanese culture, which was especially influential for audiences outside of Japan. What became emphasized in the theory was its account of subculture that focused on the differences between nations and national values, and, while oversimplified, this idea of the uniqueness of Japan in

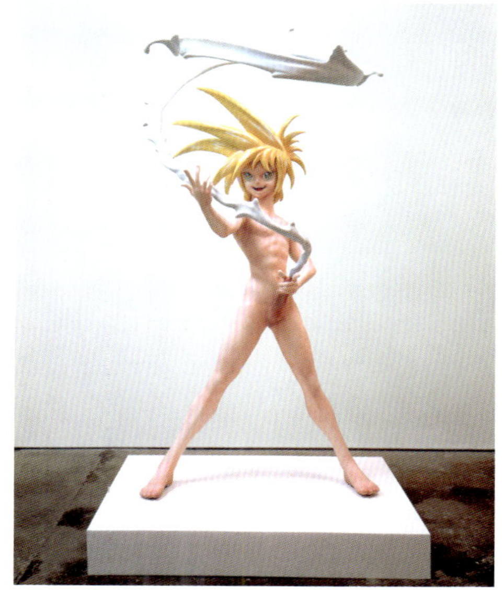

Fig. 118
Takashi Murakami,
My Lonesome Cowboy, 1998,
Oil, acrylic, fiberglass,
and iron, 100 × 46 × 35 ⅞ in.
(254 × 116.8 × 91 cm)

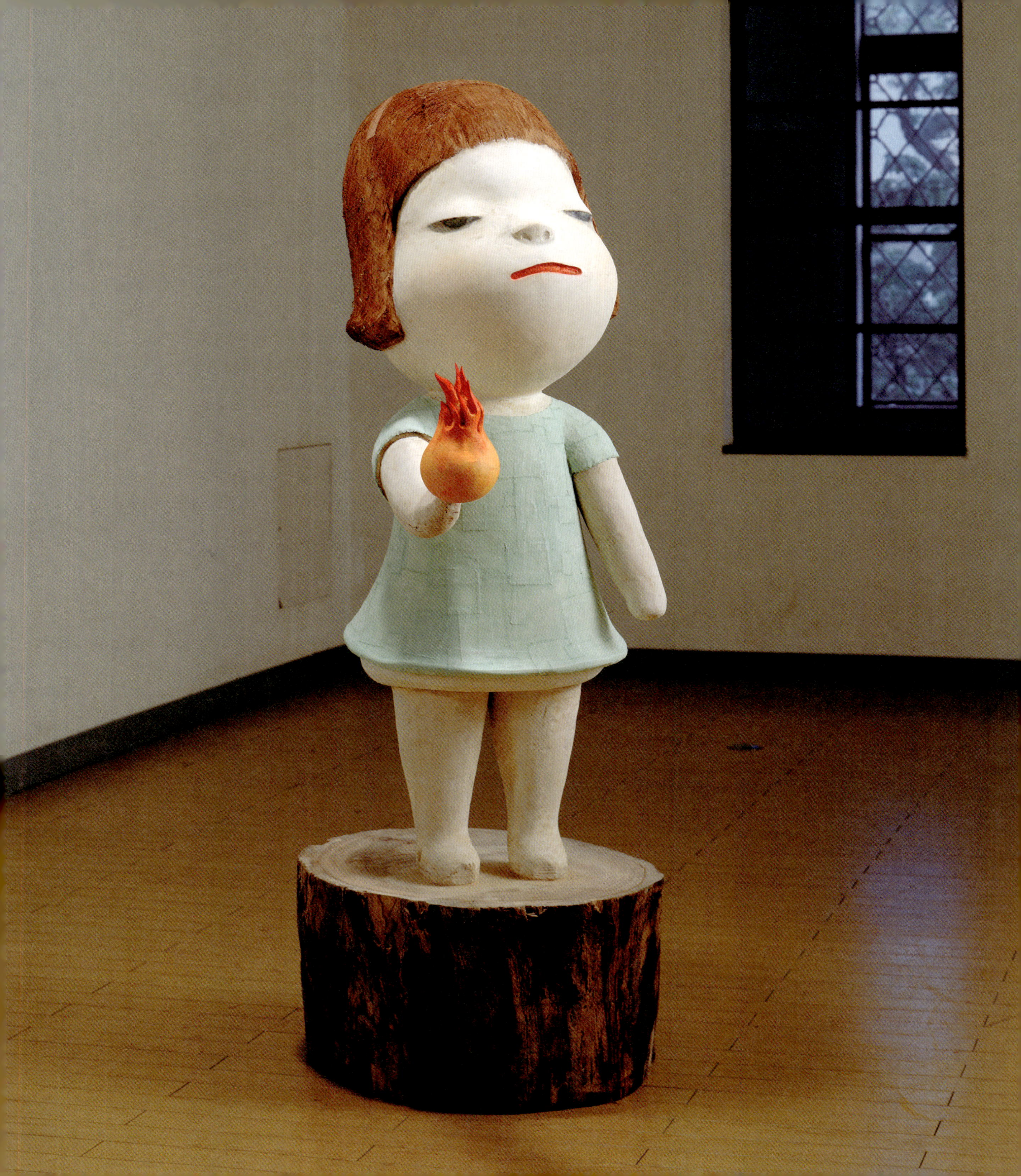

relation to the West offered a very accessible narrative. Murakami equated the *otaku* with Japaneseness in a way that fixated on the more extreme or excessive characteristics of social behavior and cultural oddity, in keeping with stereotypes of a techno-dystopian Japan seen in films such as *Blade Runner* (1982) or *Ghost in the Shell* (1995).[36] As the Superflat theory gained ground and was absorbed into mainstream use, the limits of the cultural translations of key terms such as *kawaii* and *otaku* became increasingly less relevant.[37] This resulted in a tendency for outsiders to generalize Japanese culture along these lines, a myopic ethnocentrism that overemphasized the Superflat as a form of "bizarre Japan."

In many ways, Nara would seem to inhabit the Superflat world, and in fact, by the time of Murakami's exhibition, many curators and writers had already positioned Nara within a similar postmodern Japanese art narrative by emphasizing his supposed affinity with subcultural motifs, his loyal fan base that traversed the worlds of high and low culture, and a body of work that centered on themes of childhood. For many writers, Nara's works are still often seen through the lens of Superflat; as such, it may be useful to examine more closely the relevance and limitations of the theory with respect to artworks made around the time of Murakami's exhibitions.

In a certain sense, Nara's 2001 sculpture *Light My Fire* (Fig. 119) can be regarded as the *kawaii* equivalent of Murakami's *otaku*-inspired *My Lonesome Cowboy*.[38] But Nara's engagement with visual culture in this work is not like that of Murakami, who uses pictorial codes self-reflexively to comment on conditions of cultural production. Nara made the sculpture during his tenure as a guest artist at the Tokyo University of the Arts, where, for a month, he slowly carved it from a block of wood in the company of students. The process took him back to his time as an art student, and it resurrected a motif from those days as well: a girl with fire, seen in his earlier sculpture *Flaming Head I* (1989) (Fig. 50) and the painting *Romantic Catastrophe* (1988) (Fig. 52). This consideration of the personal details of the work's creation helps situate it outside the vacuum of cultural critique that would render it Superflat. If Superflat provides a manifesto that can map cultural codes and identify a collective identity, Nara arguably resists being absorbed into this cultural map by expressing his own personal biography in his work.

Another important set of artworks is Nara's 1999 series of drawings, *In the Floating World*, in which he alters reproductions of Edo-period

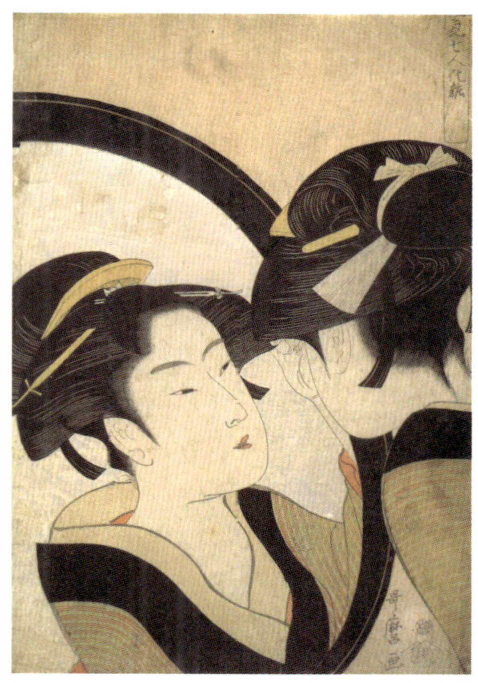

Fig. 119 (opposite)
Light My Fire, 2001,
Acrylic and cotton on carved wood, 74 × 68 ⅛ × 43 5/16 in.
(188 × 173 × 110 cm)

Fig. 120
Kitagawa Utamaro, *Naniwa Okita Admiring Herself in a Mirror*, ca. 1790–95,
Polychrome woodblock print; ink and color on paper, mica ground, 14 ½ × 9 7/8 in.
(36.8 × 25.1 cm)

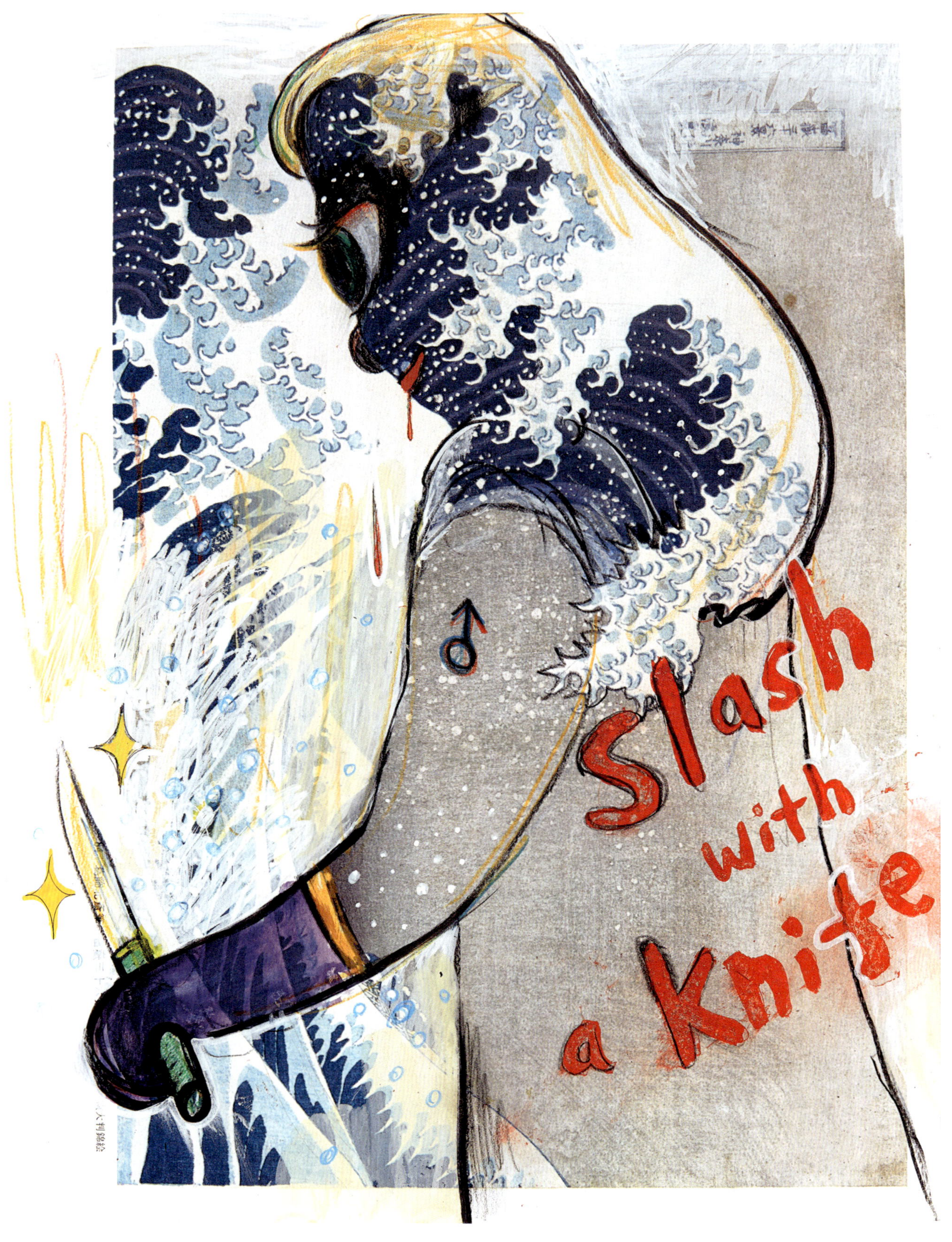

Fig. 121
Slash with a Knife (In the Floating World), 1999, Pencil, colored pencil, and acrylic on paper, 16 11/16 × 13 in. (42.4 × 33 cm)

Fig. 122 (opposite)
Mirror (In the Floating World), 1999, Pen, colored pencil, and acrylic on paper, 16 11/16 × 13 in. (42.4 × 33 cm)

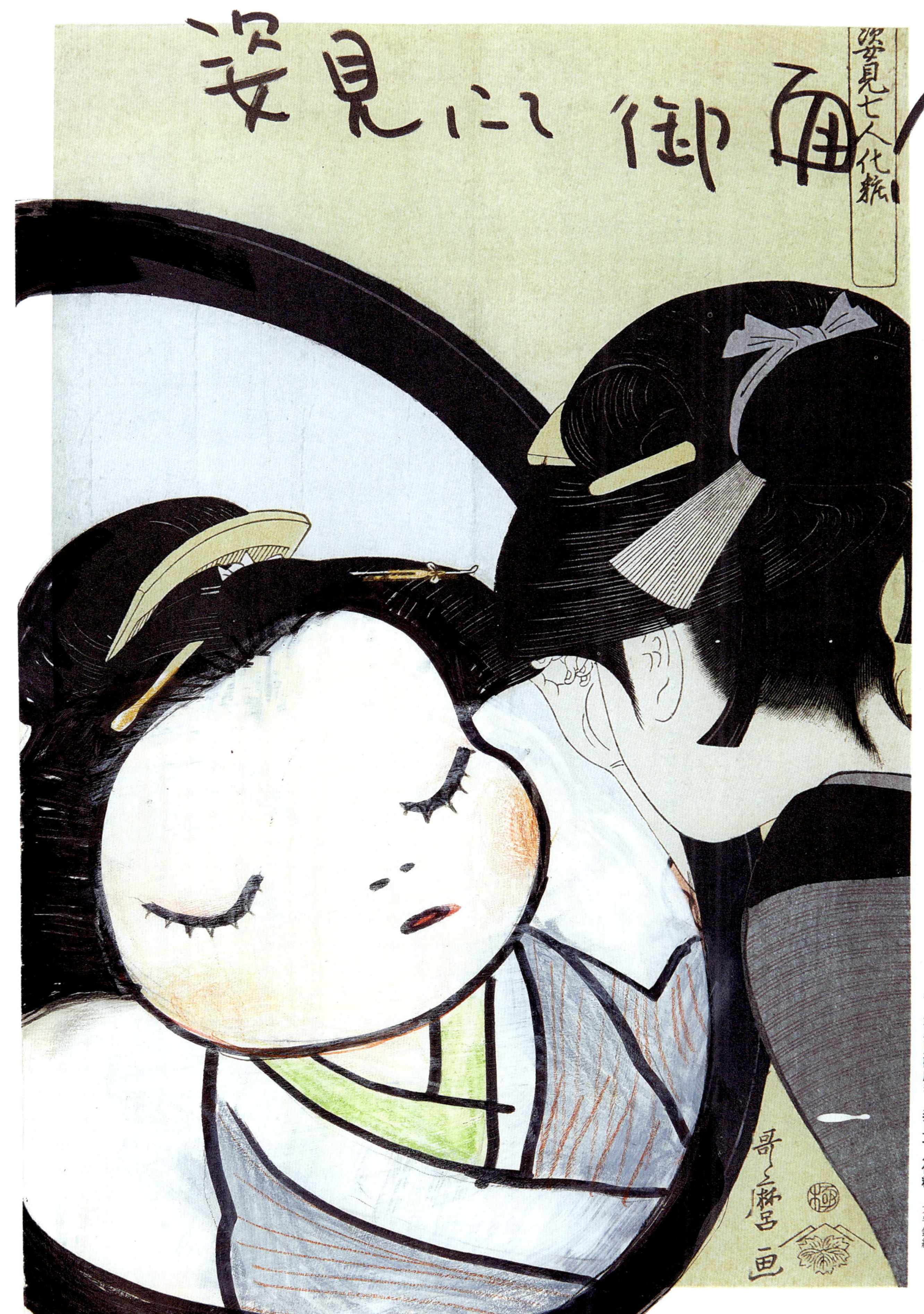

49
喜多川歌麿筆　姿見七人化粧
大判錦絵

ukiyo-e prints through erasure and graffiti. In one work, he turns the nineteenth-century master Katsushika Hokusai's famous *The Great Wave* (ca. 1830–32) on its side and superimposes upon it a giant menacing girl, with the Western male-gender symbol tattooed on her arm, slashing her way through an *ukiyo-e* world (Fig. 121). This iconoclastic gesture is only partial, for Nara never fully destroys the original *ukiyo-e* print; he often leaves the signatures and seals untouched and preserves enough of the original image to allow for a playful dialogue. For example, in *Mirror (In the Floating World)* (Fig. 122), he adds his big-headed girl as the reflection in Kitagawa Utamaro's famous print, *Naniwa-ya Okita Admiring Herself in a Mirror* (ca. 1790–95) (Fig. 120). Utamaro was a master of creating sexually charged works that captured voyeuristic glances at the beauties in Edo's floating world. Nara's black-outlined girl, clumsily drawn, intervenes in the print's circuit of gazes, and in so doing, she overturns the idealized female object—although she sits dangerously at its edge.

What is evident from this series is that Nara acknowledges, arguably even respects, the Edo past, and this, instead of flattening, opens up a space where Edo's histories become active parts of Japan's postmodern present. His rebellious young girls, in their interactions with an Edo world where women are seen as objects of male desire, push against a parallel modern history of manga and its male-dominated *otaku* universe. We have to tread carefully when proposing a feminist reading of these works—they are not intended to serve an activist role or claim a political position—but what we can see is that Nara's engagement with Edo prints is not straightforward, not least in the way it tests the rhetoric of Superflat.

Moving on: After 2001

> **I felt like I was getting swept up by a big wave that wasn't just about the art world. Nonetheless, I strove to make art with the desire I had from my Germany days, and for four or five years after the exhibition [in 2001], I stoically carried on working. But as the value of my work began to climb in the art market, the voices of those who wanted my pieces, of wanting to exhibit them, started to become too loud.**[39]

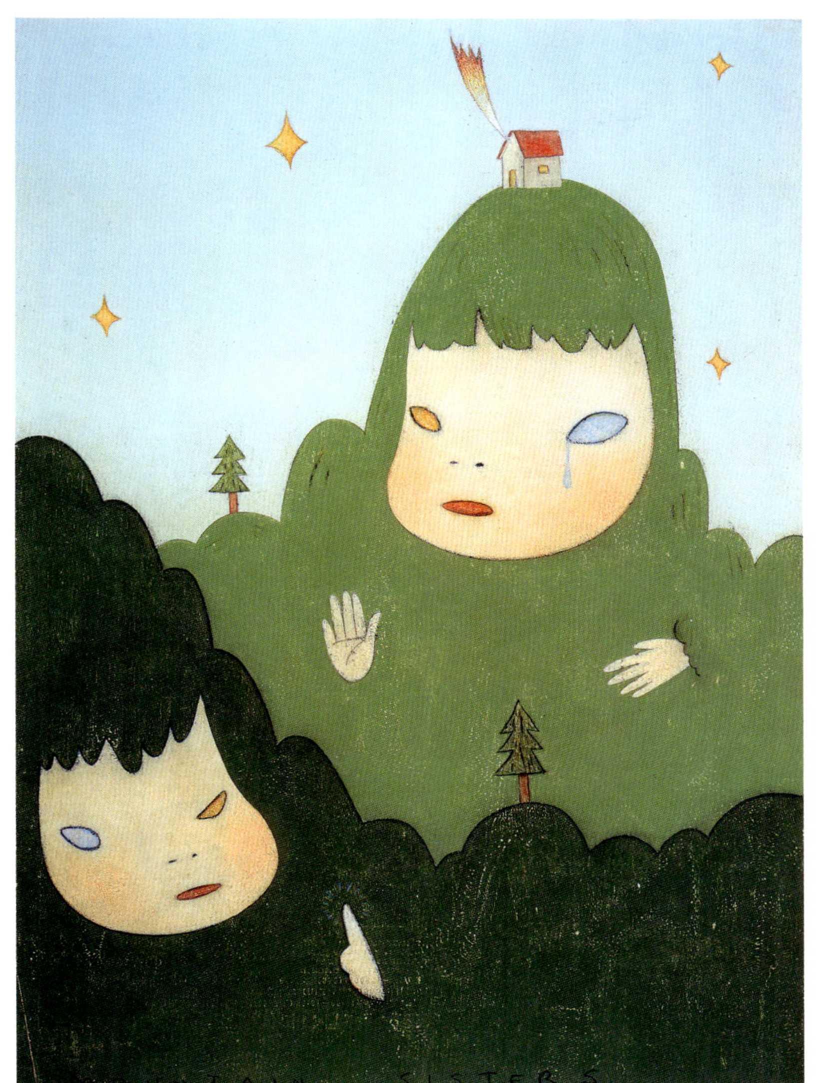

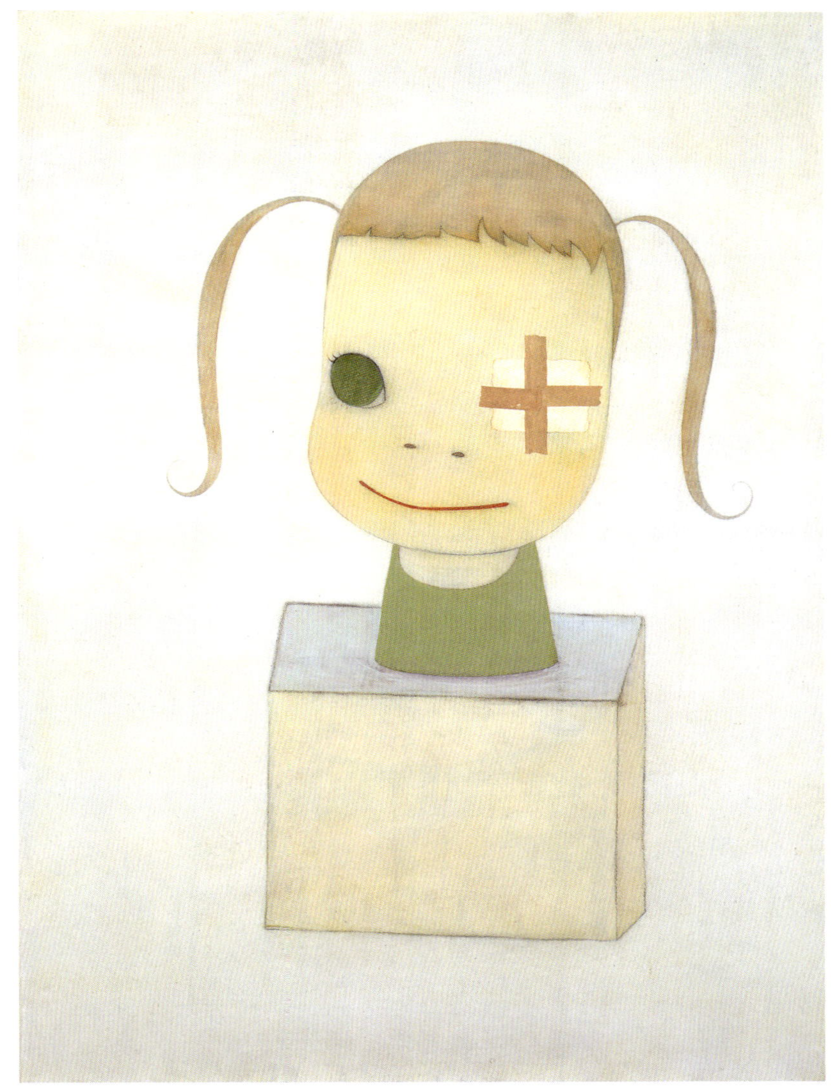

Fig. 123
Mountain Sisters, 2003,
Acrylic and colored pencil
on paper, 29 ¹⁵⁄₁₆ × 22 ¹⁄₁₆ in.
(76 × 56 cm)

Fig. 124
Sorry, Couldn't Draw the Left Eye!, 2003, Acrylic, colored
pencil, and collage on paper,
53 ¹⁵⁄₁₆ × 39 ³⁄₈ in. (137 × 100 cm)

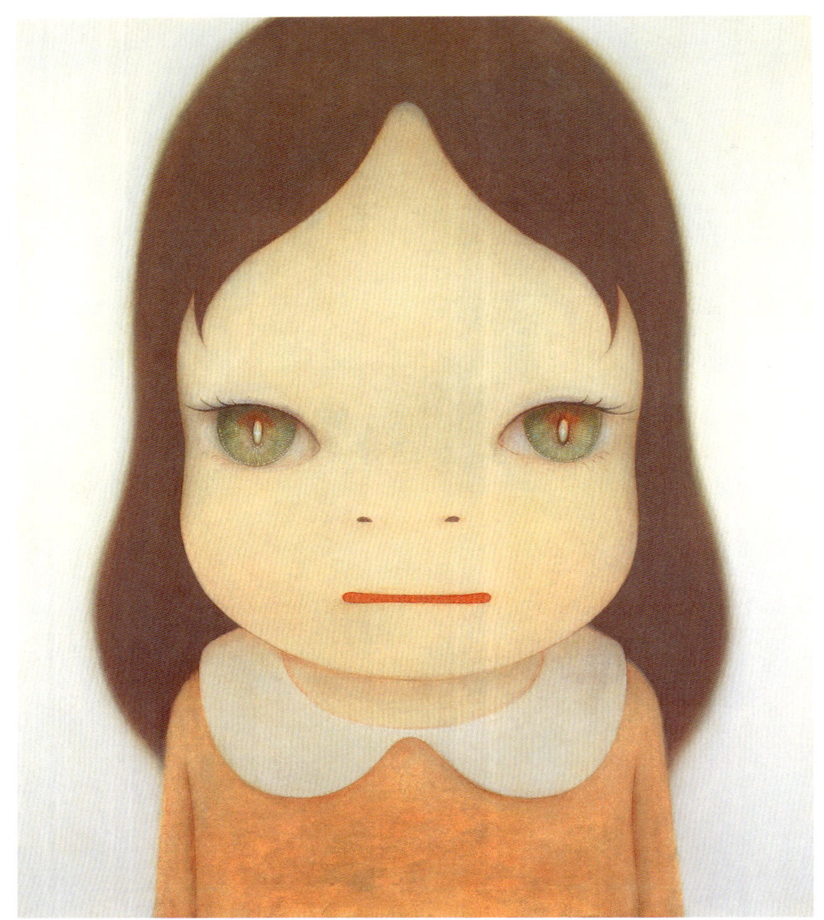

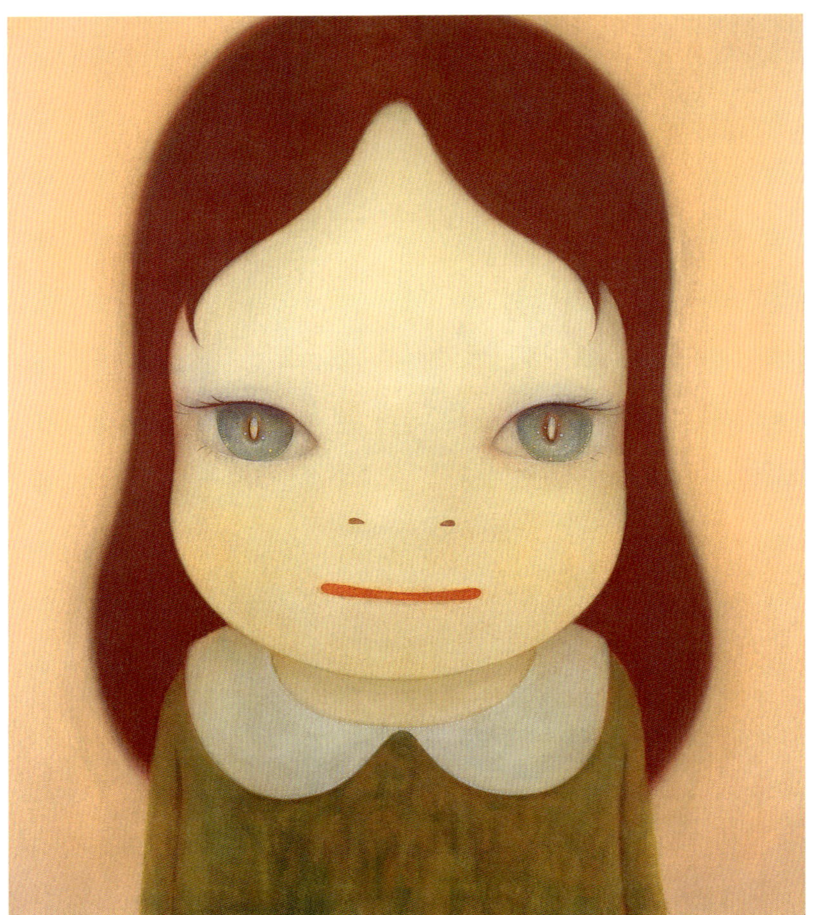

Fig. 125
Twins I, 2005, Acrylic on canvas, 46 1/16 × 39 3/8 in. (117 × 100 cm)

Fig. 126
Twins II, 2005, Acrylic on canvas, 46 1/16 × 39 3/8 in. (117 × 100 cm)

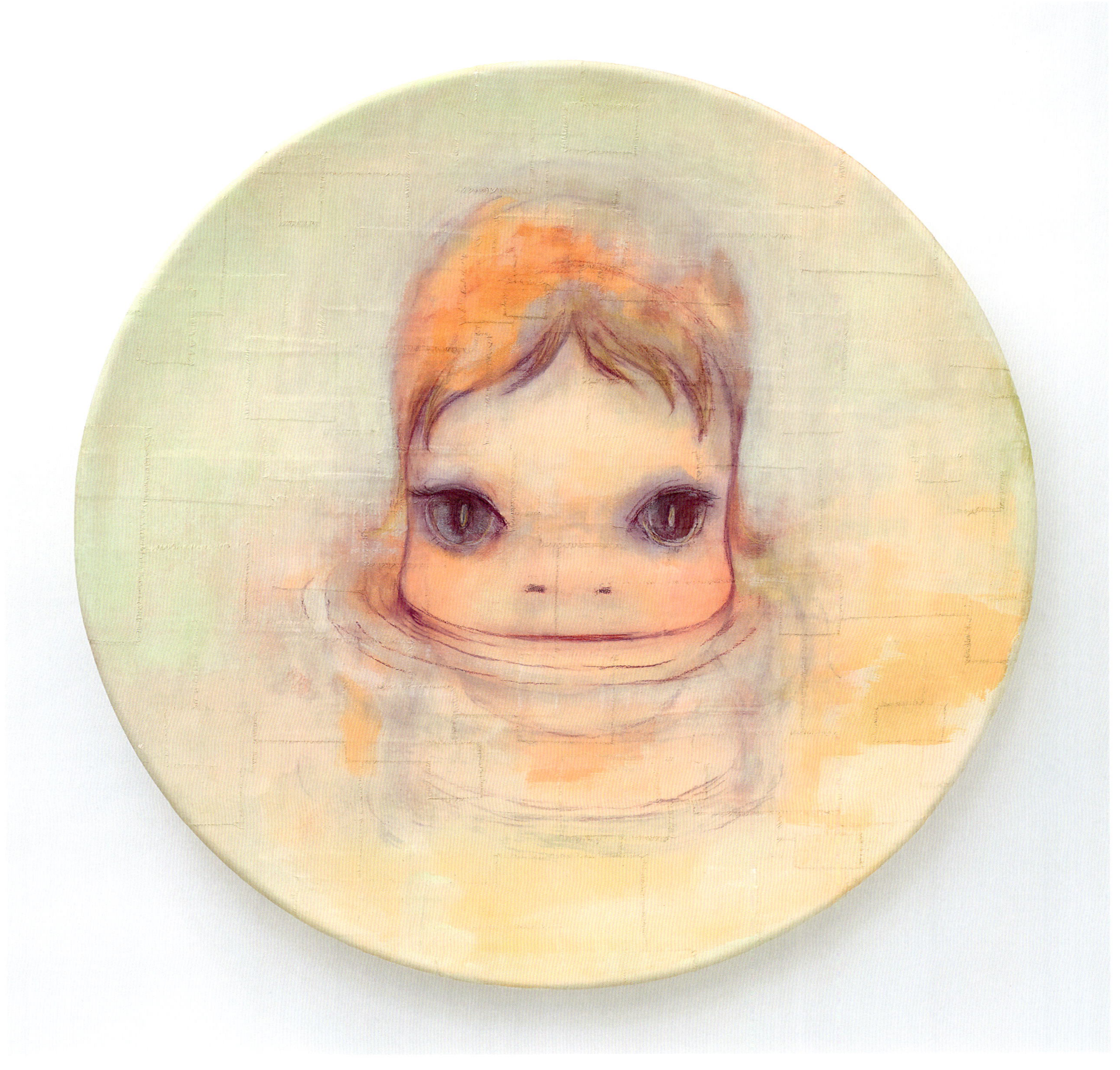

Fig. 127
Shallow Puddles 2004, 2004,
Acrylic on cotton mounted
on fiber-reinforced plastics,
diam. 37 ⅜ × d. 5 ⅞ in.
(95 cm × 15 cm)

Fig. 128 (following spread)
Shallow Puddles 2004 (detail),
2004

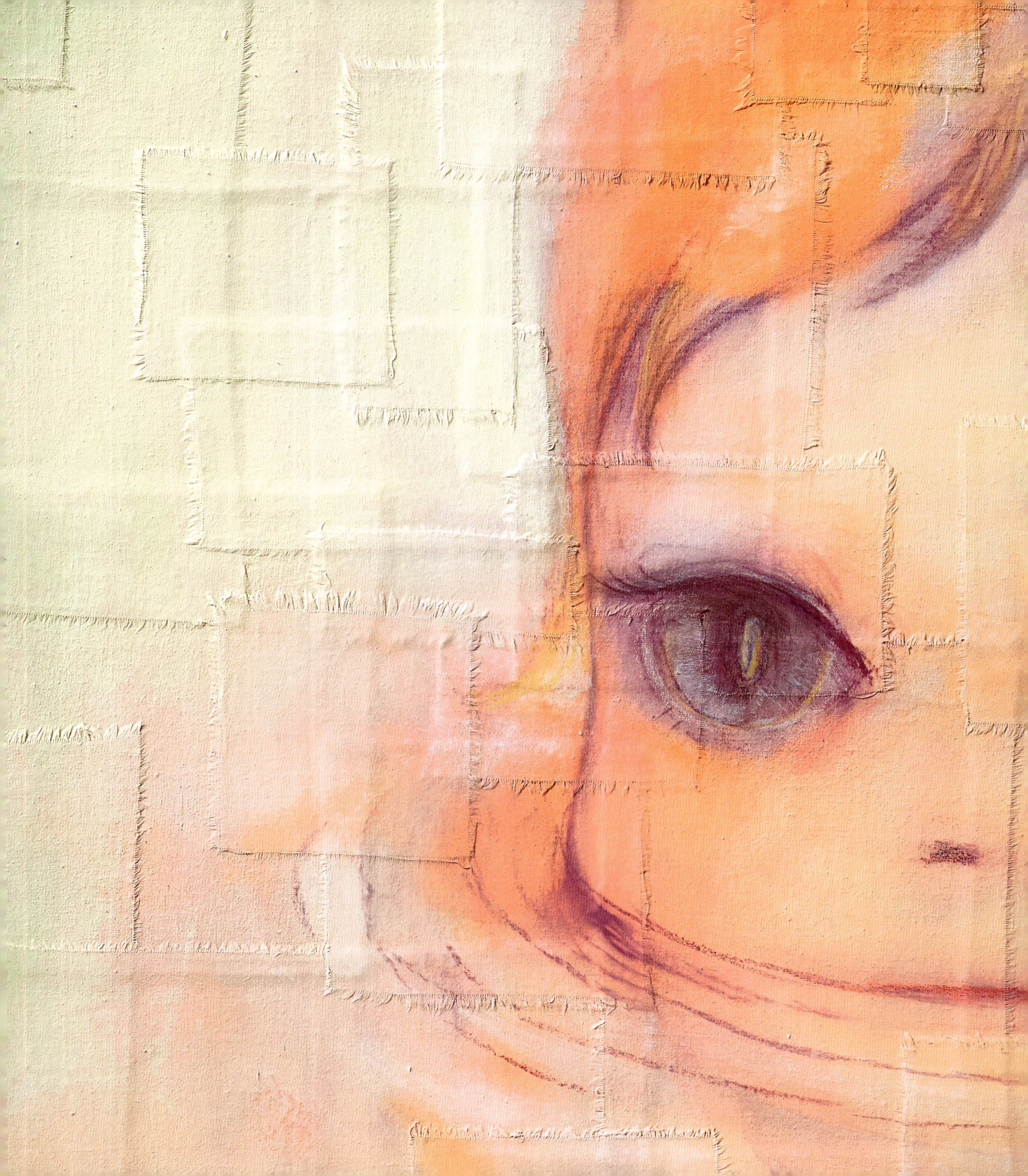

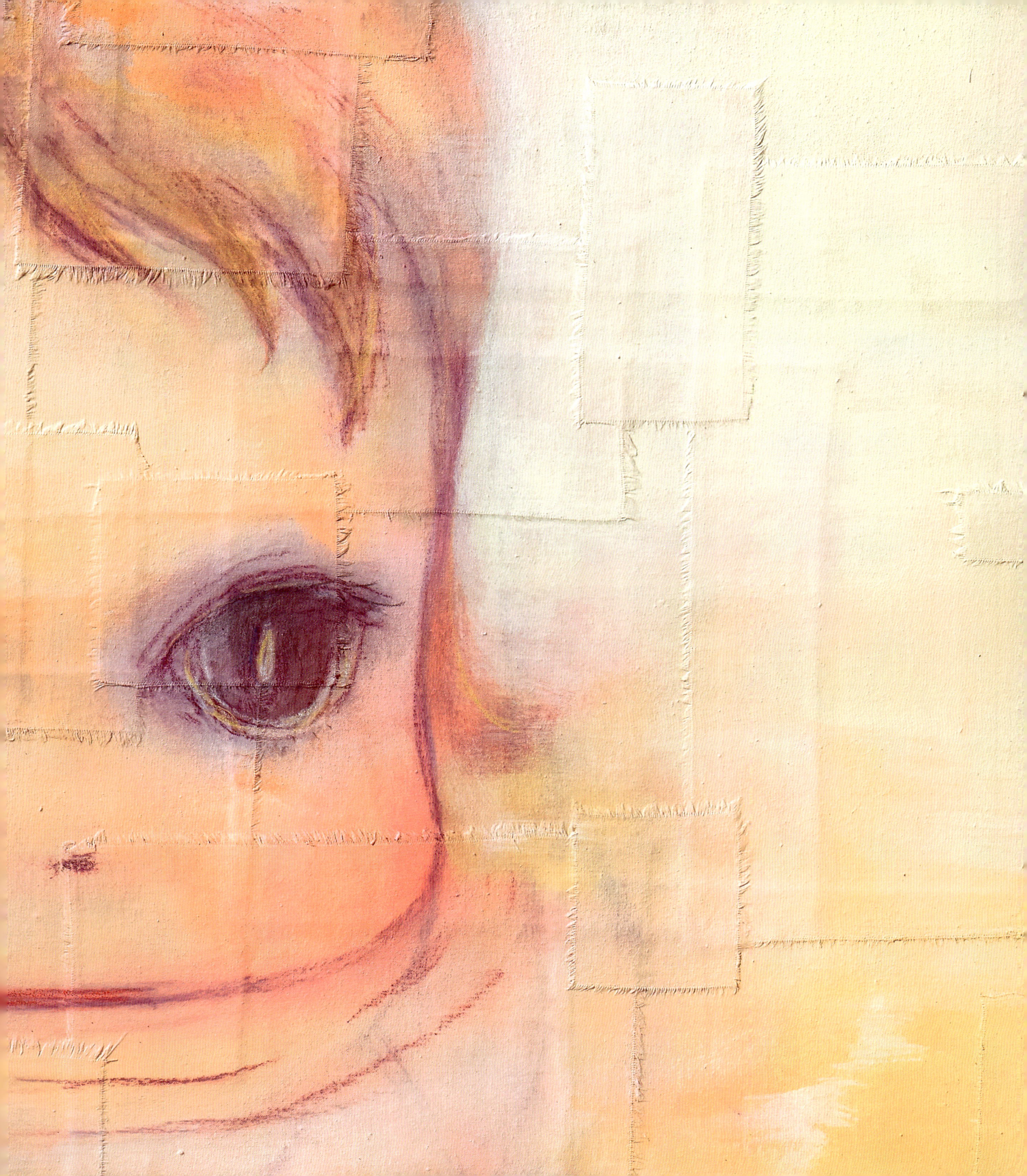

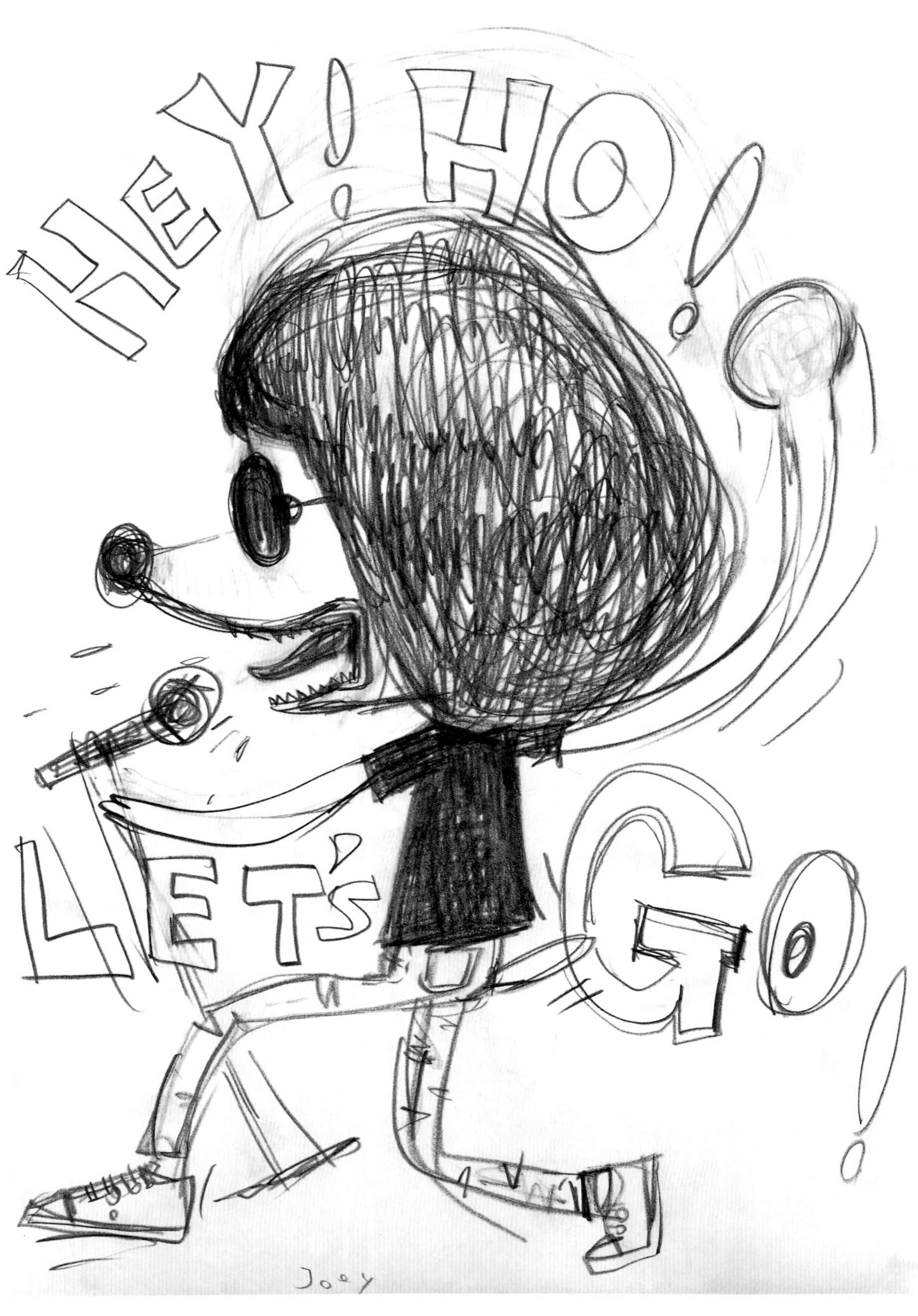

Fig. 129
Joey, 2008, Pencil on paper,
20 ¼ × 14 ⅜ in. (51.5 × 36.5 cm)

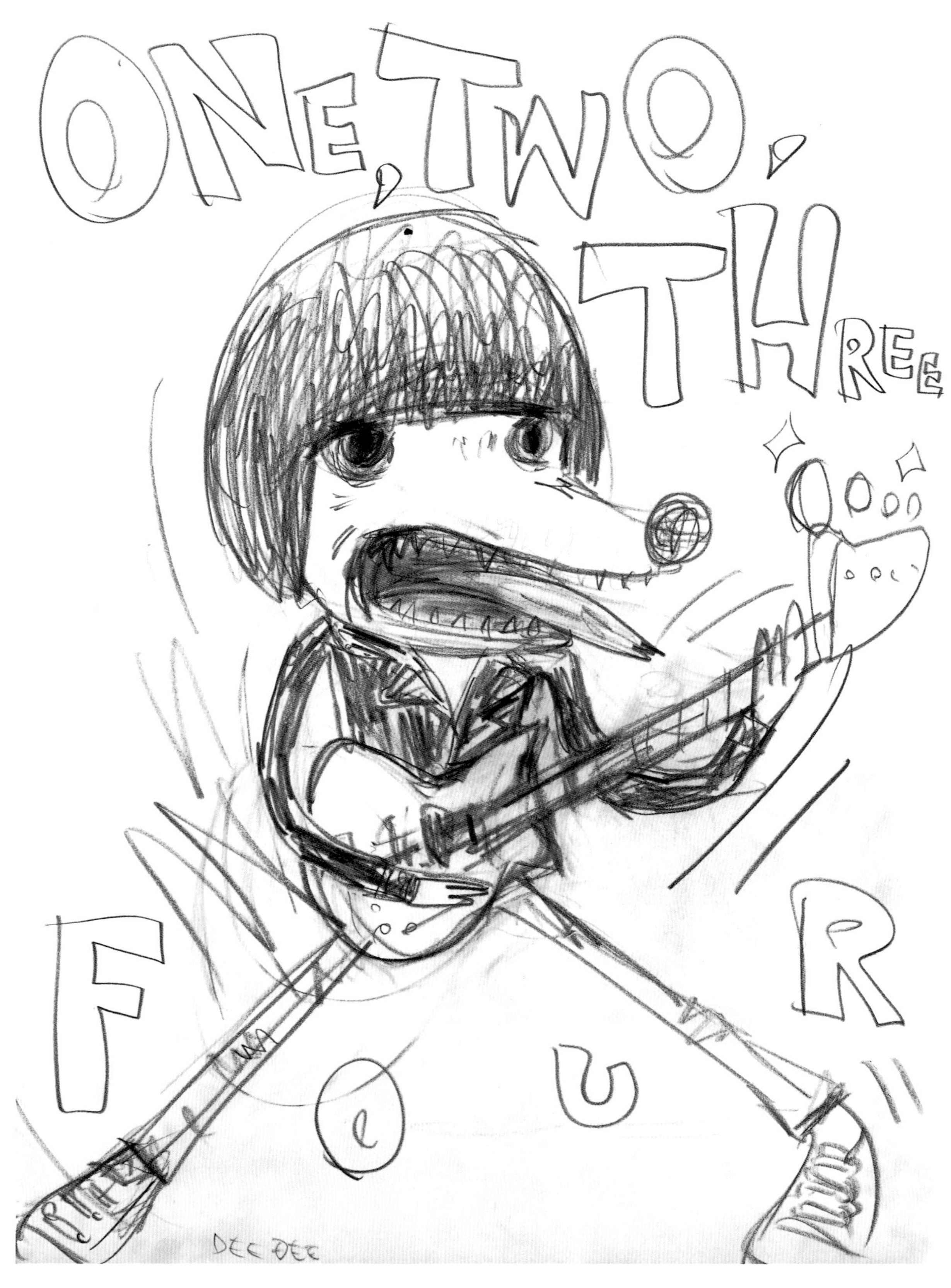

Fig. 130
Dee Dee, 2008, Pencil on paper,
20 ¼ × 14 ⅜ in. (51.5 × 36.5 cm)

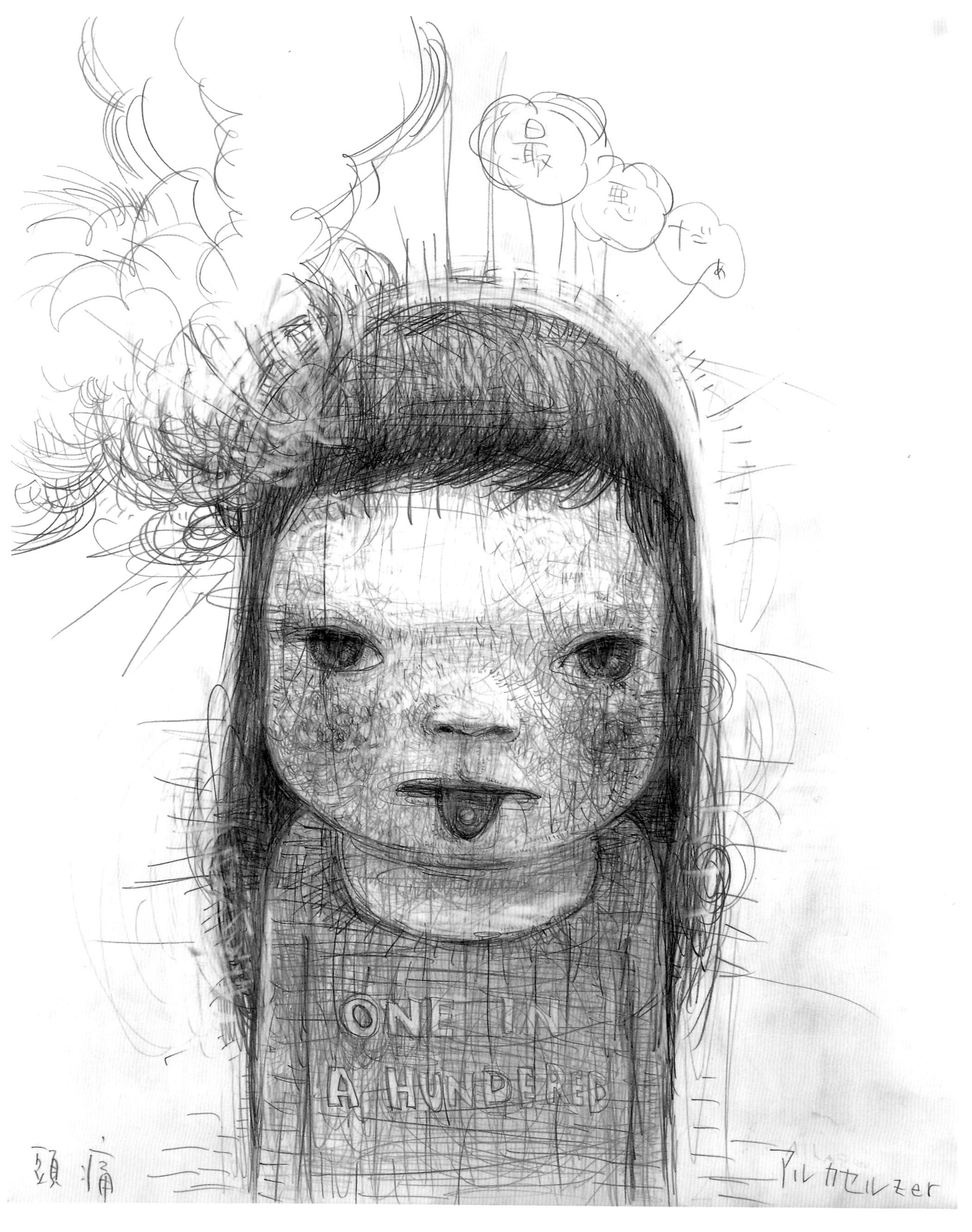

Fig. 131
Headache, 2012,
Pencil on paper,
25 9⁄16 × 19 11⁄16 in. (65 × 50 cm)

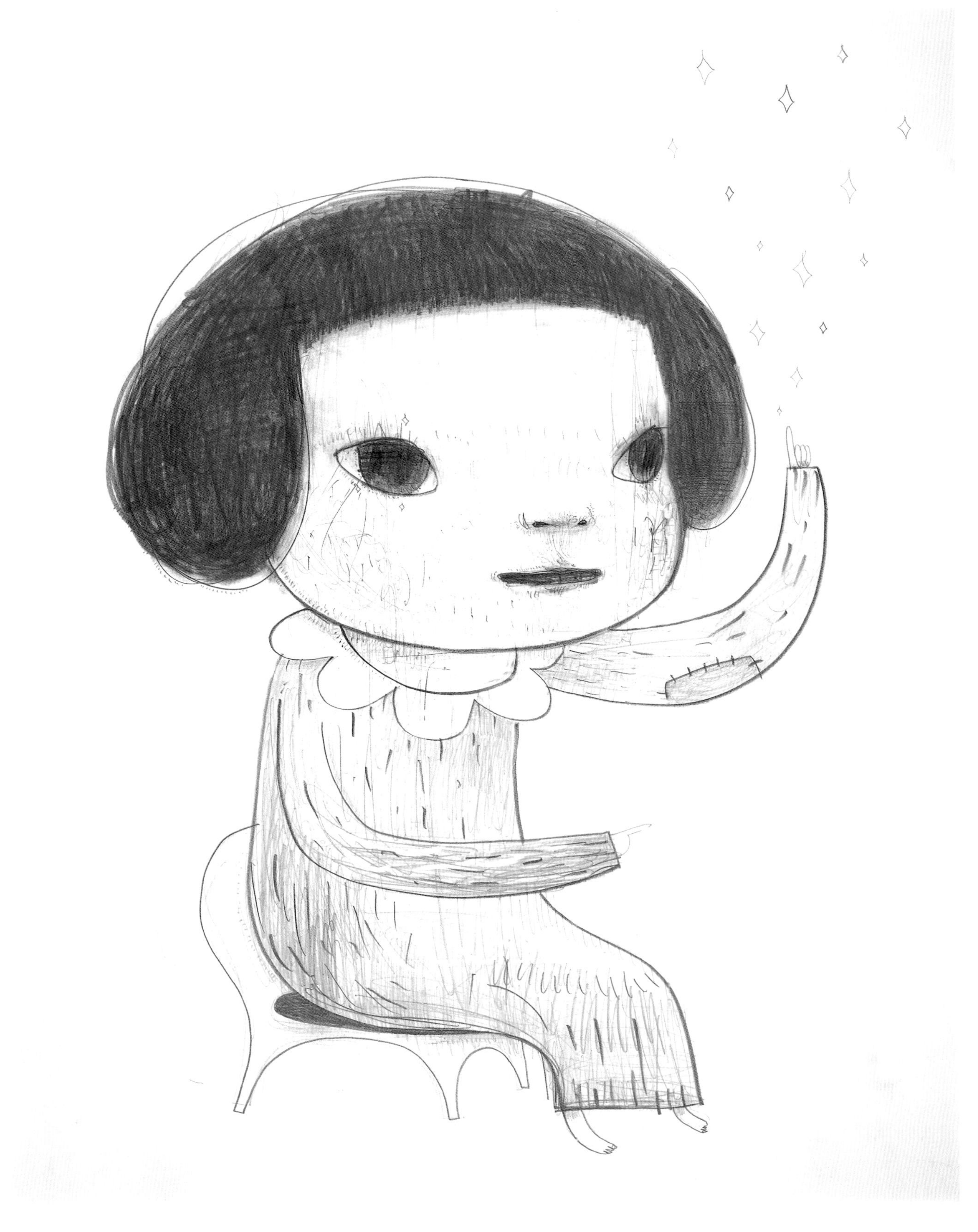

Fig. 132
News, 2011, Pencil on paper, 25 9⁄16 × 19 11⁄16 in. (65 × 50 cm)

The Yokohama exhibition was a pivotal moment in Nara's career, which took off thereafter, both at home and abroad. In the time that followed, he struggled to maintain equilibrium amid the increasing demand for new work and exhibitions. Though he found solace in projects that involved working with others (the focus of the next chapter), he continued with his paintings of big-headed girls. A key element of his solo practice after 2001 was a constant experimentation with the formal techniques of various media, whether paint or graphite pencil, as well as playing with compositions while still retaining the legibility of his now-iconic characters. The basic structure of his images from this period remains flat, limited in their use of linear perspective so that they never look more than a few inches deep. Nara's formal maturation instead comes from the expressive capacity of color on canvas and line on paper, both of which expand the affective pull of his images and engender a more intimate connection with the viewer.

Another element that remains consistent throughout the next decade is that Nara almost exclusively poses his big-headed girls in frontal portrait bust mode so that they face the viewer directly, abandoning the full-body pictures that showed them head to toe. Along with this shift, the big-headed girls, by and large, have longer hair and older faces that suggest they, too, are growing up. They exude quietness by simply sitting still; the knives, sprouts, and fires have largely disappeared. Nara's attention turns now to experimenting with the eyes of his subjects by creating small differences within a single portrait to generate a different sort of unease. One of the earliest examples dates from 2003, his drawing *Mountain Sisters* (Fig. 123), in which the subjects' eyes are mismatched in size and color; another drawing is the playfully titled *Sorry, Couldn't Draw the Left Eye!* (2003) (Fig. 124), in which one of the subject's eyes is bandaged over.

In paintings, Nara develops this theme further by creating highly detailed eyes, set in contrast to the simpler treatment of the rest of the figure's body, as seen in *Twins I* and *II* (2005) (Figs. 125 and 126). This focus on texture and contrast becomes even more distinctive when he mismatches their shapes and colors. In *Shallow Puddles 2004* (2004) (Figs. 127 and 128), painted on a dish and one in a larger series of half-submerged heads, the figure's large round eyes are depicted differently, one painted blue and the other orange, and each with small dots and strokes that add subtle texture and a sense of light. Their differences may be less obvious than those in *Mountain Sisters*,

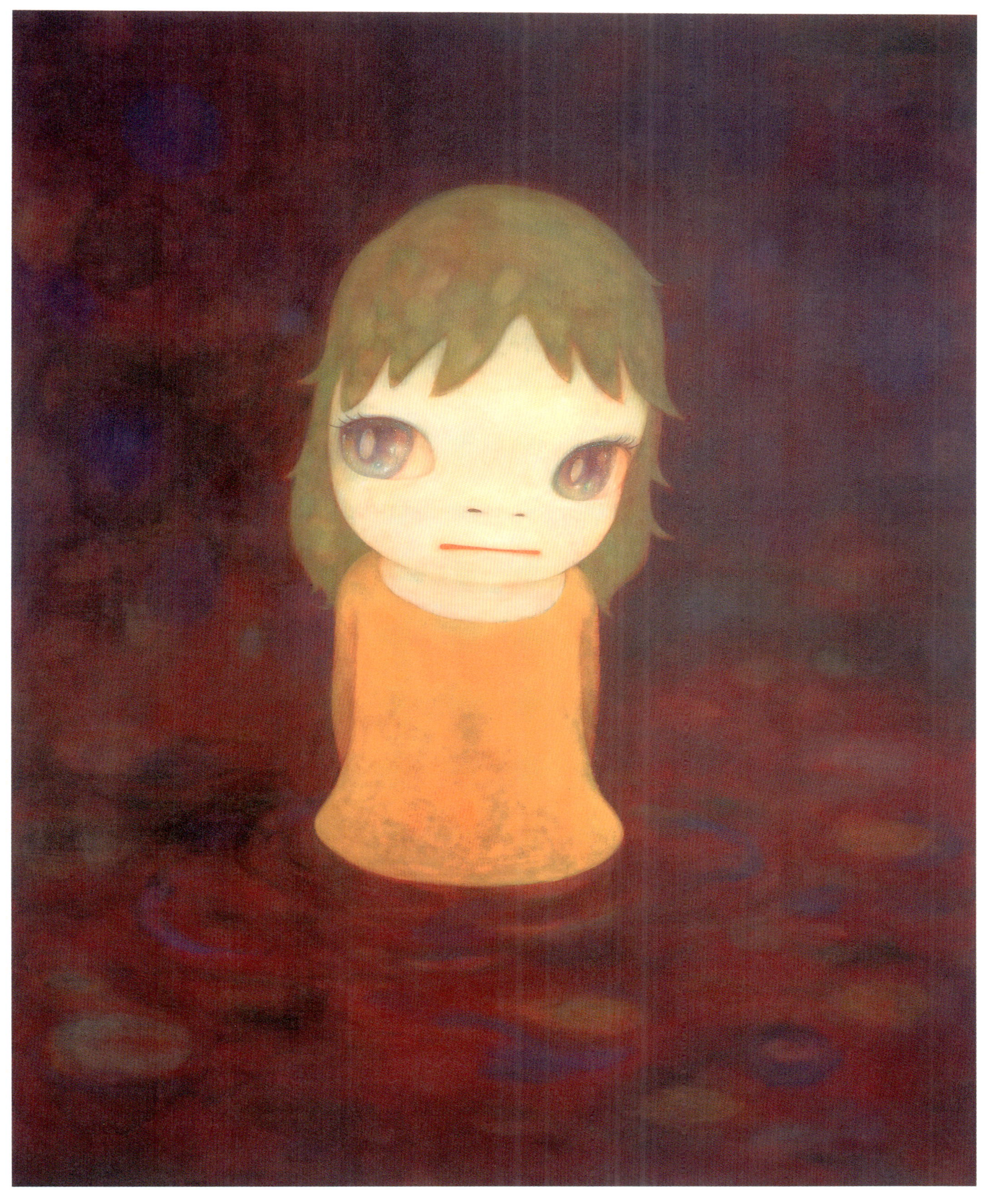

Fig. 133
After the Acid Rain, 2006,
Acrylic on canvas, 89 ⅜ × 71 ⅝ in.
(227 × 182 cm)

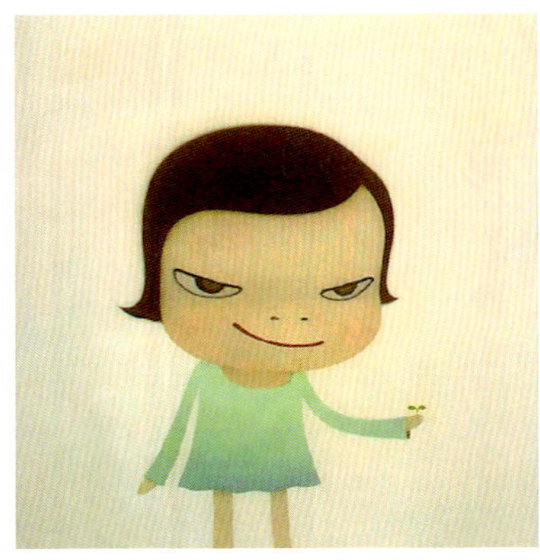 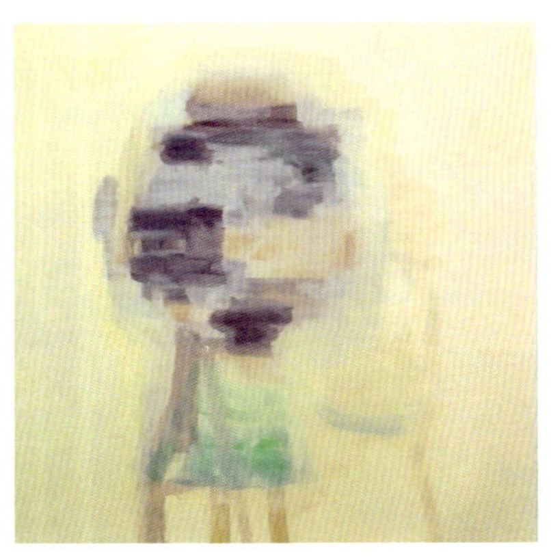 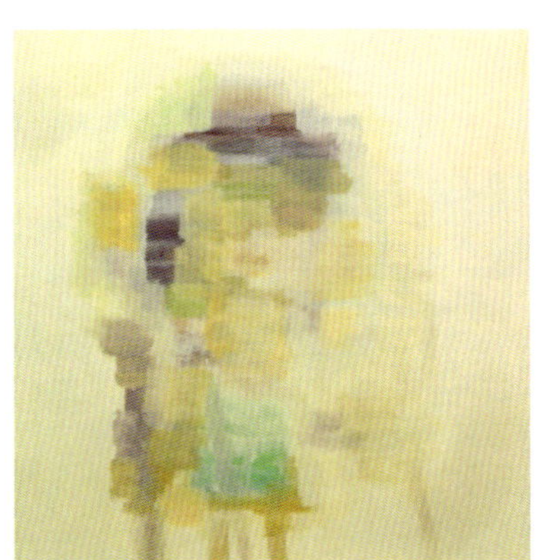 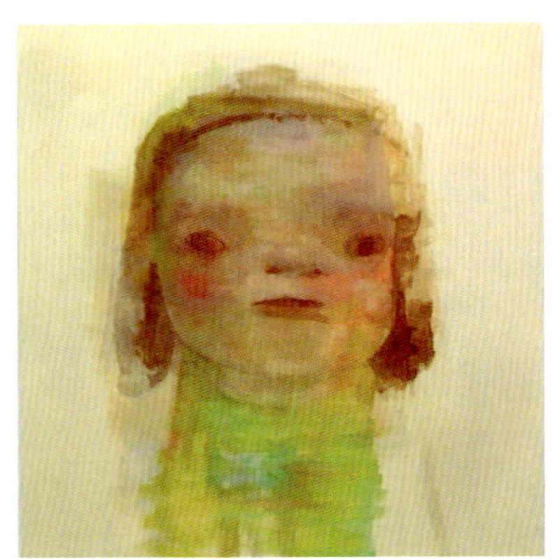

but they are enough to disrupt the stability of her posture with their look of ambivalence.

Shallow Puddles 2004 stands out from Nara's works from this period—the application of pale mauves and amber yellows, broken up to suggest the presence of an external light source, is an unusual approach for the artist. The light softens the contours of the figure's head and continues through to her reflection, which, unlike in most of his paintings of submerged heads, now stretches further, rippling across the water. This treatment of colors in association with light is part of a more general move away from his earlier graphic treatment of big-headed girls that critics associated with anime and manga aesthetics. It is possible to see this work, and others like it, as one of the ways in which Nara was pushing back against the art world's categorization of his practice.

In his drawings, Nara also focuses on the formal properties of the pencil, pushing the medium's expressiveness through a broad range of lines, tones, degrees of opacity, and movement. In *Joey* (2008) (Fig. 129) and *Dee Dee* (2008) (Fig. 130), homages to members of the Ramones, the ferocity with which he attacks the surface of the paper mirrors the abandonment of artistic restraints in punk-rock music. Two other works from this period, *Headache* (2012) (Fig. 131) and *News* (2011) (Fig. 132), further showcase the virtuosity of Nara's pencil work. *Headache* reveals a sophisticated mode of drawing that recalls his painting practice, the precise layers of lines of various lengths creating a dense network of grays articulated through circles and arcs that are reminiscent of brushstrokes. In *News*, by contrast, Nara draws long lines that sweep across the page with confident movement. These gestural marks seek to conjure a figure that has a tangible presence and that can sit within a space—a process akin to how Nara works in sculpture. The energy

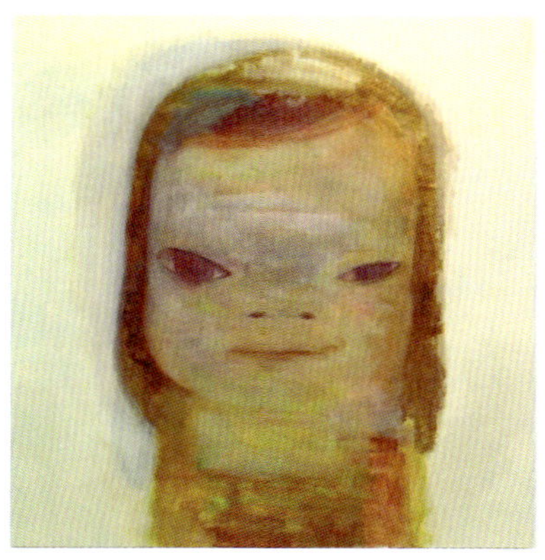
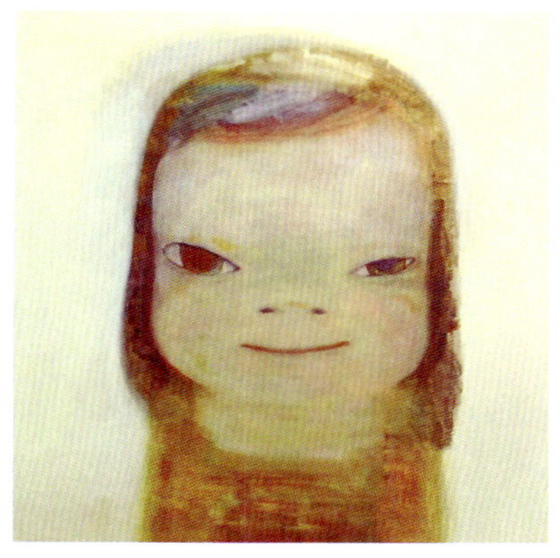
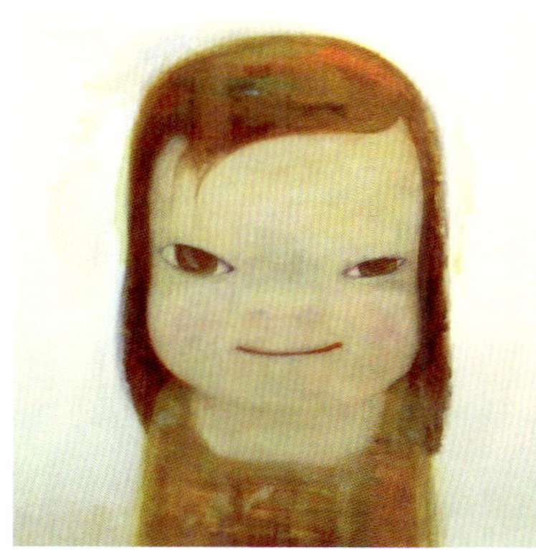
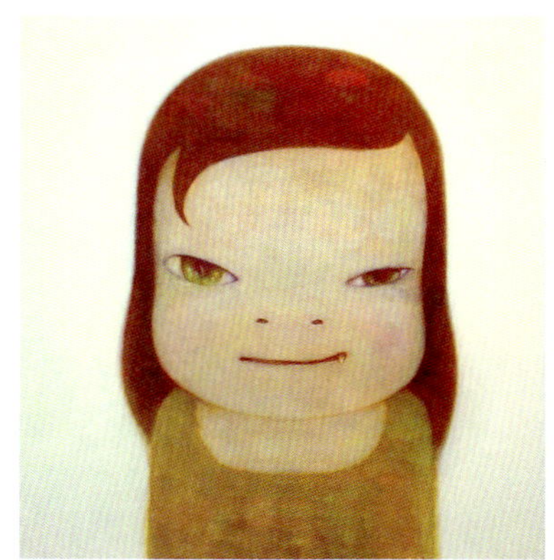

of the unfinished lines captures the internal process of an artist whose desire to create outweighs the desire for finality or completeness. If *Headache* is about surface treatment that mimics the effects of painting, *News* is about space and relates to the three-dimensionality of sculpture.

In order to understand these new directions in Nara's work, it is important to consider their development as part of his attempt to break away from his own iconic image—that rebel girl to whom he gave form in 1991. To loosen the hold she had on him, Nara frequently had to paint his big-headed girl, only to erase her before beginning anew. The 2006 work *After the Acid Rain* (Fig. 133), indicative of the rich, layered color palettes that would come to define his paintings from this period, was, in fact, painted over another figural image of a girl, which no longer exists. He continues this practice today, although only sporadically, as in his 2012 *Can't Wait 'til the Night Comes*, which lies atop a variation of his 2001 *Sprout the Ambassador* (Fig. 78). By erasing the rebel girl clutching the leaf, Nara destroys not only the underlying painting but also the memory of a work he has made many variations of before moving on to produce something new (Figs. 134a–h). If in the past, repetition was a crucial part of his practice, now erasure has become equally important. Through this iconoclastic gesture, Nara finds new ways for his big-headed girls to grow up.

Figs. 134a–h
Stages of painting *Can't Wait 'til the Night Comes*, 2012

Working with Others

I started working with other people, collaborating with other artists or doing joint projects with creative groups that I was introduced to. Collaboration meant that my personal responsibility was lower, and it taught me the joy of sweating over a project with others. Then putting together an exhibition and celebrating the opening with them was so fun that it was like a drug to me, since I had always worked alone. But there was definitely a feeling that I was running away from myself, and that made me feel guilty.[1]

The year 2001 was a major turning point in Nara's career as he rapidly became recognized as one of the leading contemporary artists in Japan.[2] It also marked a shift in his practice: he started to take on projects that involved working with people from different sectors of the art world and other creative industries. It was, as he describes it, a way of running away from himself or, rather, from the cacophony of demands that followed his success. Most of the projects were not, in the strictest sense, collaborations but endeavors in which Nara formed different types of creative connections by working closely—whether physically side by side or through a sense of artistic kinship—with artists, designers, musicians, and ceramicists. It was these creative connections, some more successful than others, that helped him regain a sense of equilibrium, reflect on his own work and practices, and learn how to negotiate his private and public worlds.

Paintings and Drawings

One of Nara's earliest collaborations was with the British artist David Shrigley between 2000 and 2002. The two knew of each other through common acquaintances and had participated in the same exhibition, *Présumés innocents: L'art contemporain et l'enfance* (Presumed Innocent: Contemporary Art and Childhood), at CAPC musée d'art contemporain de Bordeaux in 2000.[3] This was an ambitious exhibition of eighty artists that focused on how innocence is perceived in society, and it included works that were transgressive and seen by some as too controversial.[4] It was a show that placed Nara's work in a very different narrative from those that informed the more typical group exhibitions he appeared in at the time, which tended to favor a cultural approach to Japanese contemporary art.[5]

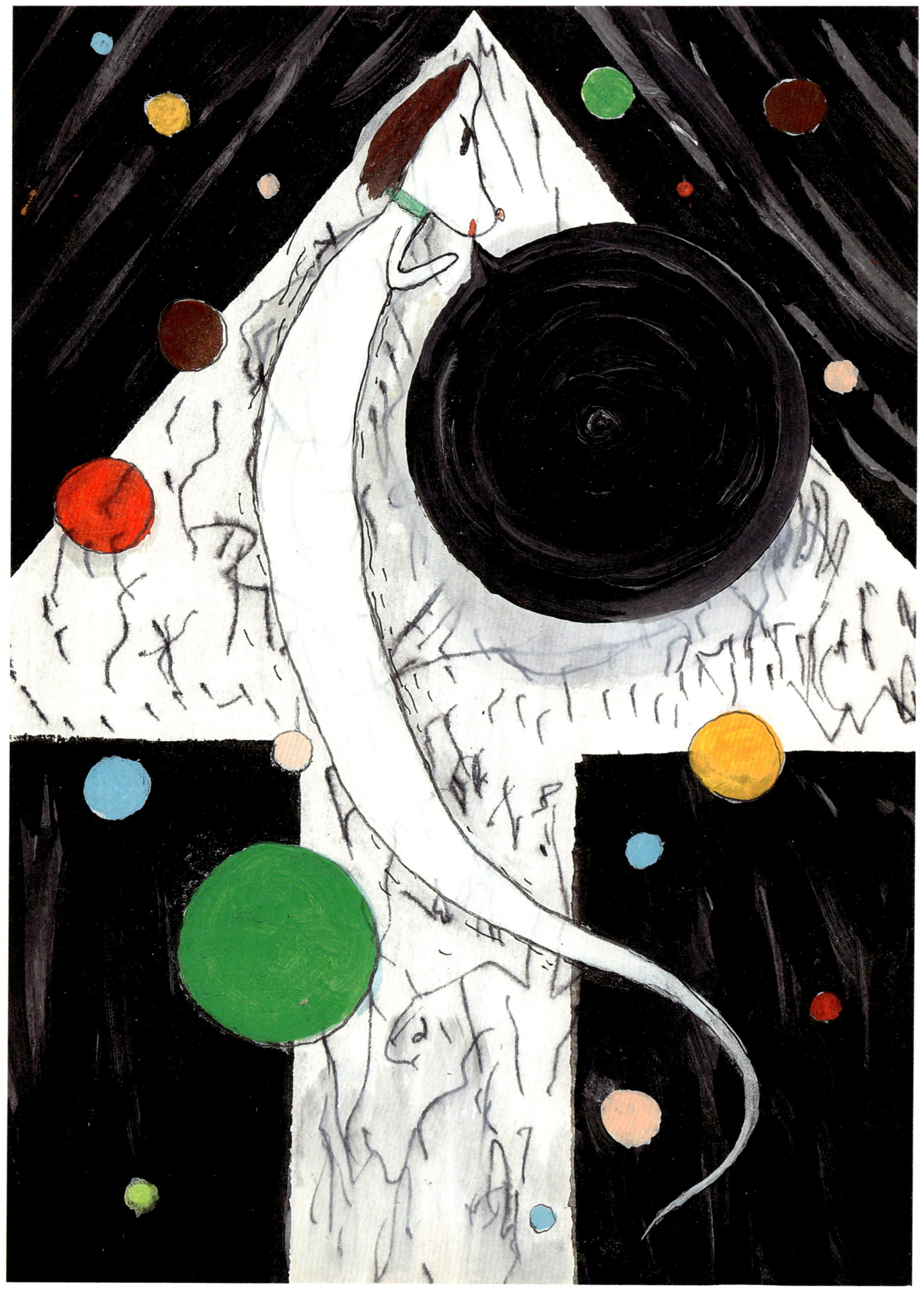

Fig. 135
Yoshitomo Nara and David Shrigley, *Untitled (Dog in Arrow)*, 2000, Acrylic and pen on paper, 7 ½ × 5 ⅛ in. (19 × 13 cm)

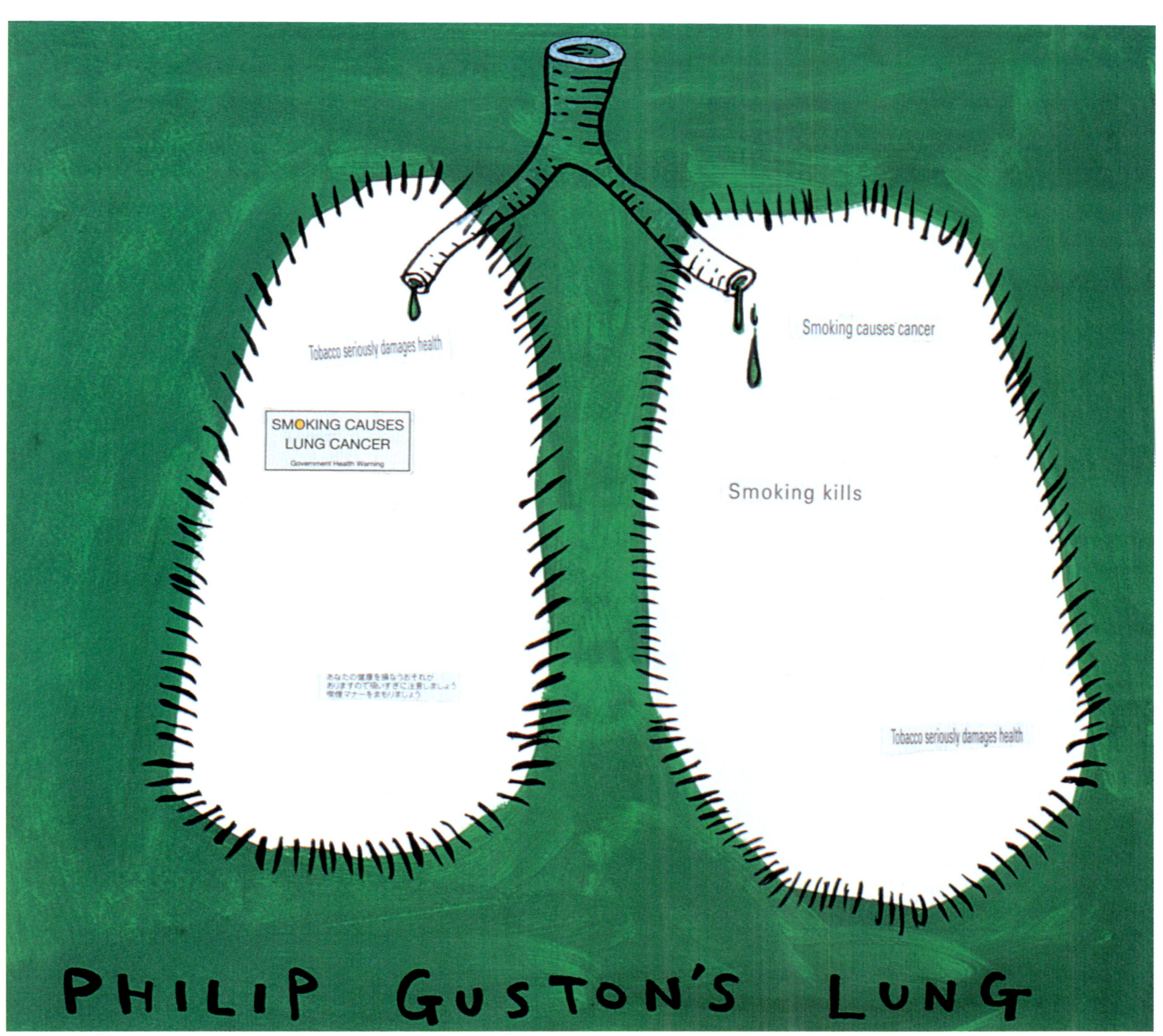

Fig. 136
Yoshitomo Nara and
David Shrigley, *Untitled*
(Philip Guston's Lung), 2002,
Acrylic and pen on paper,
16 ⅛ × 17 ⅝ in. (40.9 × 44.8 cm)

The *Presumed Innocent* exhibition also brought the works of Shrigley and Nara together in the same space and introduced the two artists to each other.

Shortly after meeting, Shrigley proposed a project in which he would send his drawings to Nara, who would then add texts or images before returning them to Shrigley to sketch some more, the process repeating until a work was deemed complete. He wanted to see what sort of dialogue could be created through interpreting each other's artistic traces as the works were passed from one set of hands to another.[6] However, Nara, who misunderstood the project's intentions, responded but did not return the drawings, thus creating a single one-way conversation. Nonetheless, the combination of the styles of two artists known for their penchant for playing with words and images resulted in a charming set of works.

Reflecting on this project today, neither artist can identify with certainty the maker of any specific element in a given drawing. The difficulty, in part, stems from Nara's tendency to have added to the drawings by mimicking or exaggerating his partner's style, blurring the line between where Shrigley's traces ended and his own began. For those familiar with Shrigley's solo works, these drawings are more open-ended, as if offering jokes without a punchline or ones so obscure that their meanings are too slippery to grasp, as seen in the absurdist drawing of a man with an apple on his head and three "missed" arrows protruding from the back of the plank against which he leans (Fig. 139). It is possible to identify components in these drawings that belong to Nara as well. There are sightings of Nara's familiar figures—his white puppies and children with menacing grins—but their presence is not as conspicuous or forceful as usual. It is as if they are conscious of sharing a space with others and shrink in size or disguise themselves within shapes in response, living, as one drawing states, "in the 2D world."

The appeal of this project is that it provides a convergence of wits of two artists for whom drawing lies at the center of their respective practices. Looking beyond their work for this project, Nara often has a playful sense of fun that can be silly, scatological, and violent but with a childlike directness and appeal (Fig. 138). Shrigley, on the other hand, plays with words and images to deliver humorous insights into human behavior with dry wit, offering ethical, social, or political insights (Fig. 137). What the two artists share is their irreverence, laughing

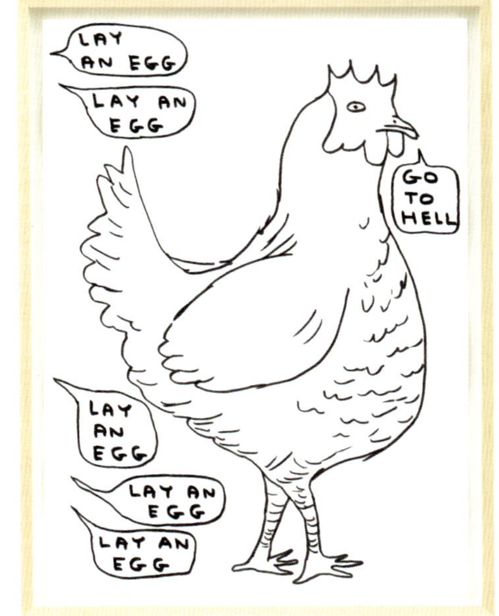

Fig. 137
David Shrigley, *Untitled*, 2018, Ink on paper, 11 ¾ × 8 ⅜ in. (29.5 × 21 cm), framed 14 ¼ × 10 ¾ in. (36 × 27 cm)

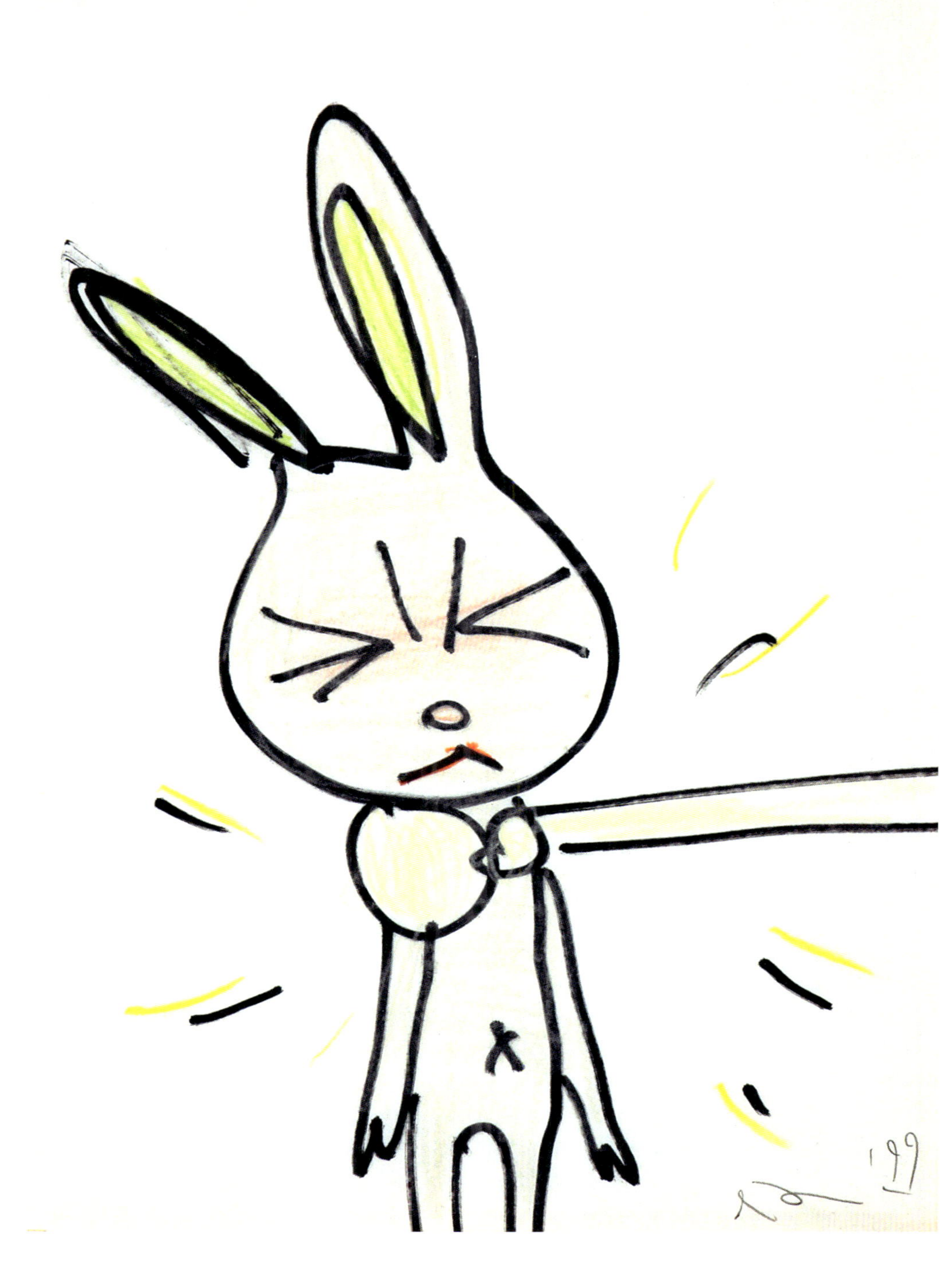

Fig. 138
Untitled, 1999, Pen and colored pencil on paper, 8 ¼ × 5 ⅞ in. (21 × 15 cm)

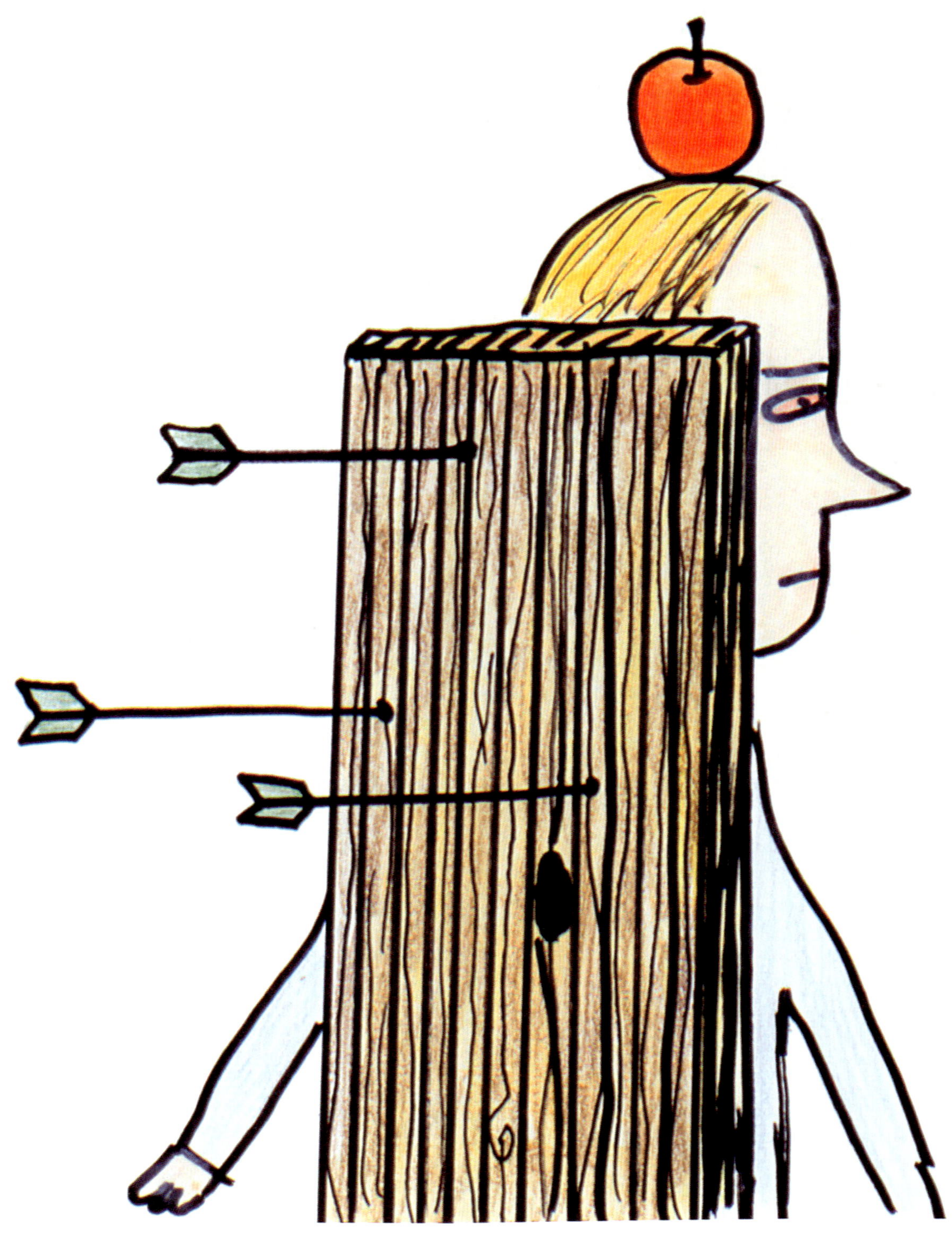

Fig. 139
Yoshitomo Nara and David Shrigley, *Untitled (William Tell with Shield)*, 2002, Pen and colored pencil on paper, 10 7/16 × 9 1/8 in. (26.5 × 23.2 cm)

BUT JUST LIVING IN THE 2D WORLD....

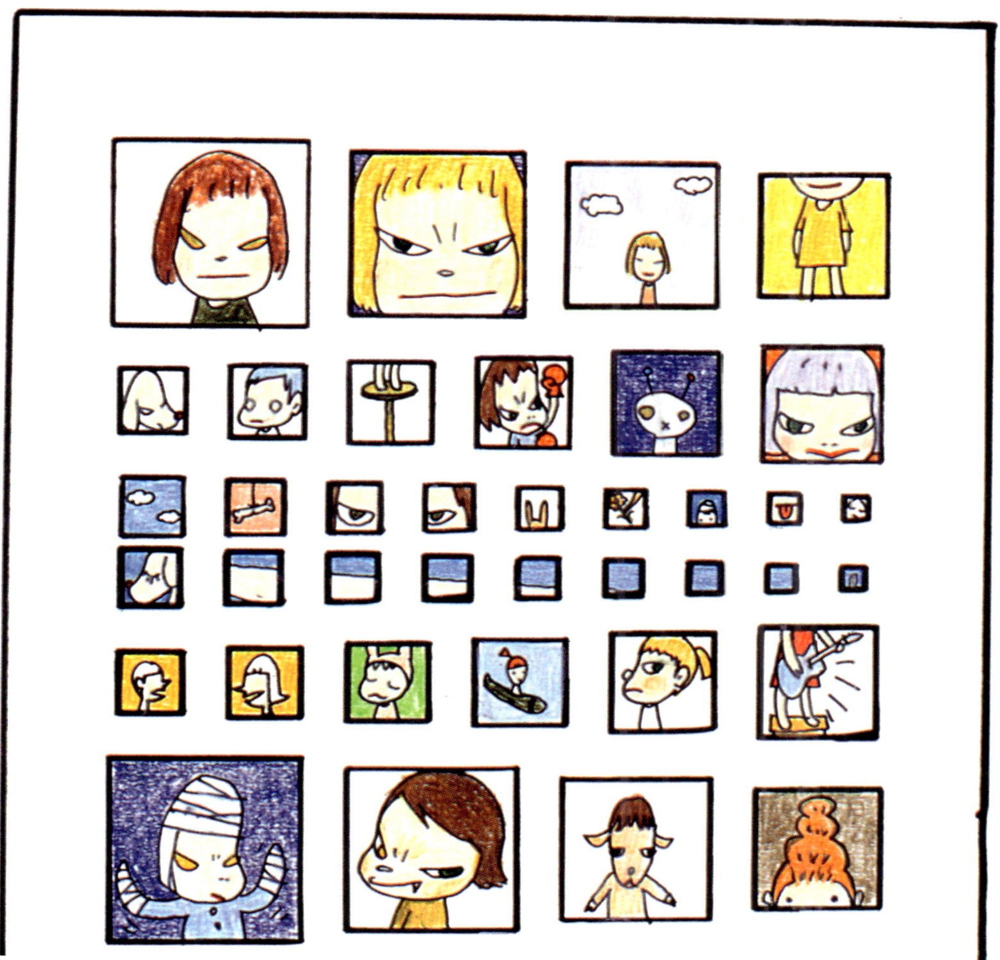

Fig. 140
Yoshitomo Nara and David Shrigley, *Untitled (But Just Living)*, 2002, Pen and colored pencil on paper, 10 15/16 × 14 13/16 in. (27.7 × 37.7 cm)

at the ridiculous expectations of modern society. As such, a disjointed connectedness, like unlikely partners in a three-legged race, makes their drawings strangely absorbing.

In 2003 Nara began a new project with Hiroshi Sugito, a former student from Aichi Prefectural University of Fine Arts and Music who had since become an established artist and a close friend. Nara invited Sugito to participate in a residency and exhibition in Vienna that would show a series of collaborative works: conversations in paint. Unlike his project with Shrigley, the plan was to paint together in the same studio over three intensive sessions in Vienna and work consecutively on a number of large canvases, aiming to complete forty to fifty works with the understanding that only a handful of them would make their way into the final show. According to Sugito, the limited studio time necessitated that they focus on their respective strengths and determine how they could best complement one another's skills. They divided their work accordingly: Nara concentrated on compositions and lines and in the first round completed about 80 percent of the work; Sugito, through his treatment of colors, added on and in the process erased about 30 percent of what Nara had done.[7] The artists continued this back-and-forth exchange until they decided the work was complete. It was a collaboration that involved a considerable degree of trust—they did not set any limits on how many times an artist could return to a work or the extent to which one was permitted to erase the work of the other.

Sugito recalls how, during their first session, Nara arrived early and had already gathered discarded panels from a construction site, prepared the primer, and stacked a neat pile of preparatory drawings on his desk. Despite this, and in his usual nonchalant way, Nara declared that he was not planning to work too hard in the session, but Sugito, who heard music playing in the background, knew that his former teacher was ready to begin.[8] It is telling that both artists remember that the music playing was by Mary Hopkin. For them, music helped process their connectedness and the intense immersive experience of a project that demanded, on the one hand, forsaking control of the painted canvas and, on the other, creating a work that could provoke a response. Sugito regularly describes their progress using analogies to music: the beginning of the project, when things were proceeding as expected, was akin to listening to the usual suspects—the Ramones or the Rolling Stones—but at a certain point,

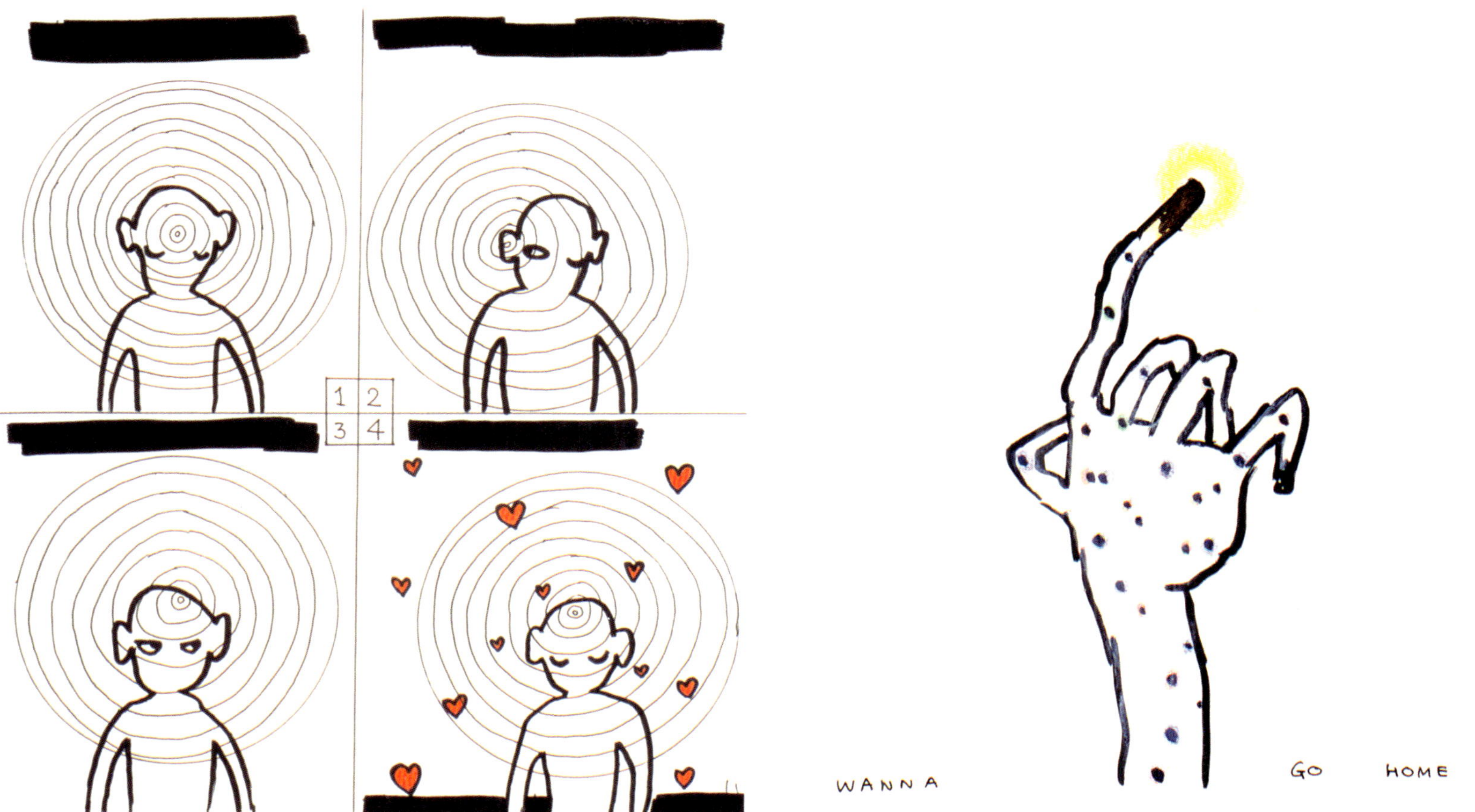

Fig. 141
Yoshitomo Nara and David Shrigley, *Untitled (1 2 3 4)*, 2002, Pen and colored pencil on paper, 10 7/16 × 9 1/8 in. (26.5 × 23.2 cm)

Fig. 142
Yoshitomo Nara and David Shrigley, *Untitled (Wanna Go Home)*, 2002, Pen and colored pencil on paper, 10 7/16 × 9 1/8 in. (26.5 × 23.2 cm)

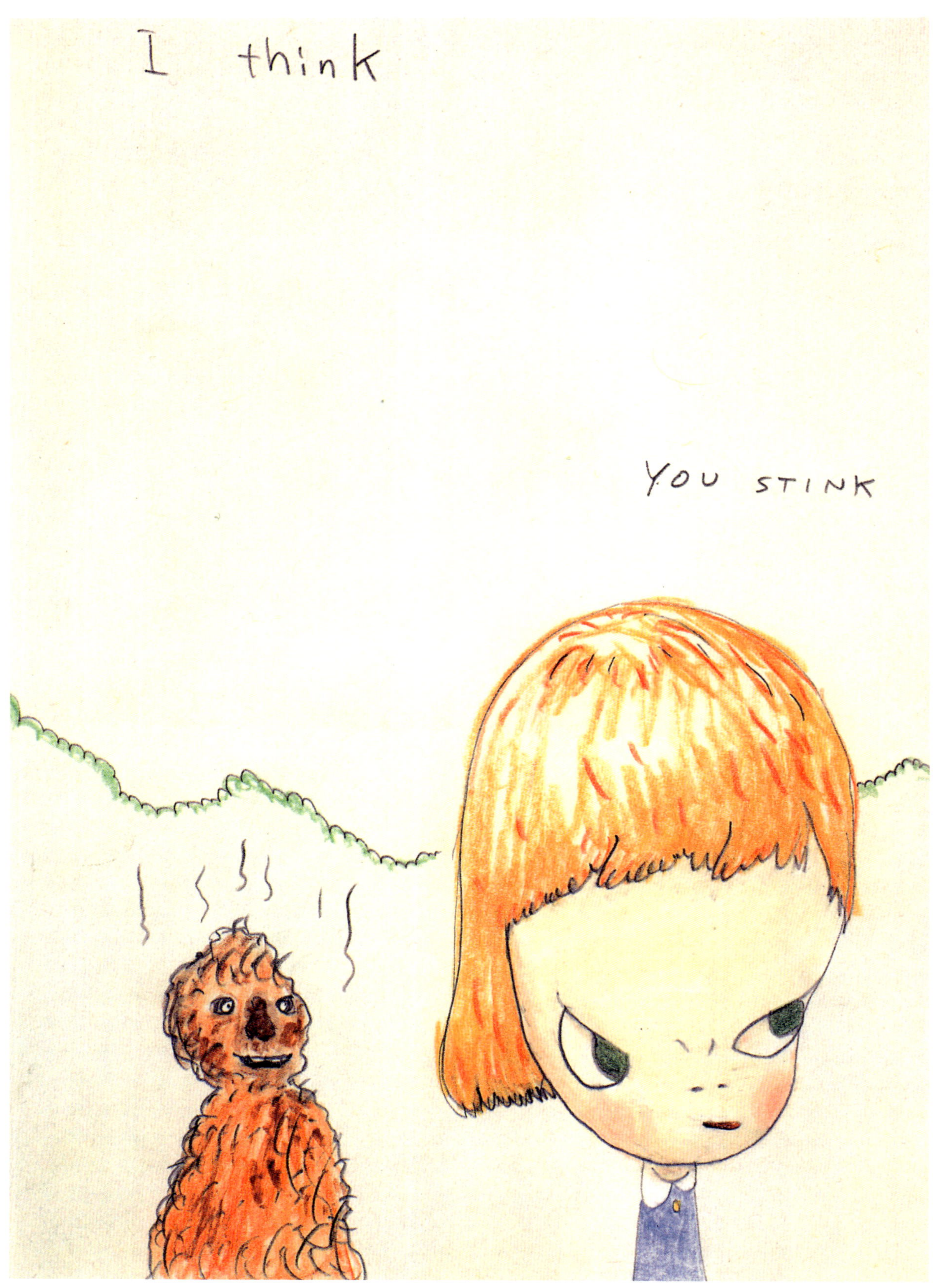

Fig. 143
Yoshitomo Nara and David Shrigley, *Untitled (I Think You Stink)*, 2000, Colored pencil and pencil on paper, 7 ½ × 5 ⅛ in. (19 × 13 cm)

the music changed to more obscure and challenging artists such as the Flaming Lips or Shinya Ohe.[9] This progression speaks to the moments when the two artists truly began to experiment, pushing each other in ways that made them confront the works in a new light. To extend the analogy, their practice was similar to a jam session, with each artist strumming a steady melody before breaking out into an amorphous musical space of improvised riffs and syncopated rhythms.

Part of the intrigue of this project lies in how two artists negotiated their individual working styles. Nara paints fast: his restless instinct is always at the fore of his painting practice, and he relies on this energy to compose forms and make instinctual decisions on lines and base colors in a work. Sugito, in contrast, needs space and time to contemplate his next moves. The two artists used these differences to set the pace of the project: Nara would attack the surface of the canvas with variations of forms and lines, and Sugito would loosen up what Nara had created. For example, when Nara used dark hues or painted large sections in a midtonal range, Sugito would then soften them with a lighter palette, applying white pigment to erase Nara's signature black lines, muting them with thin washes of paint, or creating layered textures to achieve a quality of ambivalence or uncertainty. These differences gave way to some strange combinations and, at times, created doubts—if not outright disagreements—about the direction of the project as a whole. Sugito recalls an occasion after Nara had completed his first round:

> The canvas was virtually bare so it was impossible for me to add any color. In the end, Nara himself began to apply vermillion paint in a middle tone, and as he grew increasingly impatient the vermillion halftone began to expand alarmingly, interfering with the lines and resulting in [what I thought was] the use of unnecessary color. However, [he then applied] yellow, and a purple called Bordeaux, and the subtle color adjustments in his creamy primer were inspiring, prompting me to think these would probably be the basic colors [for this painting].[10]

In Sugito's view, Nara used color in ways that were overwhelming or applied seemingly without thought. Seeing the artist in action, however, allowed Sugito to admire the fearlessness of Nara's approach.

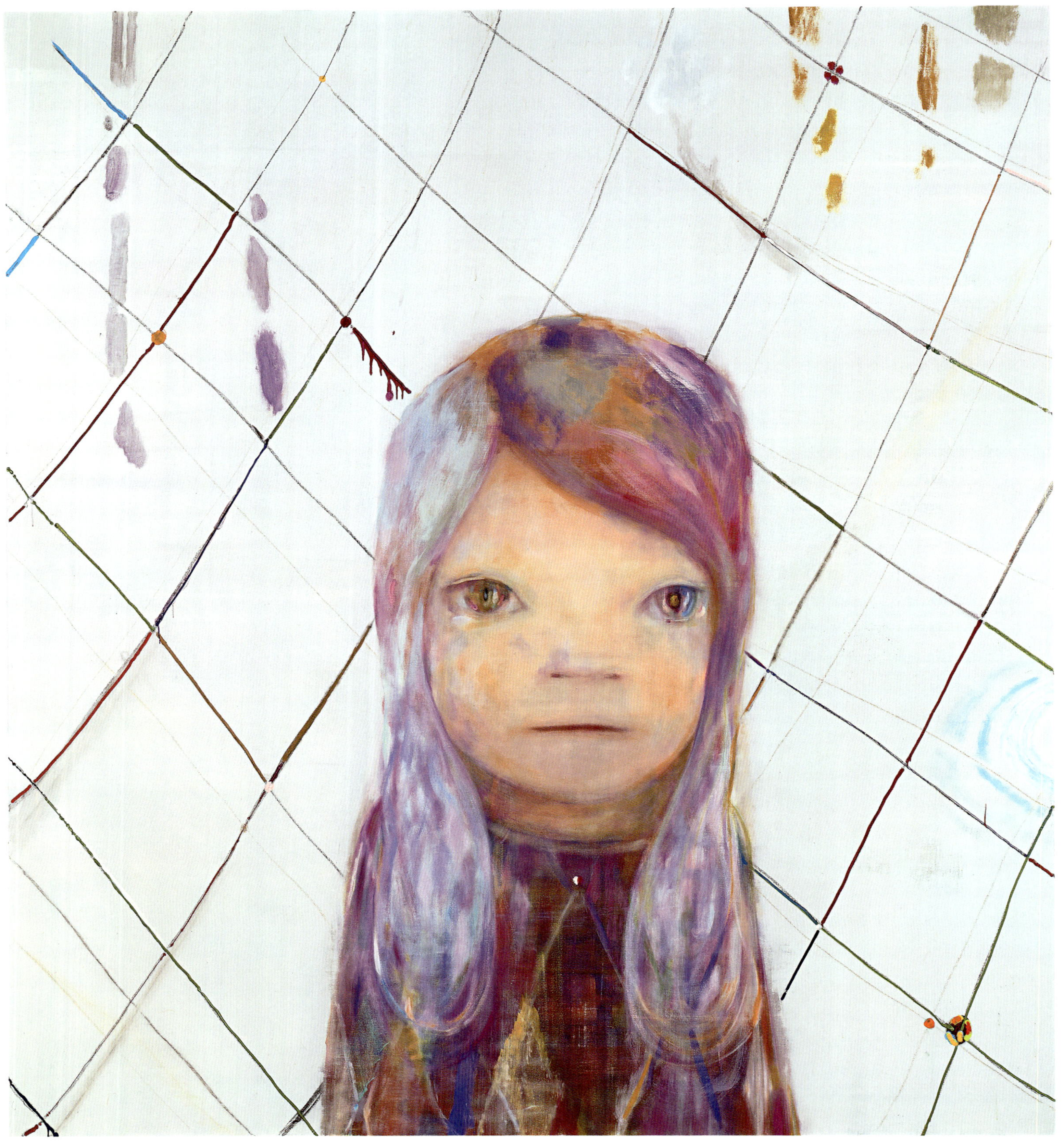

Fig. 144
Yoshitomo Nara and Hiroshi Sugito, *Rain Drops*, 2004, Acrylic on canvas, 118 5⁄16 × 106 5⁄16 in. (300.5 × 270 cm)

Nara, on the other hand, credits Sugito with helping him appreciate a slower painting process. Sugito tends to treat colors as light, as if they contain an internal luminescence that can bend and stretch the range of possible tonal qualities. This is a technique that can be seen in some of Nara's solo paintings from the time, including *Shallow Puddles 2004* (2004) (Figs. 127 and 128), in which the use of whiter shades and looser brushwork bears traces of Sugito's influence. The collaborative project coincided with a period when Nara was beginning to explore the effects of asymmetrical eyes in his solo works (a motif he also explored in the Vienna paintings with Sugito), and it is possible that the collaboration pushed these experiments further. It is as if working with someone whose approach was so different from his own made him more aware of the provocativeness of contrast and difference.

In 2008 the two artists met again to work on a smaller project for a gallery show in Tokyo.[11] This time the collaboration took a different direction with the invention of the artistic persona Chaguin, composed of the fictive characters Henri and Pierre Chaguin. Henri (Nara) was named after Henri Matisse, an artist chosen for his ability to achieve a directness with lines that pare a form down to its core, and Pierre (Sugito) after Pierre Bonnard, for his treatment of color and light. Working together, Henri and Pierre created a singular voice, eliding their differences to become one under the signature of Chaguin. In this metaworld of fictional artists, their combined Chaguin persona also borrowed the styles of Marc Chagall and Paul Gauguin (in another metaplay, *Chaguin* conflates their names). In the shadows of all this lies Paul Cézanne, acknowledged as their ultimate teacher, whose painting of apples were regarded by Chaguin as the genesis of modern European art—and a sly nod to their mentor at Aichi, Nobuya Hitsuda, whom they often joked would be Cézanne in this fabricated world.

The Chaguin project did not set any limitations on subject matter, although many of the works fall within the classical genres of still lifes, interiors, and nudes. The Chaguins, however, liked to inject a playfulness that undercut the authority of these genres. In *Le temps perdu / Youthful Days Lost* (Fig. 149), for example, a blue flower bud inches toward the voluptuous buttocks of a half-revealed nude, while a similar rounded form appears as a bulbous white vase (Fig. 148). The motif of the rounded buttocks was a remnant of their Vienna collaboration,

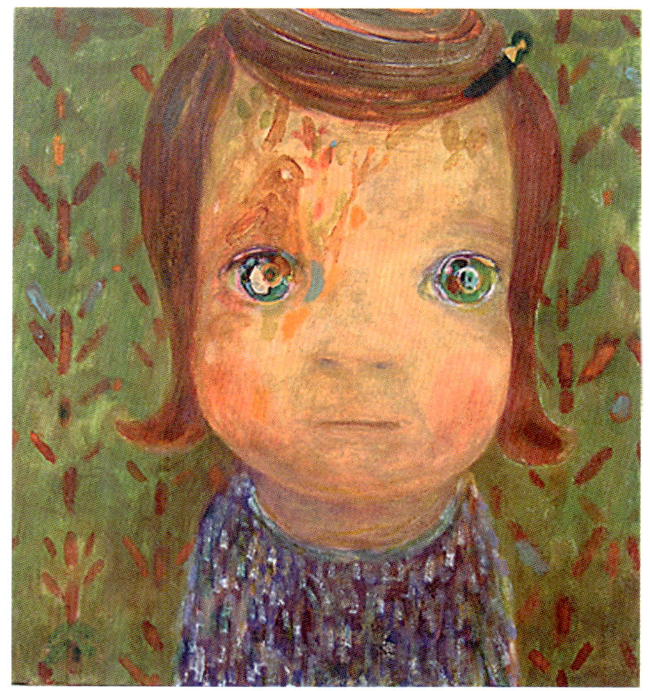

Fig. 145
Yoshitomo Nara and Hiroshi Sugito, *Untitled*, 2005, Acrylic on canvas, 22 7⁄16 × 19 11⁄16 in. (57 × 50 cm)

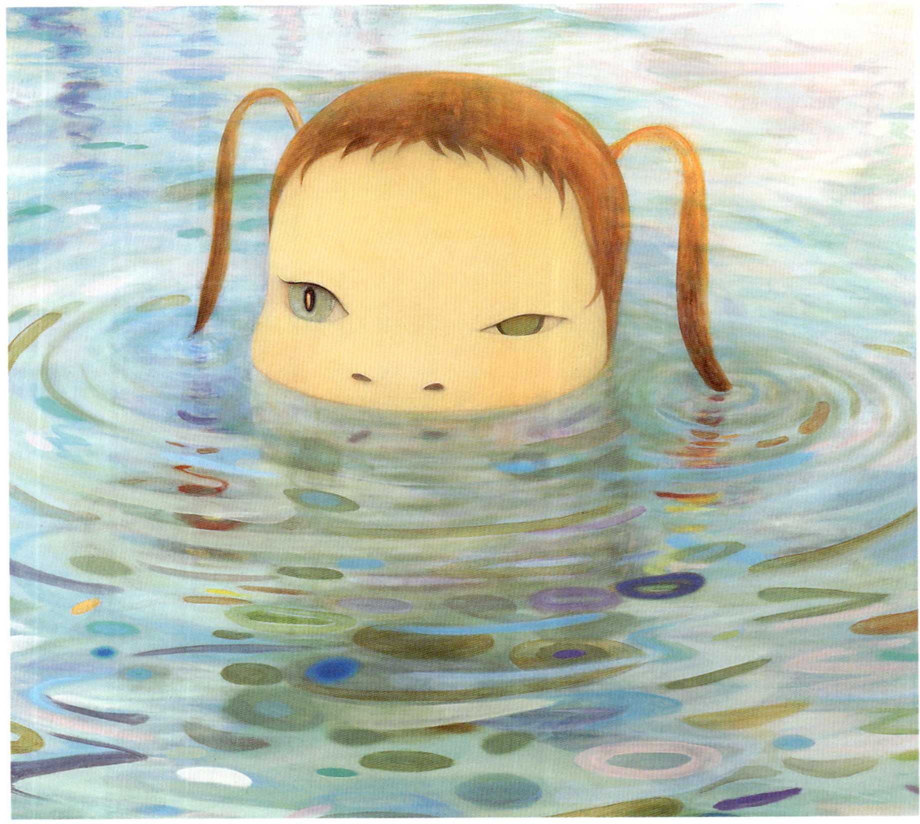

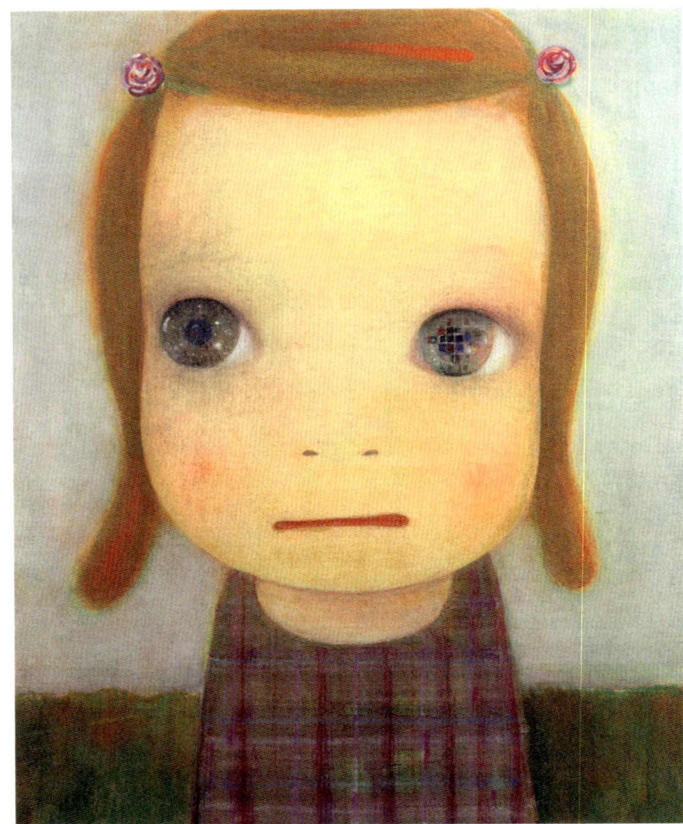

when, after their first joint session and back in their own studios in Japan, they each started making studies of Cézanne's apples as a way to help curb their own natural tendencies to draw faces with large eyes.[12] During these exercises, their apples slowly evolved into buttocks and double arcs, but the forms did not develop beyond drawings and sketches until five years later when they reintroduced the motif and the buttocks became a notable feature of their paintings, sometimes displaced onto the forms of watering cans, chairs, and other creatures (Figs. 150 and 151). Another playful reinterpretation of the classical nude was the creation of an androgynous body or anemic male figure whose erect penis was likened to the thin stems of blooming flowers (Figs. 152 and 153). In all, Chaguin produced nine paintings, and despite the short career of this imagined persona, the project allowed Nara and Sugito to indulge in transforming their many late-night expositions about art into reality.

Fig. 146
Yoshitomo Nara and Hiroshi Sugito, *Deeper than a Puddle*, 2004, Acrylic on canvas, 102 ⅜ × 110 ¼ in. (260 × 280 cm)

Fig. 147
Yoshitomo Nara and Hiroshi Sugito, *Patricia*, 2004, Acrylic on canvas, 23 ⅝ × 19 ¹¹⁄₁₆ in. (60 × 50 cm)

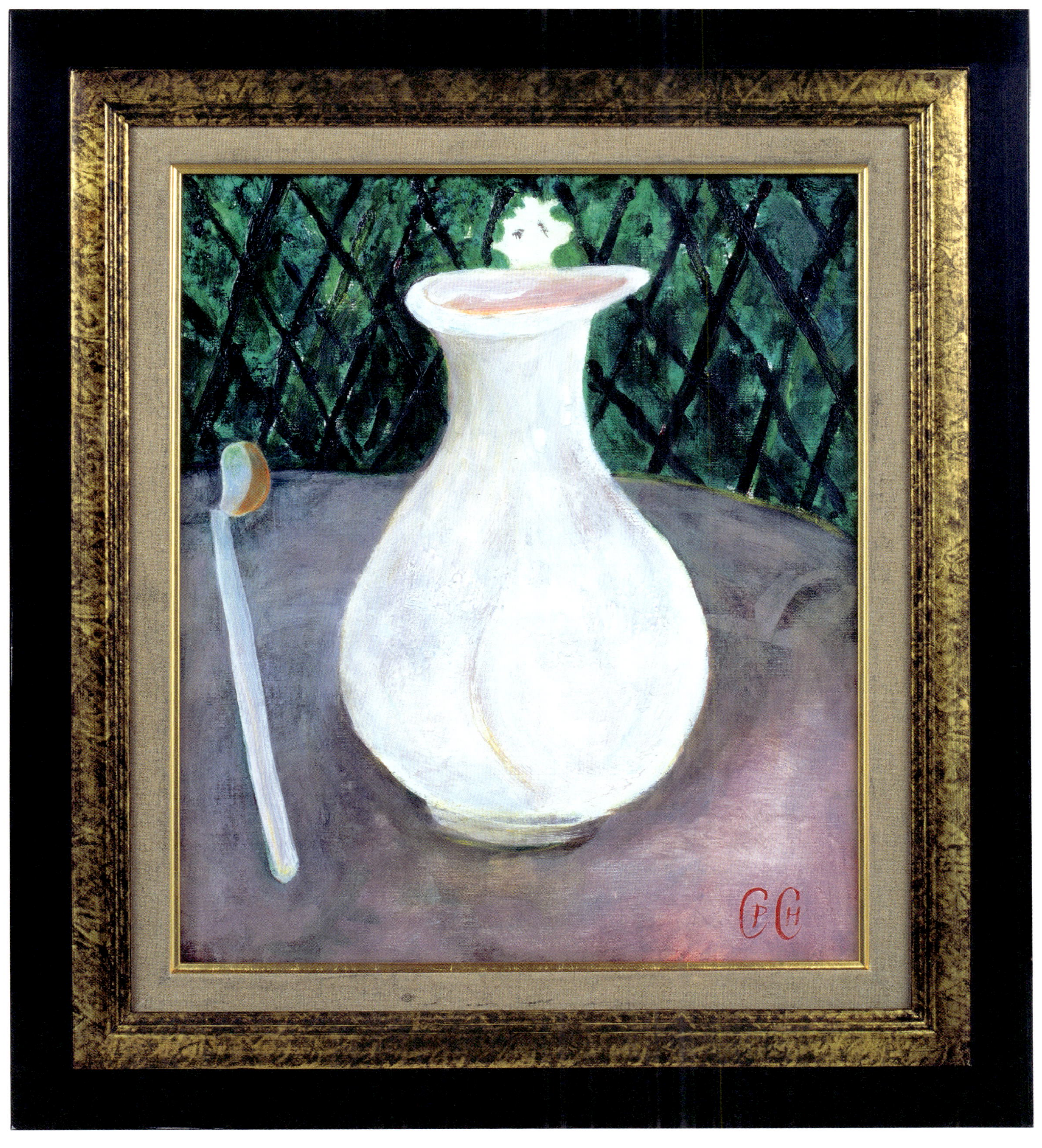

Fig. 148
Chaguin (Yoshitomo Nara and Hiroshi Sugito), *Omoutsubo*, 2008, Acrylic on canvas, 17 15⁄16 × 14 15⁄16 in. (45.5 × 38 cm)

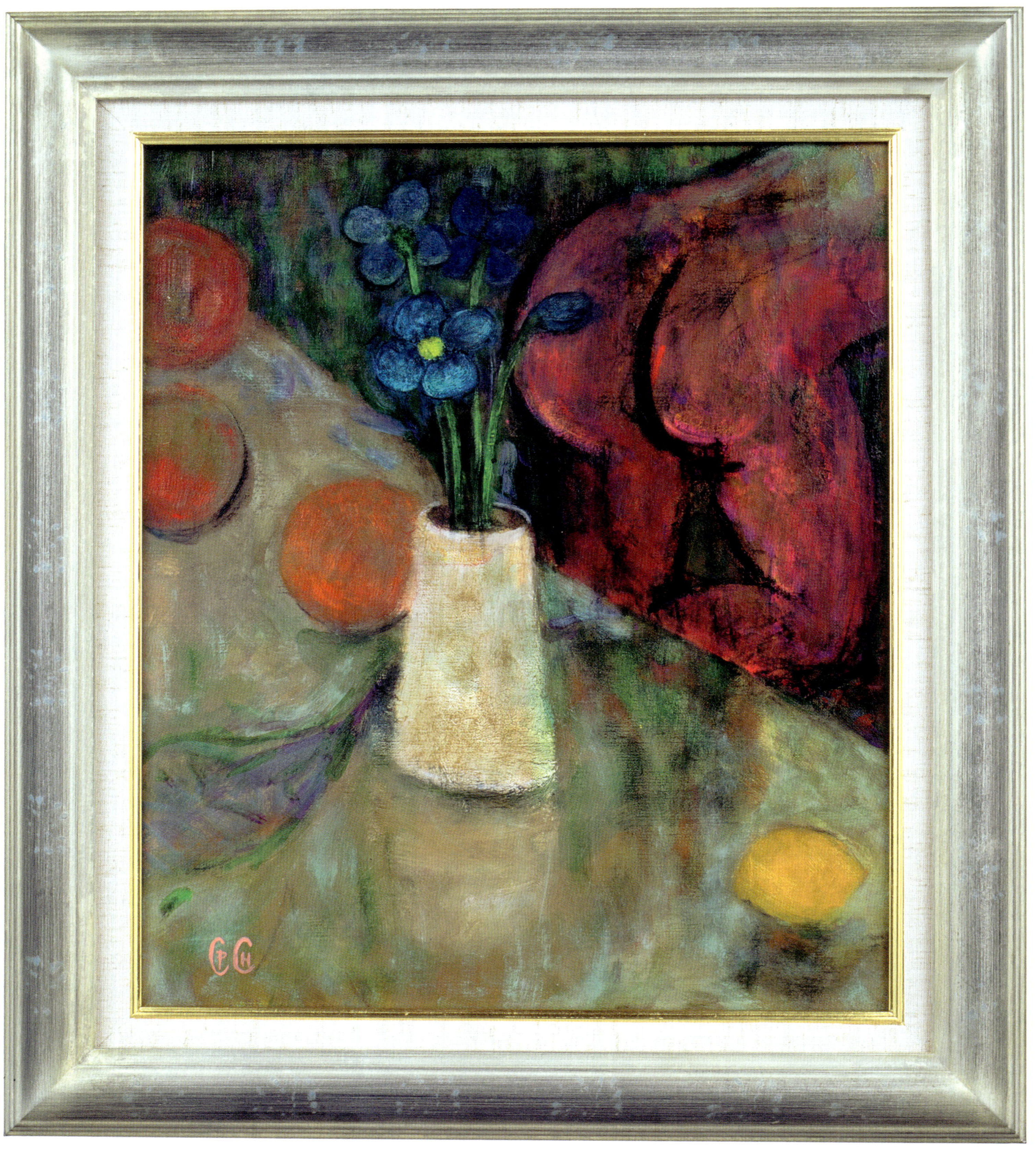

Fig. 149
Chaguin (Yoshitomo Nara and Hiroshi Sugito), *Le temps perdu / Youthful Days Lost*, 2008, Acrylic on canvas, 17 15⁄16 × 14 15⁄16 in. (45.5 × 38 cm)

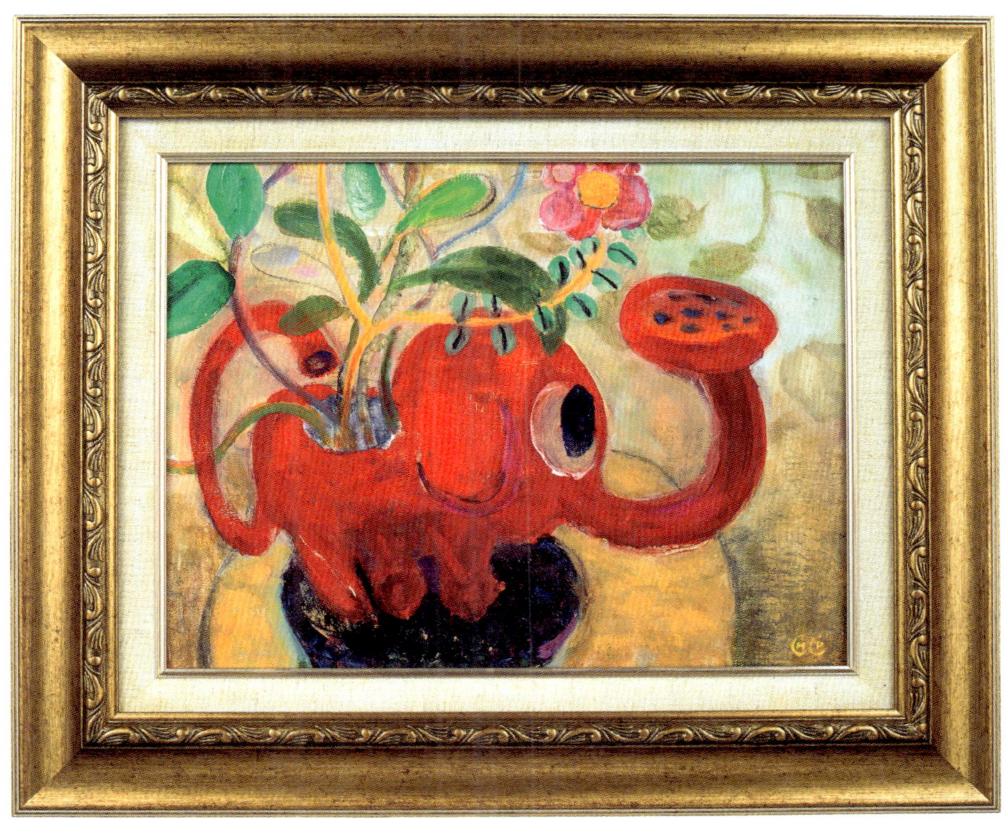

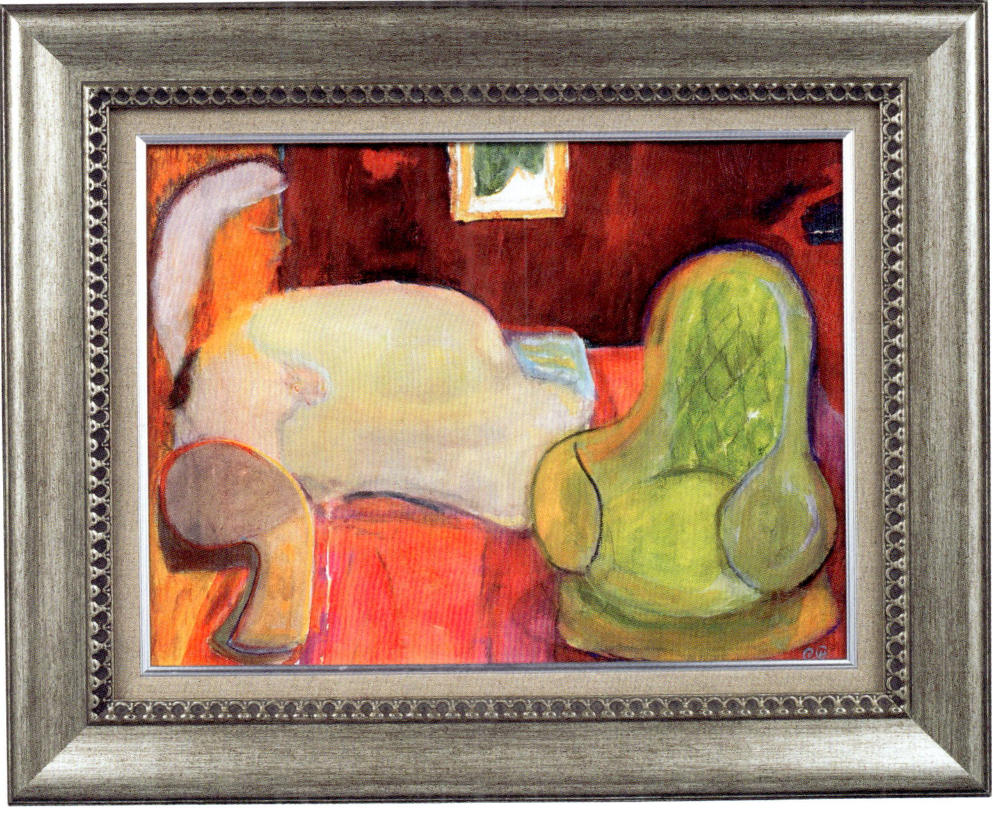

Fig. 150
Chaguin (Yoshitomo Nara and Hiroshi Sugito), *Cherchant de l'eau / In Need of Water*, 2008, Acrylic on canvas, 12 ½ × 16 ⅛ in. (31.8 × 41 cm)

Fig. 151
Chaguin (Yoshitomo Nara and Hiroshi Sugito), *Dans la salle / In the Room*, 2008, Acrylic on canvas, 12 ½ × 16 ⅛ in. (31.8 × 41 cm)

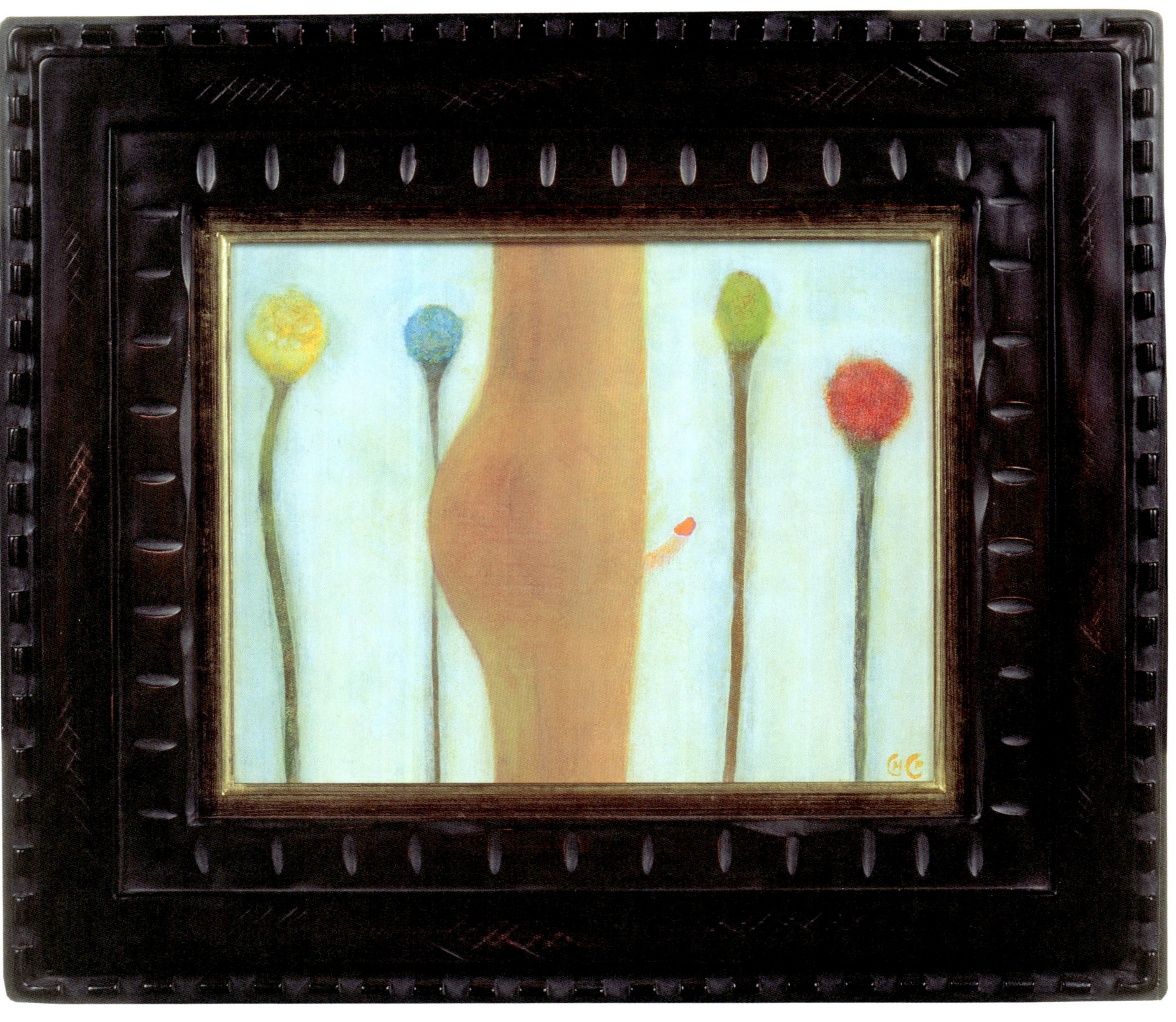

Fig. 152
Chaguin (Yoshitomo Nara and Hiroshi Sugito), *Le désir silencieux / Silent Desire*, 2008, Acrylic on canvas, 8 ¹¹⁄₁₆ × 10 ¾ in. (22 × 27.3 cm)

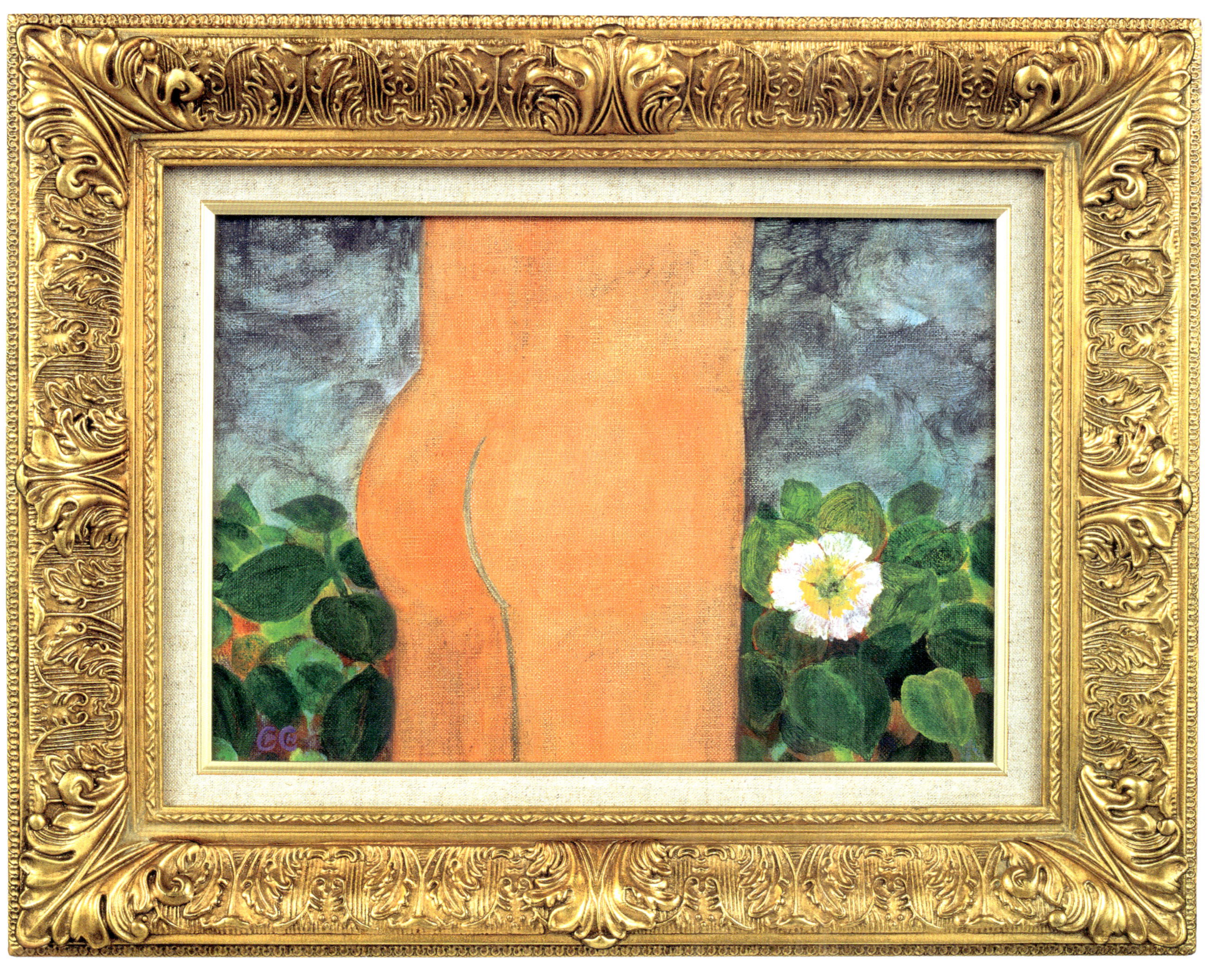

Fig. 153
Chaguin (Yoshitomo Nara and Hiroshi Sugito), *Avant l'orage / Before the Storm*, 2008, Acrylic on canvas, 9 ½ × 13 ⅛ in. (24.2 × 33.3 cm)

Designing "Houses"

In 2003 Nara presented *S.M.L.*, a set of container-style rooms in three sizes—small, medium, and large—made with members of graf, an Osaka-based design firm (Figs. 154–157). Nara's decision to collaborate with graf, and its design/architecture arm in particular, came from a desire to work with three-dimensional spaces and, specifically, to make "big" things. Until that point, his work, even his sculptures, seldom moved beyond a shallow sense of depth, and his prior experiments with sculptural installations had not always succeeded in creating compositional coherence. The *S.M.L.* project, therefore, represented a challenge he set for himself, and it also introduced a new type of working relationship that followed a workshop structure rather than a collaboration, with Nara at its epicenter. The graf team's primary role was to provide construction support, and Nara enlisted the additional help of volunteers to build the structures, together forming a motley team of professionals and amateurs. This mixture of different skill levels, especially with the inclusion of volunteers who were eager participants but not trained builders, maintained an ad hoc spirit that was in keeping with the project's aim: building structures to house Nara's drawings, sketches, and knick-knacks and installing them in exhibitions to encourage a more interactive engagement with viewers of his work.

Architecturally, the project referenced the warren of rooms and public spaces that formed graf's offices, combined with a simple external appearance that blended them into their environment. Each one of the *S.M.L.* rooms was built of found materials from local construction sites, and, as with his 2001 show at the Yokohama Museum of Art, Nara invited audiences to create dolls based on his designs. In return, he wrote notes of thanks, sometimes adding a drawing, which he would then pin onto the walls. Each of the rooms was arranged differently: a childlike space (*S*), a personal studio space (*M*), and a social gathering space (*L*). The largest room (Fig. 156) was set up like a youth club, containing a blackboard, a large sharing table, stacks of shelves, and a massive clear-acrylic antinuclear peace sign stuffed with the submitted dolls. During the week of installing and working on-site, Nara scribbled various messages and thoughts on its walls, along with displaying photographs and reflections from his recent trip to Afghanistan in 2002 (discussed in the following chapter), during which he witnessed firsthand the effects of war on

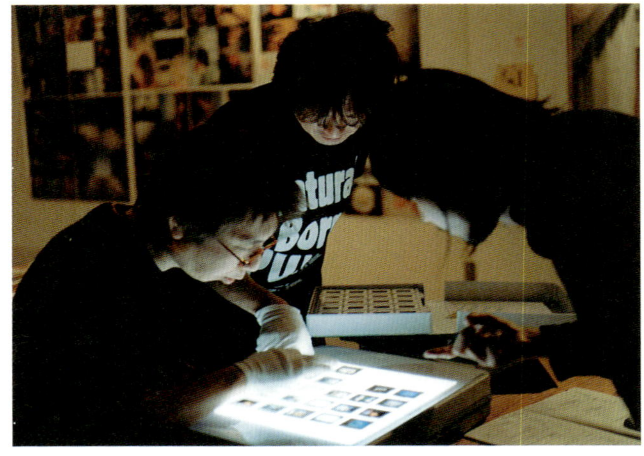

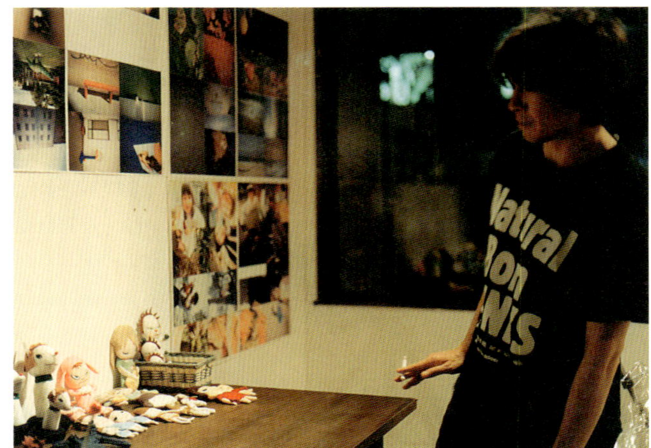

Figs. 154 and 155
Nara working on the *S.M.L.* exhibition at graf media gm, Osaka, 2003

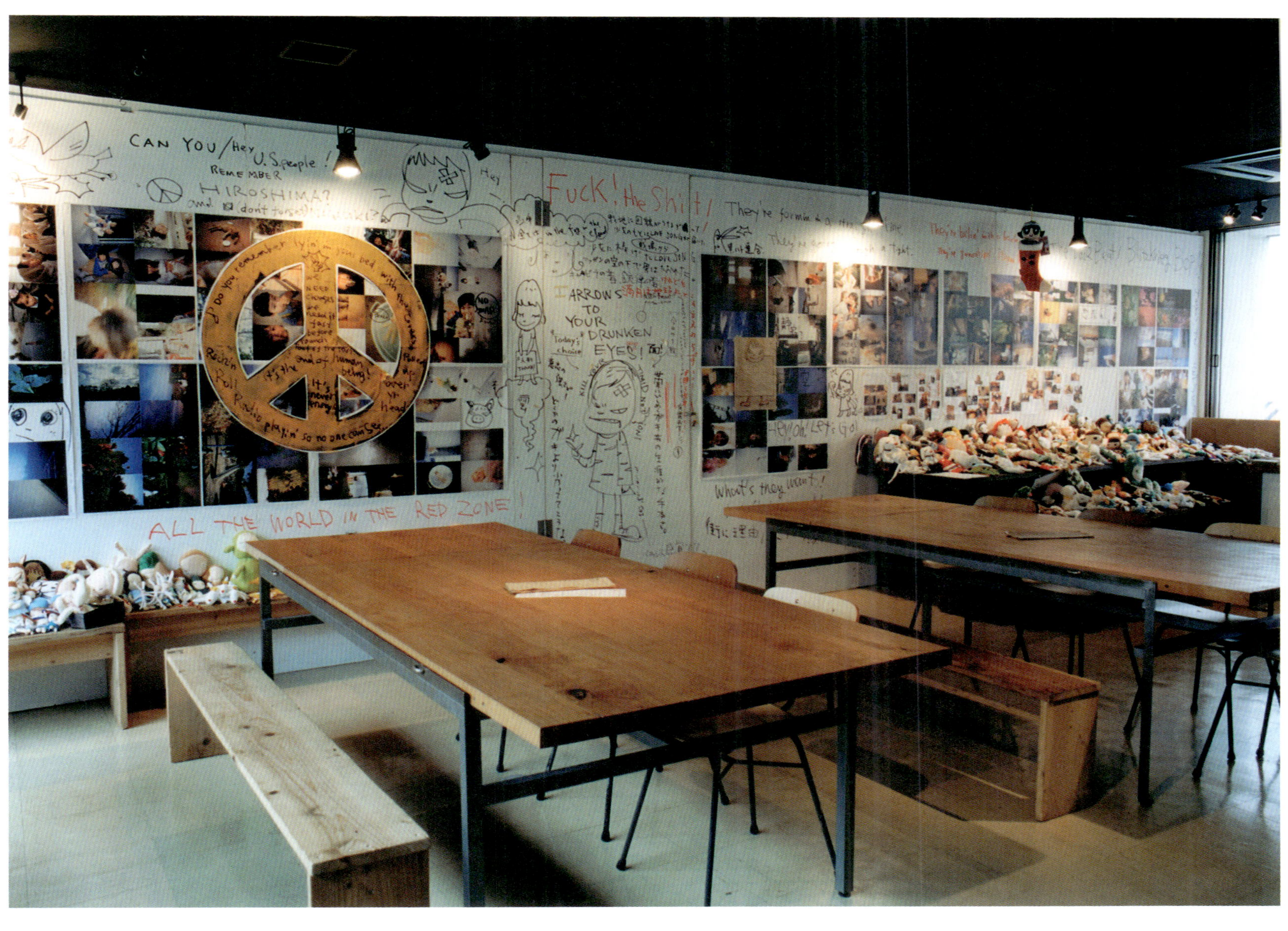

Fig. 156
Exhibition view: *S.M.L.*,
graf media gm, Osaka, 2003

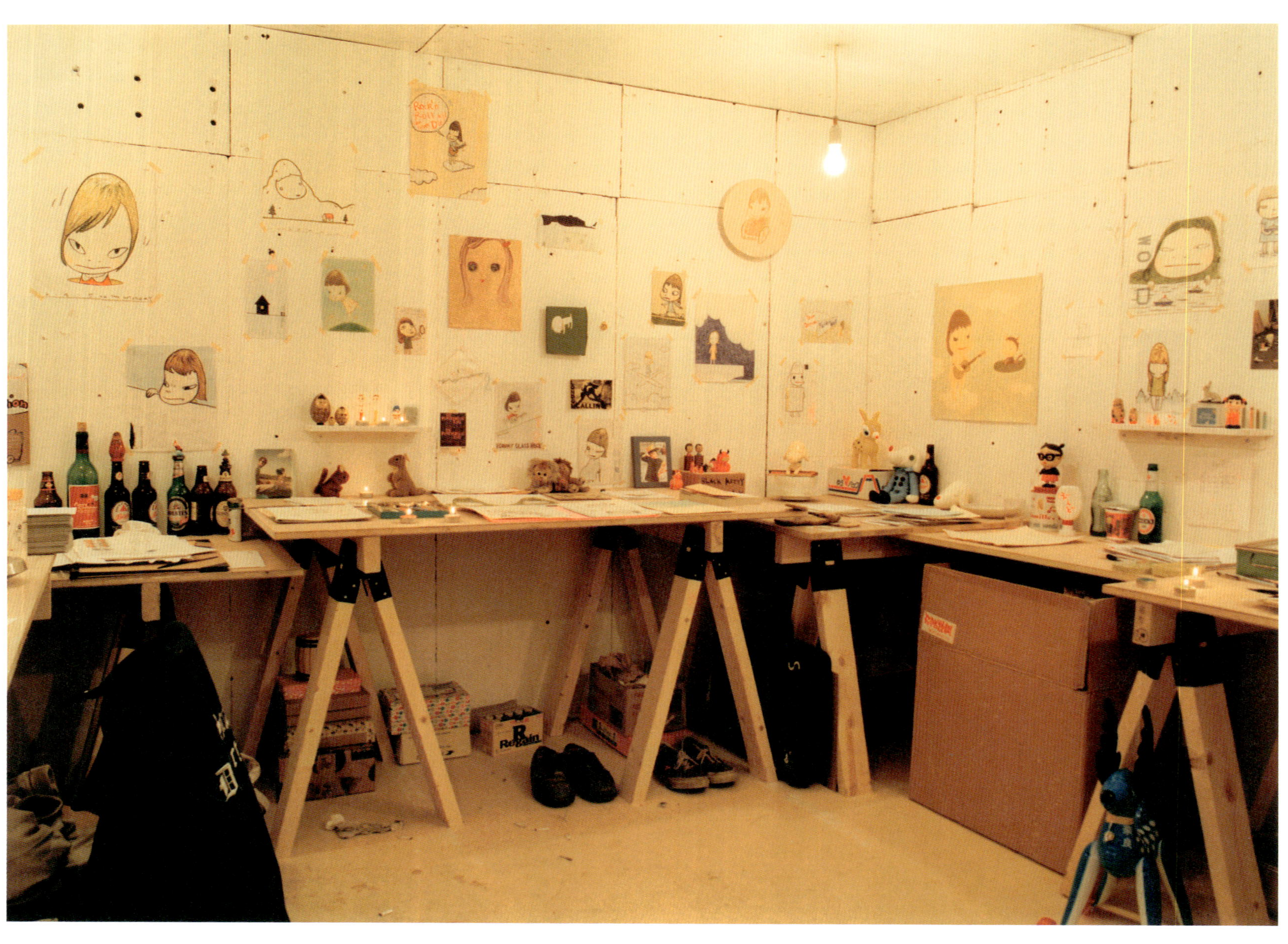

Fig. 157
Exhibition view: *S.M.L.*,
graf media gm, Osaka, 2003

a local community.[13] Room *M* (Fig. 157) was a staged space that resembled a private studio, in which every surface was covered with Nara's personal items, sketches, drawings, paintings, and sculptures. The smallest room, a child-sized version of room *M*, was designed for visitors no taller than four feet, so that most adults were required to curl and twist their bodies to gain entry, in a way becoming children again.[14]

Collectively, the rooms of *S.M.L.* can be seen to form a sort of creative autobiography that uses strategies of fiction to carefully stage scenes of personal resonance, and together they narrate Nara's own story: beginning with an imagined childlike space that, since early on, has been a source of his creativity, then leading to his private world as an artist, and finally arriving at his social side, which prefers low-key gatherings to the polished glitter of the art world. In this mixture of the candid and posed, the documentary and the aesthetic, Nara was also attempting to manage his own self-image following his explosion onto the art scene in 2001. Working harder than ever (in 2002 alone, he took part in seventeen shows), Nara received commissions, reviews, and criticisms that placed him increasingly at the center of a Neo-Pop Superflat narrative, a position that he felt falsely characterized his work. Negative reviews often followed the opinions of the highly influential critic Asada Akira, who had panned the Superflat theory as postmodern Orientalism and regarded Nara's work as a celebration of amateurism that lacked historical and technical merit.[15] Nara's desire to control his own narrative represented a way of responding to the detractions that resulted from becoming well known.

Originally, *S.M.L.* was designed to be a one-off project, but Nara and the graf team decided to carry on working together. Nara began to design different versions of these self-contained rooms/houses that varied from miniature toylike structures to glass-windowed studios facing the public street. In particular, he developed a number of spaces that he called *My Drawing Room* (Figs. 160 and 161), new iterations of his studio that found their way to Tokyo, Taipei, Seoul, Bangkok, and London. His structures also began to engage directly with their sites. For example, for his *London Mayfair House* (2006) (Fig. 162), which faced a fashionable street in the well-heeled Mayfair neighborhood of London, half of the studio was revealed to the outside world, while the other half was covered in wooden boards with two narrow openings near the bottom, which required viewers

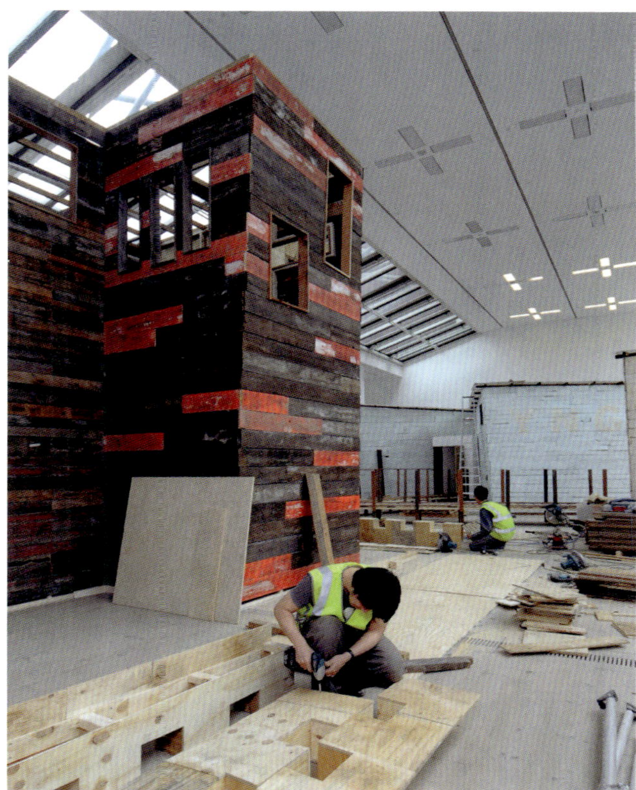

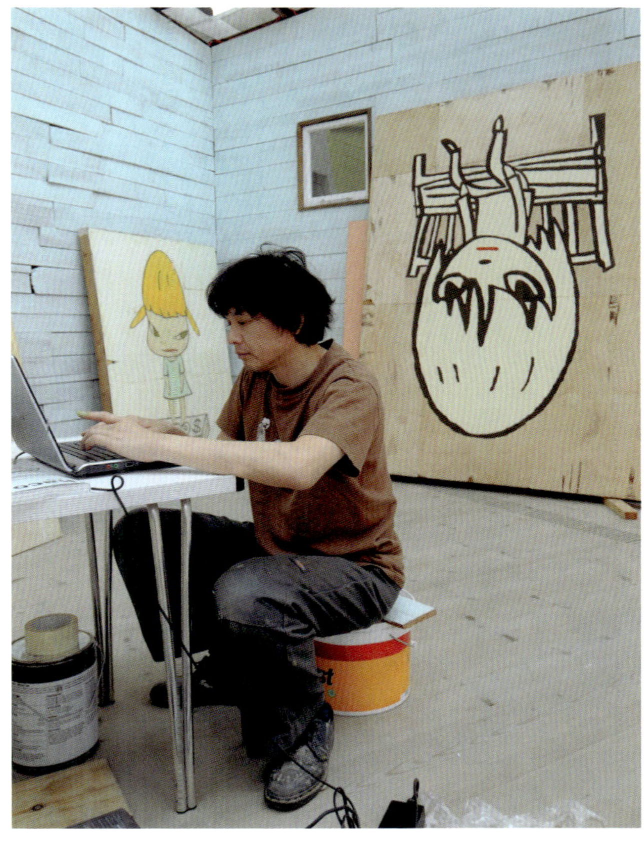

Figs. 158 and 159
Working on the exhibition *Yoshitomo Nara + graf* at BALTIC Centre for Contemporary Art, Gateshead, UK, 2008

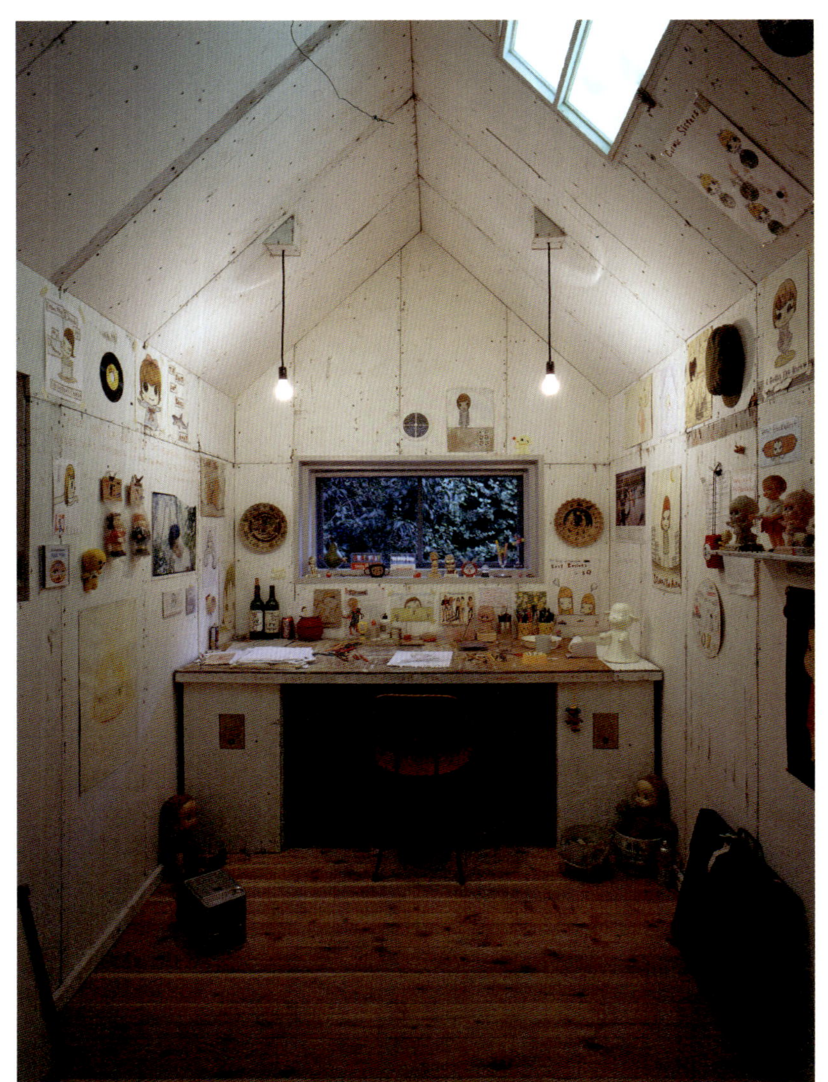

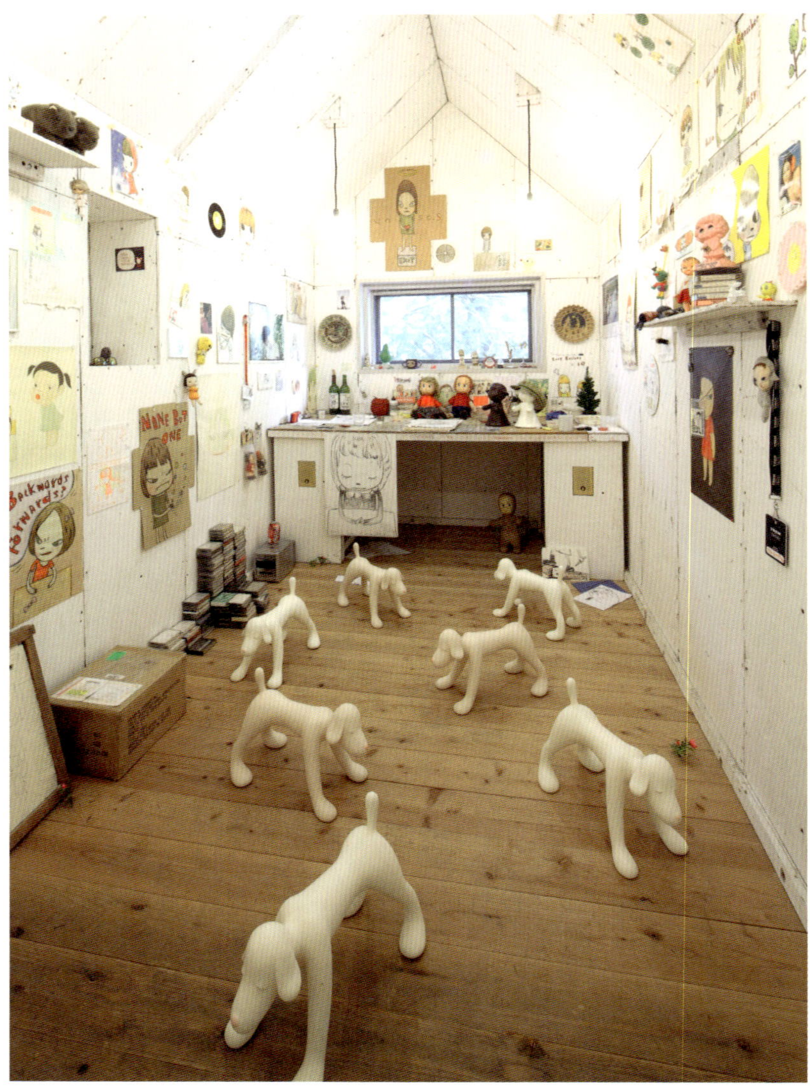

Figs. 160 and 161
My Drawing Room,
2004–ongoing, Mixed media,
122 13/16 × 78 15/16 × 176 3/8 in.
(312 × 200.5 × 448 cm)
Cooperation provided by graf

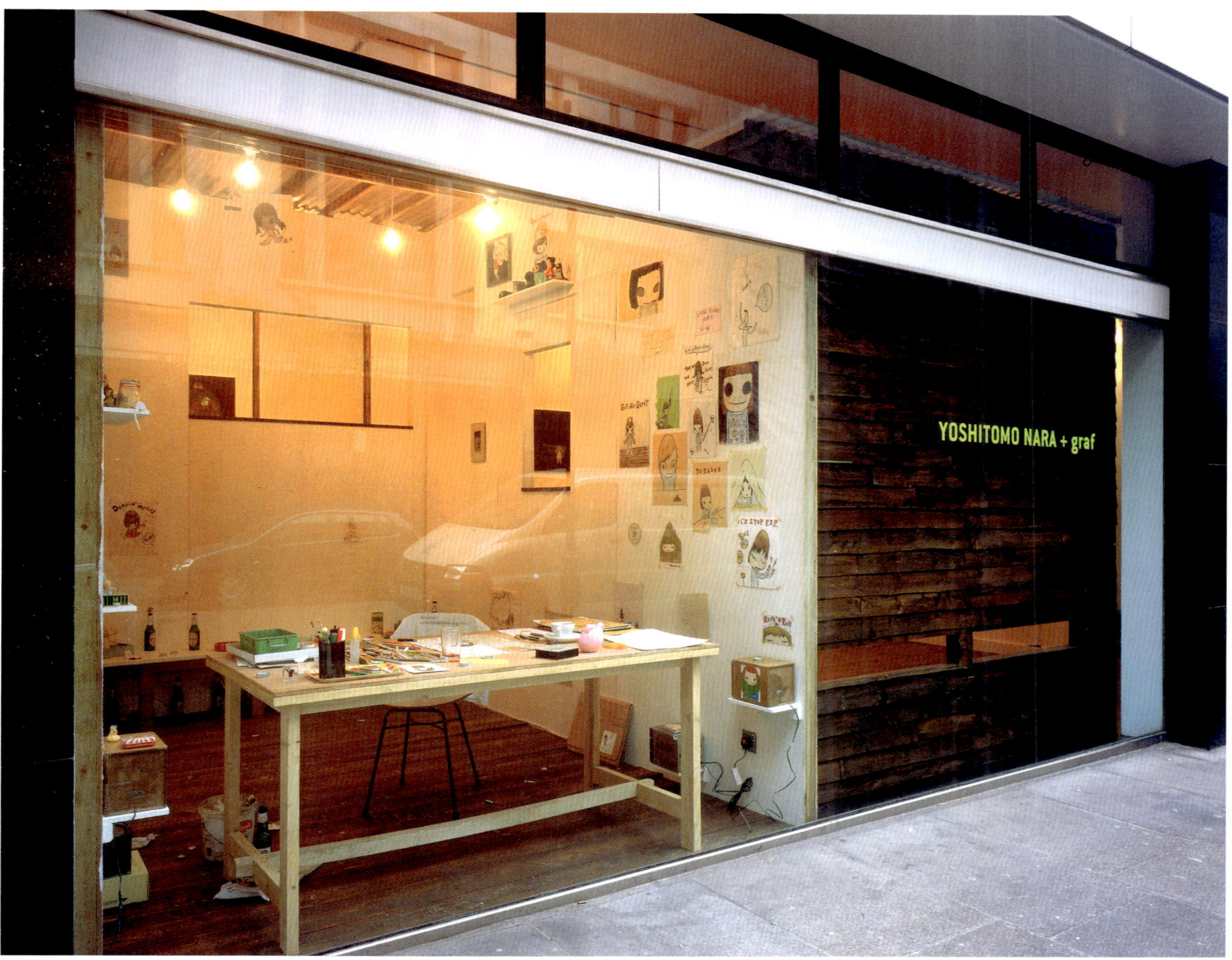

to crouch down to peer inside. For a construction at the Hara Museum of Contemporary Art in Tokyo, a former Meiji-style residential manor, a version of Nara's studio was ensconced in an upper turret room, restoring, in a small way, the building's original function as a home.

These fantastical, childlike rooms disrupted the institutional spaces of museums and galleries by challenging the traditional classifications of what is and is not considered art. In the context of their installation, the rough-and-ready aesthetics and casually presented displays of these constructed studios blur the lines between the personal (Nara), the theatrical (the staged installation), and the institutional (where it is housed). With each exhibition, a viewer's alternating experience as voyeur, consumer, or passerby becomes a part of the dislocating effect of the artwork itself.

Fig. 162
London Mayfair House,
2006, Mixed media installation,
Dimensions variable
Cooperation provided by graf

This project was at its most ambitious in Nara's *A to Z* village of 2006 (Figs. 163–165). Built inside the Yoshii Brick Brew House, the oldest brewery in Japan located in Nara's hometown of Hirosaki, the project was a massive undertaking that brought together thousands of volunteers from across the world to collectively build from the ground up a new kind of group show, led by Nara.[16] The project was composed of forty-four houses built inside the brewery, which primarily showed works by Nara but also exhibited works by nine guest artists, including Hiroshi Sugito, Rinko Kawauchi, and Atsuhiko Misawa. It was a project that operated outside a typical institutional framework by being self-funded and created with the help of a community of volunteers. Nara's aim was to realize the idea that contemporary art can operate outside the usual bureaucracy of museums and the market structures of the art world and that members of the public would willingly support this goal if one reached out to them directly. As part of this utopian vision, *A to Z* was also designed with bridges, staircases, and other architectural structures that provided different viewing positions in order to maximize the possibilities of experiencing the space so that visitors themselves became a part of the exhibition, wandering members of a new, alternative world.

Although the mobilization of voluntary labor on this scale was a departure from the intimate scale of *S.M.L.*, this type of operation was not unusual in Japan. Similar and much larger volunteer-based projects included the Echigo-Tsumari Art Triennale, which began in 2000 as a program to regenerate many of the abandoned rural spaces in Niigata prefecture by enlisting thousands of volunteers to work with artists and residents.[17] These projects targeted areas in Japan that were experiencing declining populations or stagnating economies, and *A to Z* also followed this ambition. Nara's exhibition attracted over 77,000 visitors, a substantial number for Hirosaki, allowing him to give something back to his hometown.[18]

The scope of the *A to Z* project, however, was perhaps too expansive for Nara.[19] After this massive undertaking, he began to harbor doubts about the direction of the houses and felt increasingly detached from them, even as their growing success was making them as much a signature of his practice as his portraits of big-headed girls. He began to feel the limitations of the structures: after each reconstruction, they, inevitably, lost something of their DIY origins and community-based, familial spirit, and he felt he had reached the limit of what

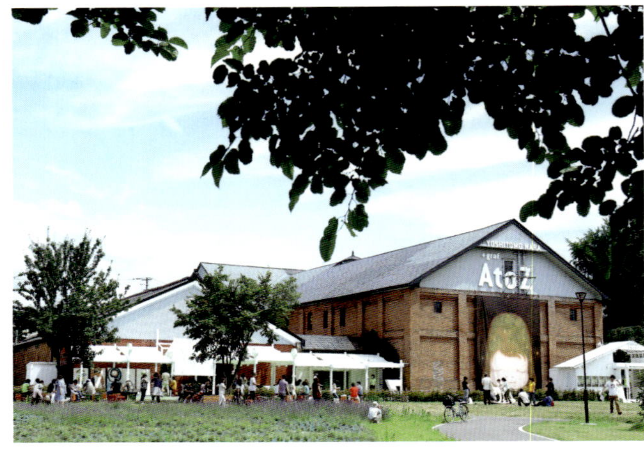

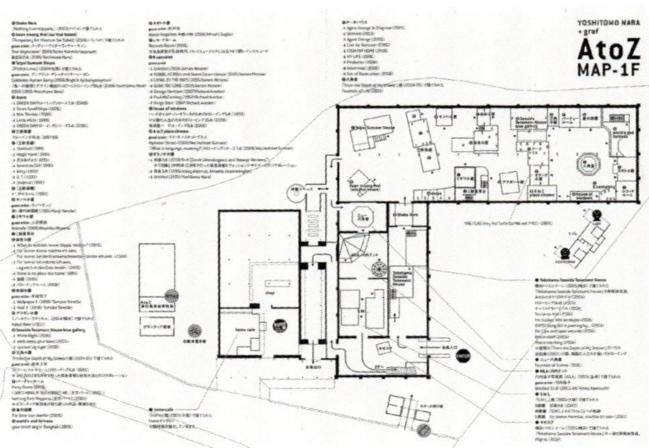

Fig. 163
Exhibition view: *Yoshitomo Nara + graf: A to Z*, Yoshii Brick Brew House, Hirosaki, Japan, 2006

Fig. 164
Floor plan of the exhibition *Yoshitomo Nara + graf* at Yoshii Brick Brew House, Hirosaki, Japan, 2006

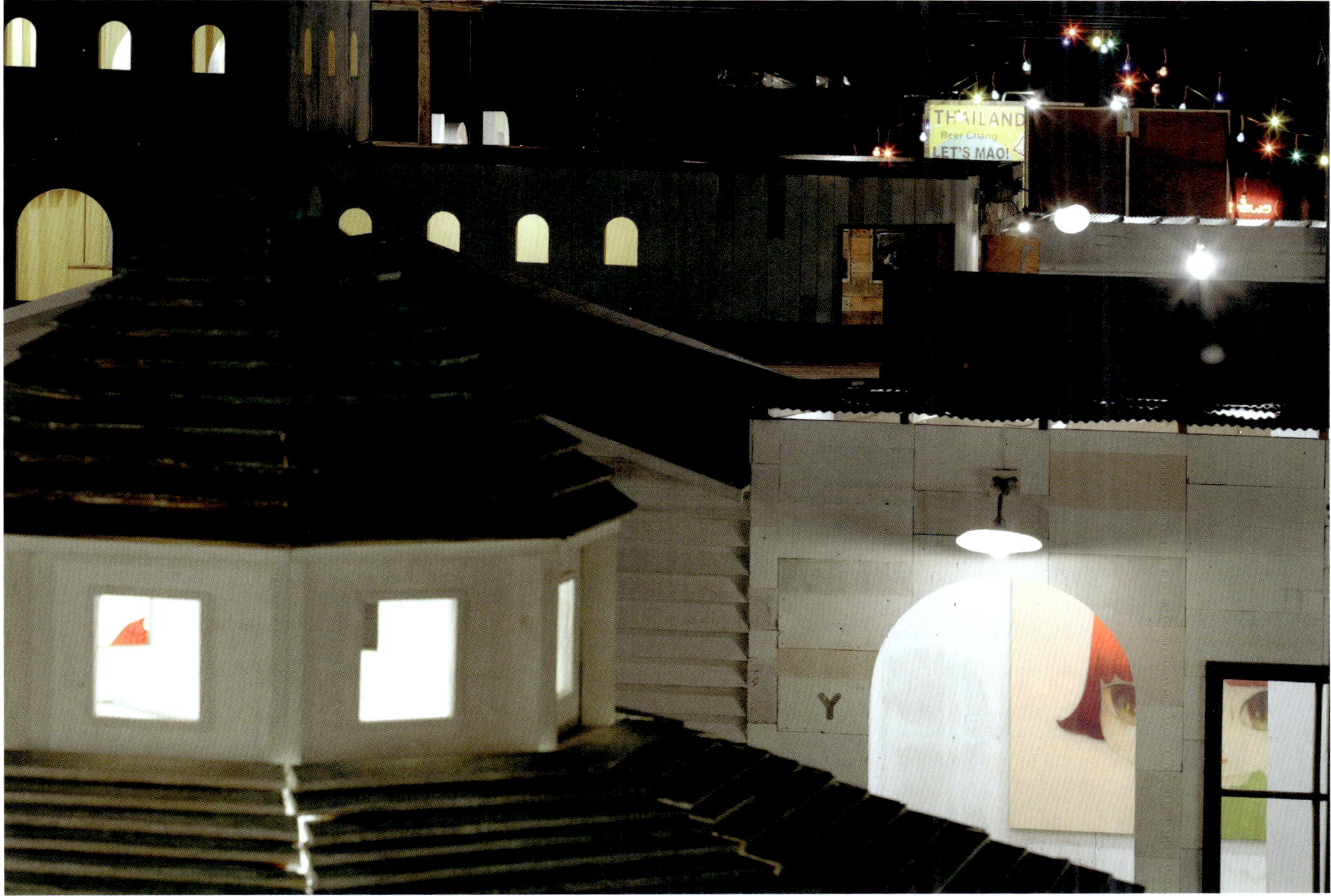

building together could achieve as a creative process. While he carried on with the house projects, he now looked for ways to push them in new directions.

One new path that Nara took was to turn the house into something more sculptural and painterly, and to bring it into the fold of his world of big-headed girls. In late 2006, for his solo exhibition *Moonlight Serenade* at the 21st Century Museum of Contemporary Art, Kanazawa, he worked with graf to build *Voyage of the Moon (Resting Moon) / Voyage of the Moon* (Figs. 166 and 167). Displayed under dim lighting, the work comprised a blue wooden house topped with the giant head of a girl staring pensively into the distance, a form akin to his fiberglass *Puff Marshie* sculptural heads from the same year (Fig. 168), one of which was also shown at his *A to Z* show in Hirosaki. Here, however, Nara painted directly onto the surface of the sculpted head, focusing especially on its eyes to achieve a painterly effect that echoes the signature style of his canvas works. The slanting slopes of the roof in *Voyage of the Moon* extend to become part of her body,

Fig. 165
Exhibition view: *Yoshitomo Nara + graf: A to Z*, Yoshii Brick Brew House, Hirosaki, Japan, 2006

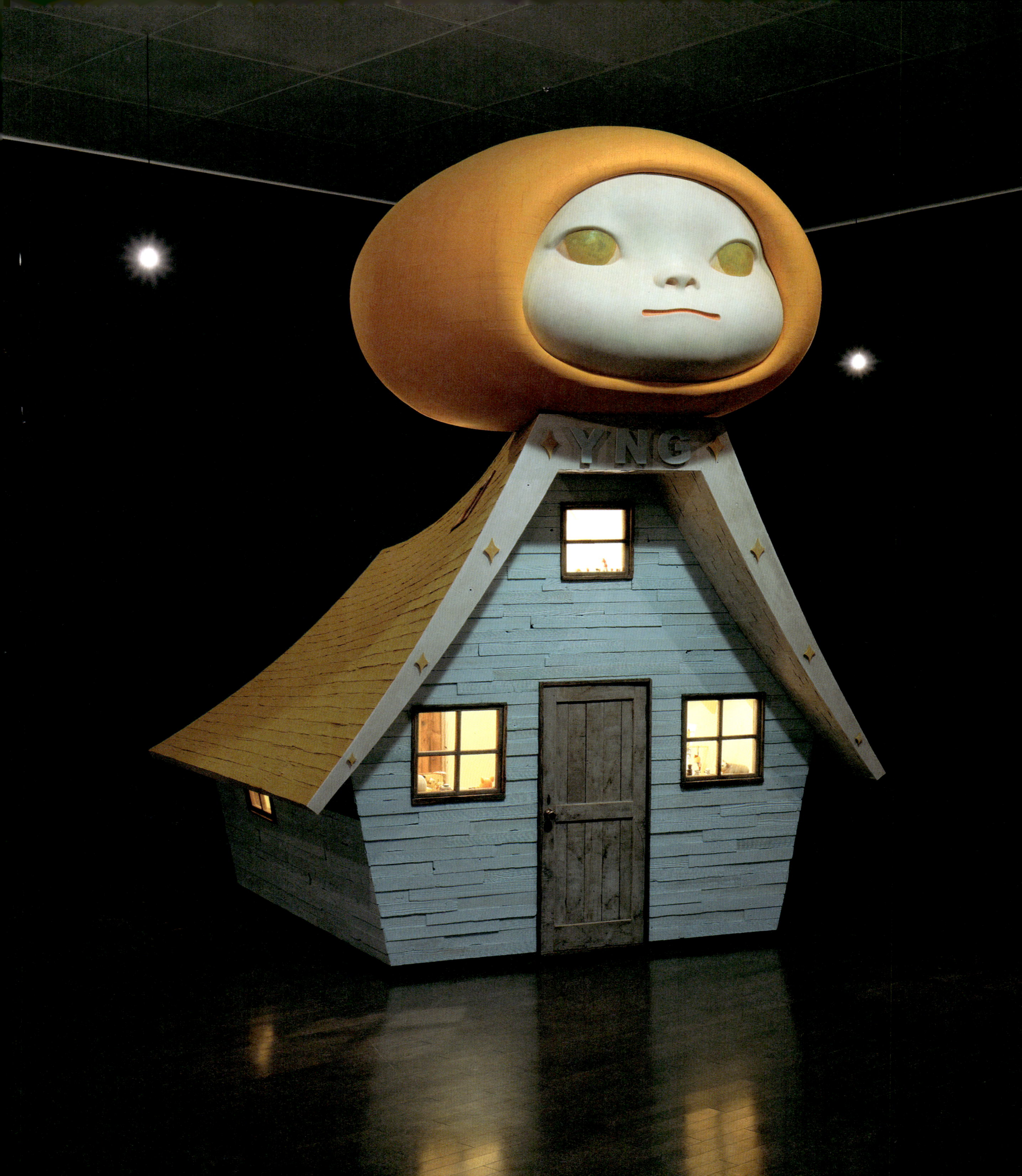
YNG

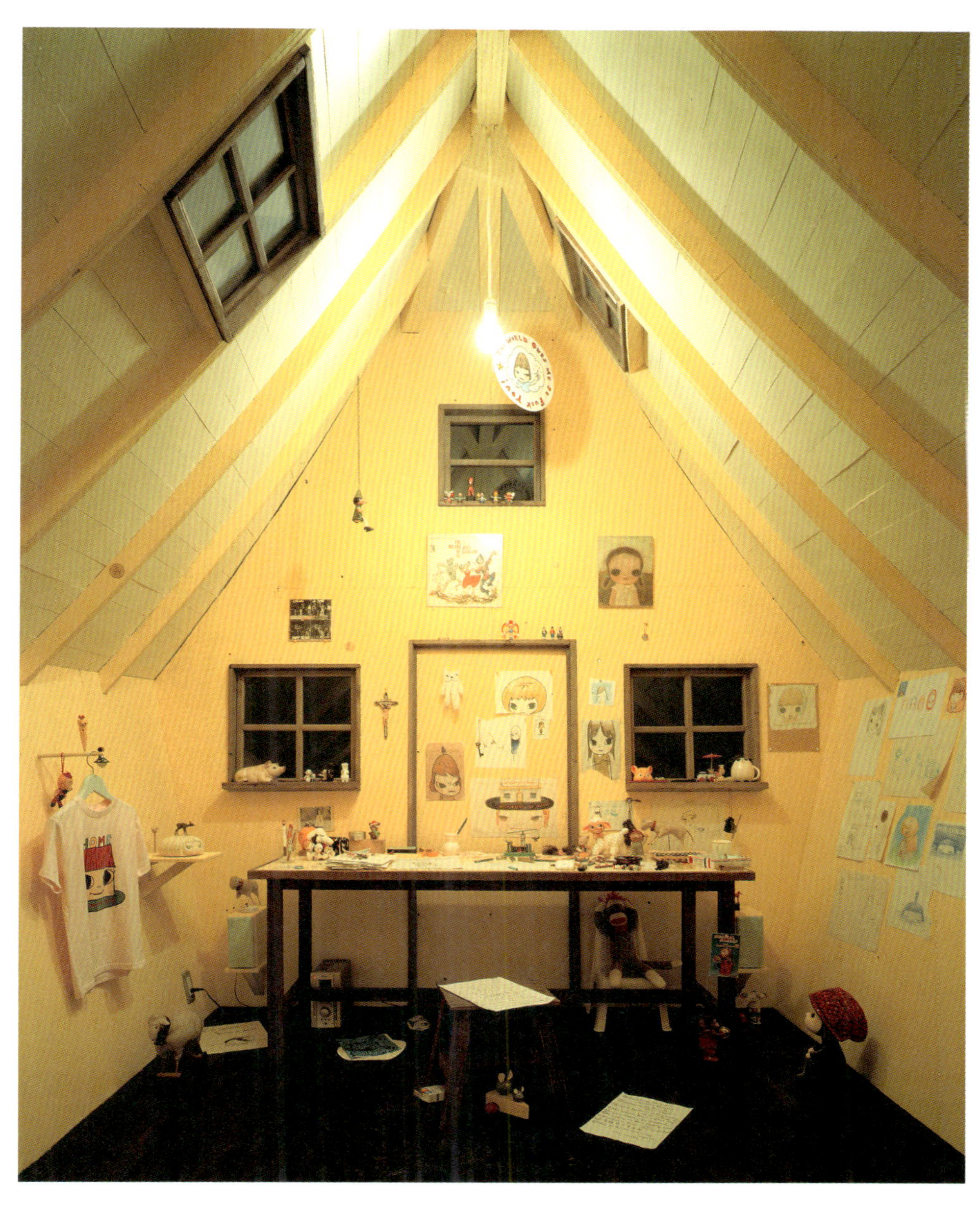

Figs. 166 and 167
Voyage of the Moon (Resting Moon) / Voyage of the Moon, 2006, Mixed media, 187 3⁄8 × 139 3⁄8 × 194 7⁄8 in. (476 × 354 × 495 cm)
Cooperation provided by graf

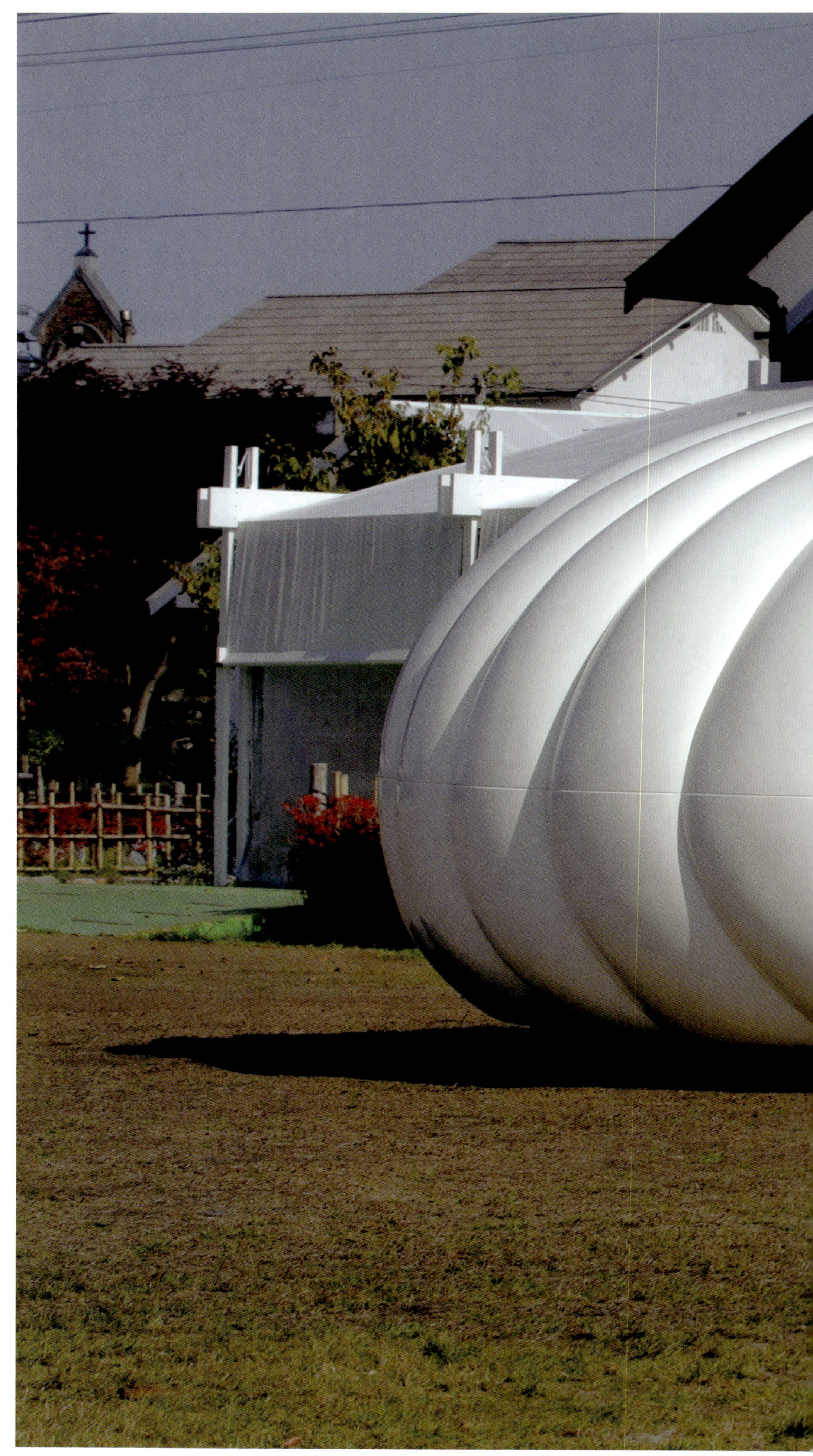

Fig. 168
Puff Marshie (Hirosaki version), 2006, Urethane on fiber-reinforced plastics, h. 59 × diam. 118 ⅛ in. (150 × 300 cm)

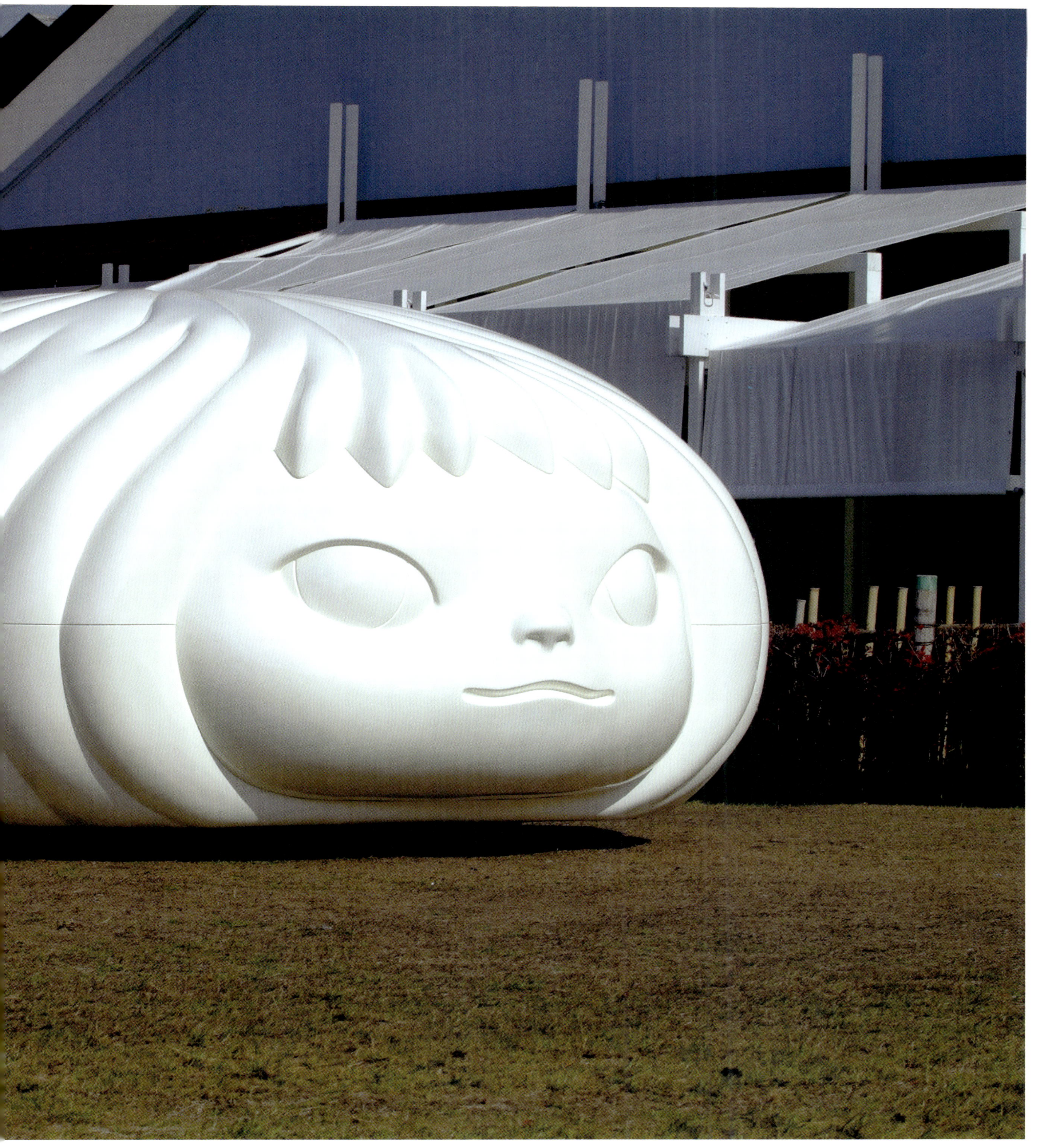

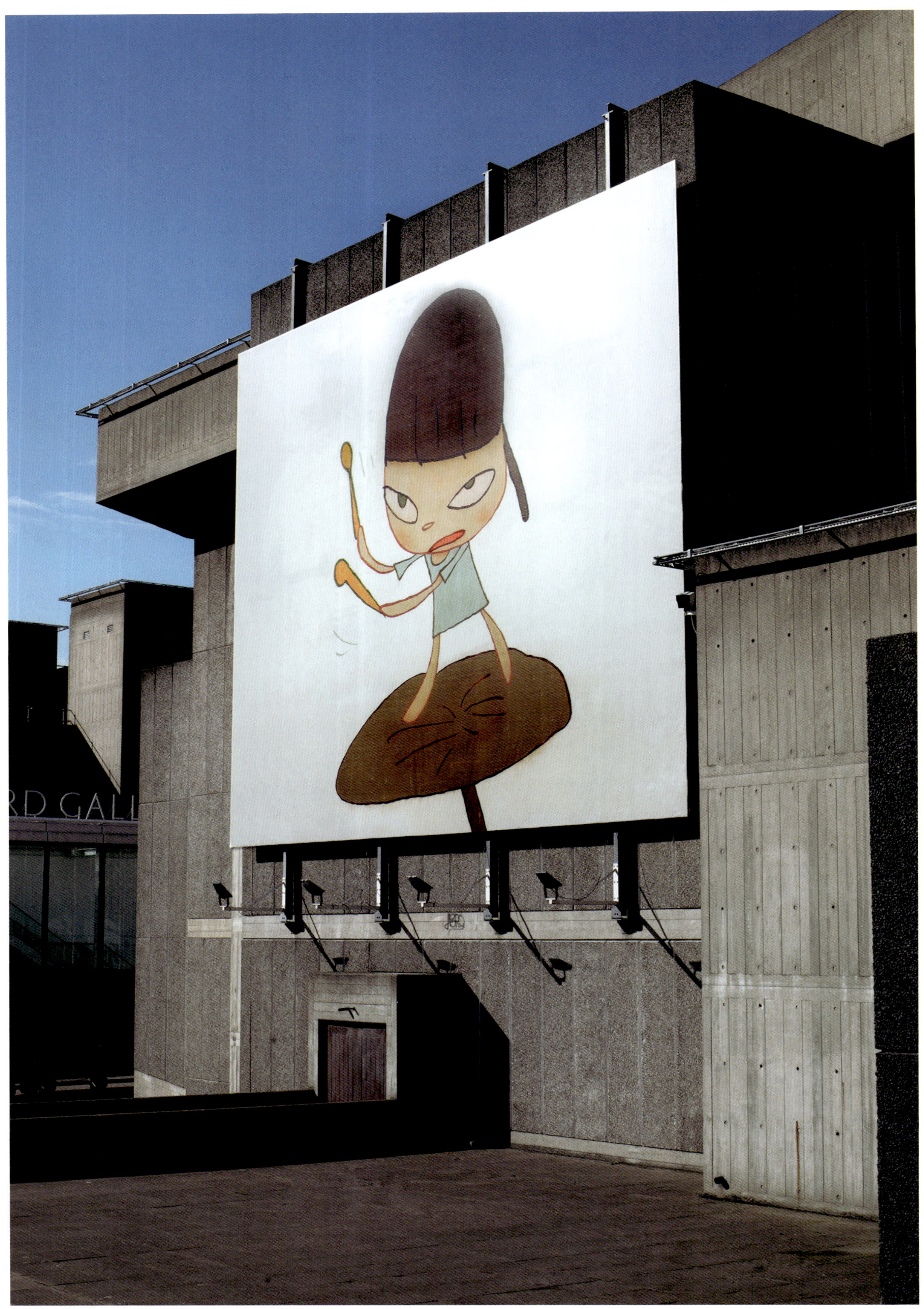
RD GALL

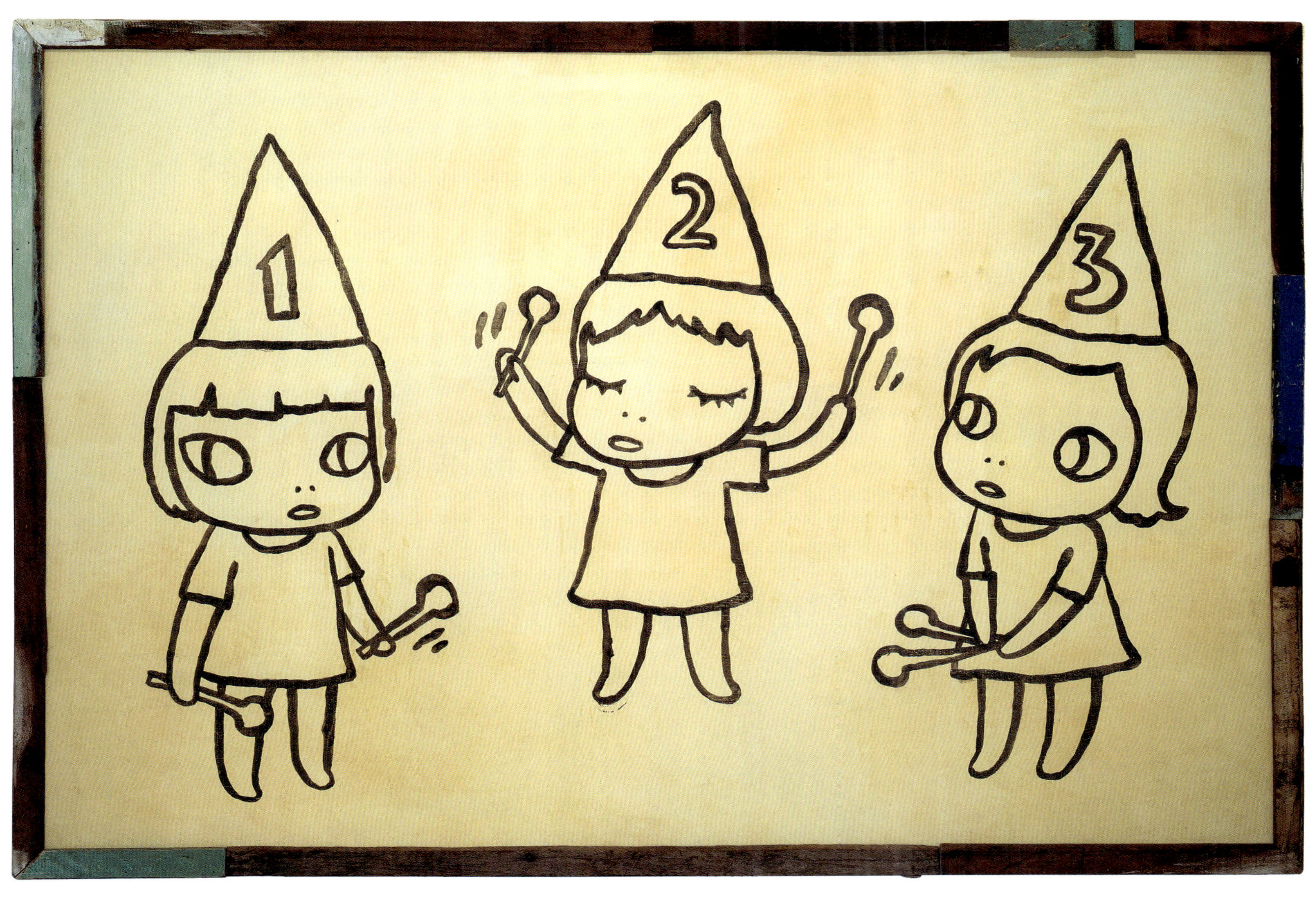

Fig. 169 (opposite)
Billboard of *Marching on the Butterbur Leaf*, 2016
Hayward Gallery Waterloo Billboard Commission, Southbank Centre, London

Fig. 170
1.2.3..., 2006, Acrylic on wood, 45 ¼ × 67 11/16 in. (115 × 172 cm)

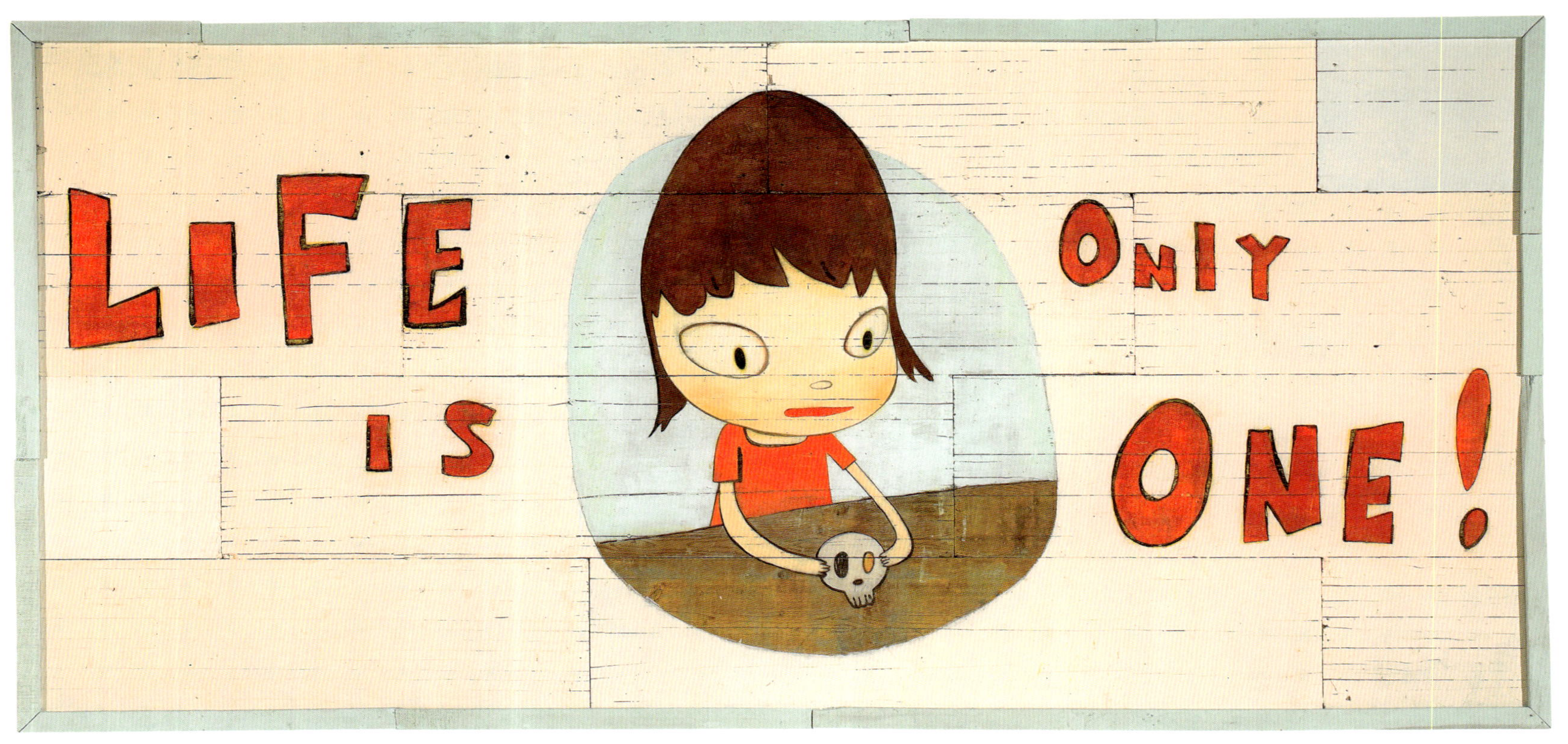

Fig. 171
Life Is Only One!, 2007,
Acrylic on wood,
76 ⅜ × 161 ⁷⁄₁₆ × 2 ¾ in.
(194 × 410 × 7 cm)

like a cape that covers the house beneath her, while inside, viewers are greeted with the scene of an untidy studio bathed in a warm glow, as if the artist has just left the room. By adding the moonlike face to the house's exterior, Nara was steering the form away from being purely functional and closer to a fantasy of nighttime adventure that recalls the work of Takeshi Motai and his children's stories (Figs. 18 and 19). It is unclear how successful *Voyage of the Moon* is in fully capturing the sculptural quality Nara was looking for, since it takes on a figural appearance only from certain angles, and the difference in material between the head and house maintains the separation between architecture and sculpture. Nonetheless, this is an important work that can be seen as a transition back to painting and sculpture, media that have always formed the foundations of Nara's childlike worlds.

It was around this time that Nara also began to create large billboard paintings for his house projects. As with the houses, these works were made of abandoned materials, and, when completed, he propped them on rooftops or along the houses' external walls. The billboard paintings are intended to subvert the primary function of the houses as containers by turning their exteriors instead into display structures. As with *Voyage of the Moon*, they show the beginnings of Nara's move away from the spatial dynamics of architecture and back to the imagistic qualities that defined his earlier focus on big-headed girls. Nevertheless, because these billboard paintings grew out of the house projects, Nara still conceived of them as three-dimensional—the frame constitutes an integral part of these works, and, as such, they lie outside his body of works on canvas. Stylistically, they differ from his paintings in their simpler designs and more graphic treatment of lines and colors that achieves a flatter surface. The themes of the billboard paintings are also more straightforward: a band of kids singing a line from one of Nara's favorite songs or featuring banal but catchy statements, such as "Life Is Only One!" (Fig. 171). As billboards, they sometimes function as public-facing advertising-like platforms (Fig. 173), and their designs are often replicated. The conceit of these works as extensions of buildings can extend in other instances to outdoor banners that adorn the sides of massive public buildings, such as in his commission for the Southbank Centre in London (Fig. 169). In these large-scale presentations, the banners communicate the playful absurdity of a giant child let loose in the city, an artist's statement broadcast to the public.

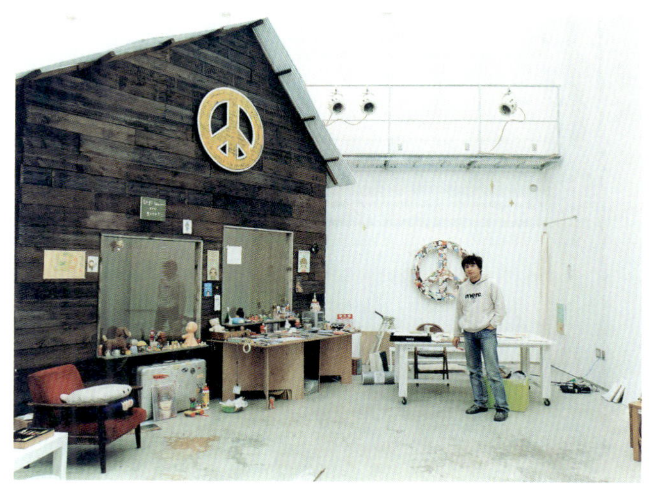

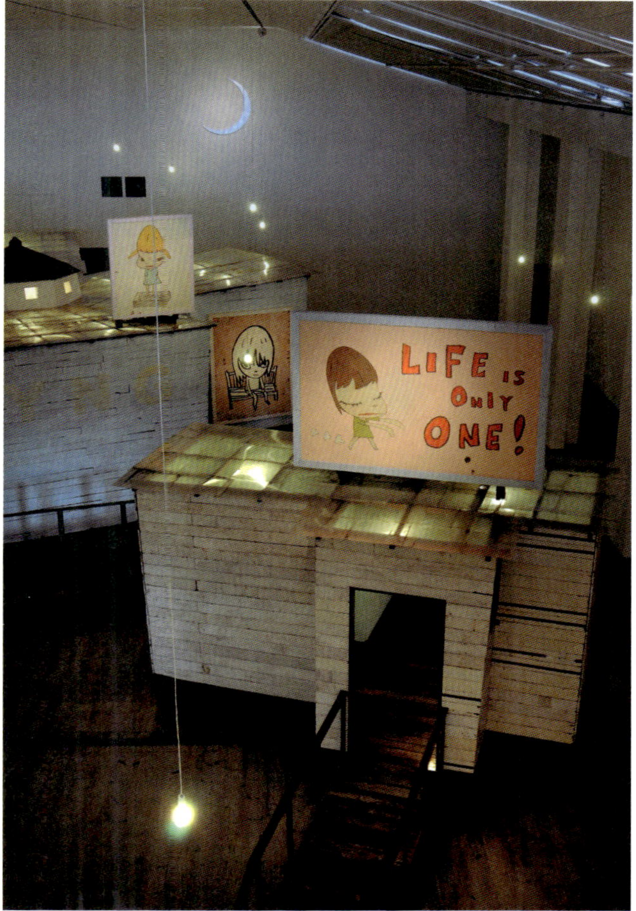

Fig. 172
Nara's open studio at the exhibition *Moonlight Serenade* at 21st Century Museum of Contemporary Art, Kanazawa, Japan, 2006

Fig. 173
Exhibition view: *Yoshitomo Nara + graf*, BALTIC Centre for Contemporary Art, Gateshead, UK, 2006

Ceramics

In 2007 Nara began an artist residency in the town of Shigaraki in the mountains outside Kyoto, home to one of six ancient kilns in Japan that have been major sites of ceramic making since at least the Kamakura period (1185–1333).[20] Shigaraki is known for its local clay, which contains high levels of feldspar and silica and produces objects with a distinctive raw and tactile surface. This quality was much prized during the Muromachi period (1392–1573), which saw the rise of Japanese tea ceremonies and the appreciation of a *wabi-sabi* aesthetic.[21]

Although Nara worked primarily on his own in Shigaraki, the community-driven artist residency program, established in 1992, provided him with a novel way of working. The place offered a spirit of community that Nara had enjoyed when he first started working with graf, before the massive workshop enterprise that demanded of Nara a managerial style of communication. Shigaraki was more like a retreat, where, during the day, everyone worked on their own projects, gathering for meals in the evenings to share updates on the progress of their work, compare techniques and ways of exploring materiality, or discuss their philosophies on art and life in general. The experience brought Nara back to an art-school environment, but here his fellow students spoke of their craft in a language of ceramics that he was only just beginning to learn. He particularly admired the dedication of the potters, who worked as if they were having a conversation with the medium, an approach he wanted to bring into his own practice.[22] As he describes it:

> It made me discover something new, and taught me how wonderful it is to work with others, especially because I usually work alone. There were younger artists, older artists, and artists from various countries, not just Japan. Some worked on a wheel to make pottery, some people were sculpting abstract works, or some would seek meaning within the act of burning the clay itself. I was not planning to use the wheel, but then once I began to know how to use it, I found it very enjoyable and ended up making plates and cups for everyday use.[23]

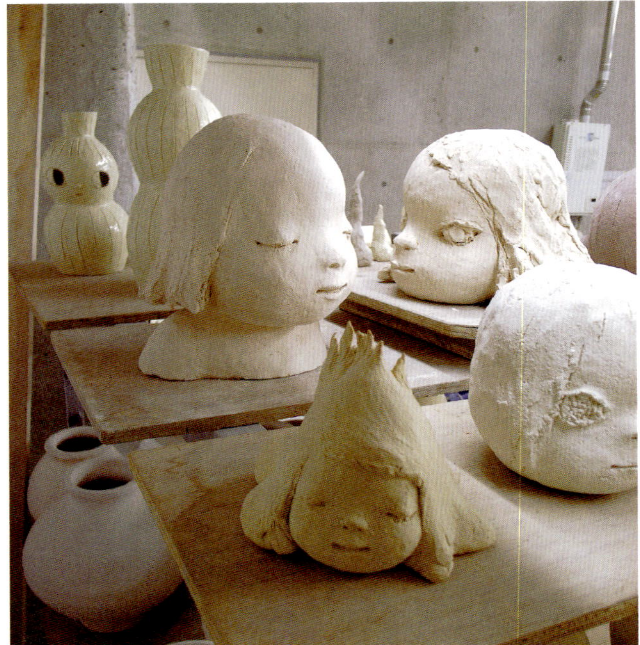

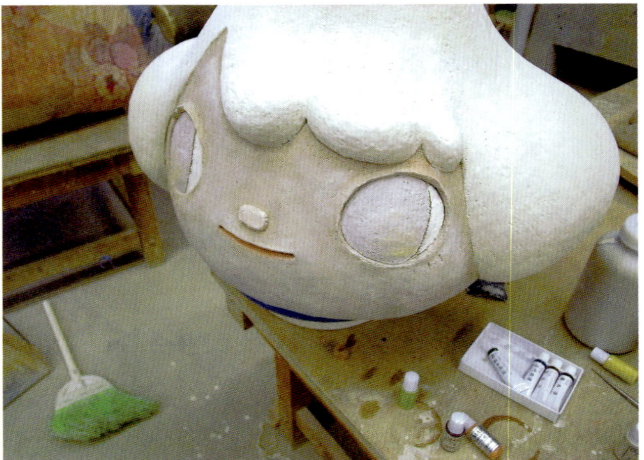

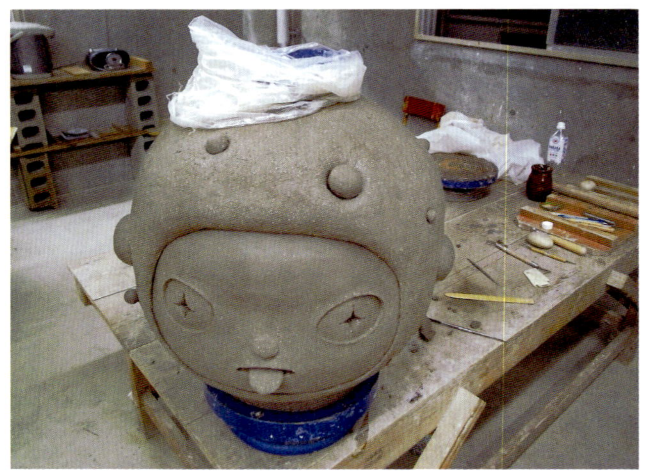

Figs. 174–176
Studio at the Shigaraki Ceramic Cultural Park, Kōka, Japan, 2010

Working in clay also introduced Nara to a new way of creating a three-dimensional form. Previously, for his fiberglass sculptures, he had produced smooth, highly polished finishes, but for this new venture into clay, he developed a more tactile approach, producing lightly textured surfaces that revealed the materiality of the medium. His earliest ceramic works from this period were small, bulbous hand-molded heads that resemble his iconic big-headed girls, some submerged in puddles and others with their tongues sticking out (Figs. 179 and 180). The heads later grew in size and in their larger forms were covered in gold or other metallic paints, but he continued to revel in the natural rawness of the material by leaving their surfaces rough and unglazed.

This focus on materiality recalls some of Nara's earliest sculptures made from abandoned pieces of wood, made when he was a student in Aichi and Düsseldorf (Figs. 45, 46, and 50). However, he took these ceramic sculptures further conceptually by referencing spiritual practices inspired by Shigaraki's history as an important Zen site, wrapping some of the larger heads with scarves to evoke Japanese religious rituals during which believers dress icons in clothing as karmic practices (Fig. 181). Other heads bear names that reference their connections to the forest (Fig. 182).

Nara tapped into that spirituality with *White Riot* (2010) (Fig. 184), a tall sculpture that combines his child and dog figures, standing with its head tilted slightly forward and gazing down at viewers with a small grin that reveals a set of sharp teeth. The work's looming presence recalls the menacing guardian deities or lion-dogs that stand at the gateways of sacred spaces at temples or shrines (Figs. 177 and 178). Nara took that image of a guardian further by making a pair of giant fiberglass versions of the *White Riot* figure, entitled *White Ghost*, which in 2010 stood on the Park Avenue median at 67th and 70th Streets in New York (Fig. 183). A public art project, *White Ghost* ran concurrently with his solo exhibition *Nobody's Fool* at Asia Society in New York. The two sculptures were arranged so that one faced south and the other north, largely for practical reasons but also in reference to early Japanese religious sites where guardian figures flank and protect the axis that runs east to west.[24]

In Shigaraki, Nara also began creating clay plates that provided him with a flat surface for painting and drawing (Figs. 185–187). These ceramics, painted in black with a broad-ended brush, often incorporate words with images, and they parallel his billboard paintings in their emphasis on graphic treatments and a focus on musical references. Many of the

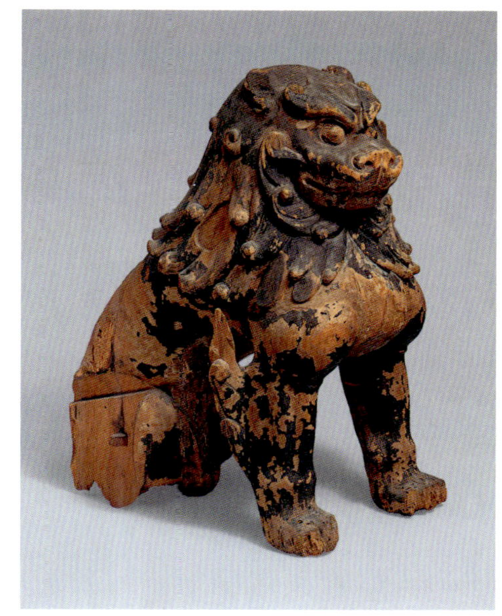

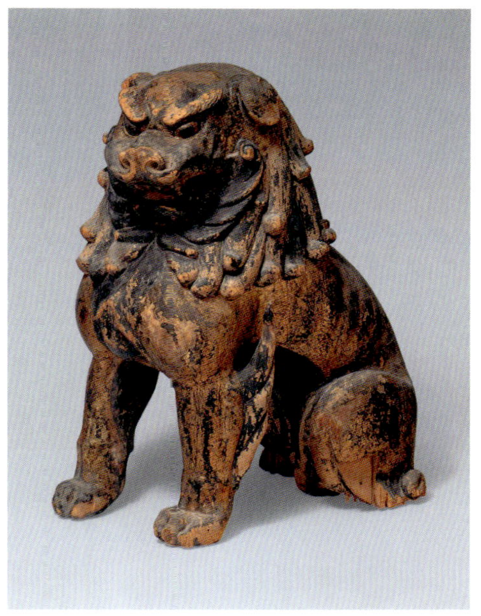

Figs. 177 and 178
Guardian Lion-Dogs,
mid-thirteenth century,
Japanese cypress with
lacquer, gold leaf, and color,
Top: h. 16 ¾ in. (42.5 cm),
Bottom: h. 18 in. (45.7 cm)

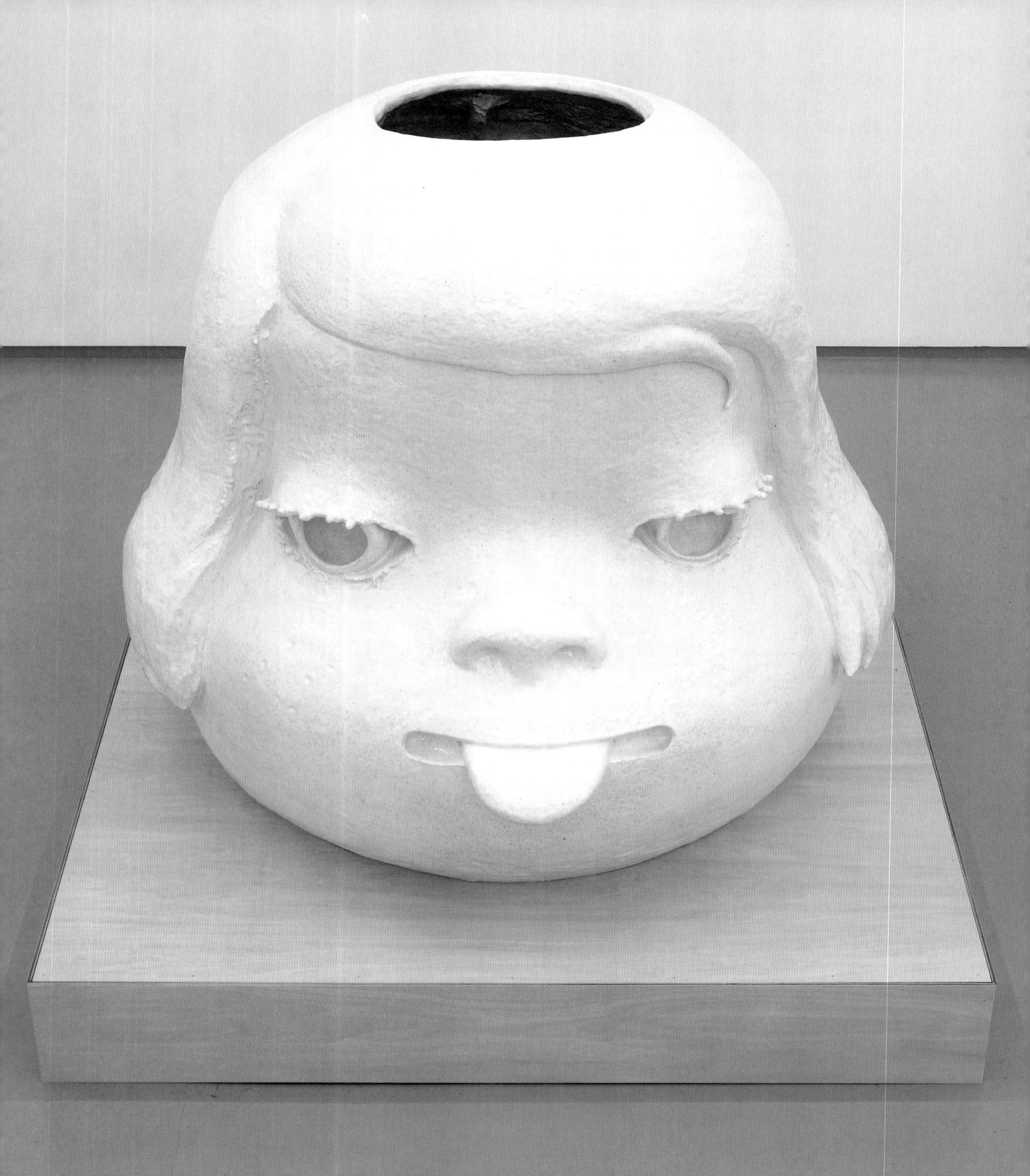

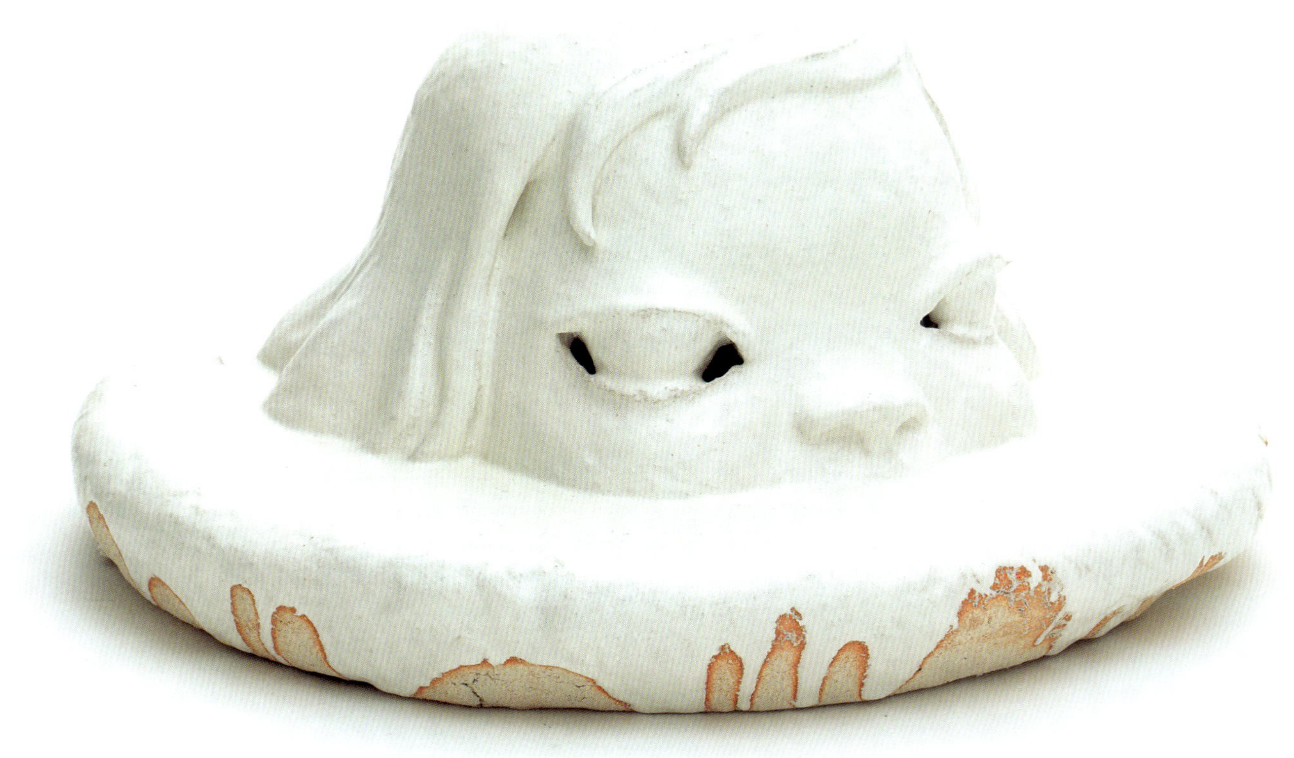

Fig. 179 (opposite)
Otafuku No. 0 (Moon-Faced Woman No. 0), 2007, Ceramic, 44 5⁄16 × 49 3⁄16 × 54 5⁄16 in. (112.5 × 125 × 138 cm)

Fig. 180
In the Puddle, 2007, Ceramic, 13 13⁄16 × 25 3⁄16 × 25 3⁄16 in. (35 × 64 × 64 cm)

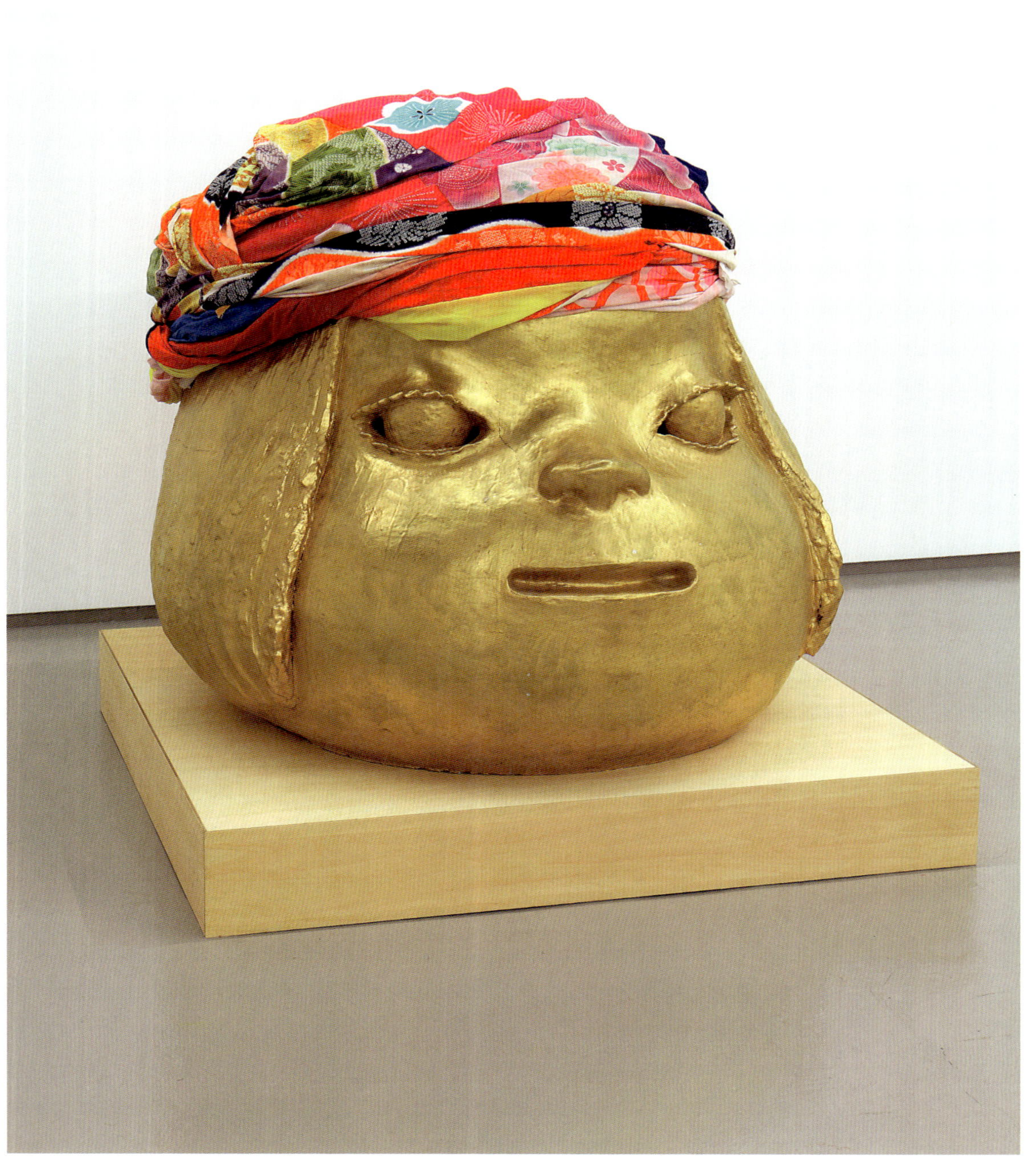

Fig. 181
Otafuku No. 1 (Moon-Faced Woman No. 1), 2010, Ceramic decorated with gold liquid and cloth, 46 7⁄16 × 49 3⁄16 × 59 1⁄16 in. (118 × 125 × 150 cm)

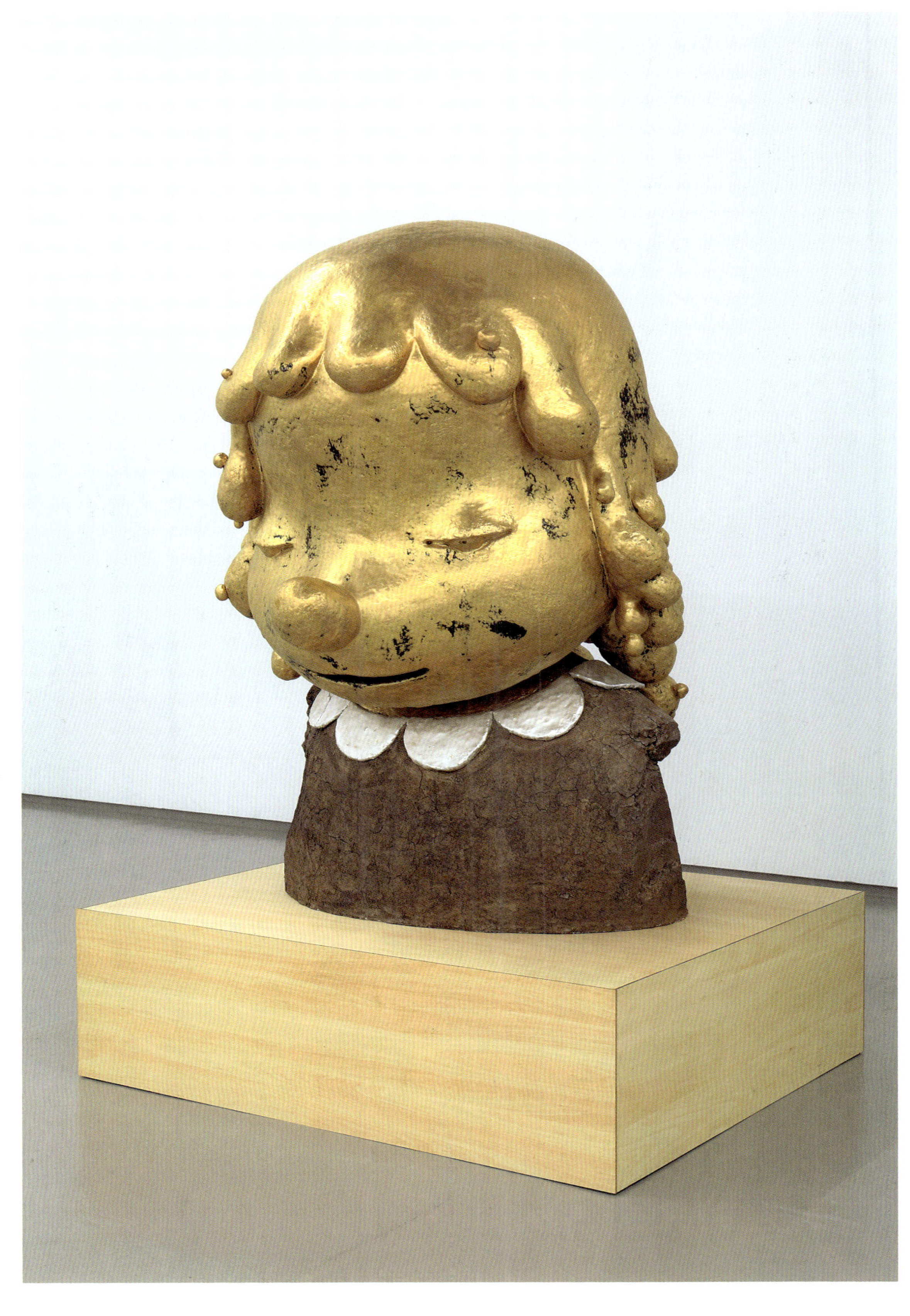

Fig. 182
Miss Forest, 2010, Ceramic decorated with platinum, gold, and silver liquid, 56 ¹¹⁄₁₆ × 40 ³⁄₁₆ × 39 ³⁄₈ in. (144 × 102 × 100 cm)

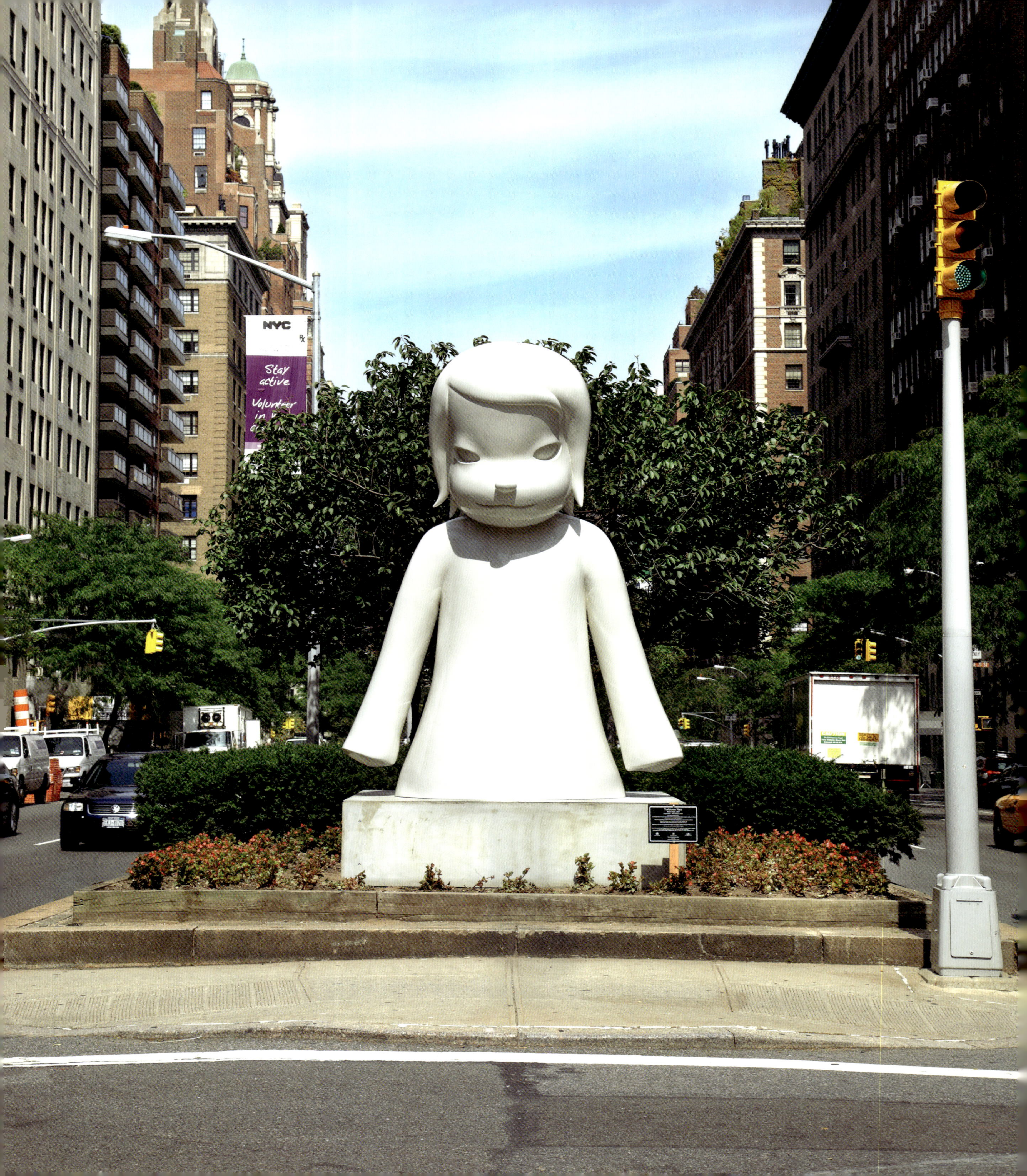
NYC
Stay
active
Volunteer

Fig. 183 (opposite)
White Ghost, 2010, Urethane on fiber-reinforced plastics, 144 × 102 × 66 in. (365.8 × 259.1 × 167.6 cm)

Fig. 184
White Riot, 2010, Ceramic, 109 7⁄16 × 69 5⁄16 × 49 5⁄8 in. (278 × 176 × 126 cm)

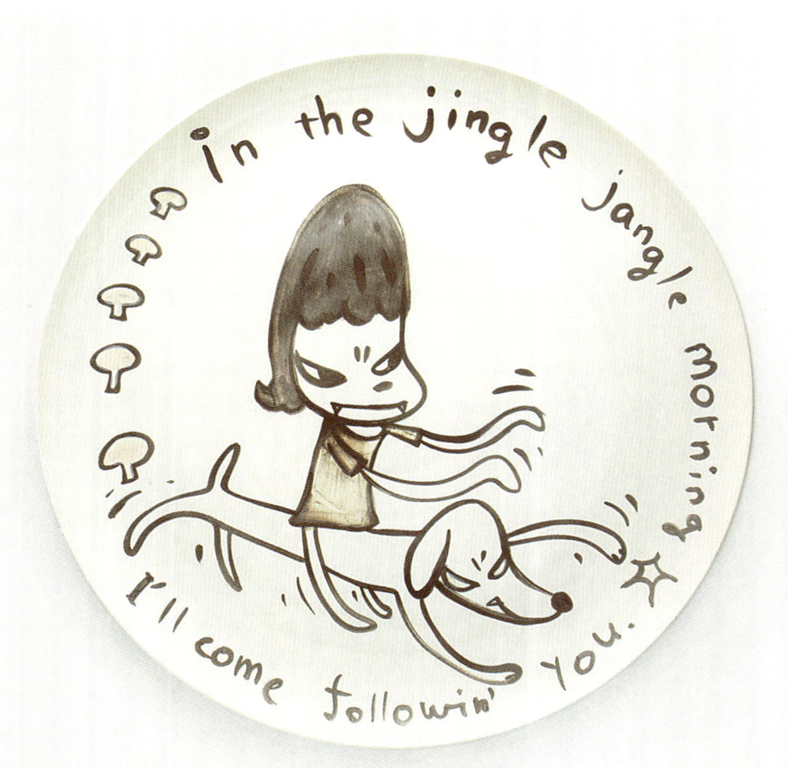

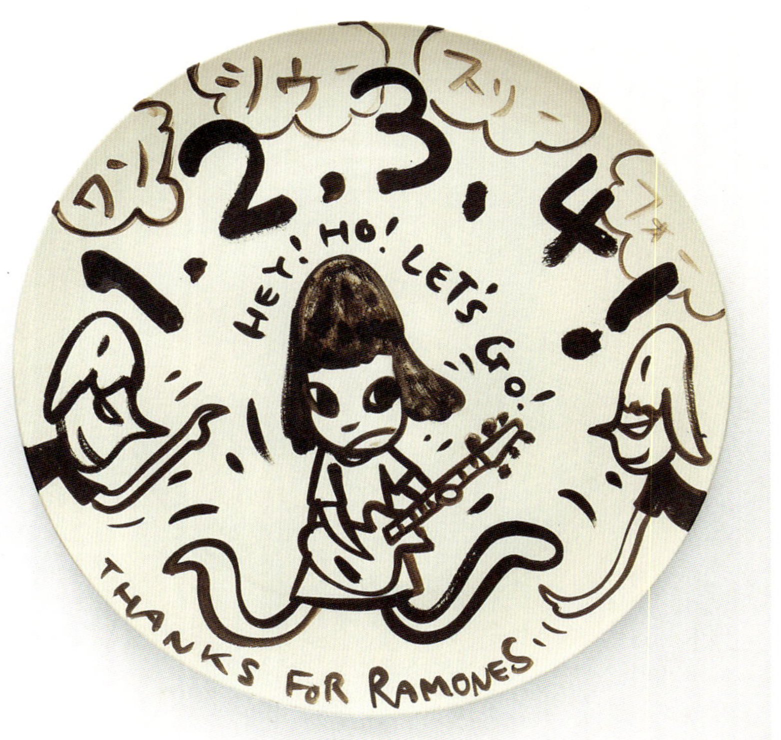

Fig. 185
In the Jingle Jangle Morning I'll Come Followin' You., 2007, Ceramic, diam. 49 ¾ × d. 3 9/16 in. (126.3 × 9 cm)

Fig. 186
1, 2, 3, 4! Hey! Ho! Let's Go!, 2007, Ceramic, diam. 33 ⅞ × d. 3 ¾ in. (86 × 9.5 cm)

Fig. 187 (opposite)
The Good, the Bad, the Average…and Unique, 2007, Ceramic, diam. 33 ⅞ × d. 3 ¾ in. (86 × 9.5 cm)

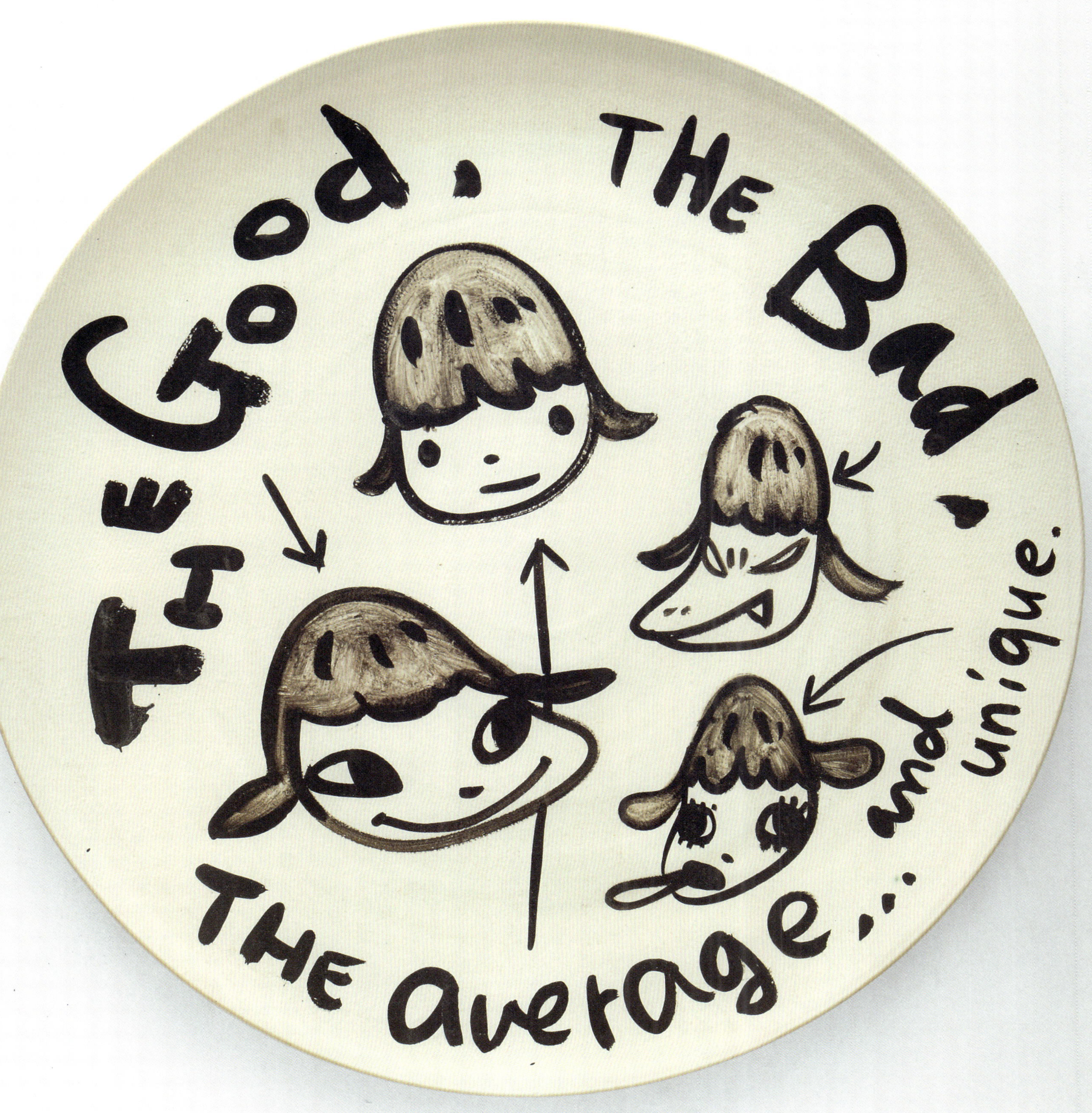
THE Good, THE Bad.
THE average... and unique.

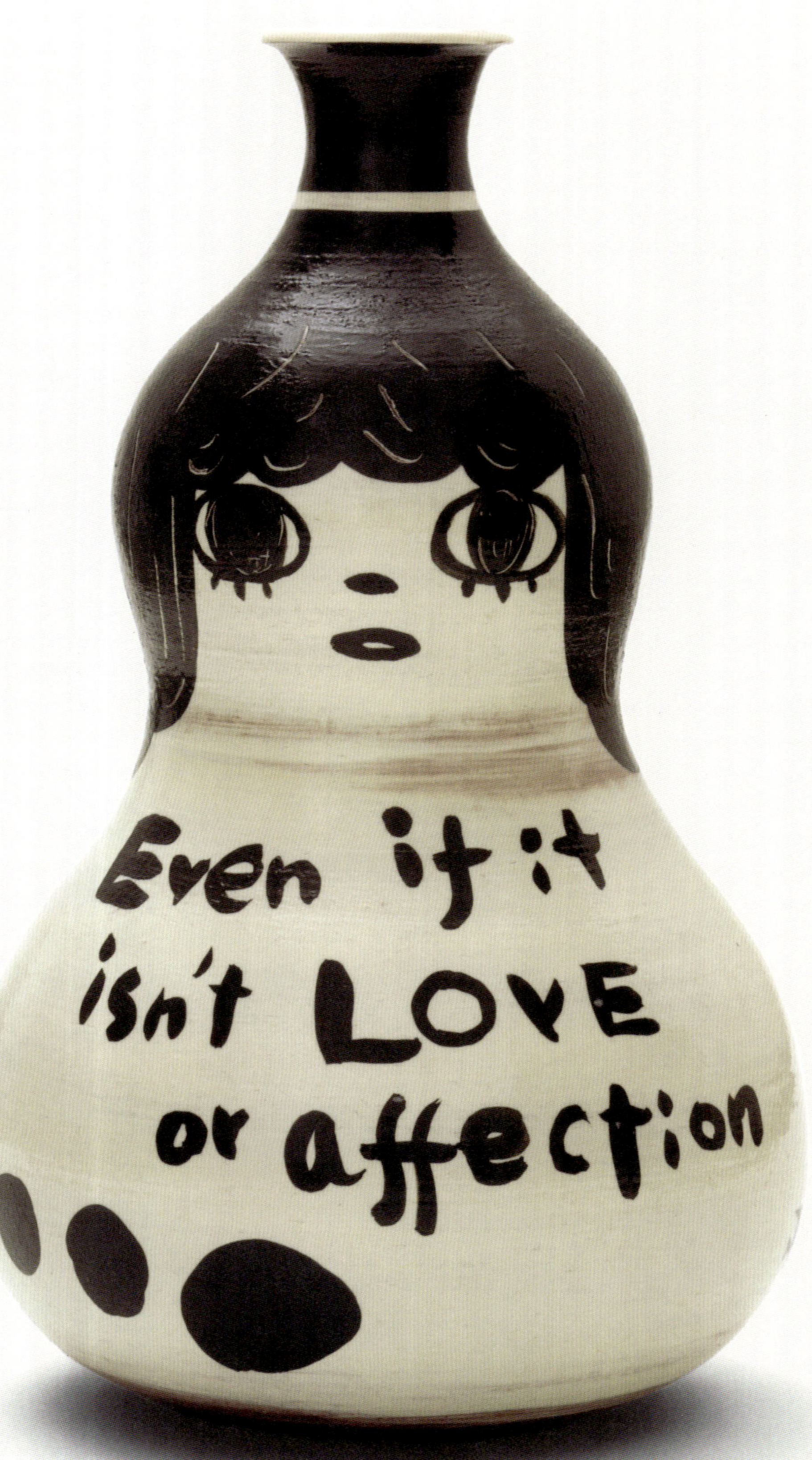
Even if it
isn't LOVE
or affection

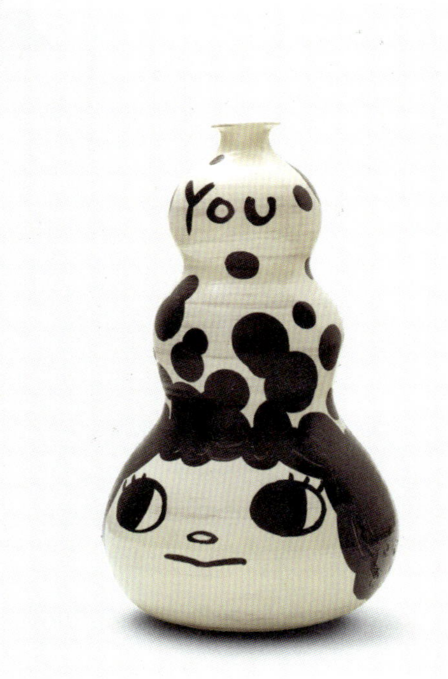

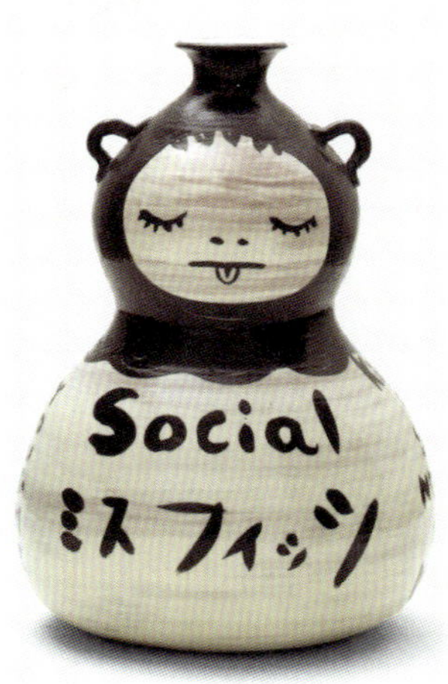

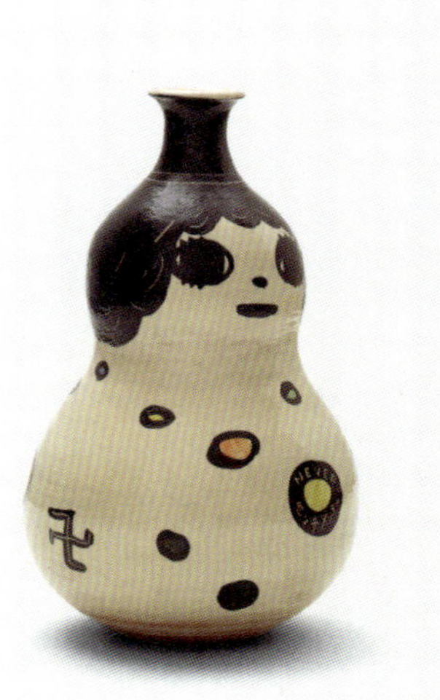

Fig. 188 (opposite)
Love or Affection, 2009, Ceramic, h. 19 11/16 × diam. 11 13/16 in. (50 × 30 cm)

Fig. 189
You & Me, 2009, Ceramic, h. 21 ¼ × diam. 13 in. (54 × 33 cm)

Fig. 190
Nobody's Fool, 2009, Ceramic, h. 17 ¾ × diam. 13 ⅜ in. (45 × 34 cm)

Fig. 191
Born to Lose, 2009, Ceramic, h. 16 15/16 × diam. 10 ¼ in. (43 × 26 cm)

designs are based on lyrics from songs, such as Bob Dylan's "Mr. Tambourine Man" or the Ramones' "Blitzkrieg Bop," or on the titles of albums, such as Carter the Unstoppable Sex Machine's *The Good, the Bad, the Average and Unique* (which is also a lyric from the band's 1992 hit "The Only Living Boy in New Cross"). Nara painted directly onto the plates, making it impossible for him to fully erase any of his markings, in a way retaining the spirit of Shigaraki, which favored a raw artisanal quality in its vessels' forms and finishes.

In 2009 Nara brought together these two areas of his ceramic practice—the drawn line on plates and the three-dimensional heads—in a series of gourd-shaped sake bottles (Figs. 188–191). For these works, he painted faces on the bodies or necks of the vessels and filled the rest of the space with words and images. The words, in Japanese, English, and German, are painted with bold, rounded strokes and often reference song titles and rock-music lyrics or contain simple doodled ponderings on basic human conditions. The cinched curvature of the gourd bottles provides a corporeal form that transforms them into anthropomorphic vessels and emphasizes the lightheartedness of the drawings that adorn them. More importantly, they capture a vernacular spirit and represent Nara's return to the basic pleasures of art making itself that helped him, after years of working collaboratively, "recover his full sense of self."[25]

The importance of working in clay would continue for Nara, especially after 2011 in the aftermath of the Great East Japan Earthquake and Fukushima Disaster, when he, like some of the other potters in Shigaraki, began to work with the medium as a way of recovering his belief in the value of creative production after the tragic destruction of northern Japan. Since 2016 he has regularly returned to Shigaraki to work alongside his fellow potters in the mountains, and although his projects are not collaborative in practice, his residencies provide him with a community that has become invaluable to his ceramic work.

Music and Musicians

Music has always been a central part of Nara's art practice, informing his artwork since the very beginning of his career. While his music-related artworks seldom involve working in physical proximity to musicians, they can be seen as collaborative through the kinship he feels with musicians both past and present. The distinction between

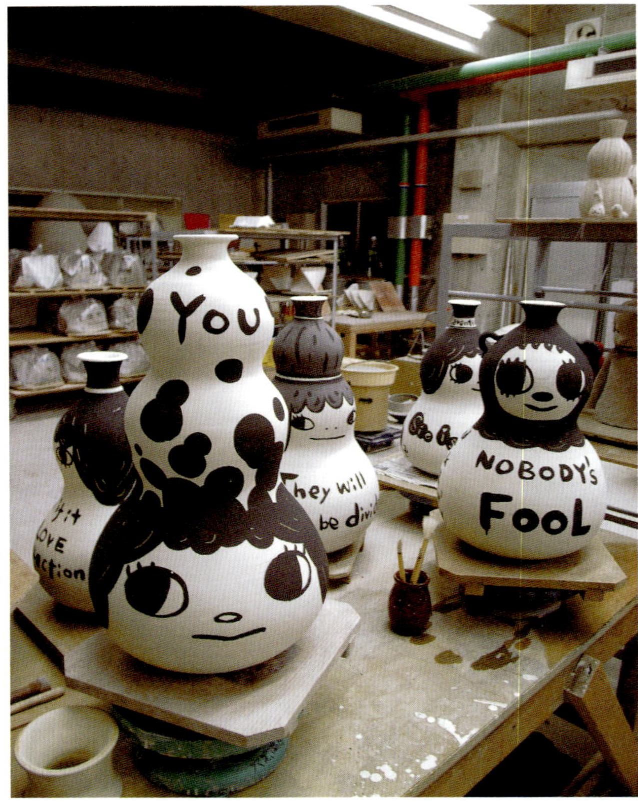

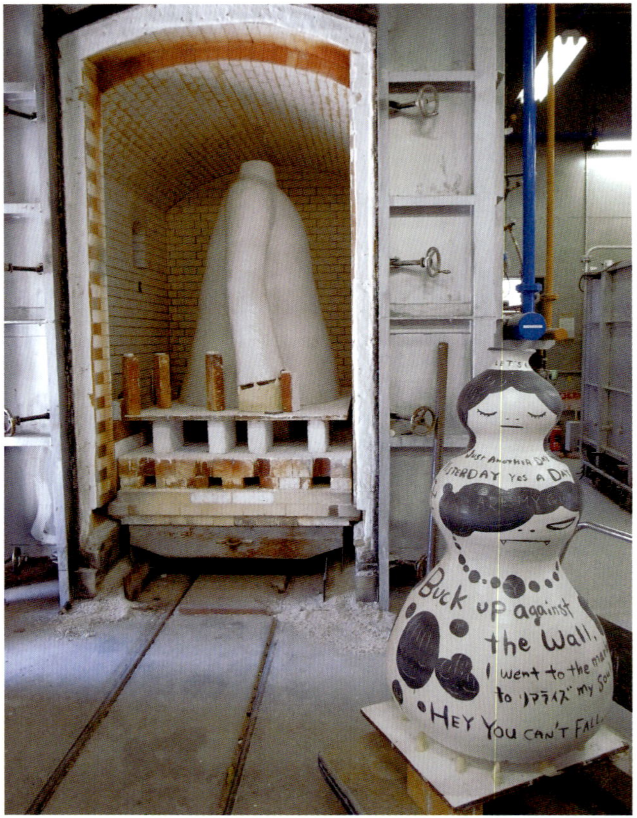

Figs. 192 and 193
Studio at the Shigaraki Ceramic Cultural Park, Kōka, Japan, 2010

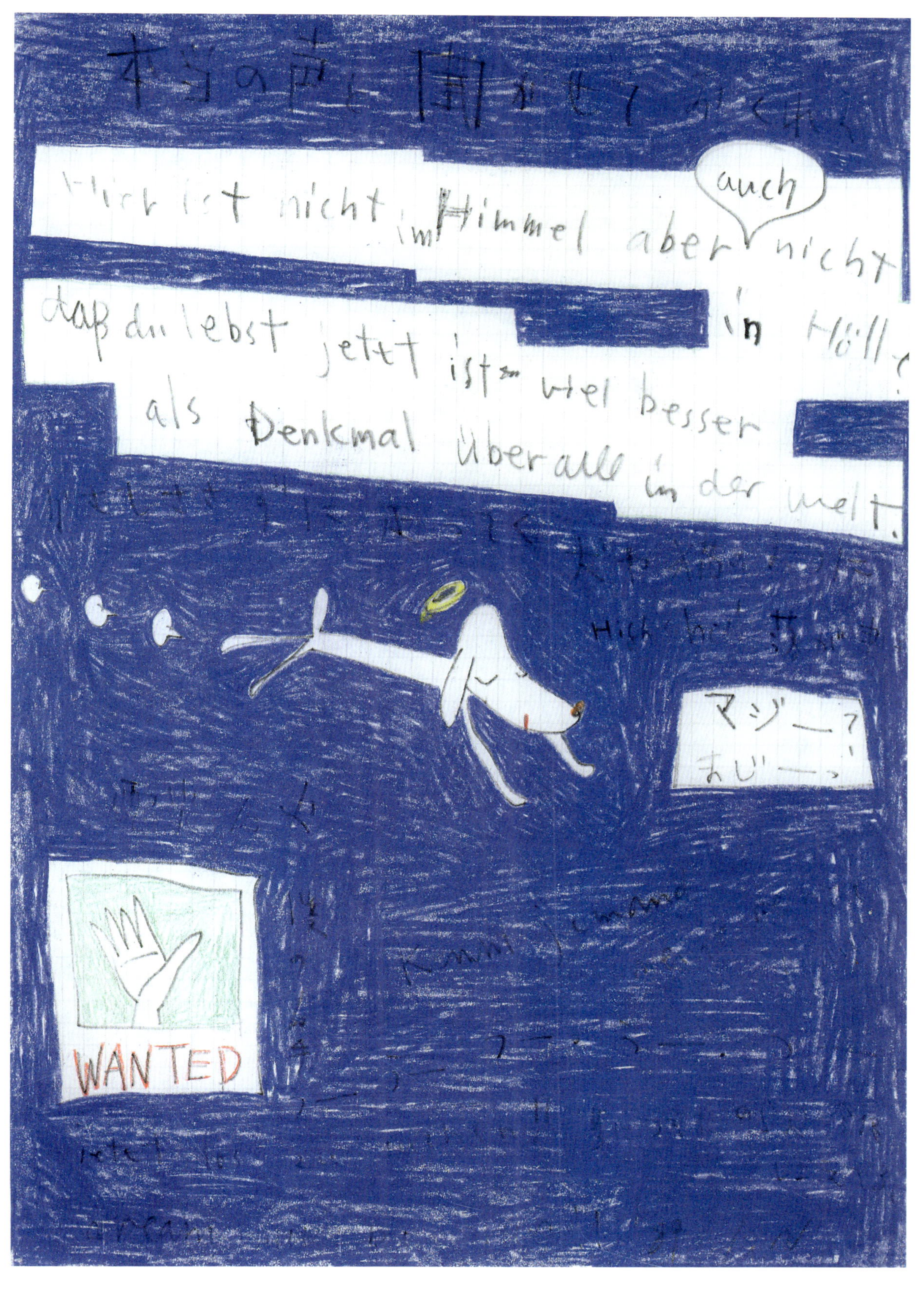

Fig. 194
Untitled, 1989, Pen and colored pencil on paper, 11 7⁄16 × 8 ¼ in. (29 × 21 cm)

musicians and the music they create is sometimes blurred for Nara, because in his eyes they cannot be separated—to speak of one is to recall the presence of the other. In a similar way, he views his music-related works not only as creative responses to another artist's vision but also as expressions of his relationships with them.

From his earliest days, Nara scribbled lyrics and doodled images on scraps of paper while listening to music, and after he moved to Germany in 1988, he began to translate lyrics from his favorite Japanese bands into German and English. Translating song lyrics is never a straightforward undertaking; at its most basic, it requires navigating between the literal and the figurative, which can risk violating the meaning of the original text. Moreover, translating poses the challenge of capturing the attitude and soul of the music itself. His drawings are, therefore, both literal and figurative, but in addition, they also contain idiosyncratic elements that visually manifest the thoughts and emotions the music arouses in Nara at that particular moment in time. As such, they are highly personal and diaristic in nature, created from the depths of Nara's interior world.

Many of Nara's early attempts to translate song lyrics into drawings were responses to the music of one of his favorite bands, the Blue Hearts, a Japanese punk group formed in 1985, which had gained a sizable following among Japanese teens before breaking up ten years later.[26] As is typical of his music-related drawings, the works are rough and raw and reflect an immediacy that mirrors the emotional spontaneity of drawing while listening to music. In an untitled sketch from 1989 (Fig. 194), he scribbled his translation of two lines from the Blue Hearts' 1988 song "Train-Train": "Hier ist nicht im Himmel aber auch nicht in Hölle. Daß du lebst jetzt ist viel besser als Denkmal uber alle in der Welt." (This is not heaven, but it is not hell. That you are alive now is better than all the monuments they've put in the world.)[27] In this sketch, Nara's familiar white dog is depicted with a halo, its legs stretched out and dreaming into the night. The scene captures another part of the song: "I want to have a surreal dream as the south wind blows me around." In the corner is a wanted poster depicting a hand that adds a Wild West element to Nara's interpretation of the overall song, specifically the lyrics that speak about having the bravery to jump on a train toward "an invisible freedom, shooting away on an invisible gun," even as the train barrels forward "to the end of earth, to its bitter end." The wanted poster is also a sly reference to the opening lyrics of

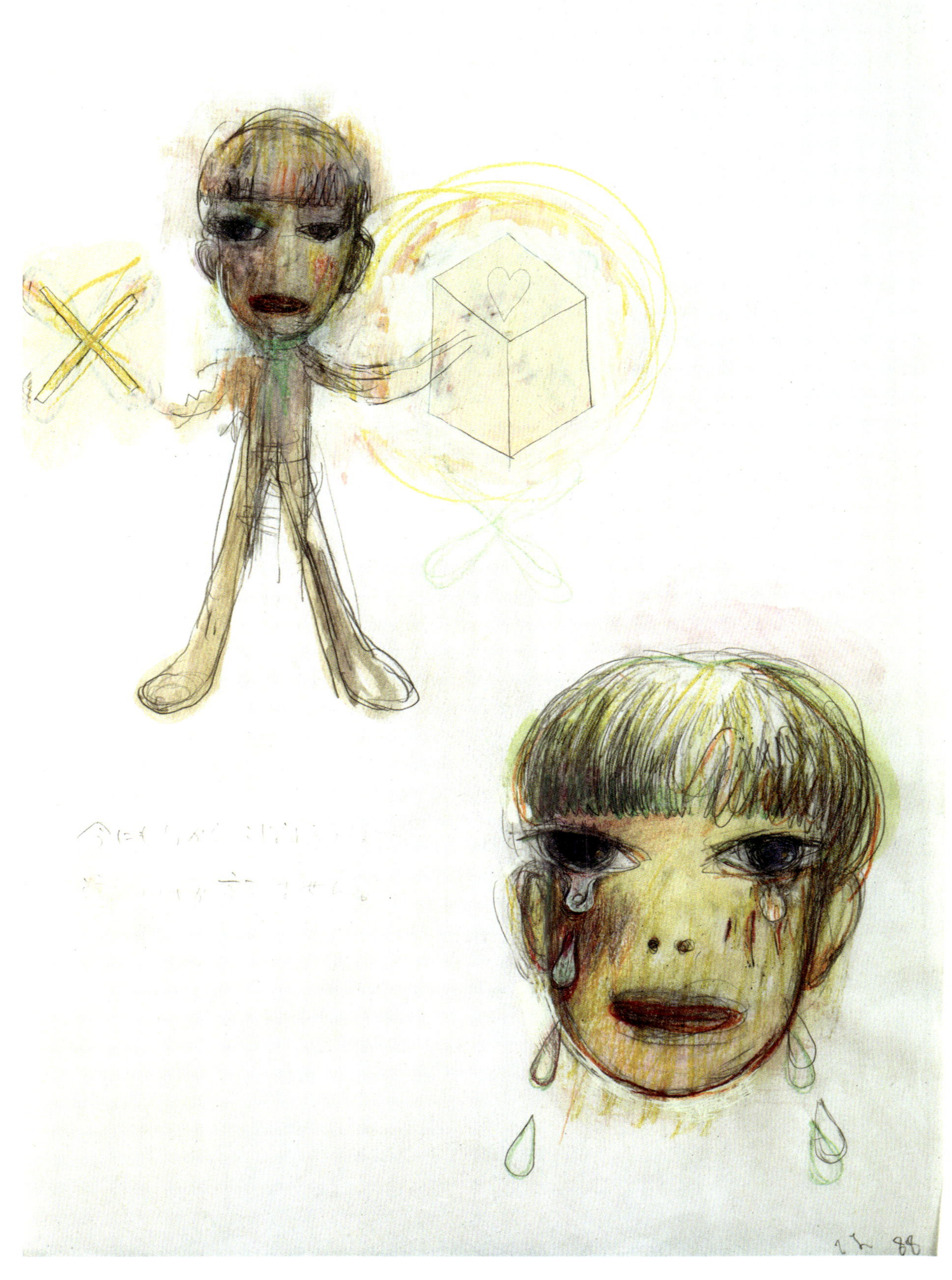

Fig. 195
I Couldn't Say the Reason Why Tears Fall from the Eyes Now., 1988, Pencil and colored pencil on paper, 11 ⅝ × 8 ¼ in. (29.5 × 21 cm)

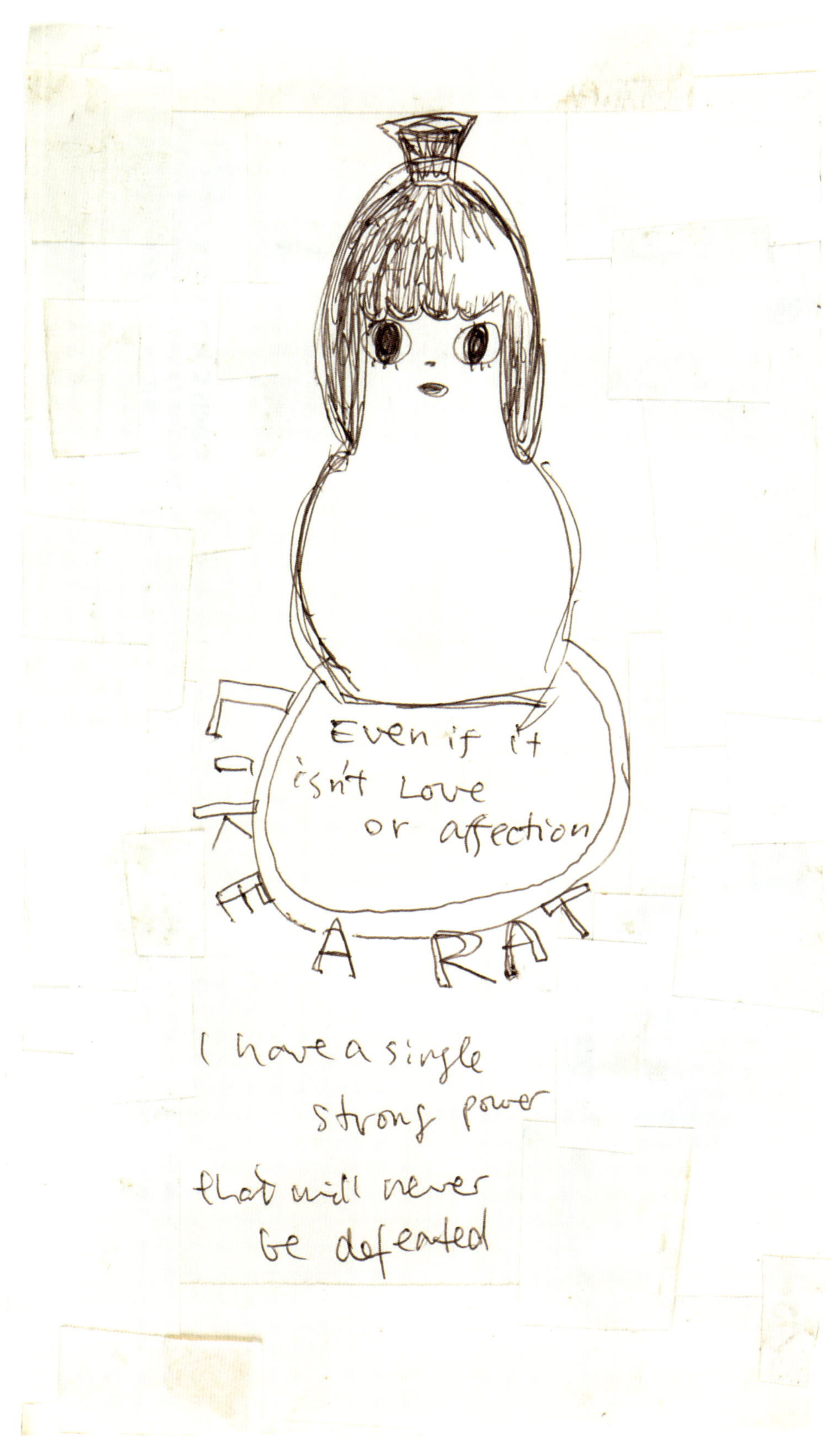

Fig. 196
Untitled sketch, 2011,
Ballpoint pen on paper,
9 ⁷⁄₁₆ × 5 ½ in. (24 × 14 cm)

"My Right Hand," another hit by the Blue Hearts from 1988: "Have you seen my right hand? It seems to have gone missing. I'll pass out wanted posters throughout the town."

Nara takes the line "I couldn't say the reason why tears fall from the eyes now" from "My Right Hand" as the inspiration for another drawing that uses the lyric as its title (Fig. 195). On the right is the face of a young boy weeping giant tears, while on the left he stands with one arm slightly raised, his hand, partially erased, in a box-shaped form. In his other hand, the boy carries a cross, a motif that appears as part of Nara's visual repertoire rather than as a representation of any part of the song lyric itself. Nara both translates and interprets the song, and as these are not always one and the same, the drawing retains a certain opacity of meaning. Despite, or possibly because of, this, many of these music-related drawings provide those with musical knowledge an additional entry point into an important part of Nara's inner world.

Many of Nara's music-related sketches are intimate works, drawn while lost in the sonic realms of his favorite bands and singers, and he has also envisioned some of the drawings as artworks in different media. One example is a raw, simple drawing that takes pride of place in Nara's studio (Fig. 196). Surrounded by patches of cut-up paper, the drawing was made in response to the Blue Hearts' 1987 song "Linda Linda," and depicts Linda as an anthropomorphic vase with large eyes and long lashes, while on her "belly" appears the phrase "Even if it isn't love or affection." Beneath her is a more unexpected phrase—"LIKE A RAT"—taken from the song's opening line, which refers to the rodent as a symbol of devoted love. This unusual starting point makes the song particularly hard to translate. Literally, it reads: "Like a rat, I want to be as beautiful because there is such a thing as beauty that cannot be captured in photographs," followed by a chorus, "Even if it's not love or affection, I have a single strong power that will never be defeated. Linda, Linda, Linda."[28] A ceramic vase made two years earlier (Fig. 188) bears striking resemblance to this sketch. Importantly, though, the drawing was not made as a reference to the vase, nor did he even have the vase in mind while drawing it. Nara, instead, wrote the lyrics on both spontaneously, showing that his interpretations of songs lie dormant in a reservoir of images that can be resurrected by the music's emotional triggers.

Part of the appeal of the Blue Hearts for Nara comes from their antinuclear and antiwar stances, sentiments that he shares but that

Fig. 197 (following spread)
I Shouldn't Give Up to Die,
1985, Acrylic and colored
pencil on paper, Size unknown

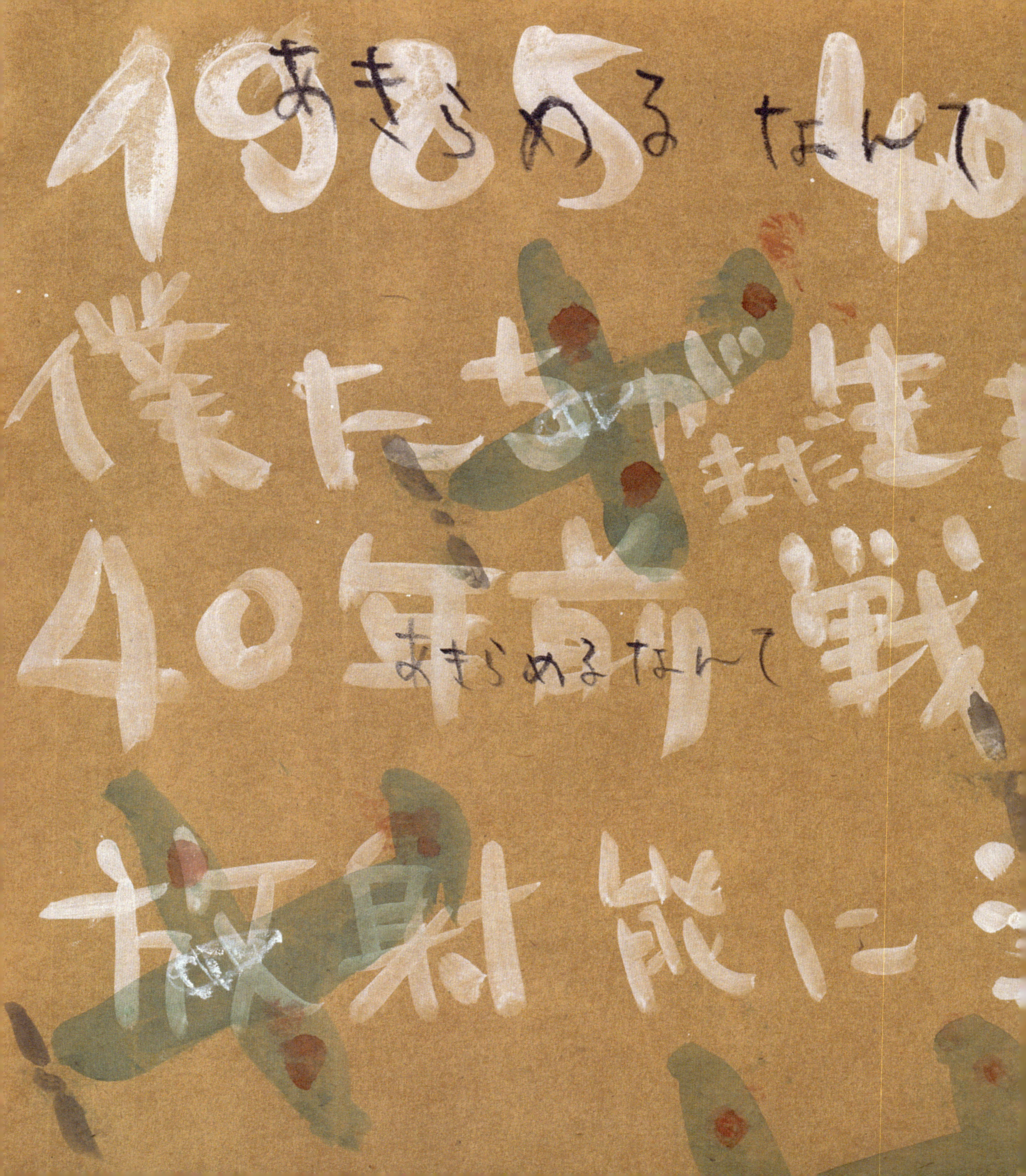
1985
あきらめる なんて
僕たち
まだ
生ま
40年前
戦
あきらめるなんて

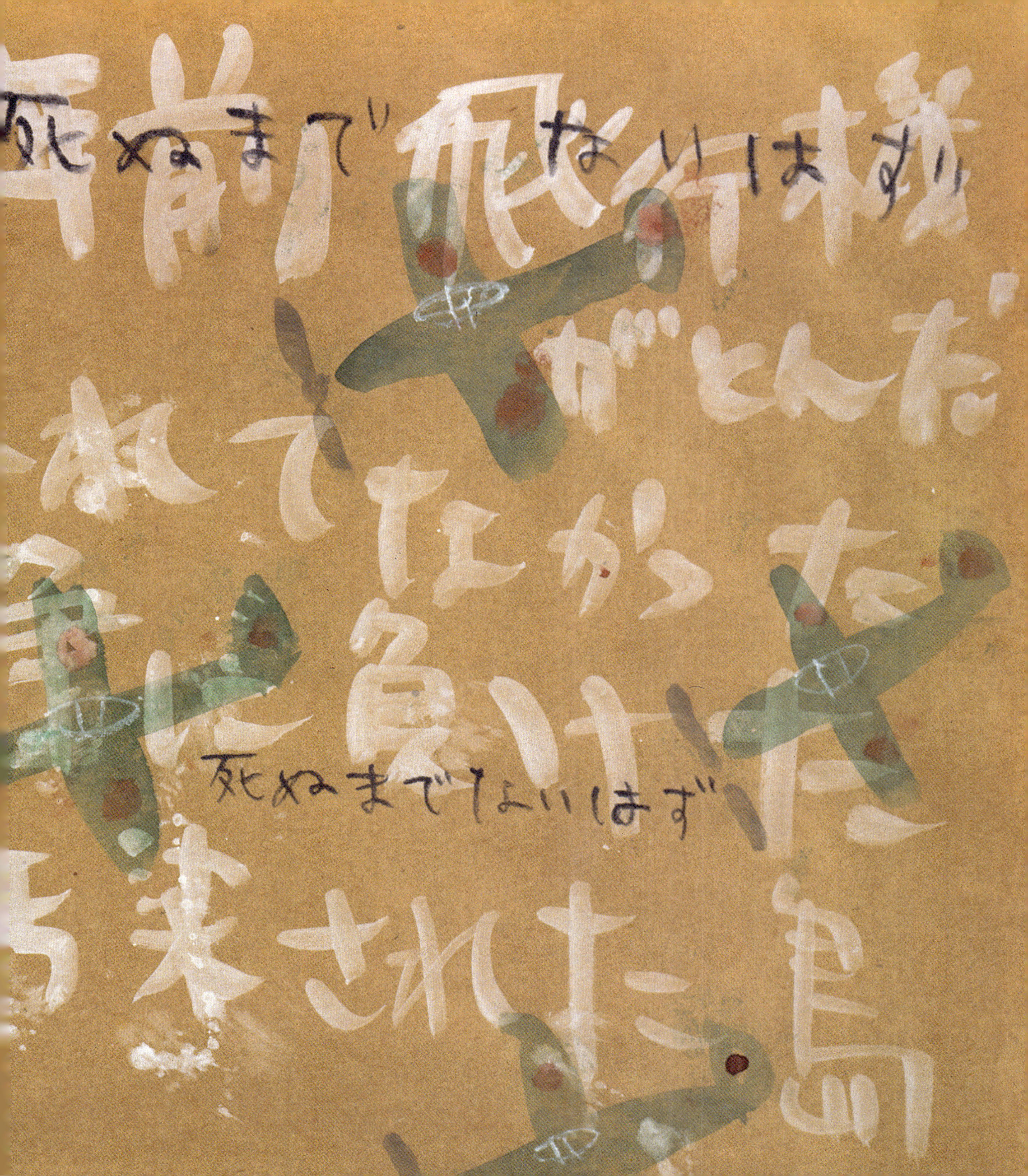
死ぬまでないはず
飛行機がとんだ
死ぬまでないはず

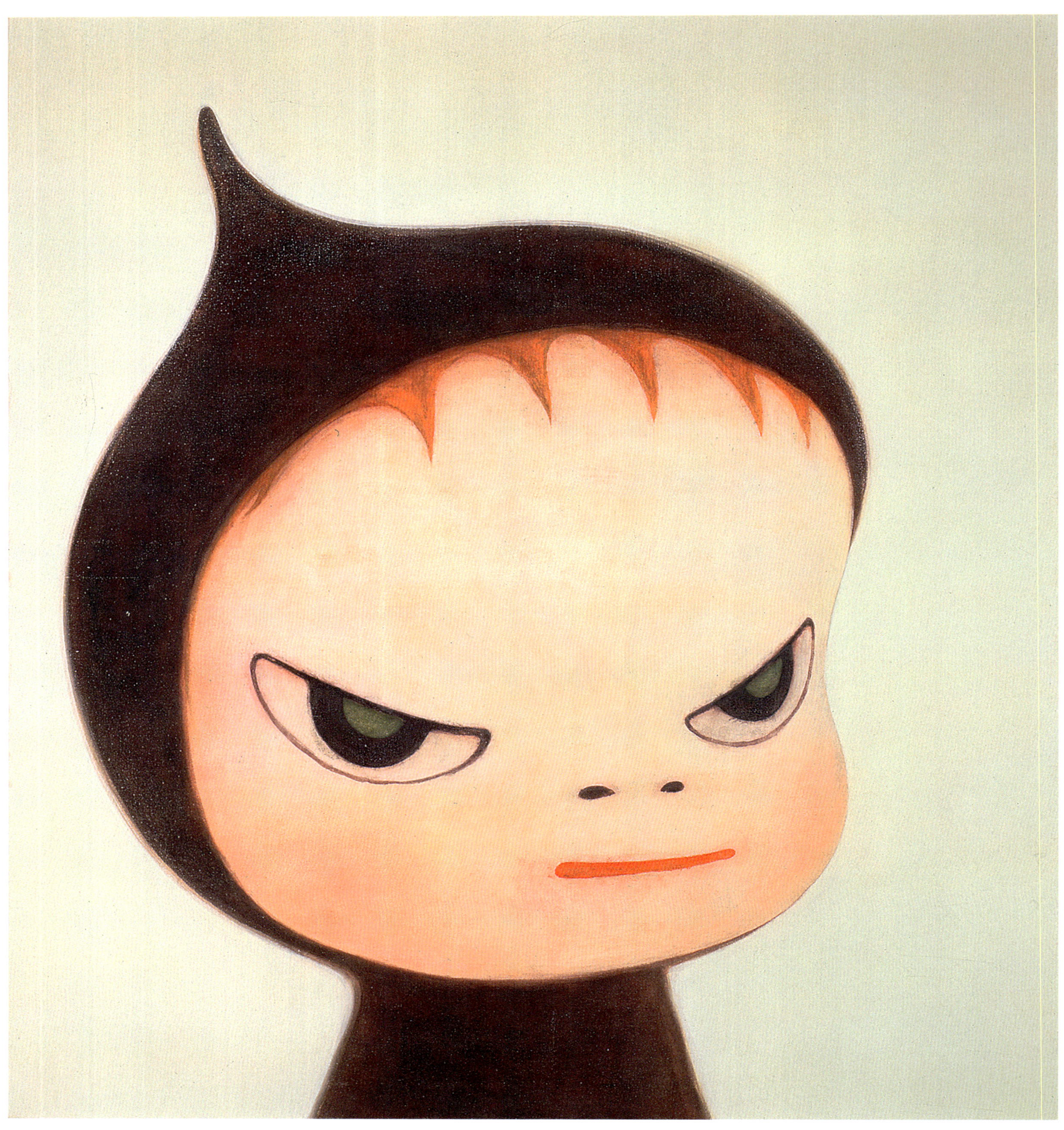

Fig. 198
Pyromaniac Day,
1999, Acrylic on canvas,
47 ¼ × 43 5⁄16 in. (120 × 110 cm)

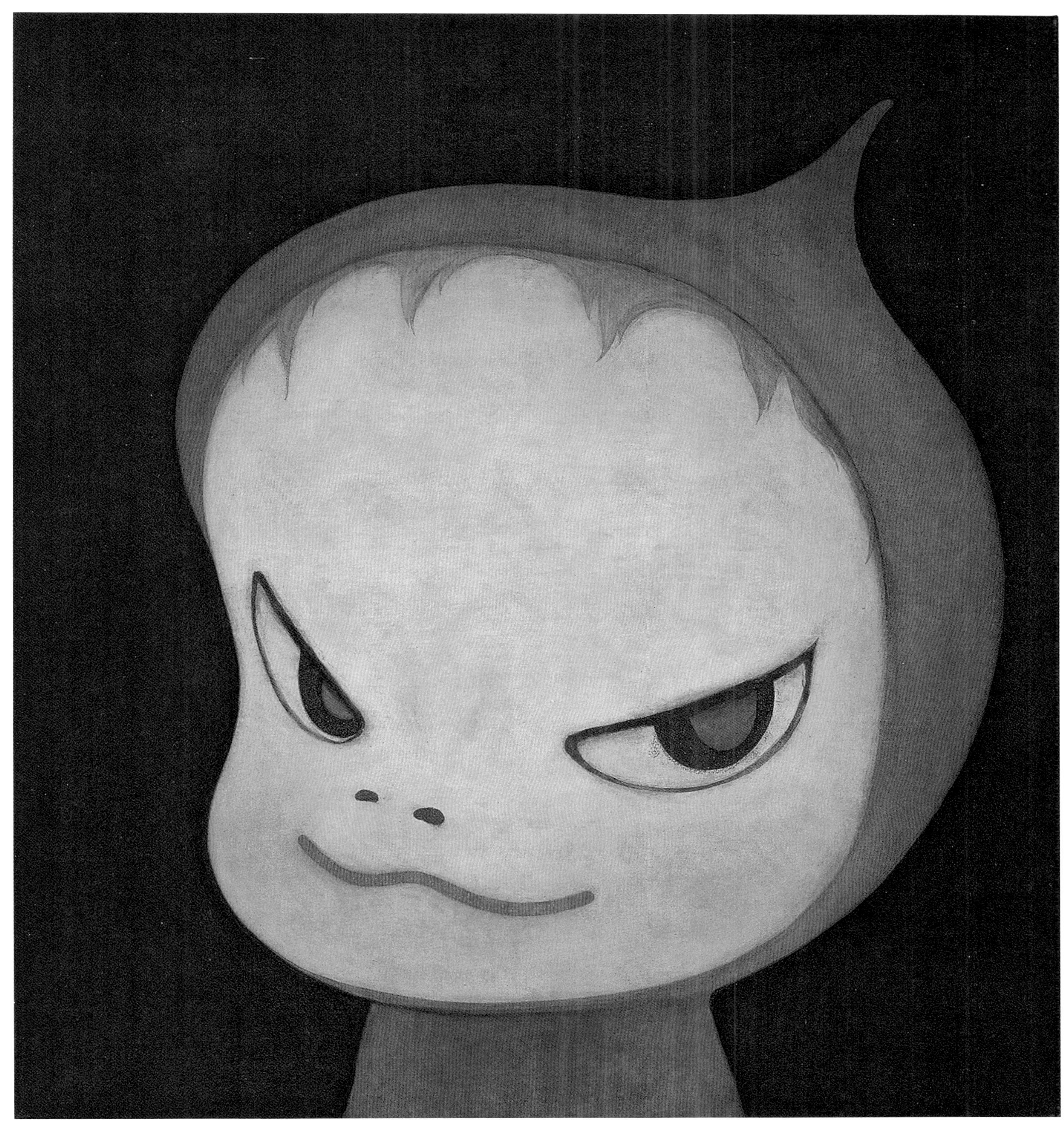

Fig. 199
Pyromaniac Dead of Night,
1999, Acrylic on canvas,
47 ¼ × 43 5⁄16 in. (120 × 110 cm)

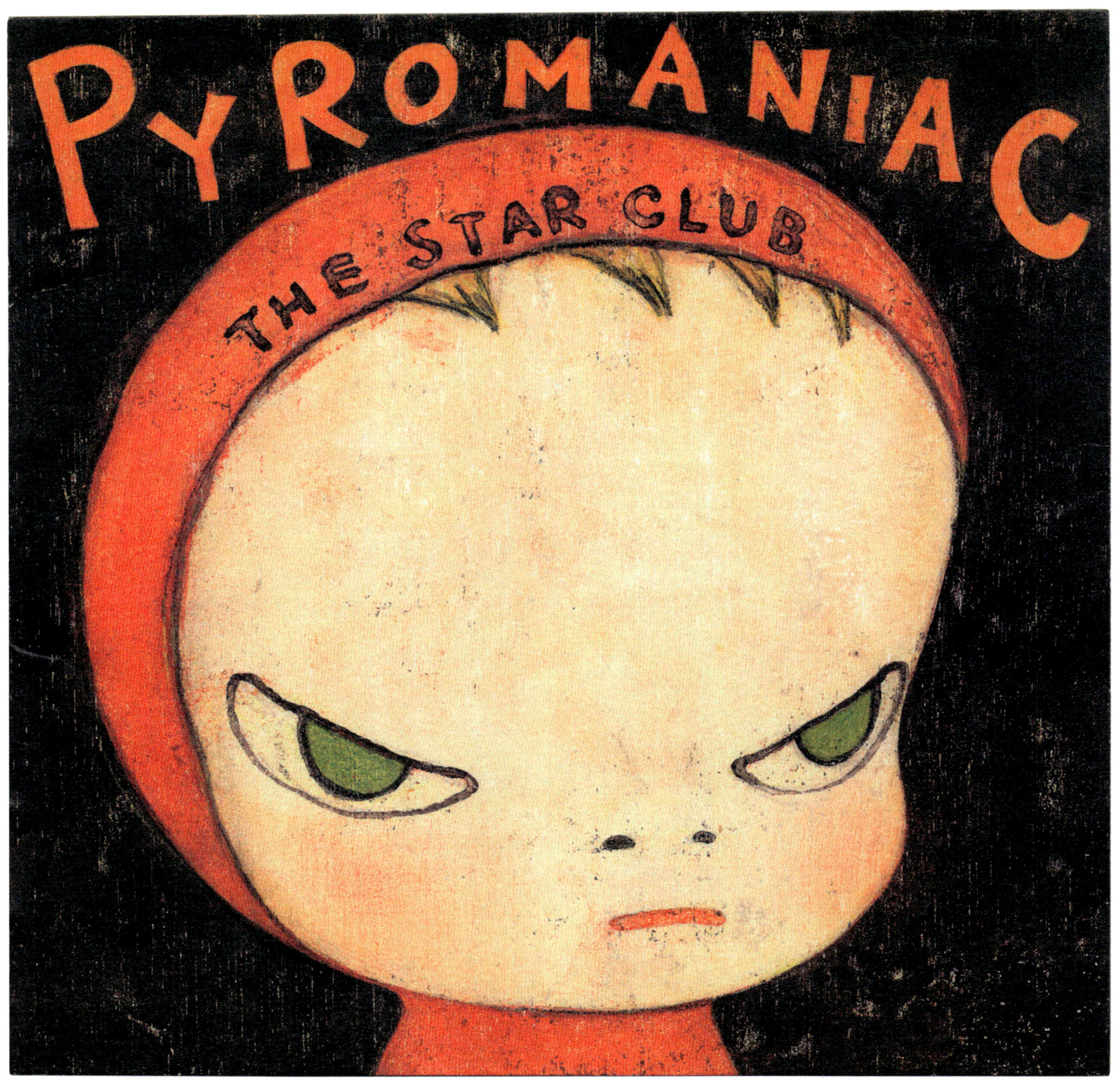

Fig. 200
The Star Club, *Pyromaniac*,
Victor Entertainment, Japan,
1999

remained largely private in his work until after his trip to Afghanistan in 2002 and that would become even more apparent in his art after the Fukushima nuclear disaster in 2011. In *I Shouldn't Give Up to Die* (1985) (Fig. 197), Nara writes the Japanese lyrics of two songs by the band, "1985" and "Blue Hearts Theme," which are layered on top of each other. The words from the latter song are particularly relevant: "Forty years ago, when we were not even born, our country lost the war and this island was marked in the history as 'island contaminated by radiation.' I shouldn't give up to die." Written over light watercolor drawings of bomber planes, the layering of scripts has a graffiti-like feel that reflects the punk energy of the song. "Blue Hearts Theme" was released as a single on a double A side with the song "Chernobyl," and it courted much public controversy for its strong stance against nuclear power, ultimately forcing the band to leave their record label. The song remained with Nara, and in 2013 he included the drawing in an installation for the *WE-LOW HOUSE* (Fig. 351), a project space made in response to the Fukushima disaster.

Nara has also sought to connect with musicians through his designs of their album covers. His first foray was in 1991 with an album by the Birdy Num Nums (Fig. 55), and since then, he has provided cover artwork for a number of musicians. Depending on the nature of the album and his relationship with the band or singer, he will either select an existing work or create a new one for the cover. Either way, he only works with musicians whose music he knows well or with whom he has had prior relationships. In supplying these works, Nara responds solely to the vision of another artist, and for this reason he always works directly with them or the music itself. Often, the projects demand endless conversations and hours of listening to music. To date, he has provided artwork for thirty-five album covers, including *Pyromaniac* (1999) by the Star Club (Fig. 200), inspired by the band's demo tape along with a pair of paintings, *Pyromaniac Day* and *Pyromaniac Dead of Night* (Figs. 198 and 199). In 2001 he provided the cover art for R.E.M.'s single "I'll Take the Rain" (Figs. 201 and 202), and his image of the dog with a crown was also adapted into an animation for the song's music video.

In 2002 Nara provided the artwork for the cover of *Splay* (Fig. 210), an album by avant-garde jazz drummer Jim Black of AlasNoAxis, and once more for Black's 2009 album *Houseplant*. In this instance, Nara was approached by the record company Winter & Winter, which was seeking artwork that would capture the progressive nature of Black's music.

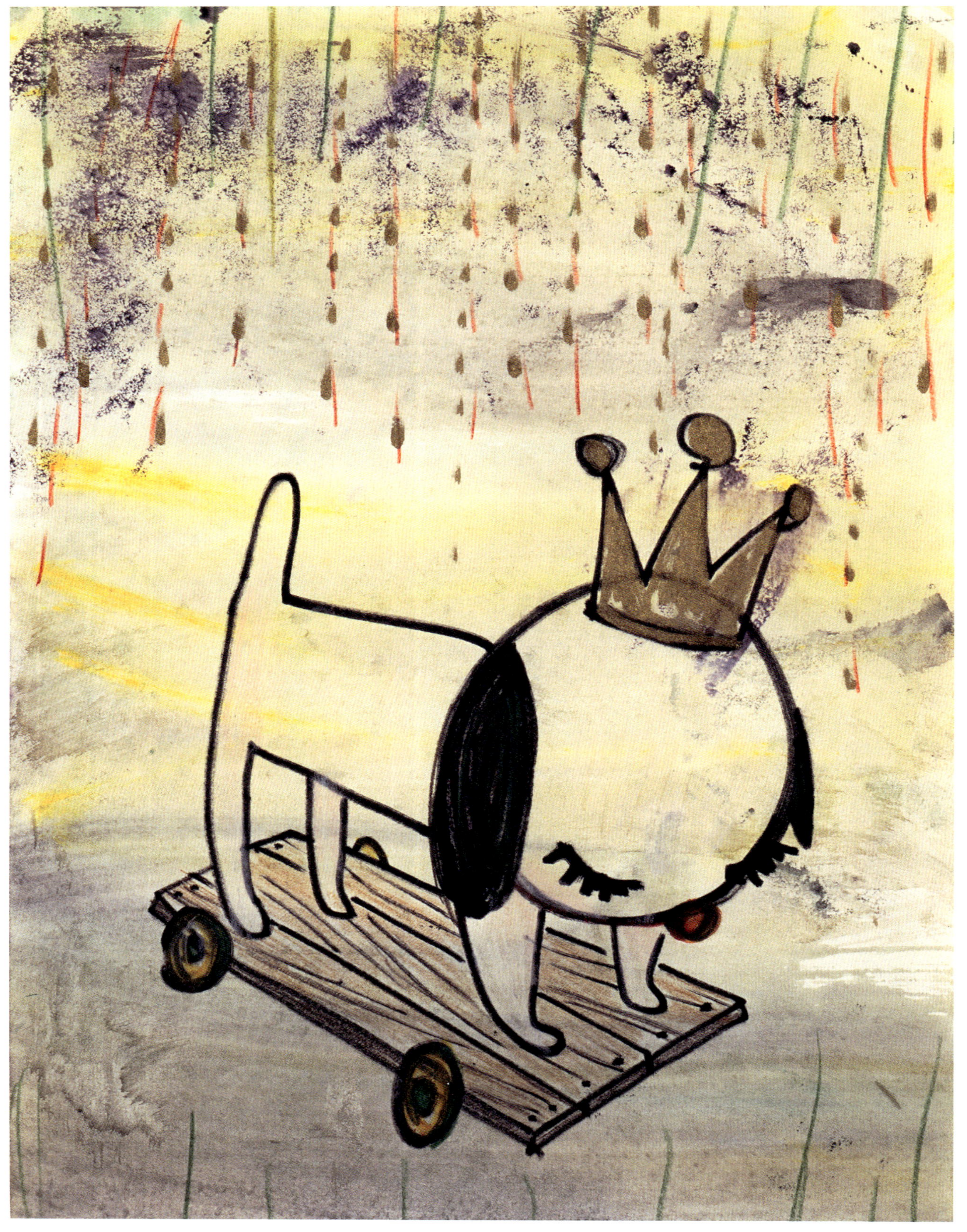

Fig. 201
Untitled, 1998, Pen, colored pencil, and acrylic on paper, 10 ¼ × 7 ¹¹⁄₁₆ in. (26 × 19.5 cm)

As with the work of Nara, Black's music cannot be easily categorized into one genre, and the combination of these two unlikely bedfellows proved fitting. On *Splay*, Black overturned conventional takes on contemporary jazz with compositions that, even in their quietest moments, hold an intensity of emotion. In response to the music, Nara made a simple drawing made on a piece of lined writing paper depicting a young girl whose light yellow eyes with darkened pointy edges offer an odd catlike gaze, embodying the album's sonic mood.

In 2005 Nara worked with his close friends, the Japanese punk band Bloodthirsty Butchers, to create the cover artwork for their album *Banging the Drum* (Figs. 203 and 204). Because of his relationship with the band, Nara felt naturally connected to the music, and it is not surprising that he responded in a way that was personal and direct. As he listened to the album, Nara was so deeply immersed in their sound that he immediately drew on a scrap of paper the image that would appear on the final cover, of a young girl banging on her drums. This spontaneous response harkens back to Nara's childhood days when he would draw as he listened to music in rock cafés, and it reveals the presence of the inner child that exists in Nara still today. The curator Takashi Azumaya perhaps best describes the artist's connection to music: "His materials are his guitar, while images are his melody, his beat."[29]

Among his many collaborators, Nara feels particularly connected to the all-female band Shonen Knife. While they have only collaborated on one album, they have supported one another in various other ways. (The band, for example, performed as part of a public program tied to Nara's exhibition at Asia Society in 2010.) His album-art project with them was in 1998, when he designed the cover of *Happy Hour* (Fig. 205), an album whose title would later be taken on as the name of his online fan club. The band, formed in 1981 by Naoko Yamano, the lead vocalist and guitarist and now the sole remaining original member of the group, is known for its distinctive edgy punk-pop sound with catchy lyrics about animals, candies, and cookies. Their song titles, varying from the banal to the outright weird, capture the group's distinctive personality: "Frogphobia," "Twist Barbie," "Banana Chips," and "Fish Eyes." Their music, with its combination of the cute and sugary with the eccentric and raw, has earned them an international cult following. For Shonen Knife's album, Nara portrayed the three band members as young girls, casting them into a dreamland of lollipops and electric guitars befitting the group's persona (Figs. 206–209).

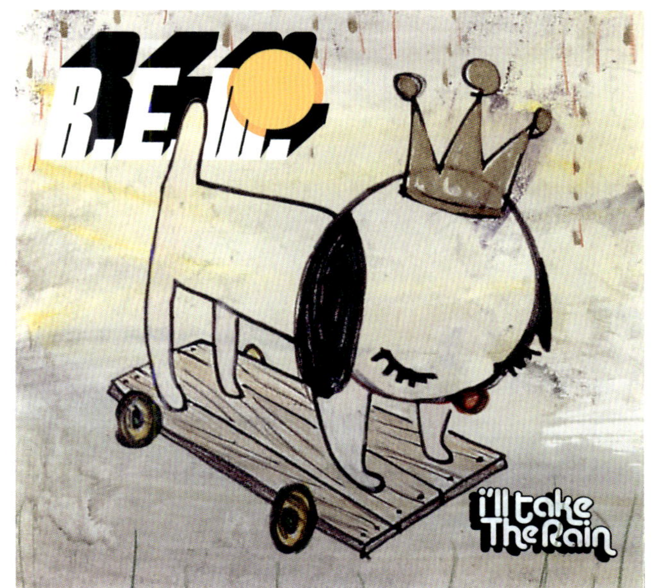

Fig. 202
R.E.M., *I'll Take the Rain* (single), Warner Bros. Records, USA, 2001

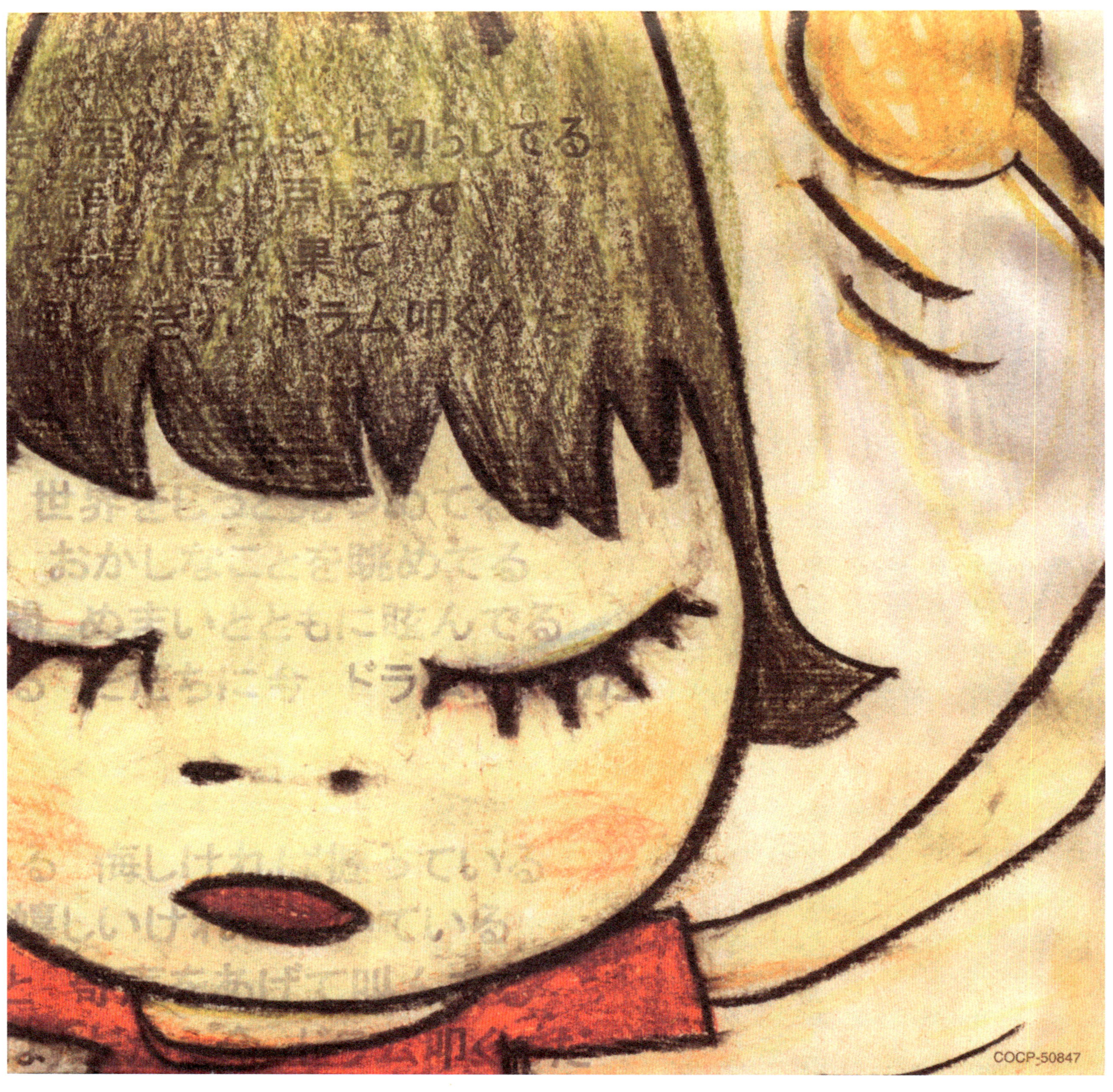

Fig. 203
Bloodthirsty Butchers,
Banging the Drum, Columbia Music Entertainment, Japan, 2005

Fig. 204 (opposite)
Banging the Drum cover foldout

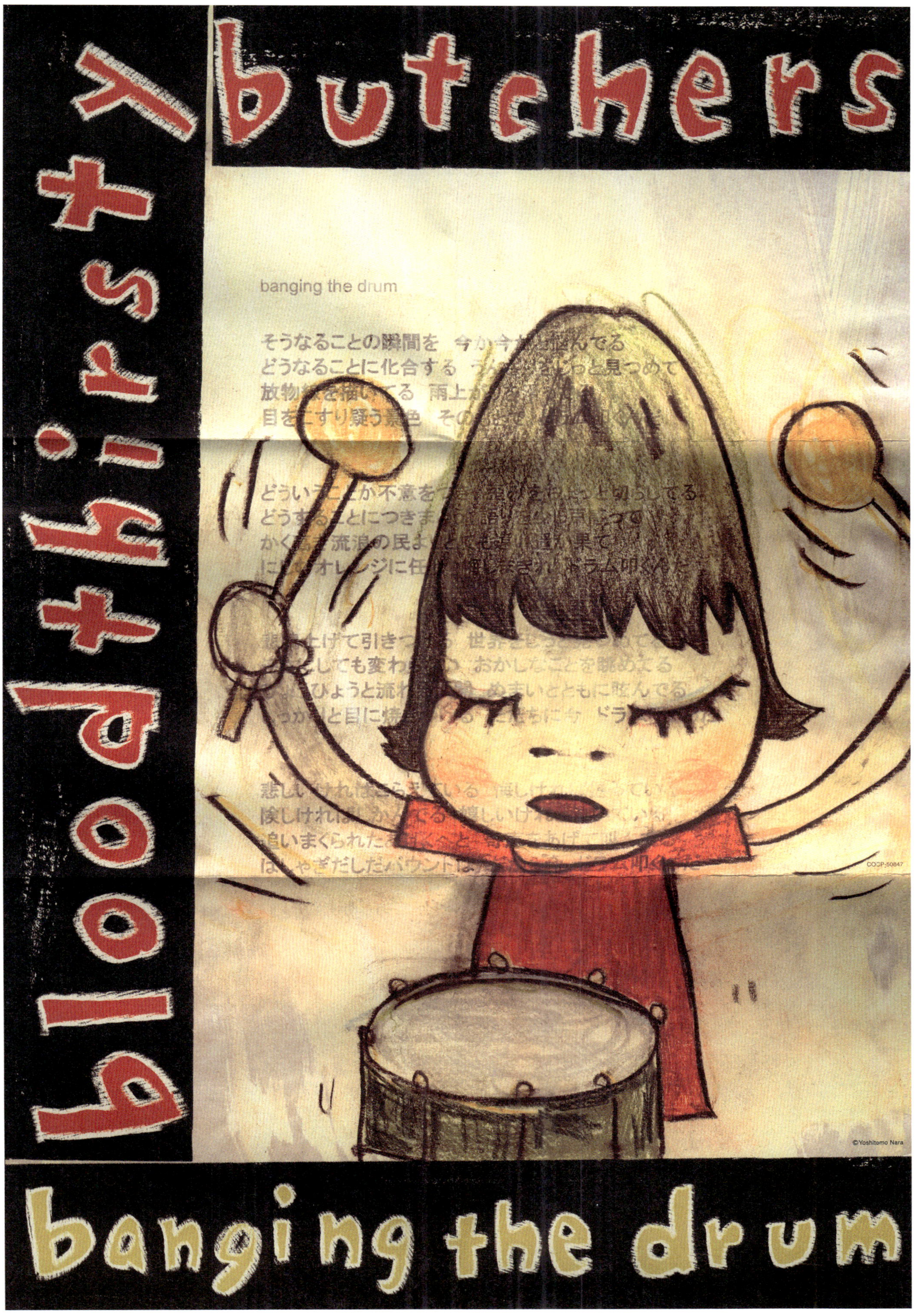

bloodthirsty
butchers
banging the drum
banging the drum
©Yoshitomo Nara

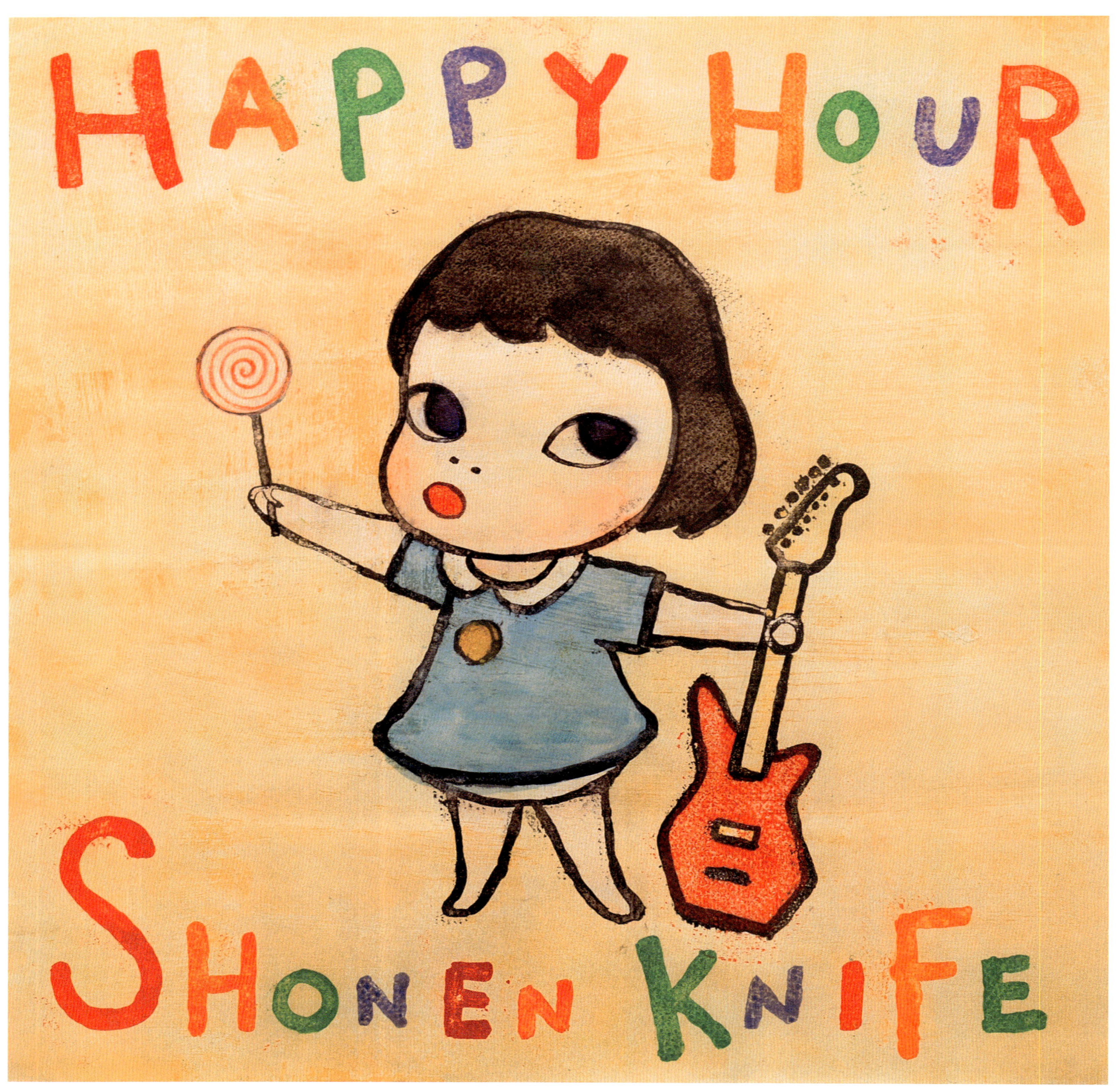

Fig. 205
Happy Hour (Japanese version), 1998, Acrylic on paper, 16 7⁄16 × 16 7⁄16 in. (41.7 × 41.7 cm)

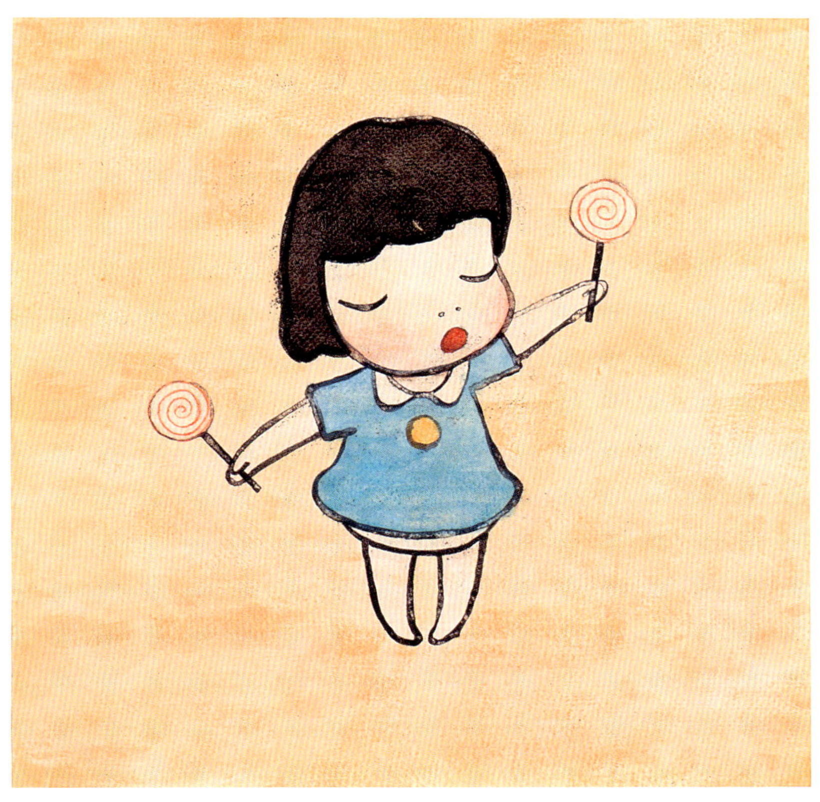

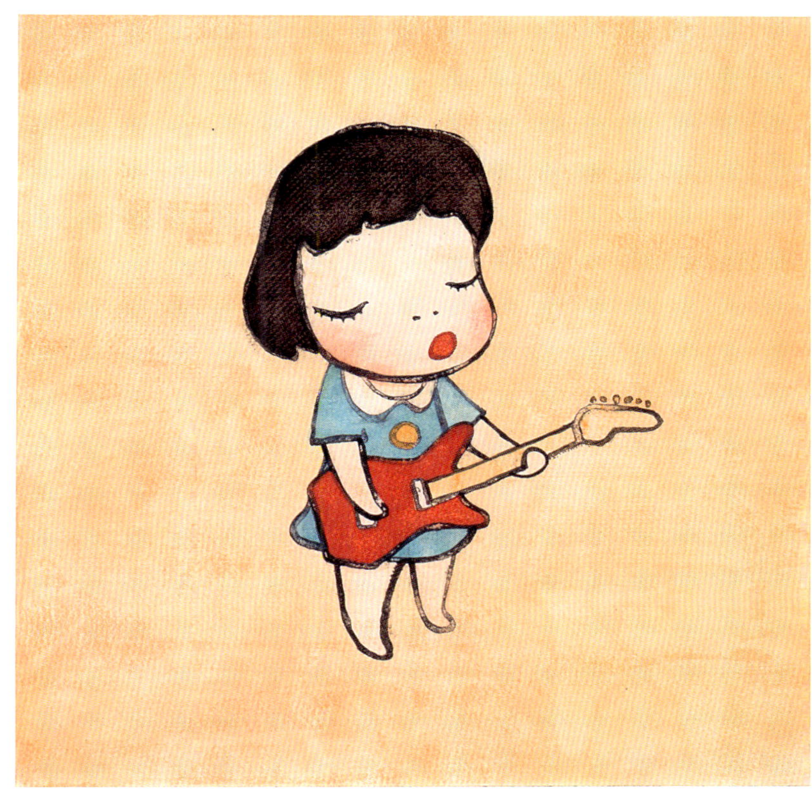

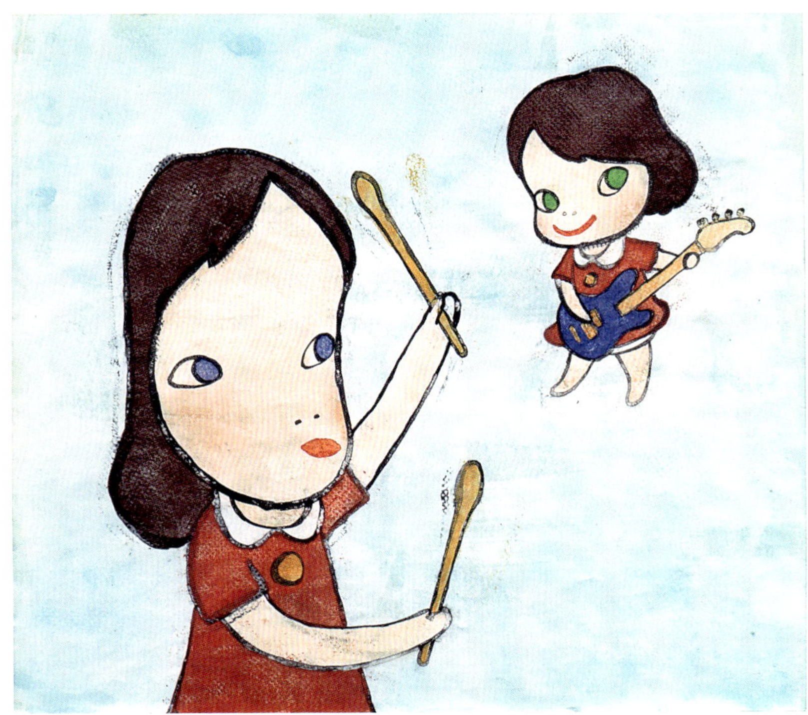

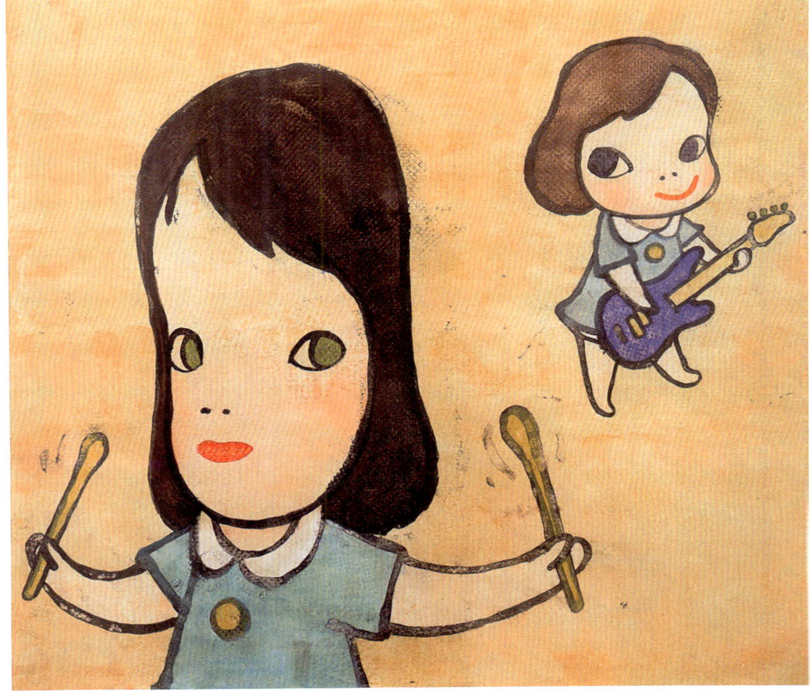

Fig. 206 (top left)
Happy Hour (English version),
1998, Acrylic on paper,
16 7/16 × 16 7/16 in. (41.7 × 41.7 cm)

Fig. 207 (top right)
Happy Hour (with Guitar),
1998, Acrylic on paper,
16 7/16 × 16 7/16 in. (41.7 × 41.7 cm)

Fig. 208 (bottom left)
Happy Hour (with Drum & Bass), 1998, Acrylic on paper,
16 7/16 × 18 1/16 in. (41.7 × 45.9 cm)

Fig. 209 (bottom right)
Happy Hour (with Drum & Bass), 1998, Acrylic on paper,
16 7/16 × 18 1/16 in. (41.7 × 45.9 cm)

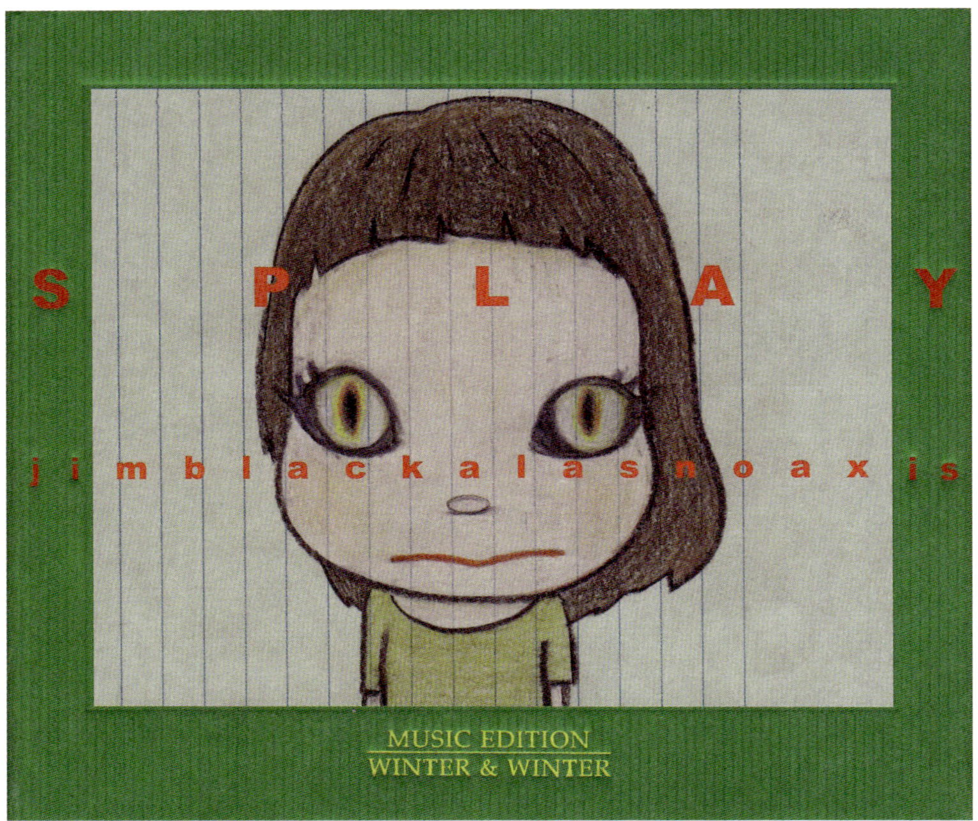

Nara vividly remembers the project's genesis. He was approached by someone at a party about making artwork for Shonen Knife's albums, a casual encounter that led to a conversation with Yamano.[30] Both artists recall how that conversation made them recognize certain shared affinities: they laughed over how they had garnered international fame despite having, in their eyes, poor language skills; their mutual interest in the incongruities of sweetness and the potential for violence (*shonen*, meaning "youth" or "young boys," is paired with *knife*); and, most importantly, the way in which both had found success by reaching out directly to audiences rather than the heads of their respective industries. They both continue to engage on that grassroots level, forming the core of their identities as artists.[31] This connection between art and the public has been particularly important for Nara, as, through his increasing success, he has been frequently accused of building a cult persona for the sole purpose of the art market, the self-fashioning of a corporate-style art maker.[32] Getting to know Shonen Knife and seeing parallels with the band's continuous engagement with the public has helped him maintain his own perspective on his career path amid the clamor of critics' harsh opinions.

Fig. 210
Jim Black/AlasNoAxis, *Splay*, Winter & Winter, Germany, 2002

Between 2016 and 2019, Nara was the host of a weekly two-hour radio show, *Radio of Shibuya*, during which he was able to share his music taste and engage in discussions about the merits of various artists. Although he enjoyed making the show, he eventually gave it up because he felt it took too much of his creative resources, and he was concerned that it would ultimately deplete the energy and imagination he needed for his art practice. This fear that concentrating on music would impact his art making shows how the two areas are deeply intertwined and gives insight into the ways in which his working connections with musicians are crucial to his development as an artist.

The spirit of kinship that comes with music once prompted Nara to make a teasing claim about one of the many playlists that he shares on his social media pages or in installations (Fig. 211). In an essay, he wrote, "If anyone knows 90 percent of this list [of albums and songs], I would be friends with that person, no questions asked."[33] It is a telling statement, for among his many different types of partnerships, music is the only creative space where the line between his private self and public persona is less guarded, where he feels most himself.

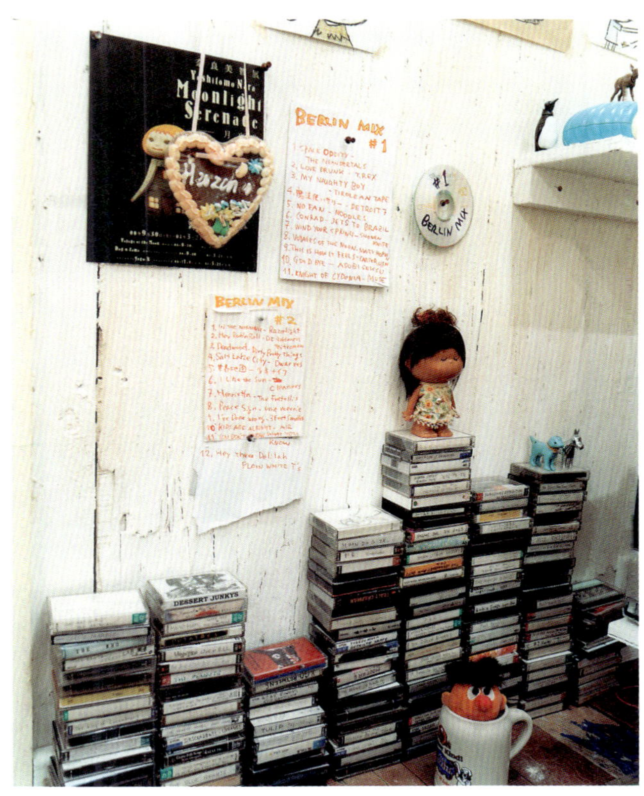

Fig. 211
Exhibition view: *Berlin Baracke*, Galerie Zink, Berlin, 2006

The playlist:
Dan Penn / Nobody's Fool
Andwella / Saint Bartholomew
Chris Smither / Lonesome Georgia Brown
Ernie Graham / Sebastian
Heron / Little Boy
Karen Dalton / Something on Your Mind
Larry McNeely / Mississippi Water
Mary Hopkin / Streets of London
Mr. Fox / Elvira Madigan
Ronnie Lane and the band "Slim Chance" / Roll On Babe
Tim Hardin / Black Sheep Boy
Vashti Bunyan / Come Wind Come Rain
Bob Martin / Captain Jesus
Marc Ellington / Oh No It Can't Be So
Donovan / Universal Soldier
Roger Tillison / Yazoo City Jail
Tony Kosinec / '48 DeSoto
Geoff & Maria Muldaur / Trials, Troubles, Tribulations
Mark LeVine / Going to the Country
Thoughts & Words / Today Has Come
Bert Jansch / Needle of Death
Eddie Mottau / Whistle a Tune
Christopher Keaney / Country Lady
Shelagh McDonald / Rod's Song
Brian Short / With You on My Side
Rosie Hardman / Four Golden Letters

Travels with the Camera

In recent years, Nara has been working in photography.[1] His results in the medium shed light on how he positions himself in relation to the people he meets and the worlds he encounters. Nara's first public body of work as a photographer came in 2002, but his interest in the medium began much earlier: he was thirteen when his parents gave him his first camera, and since then, he has clicked through endless rolls of films and filled countless memory cards.[2] For a man with restless fingers, the camera satisfies his need to jot down his thoughts and capture his impressions of the world before they escape him. The images he creates with the camera form a creative reservoir for future works in other media, but arguably just as important is the feeling of discovery he encounters from behind the lens, one that fuels his imagination. This chapter examines two photography projects, one that took Nara to Afghanistan (2002) and another to Sakhalin (2014), to explore their driving forces and understand why the medium has become so important to his larger creative practice.

Nara's desire to see the world has frequently propelled him in new directions. In 1980, as a twenty-year-old art student, he backpacked his way to Europe from Pakistan, and, three years later, after having transferred to Aichi Prefectural University of Fine Arts and Music, he visited China. The Cultural Revolution had ended in 1976, followed by Deng Xiaoping's Open Door Policy in 1978, which reopened trade systems with the outside world. In 1983, when Nara visited, there was an air of optimism as expanding manufacturing industries brought in new wealth and opportunities. Although tourism was still in its infancy and visas were difficult to obtain, Nara, with the help of a friend who worked in the foreign office, managed to get all the necessary documents to enter China, beginning his trip in the dusty industrial city of Taiyuan in Shanxi province. With fifty dollars in his pocket and a camera, aided by the kindness of friends and strangers, he explored a country whose recent history, largely shrouded in secrecy, only added to its mystique.

Nara's time there was meaningful, and it inspired him to translate his feelings into photographic images (Figs. 212–214). What he found most distinctive about China was the vast palette of earth tones, seen in the imposing concrete communist architecture, vast stretches of yellow-earthed hills in the countryside, and crowds of people all clothed in the same simple gray Mao suit. When Nara returned home, he chose to print the photographs he took in black and white, emptying the images

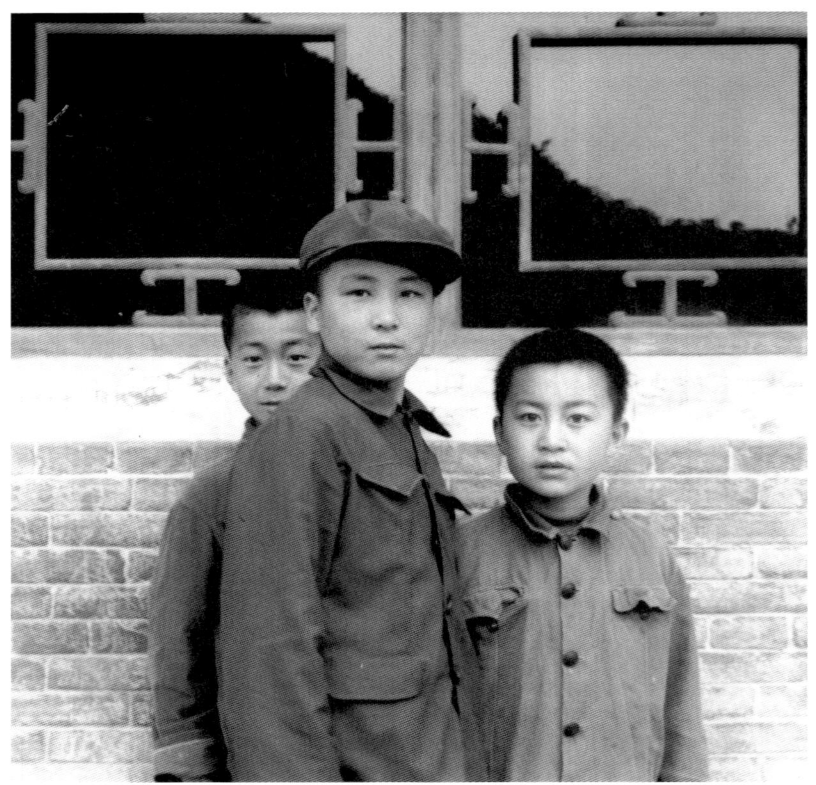

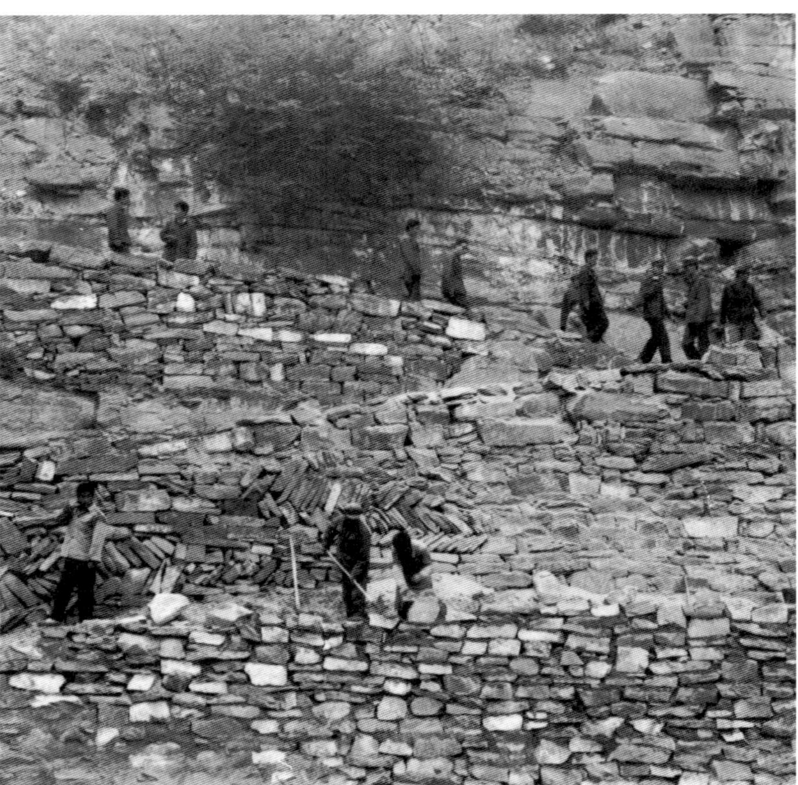

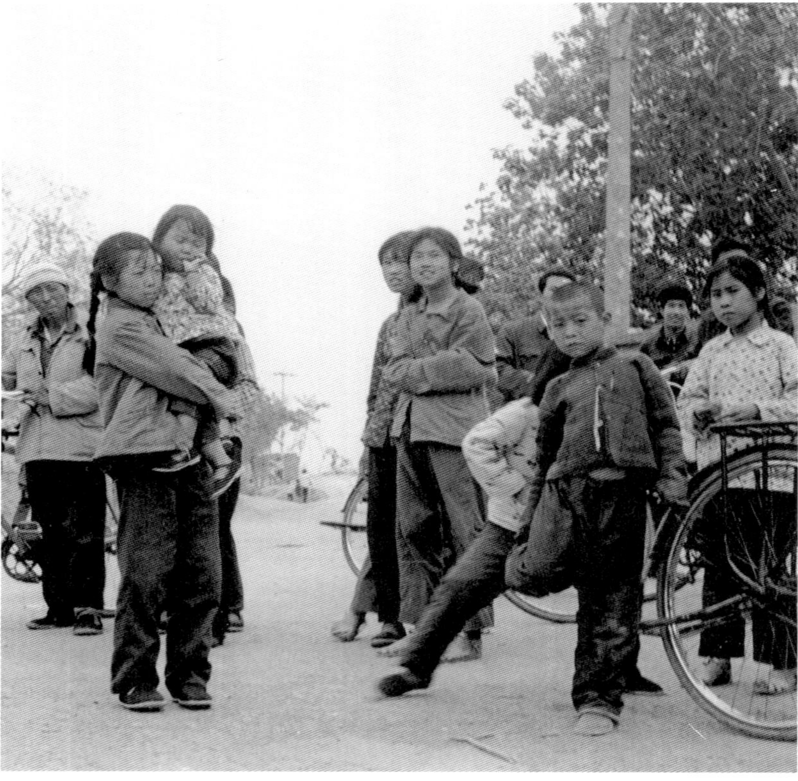

Figs. 212–214
CHINA, 1983, 1983

of color in order to emphasize, instead, the visual serenity he had witnessed in early 1980s China—surprisingly calm in contrast to the frenetic energy of Tokyo. This was a simple but powerful gesture, and it marked the first time he manipulated his photography according to an artistic choice. Whether they depict self-possessed boys in their suits or workers who blend into the stones of a hillside, the pictures reveal Nara's idiosyncratic take on the world he entered, glimpsed through the intense stares, half-grins, and quizzical glances of the subjects. It is impossible to know what these strangers might have thought of Nara with his camera and unruly mop of hair, but his photographs show an artist who empowers his subjects. He allows them—he *wants* them—to look back. With this early project, Nara set a foundation for his photographic practice, finding connections with strangers and capturing people's relationships to the places they inhabit.

In 2002 *FOIL* magazine asked Nara to take part in its inaugural issue, "No War," focusing on Afghanistan (Fig. 215). The issue paired Nara with Rinko Kawauchi, a photographer who at the time had just received the prestigious Kimura Ihei Award. He accepted the proposal, in part because it gave him an opportunity to explore a part of the world that he might not have otherwise visited and also because it allowed him to escape the demands the art world was beginning to impose on him after his successful 2001 show at the Yokohama Museum of Art (see pages 90–93). Although Nara was unsure of what to expect in Afghanistan, given its turbulent political climate, the theme of "No War," with its unabashed declaration of hope, proved appealing and promised that the trip would be a meaningful one.

The war conditions that existed in Afghanistan at the time can be traced back to the Soviet–Afghan War, a Cold War–proxy conflict between the Soviet-aligned Communist government and guerrilla rebels partially backed by the United States that began in 1979 and lasted almost a decade. With the withdrawal of the Soviet Army and later the US forces, the country was blighted by civil unrest as tensions between Afghan Marxists and Muslims escalated and various warlords swooped in to claim different parts of the region. The increasingly powerful Taliban later gained control and turned the region into an Islamic fundamentalist state that imposed strict laws on its people. The war underway by the time of Nara's travel was a US-led invasion in response to the Taliban regime's support of al-Qaeda and its alleged harboring of Osama bin Laden, who had directed the September 11

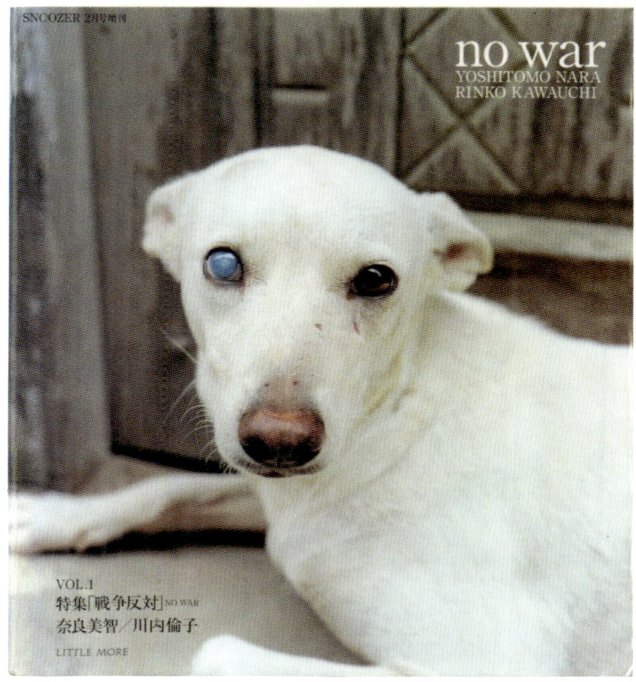

Fig. 215
FOIL, volume 1, "No War," published by Little More, Tokyo, January 2003
Cover photograph by Rinko Kawauchi

terrorist attacks on US soil.[3] American and British troops eventually expelled the Taliban soldiers, but this only marked the beginning of a long-term military engagement that continues today. In the initial wake of the Taliban's expulsion, however, there was a spirit of righteous hope as different nations gathered to discuss the future of a new democratic Afghanistan and their commitment to a larger war against terror.

In early 2002, Japan hosted the first major international conference that instigated a long-term program to restructure Afghanistan. Japan to this day continues to be a leader in organizing humanitarian aid to the region and stands second in providing funds for education, health care, agriculture, rural development, and infrastructure. This involvement is driven by its alliance with the United States and allows it to support its allies in accordance with Article 9 of Japan's post–World War II constitution, which forbids the government from deploying its own military forces.[4]

To understand the "No War" project, it is necessary to consider briefly the history of magazines and photobooks in Japan. Since the 1920s, the reproduction of photographic images in popular magazines, books, and postcards played an important role in popularizing photography in Japan's modern visual culture.[5] Magazines not only led the way in terms of modern design but also became "exhibition" spaces for experimental photography and photographic art, including photomontages, photograms, and microscopic photographs. However, during the 1930s, the state co-opted these magazines as a means of spreading wartime propaganda, a product of the systematized government support of photographers and artists in general, and as a way to promote a certain modernist style in service of an increasingly right-wing nationalist ideology.[6] Photographers' roles as artists, journalistic reporters, and designers became increasingly blurred during this period, and attempts to produce more experimental works were curtailed. After the war, in the 1950s, photography as an art form began to reemerge, catalyzed by the manufacture of locally made cameras, a rise in amateur and professional photographers, and an increase in the number of independent and commercial publishers.

The dedicated publishers, in particular, played a major role early on in helping to refine the modern photobook, experimental in style and distinct from the didactic works favored during wartime.[7] One of the most popular books from this period was *Yukiguni* (Snow Country), published in 1956 by Mainichi Shimbun-sha in association with the journal *Camera Mainichi*, which showcased the work of Hiroshi Hamaya (1915–1999) (Figs. 216 and 217).[8] Hamaya was a freelance professional photographer, who, like many other photographers during wartime, served the propaganda department. On assignment to a military training camp in Niigata prefecture, he stumbled across a remote village in Kuwadori Valley, and, over a period of ten years, he returned to take photographs of its customs and rites, an ethnographic project that resulted in the seminal photobook. With this book Hamaya introduced new ways of viewing photography, moving away from the aesthetics of earlier journals by pushing the conventions of the book format, using double-spread images that bled off the page and juxtaposing large images against smaller, related ones to create a conversation between the two. Experimenting with these various layouts, the photographer and the publisher together generated novel ways of reading and experiencing a visual narrative.

The powerful tenor of Hamaya's work would influence many later photographers, and there were several book projects thereafter that continued to focus on the anthropological documentation of places and people. More importantly, Hamaya's work signaled a shift in how images were being consumed—with pictures no longer tied to language, the images, arguably, acted as "antitext" by denying a need for verbal explanation and creating a visual language that could sustain a narrative on its own. Although these types of works initially attracted a specialized audience, the publication of photobooks and journals continued almost uninterrupted throughout the latter decades of the twentieth century, tapping into a market of readers interested not only in ethnographic histories but also in photography as an art form. For photographers, these publications provided a necessary source of income and exposure; despite the rise of independent galleries in Japan, a lingering conservative attitude toward the mechanical reproduction of prints often cast these artists as outsiders of the art establishment.[9] The market for photography publications only expanded with the advent of the more flexible and cheaper magazine format, coinciding with a widespread reevaluation of the history of Japanese photography and the establishment of the first dedicated museum of photography in Tokyo in 1995. At the same time, Japanese photography was gradually gaining attention among an international audience, and American photobooks were being distributed in larger numbers in Japan.

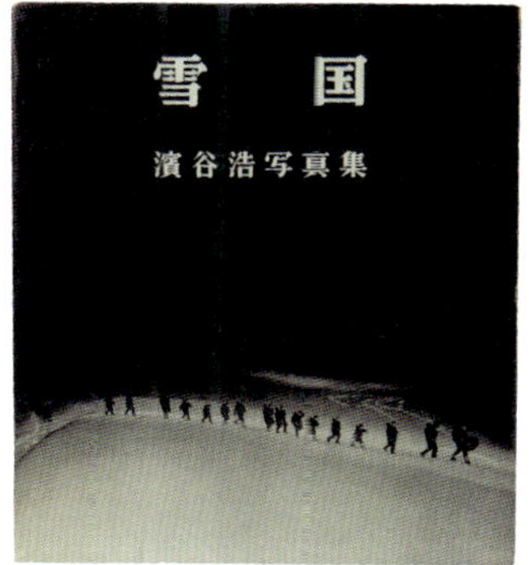

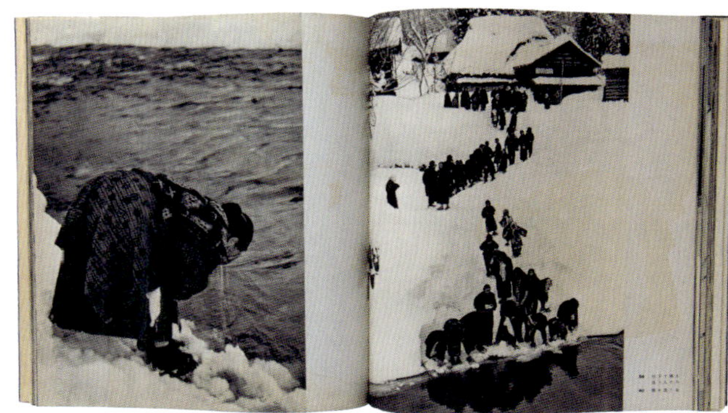

Figs. 216 and 217
Hiroshi Hamaya, *Yukiguni* (Snow Country), published by Mainichi Shimbun-sha, Tokyo, 1956

By the time of the *FOIL* commission, specialized photography magazines had an established foothold in the market and regularly promoted the works of artists made for a broader audience. The "No War" issue, however, had a unique conceit: Nara was asked to present his own photography along with a selection of paintings and drawings that would sit alongside Kawauchi's photographs. The project was also notable in its daunting undertaking of sending two established artists to a war-torn country, which involved enormous logistical organization to ensure military protection and to gain access to civilian areas that had been out of bounds to journalists and other documentarians for many years.

As their flight slowly descended into the military base, Nara was struck by the decaying, war-ravaged landscape of the country. From afar, broken planes and abandoned vehicles that littered the terrain looked like fossilized remains of dinosaurs covered in tea-colored dust.[10] Nara and Kawauchi, once on the ground, experienced a world far removed from Japan. They walked down streets strewn with discarded military vehicles, through buildings with caved-in ceilings, and along walls riddled with bullet holes. But at each destination, they were received with smiles and warm greetings. Nara was struck by this reception: children and teenagers who had never experienced lives without war welcomed them eagerly, old men on the streets waved to them, and mothers offered them food in their homes, despite the scarcity of supplies.

Although Nara is not an overtly political artist, he had, by the time of his trip, built up a body of work with antiwar and antinuclear themes—one of the many reasons why he was asked to contribute to "No War."[11] However, on his return to Japan, Nara, who had intended to produce a new painting that would be the centerpiece of his contribution, discovered himself unable to paint. He found it hard to process his conflicting emotions after witnessing, close up, the aftereffects of war. Nara had always believed in the goodness of humanity and the fundamental harmony between people and the places they inhabit, and his paintings are testaments to the importance of that empathy. Even when portraying girls in moments of mischief or anger, his rich palette emits a warmth that reaches out to the parts of us that want to believe in hope. But after spending time in Afghanistan, where he felt the traces of human violence so acutely, he began to question these long-held beliefs, complicating his ability to channel his emotions onto the canvas.

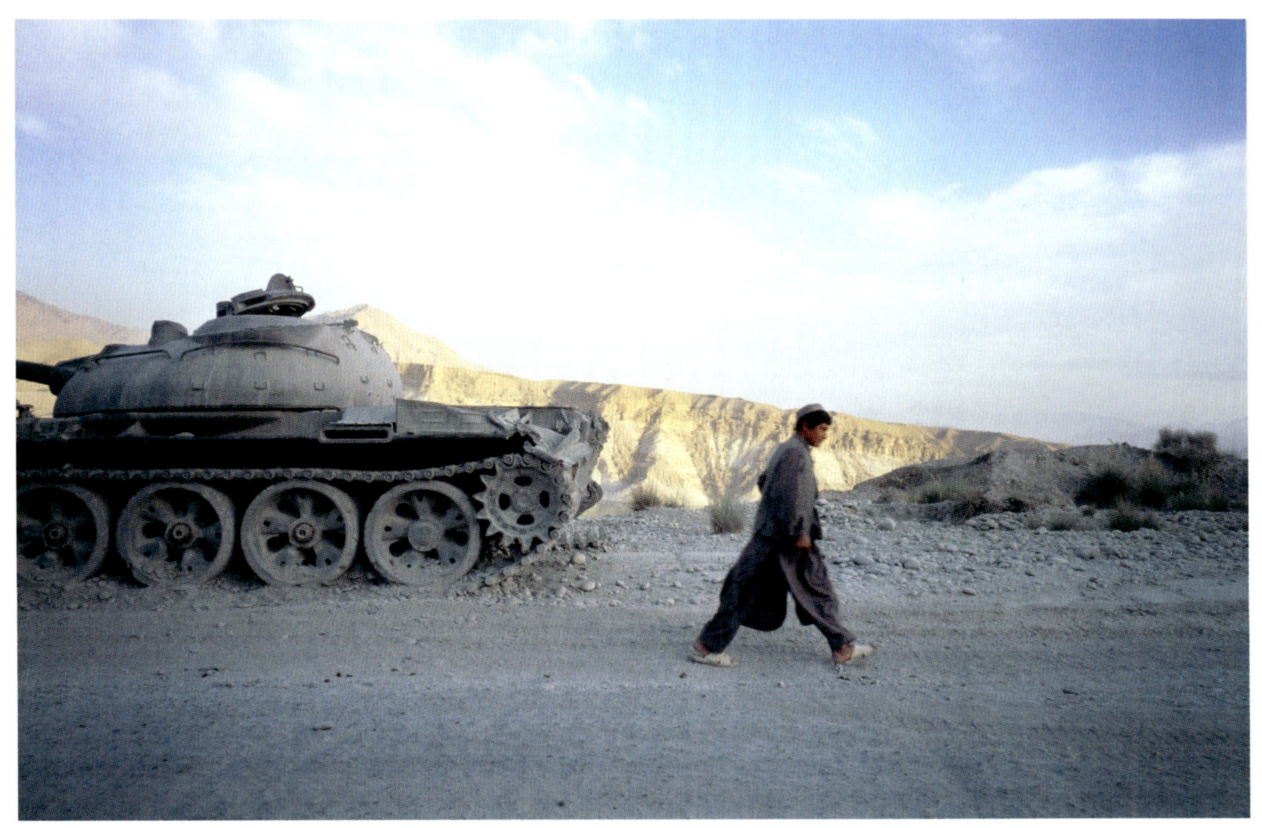

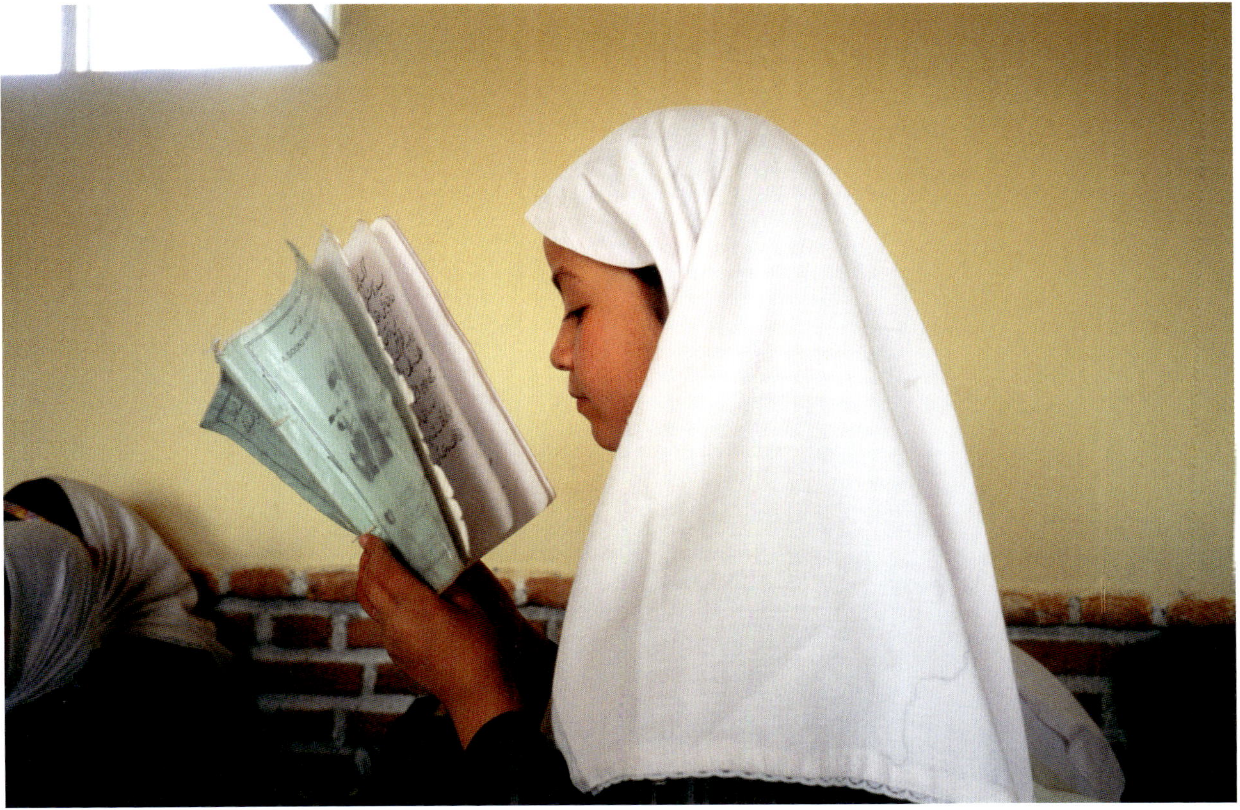

Figs. 218 and 219
Kabul Note, 2002

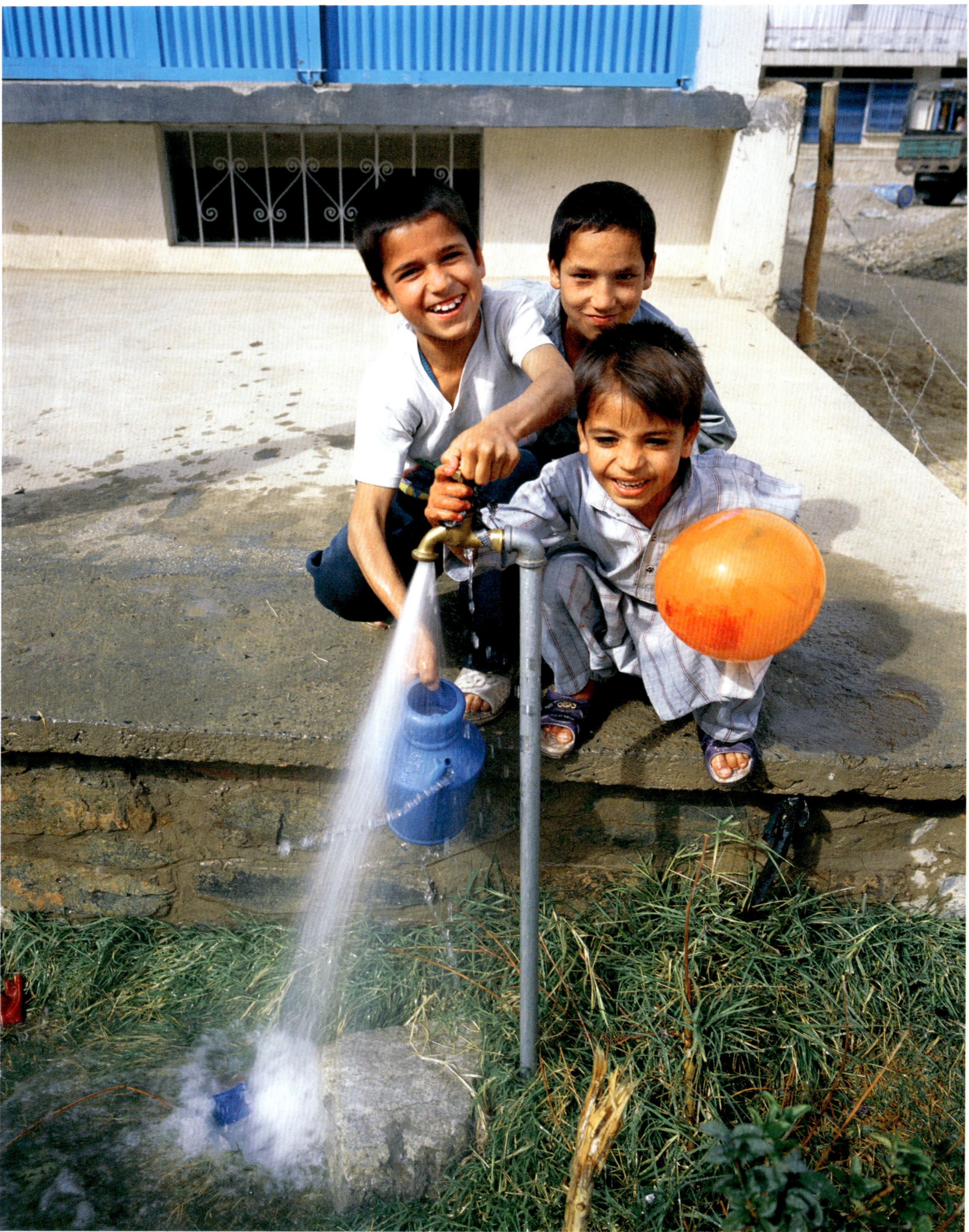

Fig. 220
Kabul Note, 2002

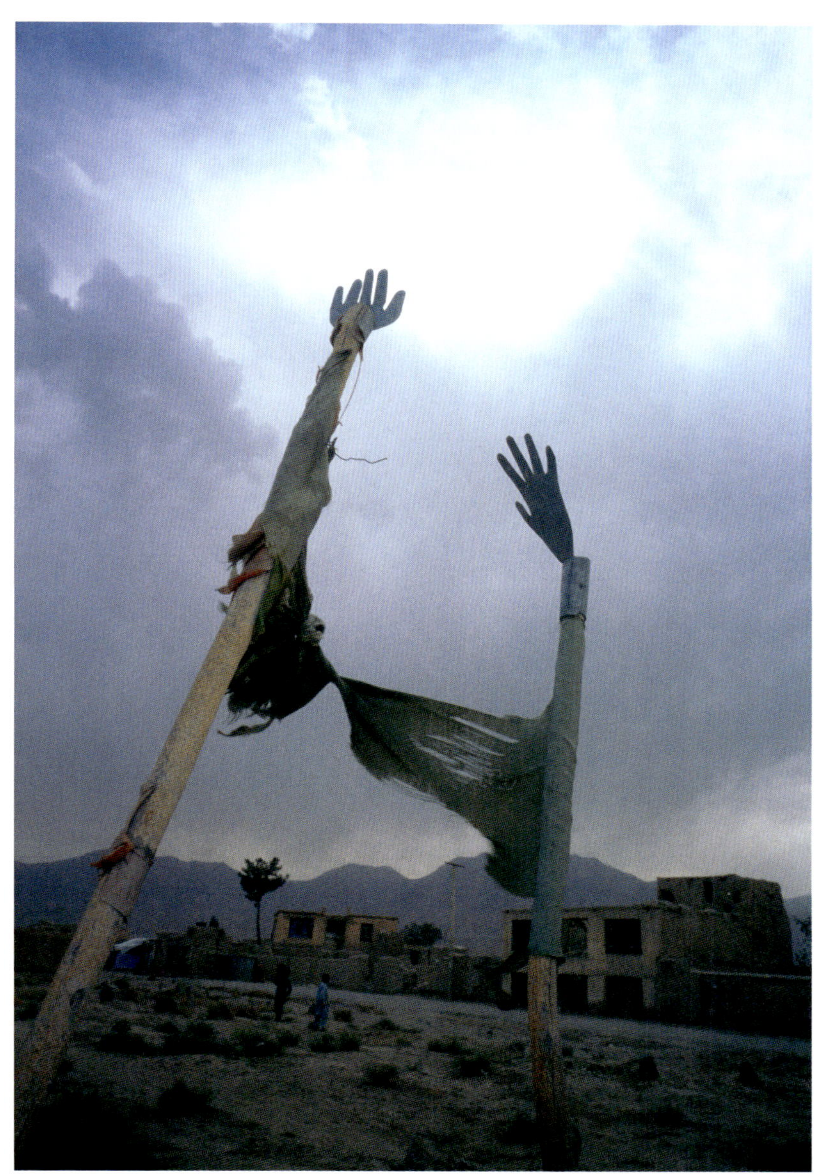

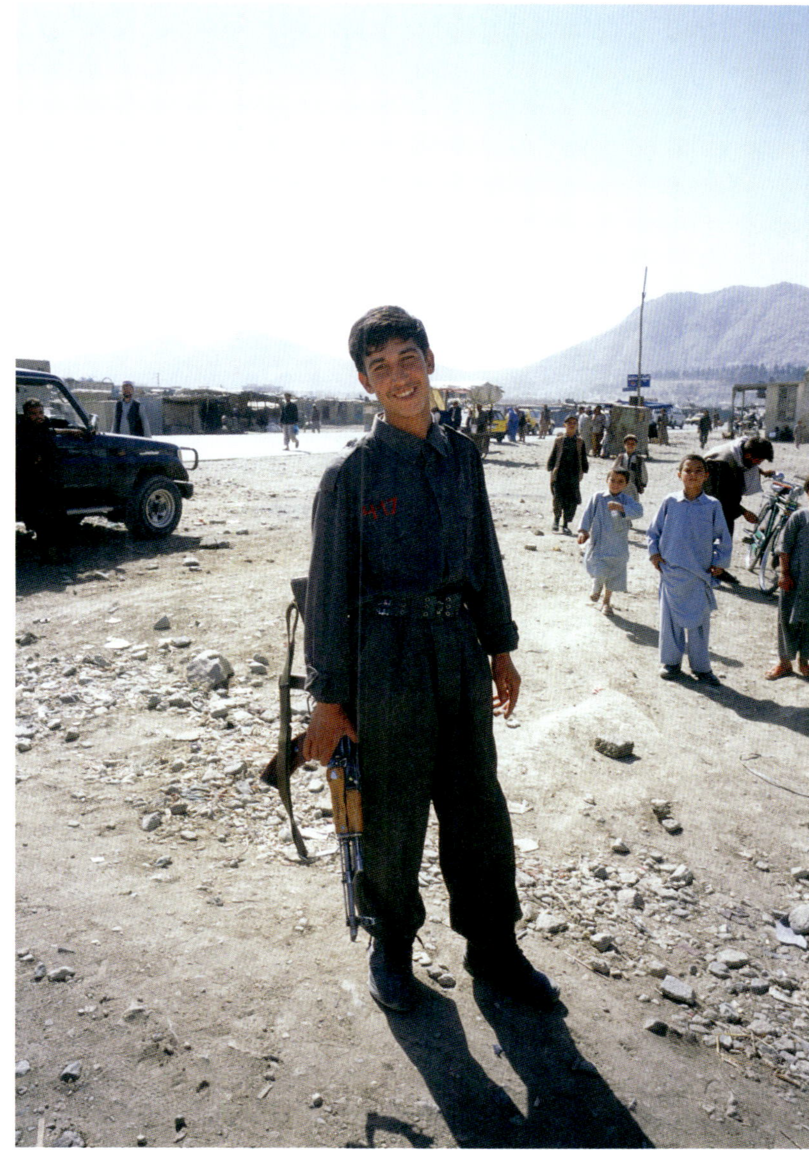

Figs. 221 and 222
Kabul Note, 2002

After staring at a blank canvas for many days, Nara decided to submit the photographs he took as his primary contribution to the issue, supported by a selection of drawings. He considered these new works emblems of his personal encounters. The big-headed girls and cheeky rebels are visible here only as glimpses. Instead, in these photographs, he showed the genuine warmth of a place that, despite its history, persevered. Nara understood that by showing pictures of the daily lives of the people he encountered and the joy they expressed, there was a danger of sidestepping politics and the realities of violence, but it was important to him to share work that was true to his experience and that embodied his hope that the will of humanity would have the strength to triumph over adversity. The end result is a photographic series that concentrates on the daily lives of the local community and on how this war-torn place maintains a feeling of home.

What is striking about Nara's photographs is how determined they are to capture embodiments of the power of life. At the butchers, hanging on green hooks, large slabs of meat with pinkish scraps cling onto bones. In a place where fresh food supplies were low during wartime, the image of the red, raw lump of meat is both vital and alive, even as it foregrounds death. In front of the shop, a child dressed in a deep blue jacket stands with arms crossed, staring back at the camera, both defiant and vulnerable (Fig. 225). It is a familiar stance in Nara's work: the child who denies our sympathies or offers of help, but here, taken in the context of a war-torn place, the gesture of independence and pride is more poignant. In another image, Nara captures a little girl in a burnt-umber dress standing on one leg, mimicking the movements of a rooster outside a house with crumbling walls splashed with shades of faded aqua green and curtains made from a mustard-yellow sheet (Fig. 226). Rendered in rich tones, the images testify to the lives of the people as something beautiful.

The pairing of Nara with Kawauchi created an interesting visual dialogue between the two artists. Both look for the extraordinary in the everyday and the wonder in the mundane, but there are substantial differences in their respective aesthetic approaches. Kawauchi seeks angles and planes that capture sparseness, heightened by a luminescence that radiates from her subjects. She has the ability to capture the light of the sun rather than its heat, resulting in a collection of images that express color in ethereal tones (Fig. 223).

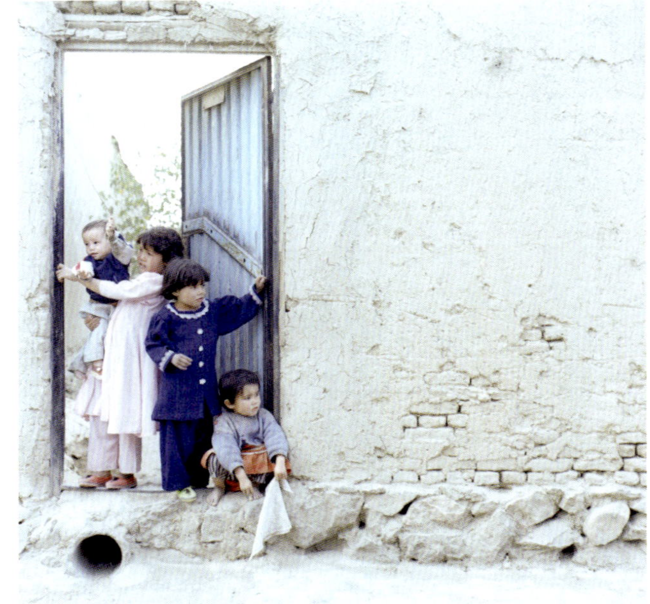

Fig. 223
Rinko Kawauchi, *Untitled*, 2003

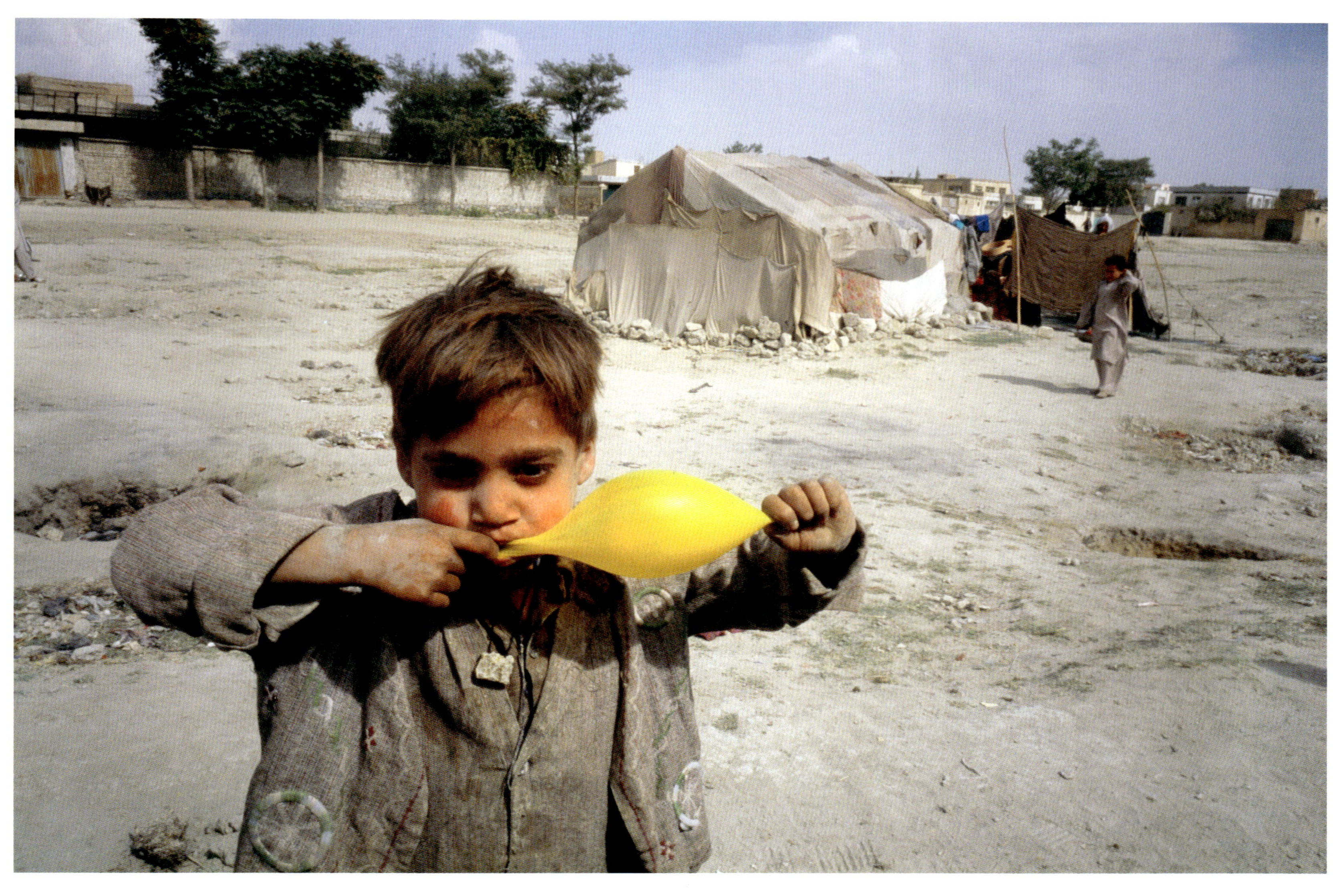

Fig. 224
Kabul Note, 2002

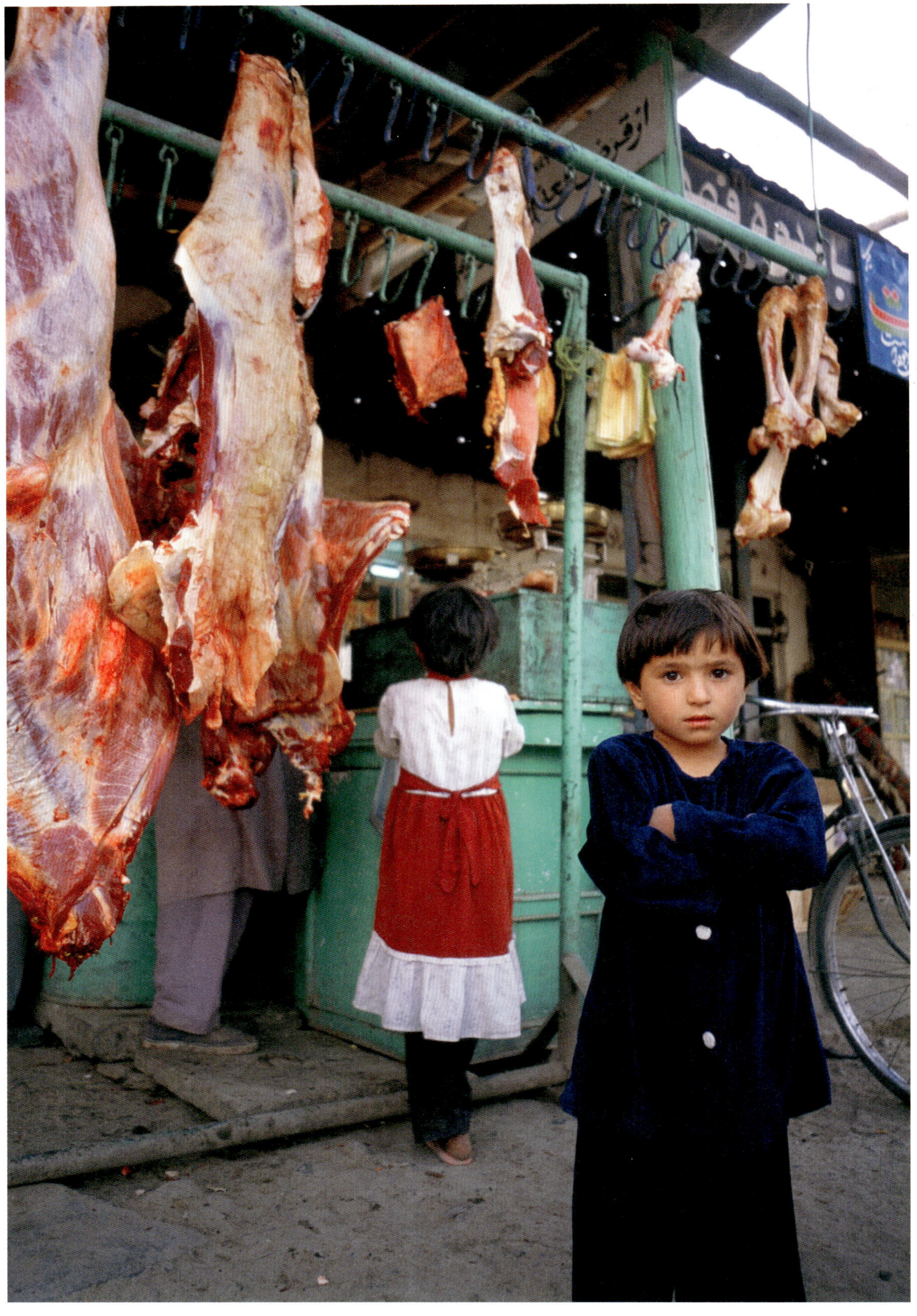

Fig. 225
Kabul Note, 2002

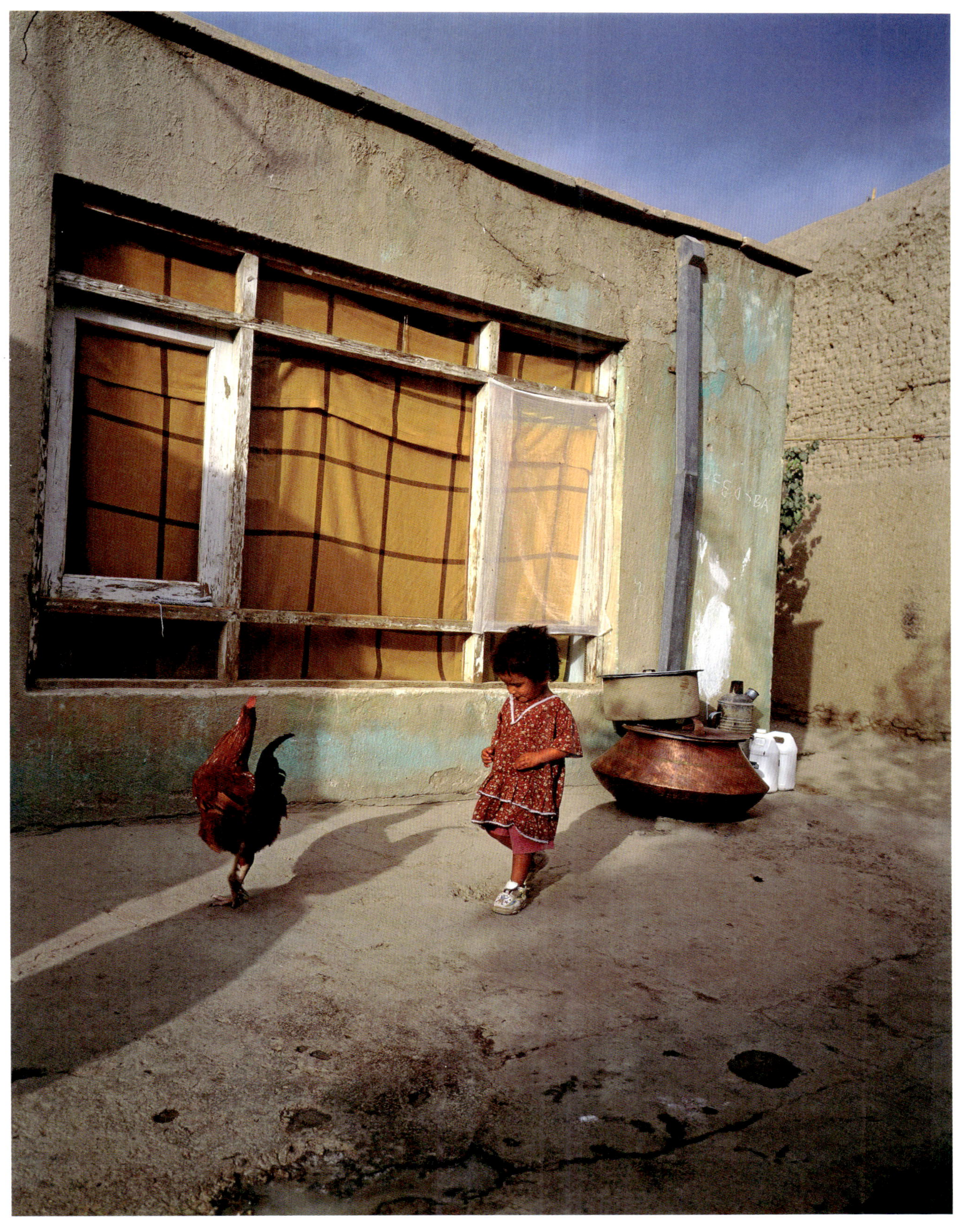

Fig. 226
Kabul Note, 2002

In contrast, Nara concentrates on the saturation of colors and uses that richness to create works that pop with life as he anchors his scenes in the present (Fig. 224).

Another difference is that Kawauchi often captures people unaware of the camera. Whereas her presence is unobtrusive, Nara engages with the people in his photographs, bringing the camera closer to his subjects and them closer to the viewer. By zooming in, he also emphasizes the minutiae of their lives. For example, one of the threads that runs through Nara's "No War" project is the connection, both physical and emotional, between the people and the land. There are many pictures of feet, dusty and bare, roaming the hot, arid ground littered with rubble. There are also images of young girls who, in their burkas and niqabs, echo the shapes of the mountainous terrain. More than anything, Nara wanted to explore the ways in which people belong to the land (Fig. 227).

Nara's drawings for this project, however, for the most part diverge from this approach, a discrepancy that speaks to the ambivalence of his experiences there. In one drawing, for example, he depicts a child looking into a deep pit of skulls as pagodas rise up from the bottom of the page (Fig. 231). It appears as if, were we to drill through the ground, we would reach another side of the world—Nara's Japan—questioning just how connected, or removed, we are from one another. That sense of disconnection is also heightened by the more subdued mood of other drawings of Afghanistan (Figs. 232–234). Nara's light pencil traces capture the solemnity of a group led by a young child walking in a line or the small scale of a young Muslim child floating on a cloud. Even when there is a suggestion of liveliness, such as a boy with a kite, the ripped edges of the page have stripped away all but his hand holding onto the spool.

If Nara's photographic portraits catch glimmers of mischief in young children, his drawings show the desolate child sitting in fear, shrinking into the corners of the page (Figs. 235 and 236). In these works on paper, Nara shows the pervasiveness of death and violence with sharper tones and bolder scales: a smiling girl on a tank above the words "Mensch panzer angreiferin" (Young Female Tank Warrior) or a ghoulish child whose eyes are ringed with darkened circles, hauntingly sad (Figs. 237 and 238). The juxtaposition of youth and death is a theme Nara had touched on before, but in this context, it has more than just metaphoric power: in these sketches, horror lies in the shadows of reality.

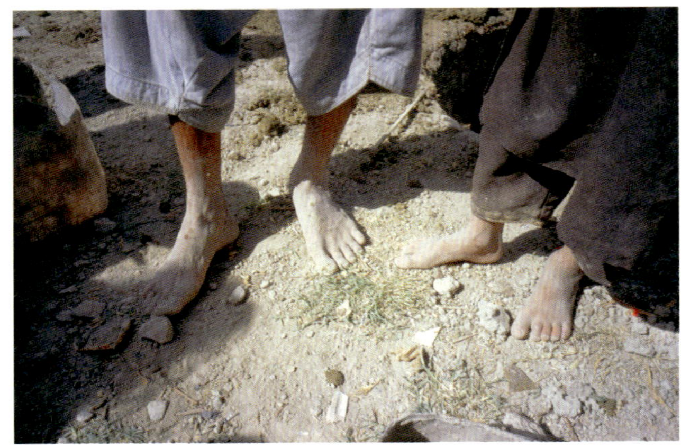

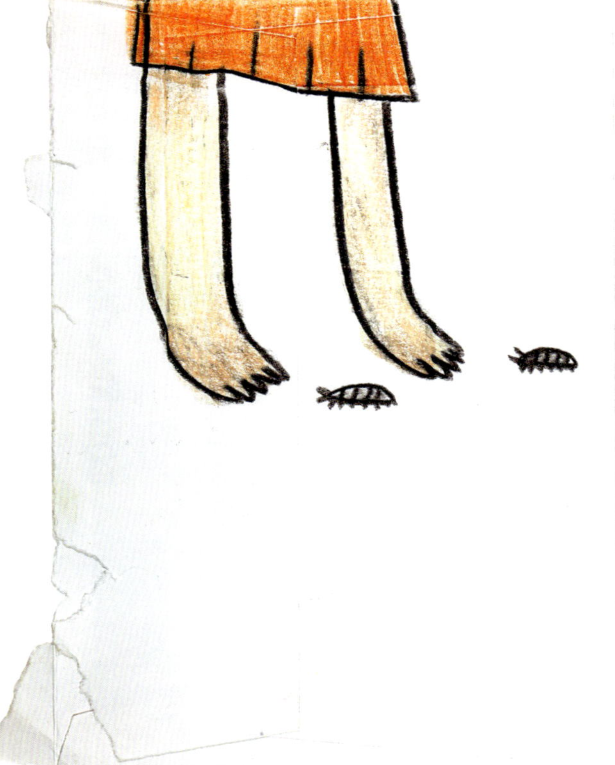

Fig. 227
Kabul Note, 2002

Fig. 228
Untitled, 2002, Colored pencil on paper, 6 ⅜ × 5 in. (16.2 × 12.7 cm)

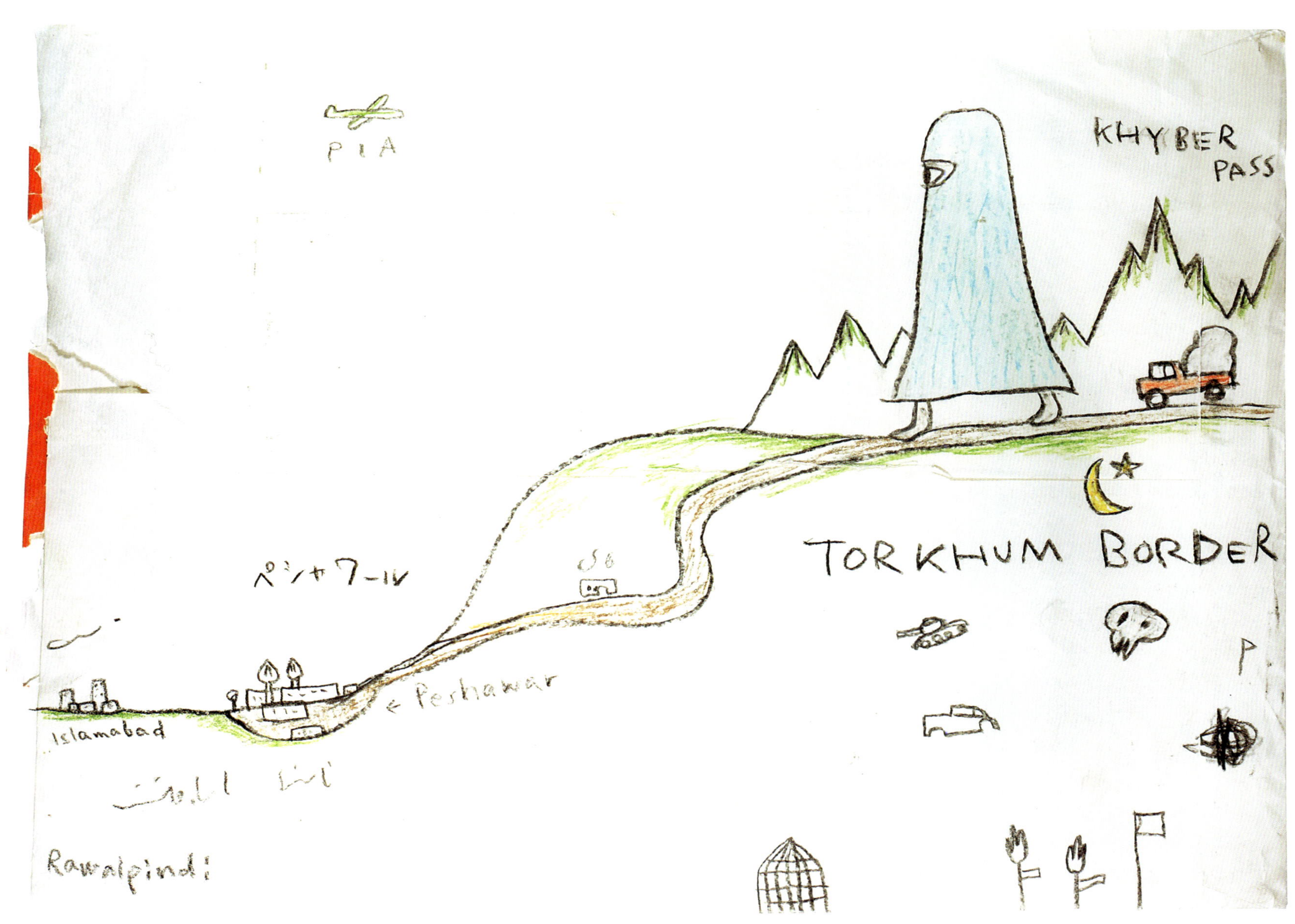

Fig. 229
Untitled, 2002, Colored pencil on paper, 9 ⅜ × 13 ¼ in. (23.8 × 33.7 cm)

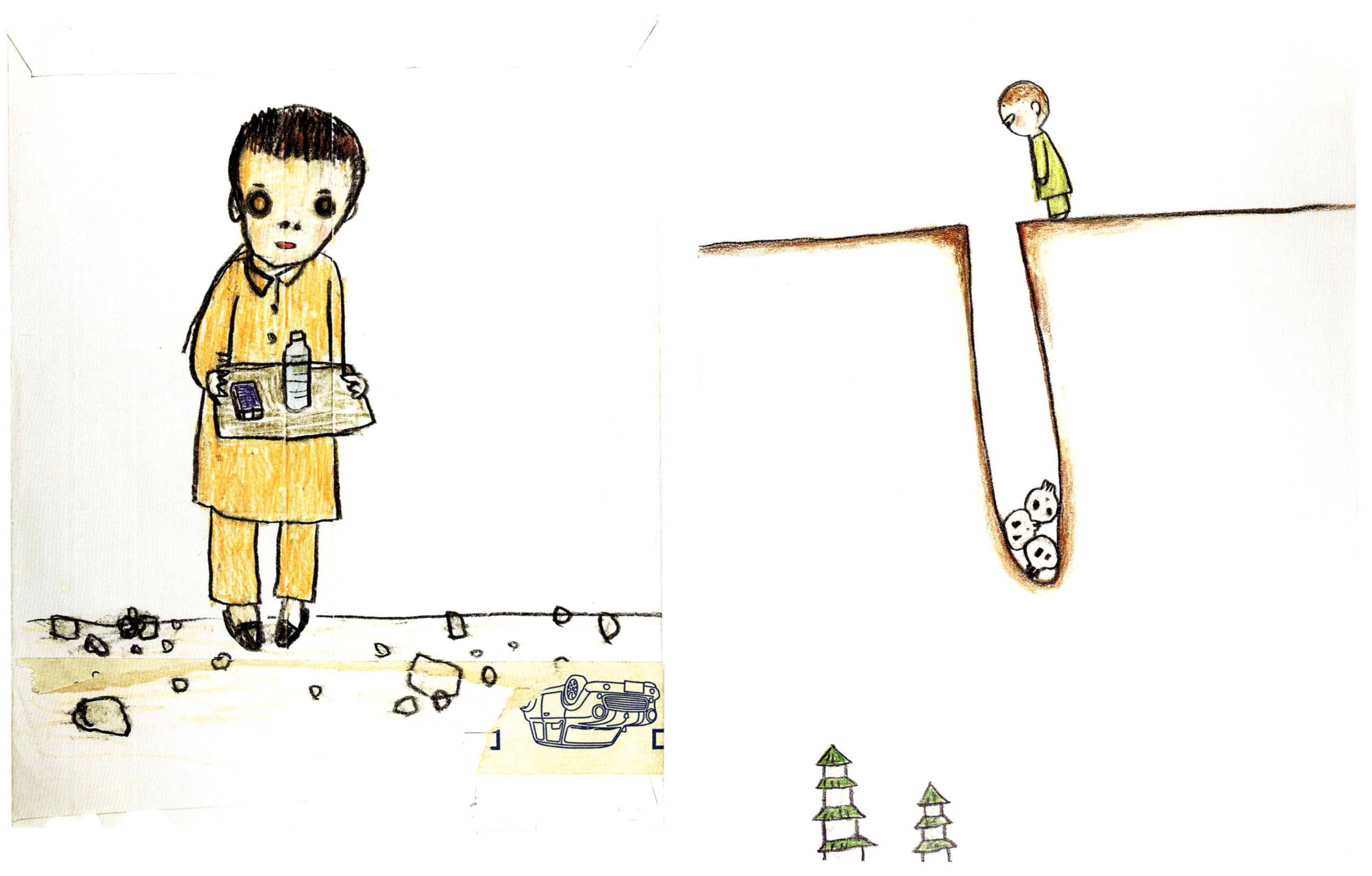

Fig. 230
Untitled, 2002, Colored pencil on paper, 10 15⁄16 × 8 ½ in. (27.8 × 21.6 cm)

Fig. 231
Untitled, 2002, Colored pencil on paper, 11 15⁄16 × 8 15⁄16 in. (30.3 × 22.7 cm)

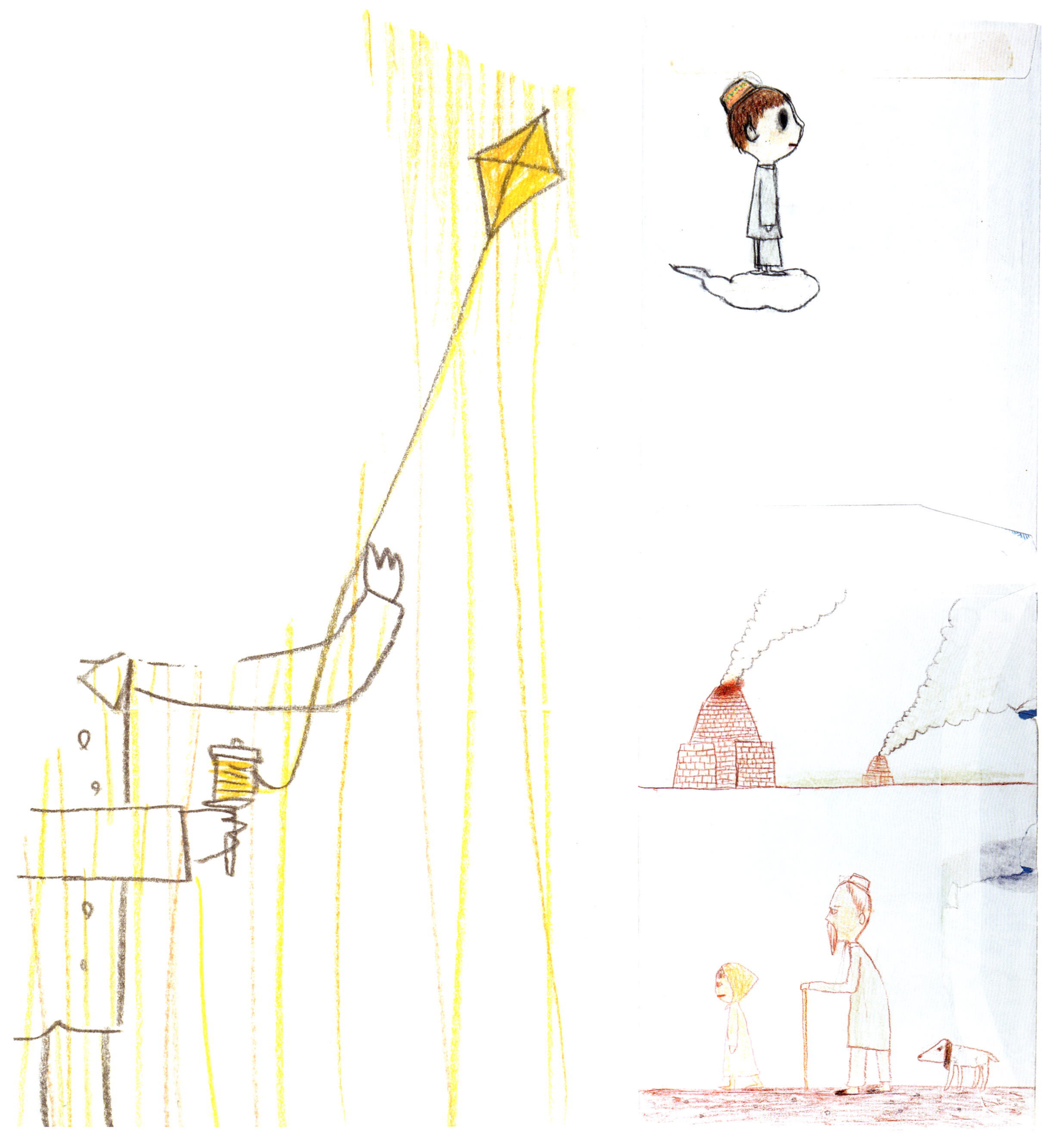

Fig. 232 (left)
Untitled, 2002, Colored pencil on paper, 10 ¾ × 6 ⅜ in. (27.3 × 16.1 cm)

Fig. 233 (top right)
Untitled, 2002, Colored pencil on paper, 9 1⁄16 × 6 5⁄16 in. (23 × 16 cm)

Fig. 234 (bottom right)
Untitled, 2002, Colored pencil on paper, 9 × 6 ⅜ in. (22.8 × 16.2 cm)

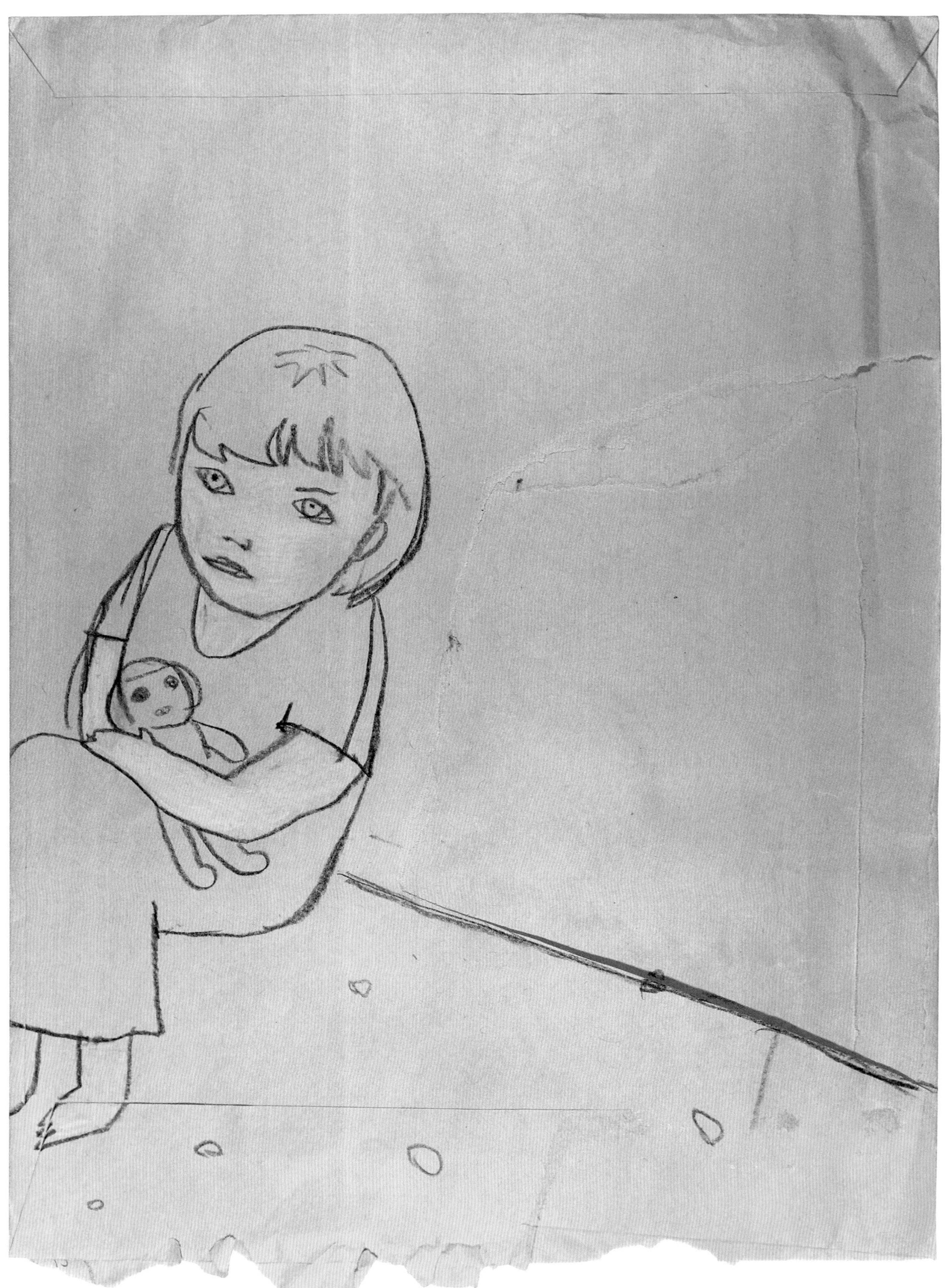

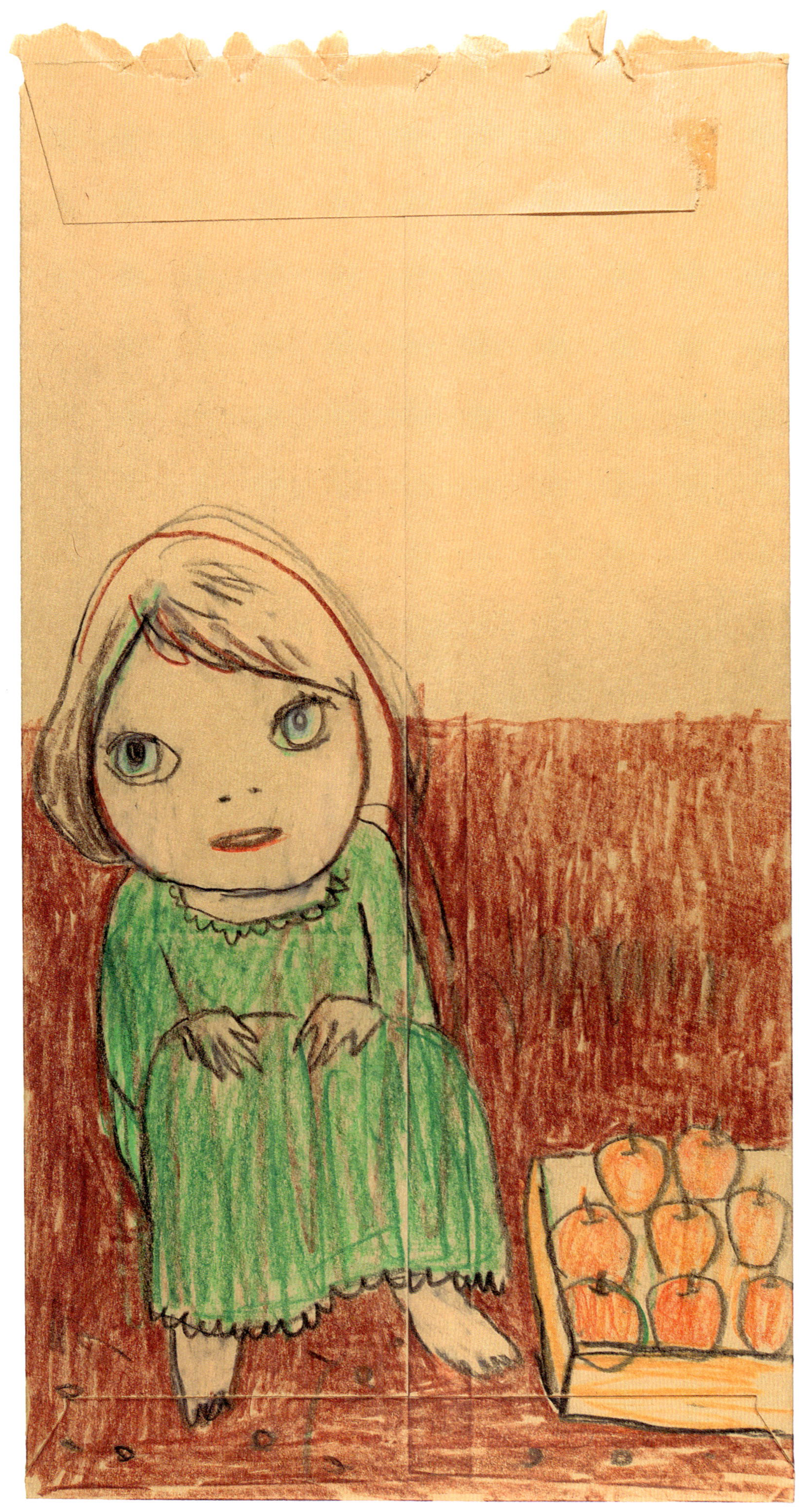

Fig. 235 (opposite)
Untitled, 2002, Colored pencil on paper, 13 5⁄16 × 9 7⁄16 in. (33.8 × 24 cm)

Fig. 236
Untitled, 2002, Colored pencil on paper, 9 7⁄16 × 4 3⁄4 in. (24 × 12 cm)

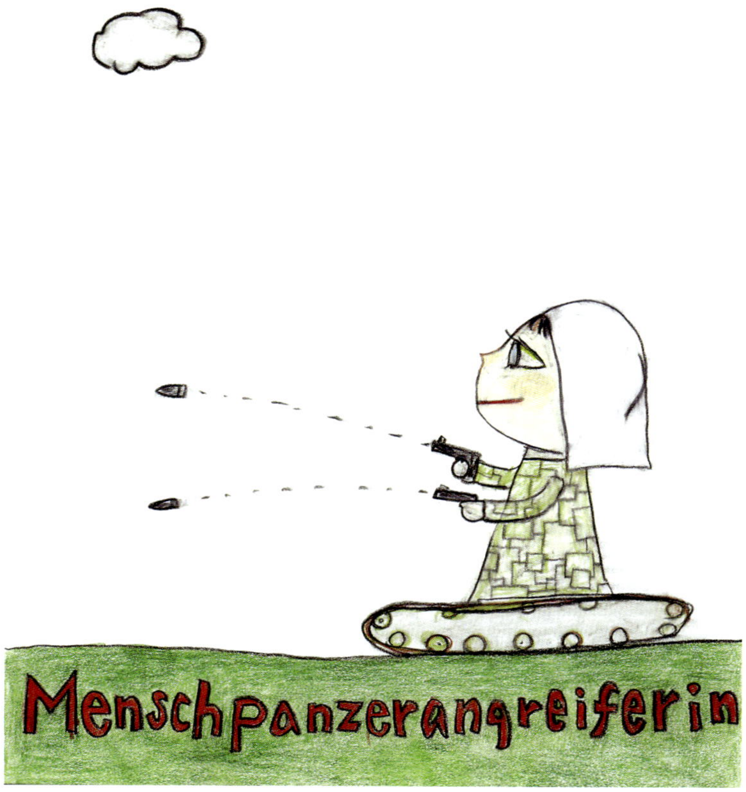

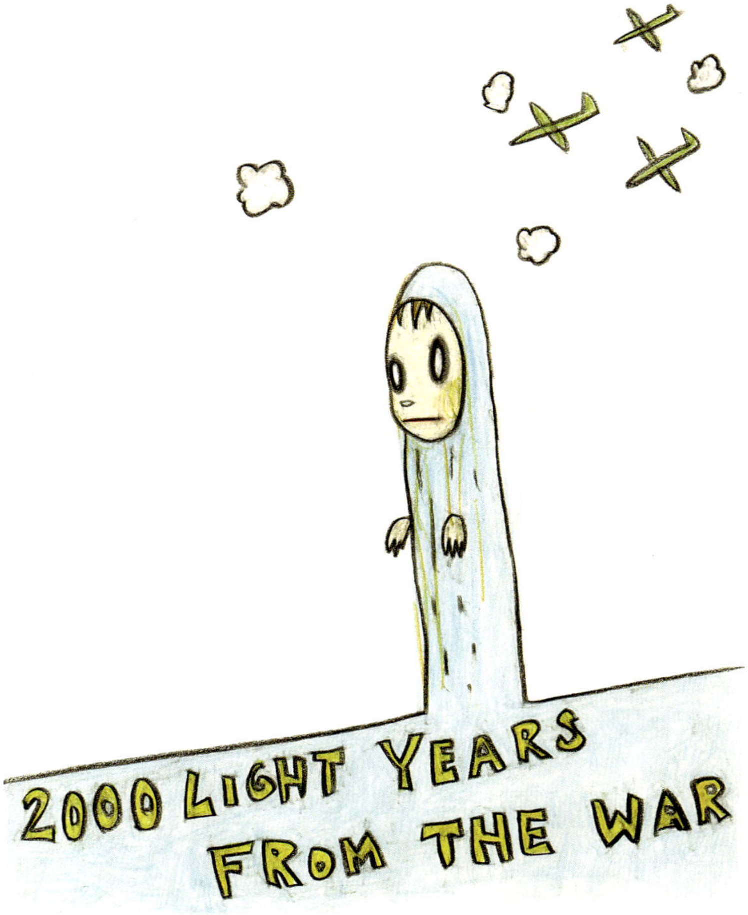

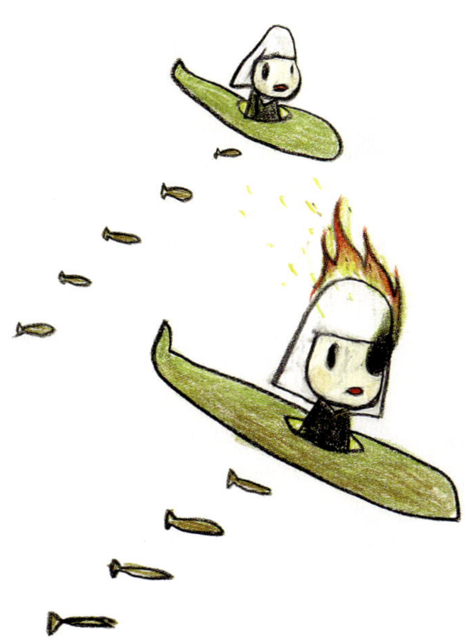

Fig. 237 (top left)
Menschpanzerangreiferin, 2002, Colored pencil on paper, 11 15⁄16 × 8 15⁄16 in. (30.3 × 22.7 cm)

Fig. 238 (top right)
2000 Light Years from the War, 2002, Colored pencil on paper, 11 15⁄16 × 8 15⁄16 in. (30.3 × 22.7 cm)

Fig. 239 (bottom)
Flying Nuns, 2002, Colored pencil on paper, 11 15⁄16 × 8 15⁄16 in. (30.3 × 22.7 cm)

The theme of war appears in Nara's other works from around this period as well, which demonstrates the enduring impact of the experience on his creative practice. The trip prompted him to revisit the histories of wars that had impacted his life, including the bombing of Hiroshima and the Vietnam War, which had fascinated him when he was young, influenced in particular by the famous 1967 image of a demonstrator placing flowers in the barrels of guns at an antiwar protest outside the Pentagon building in Arlington, Virginia (Fig. 240). Nara reflected on these histories with works that subvert traditional images of war. In *Missing in Action-Girl Meets Boy-* (Fig. 244), made at the time of the sixtieth anniversary of Hiroshima, he depicts in one of the girl's eyes the flames from Little Boy, the atomic bomb that was dropped on the city on August 6, 1945, the first nuclear weapon ever used in warfare. The following year, Nara continued the theme with *Agent Orange* (Fig. 245), a reference to the chemical weapon used by the United States during the Vietnam War. The round, smooth crown of *Agent Orange*'s head evokes the shape of a soldier's helmet, which is painted as if glowing, in an acidic orange, while her large eyes coyly stare at the viewer. The fusion of *kawaii* innocence with symbols associated with violence and modern warfare creates an unsettling sense of threat.

These artworks made between 2005 and 2006 can also be seen as responses to contemporary events regarding Japan's national security: the debates concerning the sustainability of the United States' military presence in Japan and the prospect of acquiring nuclear weapons for self-defense. After many years of tense relationships with the local community, an agreement was drawn up in 2006 to relocate the contentious Futenma Air Base from the city of Ginowan. However, this quickly turned into a political maelstrom when the incoming prime minister, Yukio Hatoyama, decided to shelve the plans. One of the major issues raised by the debates was the increasing cost of Japan's military spending. Adding fuel to that concern was Japan's role in the Middle East—in response to the escalation of violence in Afghanistan and Iraq, Japan had deployed its Ground Self-Defense Forces (GSDF) to the border between Iraq and Kuwait. Given the conditions of Article 9 of Japan's constitution outlawing the use of force to settle international disputes, this prompted heated arguments regarding the large-scale involvement of the GSDF in the region. In October

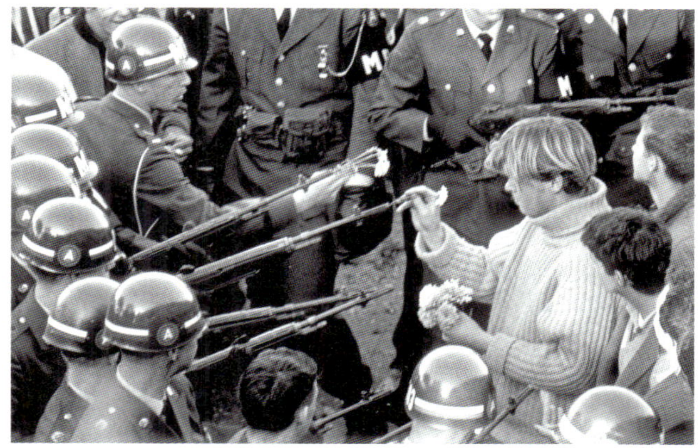

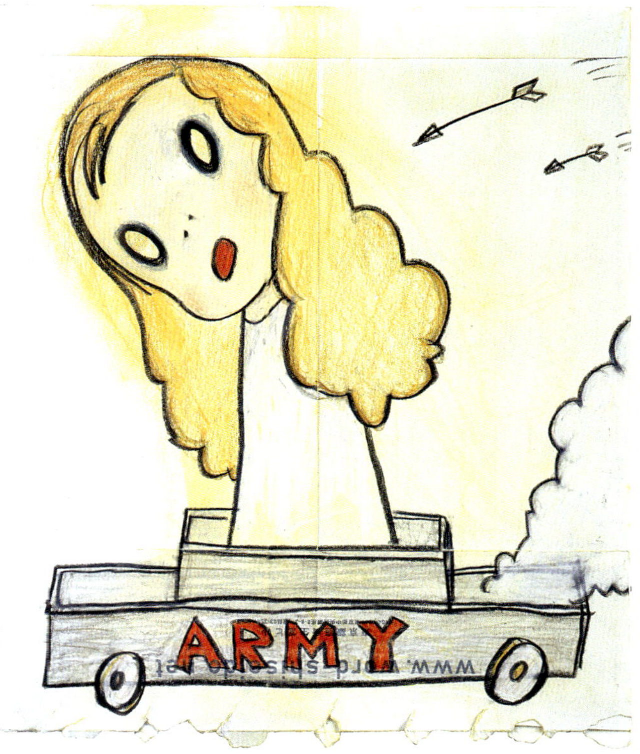

Fig. 240
Bernie Boston, *Flower Power*, 1967

Fig. 241
Untitled, 2003, Colored pencil on paper, 12 ¹⁵⁄₁₆ × 10 ⅝ in. (32.9 × 27 cm)

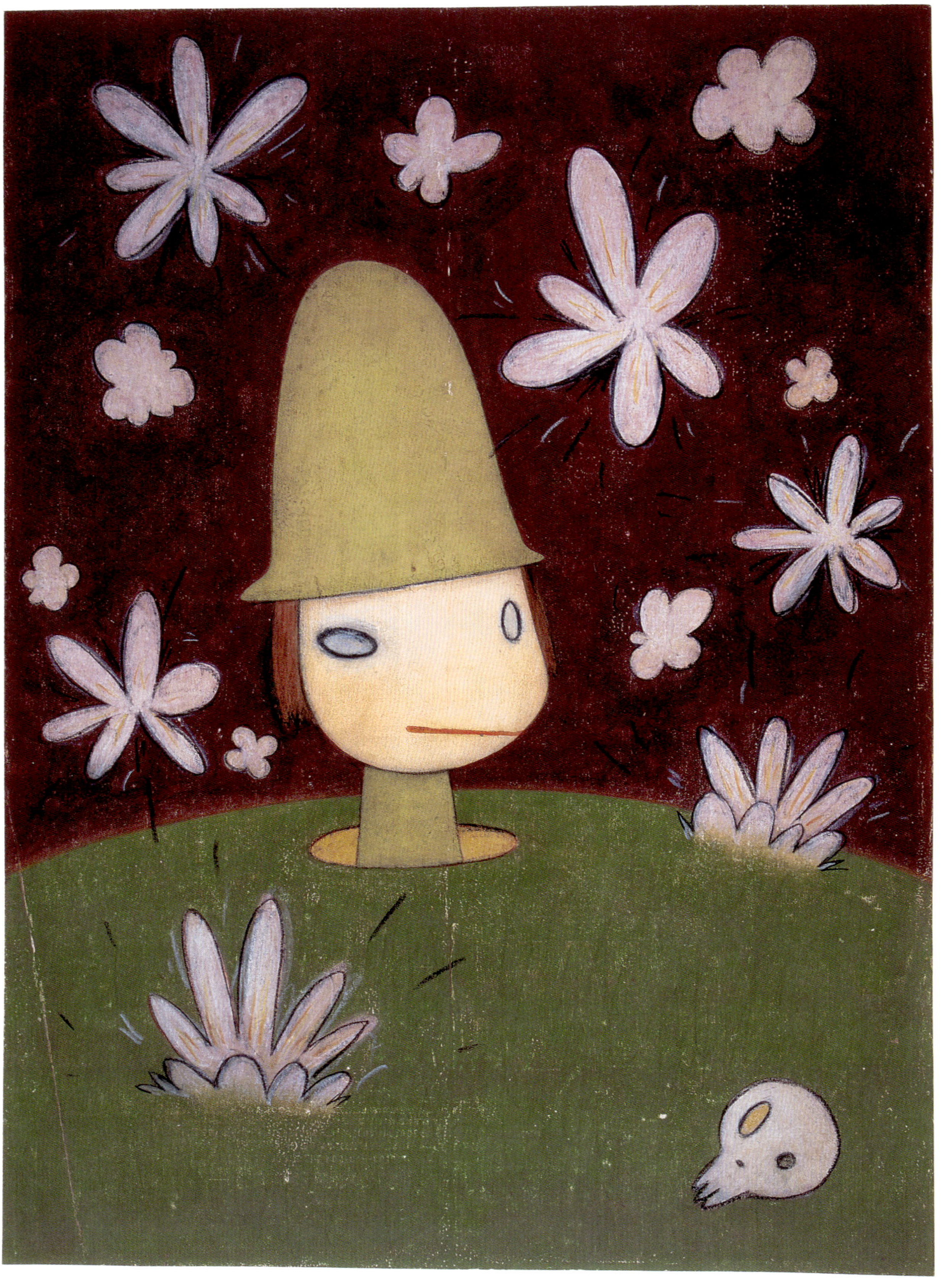

Fig. 242
Soldier, 2003, Acrylic and colored pencil on paper, 29 15⁄16 × 22 1⁄16 in. (76 × 56 cm)

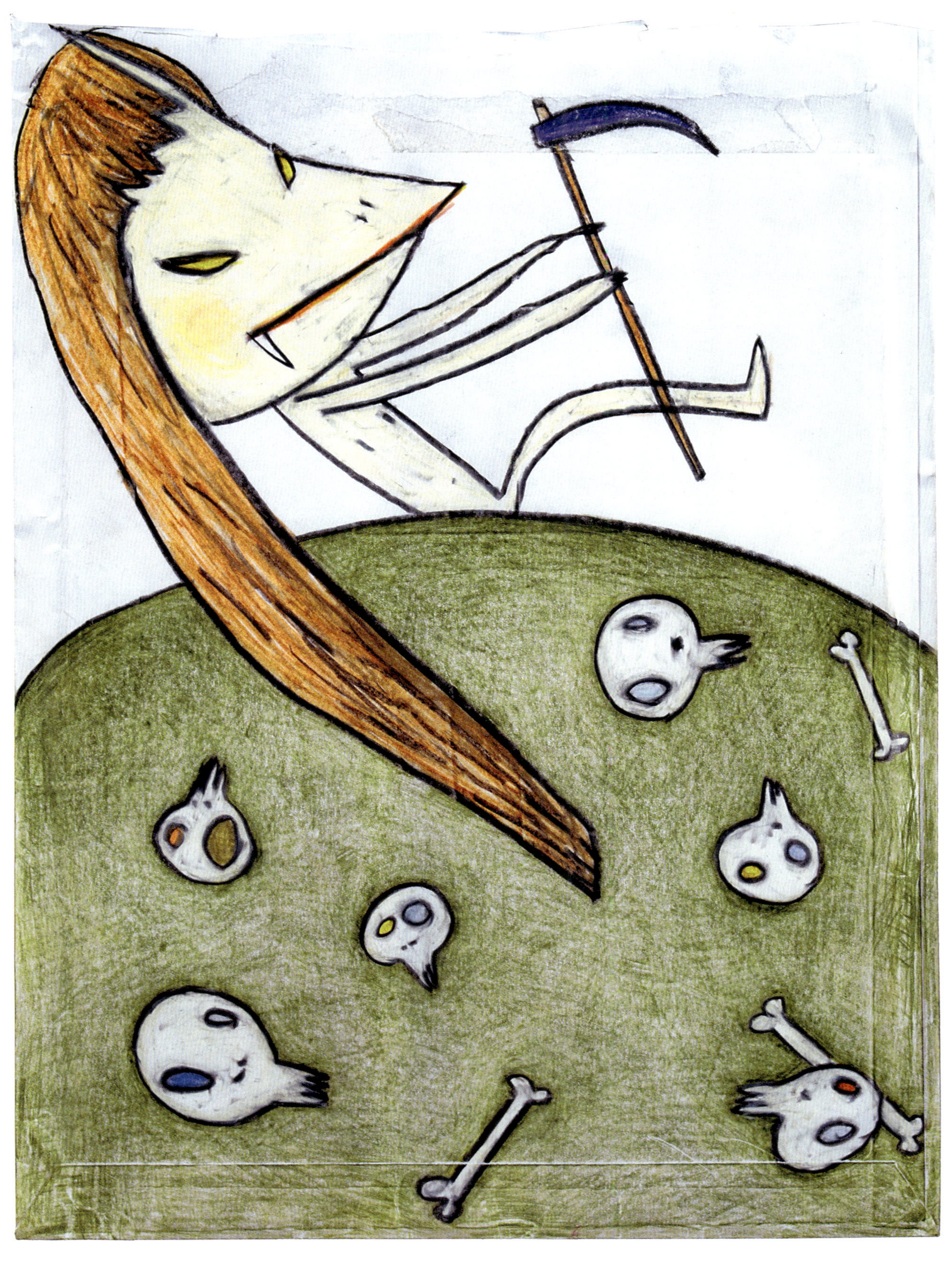

Fig. 243
Live Skulls, 2003, Colored pencil on paper, 12 15/16 × 9 7/16 in. (32.8 × 24 cm)

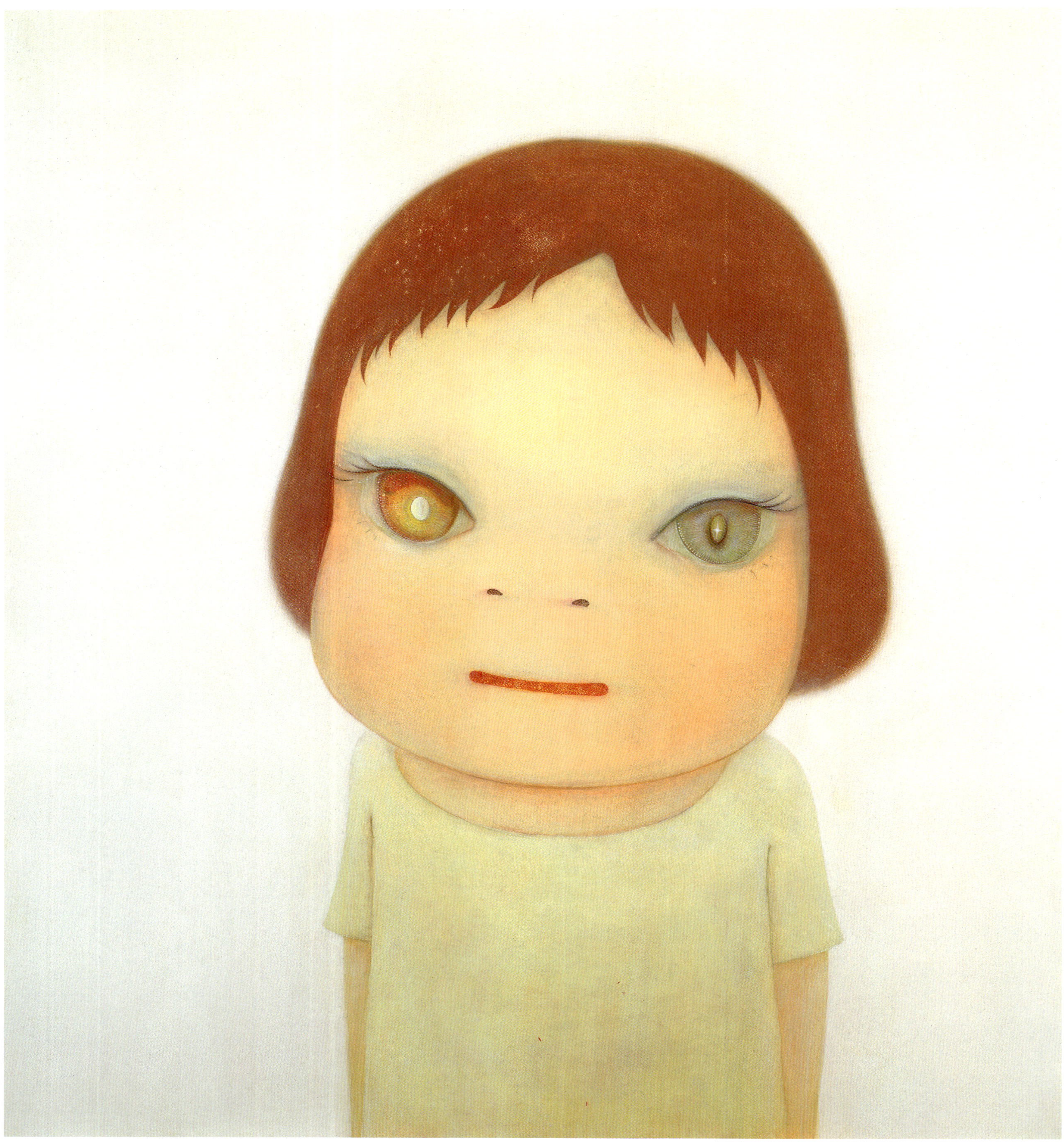

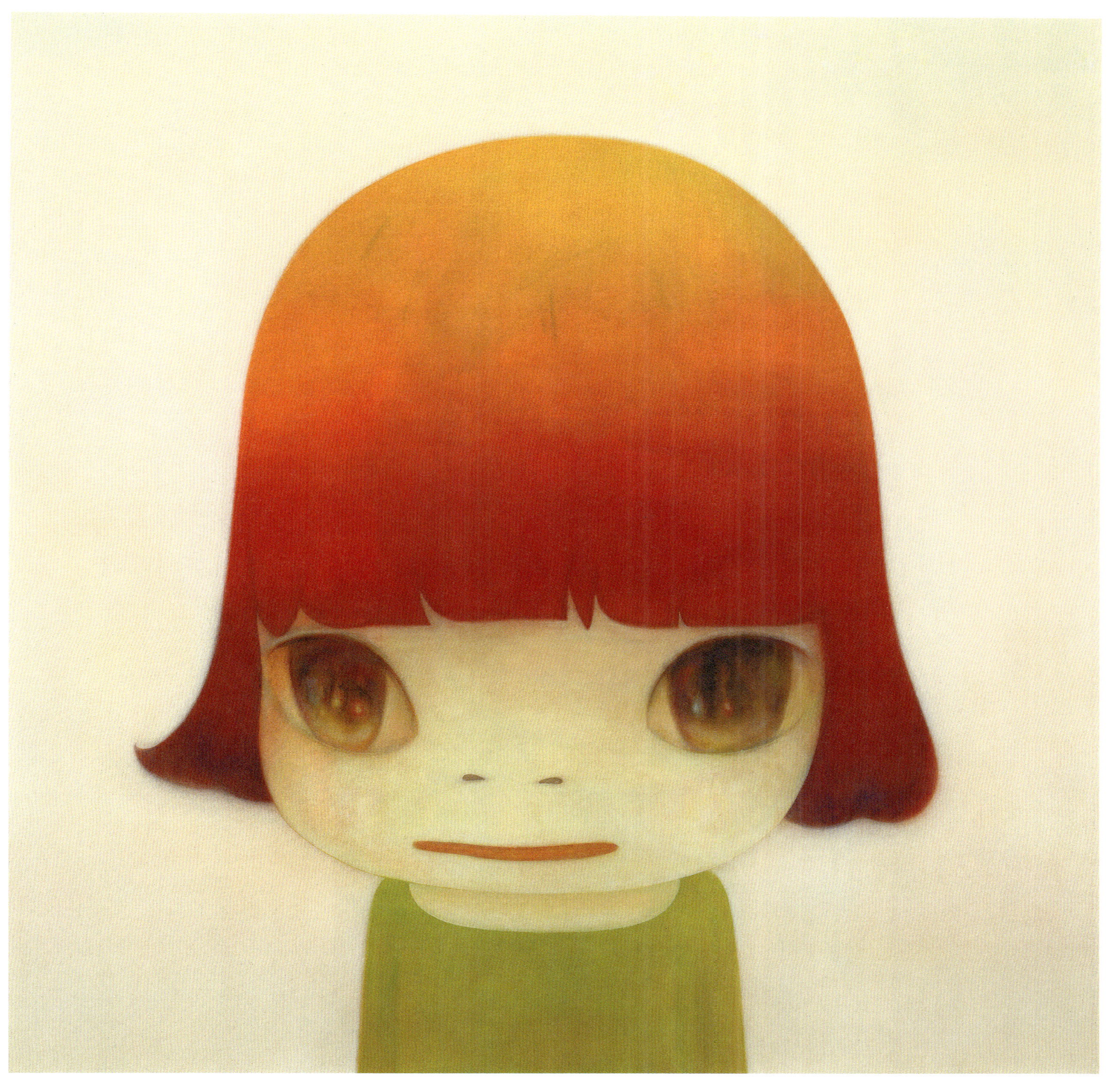

Fig. 244 (opposite)
Missing in Action–Girl Meets Boy–, 2005, Acrylic, colored pencil, and watercolor on paper, 59 1⁄16 × 53 15⁄16 in. (150 × 137 cm)

Fig. 245
Agent Orange, 2006, Acrylic on canvas, 64 × 64 in. (162.5 × 162.5 cm)

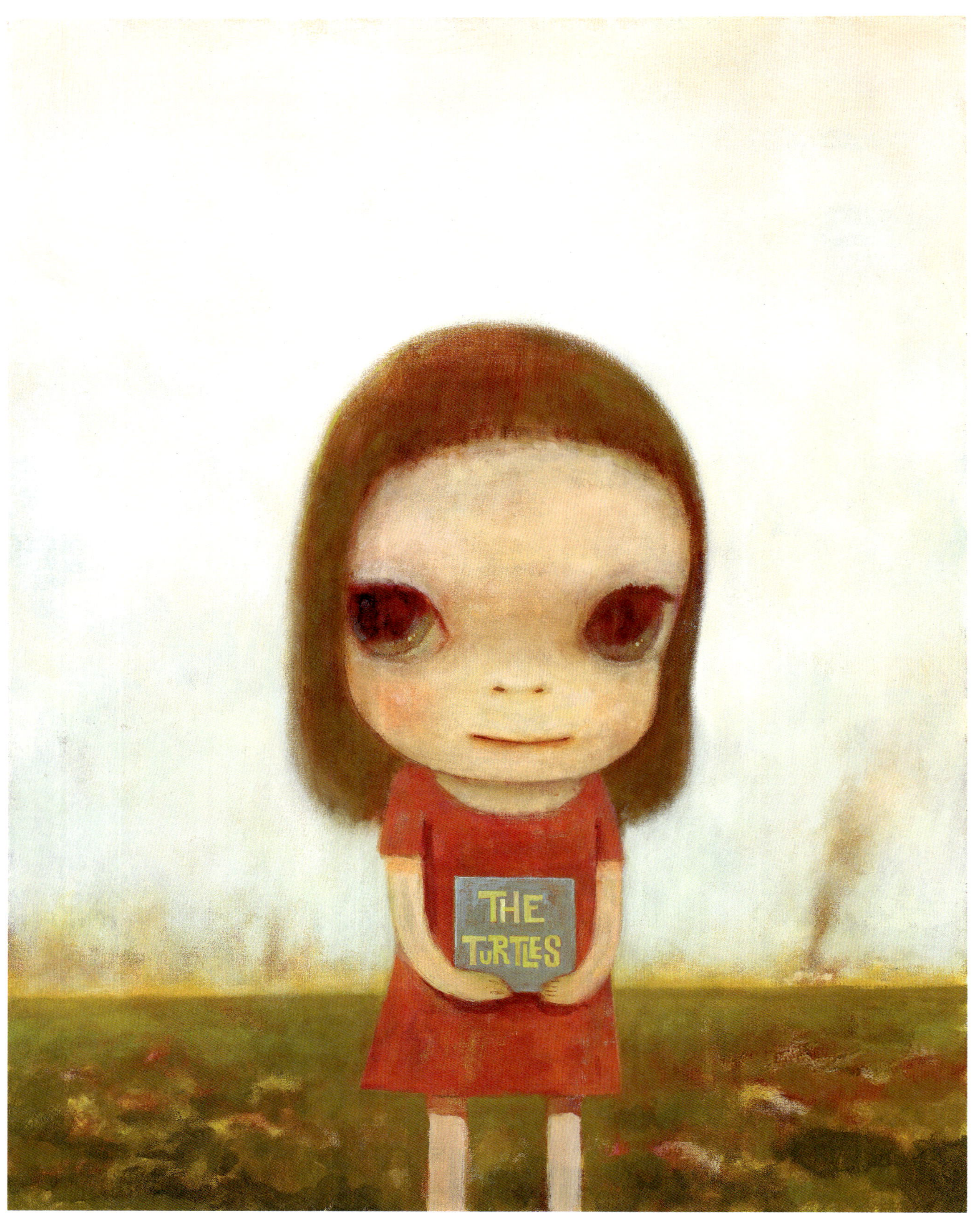

Fig. 246
Eve of Destruction,
2006, Acrylic on canvas,
46 1/16 × 35 13/16 in. (117 × 91 cm)

2006, political tensions reached a high point when North Korea tested a nuclear device in the mountains along the northeast coast of the Sea of Japan. This test raised many concerns, including whether Japan should develop nuclear weapons of its own to counter future threats or continue relying on its alliance with the United States and their joint ballistic-missile defense program.

Another seminal work, which gains greater depth of meaning once contextualized as part of Nara's response to "No War," is *Eve of Destruction* (Fig. 246), a painting he made in 2006 in homage to the 1960s band the Turtles. The title of the painting is a reference to one of the band's hit songs from 1965, a cover of P. F. Sloan's indie-folk protest song about the Vietnam War. Given the period in which this work was painted, Nara's *Eve of Destruction* is more than an homage to one the artist's favorite bands. The girl, with her large eyes and soft smile, proudly displays a Turtles album in her hands. Her countenance suggests that she is unaware of what is to come—the devastation of a war that will, according to the title of the work, begin the next day—but for the viewer, a glimpse of that future is evident: the girl is standing on a patch of grassland filled with debris. Behind her is the blurred horizon of a distant city from which a whirl of smoke drifts up high, as if the city is burning. Whether this is a depiction of the Turtles' song or a historical reflection that provides a lens onto current events, the lyrics remain a powerful anthem against war:

> Don't you understand what I'm trying to say?
> Can't you feel the fears that I'm feeling today?
> If the button is pushed, there's no running away
> There'll be no one to save with the world in a grave
> Take a look around you, boy, it's bound to scare you, boy
> And you tell me over and over and over again my friend
> Ah, you don't believe we're on the eve of destruction

In 2014 Nara began another photographic project for the Watari Museum of Contemporary Art (Fig. 247).[12] It was undertaken after the 2011 Great East Japan Earthquake and Fukushima Disaster, events that had an enormous impact on Nara, who, after 2011, took on several projects related to his northern roots. As part of this return to his origins, he began to explore areas around Hokkaido, including Sakhalin, a remote

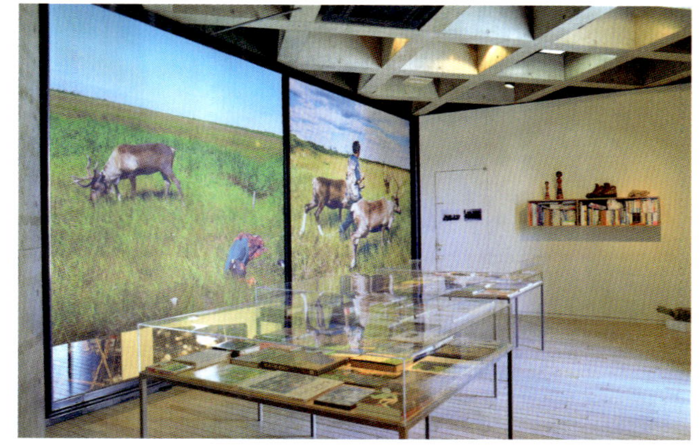

Fig. 247
Exhibition view: *to the north, from here: Naoki Ishikawa + Yoshitomo Nara*, Watari-um: The Watari Museum of Contemporary Art, Tokyo, 2015

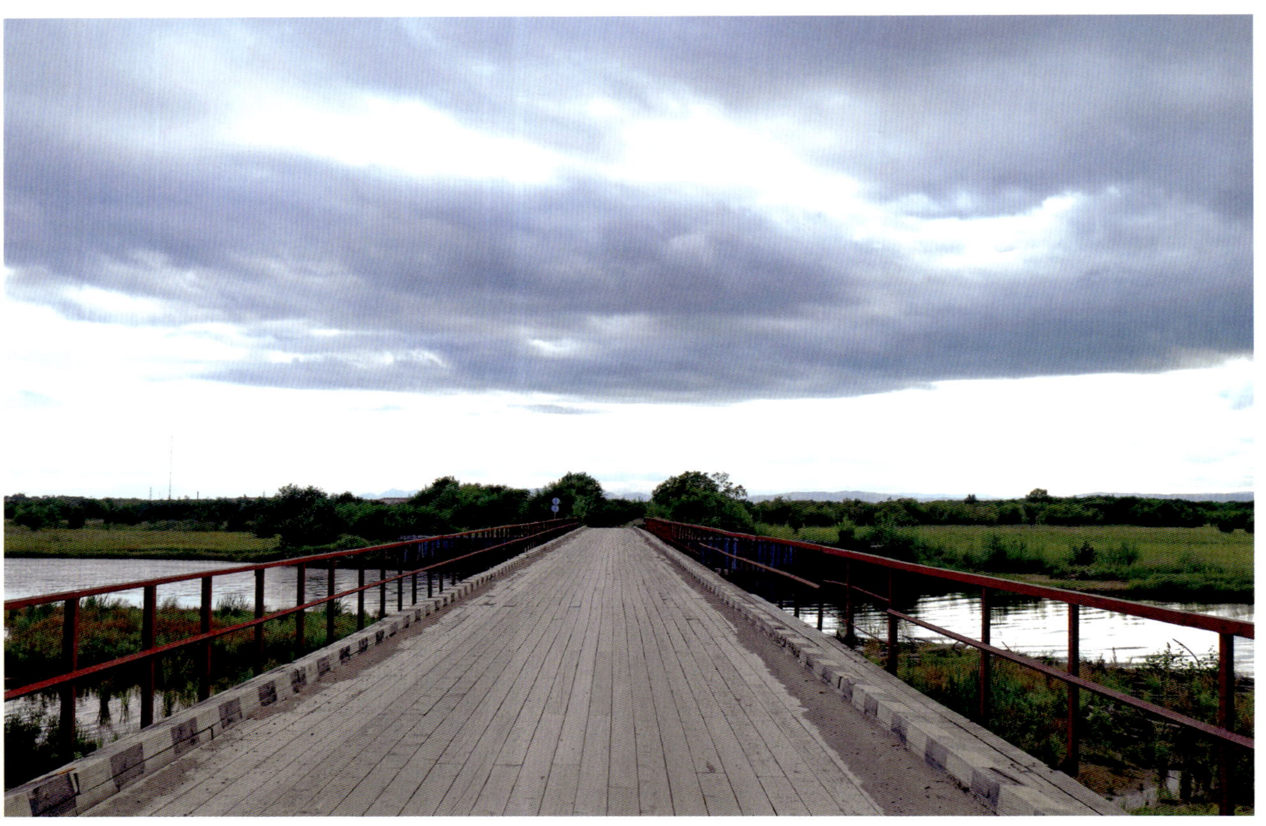

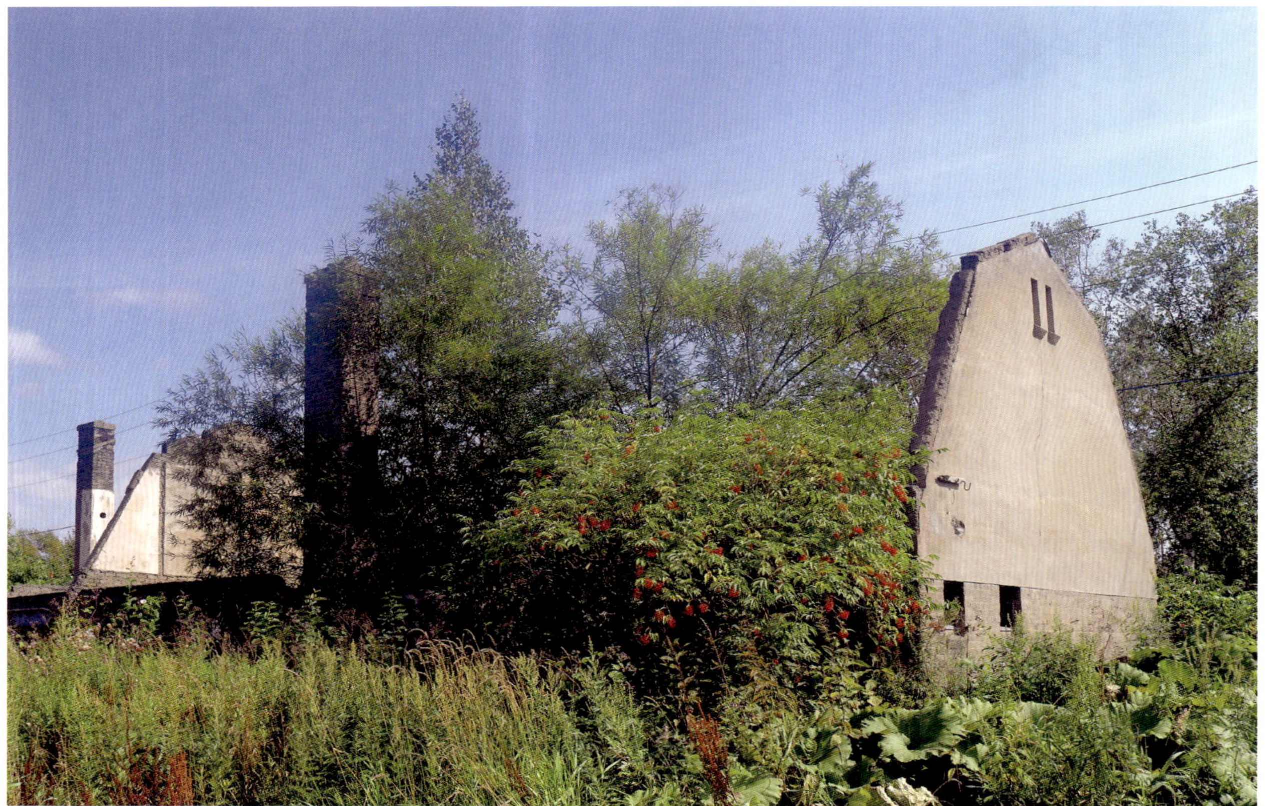

Figs. 248 and 249
SAKHALIN, 2014

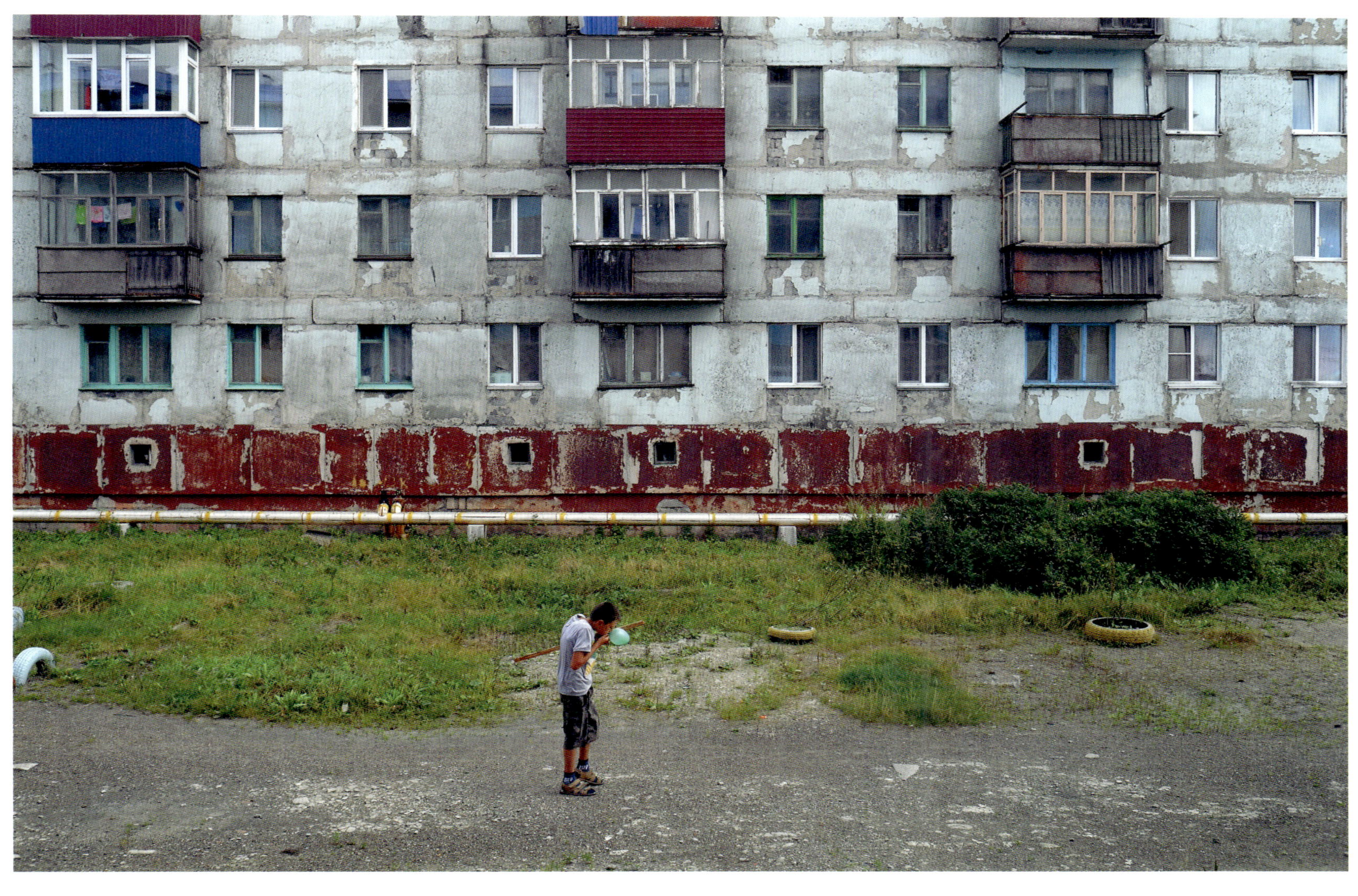

Fig. 250
SAKHALIN, 2014

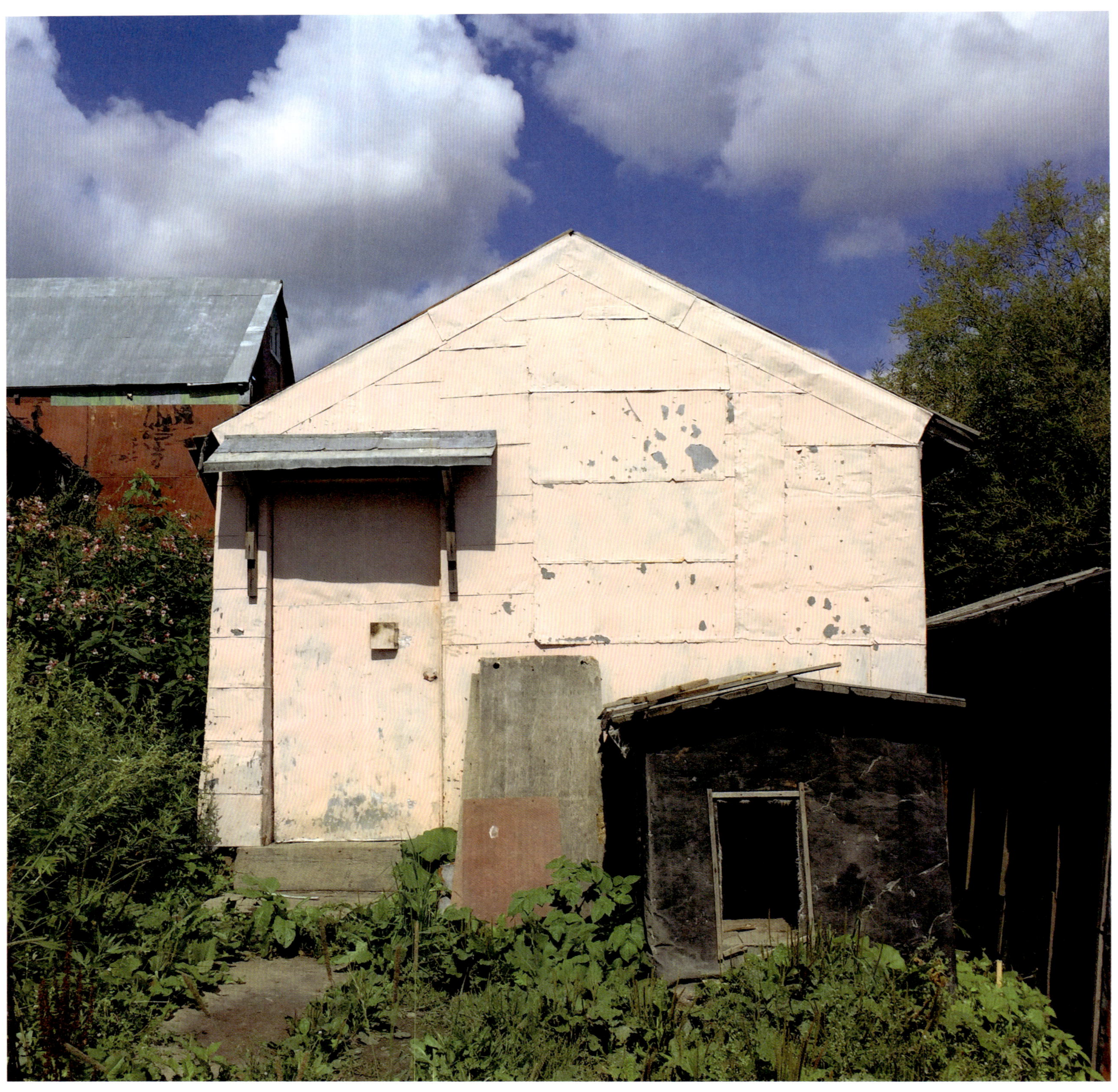

Fig. 251
SAKHALIN, 2014

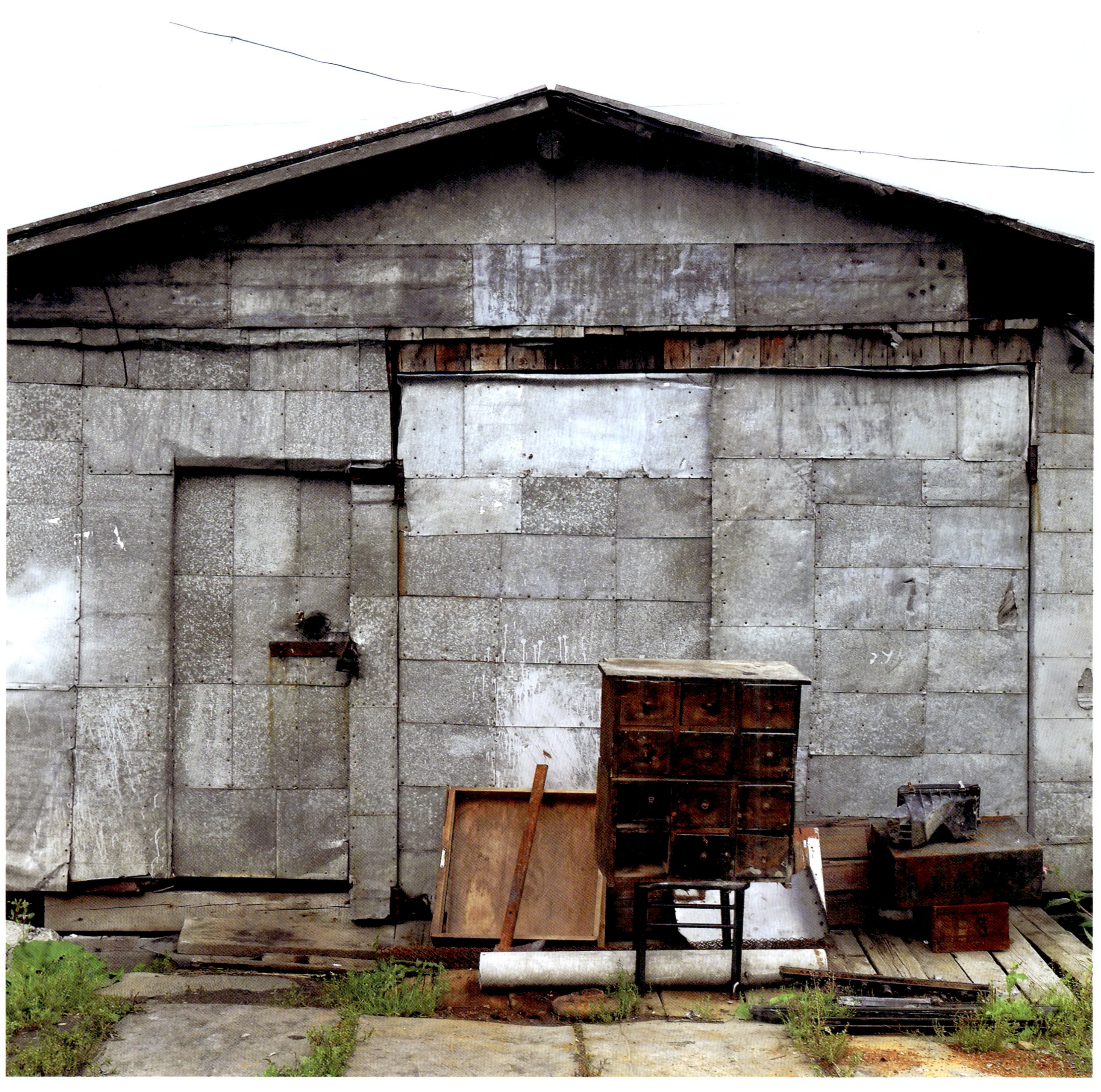

Fig. 252
SAKHALIN, 2014

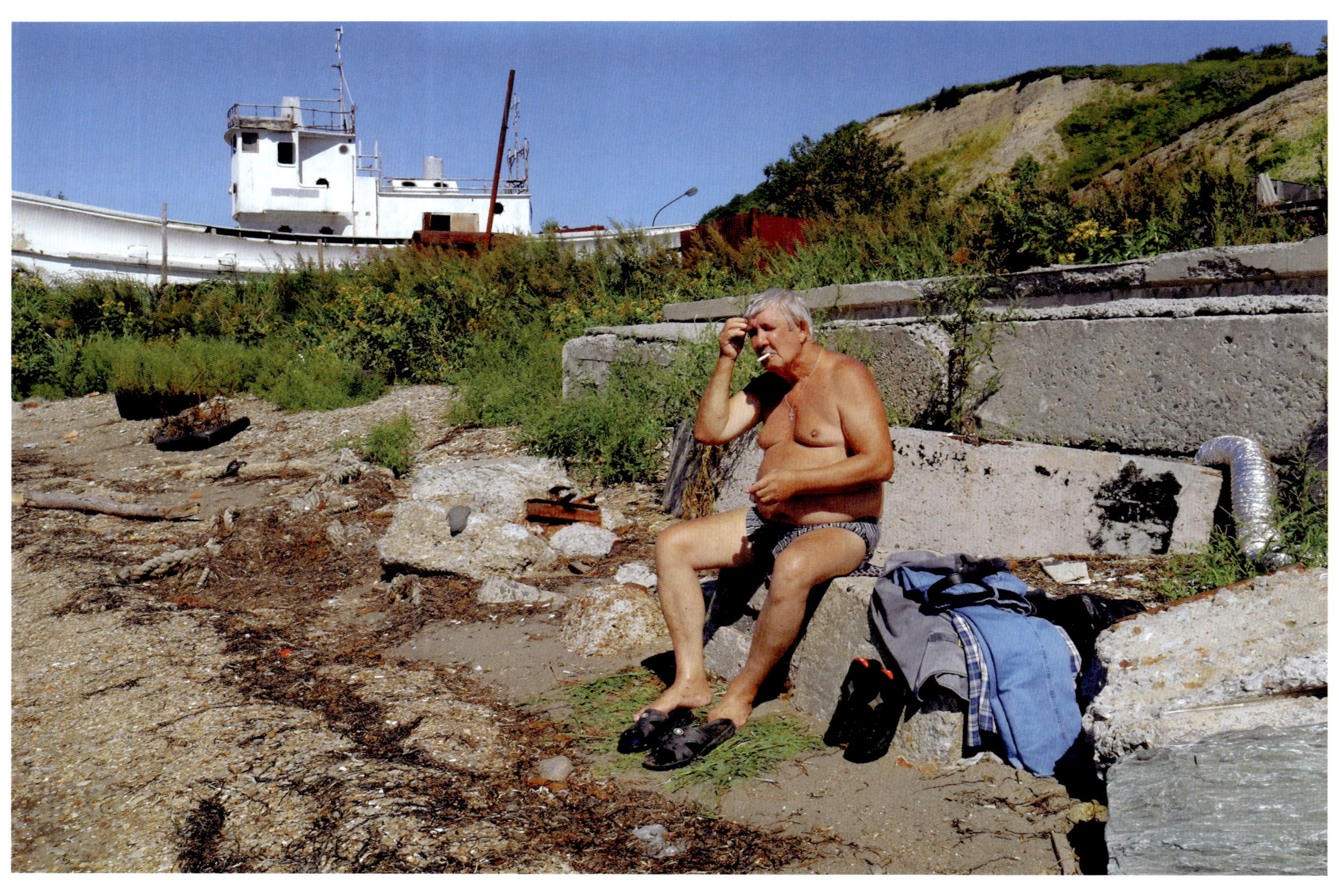

Fig. 253
SAKHALIN, 2014

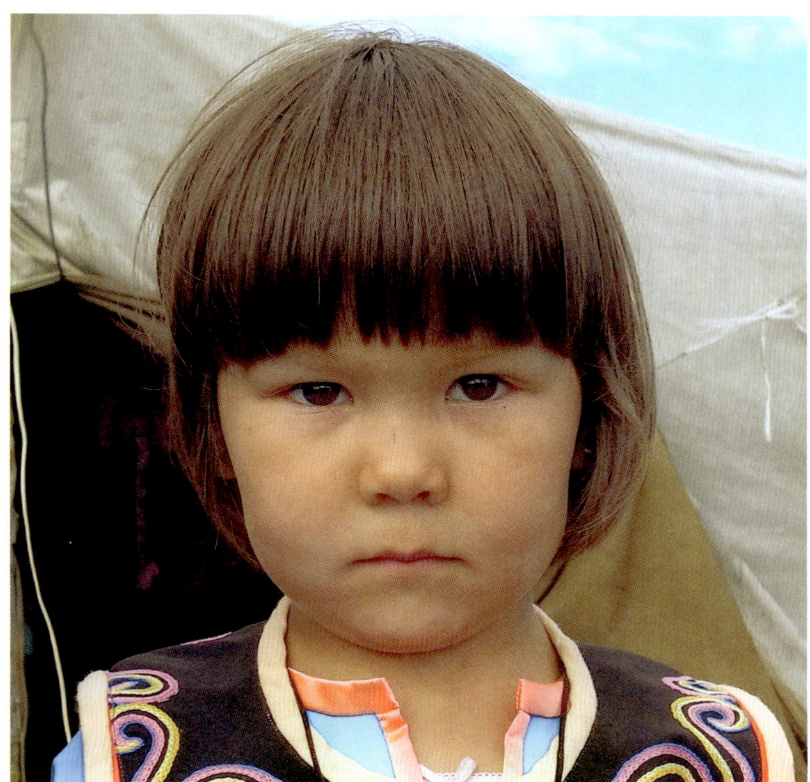

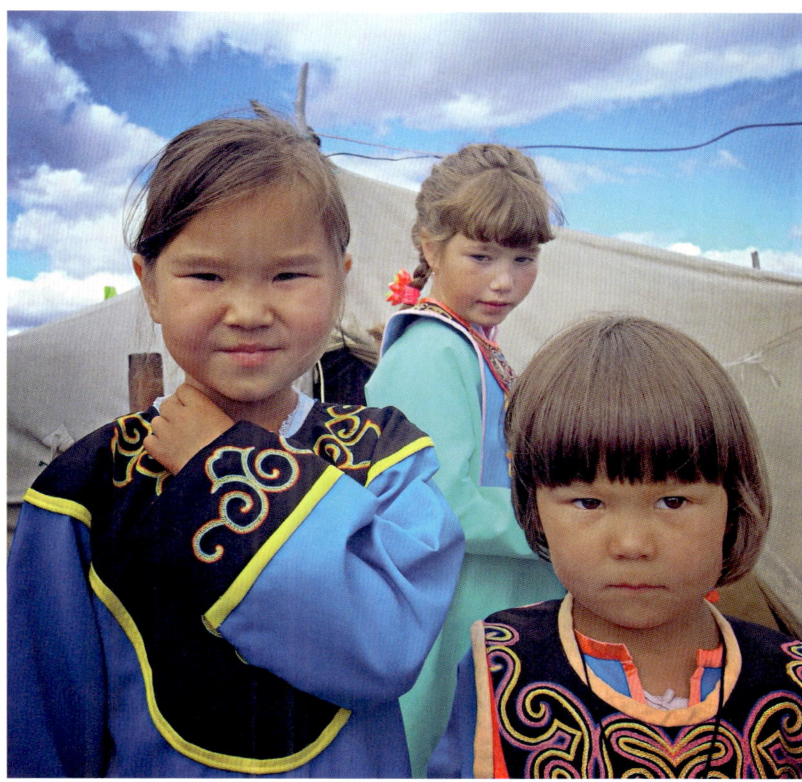

island north of Japan and south of Russia with a fragmented history of belonging to both. It is also where Nara's maternal grandfather once worked as a fisherman, and this project gave him a chance to trace a part of his heritage. Together with Naoki Ishikawa, a photographer, scholar, and explorer, Nara took the long journey to the place that Anton Chekhov, at the end of the nineteenth century, famously called "the land of intolerable suffering."[13]

Over the past two centuries, Sakhalin has seen many transformations. In the late 1800s, it was a Russian penal camp; in 1905 the southern part of the island was colonized by Japan and became Karafuto prefecture. During the forty years of Japanese colonial rule, a rail network was built to help with the extraction of local resources for the production of paper and charcoal. The Japanese government provided tax incentives as a way of attracting the necessary labor force for these expanding industries, and it was during this period that Nara's grandfather lived there. Even after the Soviet conquest of Karafuto in 1945, much of the Japanese community that had settled on the island remained, and since then, while there have been rumblings of territorial disputes, the island has retained a hybrid identity that

Figs. 254 and 255
SAKHALIN, 2014

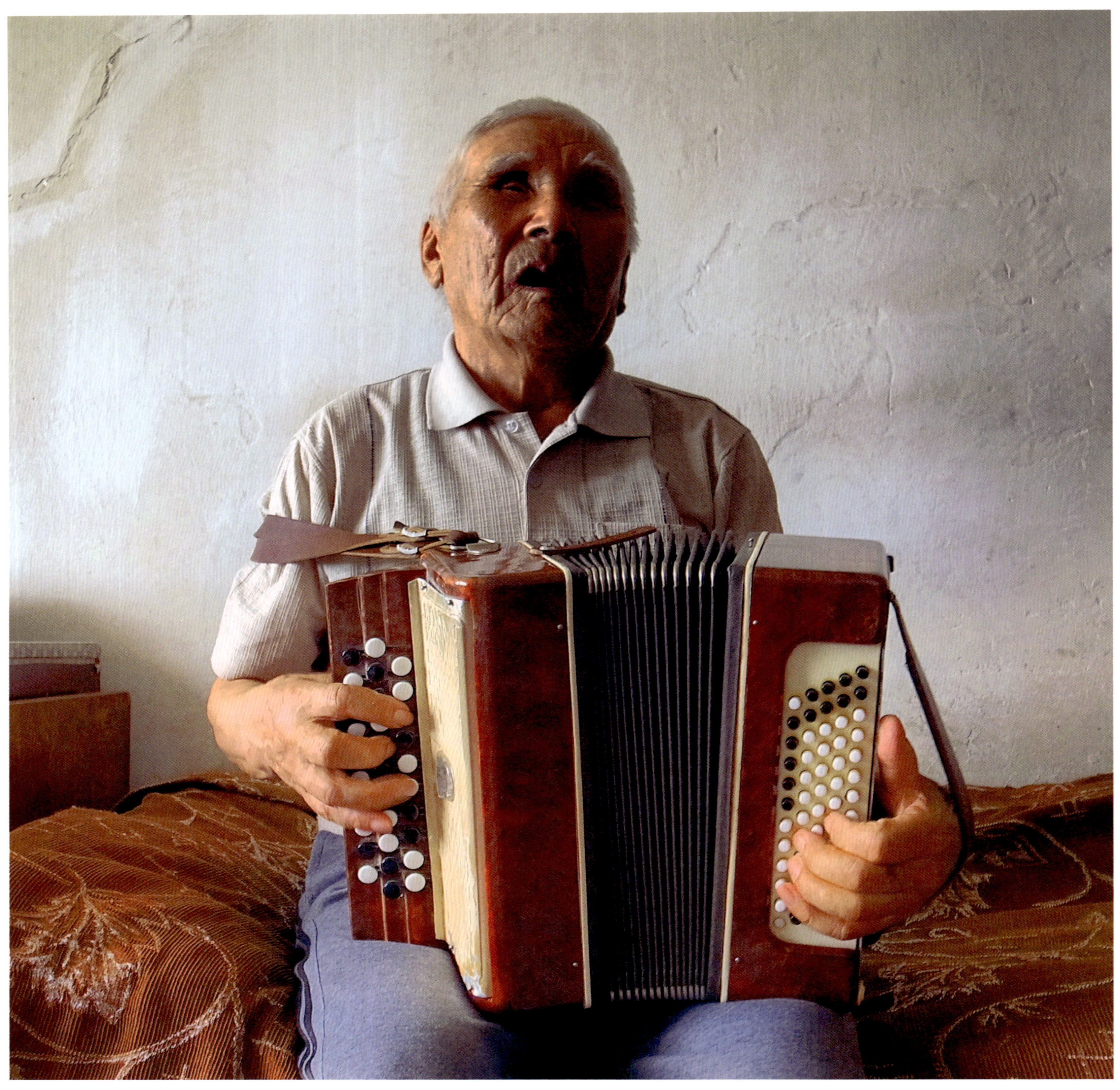

Fig. 256
SAKHALIN, 2014

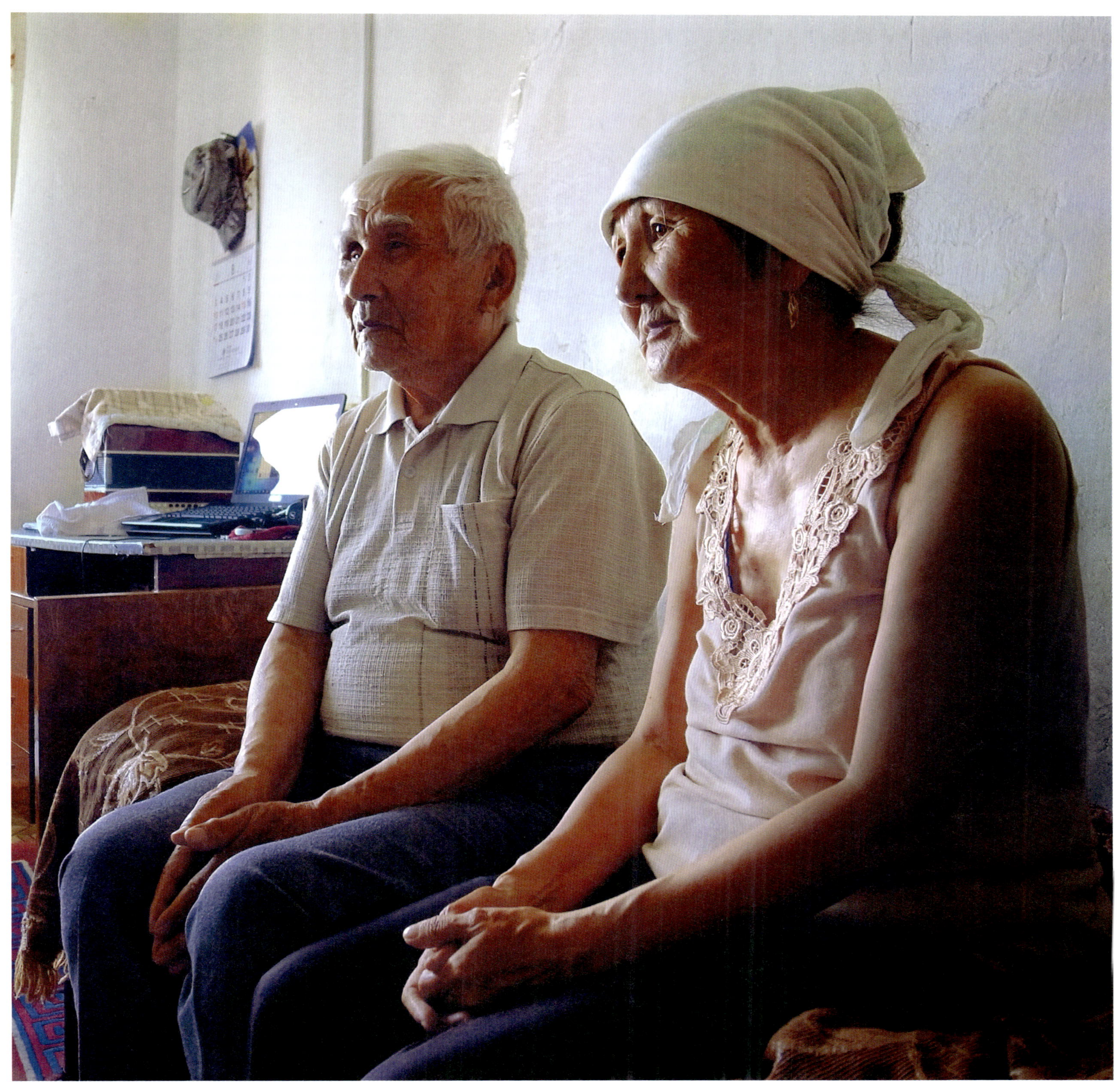

Fig. 257
SAKHALIN, 2C14

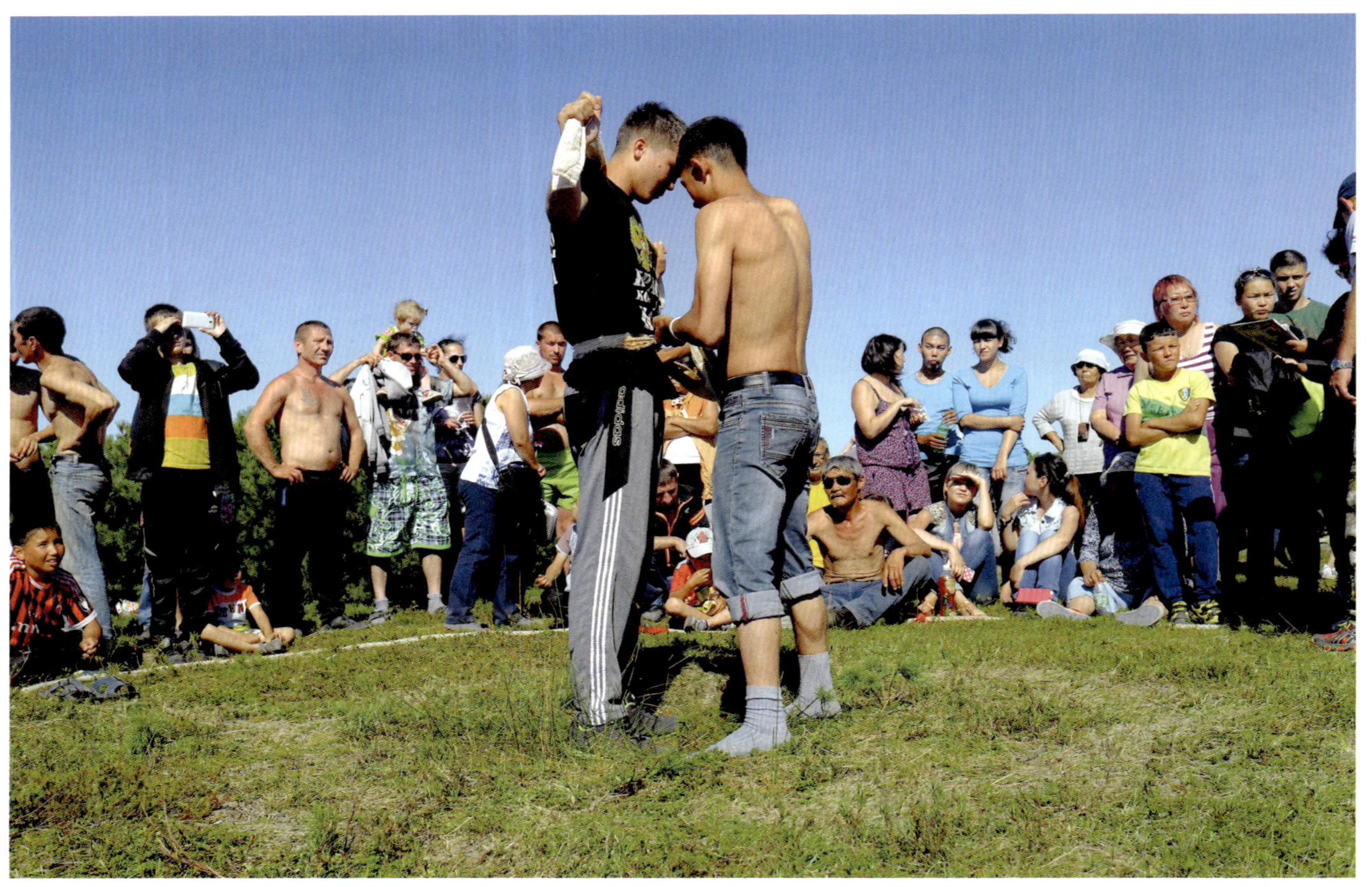

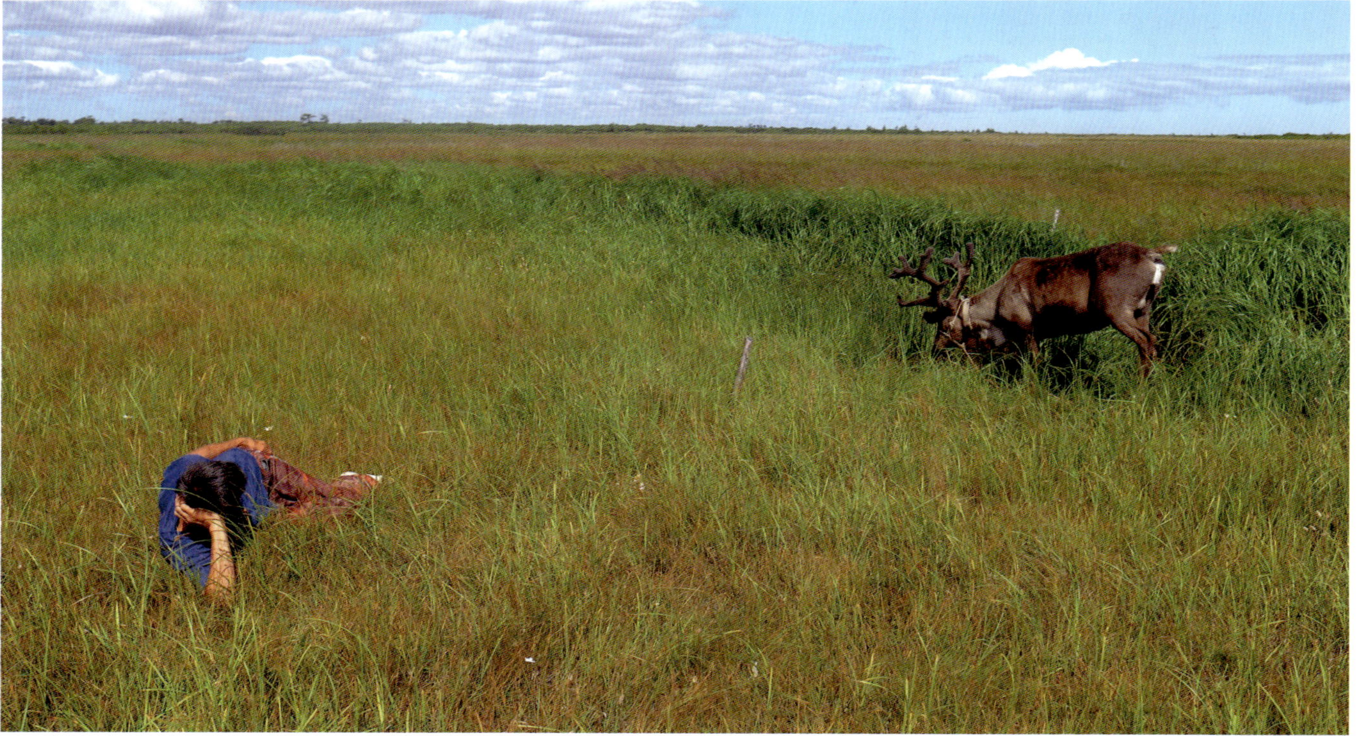

Figs. 258 and 259
SAKHALIN, 2014

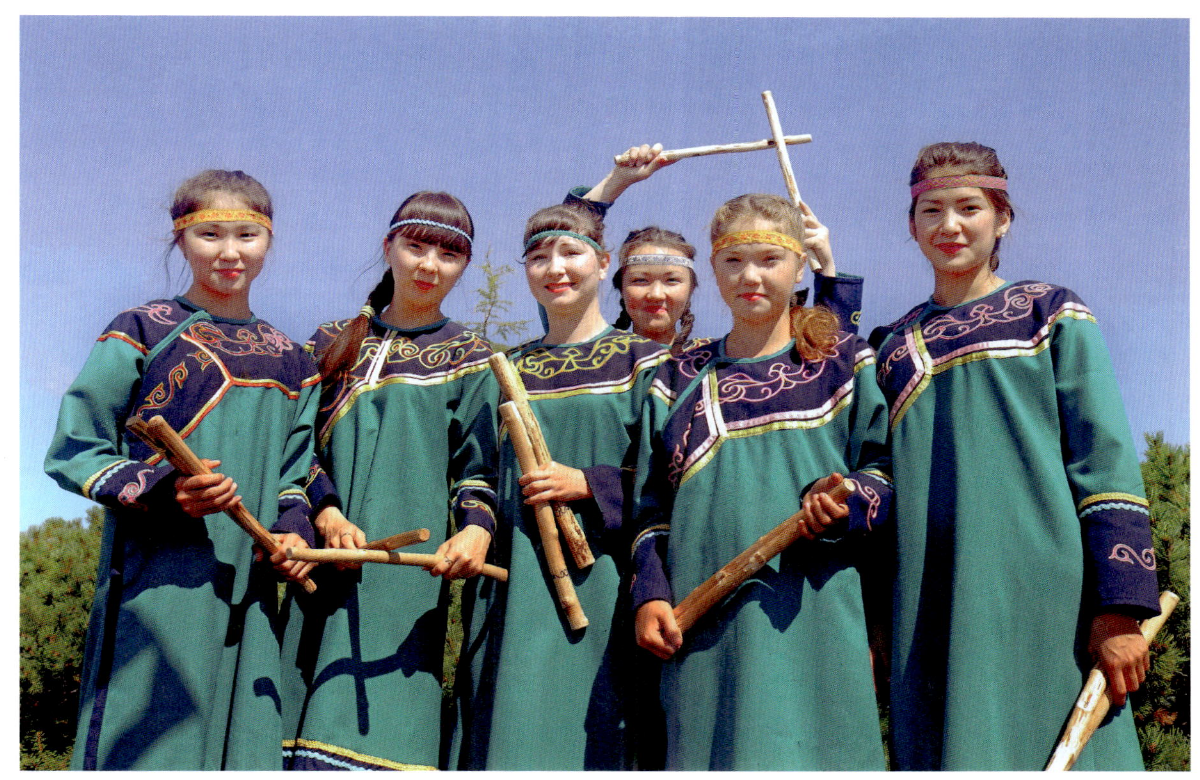

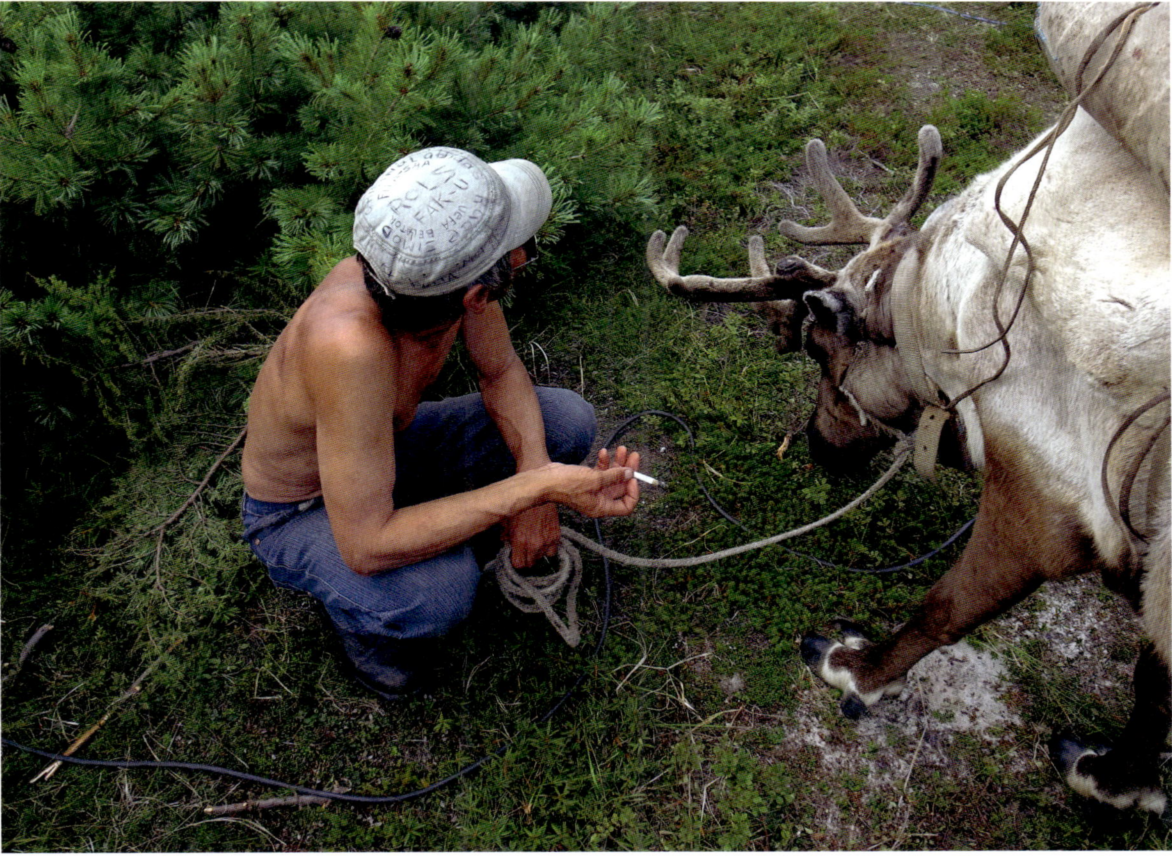

Figs. 260 and 261
***SAKHALIN*, 2014**

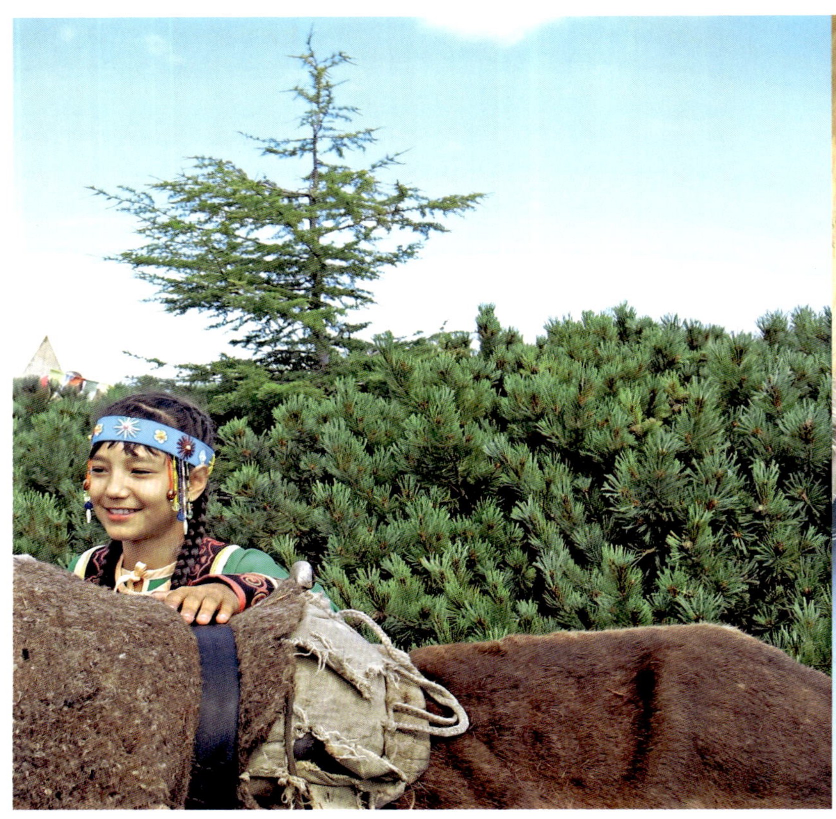

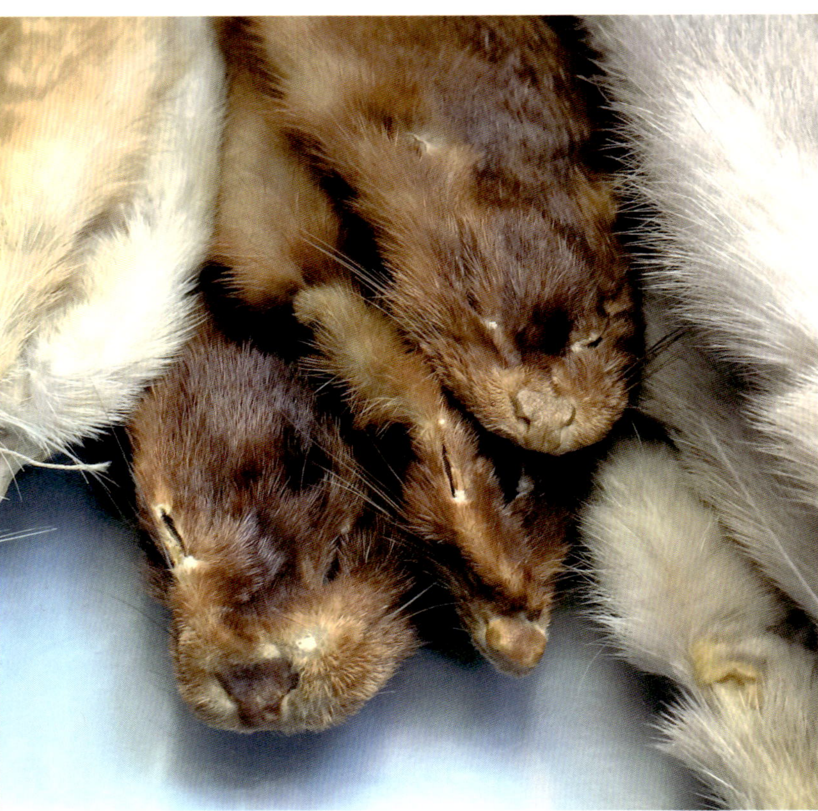

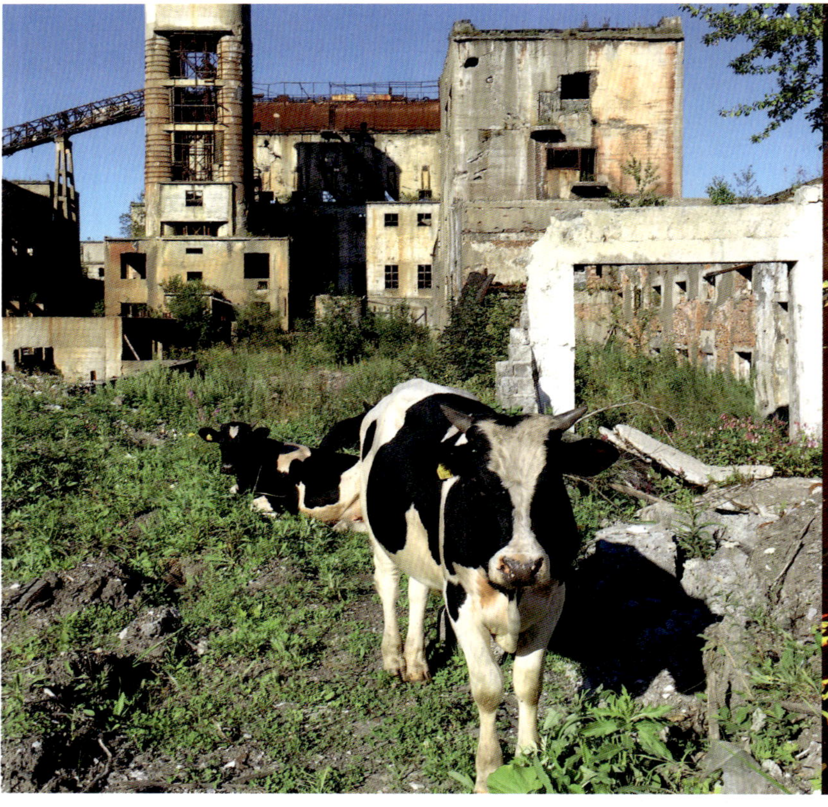

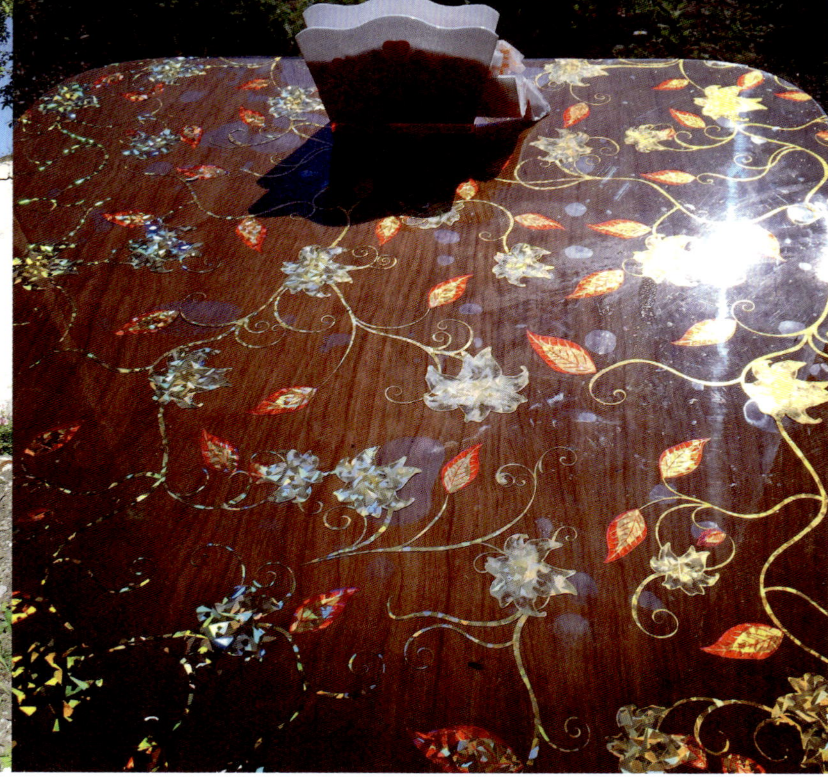

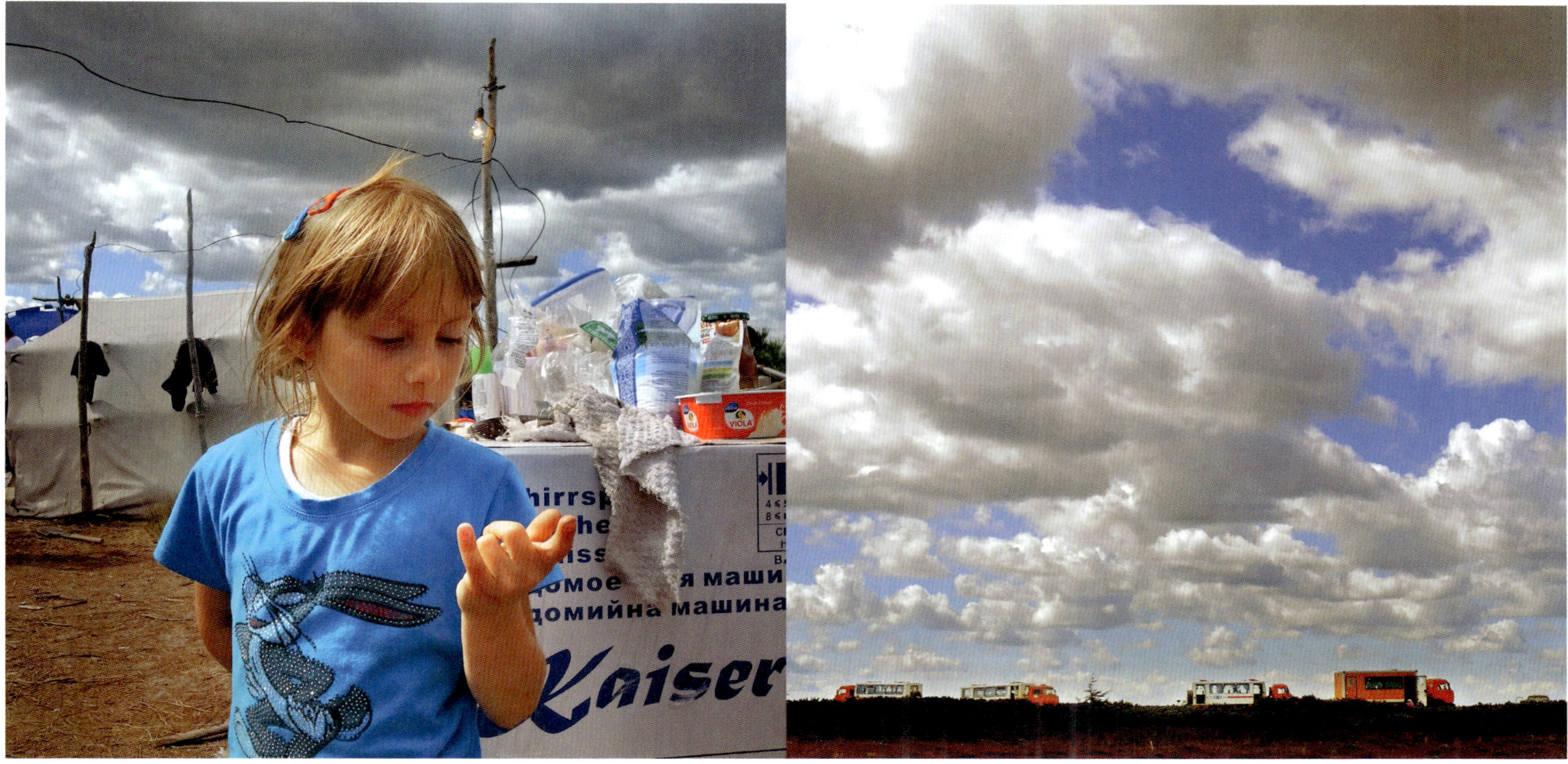

embraces the cultural histories of both countries. As is typical of those who live on the margins, they cannot be defined by either one alone.[14]

At first glance, Sakhalin appears distinctly Russian, with a gridded plan and Soviet-era concrete blocks, but beyond its urban structures, it remains a wild country: over 85 percent of its land is covered in fir trees, and bears, reindeer, and salmon are common inhabitants. There is also an underlying presence of the region's Asian roots, in its vegetation, which includes cherry blossoms typical of Japan, and through its celebrations, such as the bear festival, which has roots in Ainu culture. For the Sakhalin project, both artists capture the island's identity—the wilderness, its hybrid culture, and its colonial industrial roots. It is the island's ability to somehow defy being either Japanese or Russian that lies at the heart of their work.

Nara's portraits are his most striking works from this series. His photograph of an old man playing the accordion on his bed is not just intimate—we can almost hear his yearning lullaby, immersed in the tune of an old Japanese folk song (Fig. 256). There is also the portrait of a sulky young Nivkh girl staring back at us, her expression reminiscent of many of Nara's paintings of irreverent girls (Fig. 254). We see a man lying

Figs. 262–267
SAKHALIN, 2014

among the tall grass, keeping an eye on his grazing reindeer (Fig. 259); groups of young women inhabiting a range of ethnic identities (Figs. 255 and 260); and young men engaged in local rituals during festival time (Fig. 258). Throughout, Nara emphasizes the importance of the natural world to the daily lives of the Nivkh community, with images of a school of salmon or bloodied antlers discarded on the hills that act as reminders of the importance of hunting in Nivkh culture (Figs. 269 and 270). As with his Afghanistan project, Nara captures how the local community engages with their environment, and he is especially drawn to social customs that capture their hybrid identity. Collectively, the photographs form a diary, one that is deeply personal, connecting Nara to his grandfather through his engagement with the island.

Embarking on this project, Nara and Ishikawa were acutely aware of the dangers of constructing an identity that would essentialize their subjects as "other" to mainland Japan's inhabitants. This tension always exists when photographing a culture as an outsider, and, arguably, it is a necessary component because it alerts viewers to the ethical uncertainties that arise from conducting an ethnographic project. What is at play when you take pictures of women in their native garb? Does it reflect a desire to keep these people caught in a timeless world where their customs remain pristine for visiting outsiders? It is possible to see some of this tension in Nara's photographs, but he also sidesteps the issue by playing with different ways of juxtaposing images, whether in publications or for exhibitions, that are visually interesting side by side, thus disposing of the necessity of a thematic narrative (Figs. 262–267). By presenting his photographs with a more artistically driven eye, he avoids imposing a social reading of a place from the position of a privileged outsider. Nara has stated his position in these terms: when we seek to see from the inside how people lead their lives and what is meaningful to them, we nevertheless remain outsiders and must respect that position.[15] At the same time, the communities and topographical sites at the margins are also under threat. By giving them a visual presence, Nara hopes, their disappearance can be prevented.

Recently, Nara has adopted a new ritual with photography.[16] He has often found himself, after a long and satisfying night of painting, walking toward the large window in his study to look out at the hills

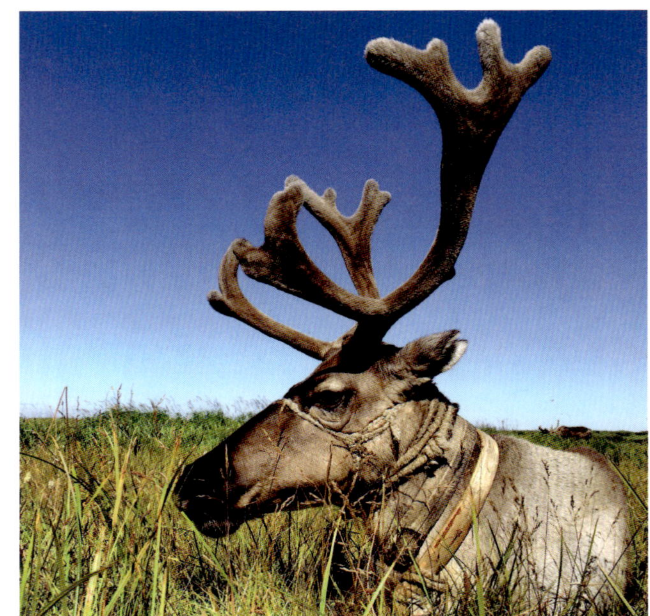

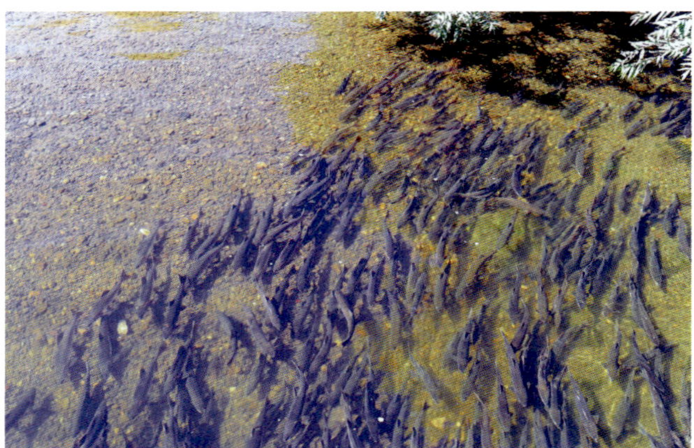

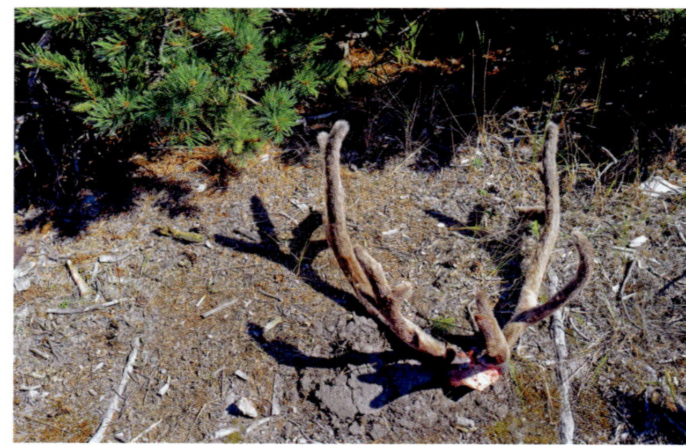

Figs. 268–270
SAKHALIN, 2014

and fields, usually just as the morning light awakens the shapes and forms in front of him: a rare quiet moment when his music is switched off and he is alone. The sense of energy and excitement that he feels after a night of painting makes him see the world differently for a split second, and he takes a photograph to capture the colors of a hazy dawn or dewy mist (Fig. 271). But he only does so when he feels he has accomplished something in the studio—not as a reward but as a ritual practice that allows him to pause from that state of creating, to step back into real life and reflect on the progress of his work. For Nara, as is true for most artists, knowing when to stop is as important as knowing how to start.

Since his Sakhalin project, Nara has expanded his photography practice. He remains drawn to places at the margins, including places associated with Japan's wartime past and its complex colonial history (Figs. 272–277) and remote areas of Hokkaido (Figs. 279–282). He continues to use the medium to connect with children who have been affected by war or disaster, including those from families displaced by the 2011 Fukushima disaster as well as Syrian refugees living in Jordan (Fig. 278). He has also embraced social media as a means of sharing his photographs, uploading new images, rediscovering old ones, and documenting the world around him in order to foster a sense of immediacy with his followers and a connectivity that dissolves the borders between the man and the artist, the artist and the viewer, the photographer and his subject. He revels in these connections, not least because they allow those who are not part of the art world to experience his work. But he is also partial to how images on social-media platforms are transitory, lending themselves to the creation of an open-ended and incomplete identity in a digital realm. This allows him to retain his privacy, which for him is just as important as sharing his work: in the moments between his posts, he allows himself to step back into his art-making mode, to his studio, his home, and his travels to places on the margins, where he can escape the noise of the art world.

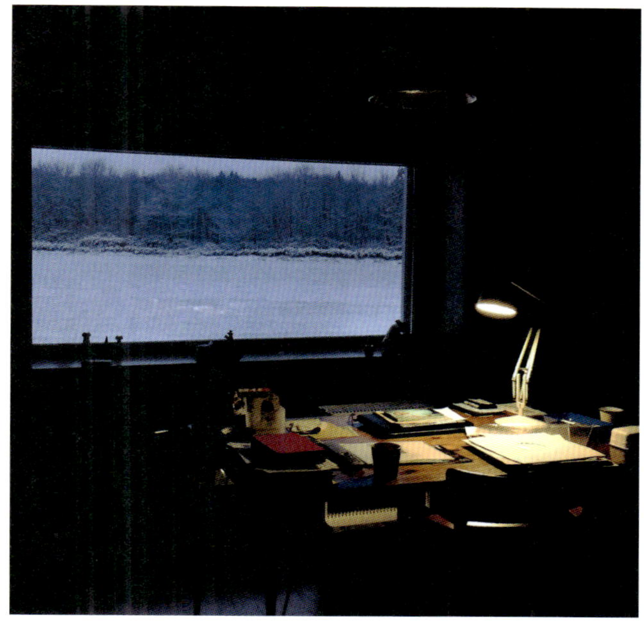

Fig. 271
View from Nara's studio, 2014

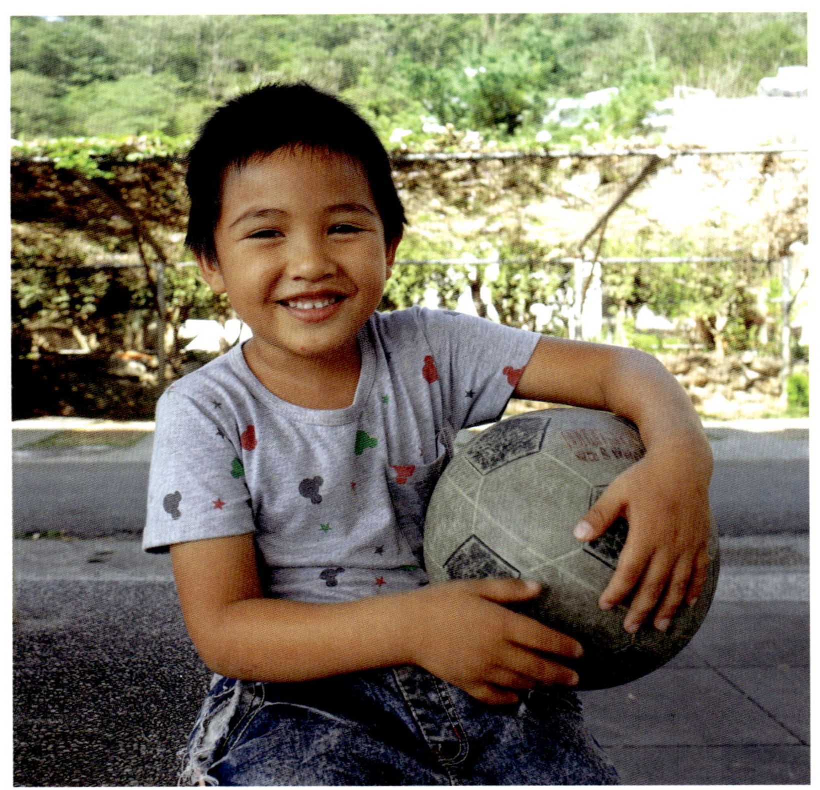
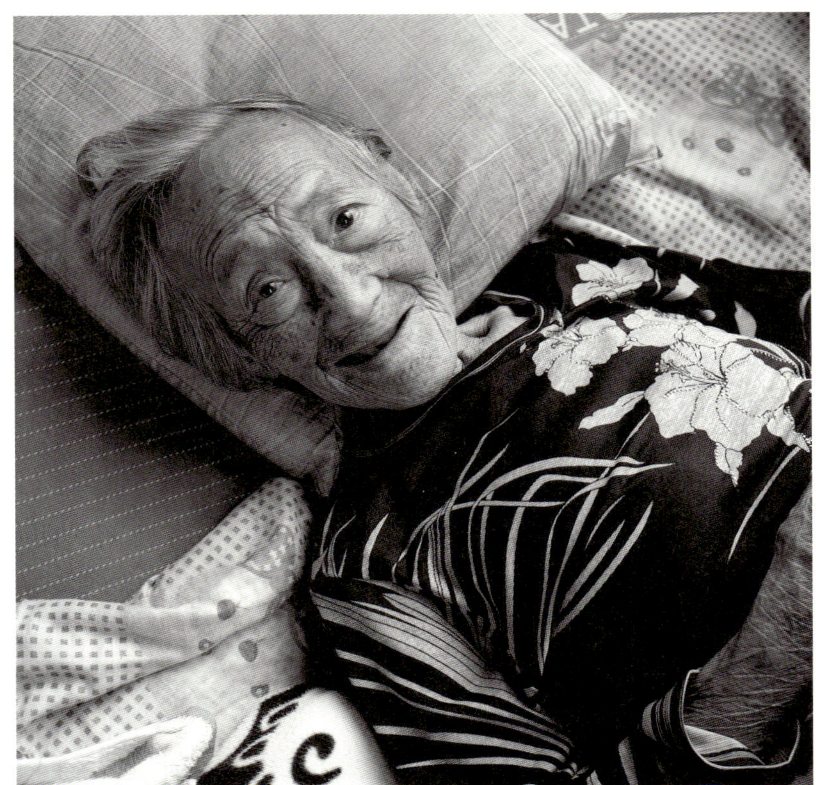
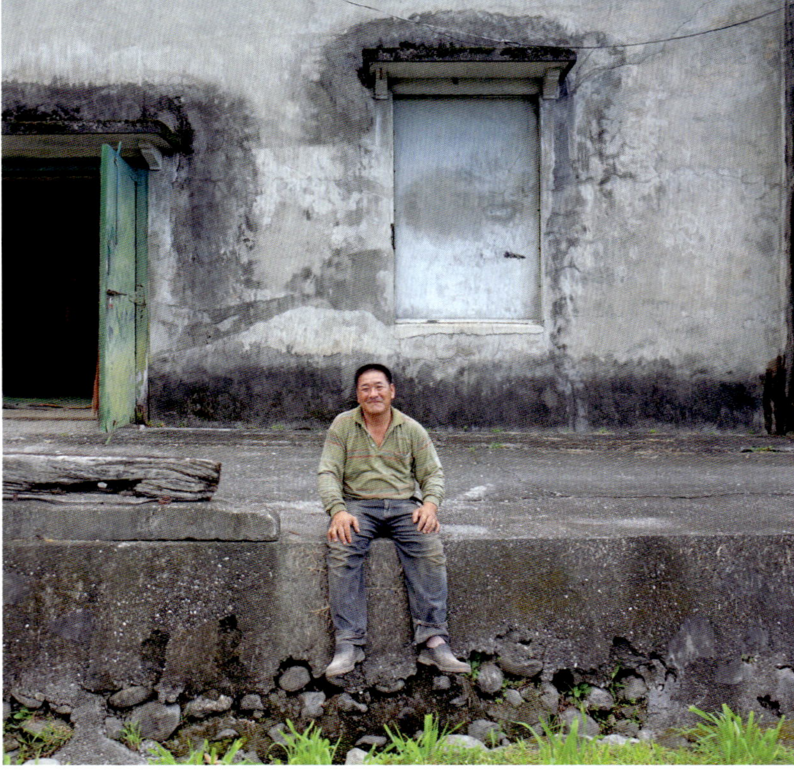
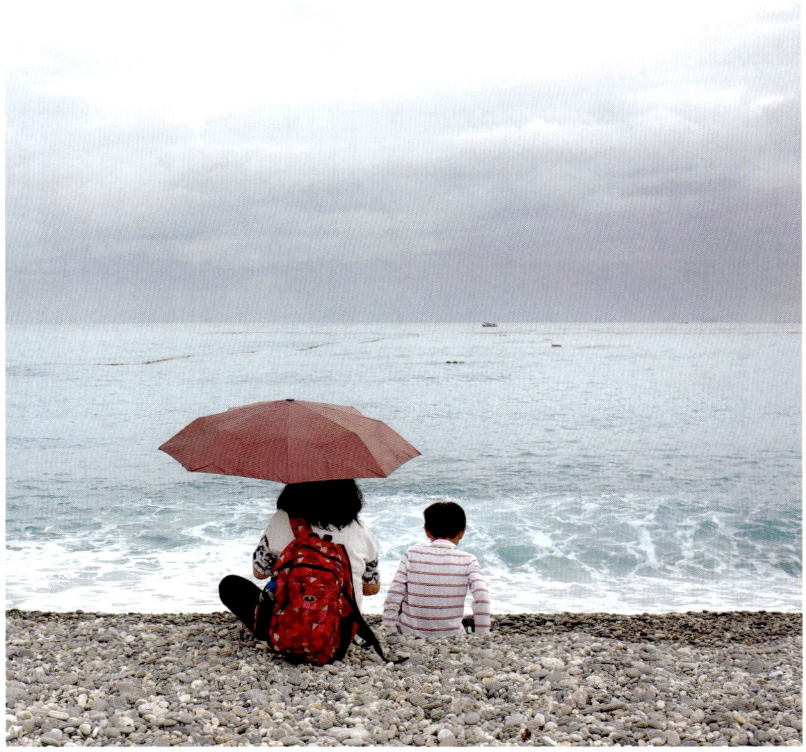

Figs. 272–275
***TAIWAN*, 2016**

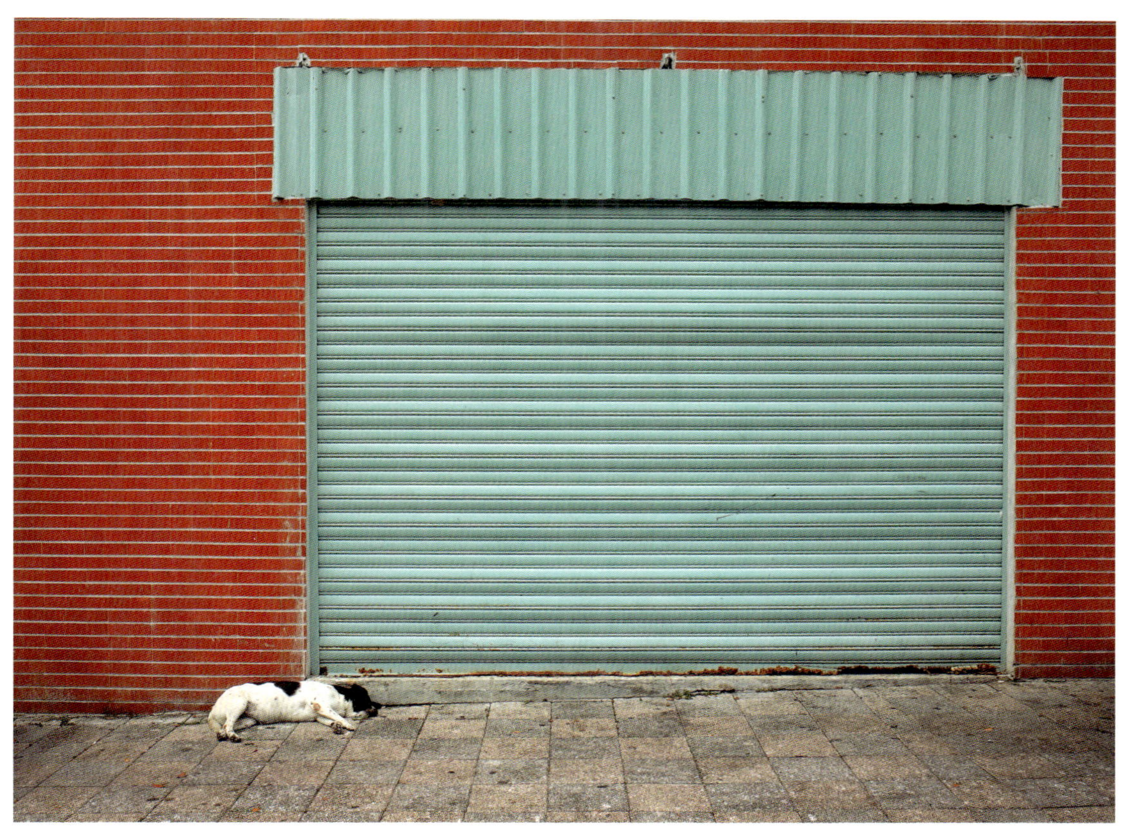

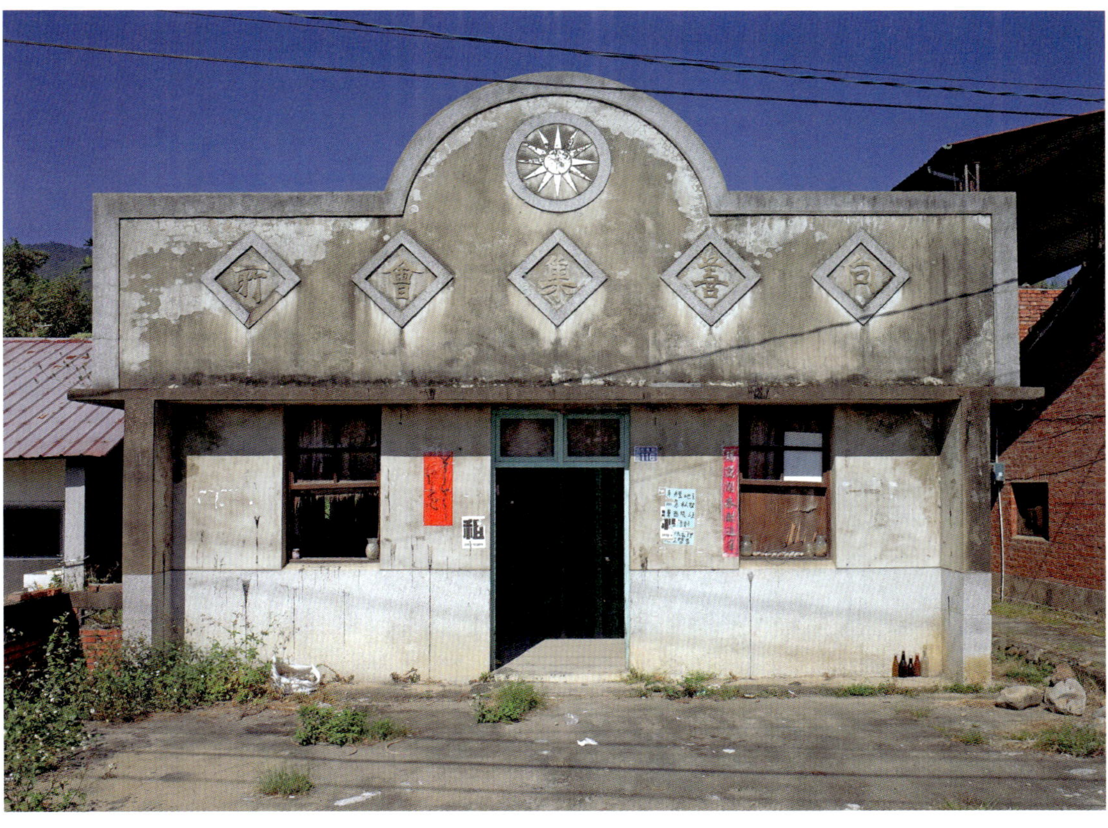

Figs. 276 and 277
TAIWAN, 2016

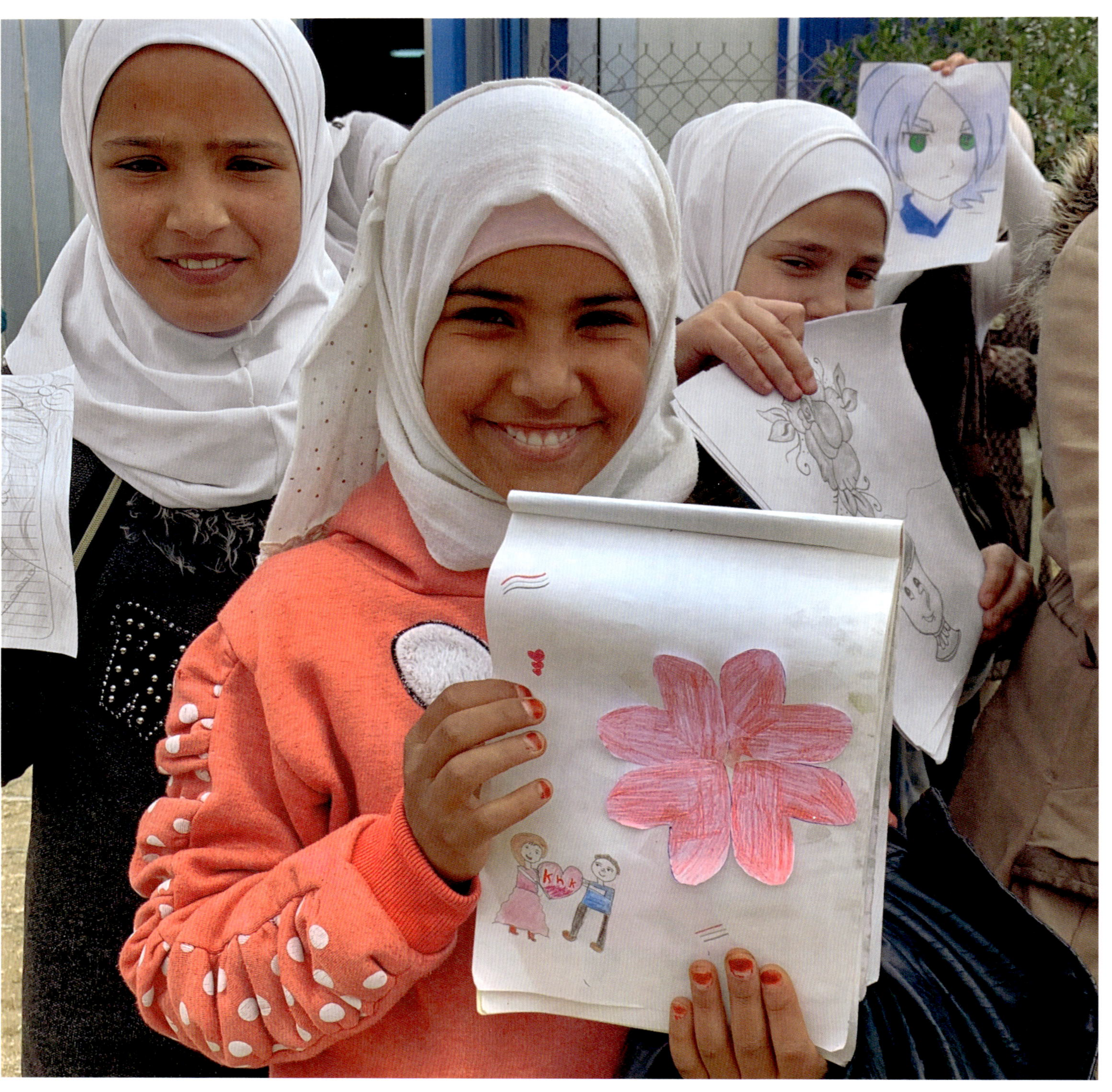

Fig. 278
Zaatari Refugee Camp, Jordan, 2019

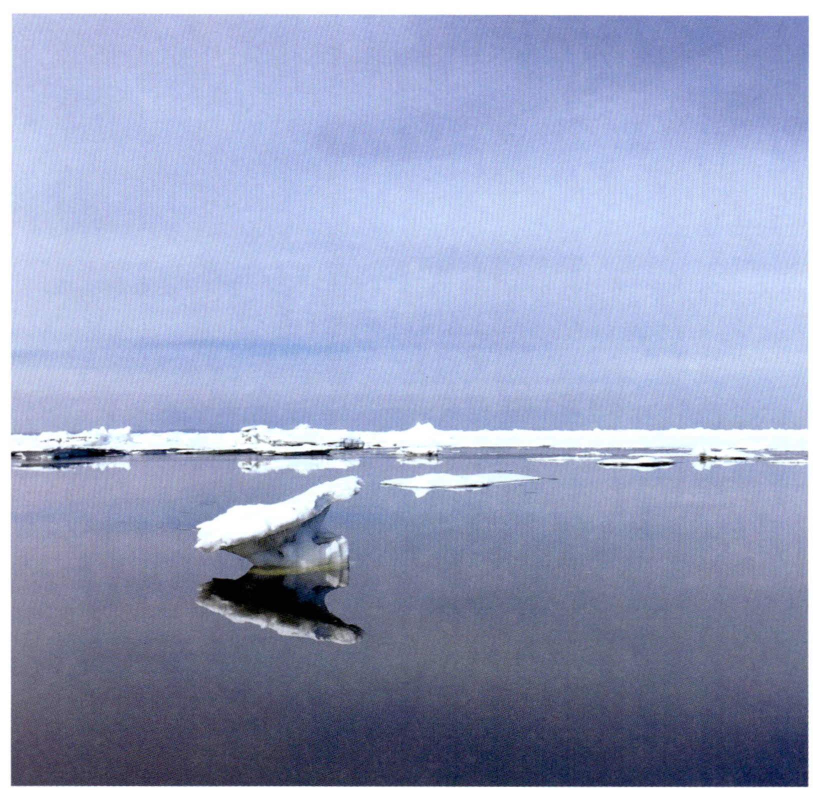

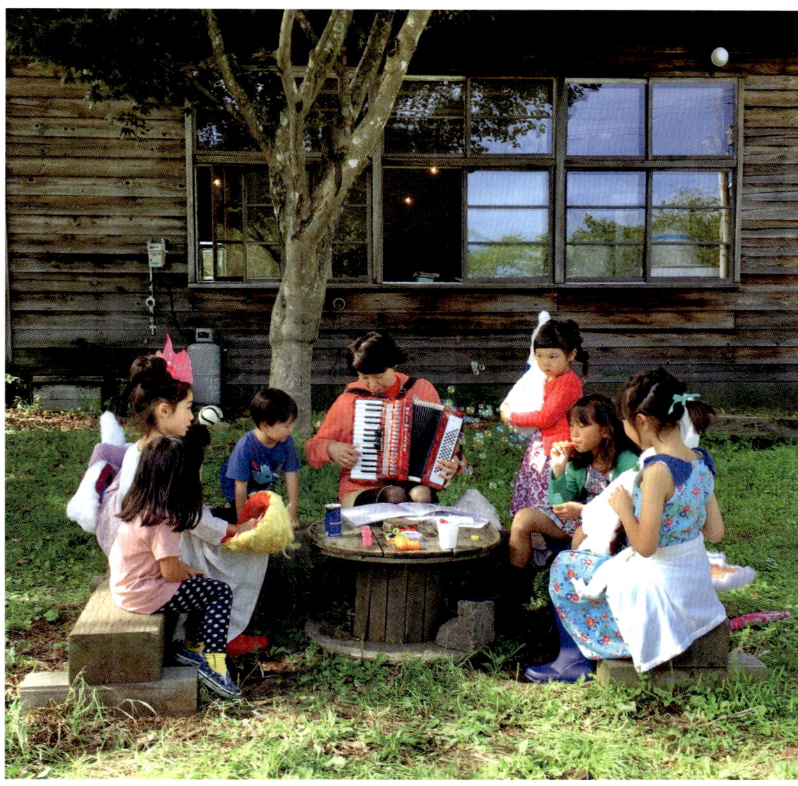

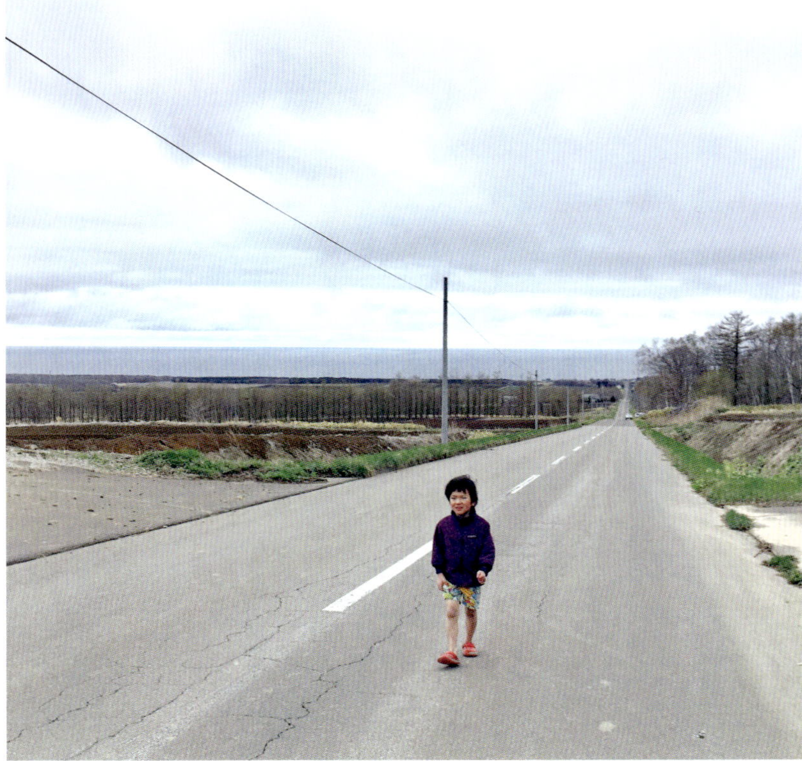

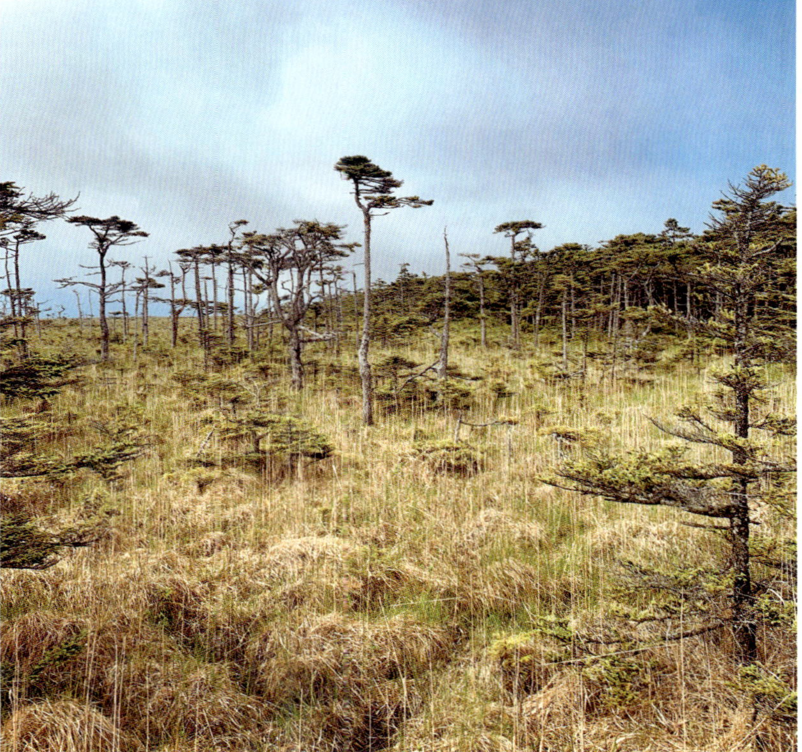

Fig. 279 (top left)
HOKKAIDO, 2017

Fig. 280 (top right)
HOKKAIDO, 2018

Fig. 281 (bottom left)
HOKKAIDO, 2018

Fig. 282 (bottom right)
HOKKAIDO, 2019

Return to the North

> **Since the day of the great earthquake, something inside of me changed. Maybe not changed exactly, but I could no longer affirm the art that I had, perhaps too easily, believed in. I am sure that the loss and helplessness I felt then was shared by everyone in Japan. I think a lot of Japanese people had to rethink their value systems, and for me that was art. Thinking about the actual victims and feeling this way made me despise art itself—to realize I have been making art without ever thinking deeply about it.**[1]

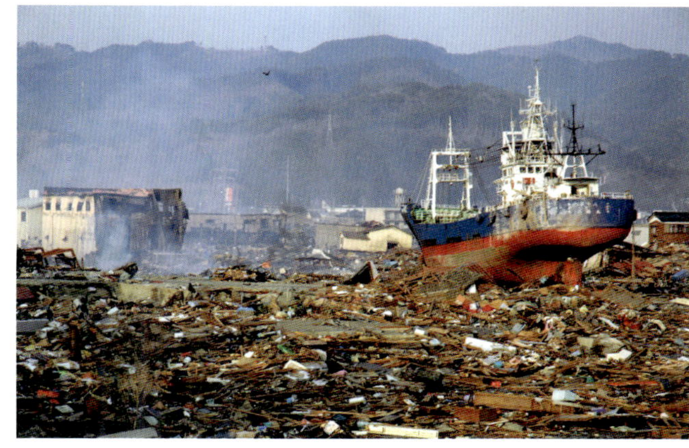

On March 11, 2011, a 9.0-magnitude earthquake triggered a tsunami that devastated the Tōhoku region in northeast Japan. The sheer force of shifting tectonic plates combined with 128-foot-high waves led to the failure of a cooling system at the Fukushima Daiichi Nuclear Power Plant, a Level 7 nuclear accident that released high quantities of radioactive discharge. The extent of the damage was enormous—more than 450,000 people were left homeless, and the death toll exceeded 18,000. The world watched, stunned, as the impact of this disaster unfolded on our screens.

In its immediate aftermath, the triple tragedy became a touchstone of heated debates on global eco-politics, disaster capitalism, and the mediatization of trauma. In an article published shortly after the disaster, social theorist Brian Massumi argued that the media was turning the public into casual spectators of catastrophes that defy human understanding. Interwoven into the media's narrative of shocking scenes, he wrote, are stories about "the personal actions of 'everyday heroes' carrying out small deeds of voluntaristic support. At this becalming pole of the affective conversion circuit, human agency is reasserted."[2] The human element helps mitigate the horror, but it also short-circuits the collective responses that reinforce a connection between natural disasters and climate change, a phenomenon rooted in global capitalism and government investment in the infrastructures of fuel production. Collective responses on the ground continue with massive government recovery operations that mobilize the military for civilian duties, while at the individual and grassroots levels, responses include the fight for fair investigations into Fukushima's preventability, compensation for those affected, and the recognition of the long-term environmental costs of nuclear-power dependency.

Fig. 283
The city of Kesennuma on March 13, 2011, two days after the Great East Japan Earthquake

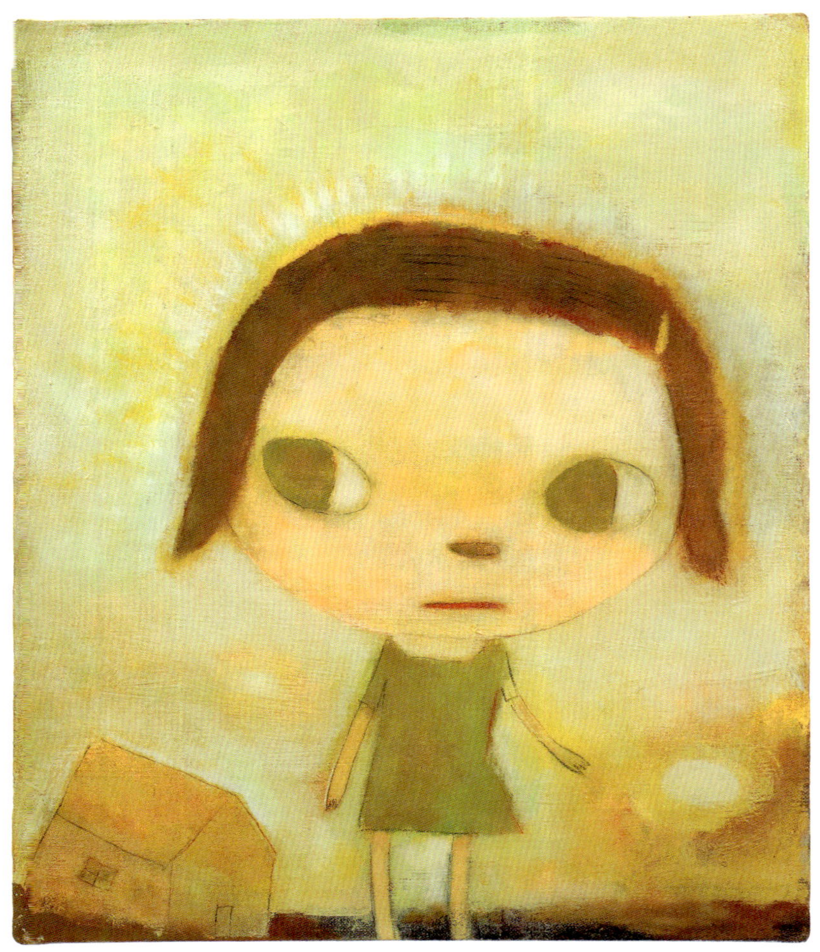

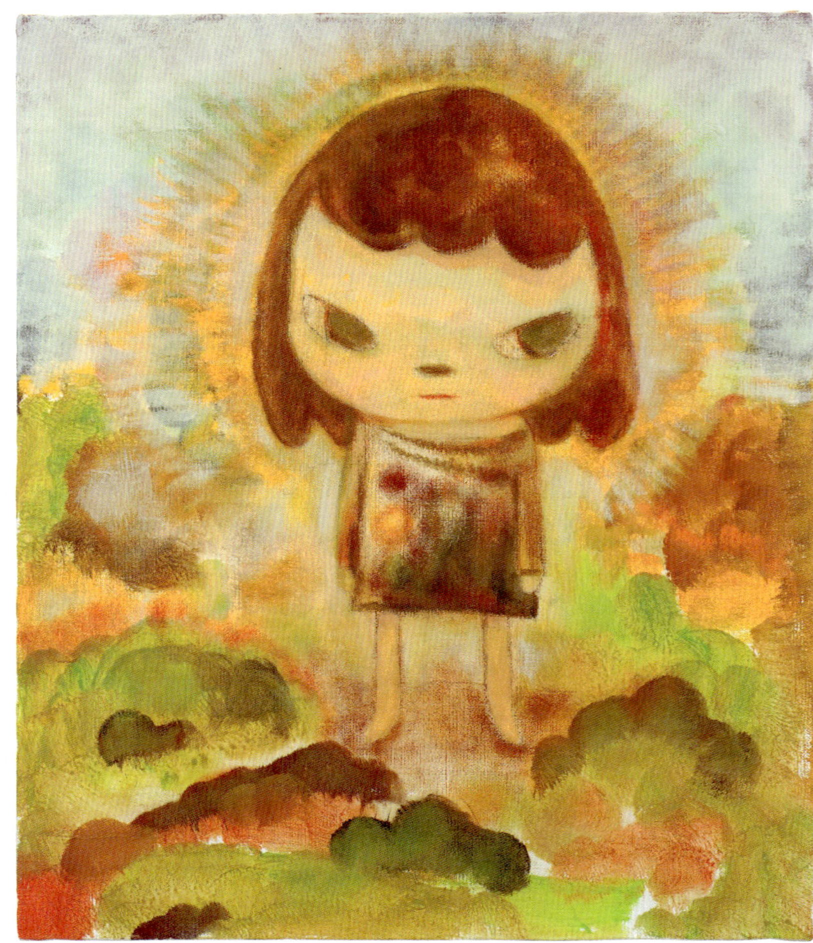

Artists reacted at the individual level to the trauma of Fukushima, interrogating the links between human agency and the natural environment, as well as the sociopolitical ethics of the response to disasters, whether on the media, state, or community level. Nobuyoshi Araki, in his 2011 series *Shakyō rōjin nikki* (*Diary of a Photo-Mad Old Man*), scratches his photographs with black lines, appearing in a rainy urban scene like acid daggers falling onto the umbrellas of unsuspecting pedestrians (Fig. 286). Chim↑Pom's *KI-AI 100* (100 Cheers, 2011) (Fig. 287) is a two-channel video of a powerful improvised performance in which the artists and the public from Sōma City huddle together among the debris of their former homes and perform 100 *kiai* yells—combat shouts that draw on the performers' inner *qi*. As the local residents try to reclaim their home city through their collective energy, they are dwarfed by the enormity of the scale of the destruction all around them, rendering their battle cries almost useless, apart from the dark humor they provide.[3]

Fig. 284
M.I.A., 2011, Acrylic and pencil on canvas, 18 1⁄16 × 14 15⁄16 in. (45.8 × 38 cm)

Fig. 285
Atomkraft Baby, 2011, Acrylic on canvas, 18 1⁄16 × 14 15⁄16 in. (45.8 × 38 cm)

Nara, however, was struggling with his work. As with his experience after Afghanistan, he found himself struck by creative inertia, but this time, the pain and confusion underlying his ennui were more personal, since the disaster had affected his hometown of Hirosaki. When the highways reopened, he made his way north to see his mother. The drive involved passing the border of Fukushima and many other small villages and towns hit by the disaster. It was a bleak journey and one that compelled him to act. As soon as he arrived home, he and his mother collected things from their house that were not being used or needed and distributed them to those affected by the disaster in the small towns of Iwate prefecture.

In April Nara completed two small paintings, *M.I.A.* (Fig. 284) and *Atomkraft Baby* (Fig. 285), for a silent auction organized by a group of Tokyo galleries to raise money for victims of the disasters.[4] In these delicate paintings of children affected by nuclear bombs, there is a softness in the treatment of colors and lines that evokes a vulnerable mood befitting the theme of the works. Nara had previously used the title *Missing in Action* for a 2005 drawing (Fig. 244) made in commemoration of the sixtieth anniversary of the nuclear attack on Hiroshima. In the 2011 painting, a small house, recalling one of Nara's earliest symbols of his childhood, appears to the left of the figure, while on the right is a circle of white light suggestive of a nuclear mushroom cloud. Caught between the two motifs, the pensive young girl stands with a halo of glowing white lines, evoking an image of a child affected by nuclear radiation. *Atomkraft Baby* is a more direct expression of the explosive energy of a nuclear bomb, with golden lines radiating from the head of an angry young girl.

It was around this time that Nara was invited to participate in a show in Fukushima organized for the people who had been displaced by the disaster, as a sort of reprieve from their daily lives in shelter camps. However, he did not feel that it was an appropriate response for him: he longed for a more direct engagement, one not centered on his art. Instead, through social media, he organized informal talks in the area, including one at the Sōma Higashi High School's art club in Fukushima, where students shared with Nara their stories of struggling through the torrential waters, hanging onto the hides of cows as the contents of their homes swept past them.[5] On other occasions, he visited gymnasiums that were serving as makeshift shelters and asked the people living there what he could do to assist

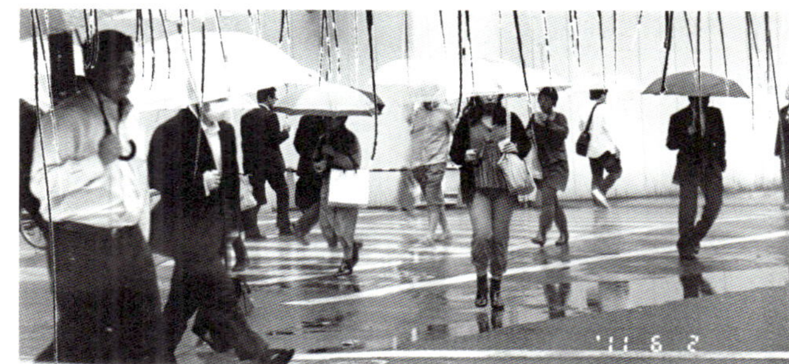

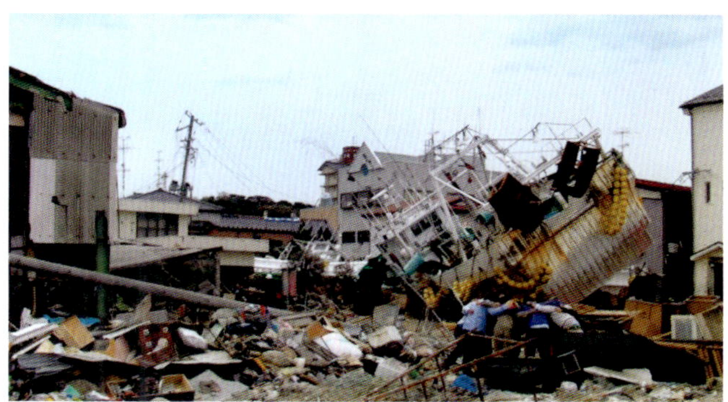

Fig. 286
Nobuyoshi Araki, *Diary of a Photo-Mad Old Man*, 2011, Gelatin silver print

Fig. 287
Chim↑Pom, *KI-AI 100*, 2011, Two-channel video, 10 min. 30 sec.

their children. Their answers were almost always the same: to help them forget, if only for a short time. He had, by chance, packed on his trip ten giant *koinobori*, streamers in the shape of a carp used in the traditional Children's Day festival in Japan. He decided to organize an art workshop, during which he helped the children fabricate costumes out of the *koinobori* and then took pictures of them, which he gifted to the children and their families (Figs. 288–290). Although Nara knew his photographs could never heal the trauma of disaster, he hoped that they would come to serve as mementos of happier moments.

After several months of restlessness, Nara knew he had to find a way to return to his art, not least because he had a major exhibition the following year at the Yokohama Museum of Art. That summer he returned to his alma mater, Aichi University of the Arts, as a visiting artist, where, among the familiar sights and smells of his old campus, he found the environment he needed to make art again. He wanted to work in a medium he could become more physically engaged with and requested space in the sculpture department rather than the painting department. As he explained, "I couldn't make pictures on a blank canvas, but I found I could confront a mass of clay. I wouldn't think about it with my mind. I would just attack it, like a sumo, with my body."[6]

When the students returned in the fall, Nara moved into a communal studio space to work alongside them (Figs. 294 and 295). He wanted to be part of their community as equals rather than as a teacher, and over the next few months, they shared meals, discussed problems, and together created a stall for a school fair. This return to student life yielded a renewed vitality in his art practice, as the materiality of his sculptures from this period show. He attacked the clay, pulled at it, dragged his hands across its surface, and coaxed it into the form of a child, embedding into the material his anxieties, anger, sorrow, and hopelessness. It was both a mental and a physical process, as if through bodily connection with the medium he was able to reach an emotional catharsis that reconciled the turmoil within himself, and only then did he feel he was making art that had something to say. In *Wicked Looking* (2012) (Figs. 292 and 293), it is possible to retrace the movements of Nara's hands as he shaped curves and swept grooves across the clay's surface and the pressure of his fingers as he formed the figure's eyelids and lips. When the final form emerged, he cast the malleable medium into cupronickel, its permanence bringing stability to a world that no longer felt as enduring as it once was.

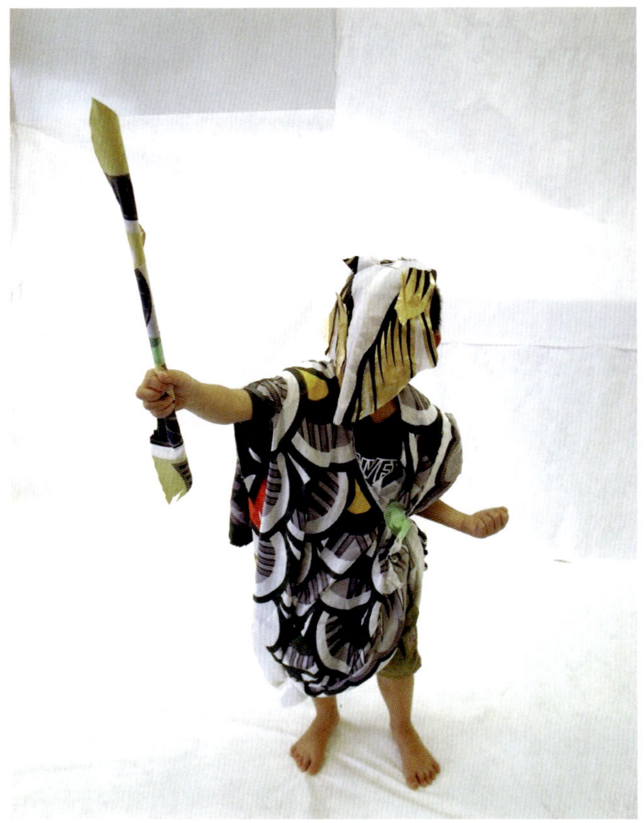

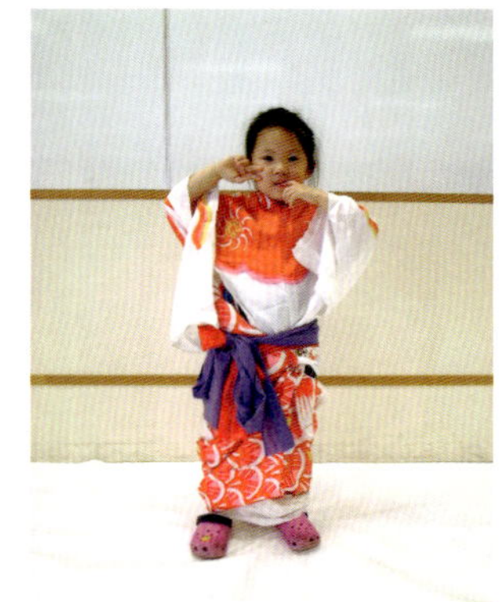

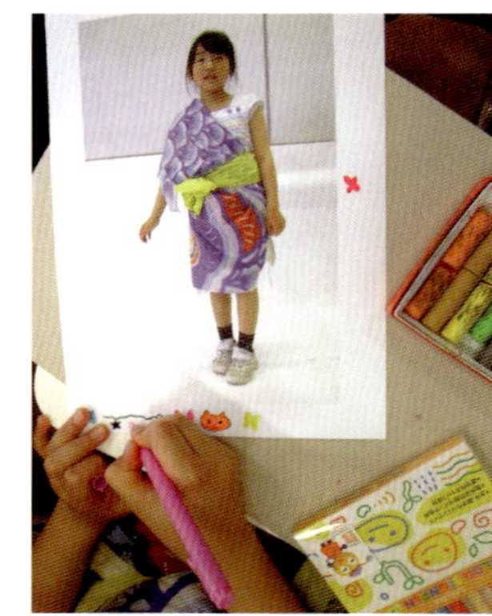

Figs. 288–290
Nara's art workshops with children in Fukushima, 2011

Fig. 291 (opposite)
Long Tall Sister, 2012,
Bronze with brass patina,
84 ⅝ × 48 13/16 × 83 ⅞ in.
(215 × 124 × 213 cm)

Fig. 292 (following spread, left)
Wicked Looking, 2012,
Cupronickel, 59 ¼ × 48 13/16 × 51 3/16 in. (150.5 × 124 × 130 cm)

Fig. 293 (following spread, right)
Wicked Looking (detail), 2012

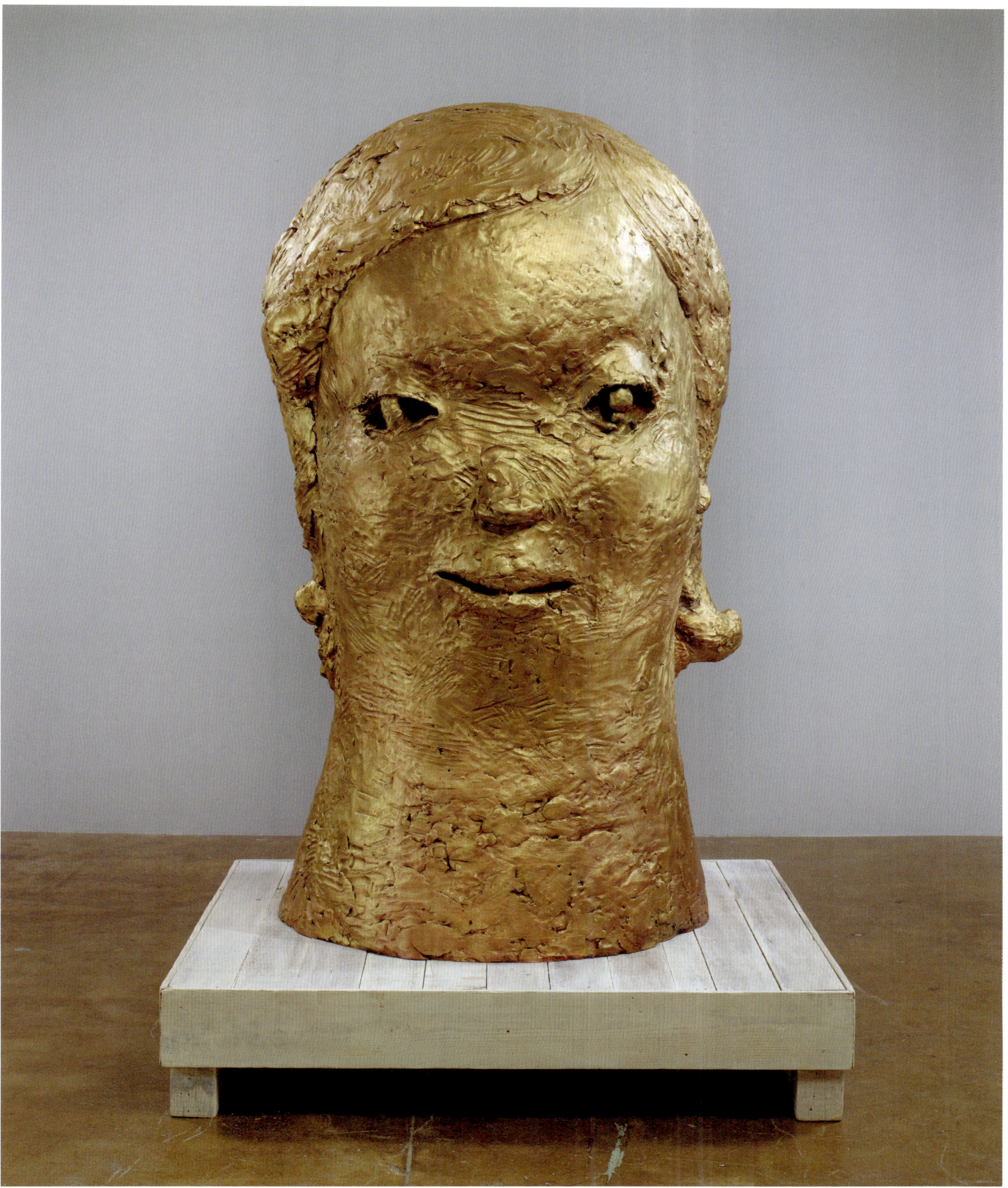

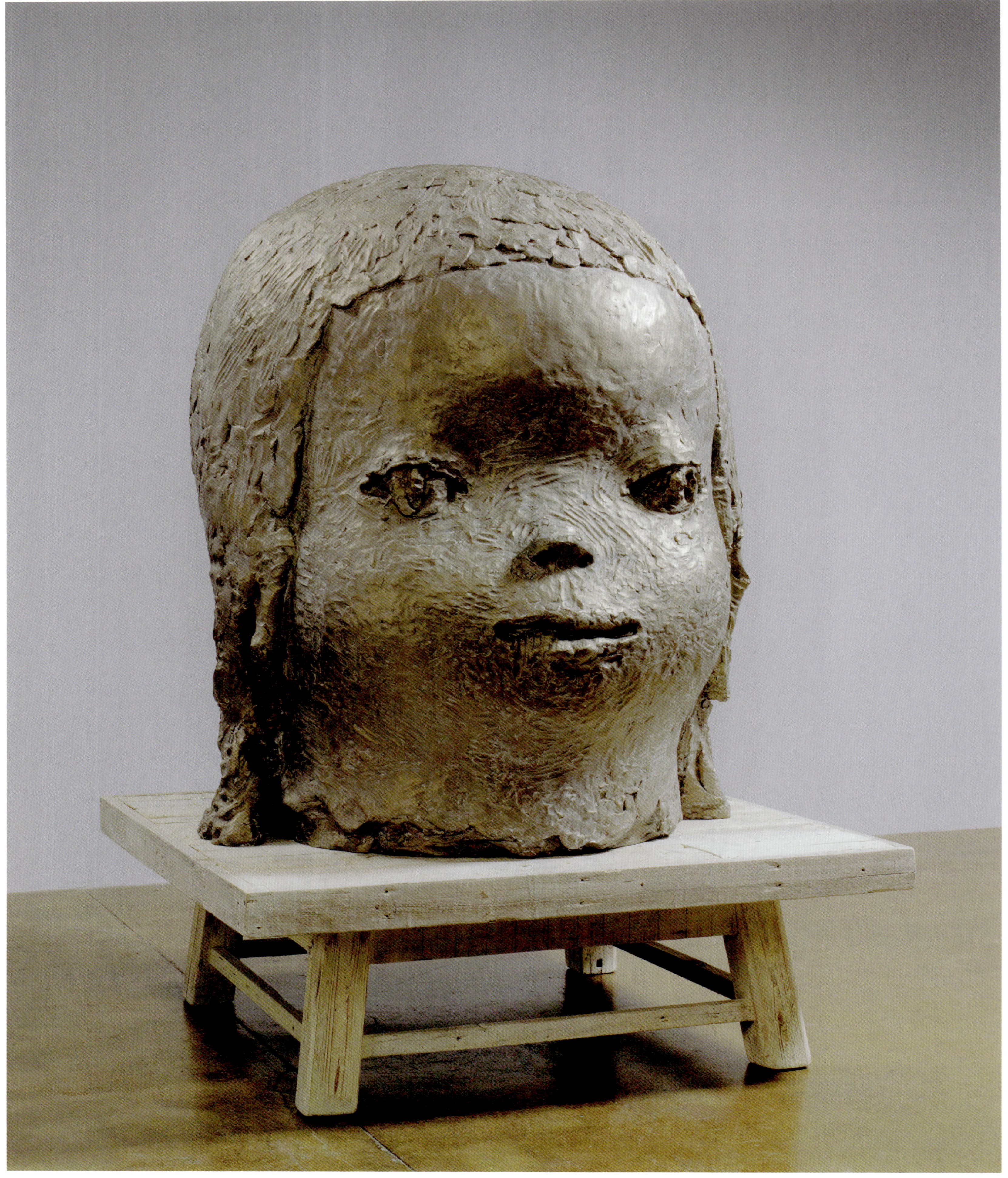

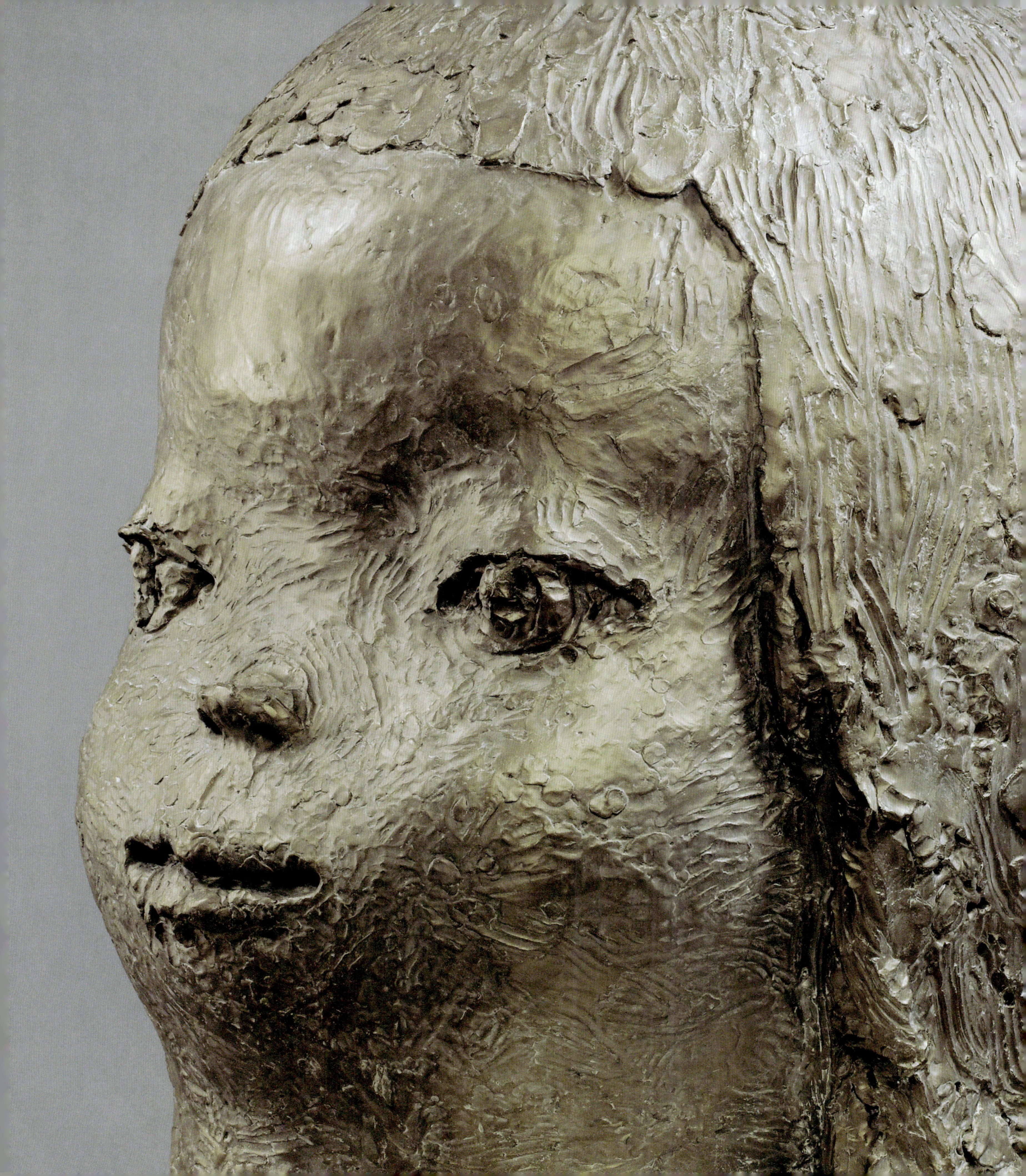

According to critical theories of trauma, the difficulty of recounting experiences—in part because of the insufficiency of language and the fallibility of memory—means that testimonies often take on creative modes, such as literature and art, in which the voice of an imagined witness can take on the task of relating traumatic events as a cathartic vehicle.[7] Viewed through this lens, it is possible to see how the emotional energy Nara invested into his sculptures effectively turned them into imagined witnesses to the unspeakable trauma of the 2011 disaster.

The making of testimonies is seldom straightforward, and often during that process, one set of experiences can be transplanted onto another. For Nara, this took the form of a reckoning with his own art-making past. What, he asked, was the value of that work now? In this reflective state, and often subconsciously, he revisited motifs from his earlier works, but these returns were not nostalgic or self-referential. Rather, his reappropriation of his own forms and styles acted as connective tissue that allowed him to process his own past as he subsumed it into the present. For example, with *Long Tall Sister* (2012) (Fig. 291), the figure's awkwardness contains echoes of his work from the late 1980s and early 1990s, when his figurative drawings took more undefined bodily shapes. *Midnight Pilgrim* (2012) (Figs. 297 and 298) can be regarded as a teenage version of *The Little Pilgrims (Night Walking)* (1999) (Fig. 102), first shown in the 1999 exhibition *ART/ DOMESTIC: Temperature of the Time*. Translated into bronze and on a grander scale, the young sleepwalker carries herself with elegiac grace.

Among the sculptures made at Aichi is *Miss Tannen* (2012) (Figs. 299 and 300), a character who would later become the model for his series of *Miss Forest* sculptures from 2016 (Fig. 301). The figure's long, pointed head is built up with lumps of clay that are impressed with deep grooves from Nara's touch. Her round face with a button nose sits beneath the cone of her head; with her eyes closed, she appears like a sleeping forest spirit. More than any other works from this period, the heads of *Miss Tannen* and *Miss Forest* resonate with the Shinto tradition Nara grew up with. They evoke the gentle presence of the Jizō sculptures that pledge to protect children and the *kami* deities who bring a primeval force to sacred lands. Nara scatters these sculptures across the world so that they effectively become protectors of nature and witnesses to its endurance. They have since found their way into the courtyards of N's YARD in Nasushiobara and the Aomori

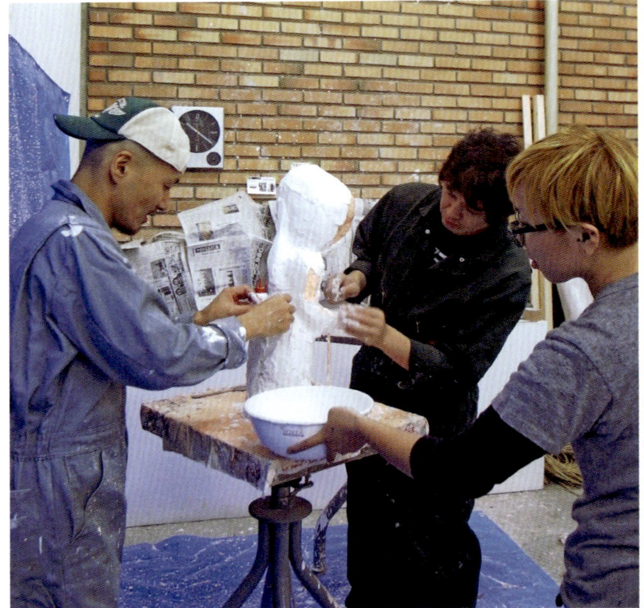

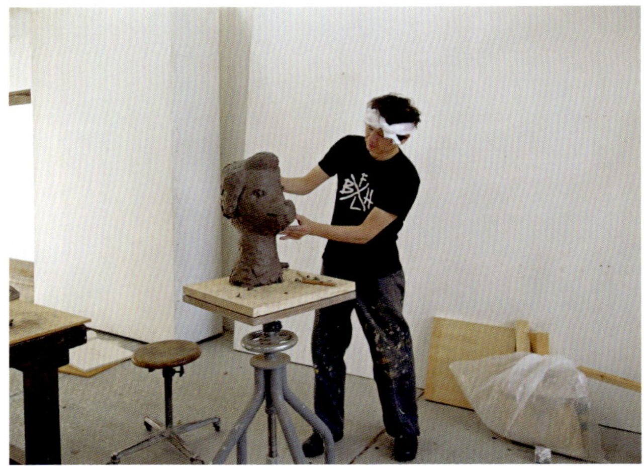

Figs. 294 and 295
Nara working in the studio at Aichi University of the Arts, Nagakute, Japan, 2011

Fig. 296 (opposite)
Thinking Sister, 2012,
Bronze, 15 ½ × 14 ⅜ × 14 5⁄16 in.
(39.3 × 36.5 × 36.4 cm)

Fig. 297 (following spread, left)
Midnight Pilgrim (detail), 2012

Fig. 298 (following spread, right)
Midnight Pilgrim, 2012,
Bronze with black patina,
62 3⁄16 × 22 13⁄16 × 25 3⁄16 in.
(158 × 58 × 64 cm)

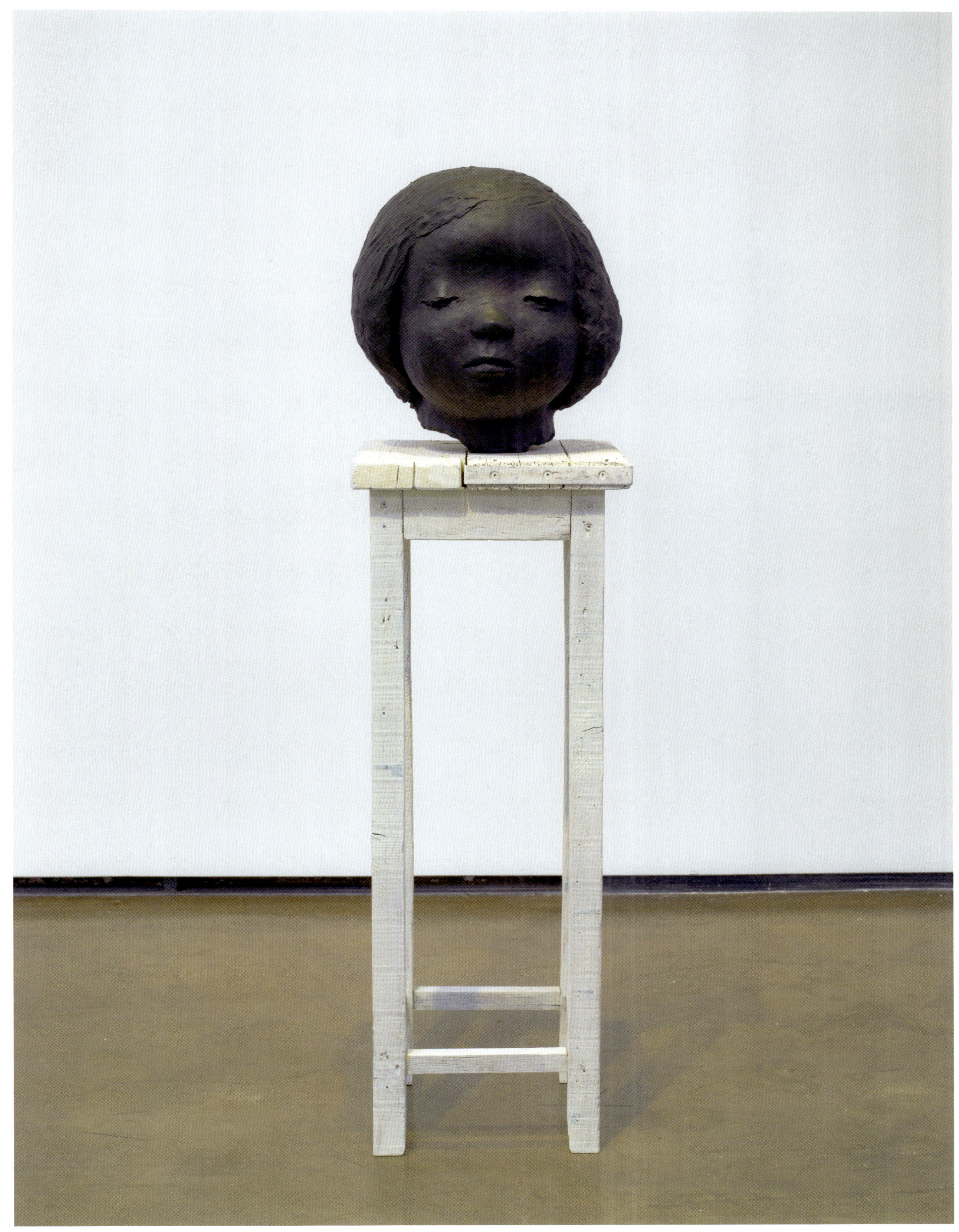

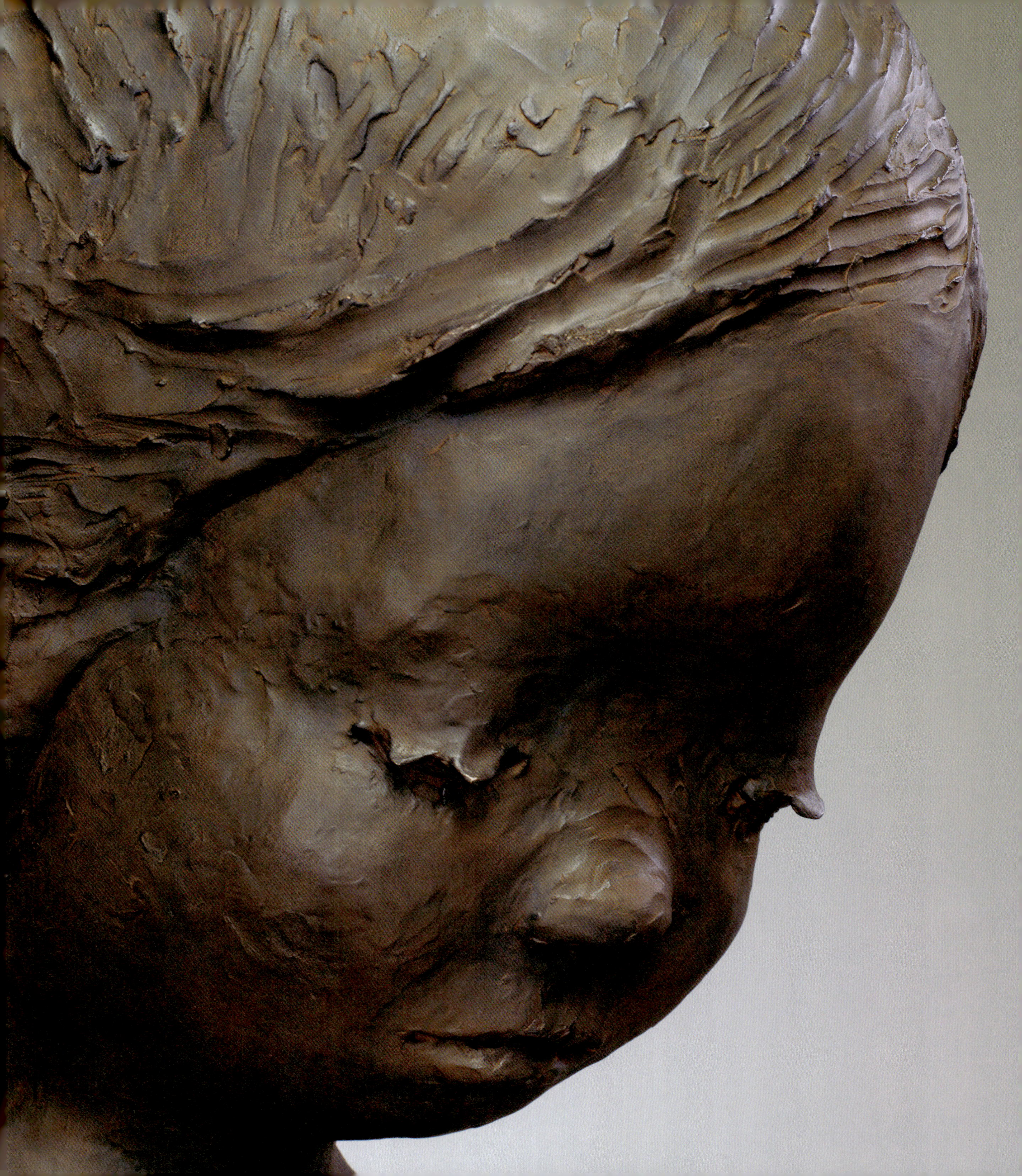

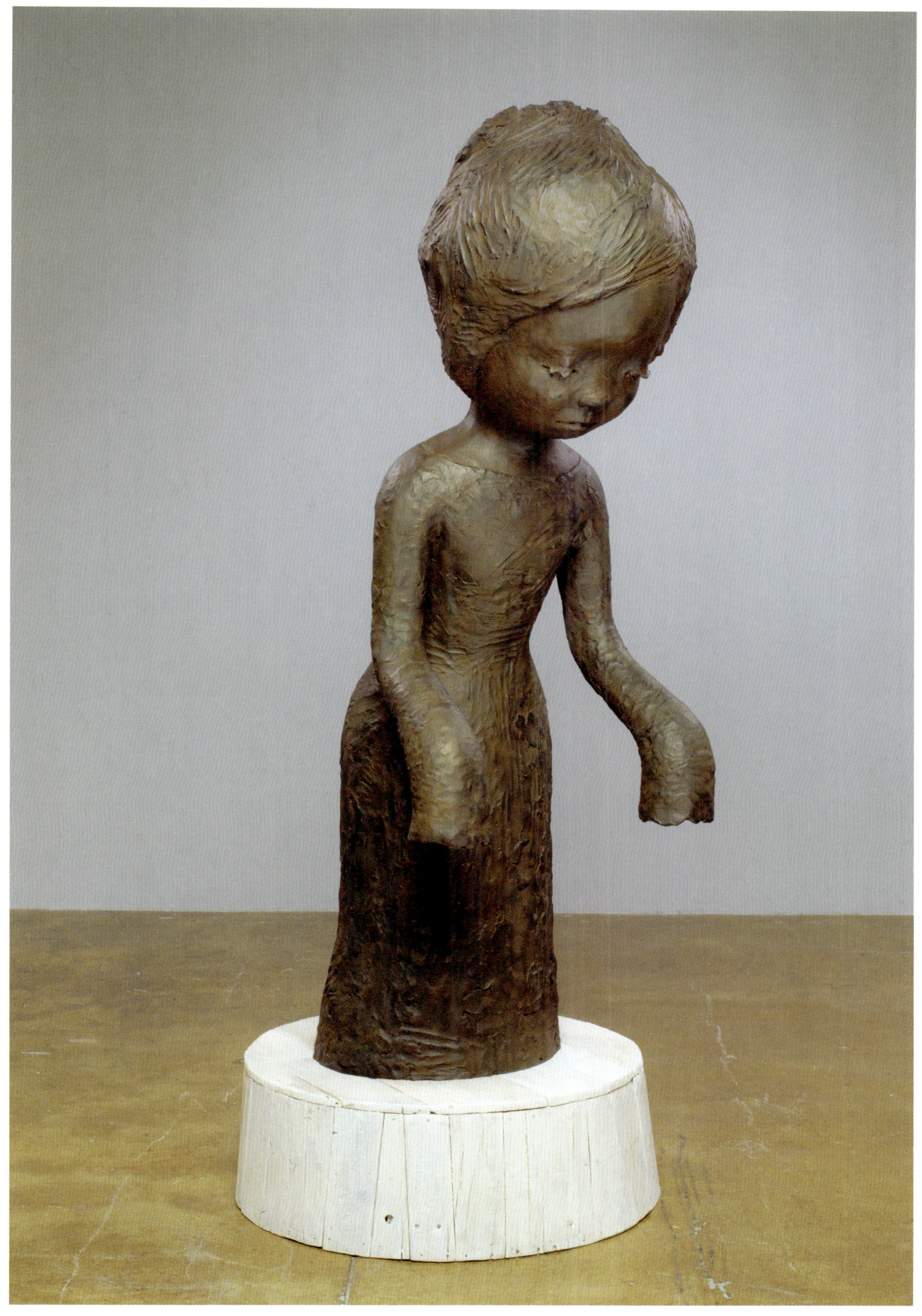

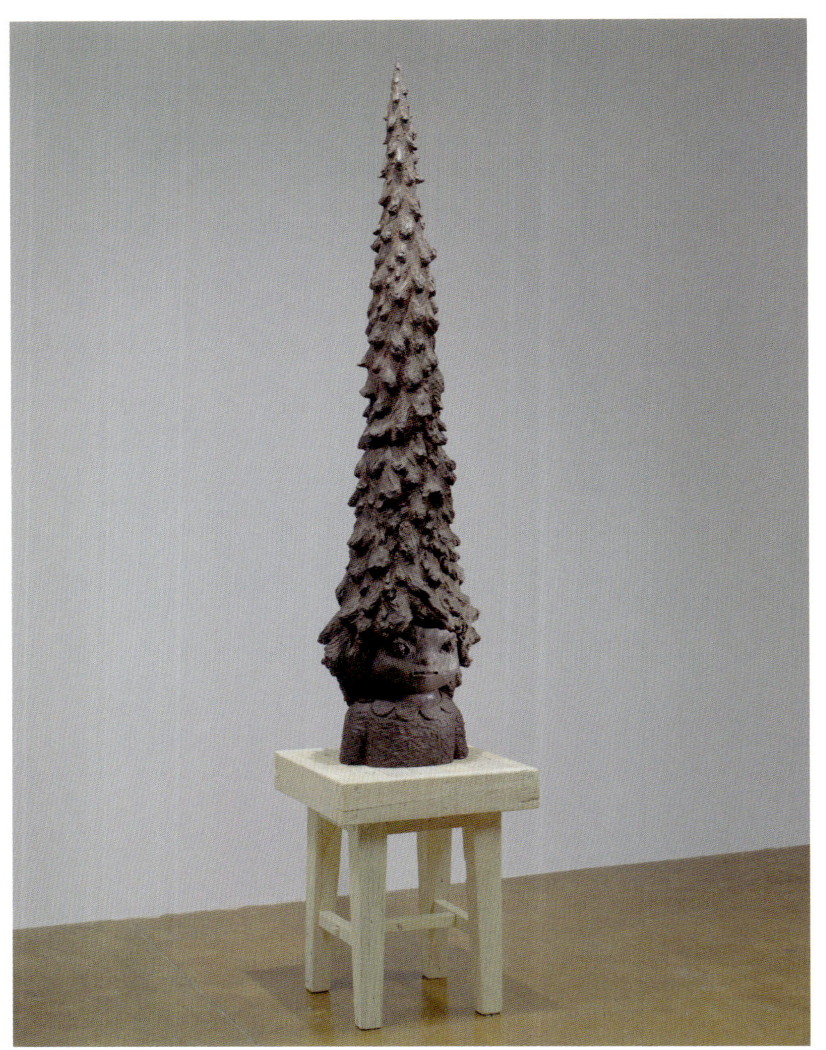

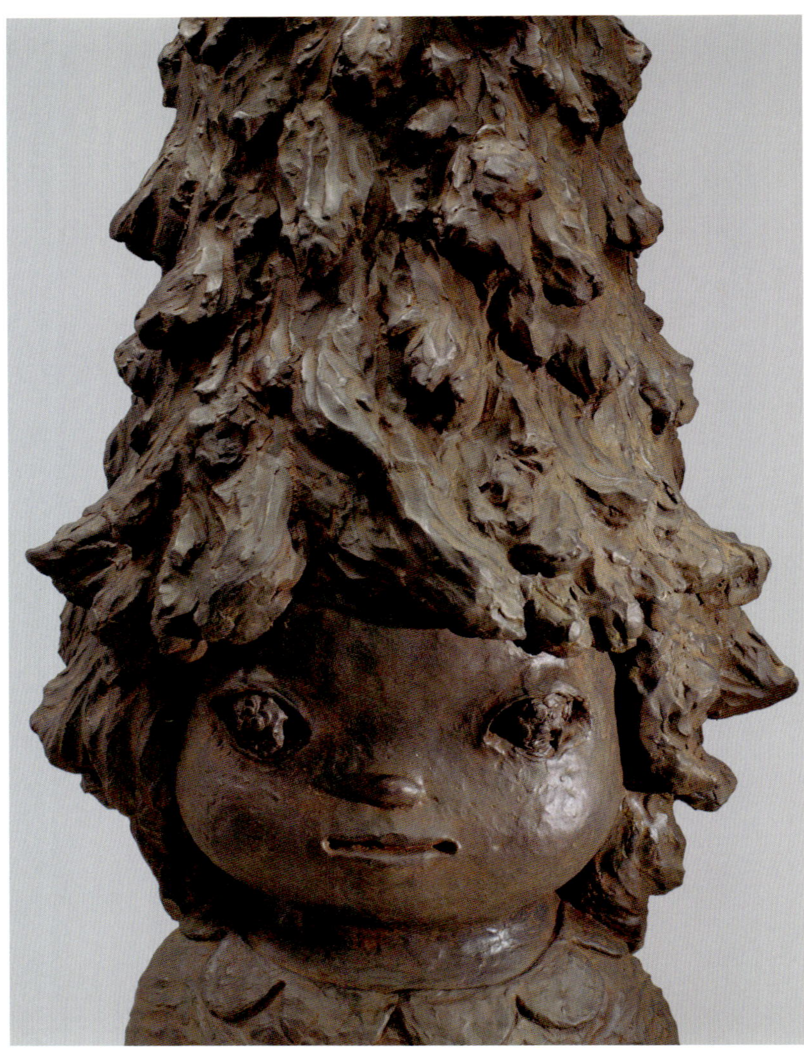

Fig. 299
Miss Tannen, 2012, Bronze with black patina, 83 ⅞ × 20 ½ × 16 ¾ in. (213 × 52 × 42.5 cm)

Fig. 300
Miss Tannen (detail), 2012

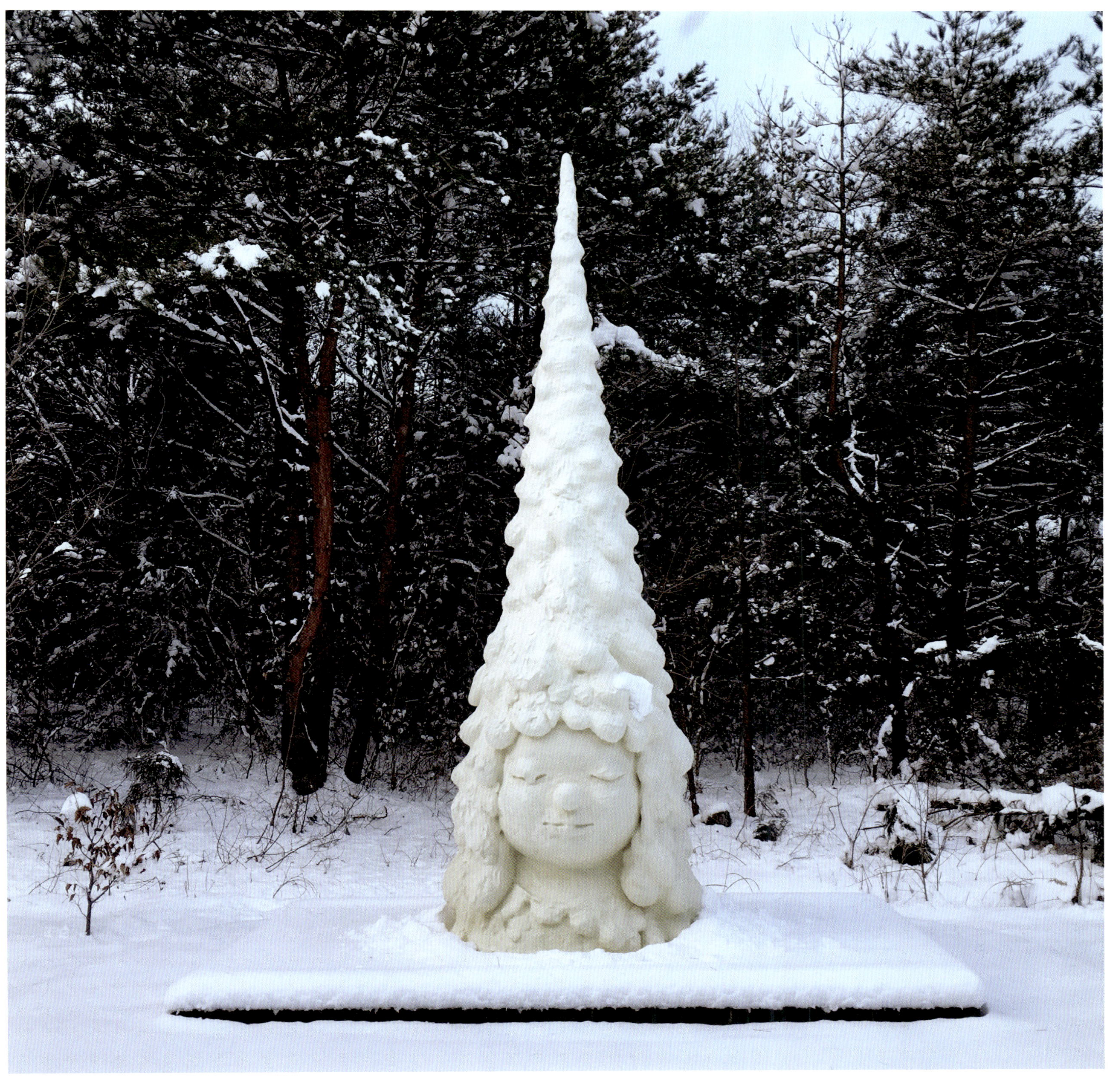

Fig. 301
Miss Forest / Thinker, 2016,
Urethane on bronze,
197 × 55 × 62 ½ in.
(500.4 × 139.7 × 158.8 cm)
Installation view: N's YARD,
Nasushiobara, Japan

Fig. 302 (following spread, left)
Lucy, 2012, Bronze with black
patina, 55 ⅞ × 61 × 59 ¹⁄₁₆ in.
(142 × 155 × 150 cm)

Fig. 303 (following spread, right)
Lucy (detail), 2012

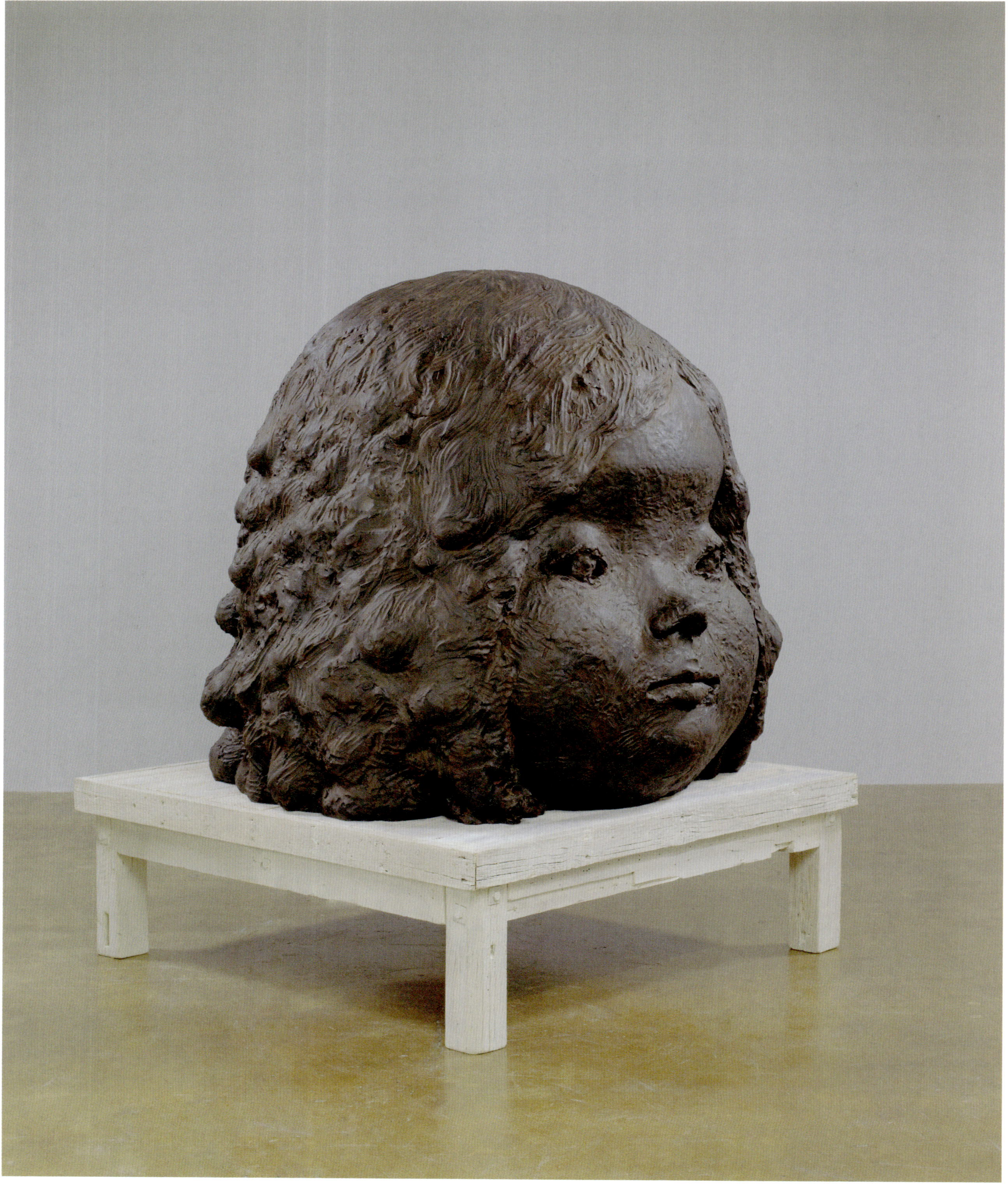

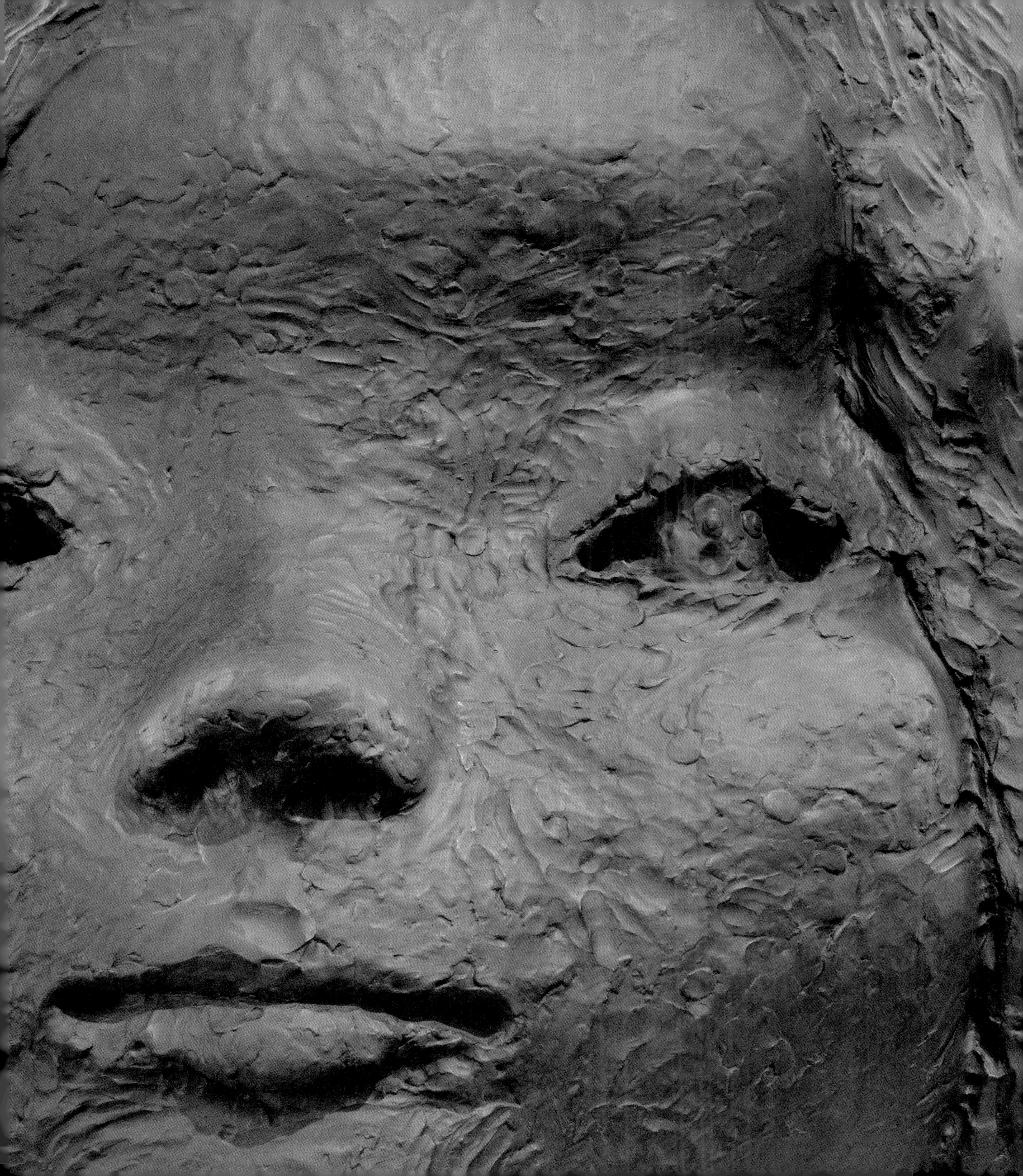

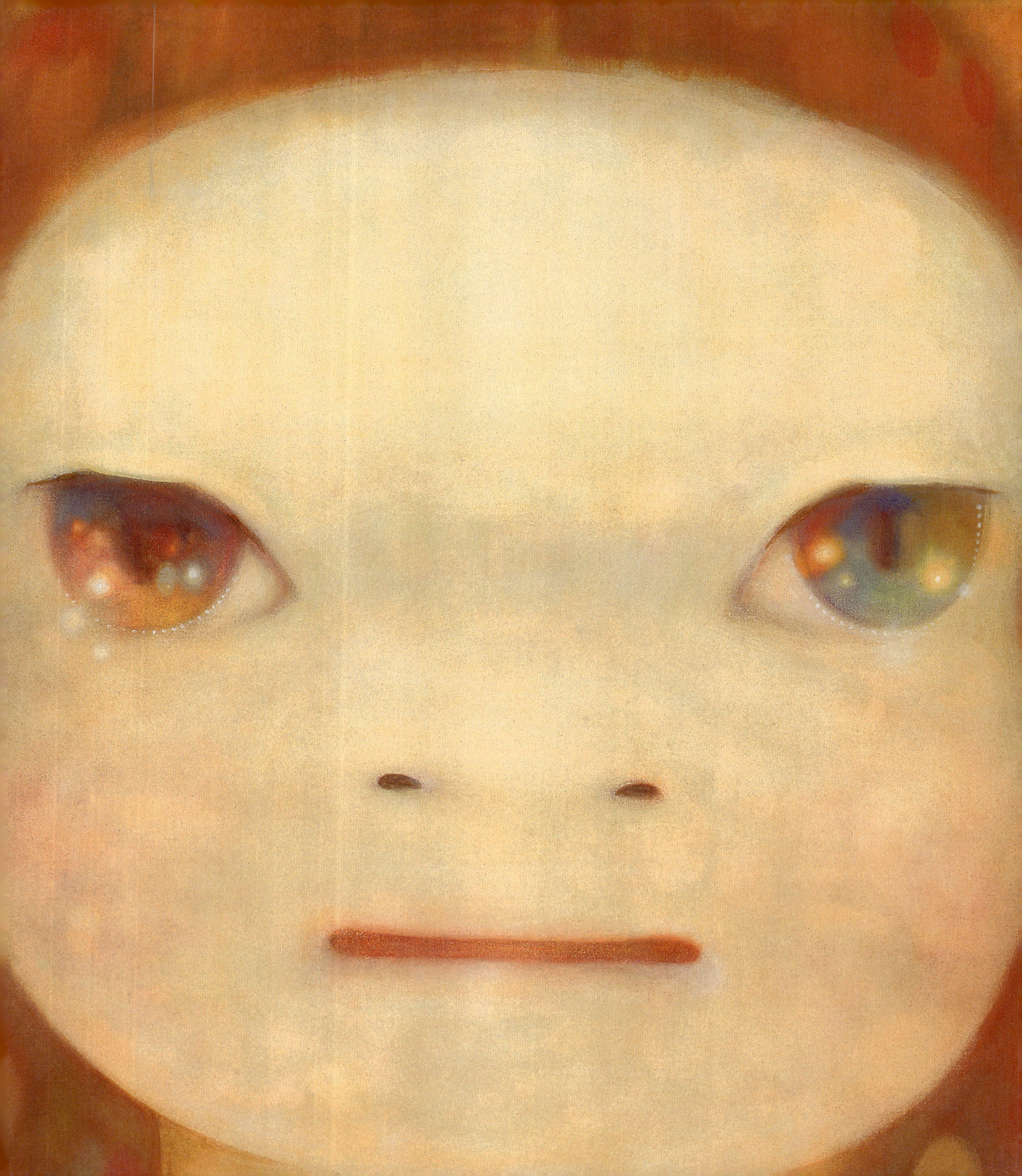

Museum of Art, as well as private homes in the United States, Turkey, Malaysia, South Korea, China, and Thailand.

By the end of his tenure at Aichi, Nara had completed thirteen sculptures, and together they form their own community of faces and figures, including *Lucy* (2012) (Figs. 302 and 303), *Thinking Sister* (2012) (Fig. 296), *Miss Tannen*, *Long Tall Sister*, and *Midnight Pilgrim*. In his 2012 Yokohama show, they stood on simple crate-like platforms in a large darkened room, invoking solemnity as well as a glimmer of hope, testaments to the complex emotions of post-2011 Japan (Figs. 305 and 306).

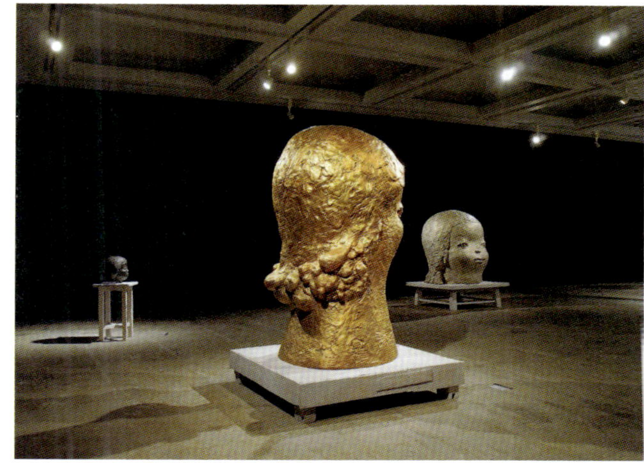

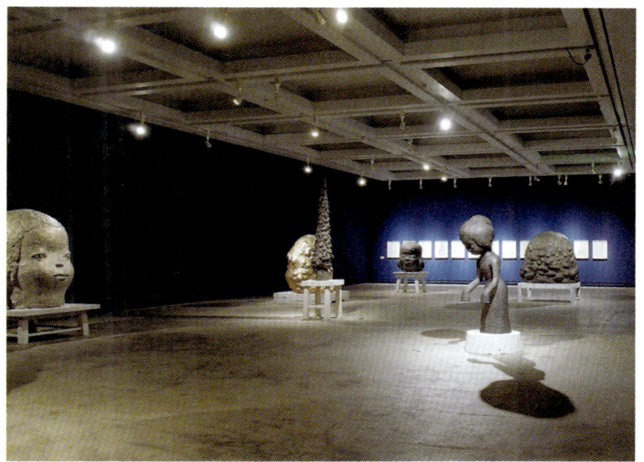

Nara returned to his studio in April 2012, at which point a noticeable shift can be detected in his paintings and drawings. Through the previous months of working in clay, engaging with local communities, and reflecting on the values of his art practice, Nara experienced a fresh surge of creative energy. He began work on a new painting, *Miss Spring* (2012) (Figs. 304 and 307), using a shade of ice-cream pink as background and employing an array of painterly textures: autumnal colored orbs suspended in the girl's hair, square swathes of jeweled colors on her sweater, and speckles of fleshy pinks and whites on her rounded cheeks. Despite this variety of shapes and colors, *Miss Spring* stands quietly, her lips pressed into a thin line and her sparkling eyes, one orange, the other blue, staring back at the viewer. It is hard to detect what she is thinking, and this opens her inner world up to interpretations that can range from diffidence to defiance.

Miss Spring can be seen as an accumulation of techniques that Nara began experimenting with in the mid-2000s and that have now evolved into a distinctive genre of bust portraits, often motionless in posture but lively in textures and colors. The painting's monumental scale invites viewers to approach the work, to view the tapestry of colors in her dress and the translucent clarity of her hair that, when seen up close, is repeated in the eyes, turning them into microcosms of the portrait itself. Nara's treatment of color is the most distinctive shift in his recent paintings. His palette feels more harmonized, even as it ranges from candy-colored concoctions of minty green and creamy pink to midtonal fields of marine blue and jeweled cerise. There is less contrast between colors and very few dark tones, and although the hues are complex and varied, there is never a sense of clutter on the canvas.

Fig. 304 (opposite)
Miss Spring (detail), 2012

Figs. 305 and 306
Exhibition views: *NARA Yoshitomo: a bit like you and me...*, Yokohama Museum of Art, Japan, 2012

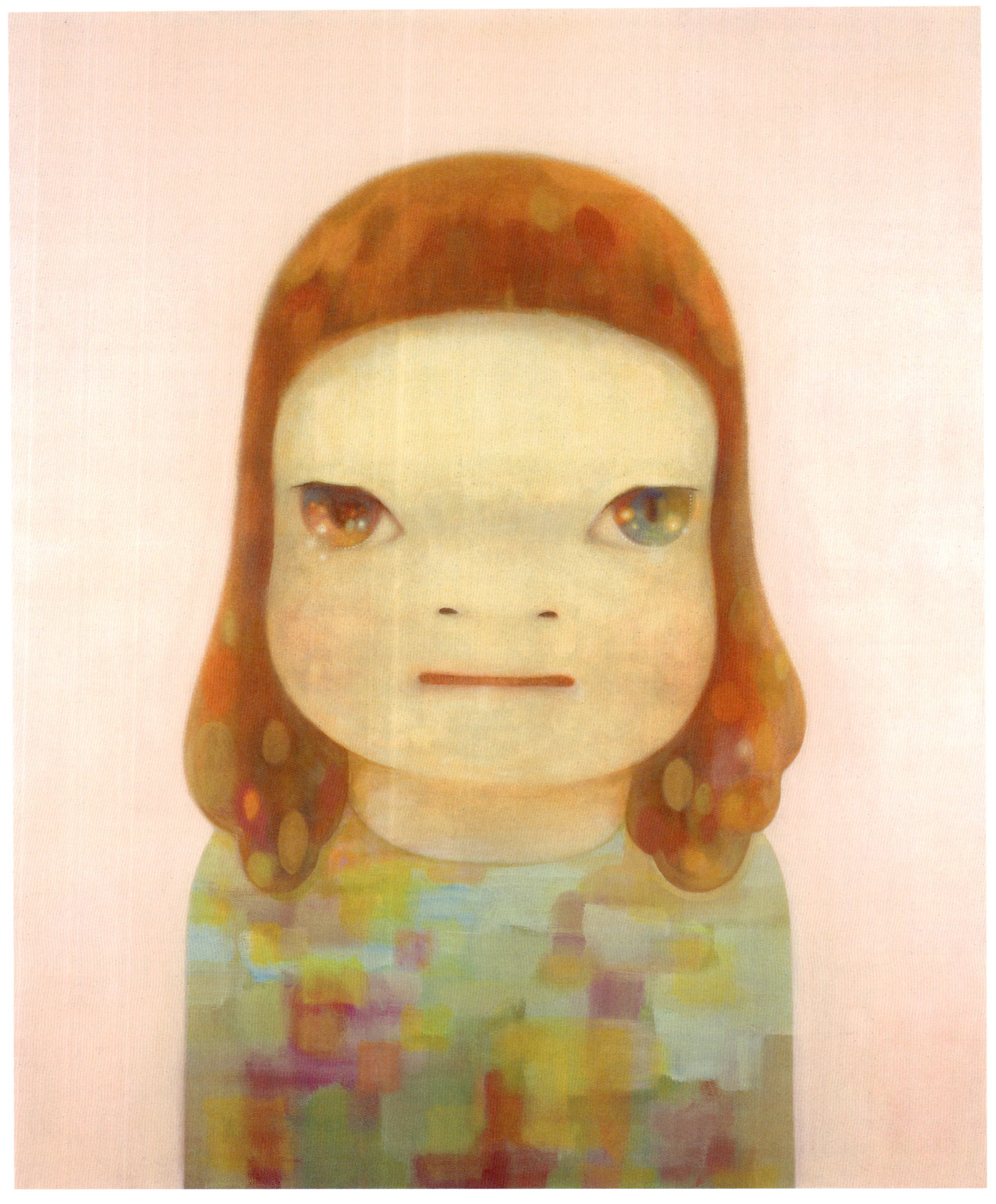

Fig. 307
Miss Spring, 2012, Acrylic on canvas, 89 ⅜ × 71 ⅝ in. (227 × 182 cm)

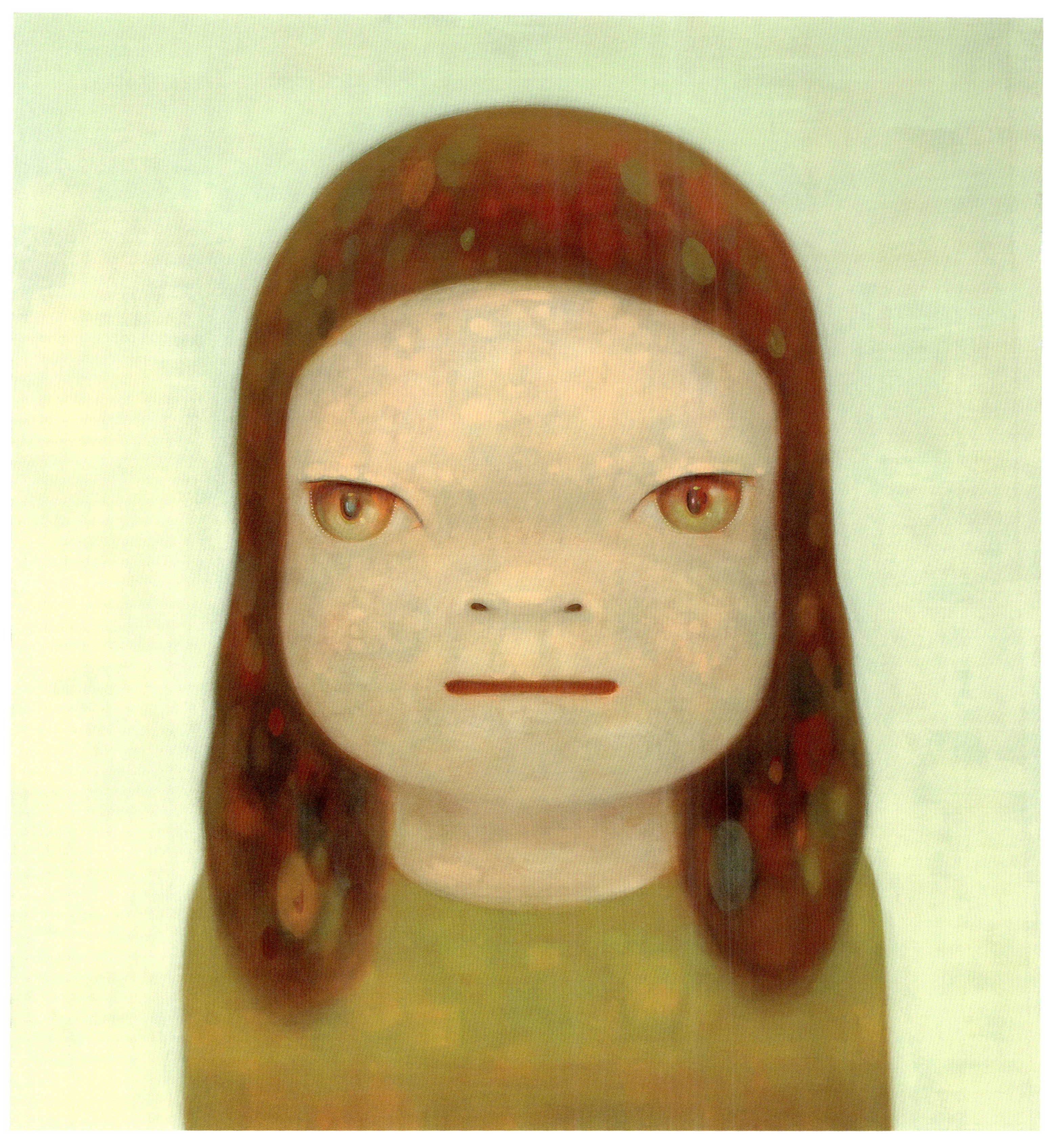

Fig. 308
Girl from North Country, 2017,
Acrylic on canvas, 86 ⅝ × 77 in.
(220 × 195.6 cm)

The formal harmony in *Miss Spring* is unexpected, because it reveals a patience in its making, one that belies the complexity of the artist's emotions after Fukushima. As with his sculptures from this time, the painting retains the material traces of its creation, and the artist rewards those who look closely beneath and in between the orbs, freckles, and swathes, where glimpses of the many layers of paint underneath are revealed. This tonal richness is only visible when the viewer stands close to the canvas—where Nara stands as he paints—to enjoy, as he does, the sensory pleasure of its colors and to revel in the sense of aliveness that comes with acknowledging the artist's painting process. Despite the difficulty in reading the internalized world of *Miss Spring*, the patterns and movements of colors suggest that she lives up to her name of growth and promise. She embodies something of the calm spirit of *Miss Tannen* silently watching, as well as of the artist's own fresh memories of inspiring children in a time of despair.

In Nara's other paintings from this period, what is on the surface of the canvas similarly makes up only a part of what comprises the work as a whole, and sometimes there is a stark contrast between what is revealed and what is concealed. Behind the pastel colors of *Girl from North Country* (2017) (Fig. 308), for example, is a layer of bright fuchsia, a color that Nara is not fond of and that he applied only so that he could paint over it with softer colors. The fuchsia acts as a jarring contrast, something he battles against to reclaim the canvas. In the end, it exists only in ghostly traces, slivers that inch their way out at the borders of the canvas and in between the soothing yellows and greens within the portrait. Nara's approach to coloring is never systematic or analytical but based on something more personal. At moments while painting, he even turns his canvas upside down to avoid being distracted by his figure's face as he focuses on the creation of rich color fields.

For Nara, the act of overpainting is not always iconoclastic. In many instances, in fact, it is a way for him to create tonal depth, to escape the flatness of the paint itself. In *Girl left behind the night* (2019) (Fig. 309), that richness of color is on full display, and by looking at the earlier stages of its progress (Figs. 310 and 311), we can glimpse how Nara built his layers of colors: a field of bright magentas, olives, marine blues, and lemony yellows are later altered with pale pinks, creamy roses, and velvety browns that he applies with greater movement until a final coherent version appears. This is a masterful work and a high point

Fig. 309
Girl left behind the night,
2019, Acrylic on canvas,
86 ⅝ × 76 ¾ in. (220 × 195 cm)

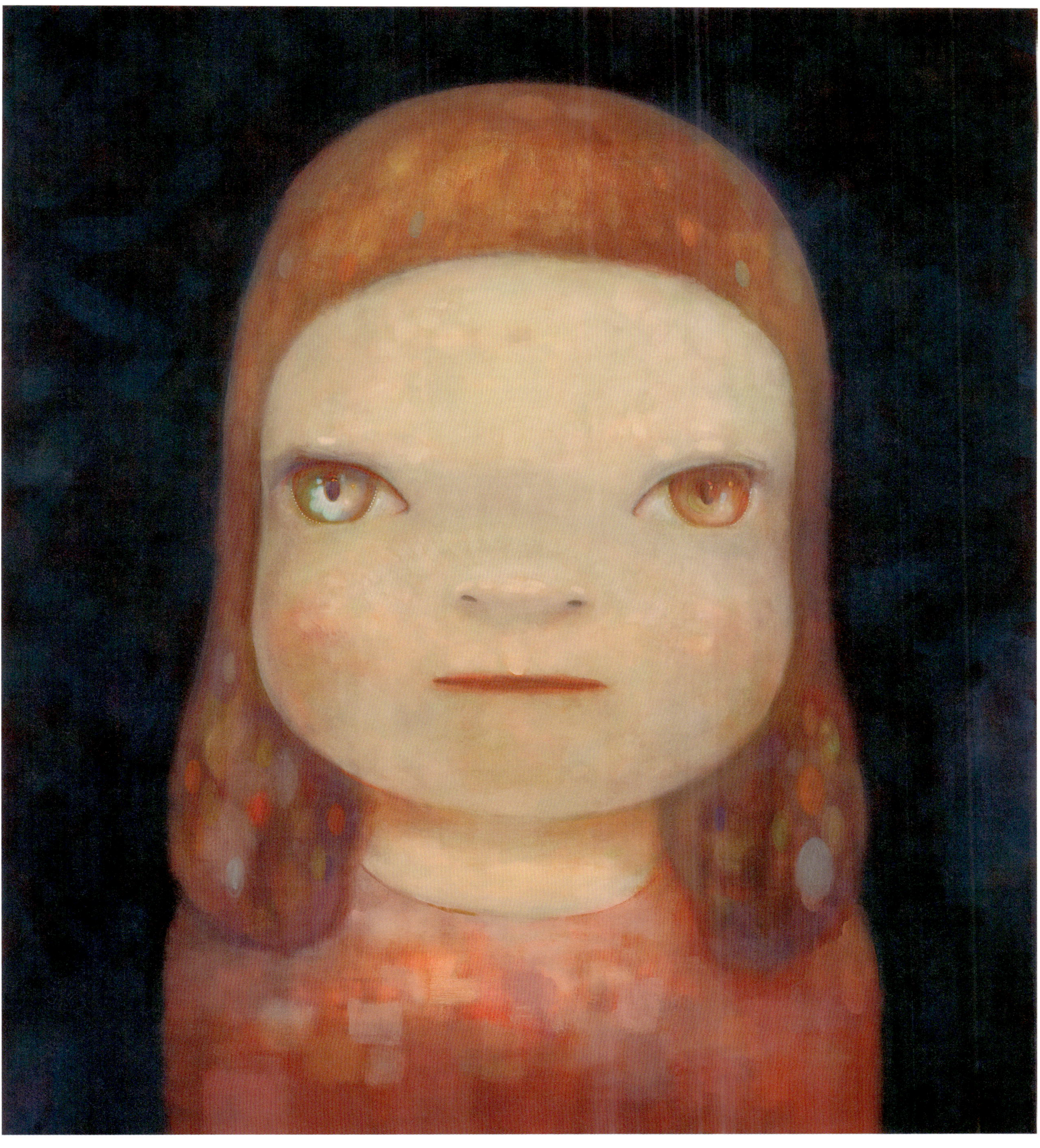

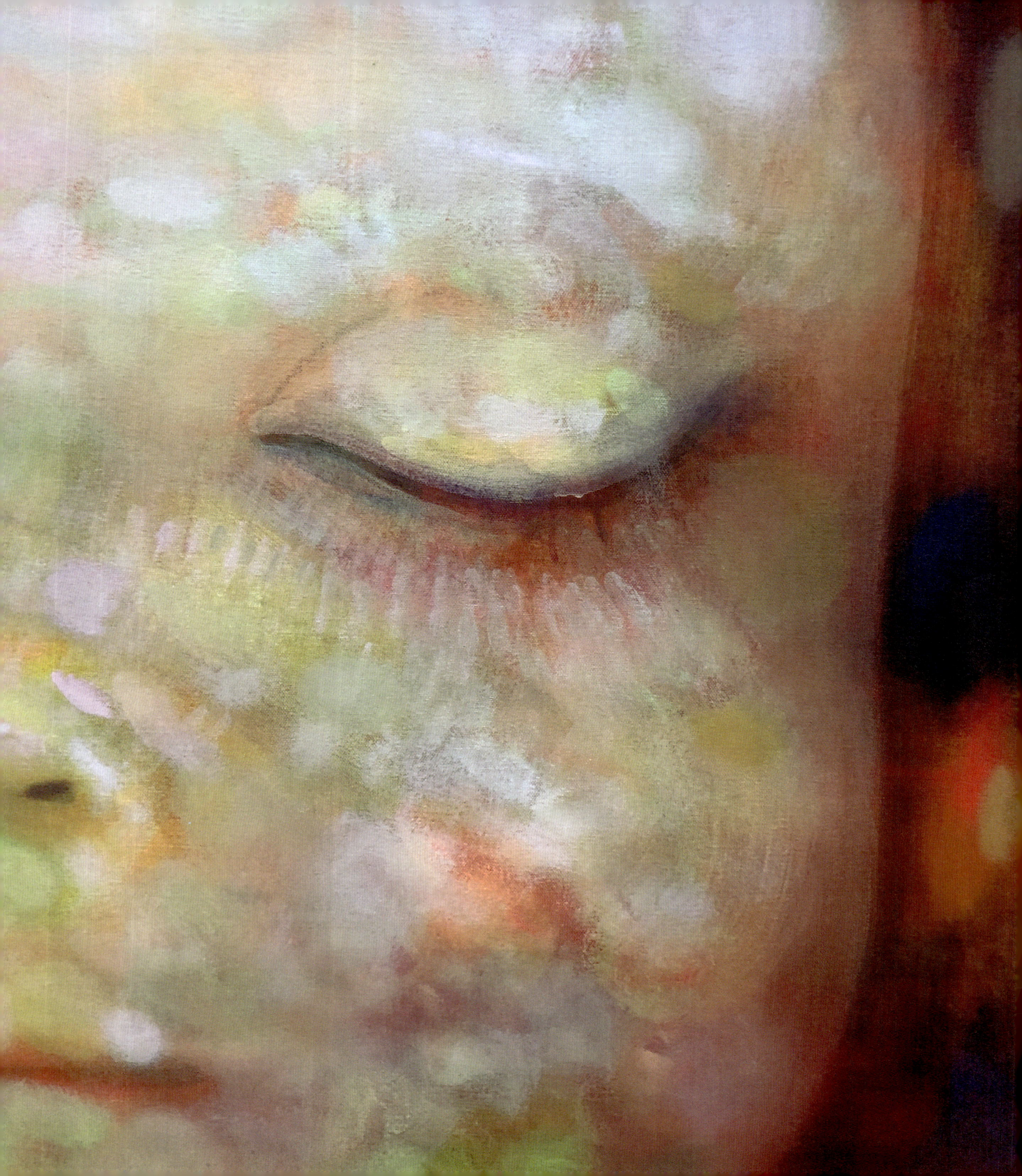

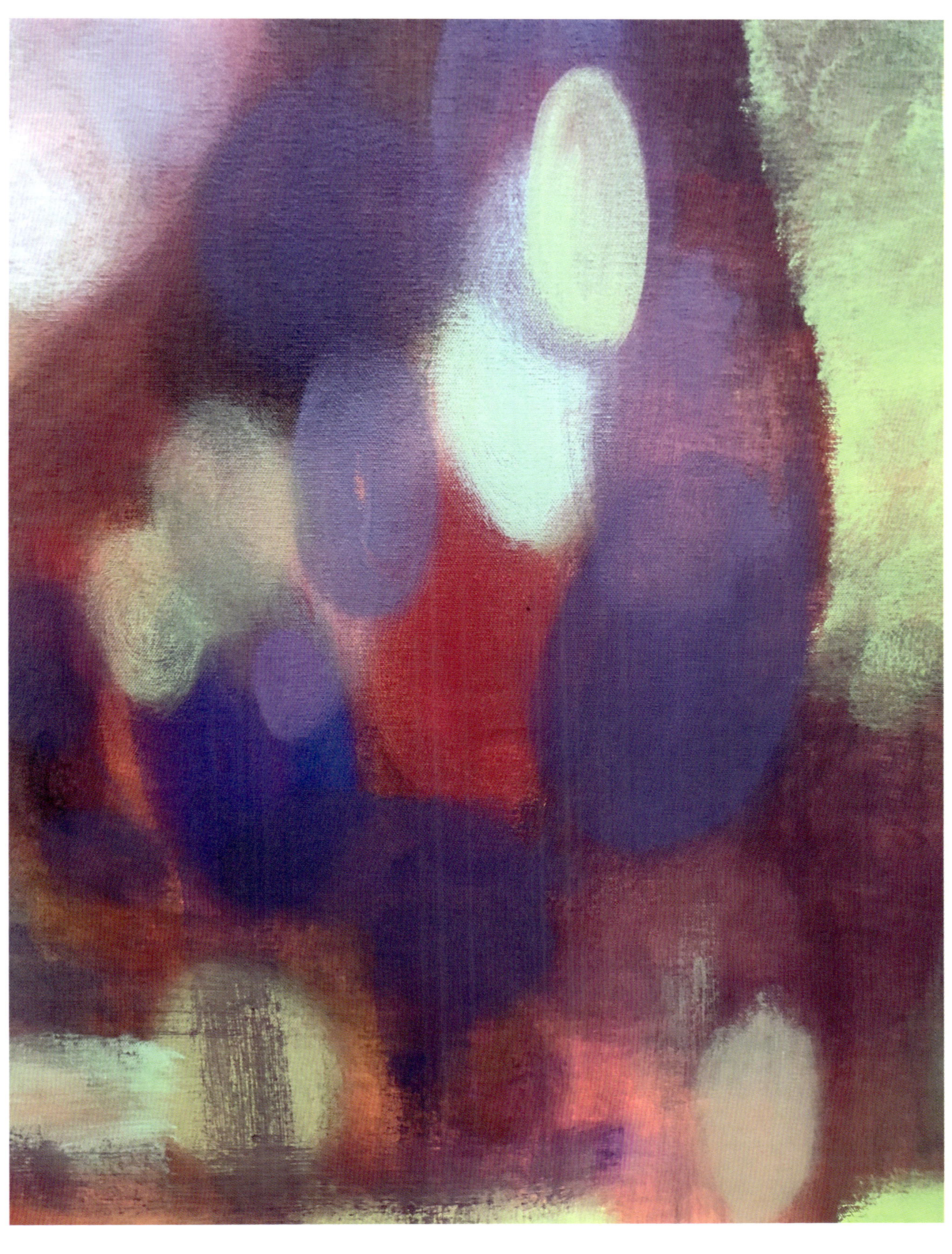

Figs. 310 and 311
Girl left behind the night
(2019) in progress

in this series of paintings that explore the effects of color; that it takes place within a representational form is incidental, or, at the very least, the child is secondary to the way in which Nara juxtaposes different values of tones, hues, highlights, and saturations, forming a puzzle of colors that lures viewers into the canvas.

Another shift in the works from this period is in how Nara processes memory. While it remains an important part of his creativity, memory is no longer employed to create a mythologized, timeless world. Rather, these later works evince a more heightened sensitivity to aging and the passing of time. Even with works whose titles indicate that Nara is drawing from early memories, such as *Girl from My Childhood* (2017) (Fig. 314), a small work of unusual tenderness, Nara leaves the edges of the figure fuzzy and indistinct as if to depict the recollection of a time past rather than childhood itself, when the world is seen through brighter eyes. In earlier works, references to his childhood acted as biographical anchors for the childlike worlds he created or, as explored in Chapter Two, as personal elements that undercut conventional readings of subcultural *kawaii* aesthetics. Now, however, the theme of childhood is used to draw attention to the act of recall itself and its impact on his present emotional state. In recent interviews, Nara has acknowledged that his references to and thoughts about childhood—both his own and in general—are often informed by his complex feelings about the Fukushima disaster and his acute awareness of the fragility of life.[8]

This change in how Nara expresses memory can perhaps be seen as a direct influence of his return to the north, a homecoming that compelled him to examine his identity as a northerner in post-2011 Japan and brought him back to some of the seminal influences in his life as an artist. In *Midnight Truth* (2017) (Fig. 313), pink, blue, and green spots of paint grace the young girl's cheeks like throbbing veins beneath translucent layers of paint, while feathered layers of color rain down onto the crown of her head. Nara made this painting with a copy of Shunsuke Matsumoto's *Standing Figure* (1942) (Fig. 312) pinned next to his canvas. Although the two paintings bear little resemblance, the inspiration Matsumoto's work provided marks a return to the group of artists that first directed Nara's pictorial experiments. Rather than functioning as an artistic reference, the older artist's work is now processed through a more subjective response. As discussed in the first chapter, Nara admired the work of Matsumoto, an artist also from northern Japan, whose paintings

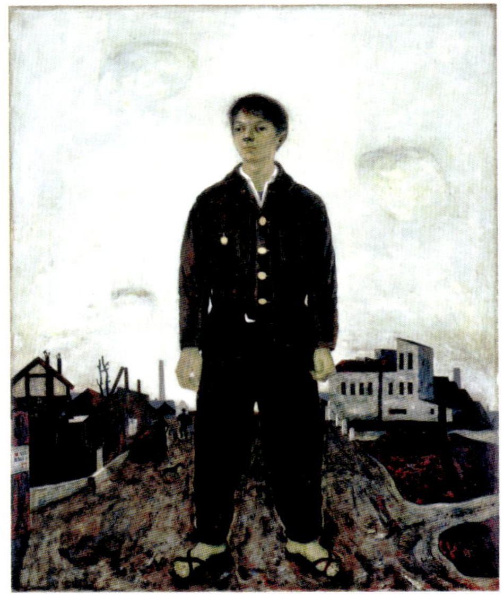

Fig. 312
Shunsuke Matsumoto,
Standing Figure, 1942,
Oil on canvas, 63 ¾ × 51 ⅜ in.
(162 × 130.5 cm)

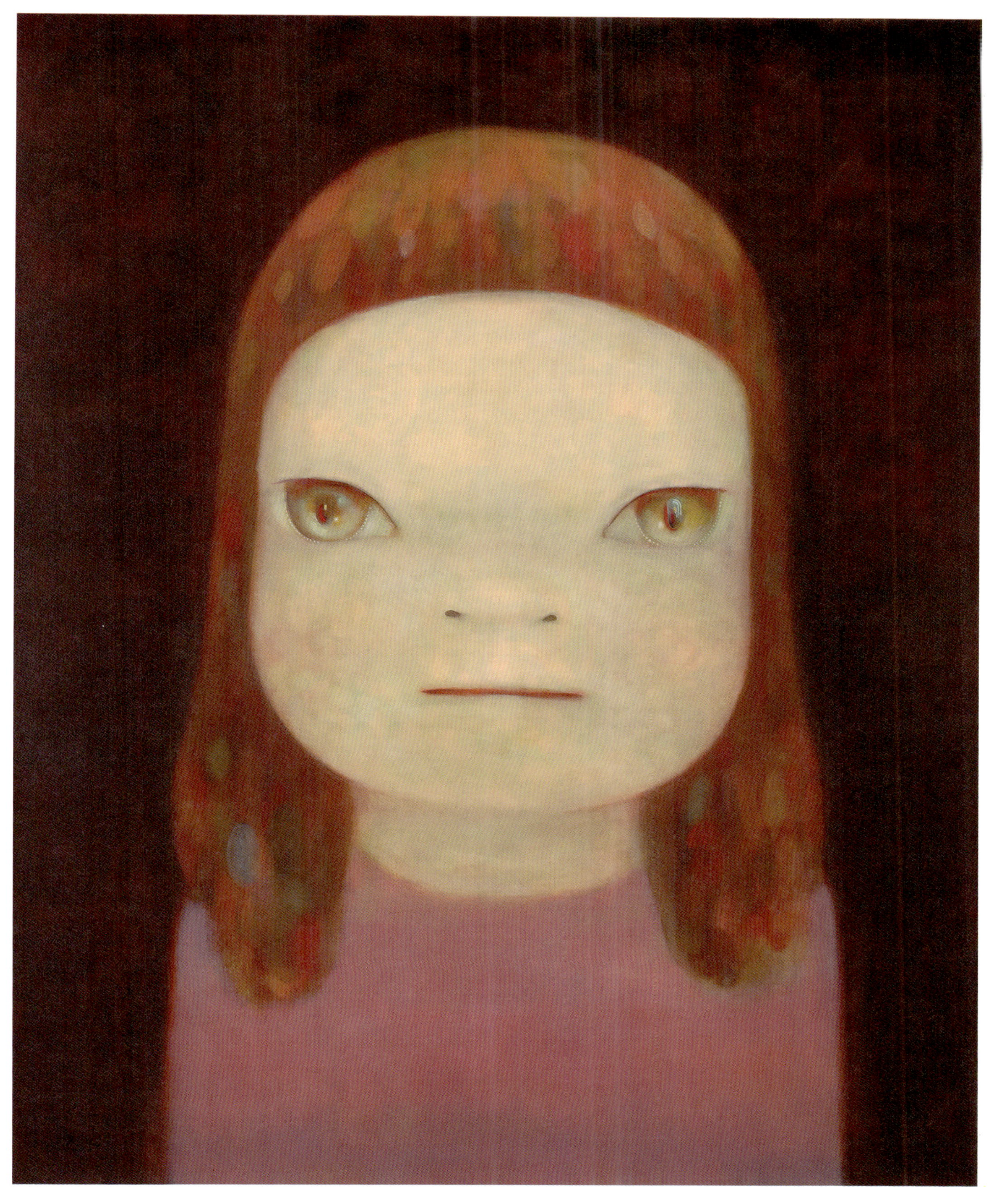

Fig. 313
Midnight Truth, 2017, Acrylic on canvas, 89 ½ × 71 ⁹⁄₁₆ in. (227.3 × 181.8 cm)

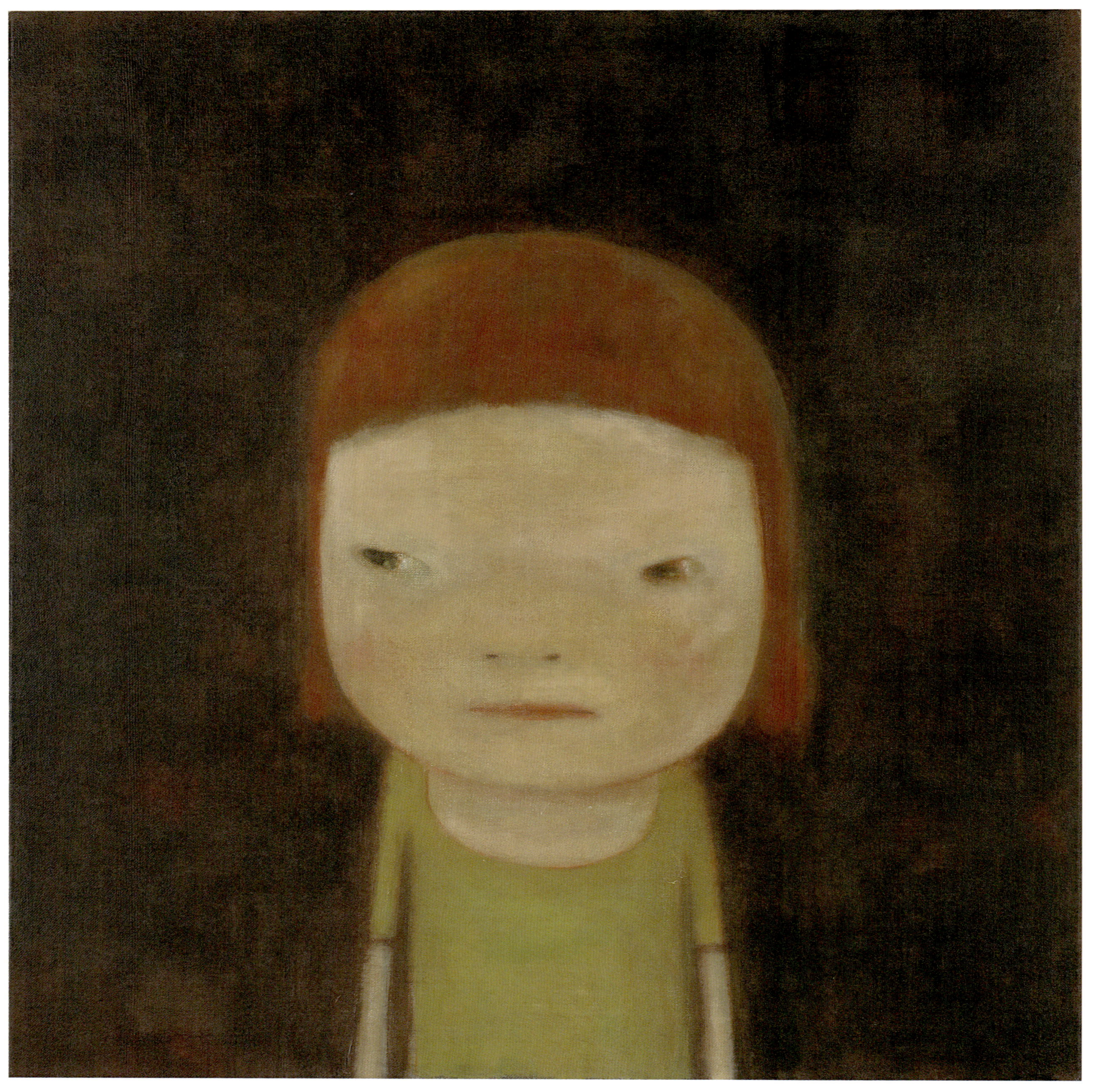

Fig. 314
Girl from My Childhood,
2017, Acrylic on canvas,
27 3/16 × 26 3/8 in. (69 × 67 cm)

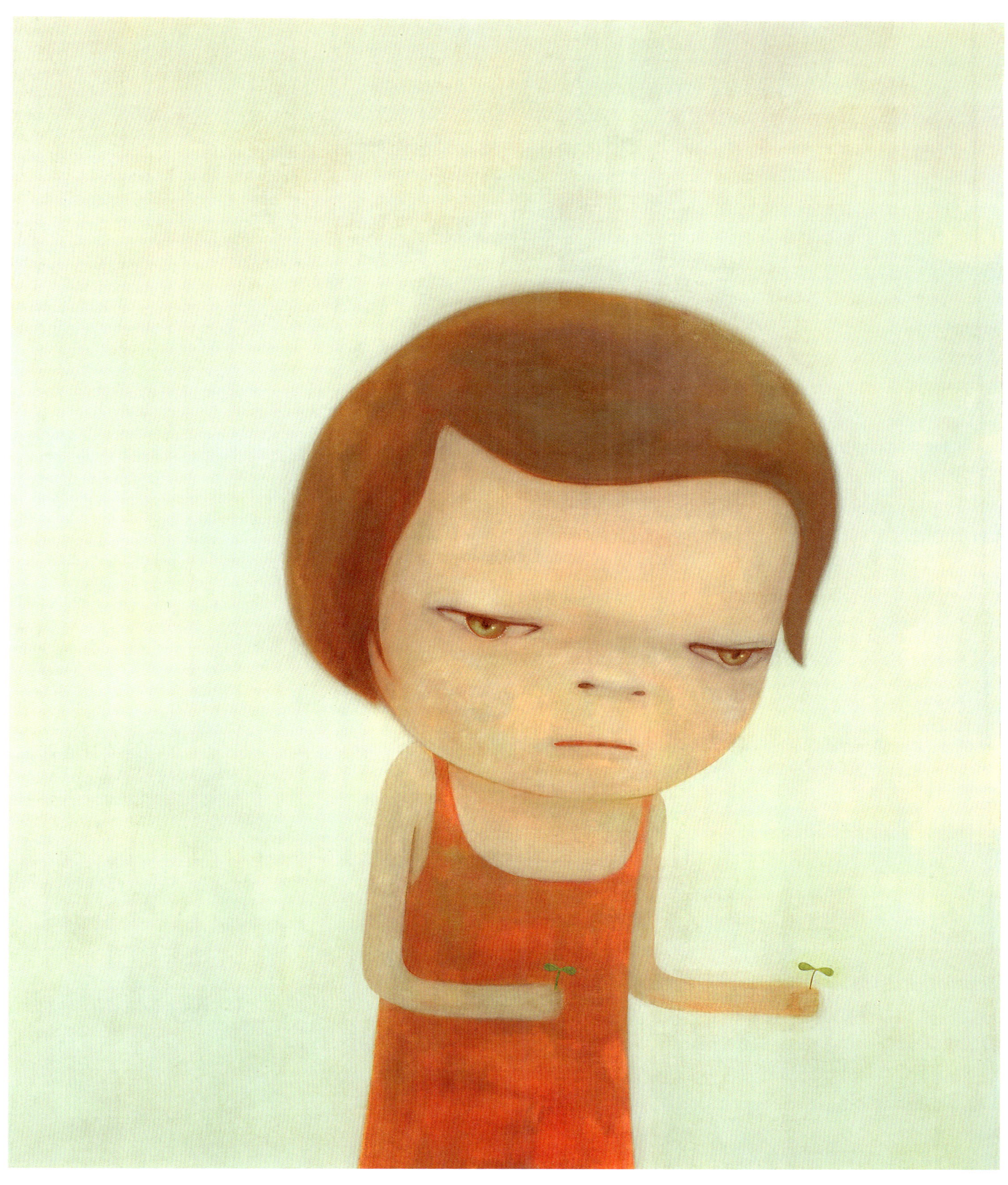

Fig. 315
Under the Hazy Sky, 2012,
Acrylic on canvas,
76 11/16 × 63 ¾ in. (194.3 × 162 cm)

often captured the internalized conflicts of young men called to arms. *Standing Figure* is a self-portrait in which the artist depicts himself in a dark green military outfit, standing proud with his feet in sandals on darkened red earth while in the near background lies a city composed of factories and traditional Japanese homes. Matsumoto's conflicted worlds are captured in this poignant image through mismatched clothing, the contrasts between modern and traditional architecture, and the overwhelming loneliness of his solitary stance. Nara relates to this sense of loneliness and internal restlessness—he, too, was struggling with a drastically changed Japan—and he attempts to channel some of this emotion in *Midnight Truth*, using a subdued palette and slow brushwork to achieve a quieter presence. The girl's eyes, with their sharp contrast of colors, refuse to engage with the audience, maintaining an emotional distance.

Nara's openness to memory went hand in hand with a greater receptiveness to his own emotional world, leading him to reflect more intimately on his relationships with the people and places that matter to him. His 2014 painting *No Means No* (Fig. 317) depicts a young person with clenched teeth whose eyes are covered with bangs, an image that recalls his punk roots. He made this painting while listening to the Bloodthirsty Butchers, an indie-punk band from Sapporo, partly in response to the untimely passing of the band's singer and guitarist, Hideki Yoshimura, who died of acute heart failure in 2013. The band, after Yoshimura's death, passed his guitar among themselves, each holding it for a period of time as an emblem of their bandmate. When *No Means No* was finished, Nara, an honorary member who was included in this circle, placed Yoshimura's guitar in front of the painting, a silent homage to a close friend (Fig. 316).

The emotional evolution of Nara's work was accompanied by a maturation of formal techniques. Where rounded edges and childlike colors, introduced in the 1991 work *The Girl with the Knife in Her Hand* (Fig. 56), once defined his portraits of big-headed girls, he now plays with their contours by diluting his signature bold outlines. In the 2018 painting *Alone in the Wind* (Fig. 318), the subject's face takes on an almost aqueous quality as it is made and unmade by the traces of Nara's brush. The insubstantial presence of the figure gives way to a wateriness that seems to break down his signature markings, a gesture that communicates the artist's own vulnerability. Nara selected *Alone in the Wind* as the cover artwork for the 2018 album *Jidai ga*

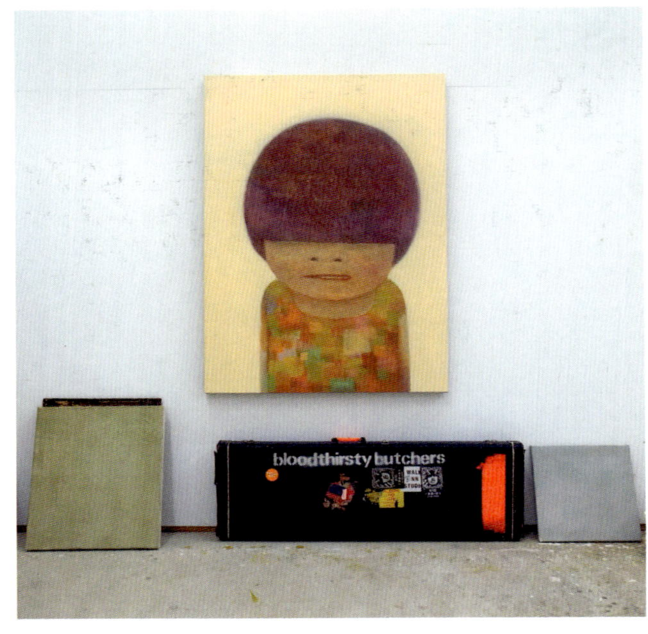

Fig. 316
No Means No (2014) in Nara's studio above Hideki Yoshimura's guitar, 2014

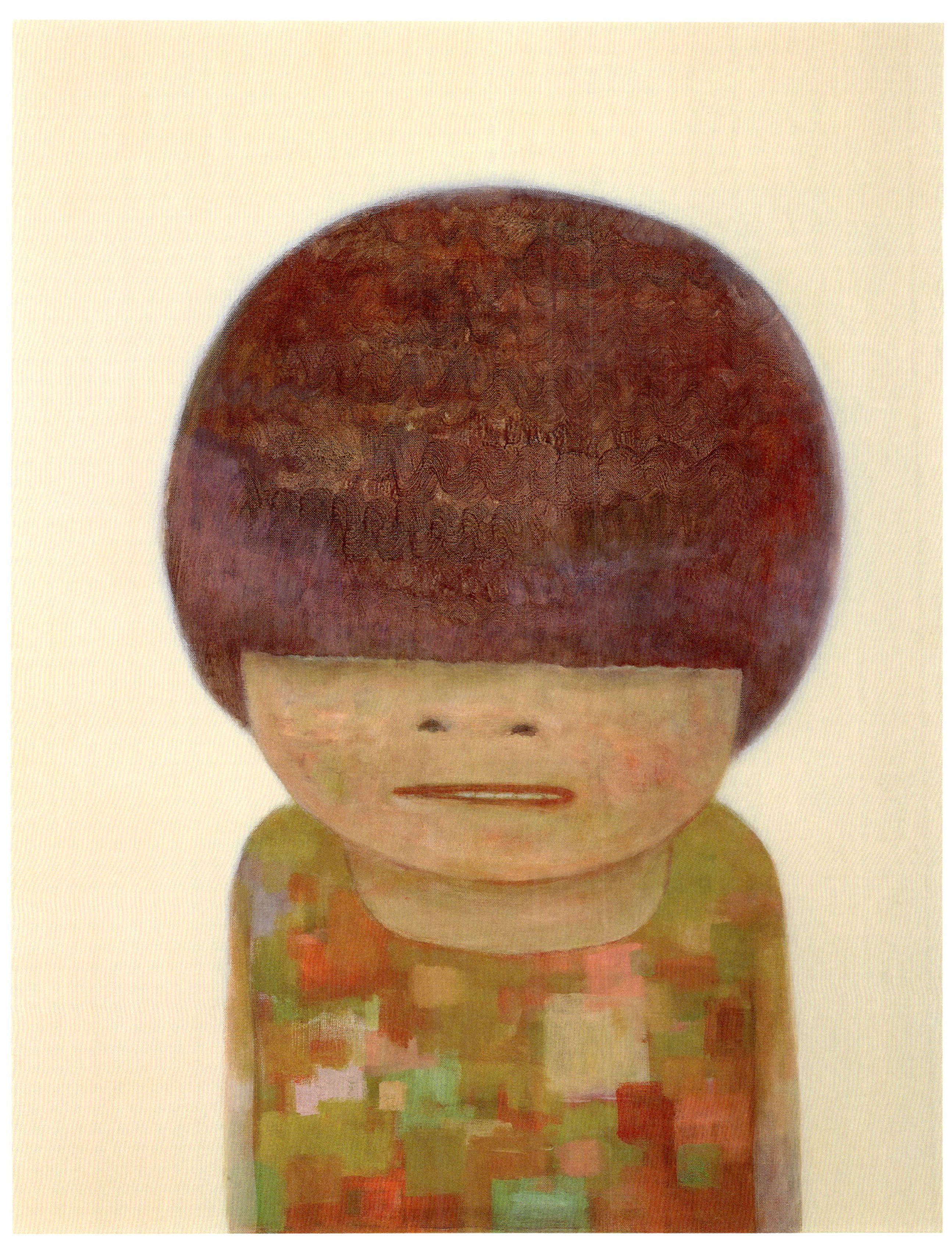

Fig. 317
No Means No, 2014, Acrylic on canvas, 51 ⁹⁄₁₆ × 38 ³⁄₁₆ in. (131 × 97 cm)

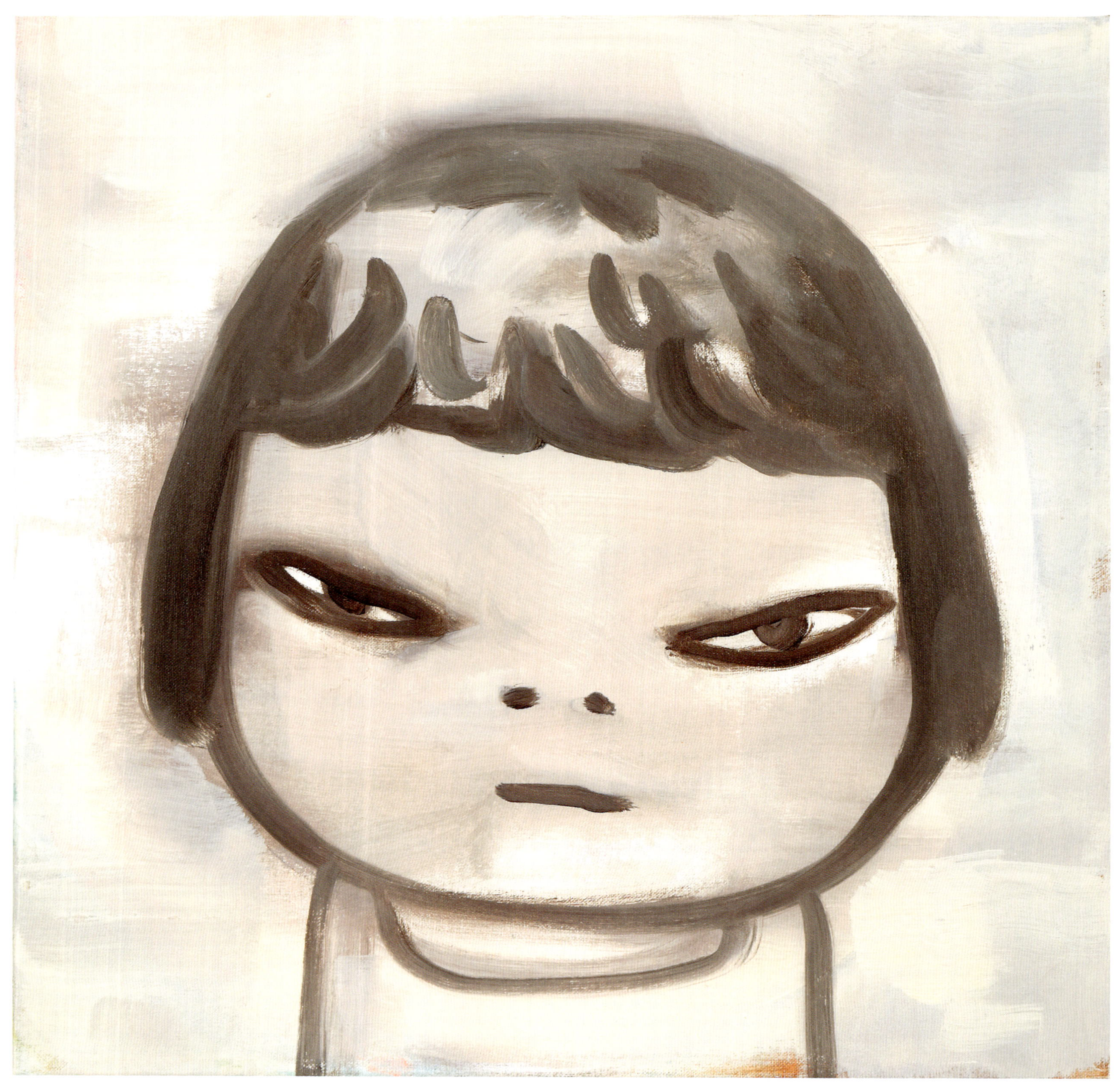

Fig. 318
Alone in the Wind, 2018, Acrylic on canvas, 20 ⅞ × 20 ⅞ in. (53 × 53 cm)

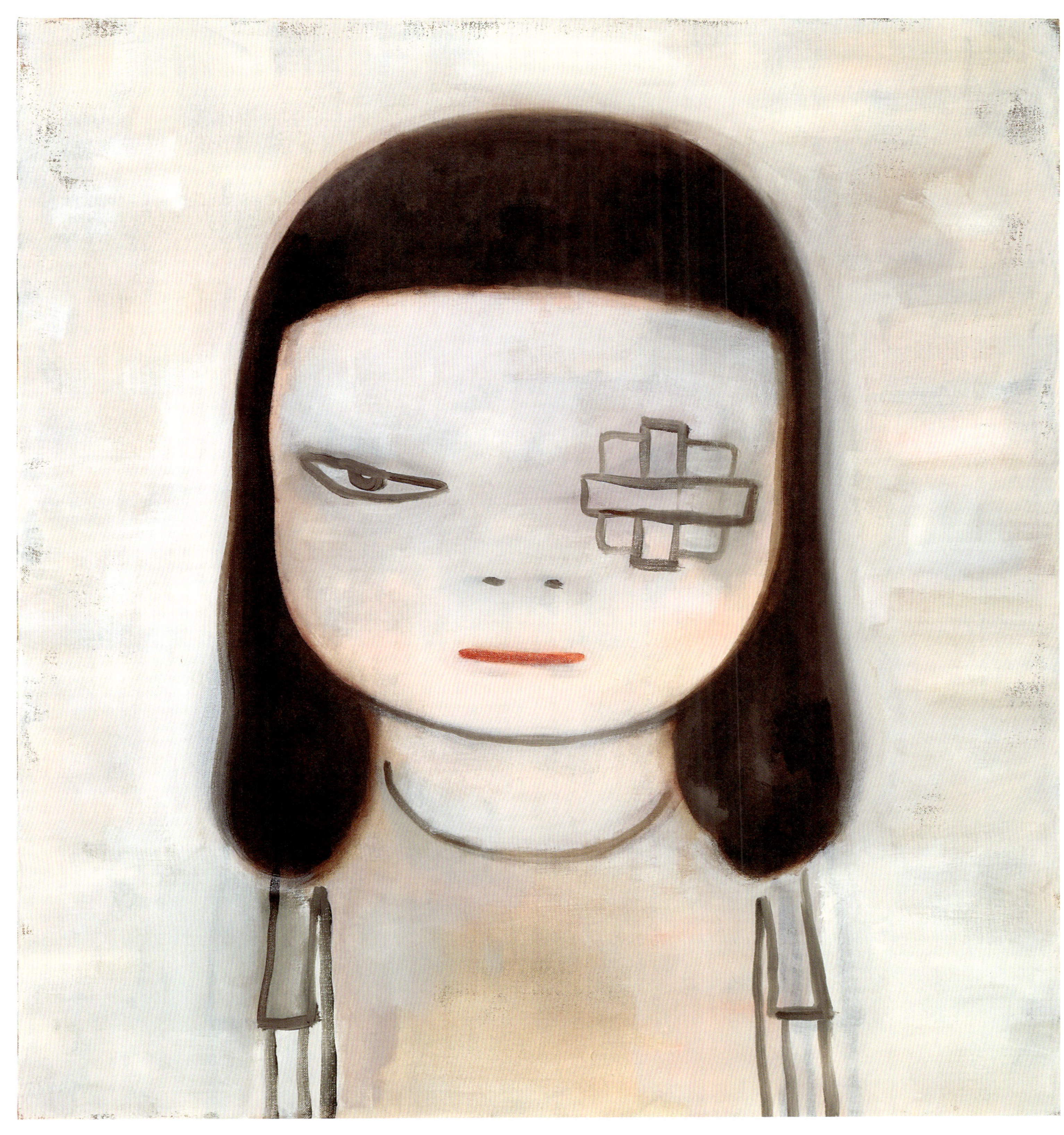

Fig. 319
Girl with Eyepatch, 2018, Acrylic on canvas, 47 ¼ × 43 5/16 in. (120 × 110 cm)

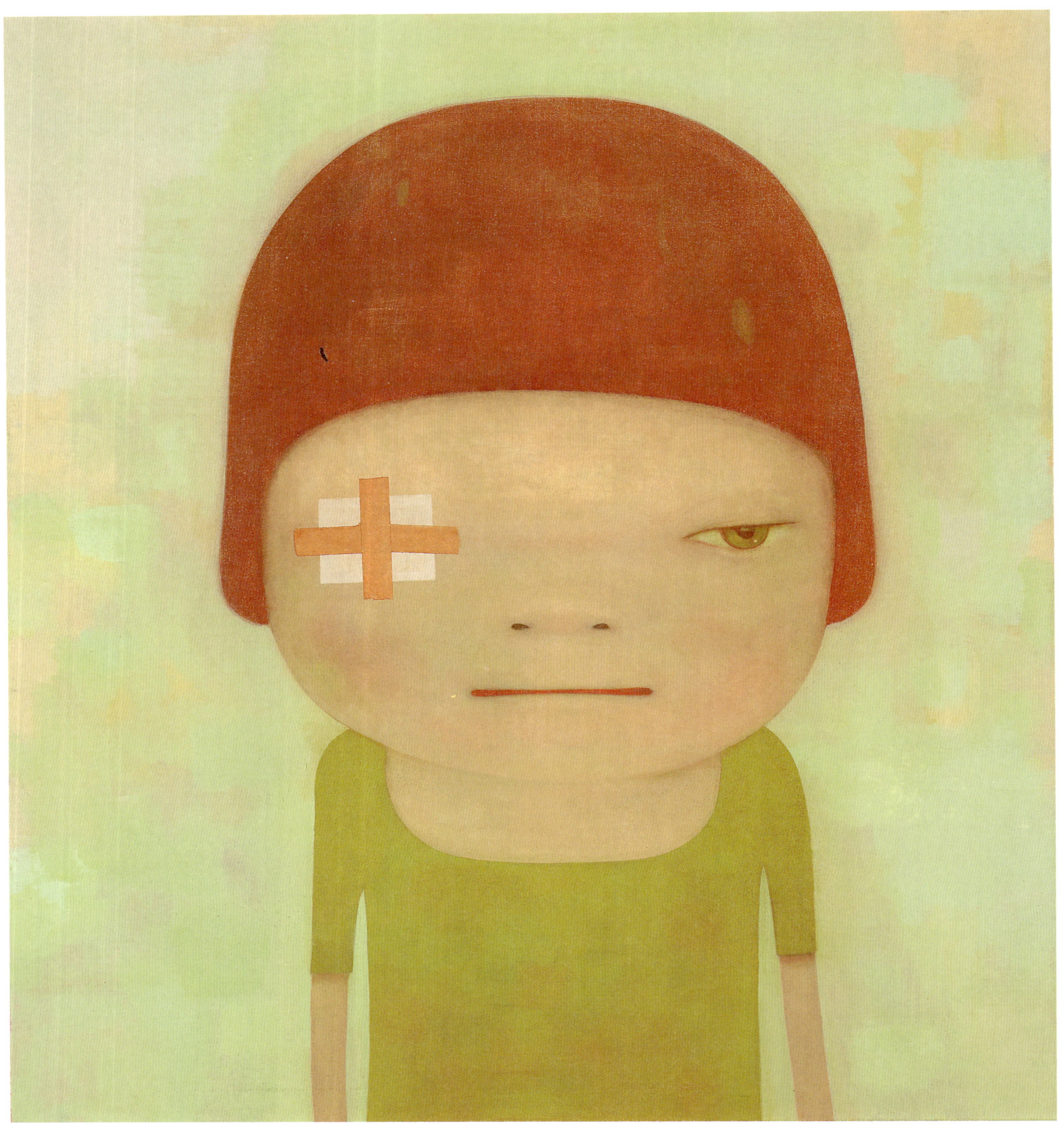

Fig. 320
Wounded, 2014, Acrylic
on canvas, 47 ¼ × 43 5⁄16 in.
(120 × 110 cm)

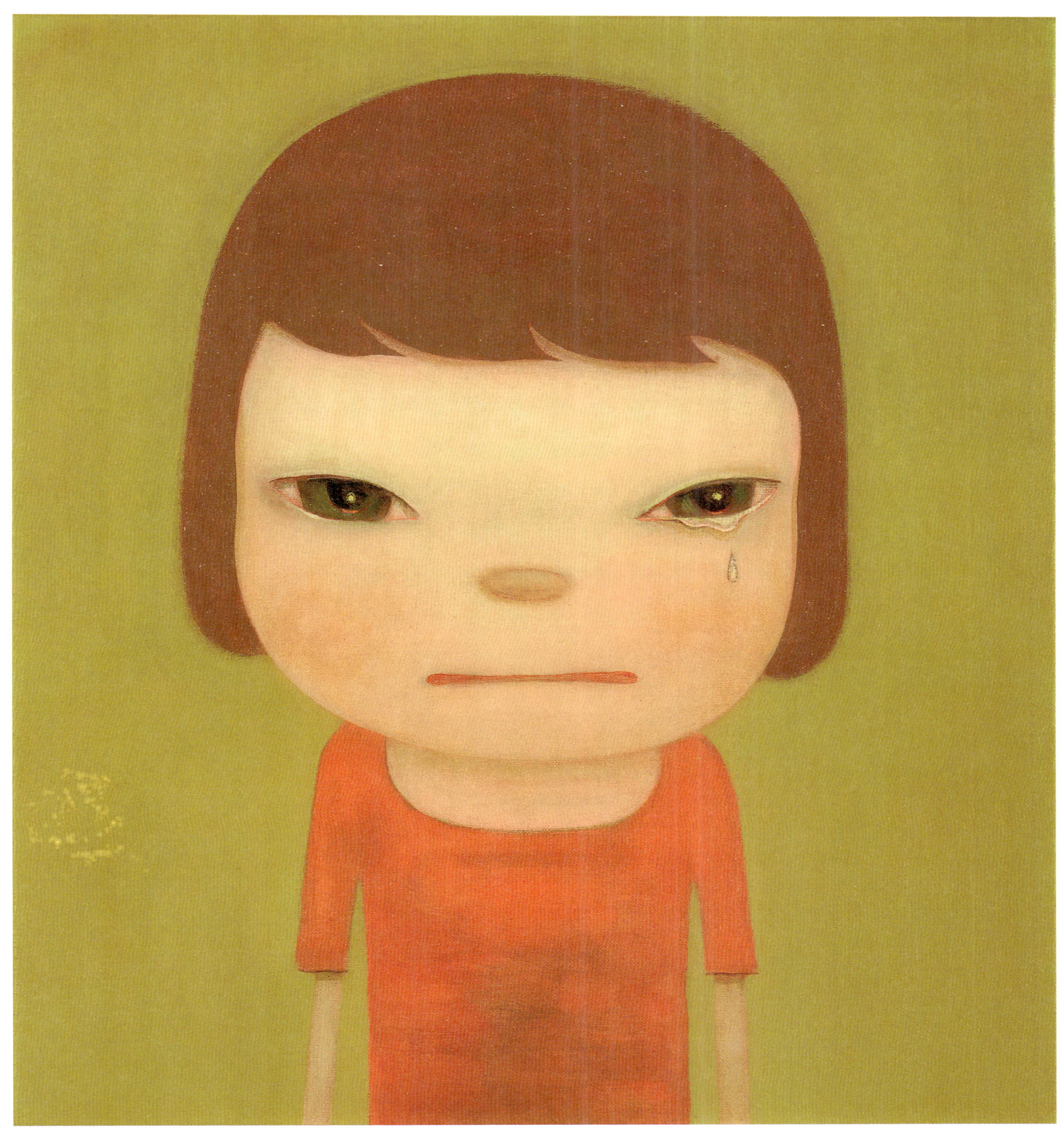

Fig. 321
Tears of Rage, 2015, Acrylic on canvas, 22 ¹⁄₁₆ × 20 ¹⁄₁₆ in. (56 × 51 cm)

fuzaketeru (A Time of Absurdity) by Kenzi Hatta, better known as Kenzi, a punk musician from Sapporo. The album commemorated the thirty-fifth anniversary of Kenzi's debut solo tour with new songs that reflected on his past. Its title comes from the first track on the album, a song that hails the importance of basic human emotions, such as love and warmth, in a time of *fuzaketeru*, or "absurdity." Other songs on the album include "Fight! Comrades!!" and "Thirty-Five Years of Hardship," which both convey ideas of never giving up hope and rejecting the hierarchies of power that strip away one's humanity. Given these nuanced messages that blend positivity with gut-punching lyrics, along with the retrospective nature of the album, it is easy to see why Nara agreed to collaborate with Kenzi and why specifically he selected *Alone in the Wind* to grace its cover. The painting continues the connection that Nara has forged between *kawaii* and punk aesthetics, a fusion that he now imbues with a delicate emotional quality.

In *Girl with Eyepatch* (2018) (Fig. 319), a similar picture from this period, Nara reincarnates one of his signature pictorial codes from the 1990s: the wounded eye. In other works, he extends this theme (Fig. 320), in one case with an eye blinded by a teary abundance of emotion (Fig. 321). These stand in contrast to his treatment of eyes in other bust portraits, which contain immersive pools of mismatched colors that invite the viewer in. With these, however, Nara turns the connection between subject and viewer on its head, the subjects' damaged eyes suggesting their yearning for social contact or, at the very least, for viewers to consider their displays of pain. Combined with the visual codes of *kawaii*, which seldom address themes of bodily harm, the works establish a tension between the outward signs of pain and the inner world of human frailty.

During this period, Nara also revisited the technique of blending drawing and painting, especially in his billboard paintings, a medium he had largely stopped working in after his 2010 exhibition *Nobody's Fool* at Asia Society in New York. He returned to it with gusto, producing a body of works that exhibits his energetic drive to reimagine past styles and practices. In his most recent billboard paintings, strong graphic lines appear with an unfinished, sketch-like quality, as seen in *Head (eyes opened)* and *Head (eyes closed)* (2017) (Figs. 322 and 323), whose abstract forms evoke those of his ceramic vases.

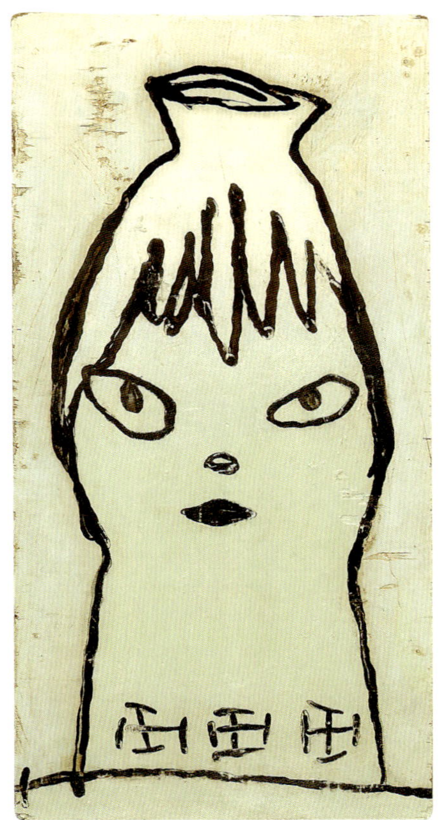

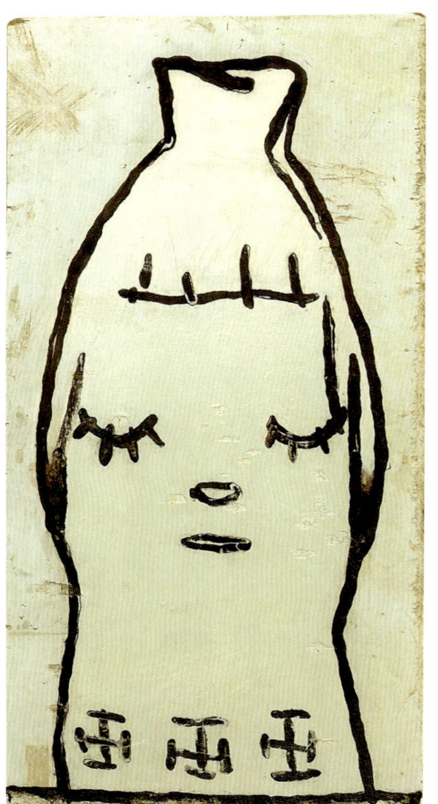

Fig. 322
Head (eyes opened), 2017, Acrylic on wood, 69 5/16 × 35 7/16 × 2 in. (176 × 90 × 5 cm)

Fig. 323
Head (eyes closed), 2017, Acrylic on wood, 69 5/16 × 35 7/16 × 2 in. (176 × 90 × 5 cm)

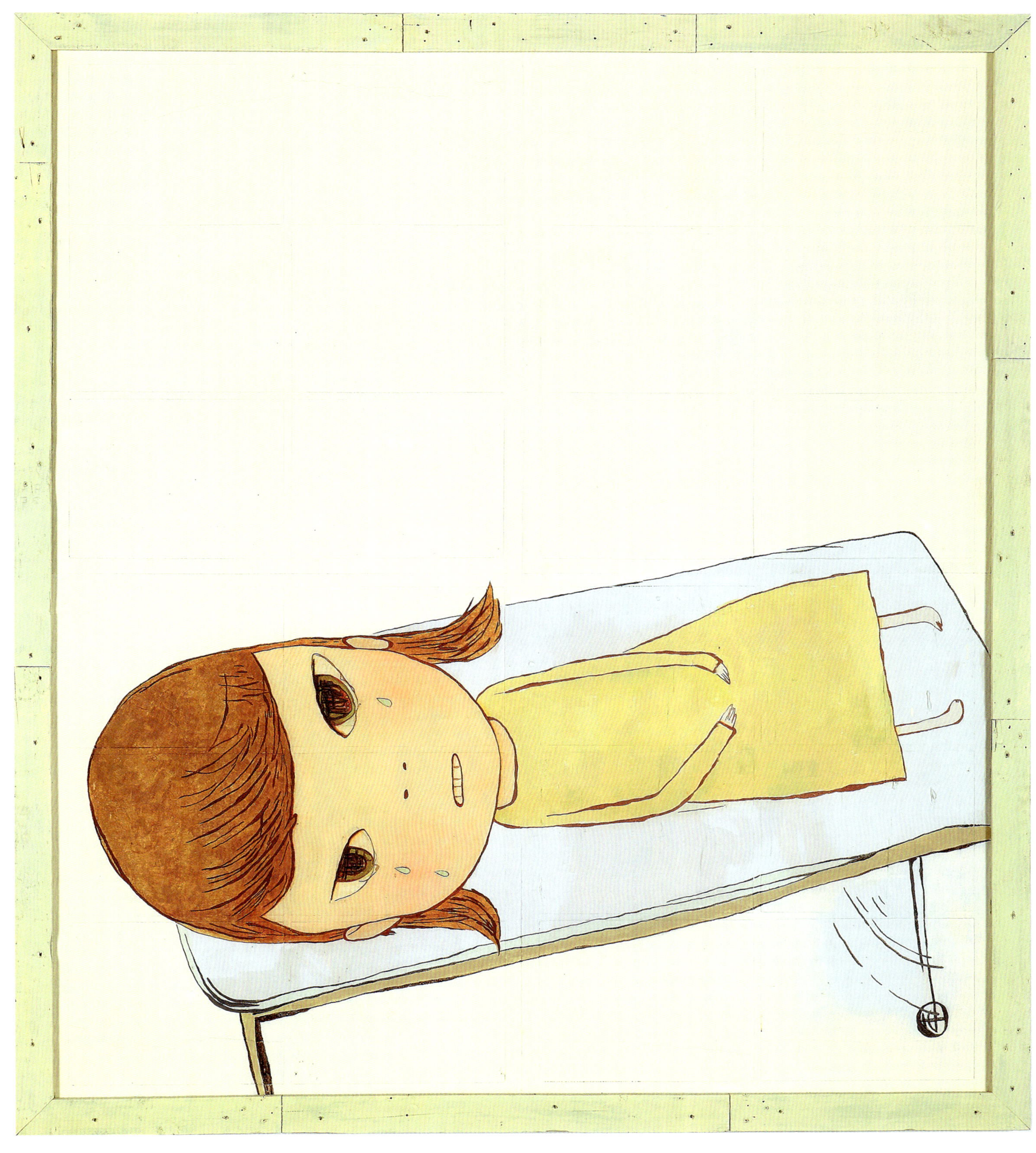

Fig. 324
Emergency, 2013, Acrylic
on wood, 83 1/16 × 73 1/4 × 3 9/16 in.
(211 × 186 × 9 cm)

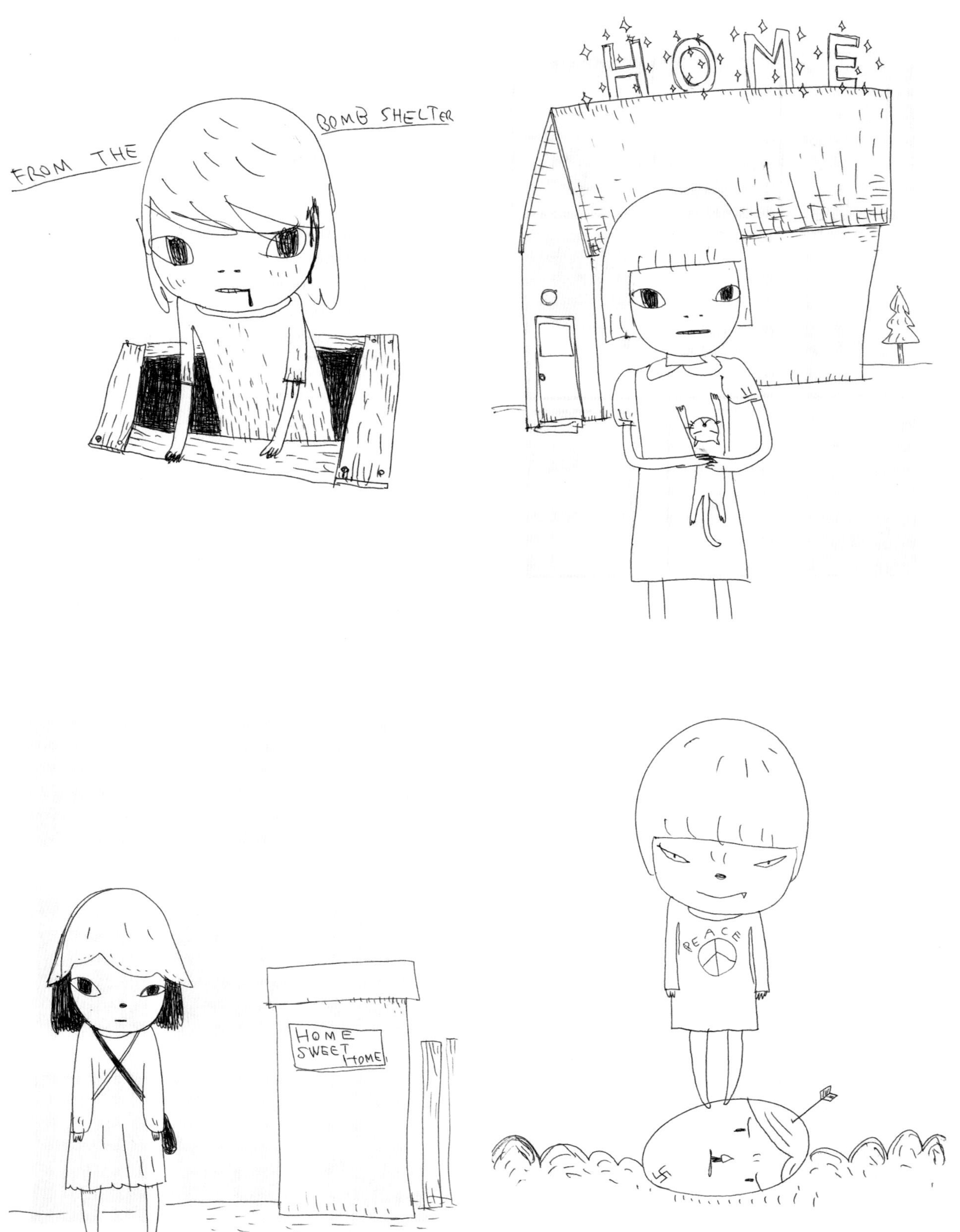

Figs. 325–328
Untitled, 2016, Ballpoint pen on paper, each 11 ¹¹⁄₁₆ × 8 ¼ in. (29.7 × 21 cm)

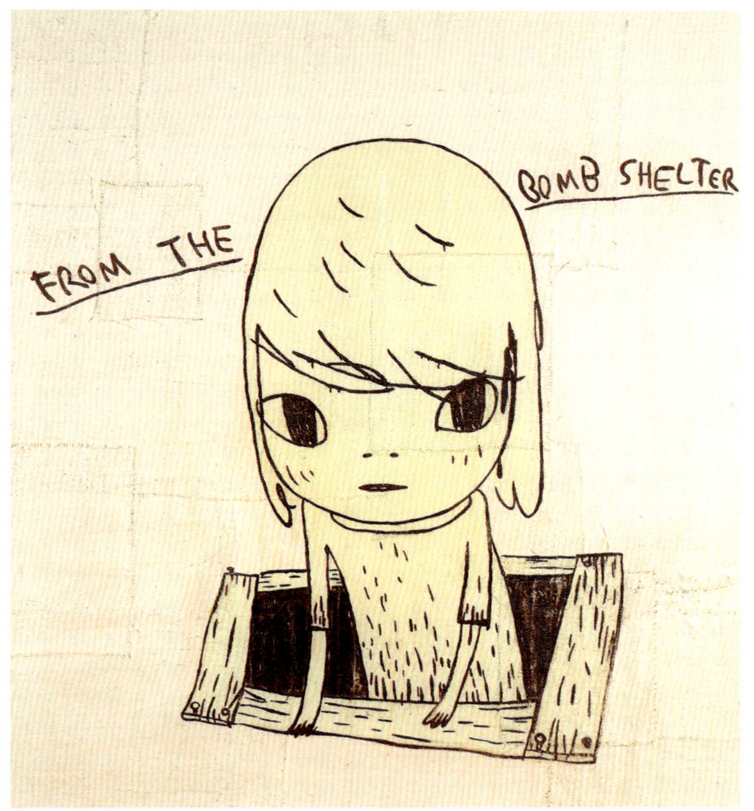

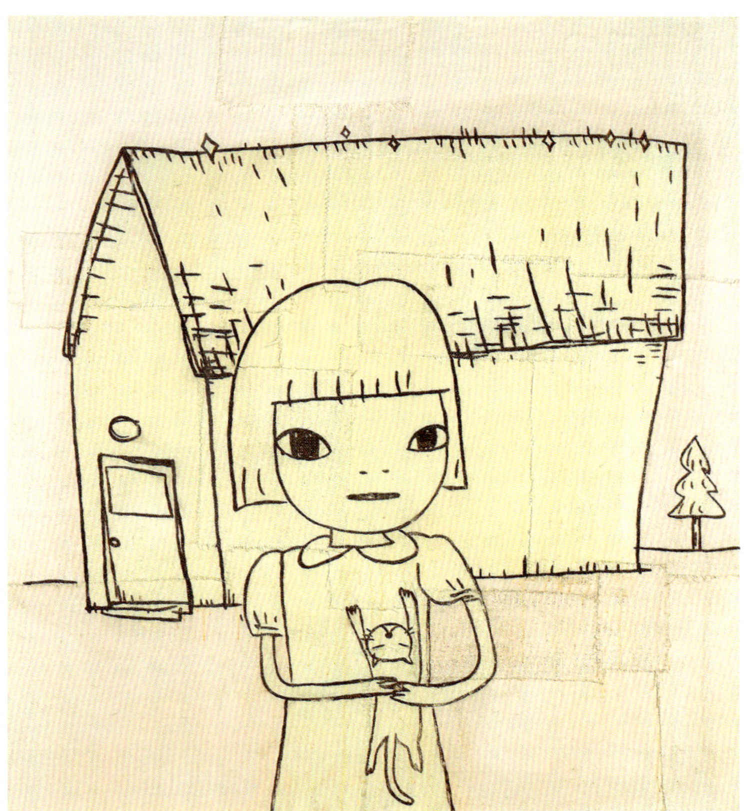

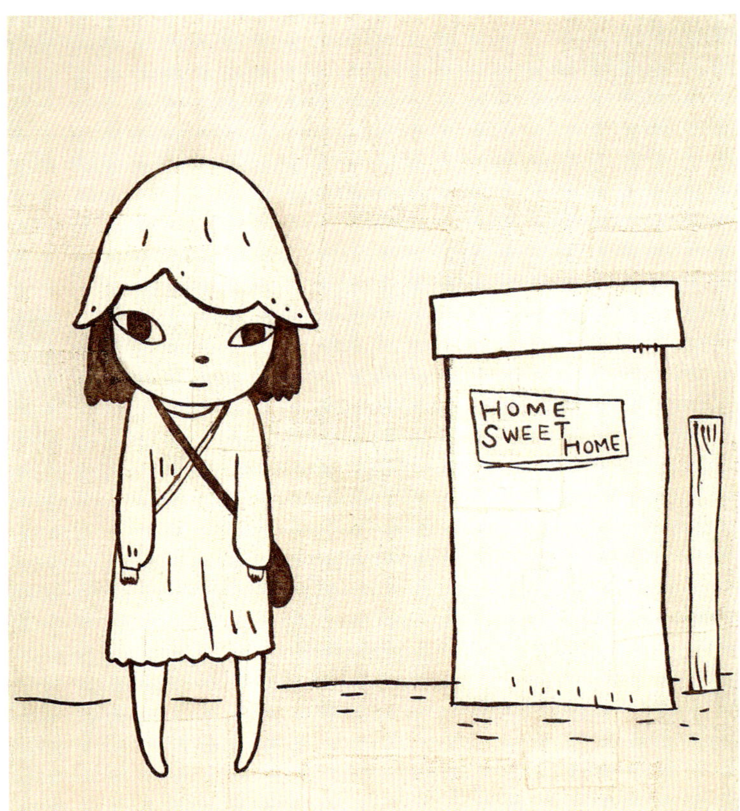

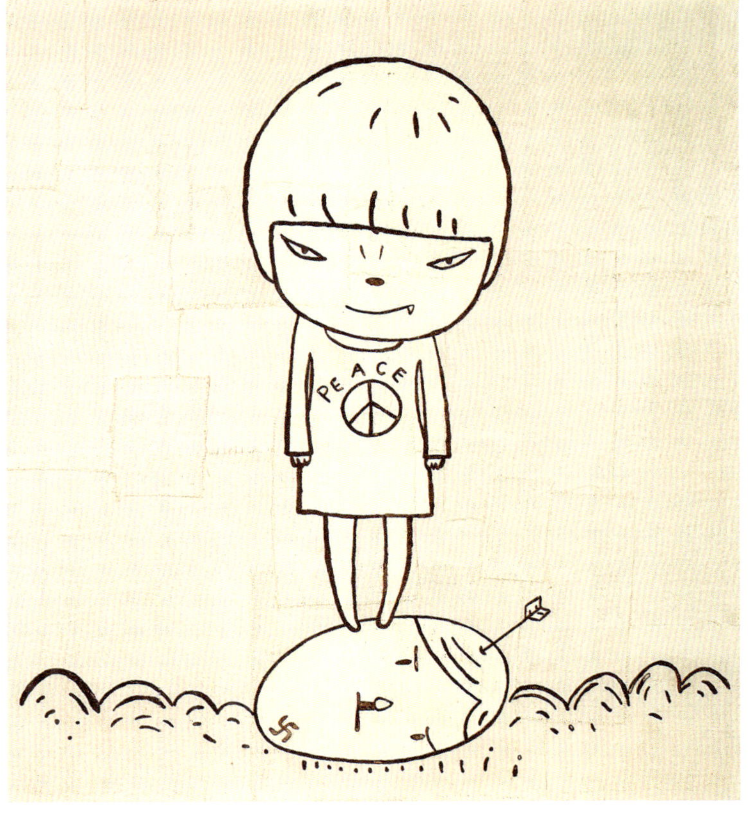

Fig. 329 (top left)
FROM THE BOMB SHELTER, 2017, Acrylic on jute mounted on wood, 71 1/16 × 63 3/16 × 1 7/8 in. (180.5 × 160.5 × 4.8 cm)

Fig. 330 (top right)
HOME, 2017, Acrylic on jute mounted on wood, 71 1/16 × 63 3/16 × 1 7/8 in. (180.5 × 160.5 × 4.8 cm)

Fig. 331 (bottom left)
SWEET HOME GATE, 2019, Acrylic on jute mounted on wood. 71 1/16 × 63 3/16 × 1 7/8 in. (180.5 × 160.5 × 4.8 cm)

Fig. 332 (bottom right)
PEACE GIRL, 2019, Acrylic on jute mounted on wood, 71 1/16 × 63 3/16 × 1 7/8 in. (180.5 × 160.5 × 4.8 cm)

At the other end of the spectrum is the 2013 work *Emergency* (Fig. 324), one of Nara's most poignant paintings on wood, in which he depicts a young girl on a gurney staring at us through gritted teeth, rendered with lines gentler than those of his other works in the medium. Like *Miss Spring*, the painting was made with the Fukushima disaster heavy on his mind, but here the message is more literal, as is typical of his billboard paintings, which exploit their inherent function as sites of public announcement. The painting also refers back to some of his earliest works that used cross-shaped compositions to depict young children lying down as if in sacrifice. But Nara's use of color—delicate washes and muted yellows and greens—departs from the haunting darkness of those works and places *Emergency* within the more hopeful world embodied by *Miss Spring*, even as it directly addresses the physical trauma of children.

Nara continued to explore this theme in a series of four billboard paintings: *FROM THE BOMB SHELTER* (Fig. 329), *HOME* (Fig. 330), *SWEET HOME GATE* (Fig. 331), and *PEACE GIRL* (Fig. 332). Each is based on a drawing (Figs. 325–328) inspired by the 1953 film *Hiroshima*, directed by Hideo Sekigawa (Fig. 333). A comparison of the drawings with the paintings shows that they largely follow their respective pen-sketch versions, with some exceptions, such as in *FROM THE BOMB SHELTER*: in the painting, the girl's wounds are absent, and instead, Nara portrays her with a steely determination. It is a posture that evokes *Abandoned Puppy* (1995) (Fig. 73), one of his seminal works, of a defiant child in a puppy outfit painted on a patchwork of cut-up canvas cloth.

The film *Hiroshima* is based on the best-selling book *Children of the Atom Bomb* (1951), a collection of 105 firsthand accounts of school children who survived the Hiroshima bombing, compiled by the author Arata Osada. Sekigawa's film was an independent production, funded by the Japanese Teachers Union (JTU) as a corrective to an earlier movie, *Children of Hiroshima*, based on the same book and directed by Kaneto Shindō in 1952, which the JTU criticized for not sufficiently addressing the political ramifications of the nuclear bomb.[9] Sekigawa's adaptation, more ambitious in scope, offered many different perspectives on the bombing and, to add to the authenticity of its accounts, included thousands of *hibakusha* (nuclear-attack survivors) as extras. The film begins with a classroom scene in which a teacher, ignorant of the legacy of the nuclear bomb and the subsequent

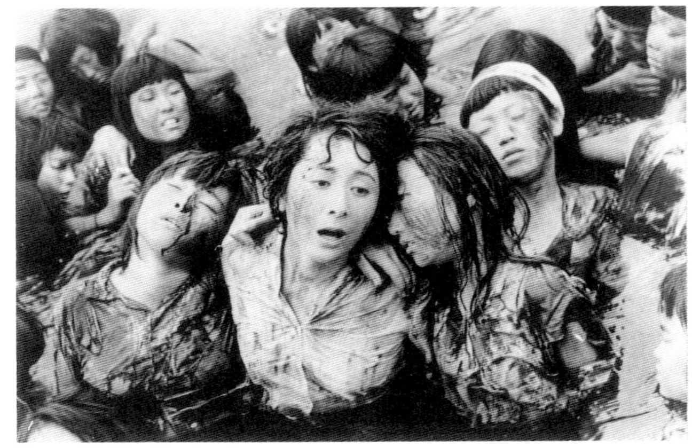

Fig. 333
Hiroshima, 1953, dir. Hideo Sekigawa, 104 min.

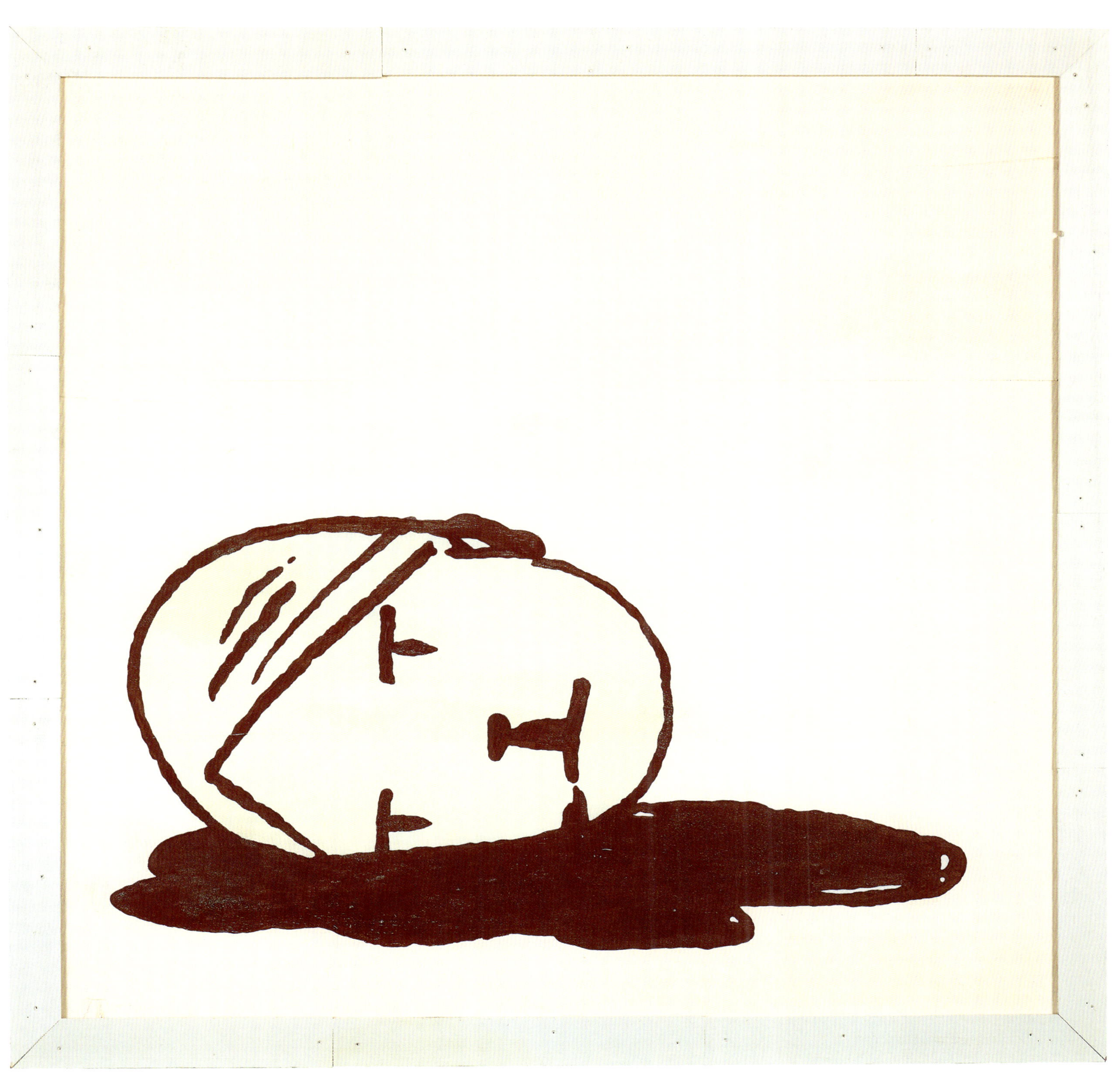

Fig. 334
Bad Head, 2014,
Acrylic on wood board,
58 1/16 × 59 7/16 × 3 9/16 in.
(147.5 × 151 × 9 cm)

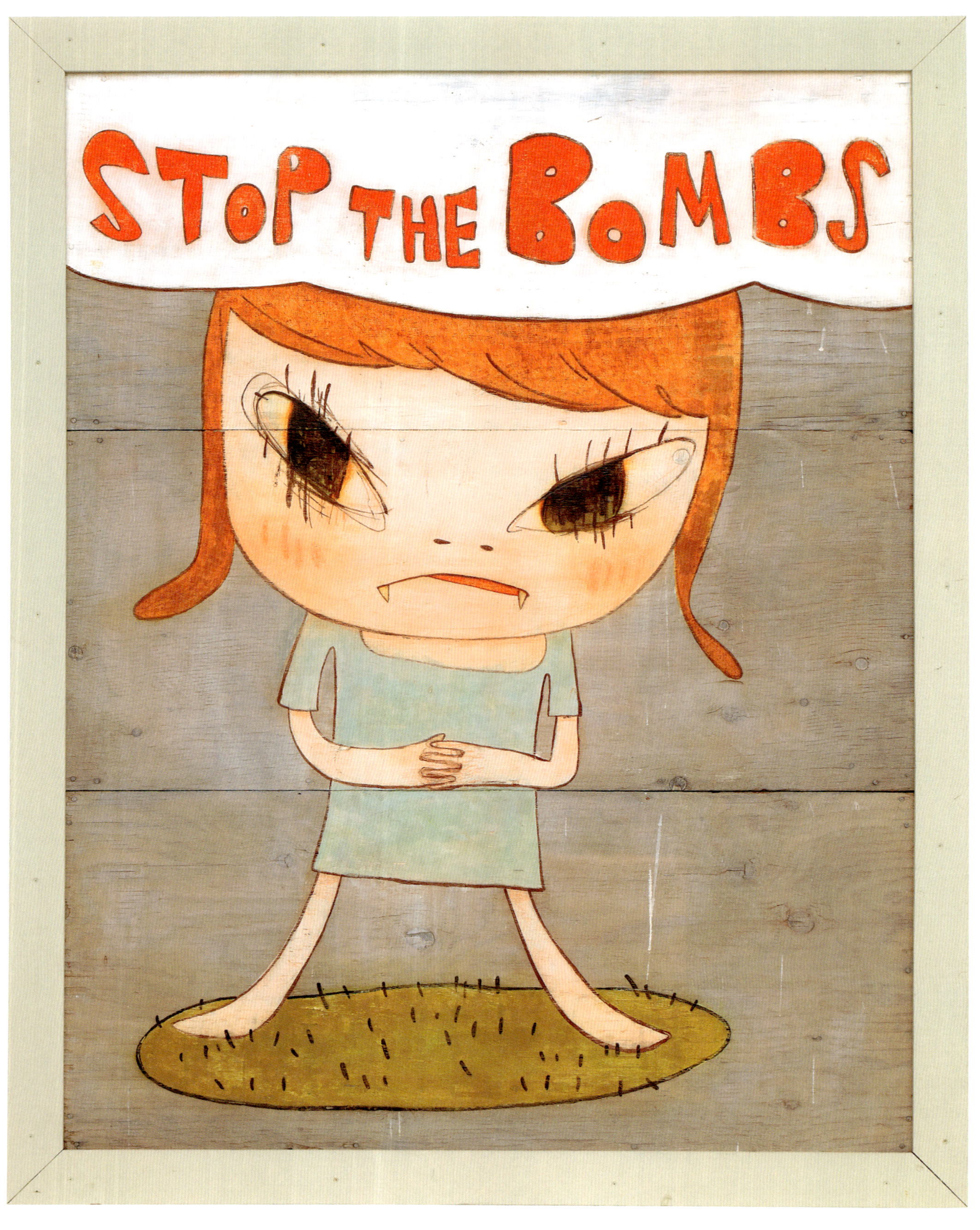

Fig. 335
STOP THE BOMBS,
2019, Acrylic on wood,
58 ⅞ × 46 ¼ × 3 in.
(149.5 × 117.5 × 7.7 cm)

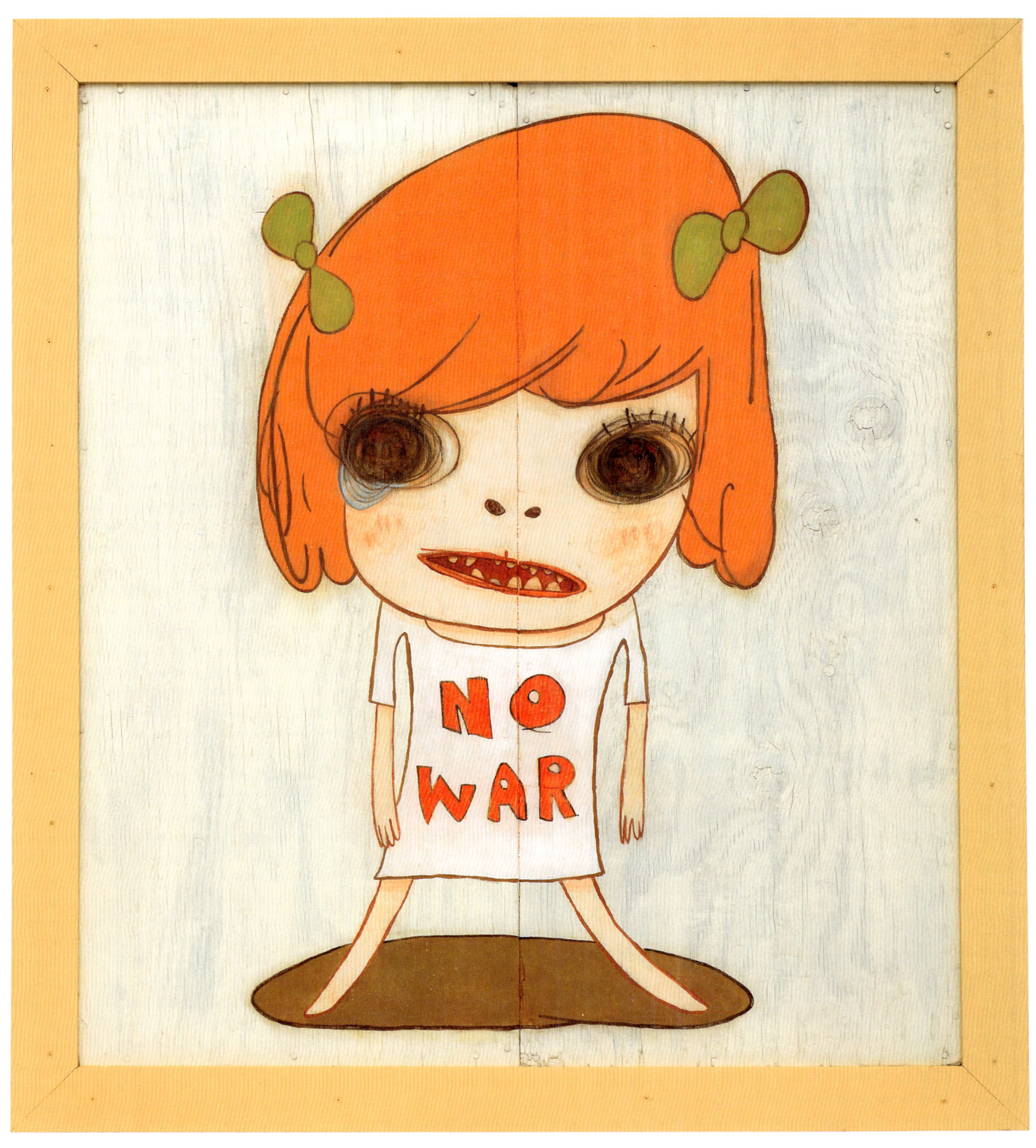

Fig. 336
NO WAR, 2019,
Acrylic on wood,
46 1⁄16 × 40 3⁄4 × 2 3⁄4 in.
(117 × 103.5 × 7 cm)

discrimination against *hibakusha*, is schooled by his pupils before the narrative shifts back in time to show the magnitude of the bomb and the human dimension of the tragedy that followed. Among the many narrative threads interwoven into this story, one of the best-known scenes shows the Japanese imperial military leadership collectively agreeing to lie to citizens that the bomb was not a nuclear weapon, in order to preserve the momentum of the war effort. At one side of the meeting table sits a nuclear scientist silently watching a moth flittering at the window, a symbol of the many who would become victims of the nuclear fallout.

In some works, Nara makes reference to the hypocrisy of wartime Japan's rightwing imperial military by drawing attention to its similarity to Nazi Germany. The fallen head of Hitler lying on its side in a pool of blood is a subject that he had explored in earlier drawings, and in *Bad Head* (2014) (Fig. 334), he turns it into a billboard painting, a genre that he associates with public statements, indicating that Nara is becoming more open about his political stances. If this billboard painting is simple in its directness, a different approach is seen in two others that mark a return to the combination of cute and menacing in his big-headed girl. However, this time he paints them with bold, politically overt vigor. With their uneven teeth and manic eyes, the girls possess a threatening energy as they pronounce messages such as "Stop the Bombs" and "No War" (Figs. 335 and 336). Although dark humor lurks behind these works, it is hard to escape the fact that these broken children also capture the nightmare of nuclear fallout.

As discussed in the previous chapter, in response to his trip to Afghanistan, Nara produced a small number of works that were critical of war and the historical militarization of chemical weapons. But after 2011, Nara's antiwar messages become far more explicit, in his billboard paintings but also on his painted canvases, as seen in two highly unusual works made as a tribute to the Georgian artist Niko Pirosmani (1862–1918) in 2018. The paintings were part of an exhibition that included artists such as Tadao Andō, Shirana Shahbazi, Andro Wekua, Pablo Picasso, and Georg Baselitz, who all made work in response to this Georgian outsider artist.[10] Pirosmani lived a short life blighted by alcoholism and poverty, a self-taught, itinerant artist who made store signs for taverns and paintings for well-heeled patrons as he wandered between cities and the Georgian countryside, equally at home painting portraits of famous actresses as he was of a herd of cows. His works have the raw emotional charge of an artist who paints with straightforward honesty and folk-style quirkiness, a style sometimes described as "primitive." Although Pirosmani had patrons and admirers within the art establishment, he was always a man on the margins. He became homeless shortly after the start of World War I when patrons stopped commissioning him; his health deteriorated, and he died before the war's end. He was later rediscovered by the art world in the 1950s, and he is now regarded as a pivotal artist of the modern art movement in Slavic Russia.

Nara, who has always been drawn to the biographies of wartime artists, has long been an admirer of Pirosmani. For this tribute show, he made two works in response to the artist: one based on *Actress Margarita* (1909) (Fig. 337) and the other on *Queen Tamar holding a scroll* (n.d.) (Fig. 338). Pirosmani's *Actress Margarita* is a painting of unrequited love. The artist had fallen passionately for the French singer and dancer to the point of losing his mind and, in an attempt to win her affection, spent all his money on flowers and laid them out on the streets outside her home. Moved by this extravagant gesture, the actress came out of her house and kissed the artist for the first and only time. Pirosmani portrays her in blazing white glory, her hands grasping the flowers as she stands, a divine presence, against a dark night on blackened earth. The painting is a besotted token of love.

Queen Tamar is a portrait of the first woman ruler of Georgia, who reigned from 1184 to 1213. Her ascension to the throne was met with opposition that she successfully neutralized through political savvy and military strength. To this day, she remains an idealized figure, and her reign stands as the pinnacle of Georgia's Golden Age. Pirosmani captures her regal bearing by depicting her standing proud wearing a fur-trimmed cloak and gold-embossed crown and carrying a long scroll, recalling Byzantine traditions of religious icons and rulers. But it is also painted in Pirosmani's signature bold, broad strokes and at an awkward scale that makes her appear more human: a thoughtful queen rather than an emblem of majesty.

Nara captures the personalities of these two women by incorporating the Georgian master's style into his two 2018 bust portraits, a hybridity that recalls his earlier collaborative project Chaguin with Hiroshi Sugito (Figs. 148–153). In *Actress Margarita, after Niko Pirosmani* (Fig. 339), Nara portrays the dynamic personality of a performer who

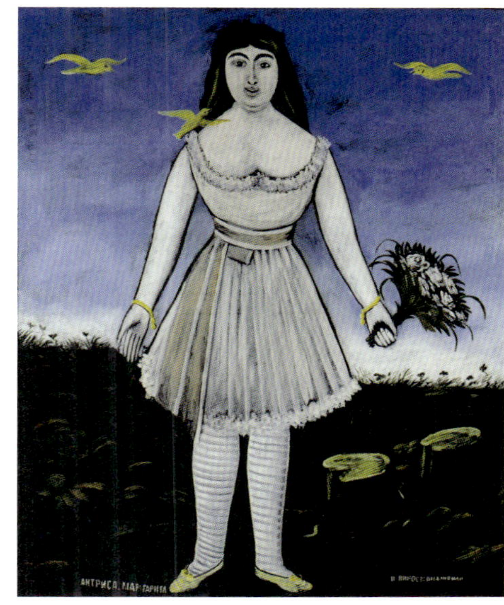

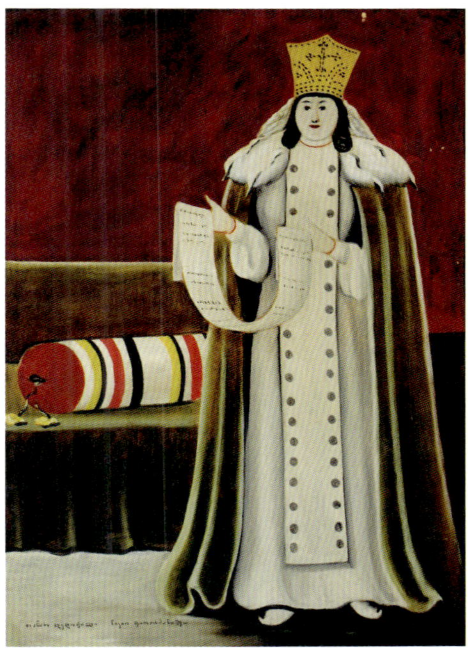

Fig. 337
Niko Pirosmani, *Actress Margarita*, 1909, Oil on oilcloth, 45 ⅞ × 36 ⅞ in. (116.5 × 93.8 cm)

Fig. 338
Niko Pirosmani, *Queen Tamar holding a scroll*, n.d., Oil on cardboard, 40 × 28 ⅛ in. (101.5 × 71.5 cm)

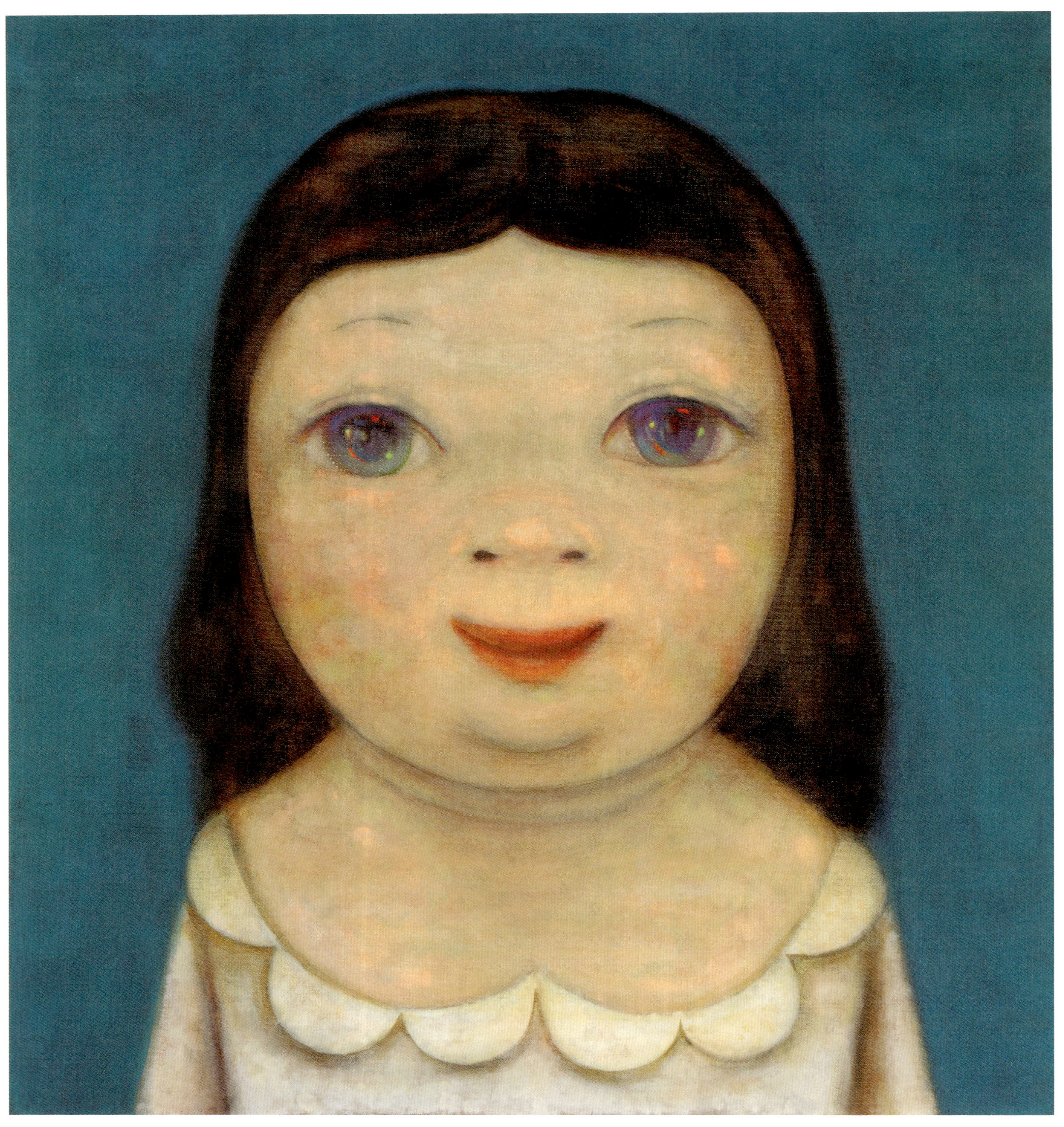

Fig. 339
Actress Margarita, after Niko Pirosmani, 2018, Acrylic on canvas, 47 ¼ × 43 5⁄16 in. (120 × 110 cm)

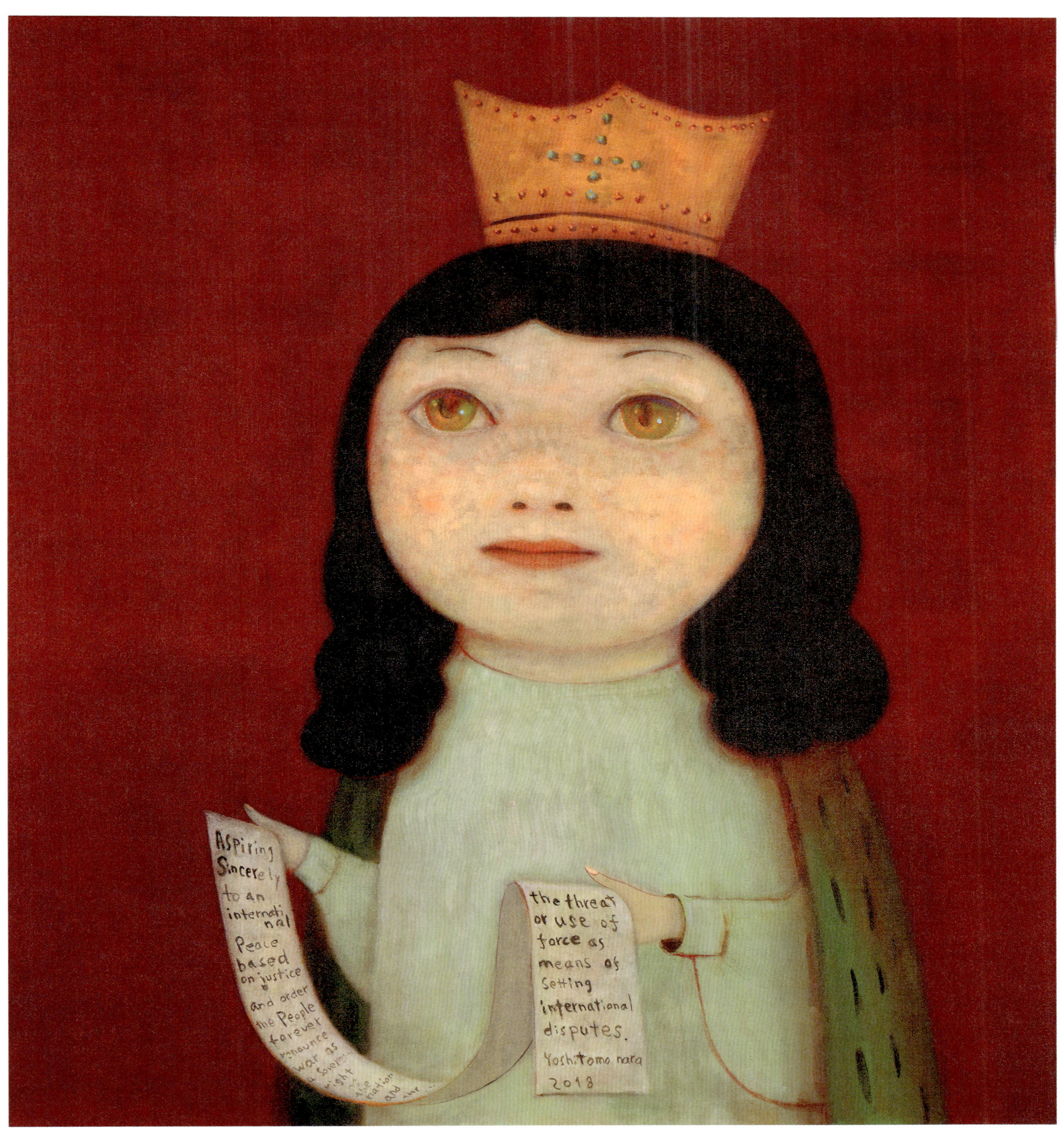

Fig. 340
Queen Tamar, after Niko Pirosmani, 2018, Acrylic on canvas, 47 ¼ × 43 5⁄16 in. (120 × 110 cm)

confronts viewers with gleeful eyes and upturned lips, carrying herself confidently in the knowledge that she is admired. The rounded contours of the actress's face, with its distinctive double chin, echo Pirosmani's portrait, as does the looser treatment of Nara's brushwork. However, his signature freckling of skin tones and rich depth of color remain his own.

In the second portrait, Nara presents a more contemplative image of Queen Tamar (Fig. 340), whose upward glance suggests a woman deep in thought. What is perhaps most intriguing about Nara's version of the painting is the scroll in her hands. The words that appear are from Article 9 of the Japanese constitution, a clause that outlaws war as a means of settling international disputes. Having taken effect on May 3, 1947, after World War II, it is a contentious point in contemporary debates over the constitution, as proponents of a militarized Japan argue that extra investment in the military is less about preparing for war than about strengthening methods of self-defense. But Nara heralds the law as exceptionally noble, depicting Georgia's most admired queen holding onto it and declaring its importance as the embodiment of good rulership.

The inclusion of Article 9 is an unusual gesture for Nara, who seldom gives direct commentary on the political administration—the degree of his political engagement is usually limited to slogans that rarely provoke serious controversy. But the political climate in Japan compelled him to make this more overt statement: recent years had seen an increased mobilization of the Japanese army, evidenced in the government's response to Fukushima, which muddied the line separating civic service and military efforts; the deployment of troops to the Middle East in support of the United States in the war on Afghanistan; and renewed parliamentary debates about the revision of Article 9 and expansion of the role and size of the Japanese military. In the context of the government's stated desire to reopen nuclear plants, concerns abounded that the line between nuclear power and nuclear weapons was becoming too fragile to maintain.

If Nara is usually more circumspect when painting on canvas, his drawings remain a powerful space to express political concerns. Those from this period reveal a vast range of subjects, from vampiric girls to mountains of skulls, wounded tears, irritated glares, agitated guitars, and streams of profanities (Figs. 341–343). He returns to his rebel girls, but they take on more sinister, violent personas: bloodthirsty or possessed

Fig. 341 (top left)
Angel, 2014, Colored pencil on paper, 12 ¼ × 9 in. (31.2 × 22.8 cm)

Fig. 342 (top right)
Untitled, 2013, Colored pencil on paper, 14 ⅜ × 10 ¼ in. (36.5 × 26 cm)

Fig. 343 (bottom)
Fuckin' Street, 2013, Colored pencil on paper, 12 ¹³⁄₁₆ × 9 ½ in. (32.5 × 24.2 cm)

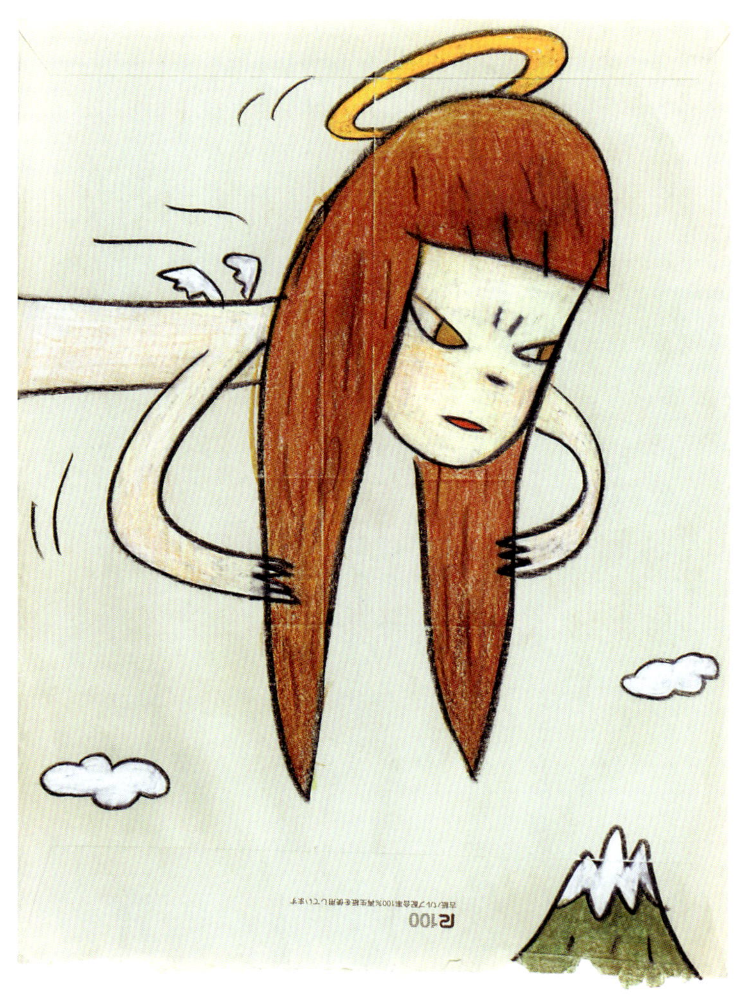

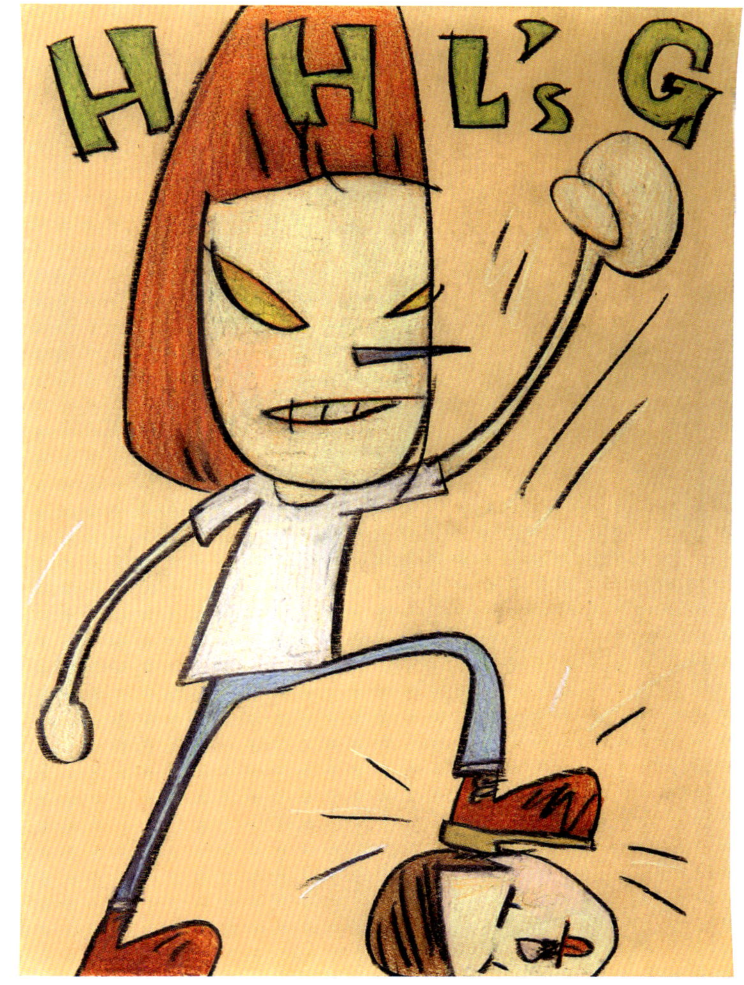
H H L's G

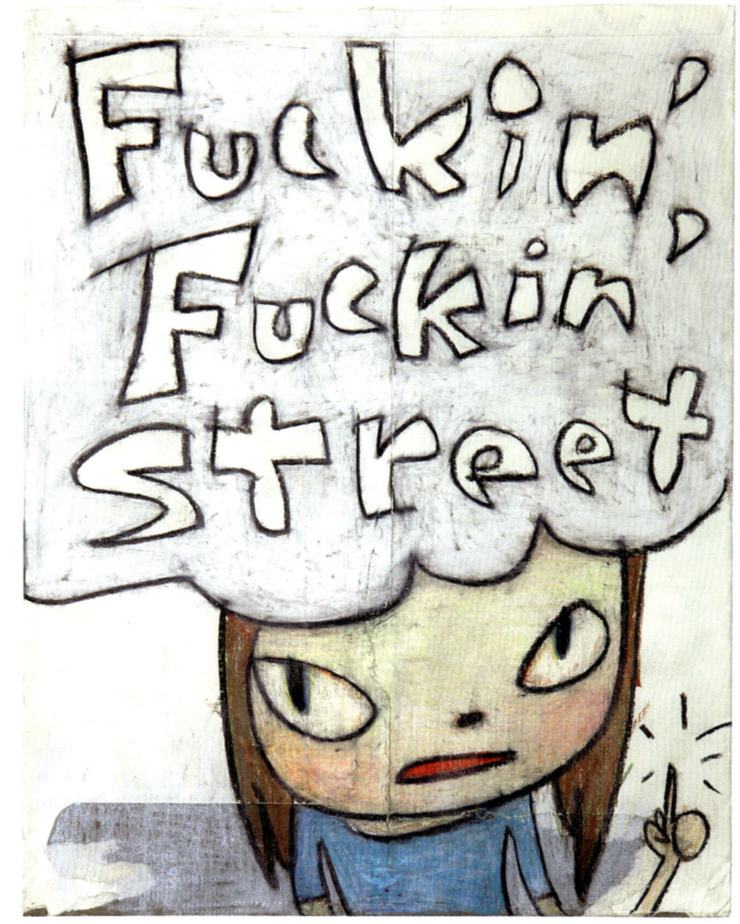
Fuckin' Fuckin' Street

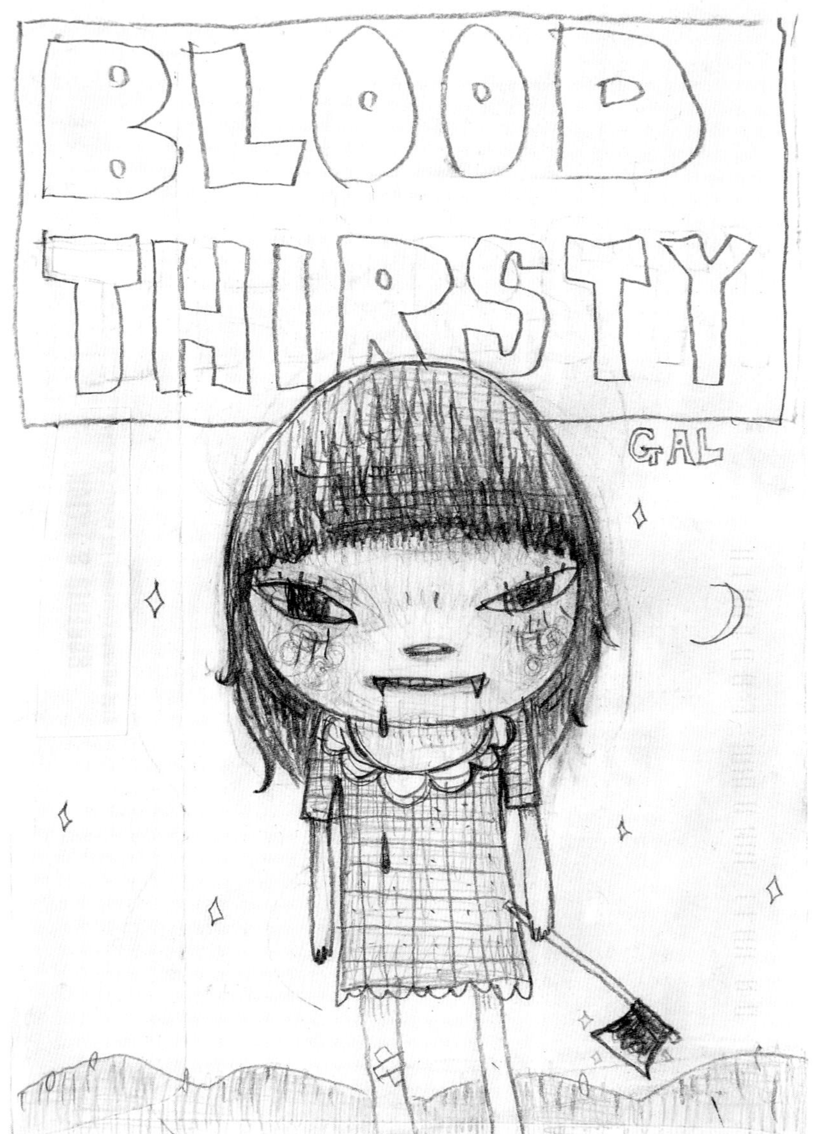

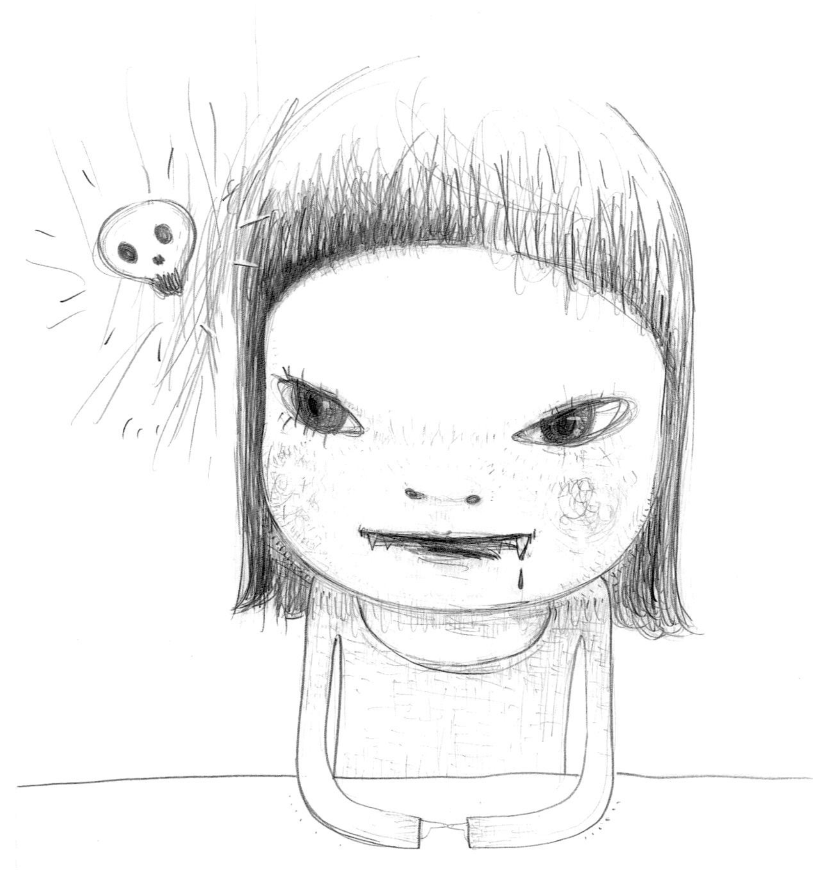

Fig. 344
Bloodthirsty Gal, 2014,
Colored pencil on paper,
9 1/16 × 6 1/8 in. (23 × 15.5 cm)

Fig. 345
The Little Vampire, 2017,
Pencil on paper, 25 5/8 × 21 5/8 in.
(65 × 55 cm)

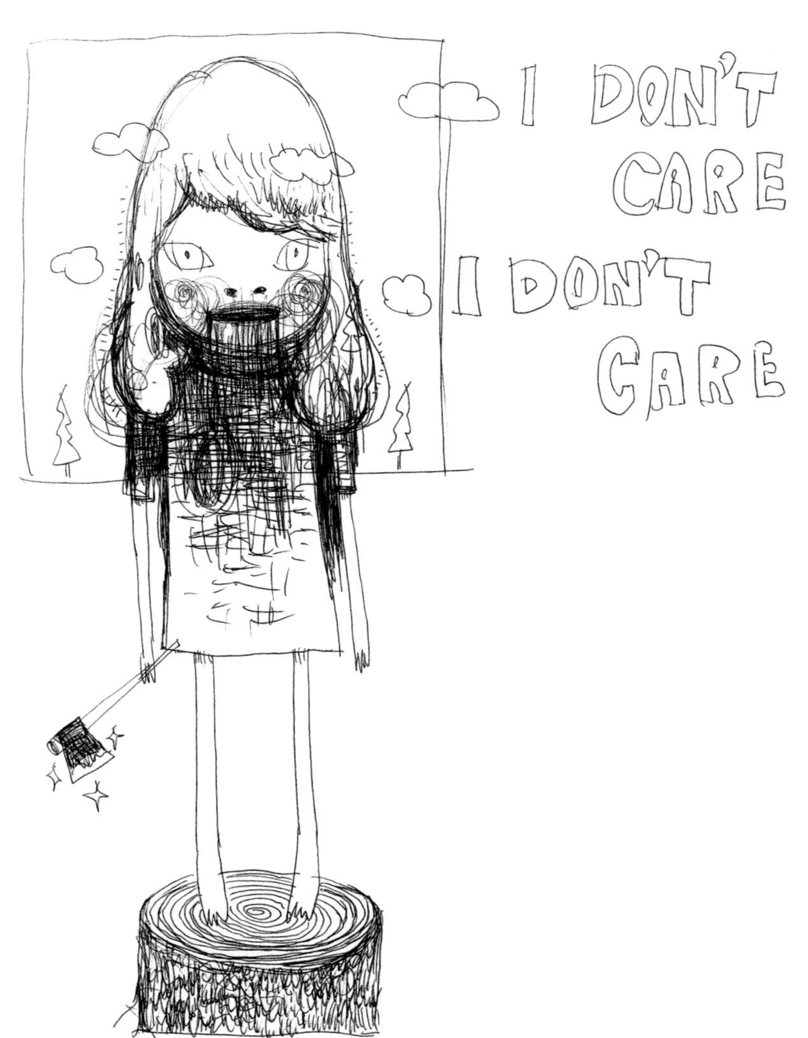

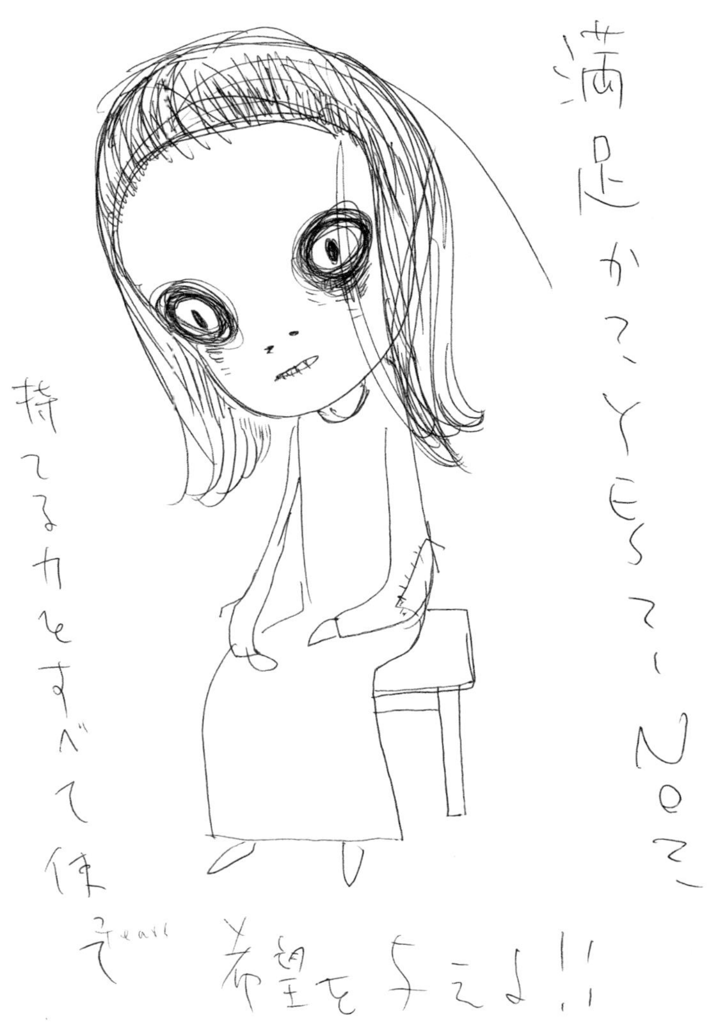

Fig. 346
I Don't Care, 2016, Ballpoint pen on paper, 11 ¹¹⁄₁₆ × 8 ¼ in. (29.7 × 21 cm)

Fig. 347
HOPE Starved, 2016, Ballpoint pen on paper, 11 ¹¹⁄₁₆ × 8 ¼ in. (29.7 × 21 cm)

with madness, not unlike those in the billboard paintings declaring "No War" or "Stop the Bombs" but now wielding axes and capable of inflicting harm on others (Figs. 344–347). These images go far beyond Nara's familiar juxtaposition of "cute/scary" rooted in the liminal spaces of Japanese subcultures. The zombie/vampire girls are closer to nightmares and horror movies, and they stand in stark contrast to the calm bust portraits he was creating at the same time. In this overspill of emotions, one wonders if the trauma of Fukushima can ever be healed.

It is now possible to see the full arc of development of Nara's big-headed girls, from his early works influenced by German Neo-Expressionism, as seen in *Romantic Catastrophe* (Fig. 52), to the bold rebel girls of the early 1990s, with their strong contour lines and bare backgrounds, and the painterly experiments of the early to mid-2000s, which, by 2011, became springboards for Nara to revisit, across media, the signature pictorial codes that had defined his career since the 1990s. Nara's big-headed girls also gained a greater sense of independence. At times, this can be seen through the titles of his works, which have evolved from descriptions to names: *Lucy*, *Miss Margaret*, *Miss Spring*.

Perhaps the greatest independence that Nara has granted his figures comes from their use by grassroots political organizations. Though he has produced a sizable portfolio of works that reflect his political positions against war and nuclear power, scholars have rarely attempted to frame them as a distinct body of work. In part, this is because he tends to express his politics from a personal standpoint rather than as part of a systematic activist intervention. In addition, curators and writers who have historically been more inclined to position him within a Neo-Pop framework tend to foreclose the possibility that his works might contain substantive political commentary. In response to the Fukushima disaster, however, Nara's antinuclear works gained public traction, and some have been co-opted by antinuclear organizations for use as signage in popular demonstrations against nuclear power.[11]

While in the immediate aftermath of 2011 Nara had felt that he was not quite ready to share his painted canvas works, he did support the use of one of his early acrylic drawings, *No Nukes*, for a protest march in 2012 (Fig. 348).[12] He made the drawing in 1998 in response

Fig. 348
No Nukes, 1998, Acrylic and colored pencil on paper, 14 $^{3}/_{16}$ × 8 $^{7}/_{8}$ in. (36 × 22.5 cm)

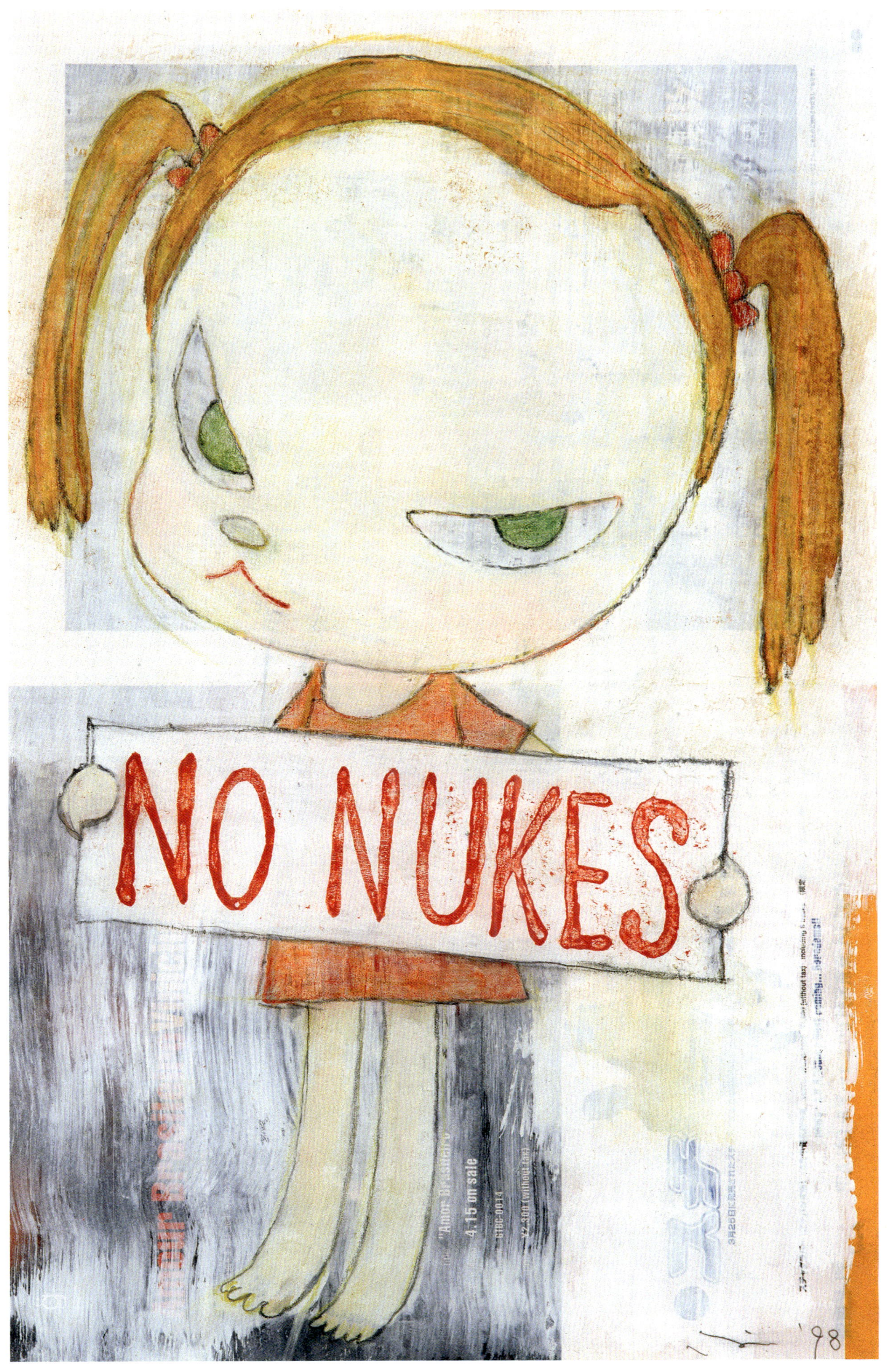
NO NUKES
'98

to his own memories of news coverage of antinuclear protests in the 1970s. During the Cold War, when the threat of the nuclear bomb had reentered discussions about nuclear power in general, the phrase “no nukes” became a rallying cry for many campaigns, including rock concerts and demonstrations that were broadcast internationally. For Nara, such news coverage was part of his early absorption of international countercultural activities, and he began using the phrase “no nukes” in some of his early works from the 1980s. The phrase reappeared in the mid-1990s and with more regularity after 2002, upon his return from Afghanistan. After the Fukushima disaster, the 1998 drawing was taken up by groups protesting the reopening of the nuclear power plant, and Nara made the work more widely available by posting a high-resolution version for download on social media.

The use of his artwork at anti–nuclear power events continued as more protests were held across the country (Fig. 349). One of the largest rallies was organized by Satoshi Kamata, a freelance journalist who has been involved in antinuclear activities since the 1970s.[13] Kamata has published several investigative books on the impact of nuclear reactors on Japanese society, including his best-known work, *Rokkasho-mura no kiroku* (The Record of the Village of Rokkasho), in 1991, which covered farmers’ protests against plans to construct a major nuclear fuel reprocessing plant in Aomori prefecture close to their land.[14] Throughout his career, Kamata has campaigned hard against nuclear power with moderate success, but with the 2011 disaster, his message garnered widespread support.

In July 2012, Kamata, along with other high-profile organizers including the writer Kenzaburō Ōe, planned a rally at Tokyo’s Yoyogi Park with the goal “to bring an end to nuclear power plants immediately.”[15] The rally, which became known as Sayonara Nuclear Power Plants, was part of a campaign to collect ten million signatures in support of closing plants across the country. Nara, long an admirer of Kamata, was asked to contribute a work of art for use in the rally, and he decided to provide an image of *Miss Spring*, which he had painted with Fukushima on his mind. While it lacks the directness of *No Nukes*, the work was quickly taken on as a visual symbol for protesters, adorning large banners raised high among the thousands of people who had gathered at the park (Fig. 350).[16] Part of its appeal is that the work, painted in his instantly recognizable style, registered Nara’s support for the campaign and thus raised its public profile with the local news media. But aside from

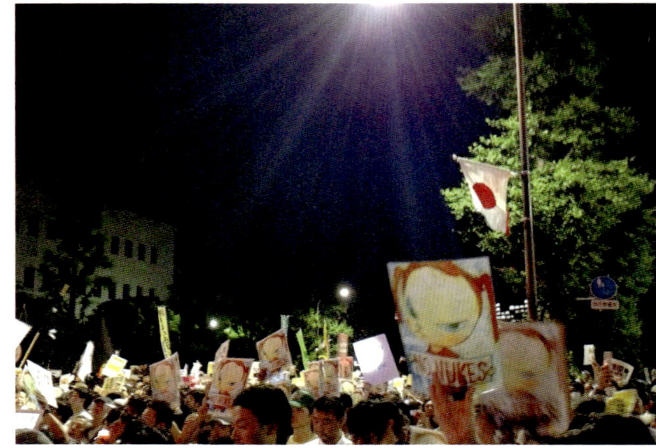

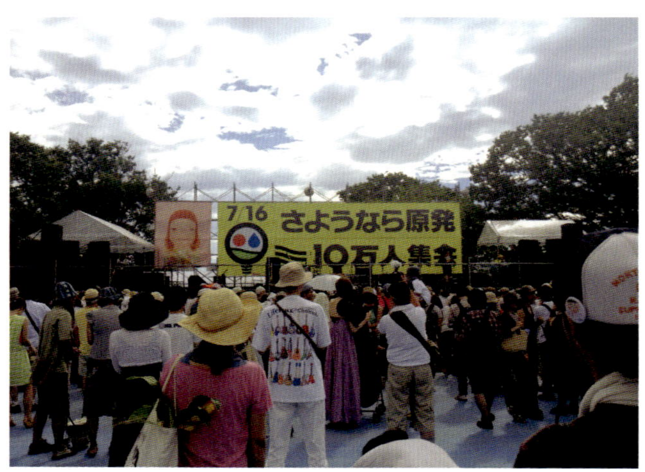

Fig. 349
Antinuclear demonstration,
June 29, 2012

Fig. 350
Sayonara Nuclear Power
Plants rally, Yoyogi Park, Tokyo,
July 16, 2012

its function as celebrity endorsement, the image of a child silently staring takes on an accusatory role when placed next to slogans denouncing plans to reopen the nuclear power plant in Fukushima. Shortly after the rally, the musician Ryuichi Sakamoto, another well-known activist, organized the No Nukes 2012 music festival (July 7–8, 2012) and printed *Miss Spring* on flyers promoting the event.[17] Along with *No Nukes*, the painting has become an indelible part of the visual landscape of contemporary antinuclear protests in Japan.

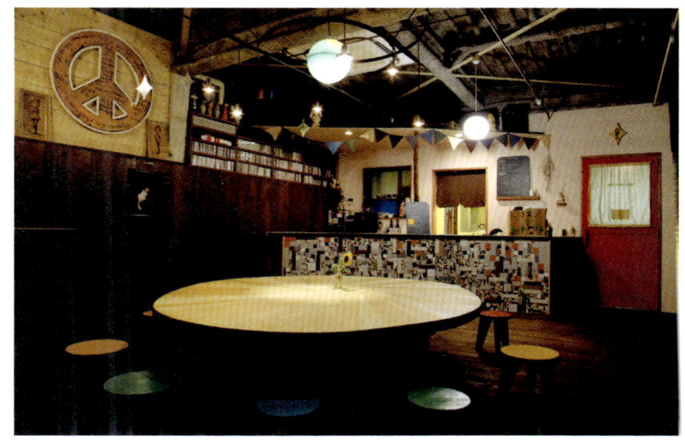

> **After I did the *A to Z* shows and their many variations in a range of different places, I thought that I needed to separate myself from society in order to keep creating. But after the earthquake, I realized that there was no need to forcibly cut myself off. I don't need to cater to everyone with my creations, but I do need to have some awareness of people.**[18]

The Great East Japan Earthquake and Fukushima Disaster brought Nara a closer spiritual connection to his home region of the north, and the events continue to influence the direction of his work. In the years since 2011, he has increasingly taken on small local projects in collaboration with individuals from northern Japan. This is not to suggest that he no longer participates in museum exhibitions and gallery shows, but more and more, he finds himself retreating to sites where he finds others like him—those who are also keen to work outside of the usual structures of the art establishment.

One of these community-focused projects was a commission for the 2013 Aichi Triennale. Instead of producing an artwork, Nara collaborated with Shin Morikita, a former student from his teaching days at Aichi, and Kazumasa Aoki, a graduate student at the university. Like Nara, Morikita and Aoki had devoted themselves to recovery efforts after the 2011 disaster, packing their cars with construction materials and sleeping bags and supplying them to families in need. For the Aichi commission, in an effort to embody that notion of community, they created the *WE-LOW HOUSE* (Fig. 351), a temporary space built in a former garage where they staged their own exhibitions and performances and set up a café for the public. The name derives from a Japanese punk band from the 1990s called the High-Lows, Morikita's favorite band, and is also a play on the

Fig. 351
THE WE-LOWS (Yoshitomo Nara + Shin Morikita + Kazumasa Aoki + Kazuhiro Koshiba + Yoko Fujita + Shiori Ishida + Yumeko Sakai), *WE-LOW HOUSE*, 2013, Mixed media installation (milk crates from Fukushima, construction waste from Aichi, audio equipment, culinary ware, miscellaneous materials), Size unknown

word *uirō*, Aoki's favorite mochi sweet.[19] The café was named Koshiba Shokudō, after a student from Nara's time at the university who had set up a guerrilla café where he cooked and served food free of charge to his peers. In this spirit, the *WE-LOW HOUSE* provided a shared space to be used by other artists and experienced by visitors from the local community and abroad, helping to foster a sense of connection and creation. Furthermore, through the project's association with Aichi University, Nara hoped to give something back to the place that had, after the disaster, inspired his return to art.

Another project, one that continues today, has taken Nara to Tobiu, a remote area in the Shiraoi district of Hokkaido. Nara's first trip to Tobiu was born of curiosity. In 2016, a new high-speed rail opened with much fanfare, for the first time connecting his home region of Aomori to the island of Hokkaido. Within a week of its opening, he bought a ticket to Muroran, a port city on the southern end of the island. Nara had heard about Tobiu and its small homegrown arts and music festival, which has attracted a diverse range of talented musicians, including OKI (Oki Kano), an Ainu musician; Yuko Ikema, an indie folk singer; and the jazz ensemble OTT. Although the festival was not taking place at the time, he wanted to see what attracted such a diverse group of musicians to a small village in the north.

Tobiu is also a place that integrates Nara's interest in borderlands in general and northern Japan more specifically. Historically, Hokkaido was inhabited by the indigenous Ainu people, but in the 1780s, the Meiji government enforced a series of assimilationist policies that brought in a larger Japanese population, which would eventually outnumber the Ainu living there.[20] Nonetheless, their culture persists, and many places in Hokkaido are still known by their Ainu names. Because the Ainu language is based on oral tradition, without a standardized writing system, many of the site names do not appear on maps of the region, seemingly absent from the Cartesian world of geographical coordinates, and when they are written, they often appear as transliterations composed of both *hiragana* and *katakana* characters, leading to variations in their pronunciation. Moreover, many Ainu place names have multiple meanings: *Tobiu*, for example, can mean both "the many places of the *chishimazasa* flower" and "place of many black birds." In short, Tobiu resists being fixed by the logics of location making in conventional society, existing instead as an organic community shaped by the imperfections of oral traditions and local knowledge.

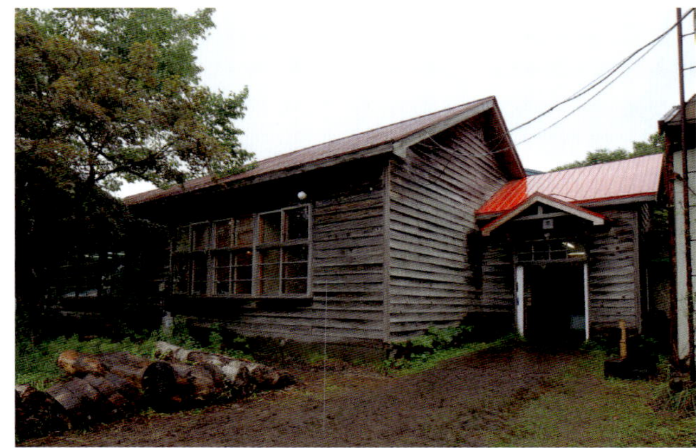

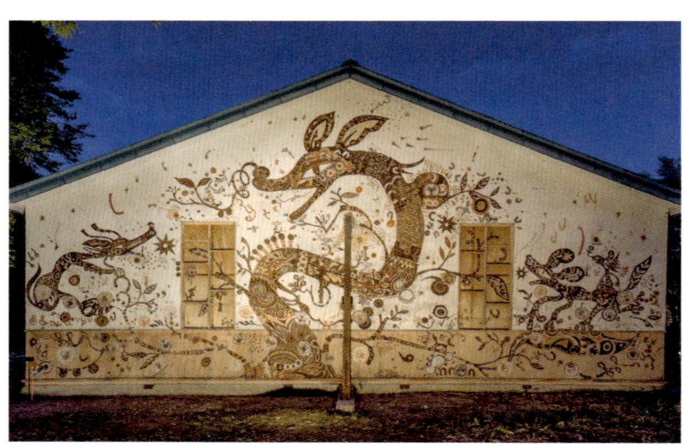

Fig. 352
Schoolhouse in Tobiu, 2011

Fig. 353
Yusuke Asai, *Seeds of Forest* (mural on the side of Tobiu gymnasium), 2015, Soil (six types), water, wood glue, and acrylic resin, 276 × 591 in. (700 × 1500 cm)

Tobiu today is home to no more than ten families, with a total population of around thirty people. Like many other places in the area, however, it was once a thriving mining village. When the state enforced a mandatory education program after the Pacific War, the local government built a small elementary school there, which quickly expanded from one classroom to a small complex with a gymnasium and an outdoor activity space carved into the forest. Like so many rural villages in Japan, its declining population is also an aging one, resulting in the abandonment of the school, which closed in 1986. The school remained deserted until Asuka Kunimatsu, a sculptor from Sapporo, moved to Tobiu with his family and turned the former school into a studio space. Although they stayed only a few years, the place left a lasting impression on Asuka's son, Kineta Kunimatsu, who also became a sculptor and later returned to the school, which remained abandoned. Like his father, Kineta rented the space to use as a studio, but he also initiated a project to clean up a clearing in the forest behind the school, calling on volunteers from nearby villages and towns to help. His choice to focus on the forest rather than the buildings was, in part, a response to the village's history and customs, as the forest had played an important part in community life: in Tobiu, all students learned to recognize different birdsongs, and taking walks through the forest was a part of their daily school activities. Kineta also refashioned parts of the deserted area into cultural spaces for artists to create work that responded to the site's environment. In addition, he organized the annual art and music festival known as Tobiu Camp and established a self-funded art-residency program. The projects he initiated have, over the years, gained a strong local reputation within the Hokkaido region.[21]

When Nara arrived in Tobiu, he found himself, unexpectedly, just in time for a volunteer restoration day, and he joined in helping clean up areas of the wilderness behind the school. The openness, the generosity, and the small-scale local initiative of giving back to the community, distinctly different from the high-profile projects of rural rejuvenation happening elsewhere in Japan at the time, immediately appealed to him, and he was invited to participate in the upcoming annual festival in September 2016.

For many visitors and residents of Tobiu, there is a certain enchantment with the site, a place with a history and traditions that inspire creative energy. This is true for Kineta, who has devoted much of his

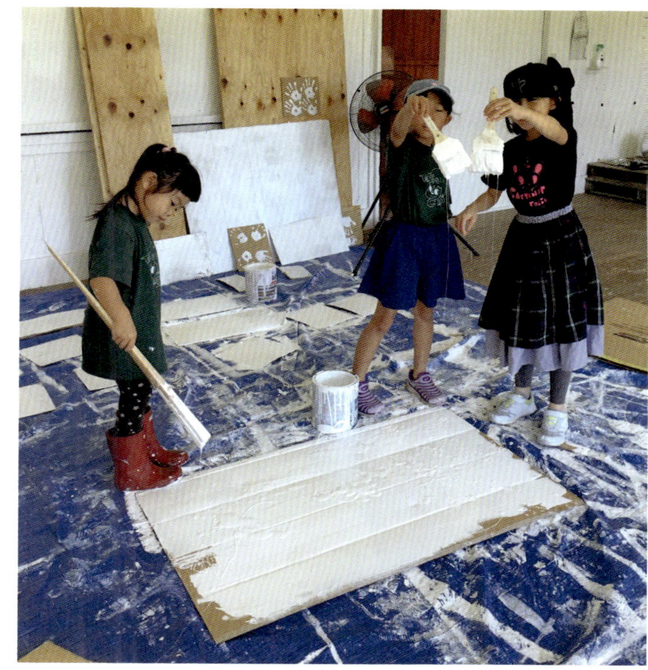

Fig. 354
Children in the abandoned school in Tobiu, 2018

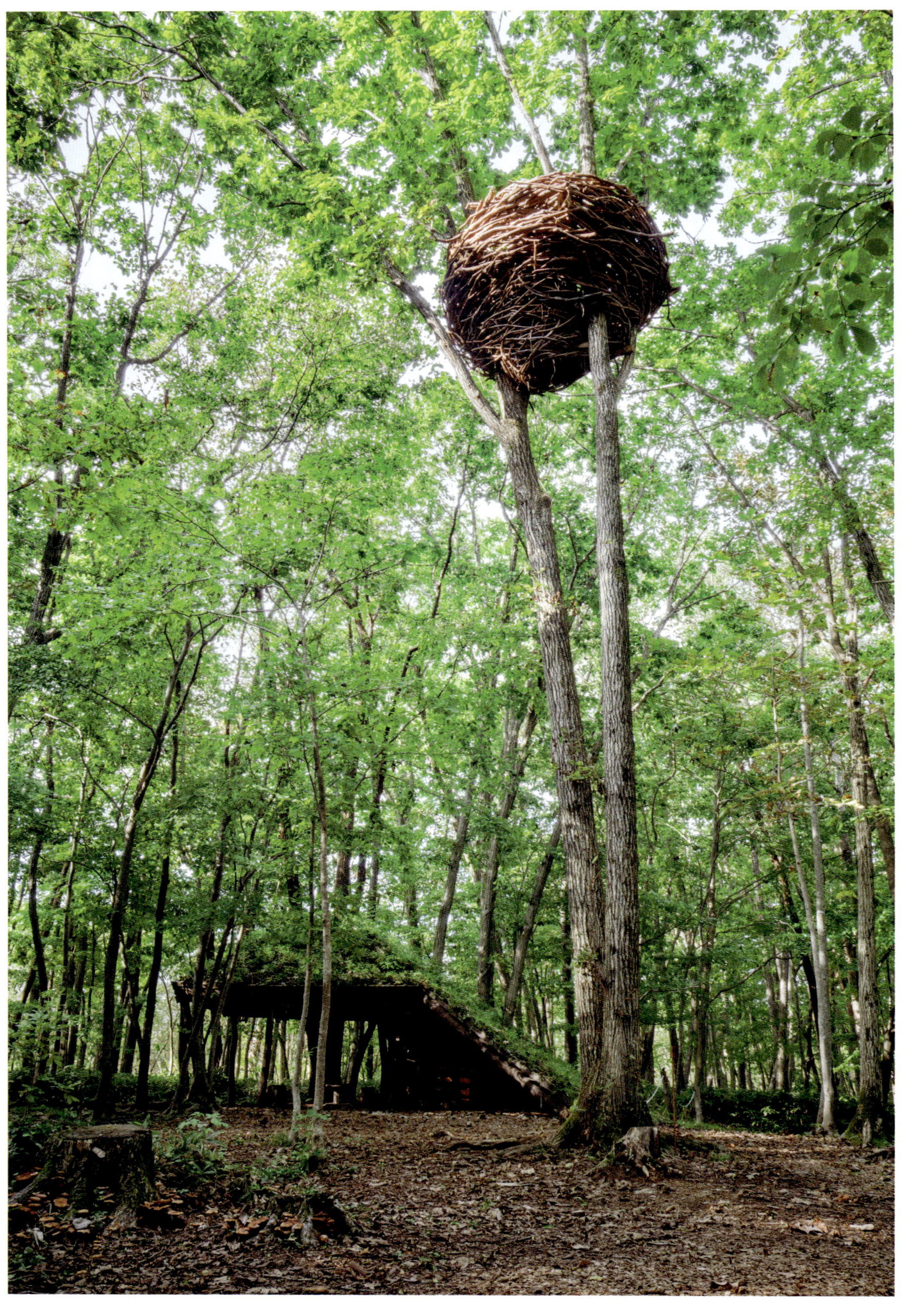

Fig. 355
Hiroyasu Kosukegawa and Kineta Kunimatsu, *Tupiu NEST*, 2016, Japanese oak, grapevine, and wood, 630 × 118 × 118 in. (1600 × 300 × 300 cm)

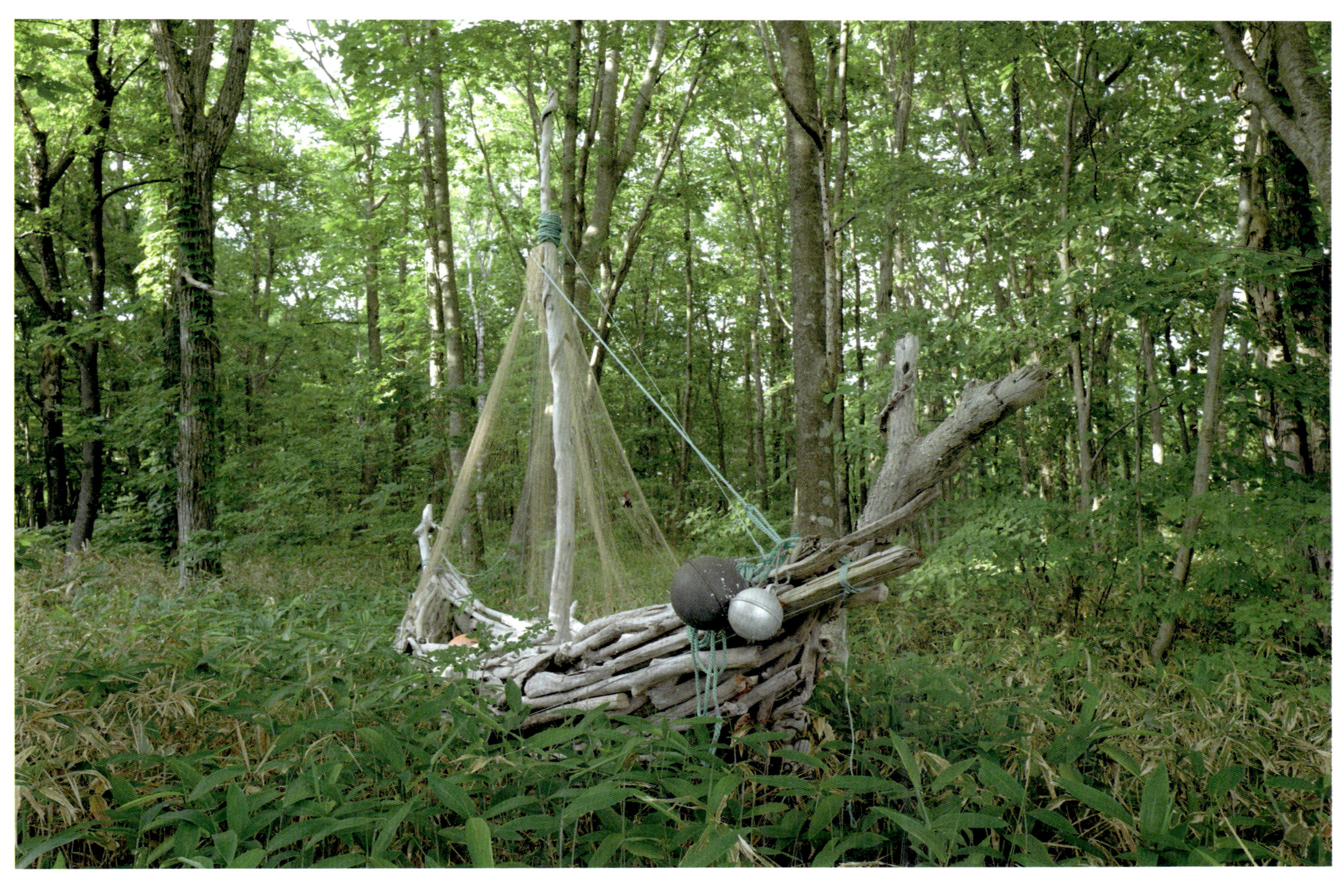

Fig. 356
Hiroyasu Kosukegawa
and Kineta Kunimatsu,
Treasure Ship, 2016,
Driftwood and miscellaneous
materials, 118 × 59 × 335 in.
(300 × 150 × 850 cm)

artistic life to both protecting the forest and making art to inhabit it. His sculptural works exist as if they are a natural part of their surroundings, seen in his giant bird's nest (Fig. 355), which sits unobtrusively in the forest, and his boat made of broken branches (Fig. 356), which rests in a partially hidden sunken pit. Other visiting artists have interacted with Tobiu's built environment, including Yusuke Asai, whose mural of a giant dragon is painted on the back of the school building (Fig. 353). Others still engage with the town's inhabitants, making art with local children or talking late into the night with audiences after live performances. It is among this range of voices that we see Nara taking part, not as an internationally renowned artist but as another participant who has fallen under Tobiu's spell.

The first time Nara took part in the Tobiu Camp festival, he showed an animated film and gave a talk about his work.[22] But he wanted to become more deeply embedded within the community and the following year, 2017, he decided to rent a space in the village and contribute as an artist-in-residence at the school for a month. Nara had in the past taken part in several different residency programs, but this one brought with it its own unique challenges, since he felt the need to properly honor the place. Wandering in the forest one day, he found a lump of dry clay and started working with it to bring it back to life, when children from nearby villages spontaneously joined in to play with the clay alongside him. He decided, through this interaction, what his project would entail: revitalizing the abandoned school by reinfusing it with the memory of its former inhabitants.

As part of the project, and for the first time since his earliest art school days, he picked up a stick of charcoal, fashioned from a dead tree in the forest, and started drawing portraits of the children who had been using the schoolroom as a play area. The five charcoal drawings are atypical for Nara, since they are not imagined depictions but realist works that return to the most basic process of art making: drawing from life. When completed, Nara hung them low on the walls of the classroom, where they evoked a ghostly illusion of life in the former school (Figs. 362–367).

In Tobiu, Nara also worked in clay, a medium that has grown in importance in his practice over the past ten years, making several palm-sized works influenced by the pottery of the Jōmon period (ca. 14000–300 BC) of ancient Japan (Fig. 358). These unearthed

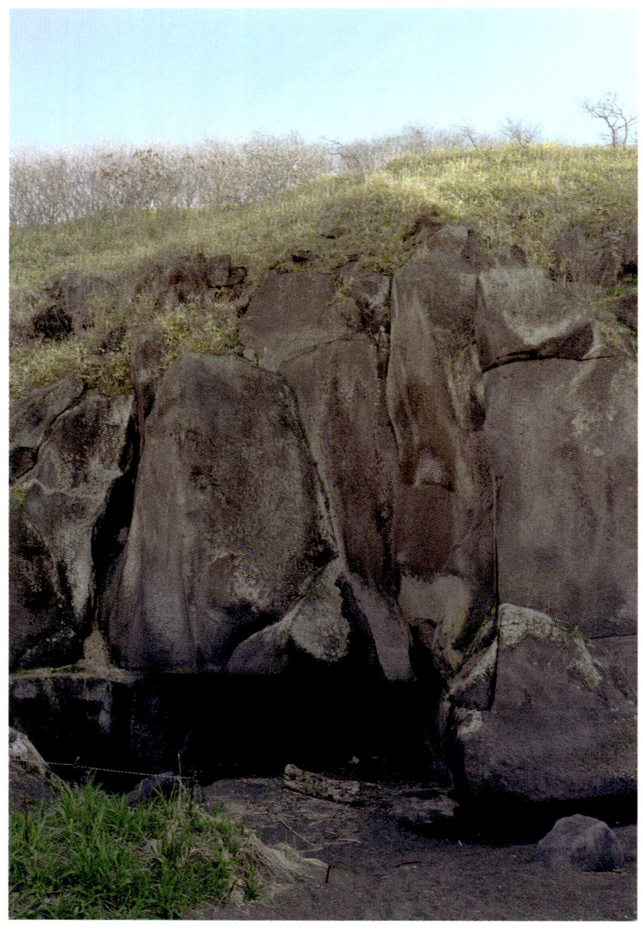

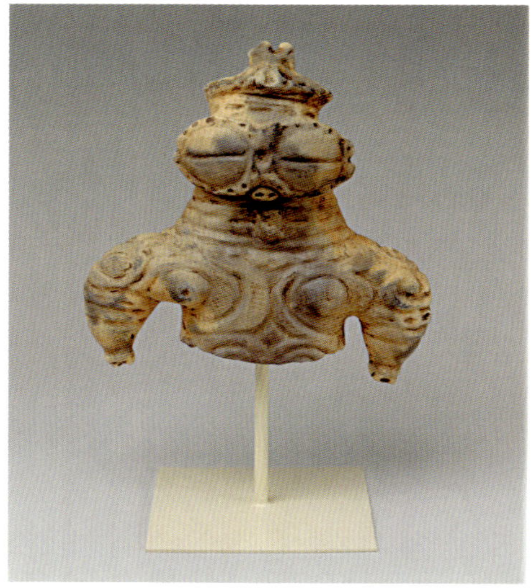

Fig. 357
Ahunrupar cave on the Shiraoi coastline

Fig. 358
Dogū (Clay Figurine), 1000–300 BC, Earthenware with cord-marked and incised decoration (Tōhoku region), 6 ½ × 6 ⅜ × 3 ⅛ in. (16.5 × 16.2 × 7.9 cm)

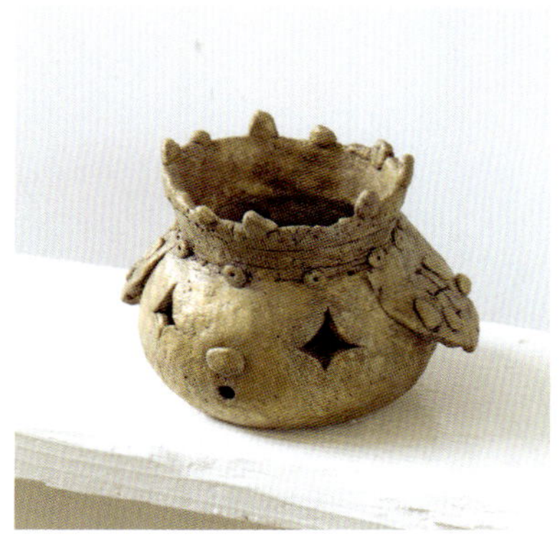
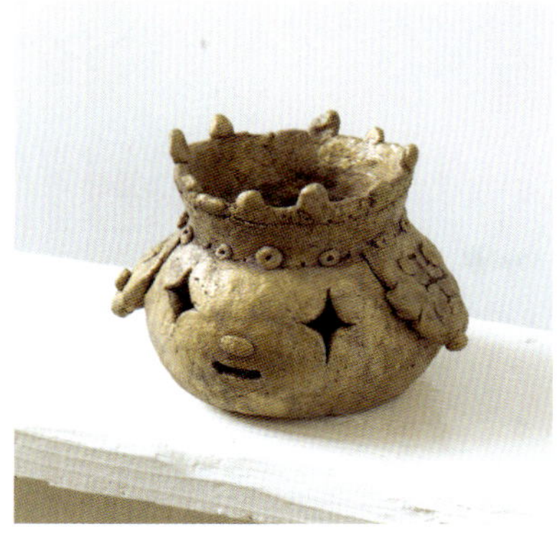
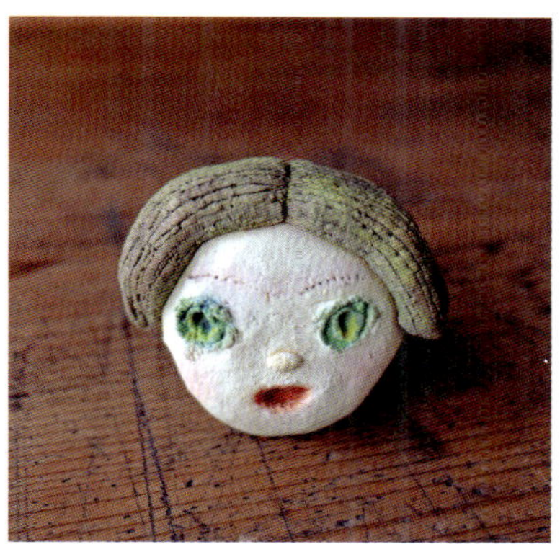
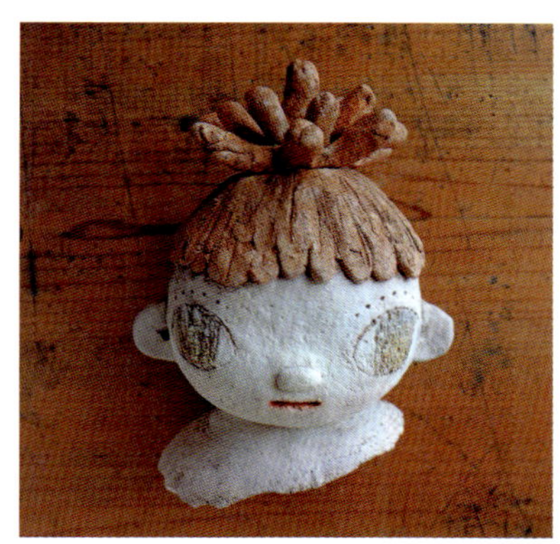

shards are among the oldest pottery objects in the world, and although they appear in many parts of Japan, some of the largest concentrations of archaeological finds are in Hokkaido and the northern areas of the Tōhoku region. One of the distinctive traits of Jōmon ware is the presence of rope patterns (giving the period its name, which translates to "rope-patterned"). Nara's response to this history is a series of small clay figurines and bust portraits, sometimes left unglazed, which bear a resemblance to his distinctive images of young girls (Figs. 359–361). He sometimes scatters these creations in the forests of Tobiu, turning them into tokens of *kami* magic.

Other works that draw on the local landscape are his *Ahunrupar* sculptures (Figs. 368 and 369). These works recall *Anymore for Anymore* (Fig. 371), Nara's 2010 ceramic vase sculpted into a head shape, on which he carefully molded the features of a young girl. In the more recent ceramic heads, Nara is still keen to capture a human presence but one that has been informed by local legends. Among the many Ainu myths is the story of Ahunrupar, an enchanted gateway hidden in a cave that leads to the playground of the gods. The locations of these magical caves are passed down through oral tradition, and many of them are in Hokkaido, including one along the nearby Shiraoi coastline (Fig. 357). This site is believed to be magical because of its face-like structure, with a protrusion resembling a nose and, beneath it, an open "mouth" leading to a shallow cave. The unusual appearance of this coastline is due to the fact that, like many in the southern regions of Hokkaido, it bears geomorphic traces of past volcanic eruptions and earthquakes. The dramatic formation is enhanced by the distinctive markings of fault lines and cracks and the darkened colors of the rock formed over the years by ash. This geological history of earthquakes also informs parts of Ainu myths, which speak of the relationship between

Figs 359a–b
Numazu Shell Mound No. 1 (Prince with Sparkling Eyes) (front and back views), 2016, Ceramic, 5 ½ × 7 1/16 × 7 1/16 in. (14 × 18 × 18 cm)

Fig. 360
Numazu Shell Mound No. 2 (Big Eyes), 2016, Ceramic, 9 13/16 × 6 5/16 × 5 1/8 in. (25 × 16 × 13 cm)

Fig. 361
Kamegaoka No. 1 (Round Eyes), 2016, Ceramic, 3 3/8 × 2 15/16 × 2 3/8 in. (8.5 × 7.5 × 6 cm)

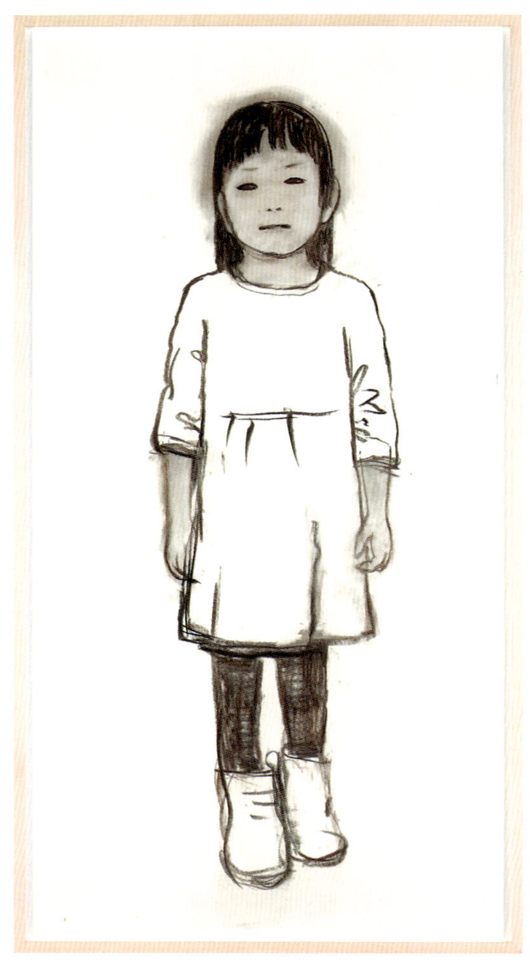

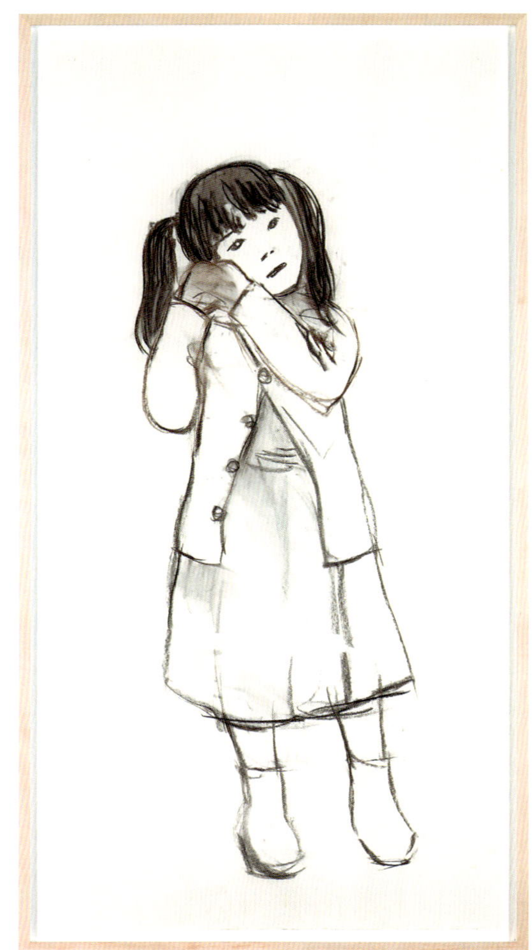

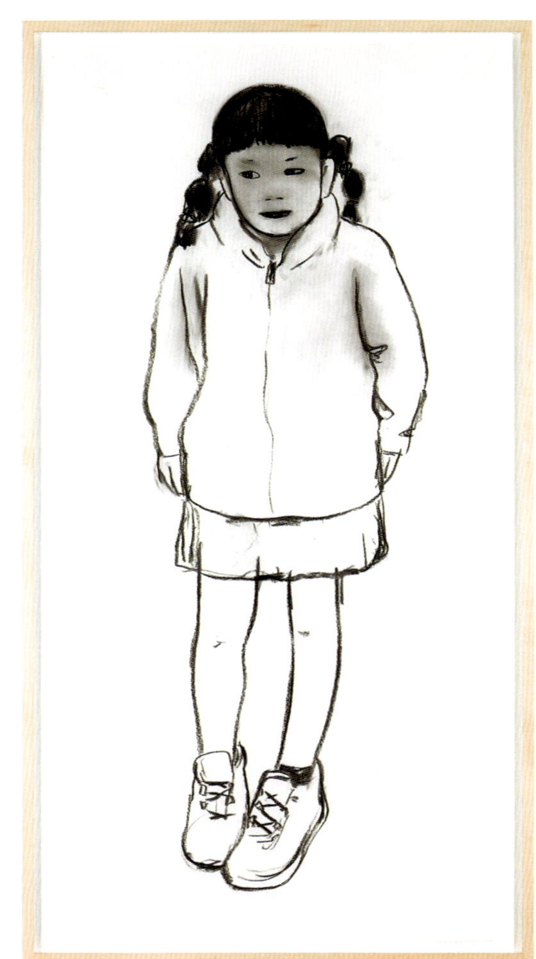

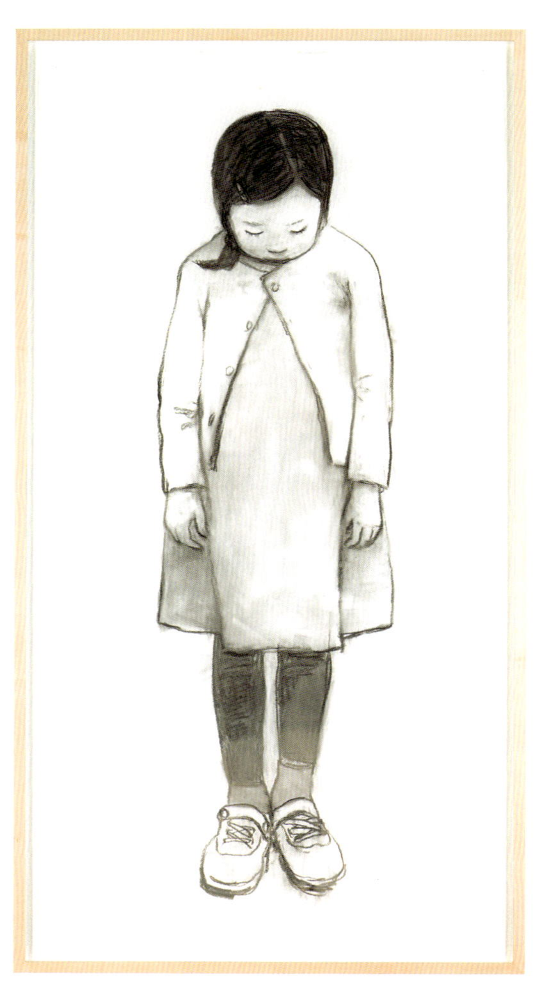

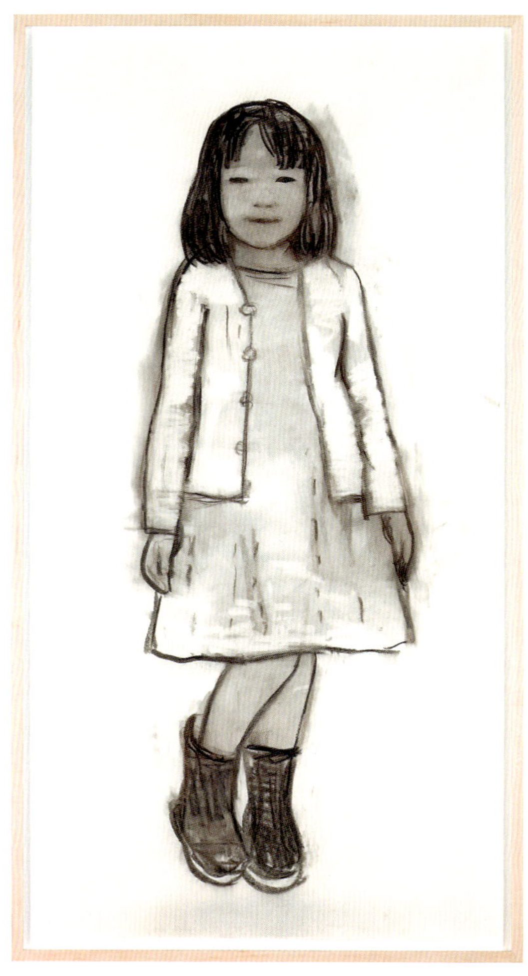

Fig. 362 (top left)
SHIU, 2017, Charcoal on paper,
71 5/8 × 35 13/16 in. (182 × 91 cm),
framed 74 × 38 3/16 in. (188 × 97 cm)

Fig. 363 (top center)
YUNOA, 2017, Charcoal on paper,
71 5/8 × 35 13/16 in. (182 × 91 cm),
framed 74 × 38 3/16 in. (188 × 97 cm)

Fig. 364 (top right)
KOU, 2017, Charcoal on paper,
71 5/8 × 35 13/16 in. (182 × 91 cm),
framed 74 × 38 3/16 in. (188 × 97 cm)

Fig. 365 (bottom left)
COCONE, 2017, Charcoal on paper,
71 5/8 × 35 13/16 in. (182 × 91 cm),
framed 74 × 38 3/16 in. (188 × 97 cm)

Fig. 366 (bottom right)
RENOA, 2017, Charcoal on paper,
71 5/8 × 35 13/16 in. (182 × 91 cm),
framed 74 × 38 3/16 in. (188 × 97 cm)

Fig. 367 (opposite)
COCONE (detail), 2017

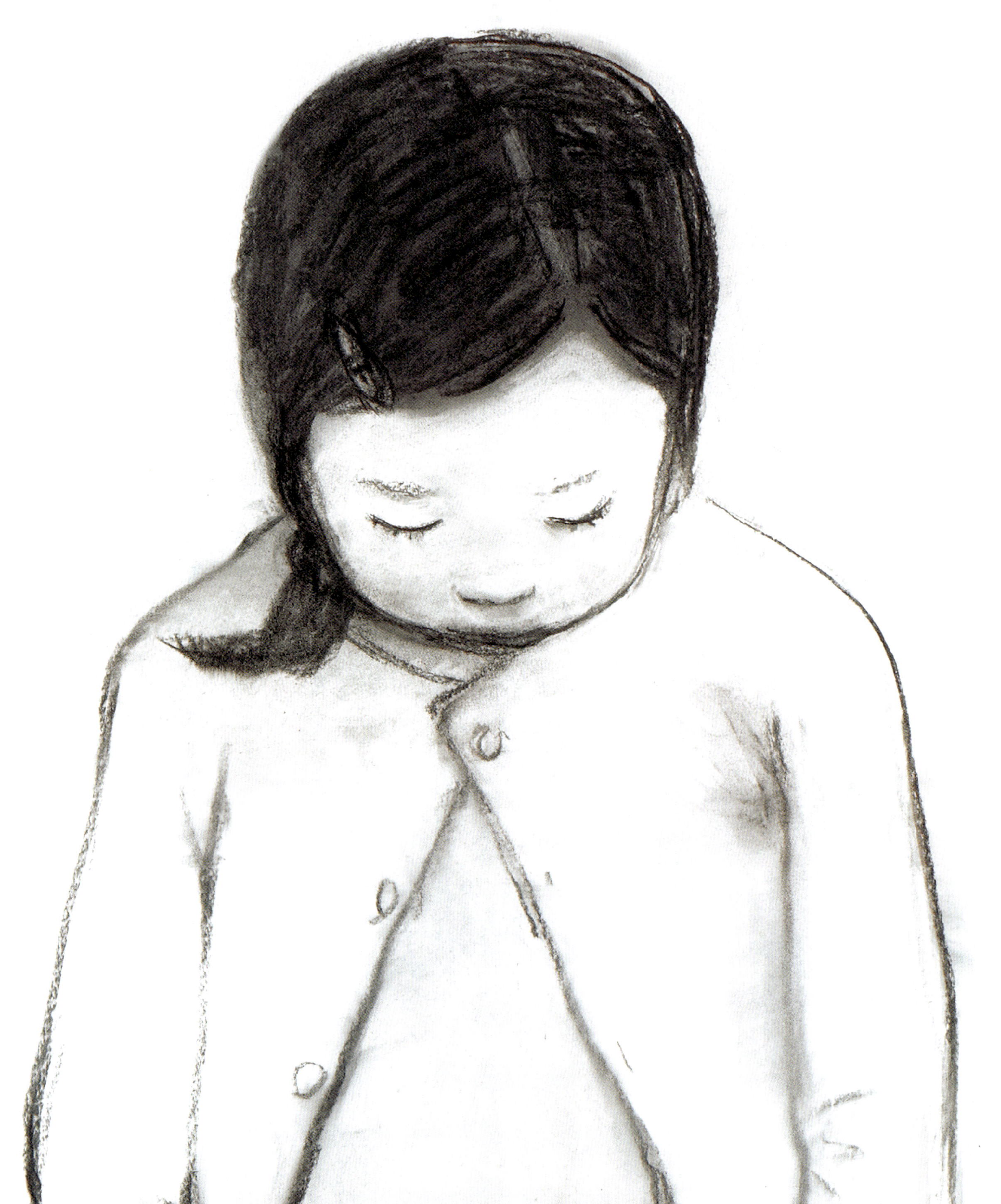

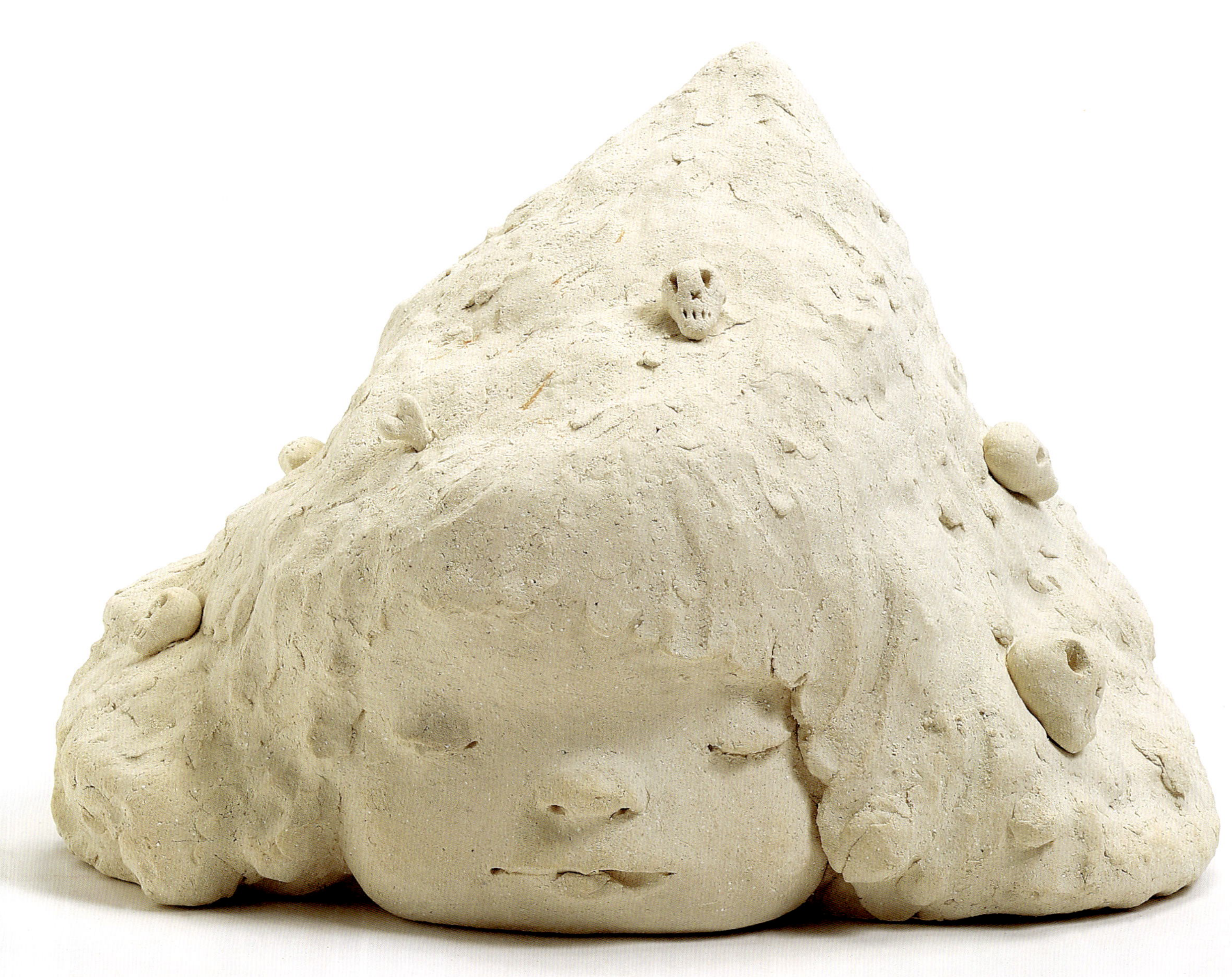

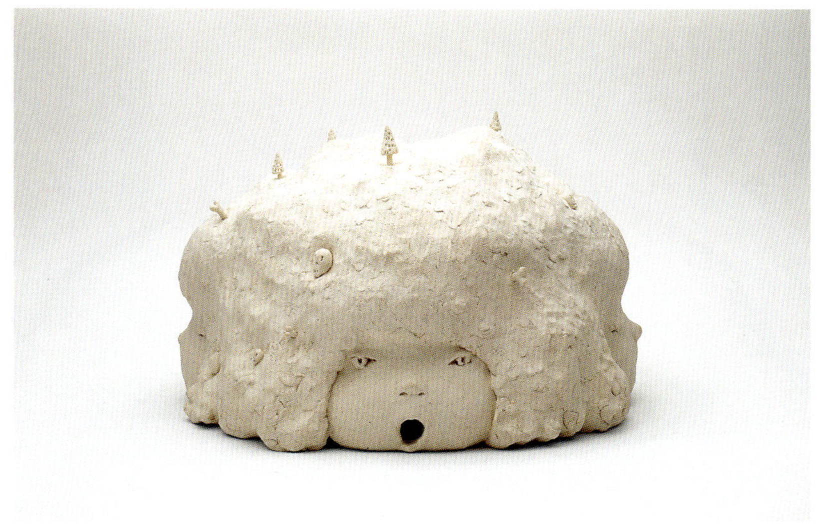

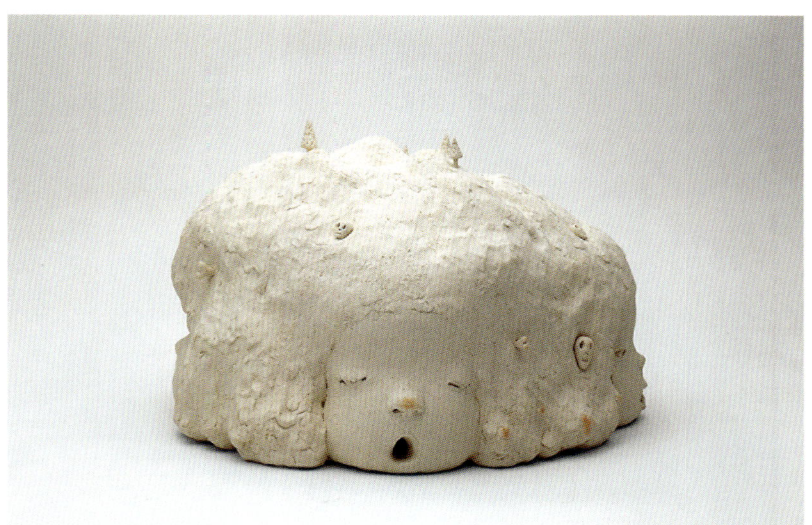

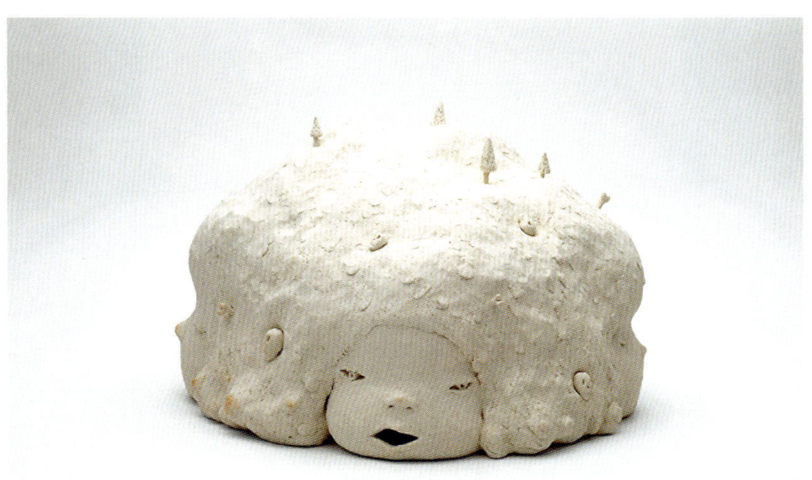

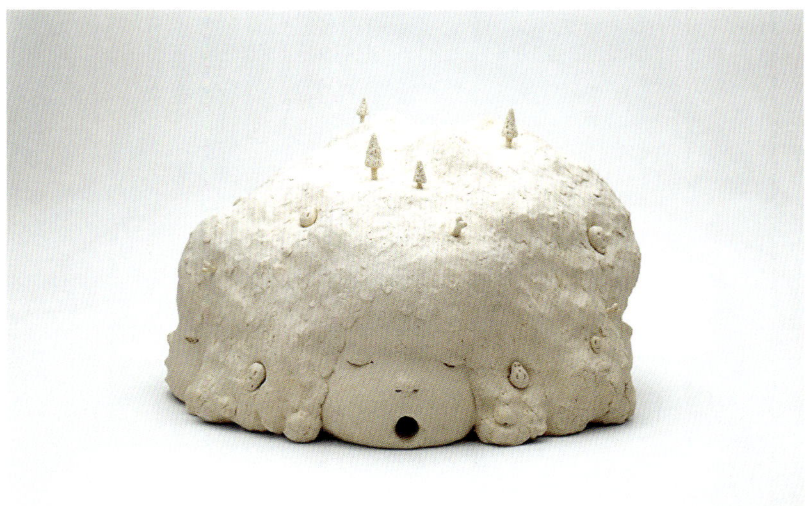

Fig. 368 (opposite)
Ahunrupar, 2018, Ceramic, 12 11/16 × 17 7/16 × 15 1/4 in. (32.3 × 44.3 × 38.8 cm)

Figs. 369a–d
Ahunrupar (multiple views), 2018, Ceramic, 13 × 17 11/16 × 18 7/8 in. (33 × 45 × 48 cm)

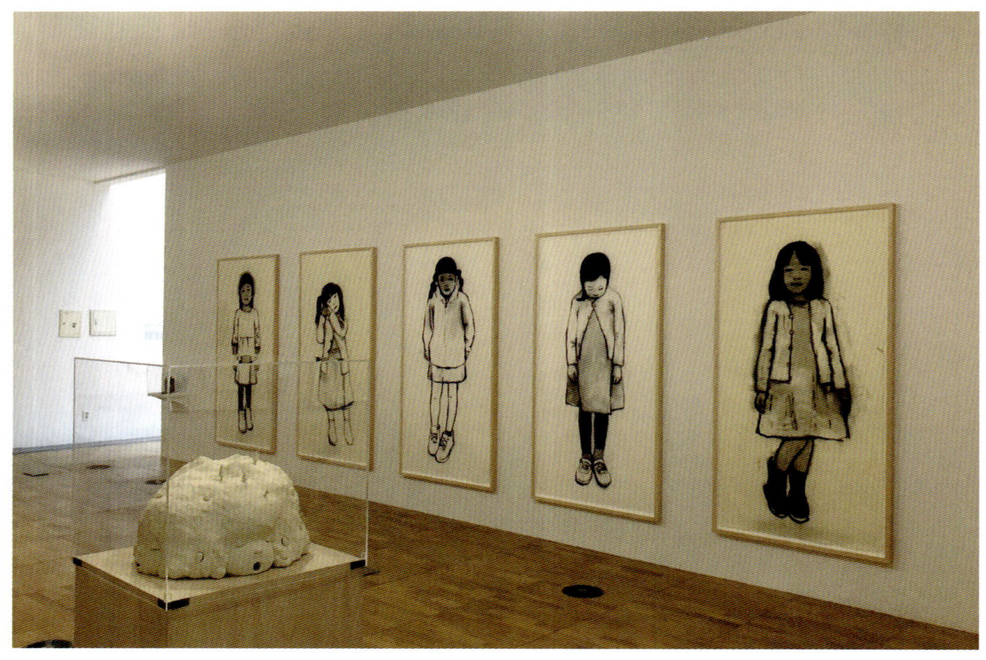

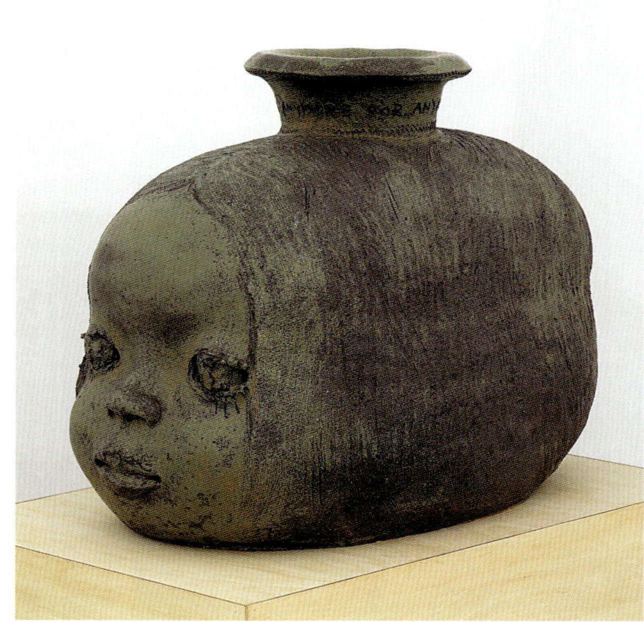

the land's transformative powers and the spiritual powers of the gods. If one is lucky enough to be able to gain entrance to Ahunrupar, one could find oneself in the realm of gods.

Nara captures the transformative power of the anthropomorphic cave at Shiraoi by creating mountain-shaped heads of clay with either two or four faces, each with their mouths and eyes opened or closed in different variations. In this way, he turns his girls into embodiments of the cave, their mouths and eyes acting as dividers between the worldly and the mythical. He emphasizes the enchantment of the body/cave by placing small trees and miniature skulls in their hair. Connected to the sculptural works are his drawings of girls' heads (Fig. 372), with various figures in their hair that can include bears (an homage to an Ainu god) or young girls carrying giant butterbur leaves (plants native to Hokkaido). These drawings, specific in their references to local lore and customs, all share a deliberately raw quality that captures a state of transformation.

For the 12th Gwangju Biennale in 2018, Nara brought these Tobiu works together—the small Jōmon-inspired clay pieces, the charcoal drawings, the drawings and sculptures of Ahunrupar, and his photographs of the place—as part of an installation called *Tobiu* (Fig. 370). The piece was his response to the exhibition *Faultlines*, a subtheme under the broader concept of the title of the Biennale, *Imagined Borders*, which examined how borders have become increasingly

Fig. 370
Exhibition view: *Faultlines*, 12th Gwangju Biennale, South Korea, 2018

Fig. 371
Anymore for Anymore, 2010, Ceramic, 28 3/8 × 23 5/8 × 28 3/8 in. (72 × 60 × 72 cm)

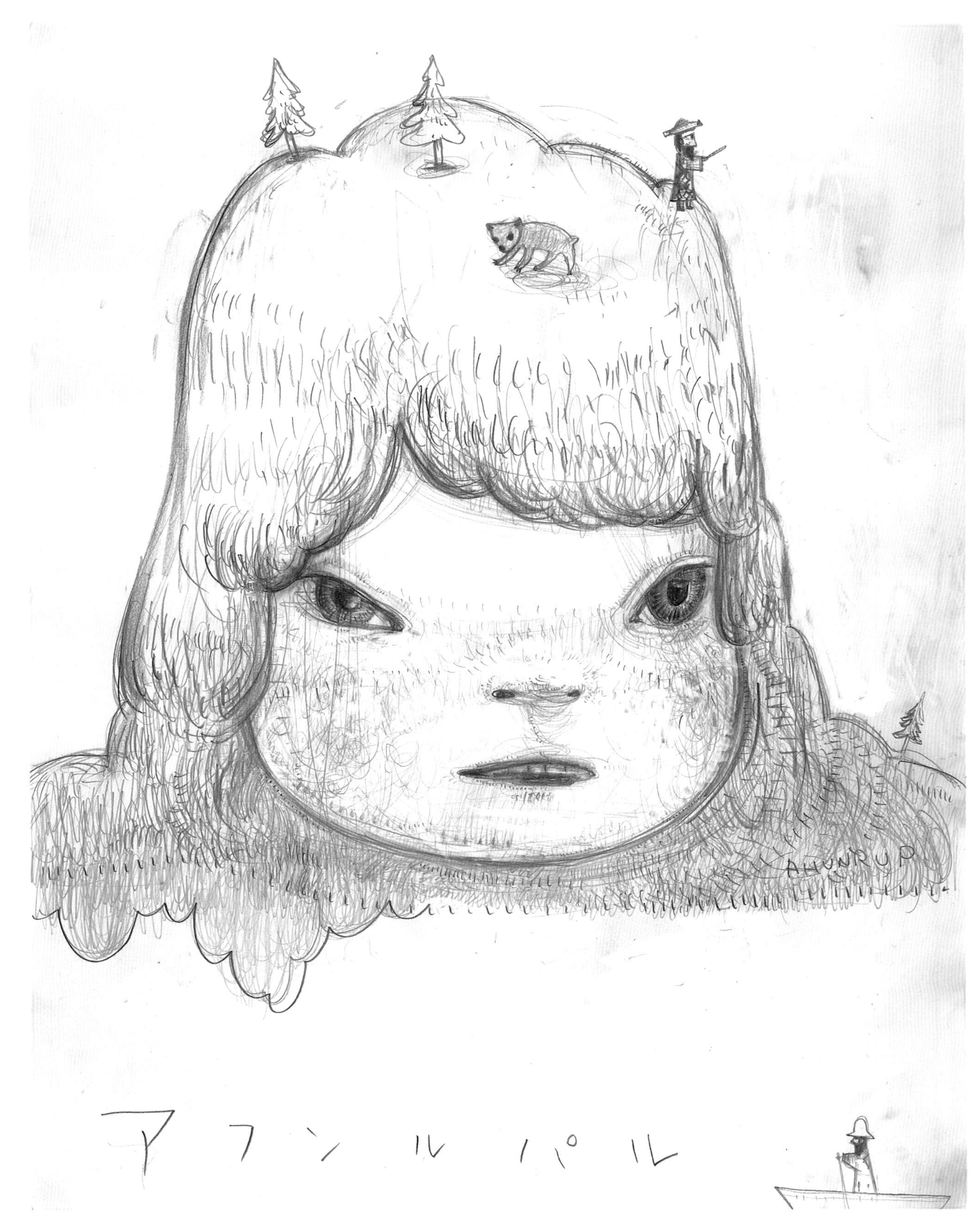

Fig. 372
Ahunrupar, 2018, Pencil on paper, 25 9/16 × 19 11/16 in. (65 × 50 cm)

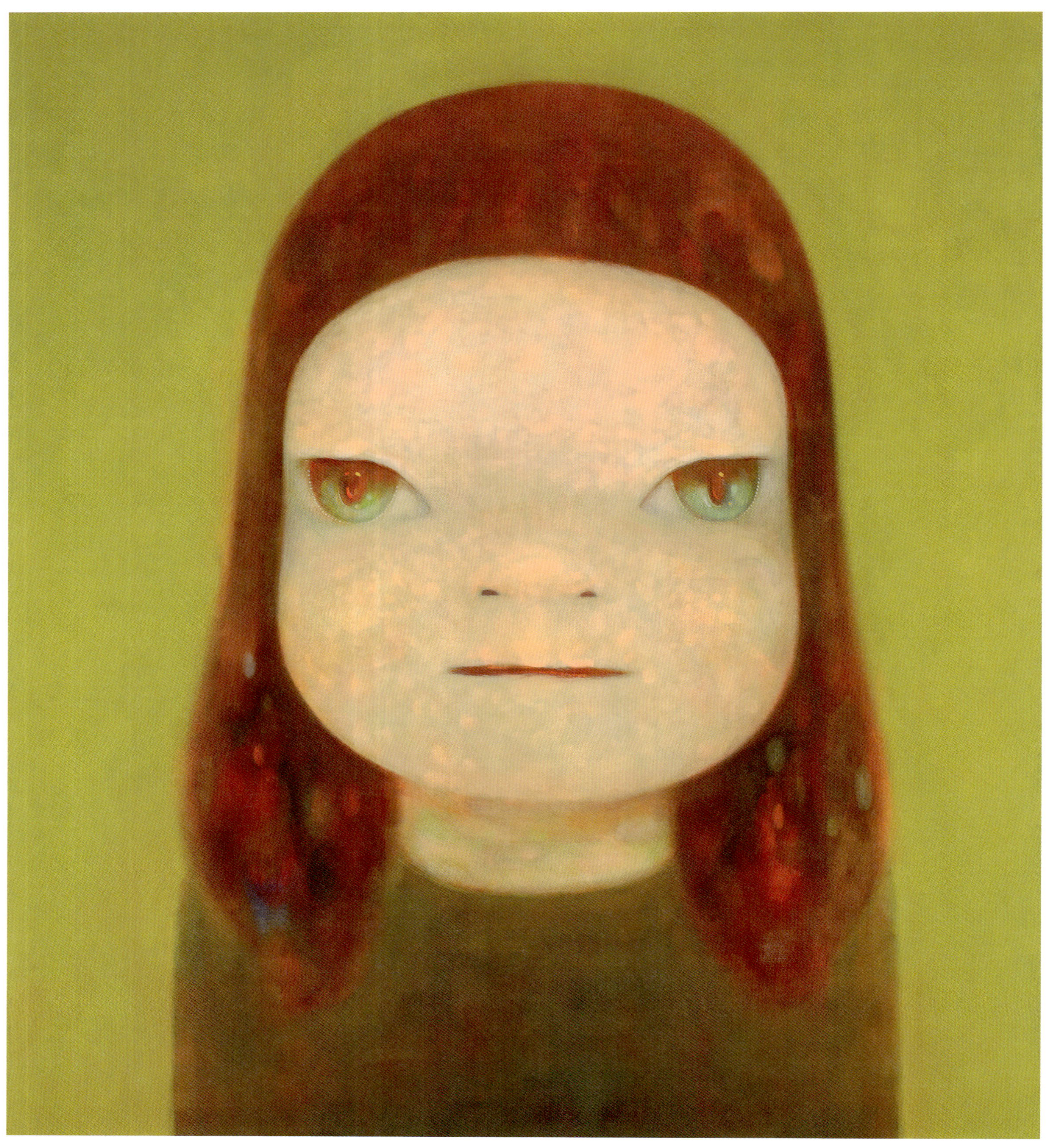

Fig. 373
I WANT TO SEE THE BRIGHT LIGHTS TONIGHT, 2017, Acrylic on canvas, 86 ⅝ × 76 ¾ in. (220 × 195 cm)

important in the geopolitical landscape of global capitalism, mass migration, and climate change, all of which are shifting the ways in which territorial borders are understood.[23] *Faultlines* looked at the different types of non-nation boundaries that define belonging today but that are also fragile or broken, embedded as they are in long histories of violence that are often ignored or forgotten. Tobiu can be seen as representative of the larger social and political issues facing northern Japan, where indigenous folktales, cultural traditions, and ethnic communities are rapidly disappearing. But at the same time, underlying these works is a hopeful vision of the regenerative nature of participation that happens on-site at Tobiu, when during "camp" time, residents and friends take part in communal activities: cleaning up the forest, painting in the schoolroom, listening to music. The vibrant sounds of community and the vitality of children playing present another side of Tobiu, one that is an active site, a place of survival rather than disappearance.

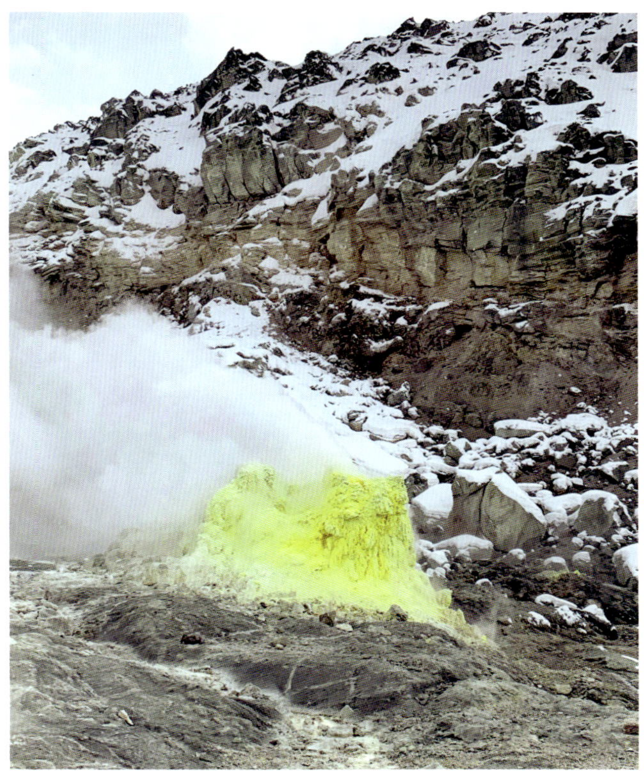

Over the last forty years, Nara has developed a distinctive voice in a career full of contradictions. He is embraced by the art establishment but finds meaning in smaller communities. His paintings project an aesthetic in which punk and cuteness go hand in hand. Categorically opposed to war, he is captivated by stories of wartime Japan. Nara revels in these contradictory positions, seeing them as a way to stake out his own marginal space where it is possible to maintain an ambiguous relationship to the establishment while at the same time rebelling against the demands of social conventions.

Recently, Nara has been traveling more and more, trekking to remote villages, spending time at Shigaraki making ceramics, and visiting Syrian refugee camps in Jordan. On these trips, he seldom thinks about his next painting or sculpture, taking only his camera and a pen to record his thoughts. They are at times travels made without aims, at others trips devoted to issues that lie close to his heart. Collectively, they give him the space to process how, as a career artist, he can maintain a balance between his private internal world and his desire for meaningful social connections, a dialectic that lies at the core of his art. His latest works reveal a greater sense of freedom, a loosening up of an artist who is, at heart, a very private person. He has become more open about being vulnerable,

Fig. 374
HOKKAIDO, 2019

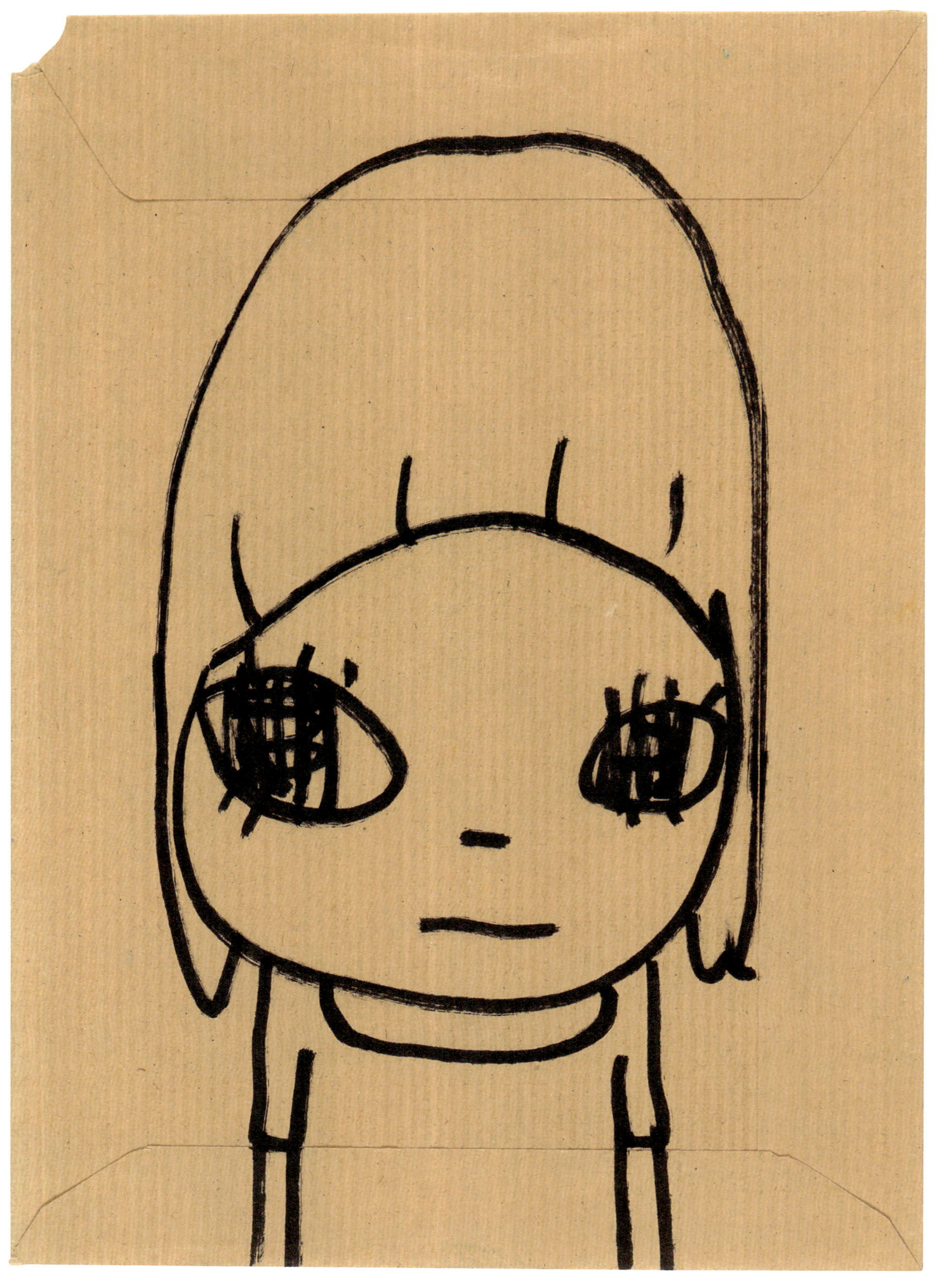

Fig. 375
Drawing for *Calendar*, 2013,
Pen on paper, Size unknown

Fig. 376 (opposite)
Invisible Vision, 2019, Acrylic
on canvas, 76 ¾ × 59 1/16 in.
(195 × 150 cm)

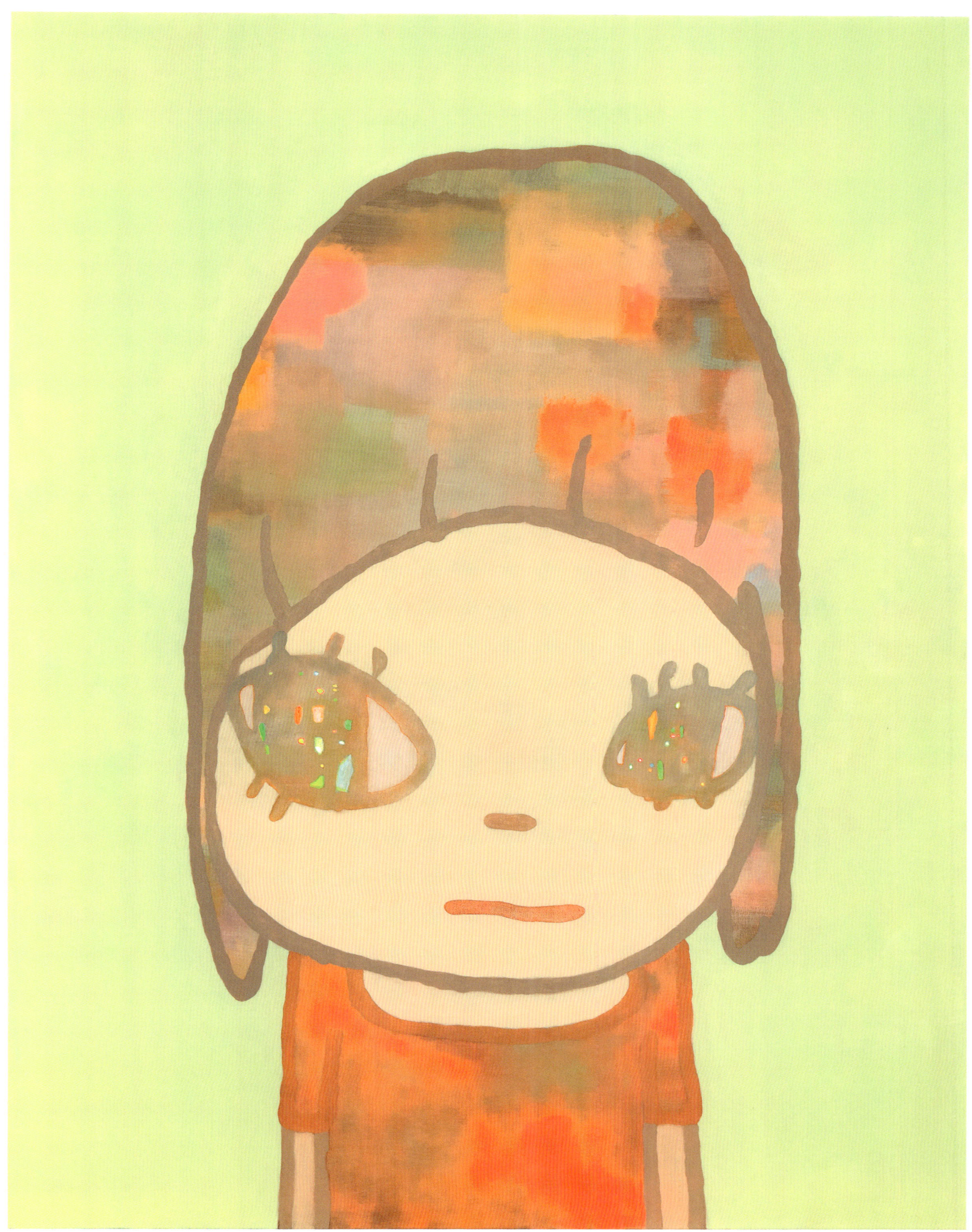

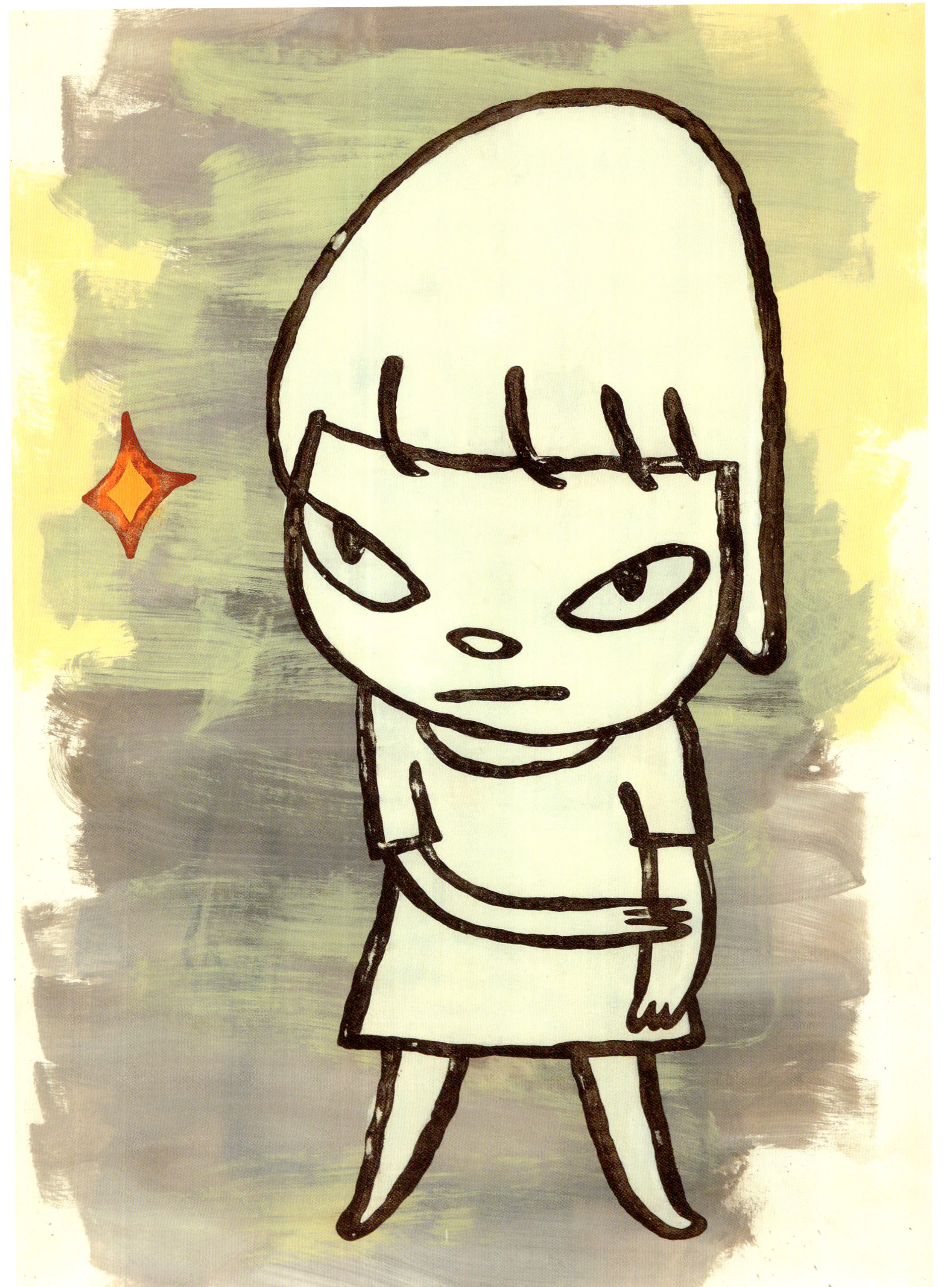

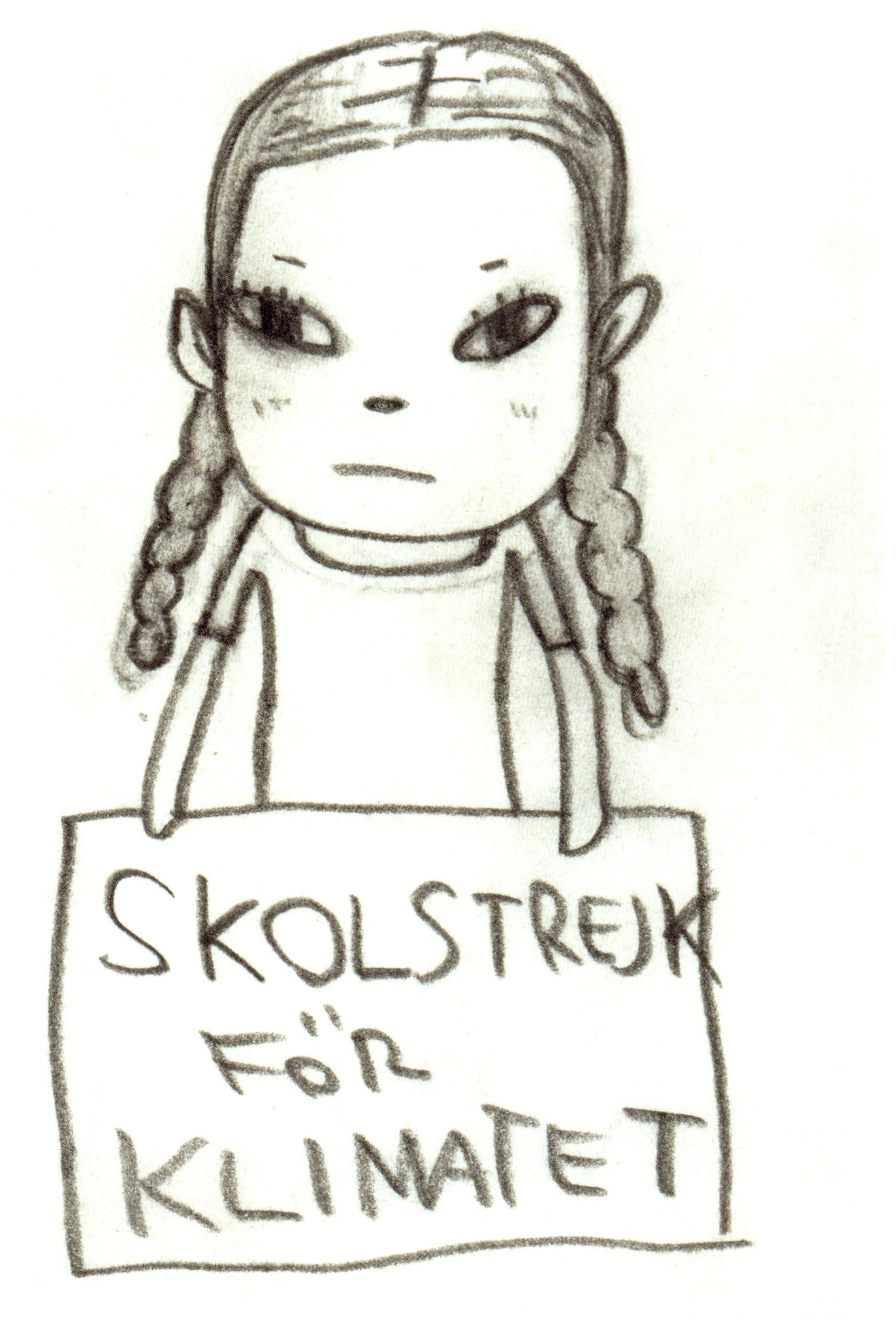

Fig. 377 (opposite)
Lone Star Girl, 2019, Acrylic on paper, 51 3⁄16 × 35 13⁄16 in. (130 × 91 cm)

Fig. 378
Untitled sketch, 2019, Pencil on paper, 6 1⁄8 × 4 5⁄16 in. (15.6 × 11 cm)

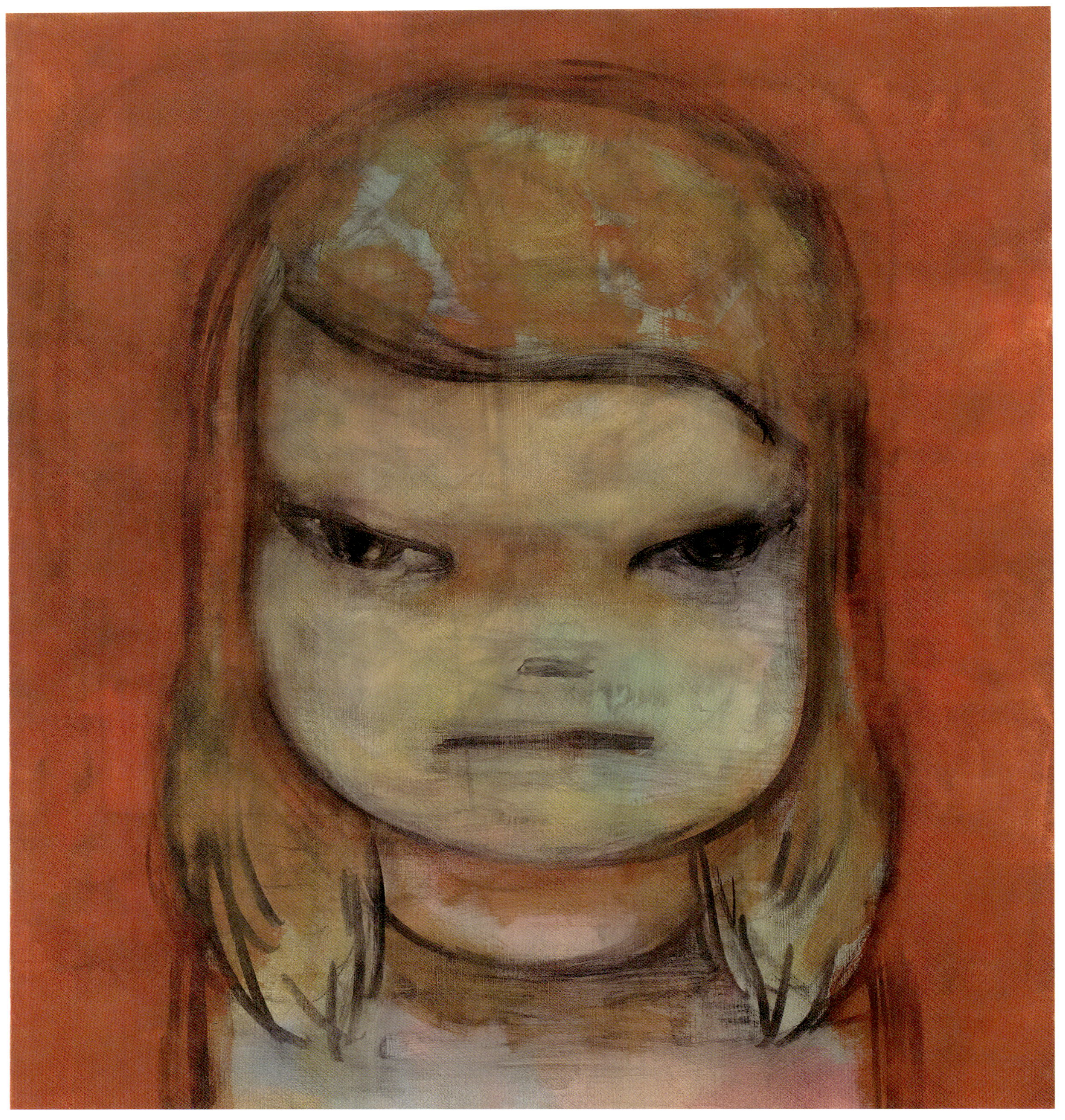

Fig. 379
Study for *Angry Sad Girl*,
2019, Acrylic on canvas,
47 ¼ × 43 ⁵⁄₁₆ in. (120 × 110 cm)

recognizing the fragility of life and of aging as he contemplates the values that matter most to his art. He paints with greater patience, although never sacrificing the pleasure of spontaneity, and he speaks up against war and nuclear power with a political voice that has always existed but has gained new resonance. His canvas bust portraits have reached a level of maturity and confidence, which means they may be on the verge of new experimentation.

Nara is currently exploring, as he had as a student in Germany, the relationship between painting and drawing, seeking different ways of achieving expressiveness by transferring some of the qualities of his penciled lines into acrylic traces or exploiting new color palettes that glimmer in between the outlines of his figures. His drawings and studies for paintings show that he is working through varied methods, whether finding new ways of portraying emotions such as anger or simply indulging in light-hearted fun. Ultimately, it is clear that he is excited by the new paths his work is taking (Figs. 375–379). For Nara, "creating is not about exhibiting. It's true that this is what ends up happening, but for me, continuing to paint is the torch that lights my existence. . . . I want to wait until the stars come out at night and howl like a wolf."[24]

Chapter 1
It Started with Music

1 Yoshitomo Nara, "Hansei (Half a Life)," in *The World of Yoshitomo Nara*, special issue, *Eureka Poetry and Critique* 49–13, no. 706 (August 2017): 236. All translations, unless stated otherwise, are adapted from translation by Chisato Uno. Any errors are the author's responsibility.

2 For a more in-depth description of life in Hirosaki and Shintoism in the Aomori region, see Ellen Schattschneider, *Immortal Wishes: Labor and Transcendence on a Japanese Sacred Mountain* (Durham, NC: Duke University Press, 2003).

3 *Oni* are eccentric spirits that are often believed to inhabit the wildest parts of the mountains. *Kami* are the embodiments of the aura found at sites believed to possess old sacred powers.

4 Shichi-Go-San is an important festival and rite of passage in Japan for girls at the ages of three and seven, and for boys at the age of five.

5 It is not unusual for Shinto shrines and to incorporate icons and temples of other religions. Jizō is venerated as the guardian of unborn, aborted, or stillborn babies, a role that is unique to him in Japan. He is also a protector of mothers, pregnant women, and young children.

6 Takeshi Terauchi (b. 1939) is a Japanese instrumental rock guitarist. He formed his first band, the Blue Jeans, in 1962, but left it in 1966 to form Takeshi Terauchi and the Bunnys. Their album *Let's Go Unmei* (1967) was the band's first hit and won the Arrangement Award at the 9th Japan Record Awards. Nara's first record purchase was the title track from this album, which was released as a single. To this day, Nara still uses the phrase "Let's Go" in many of his drawings and paintings. Despite the success of this band, Terauchi left the Bunnys and reformed the Blue Jeans in 1969.

7 Living so far north, Nara did not go to his first contemporary art museum until he was eighteen. Growing up, he had no knowledge of—let alone access to—the vibrant postwar art world in Japan. During the 1960s, there were many new artist collectives, including Hi Red Center and Zero Jigen (Zero Dimension) in Tokyo, and Yoko Ono first performed her *Cut Piece* in Kyoto (1964). For more on performance art in Japan, see Thomas R. H. Havens, *Radicals and Realists in the Japanese Nonverbal Arts: The Avant-Garde Rejection of Modernism* (Honolulu: University of Hawai'i Press, 2006).

8 Although the word *futen* is often translated as "slacker," it is closer in meaning to "hippie," as someone who is antimaterialistic, believes in peace, is informal in appearance, and has a bohemian outlook.

9 In the 1960s, distinct subcultural groups emerged in different pockets of Tokyo. The *futen-zoku* (*futen* tribe), an explicitly nonideologically driven group influenced by the American hippie movement, appeared in Shinjuku from 1967. See Taro E. F. Nettleton, "Throw Out the Books, Get Out in the Streets: Subjectivity and Space in Japanese Underground Art of the 1960s" (PhD diss., University of Rochester, 2010), 19, http://hdl.handle.net/1802/14175.

10 In Japan the definitions of, and the lines between, pop culture, subculture, and counterculture differ from Anglo-American conventions. In the West, subculture is seen as being nonnormative or marginal and follows ethnographic or sociological definitions. In Japan, subculture, or *sabukaru*, is used to define a community formed around the conventions of a medium or culture (manga, anime, or punk, for example). For more on this topic, see Anne McKnight, "Frenchness and Transformation in Japanese Subculture, 1972–2004," *Mechademia* 5 (2010): 118–37, https://muse.jhu.edu/article/400554.

11 Patricia G. Steinhoff, "Memories of New Left Protest," *Contemporary Japan* 25, no. 2 (2013): 146, https://doi.org/10.1515/cj-2013-0007.

12 There were additional events in 1970 that alienated the general populace, including the Japanese Red Army's hijacking of a passenger plane that was forced to fly to North Korea, the ritual suicide of right-wing author Yukio Mishima, and the violent murder of Toshio Ebihara, a leading member of the Japan Revolutionary Communist League, by rival leftist group Revolutionary Marxist Faction. One of the state's tactics to rein in underground political activities, including those of artists, was to stage the 1970 Osaka World Expo, which included many avant-garde artists and promoted new technology and future-oriented ideas. Although an anti-Expo movement was formed as a criticism of the state and its attempts to curtail political expression, from this period onward, there was a shift of thematic focus in the arts from Happenings to multimedia art.

13 Nara, "Hansei (Half a Life)," 237.

14 The avant-garde artist and writer Ichirō Fukuzawa (1898–1992) was instrumental in introducing European surrealism to Japan, which was quickly adopted and transformed by Japanese painters, photographers, and filmmakers in the late 1920s and early 1930s. However, as right-wing militarists gained control of the government, the state reconfigured the existing annual Ministry of Education Art Exhibition (*Teiten*) as the new Imperial Academy of Fine Arts Exhibition (*New Bunten*) in 1935 and 1937, which brought more artists from different communities under the administration of the Ministry of Education. Increasingly, the state gained more control over what types of art were to be seen and promoted. Surrealism, with its left-wing ideals and emphasis on the psyche of the individual, clashed with the rise of ultranationalism, and in 1941 Fukuzawa was arrested for promoting an "unhealthy" ideology. Traditional scholarship held the position that surrealist artists took on more conservative styles as they participated in the *New Bunten* system. However, recent studies have shown how the system also brought together artists who were working in different modes, making the boundaries between styles more fluid as members of different art communities came together. The art historian John Clark has written about the ambiguous political position of surrealism in wartime Japan: on the one hand, it offered the most explicit form of resistance to nationalism, while on the other, not many artists were willing to challenge the establishment. See Clark, "Artistic Subjectivity in the Taisho and Early Showa Avant-Garde," in *Japanese Art after 1945: Scream against the Sky*, ed. Alexandra Munroe, exh. cat. (New York: Harry N. Abrams, 1994); and Maki Kaneko, "Art in the Service of the State: Artistic Production in Japan during the Asia-Pacific War," (PhD diss., University of East Anglia, 2006).

15 It was only after the death of the Emperor Shōwa in 1989 that there was a revival of interest in Japanese wartime art. One of the major turning points was a large-scale exhibition of works by Fujita Tsuguharu in 2006 at the National Museum of Modern Art, Tokyo.

16 Mark H. Sandler, "The Living Artist: Matsumoto Shunsuke's Reply to the State," *Art Journal* 55, no. 3 (Fall 1996): 74–82, https://doi.org/10.2307/777768.

17 Ibid., 78.

18 Takeshi Motai remains an important artist to Nara, who in 2017 curated an exhibition, *Takeshi Motai the Dream Traveler*, for Chihiro Art Museum as part of the commemoration of the museum's fortieth anniversary.

19 Kenji Miyazawa's novel *Night on the Galactic Railroad* (published posthumously in 1934 and variously translated as *Night Train to the Stars* and *Milky Way Railroad*) is perhaps his best known. It is a fantasy novel about a young boy who has to care for his dying mother; his father, an explorer and geologist, is often away from home. Because of the boy's adult responsibilities, he is seen as a social outcast by his peers. One night a magical train appears, and the boy jumps on. It takes him on many adventures, during which he meets some strange people, including those on their way to the afterlife. A central theme of this story is the quest to understand true happiness. It was written after Miyazawa's beloved sister passed away, and, in mourning, he took a road trip to the remote islands of Sakhalin. This is one of the many stories that resonates with Nara, who also traveled to Sakhalin (discussed in Chapter Four). See Melissa Anne-Marie Curley, "Fruit, Fossils, Footprints: Cathecting Utopia in the Work of Miyazawa Kenji," in *Hope and the Longing for Utopia: Futures and Illusions in Theology and Narrative*, ed. Daniel Boscaljon (Cambridge: James Clarke, 2015), 96–118.

20 There is a long history of picture books in Japan, and the postwar baby boom of the 1960s ushered in a golden age of children's book publishing. This coincided with a rise in translations, which meant that children's books such as *The Little House* by Virginia Lee Burton and *Curious George* by H. A. Rey and Margret Rey became readily available.

21 Yoshitomo Nara, interview by Mika Kuraya, October 14, 2014, quoted in Mika Kuraya, "Where the Wild Children Are," in *Once in a Life: Encounters with Nara*, ed. Dominique Chan and Fumio Nanjo, exh. cat. (Hong Kong: Asia Society Hong Kong Center, 2016), 124.

22 The lone house appears in a few of Nara's later paintings and drawings, although it is often associated with destruction, such as in a series of colored pencil drawings on envelopes with houses ablaze from 2009, and *M.I.A.* (2011) (Fig. 284), which was painted in response to the Great East Japan Earthquake and Fukushima disaster. It is tempting to interpret that the erasure (and destruction) of this childhood home from his paintings reflects how Nara is letting go of certain memories of his childhood.

23 Svetlana Boym, *The Future of Nostalgia* (New York: Basic Books, 2001), 8.

24 As a struggling art student, it was not unusual for Nara to overpaint earlier works. Underneath this painting is his *Is There No Place Like Home?* (1984) (Fig. 17).

25 The left part of this painting is damaged and lost.
26 Quoted in *Yoshitomo Nara: The Complete BT Archives, 1993–2013* (Tokyo: Bijutsu Shuppan-sha, 2013), 72.
27 Nara, "Hansei (Half a Life)," 243.
28 Broadly framed as New Paintings or New Expressionism, it was a style that resonated with artistic trends in Europe and the United States. It is possible that further research into what was happening in Japan and elsewhere in Asia will reposition the Western-centric approach of art historical narratives of Neo-Expressionism.
29 Yoshitomo Nara, in conversation with the author, May 2018.

Chapter 2
Those Big-Headed Girls

1 Yoshitomo Nara, "Paint for 'What Is Being Painted,'" interview with Taku Yamashita, *Neppū Magazine*, October 2017, 18.
2 Jörg Johnen, email correspondence with the author, January 29, 2019.
3 Yoshitomo Nara, "Hansei (Half a Life)," in *The World of Yoshitomo Nara*, special issue, *Eureka Poetry and Critique* 49-13, no. 706 (August 2017): 245.
4 Translation of *kawaii* from *Nihon Kokugo Daijiten* (2000) by Hiroshi Nittono, "A Behavioral Science Framework for Understanding Kawaii" (paper presented at the Third International Workshop on Kansei, Fukuoka, Japan, February 23, 2010).
5 *Kawaii* entered the *Oxford English Dictionary* in 2011.
6 Jessika Golle, Stephanie Lisibach, Fred W. Mast, and Janek S. Lobmaier, "Sweet Puppies and Cute Babies: Perceptual Adaptation to Babyfacedness Transfers across Species," *PLoS ONE* 8, no. 3 (March 13, 2013): e58248, https://doi.org/10.1371/journal.pone.0058248.
7 Joshua Paul Dale, "Cute Studies: An Emerging Field," *East Asian Journal of Popular Culture* 2, no. 1 (April 1, 2016): 5–13, https://doi.org/10.1386/eapc.2.1.5_2.
8 For more on the Edo *ukiyo-e* world, see Donald Jenkins, *The Floating World Revisited*, exh. cat. (Portland, OR: Portland Art Museum, 1993).
9 The Mitsubishi A6M Zero was a long-range fighter aircraft used by the Imperial Japanese Navy between 1940–45. At the end of World War II, it was used in *kamikaze* suicide attacks, during which over 3,800 pilots died.
10 Marilyn Ivy's argument for seriality in Nara's work offers a different reading of how filiative identifications are made. See Marilyn Ivy, "The Art of Cute Little Things: Nara Yoshitomo's Parapolitics," *Mechademia* 5 (2010): 23, https://muse.jhu.edu/article/400548.
11 An example of this is the 1993 Biennial at the Whitney Museum of American Art in New York, curated by Thelma Golden, John G. Hanhardt, Lisa Phillips, and Elisabeth Sussman, which centered on questions of race, sexuality, and gender.
12 Nara, "Paint for 'What Is Being Painted,'" 13.
13 One of the influential writers and critics of Nara's art is Midori Matsui, who has argued for a Neo-Pop identity for Nara. See her essay "Art for Myself and Others: Yoshitomo Nara's Popular Imagination," in *Yoshitomo Nara: Nobody's Fool*, ed. Melissa Chiu and Miwako Tezuka, exh. cat. (New York: Asia Society and Abrams, 2010). Matsui takes a slightly different approach in a later essay that revises the Pop element in Nara's work as a form of "minor" art. See her essay "A Child in the White Field: Yoshitomo Nara as a Great 'Minor' Artist," in *Yoshitomo Nara: The Complete Works*, vol. 1 (San Francisco: Chronicle Books, 2011), 330–57.
14 Nara's exhibition *Nobody's Fool* at Asia Society, New York, in 2010 explored the connection between his art and music. The title of the show comes from Dan Penn's 1973 album of the same name.
15 Osamu Tezuka et al., *Tezuka Osamu ten* [The Osamu Tezuka Exhibit], exh. cat. (Tokyo: The National Museum of Modern Art, 1990).
16 Adapted from a translation by Ashley Rawlings. For Akira Asada, see "So-called Contemporary Art," *Voice*, October 2001, accessed via Critical Space Archive, http://www.kojinkaratani.com/criticalspace/old/special/asada/voice0110.html
17 In 1995, curator Fumio Nanjo, for the newly launched Shinjuku i-Land Public Art Project, commissioned several public artworks by international artists to adorn one of the busiest centers in Tokyo. The roster of artists included Robert Indiana, Roy Lichtenstein, Luciano Fabro, Katsuhito Nishikawa, and Hidetoshi Nagasawa. See Kenji Kajiya, "Japanese Art Projects in History," *FIELD: A Journal of Socially-Engaged Art Criticism* 7 (Spring 2017), http://field-journal.com/issue-7/japanese-art-projects-in-history.
18 Miwako Tezuka, "Music on My Mind: The Art and Phenomenon of Yoshitomo Nara," in Chiu and Tezuka, *Yoshitomo Nara: Nobody's Fool*, 94.
19 Yoshitomo Nara, "Rongu intabyu: Nara Yoshitomo, tabi no tochu de" [A Long Interview: Yoshitomo Nara in the Middle of His Journey], *Bijutsu techō* 52, no. 790 (July 2000): 44, quoted in Midori Matsui, "Art for Myself and Others: Yoshitomo Nara's Popular Imagination," in Chiu and Tezuka, *Yoshitomo Nara: Nobody's Fool*, 21–22.
20 Nara, "Hansei (Half a Life)," 246.
21 Here my argument veers slightly from Marilyn Ivy's. Ivy reads the subject of the I as a generalized image of the abandoned child within who has been forgotten during the transition into adulthood. Nara's work, for Ivy, is a recovery of that childlike spirit. She cites Noi Sawaragi's Lacanian reading of Nara's works as support of her argument. See Ivy, "The Art of Cute Little Things," 19–23.
22 Ibid., 17.
23 "Voices of HamaPuro Brothers & Sisters!!," *Bijutsu techō* 53, no. 813 (December 2001): 33, quoted in Ivy, "The Art of Cute Little Things," 20.
24 The *Superflat* exhibition was expanded for its run in the US. It traveled to the Museum of Contemporary Art in Los Angeles (January 14–May 27, 2001), the Walker Art Center in Minneapolis (July 15–October 14, 2001), and the Henry Art Gallery in Seattle (November 10, 2001–March 3, 2002).
25 Nara participated in the *Superflat* and *Little Boy* exhibitions.
26 Takashi Murakami, *Superflat*, exh. cat. (Tokyo: Madra Publishing, 2000). See also Michael Darling, "Plumbing the Depths of Superflatness," *Art Journal* 60, no. 3 (2001): 76–89, https://doi.org/10.1080/00043249.2001.10792079.
27 Takashi Murakami, "A Theory of Super Flat Japanese Art," in Murakami, *Superflat*, 9–25.
28 Takashi Murakami, "Earth in My Window," in *Little Boy: The Arts of Japan's Exploding Subculture*, ed. Takashi Murakami, exh. cat. (New York: Japan Society; New Haven, CT: Yale University Press, 2005), 135–36.
29 David Elliott, *Bye Bye Kitty!!!: Between Heaven and Hell in Contemporary Japanese Art*, exh. cat. (New York: Japan Society; New Haven, CT: Yale University Press, 2011), 5–7.
30 Takashi Murakami, *DOBSF: DOB in the Strange Forest* (Tokyo: Bijutsu Shuppan-sha, 1999).
31 One of the most influential works on *otaku* is by Hiroki Azuma, *Otaku: Japan's Database Animals*, trans. Jonathan E. Abel and Shion Kono (Minneapolis: University of Minnesota Press, 2009). See also Patrick W. Galbraith and Thomas Lamarre, "Otakuology: A Dialogue," *Mechademia* 5 (2010): 360–74, https://muse.jhu.edu/article/400567.
32 Setsu Shigematsu, "Dimensions of Desire: Sex, Fantasy and Fetish in Japanese Comics," in *Themes and Issues in Asian Cartooning: Cute, Cheap, Mad, and Sexy*, ed. John A. Lent (Bowling Green, OH: Bowling Green State University Popular Press, 1999), 127–64.
33 Alexandra Munroe, "Introducing Little Boy," in Murakami, *Little Boy*, 240–61.
34 Marc Steinberg, "*Otaku* Consumption, Superflat and the Return to Edo," *Japan Forum* 16, no. 3 (2004): 449–71, https://doi.org/10.1080/0955580042000257927.
35 There are many studies and exhibitions in Japan that tackle the subject of Japanese contemporary art in relation to visual culture. One influential exhibition was *Ground Zero Japan*, held at the Contemporary Art Center, Art Tower Mito in 1999–2000 and curated by preeminent art critic Noi Sawaragi. Sawaragi examined the importance of subcultures—largely the *otaku* world—in the contemporary but argued for a more complex reading of the history of American influences that have shaped contemporary Japan.
36 As Marc Steinberg has shown, many scholars, including the literary critic Hiroki Azuma, argue that the nationalist appeal to Japanese tradition made by Murakami is primarily a marketing strategy, but close readings of how Murakami appropriates *otaku* references and *ukiyo-e* suggest a certain ambivalence toward a monolithic Japanese identity. See Steinberg, "*Otaku* Consumption," 468–69.
37 The translations of these terms rarely take into account the audience's ability to process the different anime codes and narrative styles that can be conditioned by factors such as the social structure of the comic-book market. For example, in the United States, there is a sharp demarcation between the comic-book market for adults and children, which does not exist in Japan. This blurring of adult and children's markets (and sensibilities) explains, in part, how cultural differences also play a role in assessing what are considered acceptable deviant behaviors in the *otaku* and *kawaii* worlds. It is outside the scope of this book to examine the contested field of Superflat's contribution to discussions on anime culture. For an introduction to the various positions by different scholars in the field, see Kristen Sharp, "Superflatworlds: A Topography of Takashi Murakami and the Cultures of Superflat Art" (PhD diss., RMIT University, 2006). https://researchbank.rmit.edu.au/view/rmit:9886.
38 The title of Nara's work references a song by the American rock band the Doors, just as Murakami's plays on the title of the Andy Warhol film *Lonesome*

Cowboys (1968). As such, both are reflections on American influences in postwar Japan.

39 Nara, "Hansei (Half a Life)," 247.

Chapter 3
Working with Others

1 Yoshitomo Nara, "Hansei (Half a Life)," in *The World of Yoshitomo Nara*, special issue, *Eureka Poetry and Critique* 49-13, no. 706 (August 2017): 247.

2 The success of Nara and Murakami led to the term *Narakami*. See Kay Itoi, "Japan's Year of Narakami," *Artnet Magazine*, October 22, 2001, http://www.artnet.com/magazine/features/itoi/itoi10-22-01.asp.

3 At the time of the project, the artists were also both represented by Stephen Friedman Gallery in London.

4 The show's curators, Marie-Laure Bernadac and Stéphanie Moisdon, both faced judicial inquiry after accusations from a local children's organization that they were showing child pornography. Although twenty-one artworks were cited as being pornographic, only two artists were brought up for investigation: Elke Krystufek, for the installation *The Tunnel*, which showed the artist masturbating, and Ugo Rondinone. When Krystufek was questioned, the artist said the installation had been destroyed and thus could not be provided as evidence. The charges were later dropped. See Jennifer Allen, "'Kiddie Porn' Curators Questioned," *Artforum*, January 8, 2007, https://www.artforum.com/news/curators-questioned-over-child-porn-porn-in-german-journals-journal-des-arts-and-zkm-celebrate-milestones-luxembourg-s-cultural-capital-more-documenta-artists-12339.

5 It is from this period that Nara began participating in a number of exhibitions, both in Japan and internationally. Many of these exhibitions focused on themes that promoted the image of a "cool Japan" as well as Japanese pop culture, which, aside from the important series of Superflat shows, also included *Dark Mirrors of Japan* (2000) at de Appel Foundation in Amsterdam, *Tokyo Pop* (2001) at Kansas City Jewish Museum in Overland Park, KS, *My Reality: Contemporary Art and the Culture of Japanese Animation* (2001) at Des Moines Art Center and other venues in the US, and *Pop! Pop! Pop!* (2002) at the Museum of Modern Art, Ibaraki, in Mito, Japan.

6 David Shrigley, interview with the author, March 2019.

7 Hiroshi Sugito, "Baby-Blue Jeans and Fragrant Orange Tea Olive," in *Yoshitomo Nara: The Complete Works*, vol. 1 (San Francisco: Chronicle Books, 2011), 241–42.

8 Ibid.

9 Yoshimoto Nara, interview with the author, April 4, 2019.

10 Sugito, "Baby-Blue Jeans," 242.

11 The show *Chaguin* was held at Misako & Rosen, February 26 through March 23, 2008. The gallery's introduction recalls how this show came about:

> Chaguin – Henri and Pierre Chaguin. In 2004, in the old capital city of Vienna Henri made a stop and began to create new artworks; at this time he contacted his good old friend, Pierre, entreating him to visit and to try working together—at this time their collaboration began. Their joint creation was the result of pure joy in work and working together so they decided to avoid a typical exhibition.
>
> 2008: Pierre phones to Henri from his studio in Aichi, Japan: "Henri, Here there is the sunlight observed by Cézanne in Aix-en-Provence!"
>
> "The time is here! Let's sketch apples together!"
>
> "Ok Pierre! I will be there soon!"
>
> "I can't hold back!—come, come now! I can't wait any longer!"
>
> "Please don't do a thing until I arrive! I am coming soon!"
>
> One month of creation by the two artists again commenced. Afternoon, evening—they paid no mind and continued to feverishly work.

"Chaguin," Misako & Rosen website, accessed May 2019, https://www.misakoandrosen.jp/en/exhibitions/08/02/.

12 Yoshimoto Nara, email exchange with the author, May 4, 2019.

13 For example, above a collage of photos from Afghanistan, Nara wrote, "Can you / Hey US people! Remember Hiroshima, and don't forget Nagasaki." See Masako Nagano et al., *This Is a Time of...S.M.L.*, exh. cat. (Kyoto: Seigensha, 2004), n.p.

14 Hisako Hara, "Ten Days in Winter," trans. Linda Yabushita, in Nagano et al., *This Is a Time of...S.M.L.*, n.p.

15 For an example of how Nara's artworks were seen as showing a world of children and animals who were emotionally detached, see Michael Darling, "Plumbing the Depths of Superflatness," *Art Journal* 60, no. 3 (2001): 76–89, https://doi.org/10.1080/00043249.2001.10792079. For Akira Asada's critique, see "So-called Contemporary Art," *Voice*, October 2001, accessed via Critical Space Archive, http://www.kojinkaratani.com/criticalspace/old/special/asada/voice0110.html.

16 According to an unpublished report made by the A-Z Committee, there were 850 registered volunteers and a total number of 77,343 visitors. However, the report also notes that the total number of volunteers was 13,359, but this is a total sum of volunteers per day over the period of the exhibition, and as some volunteers worked multiple days, they were counted more than once. This accounts for why the figures cited here differ from those in other writings.

17 See Adrian Favell, "Socially Engaged Art in Japan: Mapping the Pioneers," in *FIELD: A Journal of Socially-Engaged Art Criticism* 7 (Spring 2017), http://field-journal.com/issue-7/socially-engaged-art-in-japan-mapping-the-pioneers.

18 Midori Matsui, *"A to Z," Artforum*, December 2006, 328.

19 The utopian ideal of this project was always difficult to achieve—it relied on Nara's fame in order to attract volunteers and funding, but this also meant that the other artists had less presence, thus overturning the democratic ambition of the project. See Matsui, *"A to Z."*

20 Louise Allison Cort, *Shigaraki: Potters' Valley* (Tokyo: Kodansha International, 1979).

21 In the sixteenth century, the tea master and Zen priest Sen no Rikyū introduced a more austere and rustic form of tea ceremony, which incorporated the use of ceramic vessels of unrefined, natural, and imperfect forms. This was a quality known as *wabi*. The term *sabi* originally meant "withered" or "lean," with connotations of being humble. It is unclear when the two terms were combined. For additional information about sixteenth-century aesthetics and tea culture, see Paul Varley and Kumakura Isao, eds., *Tea in Japan: Essays on the History of Chanoyu* (Honolulu: University of Hawai'i Press, 1989).

22 Nara, "Hansei (Half a Life)," 248.

23 Quoted in Sam Phillips, "Tokyo Pop in Clay," *Ceramic Review*, no. 250 (July/August 2011): 54.

24 See Edwina Palmer, "Land of the Rising Sun: The Predominant East-West Axis Among the Early Japanese," *Monumenta Nipponica* 46, no. 1 (Spring 1991): 69–90, https://doi.org/10.2307/2385147.

25 Nara, "Hansei (Half a Life)," 248.

26 After breaking up, three of the four original members of the Blue Hearts formed a new band, the High-Lows, which would later inspire the name of Nara's café project, *WE-LOW HOUSE*, discussed in Chapter Five.

27 These two lines are from the first part of the song: "This might not be heaven, but it's not hell either / It's not full of good people, but it's not only bad people either." Translation by the author assisted by Yoshiko Nakano.

28 Another translation of this line is: "In the manner of a sewer rat / Is the way I want to be beautiful / Because there is a type of beauty that a photograph can never show." The key line in the chorus, "Even if it's not love or affection, I have a single strong power / that will never be defeated. Linda, Linda, Linda," is the hardest section to translate, and it is possible to find variations. The translation here is Nara's own.

29 Takashi Azumaya, "Yoshitomo Nara: His Gothic Innocent World," in *Yoshitomo Nara: From the Depth of My Drawer*, exh. cat. (Seoul: Leeum, Samsung Museum of Art, 2005), 50, quoted in Tezuka, "Music on My Mind," 93.

30 "Sound by Vision," interview between Shonen Knife and Yoshitomo Nara, *COMPOSITE*, June 1998, 73.

31 Ibid.

32 One of the harshest criticisms lobbied at Nara comes from a controversial study on contemporary Japanese art by Adrian Favell, *Before and After Superflat: A Short History of Japanese Contemporary Art 1990–2011* (Hong Kong: Blue Kingfisher, 2011). Related to this study was a short article for the website *ART iT* entitled "Yoshitomo Nara as a Businessman," which Favell later requested to have taken off the website. However, in a rare response by Nara, who questioned the factuality of Favell's claims, sections of Favell's original post have been reposted. See "Response from Yoshitomo Nara to the article 'Yoshitomo Nara as a Businessman,'" *ART iT*, August 14, 2012, https://www.art-it.asia/en/u/admin_ed_sp2_e/response-from-yoshitomo-nara-to-the-article-yoshitomo-nara-as-a-businessman.

33 Yoshitomo Nara, *NARA LIFE: The Days of Yoshitomo Nara* (Kyoto: FOIL, 2012), 261.

Chapter 4
Travels with the Camera

1 This chapter is an expansion of an earlier essay by the author, "The Artist behind the Camera," in *Once in a Life: Encounters with Nara*, ed. Dominique Chan and Fumio Nanjo, exh. cat. (Hong Kong: Asia Society Hong Kong Center, 2016), 83–99.

2 Nara's first public showing of his photography was for a special supplement, "Photography Talks," for the Japanese edition of *Esquire* magazine in 2002.

3 The September 11 attacks consisted of a series of four coordinated attacks by the Islamic terrorist group al-Qaeda against the United States. Despite the expulsion of the Taliban, the war in Afghanistan continues today, largely centered on battling Taliban insurgents. To date, it is the longest war in US history.
4 Japan provided naval ships from its Ground Self-Defense Forces to help refuel ships and deliver water. This is still in keeping with Article 9 of the Japanese constitution, which allows Japan to provide humanitarian aid in international disputes.
5 Gennifer Weisenfeld, "Japanese Modernism and Consumerism: Forging the New Artistic Field of '*Shōgyō Bijutsu*' (Commercial Art)," in *Being Modern in Japan: Culture and Society from the 1910s to the 1930s*, ed. Elise K. Tipton and John Clark (Honolulu: University of Hawai'i Press, 2000), 75–98.
6 There were many different types of modern art that came under attack by the government as it became increasingly involved in censoring the art world, such as surrealism and Dada, as discussed in Chapter One.
7 Gennifer Weisenfeld, "Publicity and Propaganda in 1930s Japan: Modernism as Method," *Design Issues* 25, no. 4 (Autumn 2009): 13–28, https://doi.org/10.1162/desi.2009.25.4.13.
8 John Clark, "Hamaya Hiroshi (1915–1999) and Photographic Modernism in Japan," *TAP: Trans-Asia Photography Review* 7, no. 1 (Fall 2016), http://hdl.handle.net/2027/spo.7977573.0007.102.
9 In the 1980s and 1990s, there was a short lull in the publication of photographic books, as some of the more traditional publishers closed down. There has been a resurgence of interest since the 1990s, when artists such as Yasumasa Morimura, Nobuyoshi Araki, and Hiroshi Sugimoto began to gain a presence on the international stage. Although their works are often presented in single-sheet forms, their photographic books are considered to be highly significant and influential within the genre. To see the importance of the photobook in the early careers of Japanese photographers, see Russet Lederman, "Then and Now: Japanese Women Photographers of the 1970s and '80s Revealed Through Their Photobooks," *Art and Vernacular Photographies in Asia* 8, no. 1 (Fall 2017), http://hdl.handle.net/2027/spo.7977573.0008.102.
10 Yoshitomo Nara, *The Little Star Dweller*, trans. Wang Xiaoling and Huang Bijun (Taipei: Locus Publishing, 2004), 108.
11 Nara's antiwar stance is discussed in more detail in the following chapter. After the Great Tōhoku Earthquake, he becomes more open about his position on war and nuclear power, and in 2014, on the seventieth anniversary of the end of World War II, he produced a book entitled *NO WAR!*, showing select works made throughout his career on this theme. See Yoshitomo Nara, *NO WAR!* (Tokyo: Bijutsu Shuppan-sha, 2014).
12 The Watari Museum of Contemporary Art in Tokyo approached Nara for a solo show at a time when he was already traveling in Sakhalin with Naoki Ishikawa. Nara proposed that he would do a joint exhibition with Ishikawa based on their trip. The show, *to the north, from here*, ran January 25–May 10, 2015.
13 Anton Chekhov's *Ostrov Sakhalin* (Sakhalin Island), written in 1890, was published in 1895, although one of its chapters was released in 1892 to help raise relief funds for the Russian famine of 1891–92. The book is a journalistic investigation of the prison conditions in Siberia, told with the clarity of reportage but with the human compassion of prose fiction.
14 For an interesting study on the complexity of identities during the Japanese occupation of Sakhalin, see Tessa Morris-Suzuki, "Northern Lights: The Making and Unmaking of Karafuto Identity," *Journal of Asian Studies* 60, no. 3 (August 2001): 645–71, https://doi.org/10.2307/2700105.
15 Yoshitomo Nara, in conversation with the author, April 3, 2019.
16 Ibid.

Chapter 5
Return to the North

1 Yoshitomo Nara, "Hansei (Half a Life)," in *The World of Yoshitomo Nara*, special issue, *Eureka Poetry and Critique* 49-13, no. 706 (August 2017): 250.
2 Brian Massumi, "The Half-Life of Disaster," *Guardian*, April 15, 2011, https://www.theguardian.com/commentisfree/2011/apr/15/half-life-of-disaster.
3 *Kiai* is a martial arts term that describes the short intake of breath and release of energy before one confronts an opponent. Chim↑Pom is one of the most active artist collectives responding to the Fukushima disaster, with many of its activist projects relating to nuclear power and its long-term harm.
4 "Kiyosumi Gallery Complex Silent Auction," *ITmedia Online*, April 8, 2011, https://www.itmedia.co.jp/style/articles/1104/08/news066.html.
5 Nara, "Hansei (Half a Life)," 250.
6 Edan Corkill, "Yoshitomo Nara Puts the Heart Back in Art," *Japan Times*, July 20, 2012, https://www.japantimes.co.jp/culture/2012/07/20/arts/yoshitomo-nara-puts-the-heart-back-in-art.
7 Shoshana Felman and Dori Laub, *Testimony: Crises of Witnessing in Literature, Psychoanalysis, and History* (New York: Routledge, 1992), 82.
8 Robert Ayers, "'I Was Really Unthinking Before': Yoshitomo Nara on His Recent Work and His Show at Pace Gallery in New York," *ARTnews*, April 14, 2017, http://www.artnews.com/2017/04/14/i-was-really-unthinking-before-yoshitomo-nara-on-his-recent-work-and-his-show-at-pace-gallery-in-new-york/.
9 The Japanese Teachers Union, established in 1947, was one of the key groups that promoted works, including films, that critically examined the role of the Japanese Imperial Army and right-wing politicians in the bombing of Hiroshima, a topic that had been taboo for many years.
10 The exhibition *Niko Pirosmani* was hosted by the Albertina Museum in Vienna (October 26, 2018–January 27, 2019) in partnership with the Infinitart Foundation, Fondation Vincent van Gogh Arles, and the Georgian National Museum.
11 Large-scale demonstrations against nuclear power have multiplied in the years since the Fukushima disaster. On June 11, 2011, thousands of activists occupied the east-exit plaza of the Shinjuku train station and renamed it No Nukes Plaza. On June 29, 2012, an estimated 200,000 people protested against the reopening of the nuclear reactor at Ōi in Fukui prefecture, making it the largest street demonstration to take place in post–World War II Japan. In July 2018, the three hundredth such protest was held in front of the prime minister's office in Chiyoda Ward.
12 Alexander Brown and Vera Mackie, "Introduction: Art and Activism in Post-Disaster Japan," *Asia-Pacific Journal* 13, no. 7 (February 16, 2015), https://apjjf.org/2015/13/6/Vera-Mackie/4277.html.
13 Satoshi Kamata has also published numerous investigative journalistic articles and books on labor rights, and the US military in Japan, some of which have been translated into English, including *Japan in the Passing Lane: An Insider's Account of Life in a Japanese Auto Factory*, trans. Tatsuru Akimoto (New York: Pantheon Books, 1982).
14 This book would later win the prestigious Mainichi Publications Culture Prize.
15 This was part of the opening statement made by Satoshi Kamata at the rally, reported by Kyodo News, *Mainichi Shimbun*, July 16, 2012.
16 According to news reports, organizers estimated a crowd of 170,000–200,000 people, but the Metropolitan Police Department put the total count at 17,000.
17 The two-day rock concert was held in the Makuhari Messe Convention Center in Chiba, featuring twenty-five bands.
18 Masue Kato, "Interview: Yoshitomo Nara, Reflecting Back on his Career," in *Yoshitomo Nara: The Complete BT Archives, 1993–2013* (Tokyo: Bijutsu Shuppan-sha, 2013), 265.
19 Two members of the High-Lows, Hiroto Kōmoto and Masatoshi Mashima, were formerly in the punk band the Blue Hearts, one of Nara's favorite bands, which inspired many of his drawings.
20 The word *ainu* means "human being" in the Ainu language. The Ainu land, *Ainu moshir* (land of men), originally encompassed present-day Hokkaido, the Kuril Islands, Sakhalin, southern Kamchatka, and the Amur River estuary region, before they were incorporated into nation states. For an introduction to Ainu culture, see William W. Fitzhugh and Chisato O. Dubreuil, eds., *Ainu: Spirit of a Northern People*, exh. cat. (Washington, DC: Arctic Studies Center, National Museum of Natural History, Smithsonian Institute in association with University of Washington Press, 1999).
21 Kineta Kunimatsu, interview with the author, May 29, 2018.
22 The animation was adapted from a segment of *Playground* (2009), a documentary on child sex trafficking directed by Libby Spears. Spears had asked Nara to create images that were then animated for the film's closing credits. He later extracted the segment and added his own selection of music to it which he showed at Tobiu Camp in 2016.
23 *Faultlines* was cocurated by this author, Yeewan Koon, with Yeon Shim Chung. The 12th Gwangju Biennale (September 7–November 11, 2018) was formed of six main exhibitions with a collective of eleven curators. The driving concept of *Beyond Borders* is a reference to both Benedict Anderson's book *Imagined Communities* (1983) and the theme of the inaugural biennale, *Beyond Borders*, held in 1995.
24 Nara, "Hansei (Half a Life)," 255.

List of Works

All dimensions, unless otherwise noted, listed h. × w. × d.

CHINA, 1983, 1983
Figs. 212–214

Futaba House, Waiting for Rain Drops, 1984
Acrylic and colored pencil on wood board
each 17 11/16 × 14 3/16 in. (45 × 36 cm)
Collection of Aomori Museum of Art, Japan
Figs. 22a–b

Is There No Place Like Home?, 1984
Acrylic on canvas
51 3/16 × 76 ⅜ in. (130 × 194 cm)
Fig. 17

Lost Memory, 1984
Acrylic and colored pencil on paper mounted on board
Size unknown
Fig. 20

Untitled, 1984
Acrylic and collage on paper mounted on board
Size unknown
Fig. 21

I Shouldn't Give Up to Die, 1985
Acrylic and colored pencil on paper
Size unknown
Fig. 197

All Alone, 1986
Acrylic and colored pencil on canvas
76 × 51 5/16 in. (193 × 130.3 cm)
Fig. 24

Innocent Being, 1986
Acrylic and colored pencil on canvas
76 ⅜ × 51 5/16 in. (194 × 130.3 cm)
Collection of Aichi University of the Arts, Nagakute, Japan
Fig. 23

Somewhere Somewhere, 1986
Pen on paper
7 3/16 × 5 1/16 in. (18.2 × 12.8 cm)
Fig. 30

Untitled, 1986
Acrylic on canvas
h. 63 ¾ in. (162 cm)
[left side broken and lost]
Fig. 25

Untitled, 1986
Acrylic and colored pencil on carved wood
Size unknown
Fig. 46

Merry-Go-Round, 1987
Acrylic on canvas
51 5/16 × 51 5/16 in. (130.3 × 130.3 cm)
Fig. 27

Untitled [after overpainting], 1987–97
Acrylic on paper and wood
35 1/16 × 24 13/16 × 3 ⅜ in. (89 × 63 × 8.5 cm)
Fig. 34

Drawings, 1988
Acrylic, colored pencil, and pencil on paper
each 8 ¼ × 5 11/16 in. (21 × 14.5 cm)
Entrusted to Toyota Municipal Museum of Art, Japan
Fig. 44

I Couldn't Say the Reason Why Tears Fall from the Eyes Now., 1988
Pencil and colored pencil on paper
11 ⅝ × 8 ¼ in. (29.5 × 21 cm)
Fig. 195

Romantic Catastrophe, 1988
Acrylic and colored pencil on canvas
45 15/16 × 35 13/16 in. (116.7 × 90.9 cm)
Fig. 52

Sorry, Just Not Big Enough, 1988
Acrylic and tempera on board
35 13/16 × 28 ⅝ in. (90.9 × 72.7 cm)
Fig. 53

Untitled, 1988
Acrylic on canvas
Size unknown
Fig. 26

Untitled, 1988
Acrylic, colored pencil, and pencil on paper
11 ⅝ × 8 ¼ in. (29.5 × 21 cm)
Fig. 28

Untitled, 1988
Colored pencil and pen on paper
overall 14 9/16 × 10 13/16 in. (37 × 27.5 cm)
Figs. 29a–c

Untitled, 1988
Acrylic and colored pencil on carved wood
h. 38 3/16 in. (97 cm)
Fig. 45

Flaming Head I, 1989
Acrylic on wood
60 ⅞ × 9 ⅛ × 10 13/16 in. (154.7 × 23.2 × 27.5 cm)
Fig. 50

Hannya Neko (Hannya Cat), 1989
Acrylic on canvas
23 ⅝ × 39 ⅜ in. (60 × 100 cm)
Collection of Aomori Museum of Art, Japan
Fig. 43

I Can't Bite., 1989
Watercolor, colored pencil, and pencil on paper
8 1/16 × 5 11/16 in. (20.5 × 14.5 cm)
Collection of Aomori Museum of Art, Japan
Fig. 35

Irrlichter, 1989
Acrylic on canvas
25 9/16 × 25 9/16 in. (65 × 65 cm)
Fig. 42

People on the Cloud, 1989
Acrylic on canvas
39 ⅜ × 39 ⅜ in. (100 × 100 cm)
Fig. 49

Untitled, 1989
Acrylic on paper
19 ½ × 13 11/16 in. (49.5 × 34.7 cm)
Fig. 36

Untitled, 1989
Acrylic on paper
13 ⅜ × 9 7/16 in. (34 × 24 cm)
Fig. 37

Untitled, 1989
Acrylic on paper
19 ½ × 13 9/16 in. (49.5 × 34.5 cm)
Fig. 38

Untitled, 1989
Acrylic on paper
19 ½ × 13 9/16 in. (49.5 × 34.5 cm)
Fig. 39

Untitled, 1989
Acrylic on paper
13 ⅜ × 9 7/16 in. (34 × 24 cm)
Fig. 40

Untitled, 1989
Acrylic on paper
19 ½ × 13 9/16 in. (49.5 × 34.5 cm)
Fig. 41

Untitled, 1989
Acrylic and colored pencil on paper
14 ⅛ × 9 ⅜ in. (35.8 × 23.8 cm)
Fig. 86

Untitled, 1989
Pen and colored pencil on paper
11 7/16 × 8 ¼ in. (29 × 21 cm)
Fig. 194

Give You the Flower, 1990
Acrylic on canvas
43 11/16 × 36 3/16 in. (111 × 92 cm)
Fig. 47

Make the Road, Follow the Road, 1990
Acrylic on canvas
39 ⅜ × 39 ⅜ in. (100 × 100 cm)
Fig. 48

Pandora's Box, 1990
Acrylic on canvas
35 7/16 × 35 7/16 in. (90 × 90 cm)
Fig. 54

The Girl with the Knife in Her Hand, 1991
Acrylic on canvas
59 ¼ × 55 ⅛ in. (150.5 × 140 cm)
Collection of Vicki and Kent Logan, fractional and promised gift to the San Francisco Museum of Modern Art
Fig. 56

Hundeberg als Trugbild, 1991
Acrylic on canvas
64 × 25 ⅜ in. (162.5 × 64.5 cm)
Collection of Aomori Museum of Art, Japan
Fig. 85

Pray, 1991
Acrylic on papier-mâché and canvas collage
h. 26 ¾ in. (68 cm)
Fig. 51

Rock'n Roll Suicide, 1992
Acrylic on canvas
35 7/16 × 35 7/16 in. (90 × 90 cm)
Fig. 68

For the People, 1992–2000
Pencil and colored pencil on paper
11 ¾ × 8 ¼ in. (29.8 × 21 cm)
Collection of the Museum of Modern Art, New York
Fig. 83

The Girl with the Knife II, 1993
Acrylic on canvas
39 ⅜ × 31 ½ in. (100 × 80 cm)
Fig. 57

Lampflowers, 1993
Acrylic on canvas
59 1/16 × 78 ¾ in. (150 × 200 cm)
Collection of Aomori Museum of Art, Japan
Fig. 58

Untitled, 1993
Acrylic on canvas
34 ⅝ × 34 ⅝ in. (88 × 88 cm)
Fig. 60

Walk On I, 1993
Acrylic on canvas
39 ⅜ × 29 ½ in. (100 × 75 cm)
Fig. 61

Don't Cry, No Tears, Love Me, 1994
Mixed media
9 1/16 × 27 15/16 × 5 ½ in. (23 × 71 × 14 cm)
Fig. 64

Harmless Kitty, 1994
Acrylic on canvas
59 1/16 × 55 1/8 in. (150 × 140 cm)
Collection of the National Museum of Modern Art, Tokyo
Fig. 72

Hula Hula Garden, 1994
Mixed media
Dimensions variable
Figs. 66 and 67

Monkey Brothers, 1994
Mixed media
Dimensions variable
Fig. 63

One Way Dog, 1994
Mixed media
Dog: 90 1/2 × 129 7/8 × 66 7/8 in.
(230 × 330 × 170 cm)
Home: 41 × 31 1/2 × 39 3/8 in.
(104 × 80 × 100 cm)
Fig. 90

Telepathy, 1994
Mixed media
5 1/4 × 5 11/16 × 4 5/16 in. (13.3 × 14.5 × 11 cm)
Fig. 65

Yellow in Blue, 1994
Acrylic on canvas
70 7/8 × 59 1/16 in. (180 × 150 cm)
Fig. 98

Abandoned Puppy, 1995
Acrylic on cotton mounted on canvas
47 1/4 × 43 5/16 in. (120 × 110 cm)
Fig. 73

Dog in Boy, 1995
Acrylic on canvas
25 × 19 in. (63.5 × 48.3 cm)
Fig. 74

In the Deepest Puddle II, 1995
Acrylic on cotton mounted on canvas
47 1/4 × 43 5/16 in. (120 × 110 cm)
Takahashi Collection, Tokyo
Fig. 69

The Longest Night, 1995
Acrylic on canvas
47 1/4 × 43 5/16 in. (120 × 110 cm)
Collection of the National Museum of Art, Osaka, Japan
Fig. 71

There Is No Place Like Home, 1995
Painting: Acrylic on canvas
16 1/4 × 19 3/4 in. (41.3 × 50.2 cm)
Sculpture: Mixed media
9 7/8 × 47 1/4 × 15 3/4 in. (25.1 × 120 × 40 cm)
Fig. 75

Dog from Your Childhood (prototype), 1997
Acrylic and cotton on Styrofoam
16 1/8 × 16 9/16 × 18 7/8 in. (41 × 42 × 48 cm)
Fig. 91

Sleepless Night (Sitting), 1997
Acrylic on canvas
47 1/4 × 43 5/16 in. (120 × 110 cm)
Rubell Museum, Miami
Fig. 76

Happy Hour (English version), 1998
Acrylic on paper
16 7/16 × 16 7/16 in. (41.7 × 41.7 cm)
Fig. 206

Happy Hour (Japanese version), 1998
Acrylic on paper
16 7/16 × 16 7/16 in. (41.7 × 41.7 cm)
Fig. 205

Happy Hour (with Drum & Bass), 1998
Acrylic on paper
16 7/16 × 18 1/16 in. (41.7 × 45.9 cm)
Fig. 208

Happy Hour (with Drum & Bass), 1998
Acrylic on paper
16 7/16 × 18 1/16 in. (41.7 × 45.9 cm)
Fig. 209

Happy Hour (with Guitar), 1998
Acrylic on paper
16 7/16 × 16 7/16 in. (41.7 × 41.7 cm)
Fig. 207

No Nukes, 1998
Acrylic and colored pencil on paper
14 3/16 × 8 7/8 in. (36 × 22.5 cm)
Fig. 348

Untitled, 1998
Pen, colored pencil, and acrylic on paper
10 1/4 × 7 11/16 in. (26 × 19.5 cm)
Fig. 201

Time of My Life 2001, 1998–2001
Pen and colored pencil on paper
10 1/2 × 9 3/8 in. (26.7 × 23.9 cm)
Fig. 104

Dogs from Your Childhood, 1999
Acrylic, lacquer, and urethane on fiber-reinforced plastics, wood
each 59 13/16 × 36 1/4 × 39 3/4 in.
(152 × 92 × 101 cm)
Fig. 93

The Little Pilgrims (Night Walking), 1999
Acrylic, lacquer, and cotton on fiber-reinforced plastics
Set of five, each 28 3/8 × 19 11/16 × 16 3/4 in.
(72 × 50 × 42.5 cm)
Collection of Takamatsu City Museum of Art, Japan
Fig. 102

Mirror (In the Floating World), 1999
Pen, colored pencil, and acrylic on paper
16 11/16 × 13 in. (42.4 × 33 cm)
Fig. 122

Night Cat, 1999
Acrylic on canvas
23 7/16 × 19 11/16 in. (59.5 × 50 cm)
Fig. 77

Pyromaniac Day, 1999
Acrylic on canvas
47 1/4 × 43 5/16 in. (120 × 110 cm)
Fig. 198

Pyromaniac Dead of Night, 1999
Acrylic on canvas
47 1/4 × 43 5/16 in. (120 × 110 cm)
Fig. 199

Quiet, Quiet, 1999
Lacquer on fiber-reinforced plastics
h. 78 3/4 × diam. 35 13/16 in. (200 × 91 cm)
Fig. 97

Slash with a Knife (In the Floating World), 1999
Pencil, colored pencil, and acrylic on paper
16 11/16 × 13 in. (42.4 × 33 cm)
Fig. 121

Untitled, 1999
Pen and colored pencil on paper
8 1/4 × 5 7/8 in. (21 × 15 cm)
Fig. 138

Dog from Your Childhood, 2000
Fiber-reinforced plastics, plywood, cotton, and acrylic
63 3/16 × 23 1/8 × 97 5/8 in.
(106.5 × 58.8 × 248 cm)
Figs. 109 and 110

Only Faces Appear in My Mind, 2000
Acrylic and colored pencil on paper
79 5/16 × 80 1/8 in. (201.5 × 203.5 cm)
Fig. 116

Untitled (Dog in Arrow), 2000
Acrylic and pen on paper
7 1/2 × 5 1/8 in. (19 × 13 cm)
Collaboration with David Shrigley
Fig. 135

Untitled (I Think You Stink), 2000
Colored pencil and pencil on paper
7 1/2 × 5 1/8 in. (19 × 13 cm)
Collaboration with David Shrigley
Fig. 143

Fountain of Life, 2001
Lacquer and urethane on fiber-reinforced plastics, motor, and water
h. 68 7/8 × diam. 70 7/8 in. (175 × 180 cm)
Figs. 95 and 96

Fountain of Sorrow, 2001
Lacquer and urethane on fiber-reinforced plastics, motor, and water
h. 26 3/8 × diam. 70 7/8 in. (67 × 180 cm)
Fig. 94

I DON'T MIND, IF YOU FORGET ME., 2001
Plexiglass, stuffed animals and figurines, plywood, and various playthings
Top: 22 1/2 × 293 1/4 × 4 in.
(57 × 745 × 10 cm)
Bottom: 21 1/4 × 293 1/4 × 13 1/4 in.
(54 × 745 × 33.5 cm)
Figs. 111–113

Keep Your Chin Up, 2001
Acrylic on canvas
76 3/8 × 102 1/16 in. (194 × 259.3 cm)
Fig. 88

Light My Fire, 2001
Acrylic and cotton on carved wood
74 × 68 1/8 × 43 5/16 in. (188 × 173 × 110 cm)
Fig. 119

Pee "Dead of Night," 2001
Acrylic on canvas
31 11/16 × 35 7/8 in. (80.5 × 91.2 cm)
Fig. 82

Princess of Snooze, 2001
Acrylic on canvas
113 3/8 × 71 9/16 in. (288 × 181.8 cm)
Fig. 79

Ready to Scout, 2001
Acrylic on cotton mounted on fiber-reinforced plastics
diam. 70 × d. 10 in. (177.8 × 25.4 cm)
Fig. 80

Spin • Kids / Houka, 2001
Acrylic and colored pencil on paper
19 5/16 × 13 5/8 in. (49 × 34.6 cm)
Fig. 106

Spin • Kids / Pi-ta, 2001
Acrylic and colored pencil on paper
19 5/16 × 13 5/8 in. (49 × 34.6 cm)
Fig. 105

Sprout the Ambassador, 2001
Acrylic on canvas
82 × 78 in. (208.3 × 198.1 cm)
Fig. 78

Sprout the Ambassador, 2001
Acrylic on cotton mounted on fiber-reinforced plastics
diam. 70 ⅞ × d. 10 ¼ in. (180 × 26 cm)
Fig. 81

Thinker, 2001
Acrylic on cotton mounted on plywood
14 1/16 × 5 3/16 in. (35.7 × 14.7 cm)
Fig. 87

Time of My Life, 2001
93 drawings, plywood, water paint, and light bulbs
118 ¾ × 217 ¾ × 212 ⅝ in.
(301.5 × 553 × 540 cm)
Figs. 107 and 108

Too Young to Die, 2001
Acrylic on cotton mounted on fiber-reinforced plastics
diam. 70 × d. 10 in. (177.8 × 25.4 cm)
Rubell Museum, Miami
Fig. 84

YOUR CHILDHOOD, 2001
Plywood, water paint, fiber-reinforced plastics, acrylic on cotton mounted on plywood, vinyl sheets, mirrors, stuffed animals, and figurines
Plywood walls: 94 ½ × 236 ¼ × 31 ½ in.
(240 × 600 × 80 cm)
Dog (not pictured): 43 ⅞ × 39 ⅛ × 29 ½ in.
(111.5 × 99.5 × 75 cm)
Letters: 21 ⅝ × 233 ½ in. (55 × 593 cm)
Fig. 114

2000 Light Years from the War, 2002
Colored pencil on paper
11 15/16 × 8 15/16 in. (30.3 × 22.7 cm)
Fig. 238

Flying Nuns, 2002
Colored pencil on paper
11 15/16 × 8 15/16 in. (30.3 × 22.7 cm)
Fig. 239

Kabul Note, 2002
Figs. 218–222, 224–227

Menschpanzerangreiferin, 2002
Colored pencil on paper
11 15/16 × 8 15/16 in. (30.3 × 22.7 cm)
Fig. 237

Untitled, 2002
Colored pencil on paper
6 ⅜ × 5 in. (16.2 × 12.7 cm)
Fig. 228

Untitled, 2002
Colored pencil on paper
9 ⅜ × 13 ¼ in. (23.8 × 33.7 cm)
Fig. 229

Untitled, 2002
Colored pencil on paper
10 15/16 × 8 ½ in. (27.8 × 21.6 cm)
Fig. 230

Untitled, 2002
Colored pencil on paper
11 15/16 × 8 15/16 in. (30.3 × 22.7 cm)
Fig. 231

Untitled, 2002
Colored pencil on paper
10 ¾ × 6 ⅜ in. (27.3 × 16.1 cm)
Fig. 232

Untitled, 2002
Colored pencil on paper
9 1/16 × 6 5/16 in. (23 × 16 cm)
Fig. 233

Untitled, 2002
Colored pencil on paper
9 × 6 ⅜ in. (22.8 × 16.2 cm)
Fig. 234

Untitled, 2002
Colored pencil on paper
13 5/16 × 9 7/16 in. (33.8 × 24 cm)
Fig. 235

Untitled, 2002
Colored pencil on paper
9 7/16 × 4 ¾ in. (24 × 12 cm)
Fig. 236

Untitled (1 2 3 4), 2002
Pen and colored pencil on paper
10 7/16 × 9 ⅛ in. (26.5 × 23.2 cm)
Collaboration with David Shrigley
Fig. 141

Untitled (But Just Living), 2002
Pen and colored pencil on paper
10 15/16 × 14 13/16 in. (27.7 × 37.7 cm)
Collaboration with David Shrigley
Fig. 140

Untitled (Philip Guston's Lung), 2002
Acrylic and pen on paper
16 ⅛ × 17 ⅝ in. (40.9 × 44.8 cm)
Collaboration with David Shrigley
Fig. 136

Untitled (Wanna Go Home), 2002
Pen and colored pencil on paper
10 7/16 × 9 ⅛ in. (26.5 × 23.2 cm)
Collaboration with David Shrigley
Fig. 142

Untitled (William Tell with Shield), 2002
Pen and colored pencil on paper
10 7/16 × 9 ⅛ in. (26.5 × 23.2 cm)
Collaboration with David Shrigley
Fig. 139

Live Skulls, 2003
Colored pencil on paper
12 15/16 × 9 7/16 in. (32.8 × 24 cm)
Fig. 243

Mountain Sisters, 2003
Acrylic and colored pencil on paper
29 15/16 × 22 1/16 in. (76 × 56 cm)
Fig. 123

Soldier, 2003
Acrylic and colored pencil on paper
29 15/16 × 22 1/16 in. (76 × 56 cm)
Fig. 242

Sorry, Couldn't Draw the Left Eye!, 2003
Acrylic, colored pencil, and collage on paper
53 15/16 × 39 ⅜ in. (137 × 100 cm)
Fig. 124

Untitled, 2003
Colored pencil on paper
12 15/16 × 10 ⅝ in. (32.9 × 27 cm)
Fig. 241

Deeper than a Puddle, 2004
Acrylic on canvas
102 ⅜ × 110 ¼ in. (260 × 280 cm)
Collaboration with Hiroshi Sugito
Fig. 146

Patricia, 2004
Acrylic on canvas
23 ⅝ × 19 11/16 in. (60 × 50 cm)
Collaboration with Hiroshi Sugito
Fig. 147

Rain Drops, 2004
Acrylic on canvas
118 5/16 × 106 5/16 in. (300.5 × 270 cm)
Collaboration with Hiroshi Sugito
Fig. 144

Shallow Puddles 2004, 2004
Acrylic on cotton mounted on fiber-reinforced plastics
diam. 37 ⅜ × d. 5 ⅞ in. (95 cm × 15 cm)
Figs. 127 and 128

My Drawing Room, 2004–ongoing
Mixed media
122 13/16 × 78 15/16 × 176 ⅜ in.
(312 × 200.5 × 448 cm)
Cooperation provided by graf
Collection of Hara Museum of Contemporary Art, Tokyo
Figs. 160 and 161

Aomori-ken (Aomori Dog), 2005
Reinforced concrete
334 ⅝ × 263 ¾ × 354 ⅜ in.
(850 × 670 × 900 cm)
Collection of Aomori Museum of Art, Japan
Fig. 92

Missing in Action-Girl Meets Boy-, 2005
Acrylic, colored pencil, and watercolor on paper
59 1/16 × 53 15/16 in. (150 × 137 cm)
Collection of Hiroshima City Museum of Contemporary Art, Japan
Fig. 244

Twins I, 2005
Acrylic on canvas
46 1/16 × 39 ⅜ in. (117 × 100 cm)
Collection of Leeum, Samsung Museum of Art, Seoul
Fig. 125

Twins II, 2005
Acrylic on canvas
46 1/16 × 39 ⅜ in. (117 × 100 cm)
Collection of Leeum, Samsung Museum of Art, Seoul
Fig. 126

Untitled, 2005
Acrylic on canvas
22 7/16 × 19 11/16 in. (57 × 50 cm)
Collaboration with Hiroshi Sugito
Fig. 145

1.2.3..., 2006
Acrylic on wood
45 ¼ × 67 11/16 in. (115 × 172 cm)
Fig. 170

After the Acid Rain, 2006
Acrylic on canvas
89 ⅜ × 71 ⅝ in. (227 × 182 cm)
Fig. 133

Agent Orange, 2006
Acrylic on canvas
64 × 64 in. (162.5 × 162.5 cm)
Fig. 245

Eve of Destruction, 2006
Acrylic on canvas
46 1/16 × 35 13/16 in. (117 × 91 cm)
Collection of Hara Museum of Contemporary Art, Tokyo
Fig. 246

London Mayfair House, 2006
Mixed media installation
Dimensions variable
Cooperation provided by graf
Fig. 162

Puff Marshie (Hirosaki version), 2006
Urethane on fiber-reinforced plastics
h. 59 × diam. 118 ⅛ in. (150 × 300 cm)
Fig. 168

Voyage of the Moon (Resting Moon) / Voyage of the Moon, 2006
Mixed media
187 ⅜ × 139 ⅜ × 194 ⅞ in.
(476 × 354 × 495 cm)
Cooperation provided by graf
Collection of 21st Century Museum of Contemporary Art, Kanazawa, Japan
Figs. 166 and 167

1, 2, 3, 4! Hey! Ho! Let's Go!, 2007
Ceramic
diam. 33 ⅞ × d. 3 ¾ in. (86 × 9.5 cm)
Fig. 186

The Good, the Bad, the Average...and Unique, 2007
Ceramic
diam. 33 ⅞ × d. 3 ¾ in. (86 × 9.5 cm)
Fig. 187

In the Jingle Jangle Morning I'll Come Followin' You., 2007
Ceramic
diam. 49 ¾ × d. 3 9/16 in. (126.3 × 9 cm)
Fig. 185

In the Puddle, 2007
Ceramic
13 13/16 × 25 3/16 × 25 3/16 in. (35 × 64 × 64 cm)
Fig. 180

Life Is Only One!, 2007
Acrylic on wood
76 ⅜ × 161 7/16 × 2 ¾ in. (194 × 410 × 7 cm)
Fig. 171

Otafuku No. 0 (Moon-Faced Woman No. 0), 2007
Ceramic
44 5/16 × 49 3/16 × 54 5/16 in.
(112.5 × 125 × 138 cm)
Fig. 179

Avant l'orage / Before the Storm, 2008
Acrylic on canvas
9 ½ × 13 ⅛ in. (24.2 × 33.3 cm)
Collaboration with Hiroshi Sugito (as Chaguin)
Fig. 153

Cherchant de l'eau / In Need of Water, 2008
Acrylic on canvas
12 ½ × 16 ⅛ in. (31.8 × 41 cm)
Collaboration with Hiroshi Sugito (as Chaguin)
Fig. 150

Dans la salle / In the Room, 2008
Acrylic on canvas
12 ½ × 16 ⅛ in. (31.8 × 41 cm)
Collaboration with Hiroshi Sugito (as Chaguin)
Fig. 151

Dee Dee, 2008
Pencil on paper
20 ¼ × 14 ⅜ in. (51.5 × 36.5 cm)
Fig. 130

Joey, 2008
Pencil on paper
20 ¼ × 14 ⅜ in. (51.5 × 36.5 cm)
Fig. 129

Le désir silencieux / Silent Desire, 2008
Acrylic on canvas
8 11/16 × 10 ¾ in. (22 × 27.3 cm)
Collaboration with Hiroshi Sugito (as Chaguin)
Fig. 152

Le temps perdu / Youthful Days Lost, 2008
Acrylic on canvas
17 15/16 × 14 15/16 in. (45.5 × 38 cm)
Collaboration with Hiroshi Sugito (as Chaguin)
Fig. 149

Omoutsubo, 2008
Acrylic on canvas
17 15/16 × 14 15/16 in. (45.5 × 38 cm)
Collaboration with Hiroshi Sugito (as Chaguin)
Fig. 148

Untitled, 2008
Colored pencil and acrylic on paper
13 × 9 in. (33 × 22.9 cm)
Fig. 99

Born to Lose, 2009
Ceramic
h. 16 15/16 × diam. 10 ¼ in. (43 × 26 cm)
Fig. 191

Love or Affection, 2009
Ceramic
h. 19 11/16 × diam. 11 13/16 in. (50 × 30 cm)
Fig. 188

Nobody's Fool, 2009
Ceramic
h. 17 ¾ × diam. 13 ⅜ in. (45 × 34 cm)
Fig. 190

You & Me, 2009
Ceramic
h. 21 ¼ × diam. 13 in. (54 × 33 cm)
Fig. 189

Anymore for Anymore, 2010
Ceramic
28 ⅜ × 23 ⅝ × 28 ⅜ in. (72 × 60 × 72 cm)
Fig. 371

Miss Forest, 2010
Ceramic decorated with platinum, gold, and silver liquid
56 11/16 × 40 3/16 × 39 ⅜ in.
(144 × 102 × 100 cm)
Collection of Leeum, Samsung Museum of Art, Seoul
Fig. 182

Otafuku No. 1 (Moon-Faced Woman No. 1), 2010
Ceramic decorated with gold liquid and cloth
46 7/16 × 49 3/16 × 59 1/16 in. (118 × 125 × 150 cm)
Fig. 181

White Ghost, 2010
Urethane on fiber-re nforced plastics
144 × 102 × 66 in. (365.8 × 259.1 × 167.6 cm)
Fig. 183

White Riot, 2010
Ceramic
109 7/16 × 69 5/16 × 49 ⅝ in.
(278 × 176 × 126 cm)
Fig. 184

Atomkraft Baby, 2011
Acrylic on canvas
18 1/16 × 14 15/16 in. (45.8 × 38 cm)
Fig. 285

M.I.A., 2011
Acrylic and pencil cn canvas
18 1/16 × 14 15/16 in. (45 8 × 38 cm)
Fig. 284

News, 2011
Pencil on paper
25 9/16 × 19 11/16 in. (65 × 50 cm)
Fig. 132

Untitled sketch, 2011
Ballpoint pen on paper
9 7/16 × 5 ½ in. (24 × 14 cm)
Fig. 196

Headache, 2012
Pencil on paper
25 9/16 × 19 11/16 in. (65 × 50 cm)
Fig. 131

Long Tall Sister, 2012
Bronze with brass patina
84 ⅝ × 48 13/16 × 83 ⅞ in.
(215 × 124 × 213 cm)
Fig. 291

Lucy, 2012
Bronze with black patina
55 ⅞ × 61 × 59 1/16 in. (142 × 155 × 150 cm)
Figs. 302 and 303

Midnight Pilgrim, 2012
Bronze with black patina
62 3/16 × 22 13/16 × 25 3/16 in.
(158 × 58 × 64 cm)
Figs. 297 and 298

Miss Spring, 2012
Acrylic on canvas
89 ⅜ × 71 ⅝ in. (227 × 182 cm)
Collection of Yokohama Museum of Art
Figs. 304 and 307

Miss Tannen, 2012
Bronze with black patina
83 ⅞ × 20 ½ × 16 ¾ in. (213 × 52 × 42.5 cm)
Figs. 299 and 300

Thinking Sister, 2012
Bronze
15 ½ × 14 ⅜ × 14 5/16 in. (39.3 × 36.5 × 36.4 cm)
Fig. 296

Under the Hazy Sky, 2012
Acrylic on canvas
76 11/16 × 63 ¾ in. (194.8 × 162 cm)
Fig. 315

Wicked Looking, 2012
Cupronickel
59 ¼ × 48 13/16 × 51 3/16 in.
(150.5 × 124 × 130 cm)
Figs. 292 and 293

Drawing for *Calendar*, 2013
Pen on paper
Size unknown
Fig. 375

Emergency, 2013
Acrylic on wood
83 1/16 × 73 ¼ × 3 9/16 in. (211 × 186 × 9 cm)
Fig. 324

Fuckin' Street, 2013
Colored pencil on paper
12 13/16 × 9 ½ in. (32.5 × 24.2 cm)
Fig. 343

Untitled, 2013
Colored pencil on paper
14 ⅜ × 10 ¼ in. (36.5 × 26 cm)
Fig. 342

Angel, 2014
Colored pencil on paper
12 ¼ × 9 in. (31.2 × 22.8 cm)
Fig. 341

Bad Head, 2014
Acrylic on wood board
58 1⁄16 × 59 7⁄16 × 3 9⁄16 in. (147.5 × 151 × 9 cm)
Fig. 334

Bloodthirsty Gal, 2014
Colored pencil on paper
9 1⁄16 × 6 1⁄8 in. (23 × 15.5 cm)
Fig. 344

No Means No, 2014
Acrylic on canvas
51 9⁄16 × 38 3⁄16 in. (131 × 97 cm)
Fig. 317

SAKHALIN, 2014
Figs. 248–270

Wounded, 2014
Acrylic on canvas
47 1⁄4 × 43 5⁄16 in. (120 × 110 cm)
Fig. 320

Tears of Rage, 2015
Acrylic on canvas
22 1⁄16 × 20 1⁄16 in. (56 × 51 cm)
Fig. 321

HOPE Starved, 2016
Ballpoint pen on paper
11 11⁄16 × 8 1⁄4 in. (29.7 × 21 cm)
Fig. 347

I Don't Care, 2016
Ballpoint pen on paper
11 11⁄16 × 8 1⁄4 in. (29.7 × 21 cm)
Fig. 346

Kamegaoka No. 1 (Round Eyes), 2016
Ceramic
3 3⁄8 × 2 15⁄16 × 2 3⁄8 in. (8.5 × 7.5 × 6 cm)
Fig. 361

Miss Forest / Thinker, 2016
Urethane on bronze
197 × 55 × 62 1⁄2 in.
(500.4 × 139.7 × 158.8 cm)
Fig. 301

Numazu Shell Mound No. 1 (Prince with Sparkling Eyes), 2016
Ceramic
5 1⁄2 × 7 1⁄16 × 7 1⁄16 in. (14 × 18 × 18 cm)
Figs. 359a–b

Numazu Shell Mound No. 2 (Big Eyes), 2016
Ceramic
9 13⁄16 × 6 5⁄16 × 5 1⁄8 in. (25 × 16 × 13 cm)
Fig. 360

TAIWAN, 2016
Figs. 272–277

Untitled, 2016
Ballpoint pen on paper
each 11 11⁄16 × 8 1⁄4 in. (29.7 × 21 cm)
Figs. 325–328

COCONE, 2017
Charcoal on paper
71 5⁄8 × 35 13⁄16 in. (182 × 91 cm)
framed 74 × 38 3⁄16 in. (188 × 97 cm)
Figs. 365 and 367

FROM THE BOMB SHELTER, 2017
Acrylic on jute mounted on wood
71 1⁄16 × 63 3⁄16 × 1 7⁄8 in.
(180.5 × 160.5 × 4.8 cm)
Fig. 329

Girl from My Childhood, 2017
Acrylic on canvas
27 3⁄16 × 26 3⁄8 in. (69 × 67 cm)
Fig. 314

Girl from North Country, 2017
Acrylic on canvas
86 5⁄8 × 77 in. (220 × 195.6 cm)
Collection of Los Angeles County Museum of Art
Fig. 308

Head (eyes closed), 2017
Acrylic on wood
69 5⁄16 × 35 7⁄16 × 2 in. (176 × 90 × 5 cm)
Fig. 323

Head (eyes opened), 2017
Acrylic on wood
69 5⁄16 × 35 7⁄16 × 2 in. (176 × 90 × 5 cm)
Fig. 322

HOKKAIDO, 2017
Fig. 279

HOME, 2017
Acrylic on jute mounted on wood
71 1⁄16 × 63 3⁄16 × 1 7⁄8 in.
(180.5 × 160.5 × 4.8 cm)
Fig. 330

I WANT TO SEE THE BRIGHT LIGHTS TONIGHT, 2017
Acrylic on canvas
86 5⁄8 × 76 3⁄4 in. (220 × 195 cm)
Fig. 373 and cover

KOU, 2017
Charcoal on paper
71 5⁄8 × 35 13⁄16 in. (182 × 91 cm)
framed 74 × 38 3⁄16 in. (188 × 97 cm)
Fig. 364

The Little Vampire, 2017
Pencil on paper
25 5⁄8 × 21 5⁄8 in. (65 × 55 cm)
Fig. 345

Midnight Truth, 2017
Acrylic on canvas
89 1⁄2 × 71 9⁄16 in. (227.3 × 181.8 cm)
Collection of the National Gallery of Art, Washington, DC
Fig. 313

RENOA, 2017
Charcoal on paper
71 5⁄8 × 35 13⁄16 in. (182 × 91 cm)
framed 74 × 38 3⁄16 in. (188 × 97 cm)
Fig. 366

SHIU, 2017
Charcoal on paper
71 5⁄8 × 35 13⁄16 in. (182 × 91 cm)
framed 74 × 38 3⁄16 in. (188 × 97 cm)
Fig. 362

YUNOA, 2017
Charcoal on paper
71 5⁄8 × 35 13⁄16 in. (182 × 91 cm)
framed 74 × 38 3⁄16 in. (188 × 97 cm)
Fig. 363

Actress Margarita, after Niko Pirosmani, 2018
Acrylic on canvas
47 1⁄4 × 43 5⁄16 in. (120 × 110 cm)
Fig. 339

Ahunrupar, 2018
Ceramic
12 11⁄16 × 17 7⁄16 × 15 1⁄4 in.
(32.3 × 44.3 × 38.8 cm)
Fig. 368

Ahunrupar, 2018
Ceramic
13 × 17 11⁄16 × 18 7⁄8 in. (33 × 45 × 48 cm)
Figs. 369a–d

Ahunrupar, 2018
Pencil on paper
25 9⁄16 × 19 11⁄16 in. (65 × 50 cm)
Fig. 372

Alone in the Wind, 2018
Acrylic on canvas
20 7⁄8 × 20 7⁄8 in. (53 × 53 cm)
Fig. 318

Girl with Eyepatch, 2018
Acrylic on canvas
47 1⁄4 × 43 5⁄16 in. (120 × 110 cm)
Fig. 319

HOKKAIDO, 2018
Figs. 280 and 281

Queen Tamar, after Niko Pirosmani, 2018
Acrylic on canvas
47 1⁄4 × 43 5⁄16 in. (120 × 110 cm)
Fig. 340

Study for *Angry Sad Girl*, 2019
Acrylic on canvas
47 1⁄4 × 43 5⁄16 in. (120 × 110 cm)
Fig. 379

Girl left behind the night, 2019
Acrylic on canvas
86 5⁄8 × 76 3⁄4 in. (220 × 195 cm)
Fig. 309

HOKKAIDO, 2019
Figs. 282 and 374

Invisible Vision, 2019
Acrylic on canvas
76 3⁄4 × 59 1⁄16 in. (195 × 150 cm)
Fig. 376

Lone Star Girl, 2019
Acrylic on paper
51 3⁄16 × 35 13⁄16 in. (130 × 91 cm)
Fig. 377

NO WAR, 2019
Acrylic on wood
46 1⁄16 × 40 3⁄4 × 2 3⁄4 in. (117 × 103.5 × 7 cm)
Fig. 336

PEACE GIRL, 2019
Acrylic on jute mounted on wood
71 1⁄16 × 63 3⁄16 × 1 7⁄8 in. (180.5 × 160.5 × 4.8 cm)
Fig. 332

STOP THE BOMBS, 2019
Acrylic on wood
58 7⁄8 × 46 1⁄4 × 3 in. (149.5 × 117.5 × 7.7 cm)
Fig. 335

SWEET HOME GATE, 2019
Acrylic on jute mounted on wood
71 1⁄16 × 63 3⁄16 × 1 7⁄8 in.
(180.5 × 160.5 × 4.8 cm)
Fig. 331

Untitled sketch, 2019
Pencil on paper
6 1⁄8 × 4 5⁄16 in. (15.6 × 11 cm)
Fig. 378

Zaatari Refugee Camp, Jordan, 2019
Fig. 278

Artist Biography

Born in Hirosaki, Japan, 1959
Lives and works in Japan

Education

BFA, Aichi Prefectural University of Fine Arts and Music, Nagakute, Japan
MFA, Aichi Prefectural University of Fine Arts and Music, Nagakute, Japan
Kunstakademie Düsseldorf

Solo Exhibitions

2020
Yoshitomo Nara, Los Angeles County Museum of Art; Yuz Museum Shanghai; Guggenheim Museum Bilbao, Spain; Kunsthal Rotterdam, Netherlands
Yoshitomo Nara, Dallas Contemporary

2019
Drawings—Last 31 Years, Château la Coste, Le Puy-Sainte-Réparade, France
En/trance, Japan Society, New York (installation)

2018
Ceramic Works and..., Pace Gallery, Hong Kong (cat. with *Thinker*, Pace Gallery, New York, 2017)
Drawings: 1988–2018, Kaikai Kiki Gallery, Tokyo
Your Dog, Asian Art Museum, San Francisco (installation)
Sixteen springs and sixteen summers gone—Take your time, it won't be long now, Taka Ishii Gallery Photography/Film, Tokyo (cat.)
all things must pass, but nothing is lost / precious days around me, sometimes farther along, sometimes under my feet, Pace/MacGill Gallery, New York

2017
Thinker, Pace Gallery, New York (cat. with *Ceramic Works and...*, Pace Gallery, Hong Kong, 2018)
for better or worse: Works 1987–2017, Toyota Municipal Museum of Art, Japan (cat.)
At Tobiu, Tobiu Art Community, Shiraoi, Japan
Will the Circle Be Unbroken, Daikanyama Hillside Plaza, Tokyo (cat.)

2016
New Works, Stephen Friedman Gallery, London (cat.)

2015
Shallow Puddles, Blum & Poe, Tokyo (cat.)
stars, Pace Gallery, Hong Kong (cat.)
Life is Only One: Yoshitomo Nara, Asia Society Hong Kong Center (cat.)
Johnen Galerie, Berlin
to the north, from here: Naoki Ishikawa + Yoshitomo Nara, Watari-um: The Watari Museum of Contemporary Art, Tokyo

2014
A 3-Day Drawing Show, Sawada Mansion Gallery room38, Kōchi, Japan
Greetings from a Place in My Heart, Dairy Art Centre, London (cat.)
Print Works, Satellite, Okayama, Japan
Blum & Poe, Los Angeles (cat.)

2013
Pace Gallery, New York (cat.)

2012
a bit like you and me..., Yokohama Museum of Art; traveled to Aomori Museum of Art; Contemporary Art Museum, Kumamoto, Japan (cat.)
The Little Little House in the Blue Woods, Towada Art Center, Japan
Yoshitomo Nara Prints, 8/Art Gallery/Tomio Koyama Gallery, Tokyo

2011
Print Works, Roppongi Hills A/D Gallery, Tokyo

2010
Ceramic Works, Tomio Koyama Gallery, Tokyo (cat.)
Nobody's Fool, Asia Society, New York (cat.)
New Editions, Pace Prints, New York

2009
Marianne Boesky Gallery, New York
The Crated Rooms in Iceland – Yoshitomo Nara + YNG, Reykjavík Art Museum (cat.)

2008
Yoshitomo Nara with Installation by YNG, Blum & Poe, Los Angeles
Yoshitomo Nara + graf, BALTIC Centre for Contemporary Art, Gateshead, UK (cat.)
Galerie Zink, Munich
Galerie Meyer Kainer, Vienna
Chaguin, Misako & Rosen, Tokyo (collaboration with Hiroshi Sugito)

2007
Yoshitomo Nara + graf: Torre de Málaga, Centro de arte contemporáneo de Málaga, Spain (cat.)
Yoshitomo Nara + graf, GEM, Museum of Contemporary Art, The Hague
Johnen + Schöttle, Cologne, Germany
Yoshitomo Nara + graf: Berlin Baracke, Galerie Zink, Berlin

2006
Moonlight Serenade, 21st Century Museum of Contemporary Art, Kanazawa, Japan (cat.)
Yoshitomo Nara + graf: A to Z, Yoshii Brick Brew House, Hirosaki, Japan (cat.)
Yoshitomo Nara + graf, Stephen Friedman Gallery, London

2005
home, graf media gm, Osaka, Japan
Marianne Boesky Gallery, New York

2004
From the Depth of My Drawer, Hara Museum of Contemporary Art, Tokyo; traveled to Kanaz Forest of Creation, Awara, Japan; Yonago City Museum of Art, Japan; Yoshii Brick Brew House, Hirosaki, Japan; Rodin Gallery, Seoul (cat.)
Galerie Meyer Kainer, Vienna
Nowhere Land, Johnen + Schöttle, Cologne, Germany
new works 2004, Blum & Poe, Los Angeles
Somewhere..., Galerie Zink & Gegner, Munich (collaboration with Hiroshi Sugito)
Shadow Puddles, graf media gm, Osaka, Japan
Over the Rainbow: Yoshitomo Nara and Hiroshi Sugito, Pinakothek der Moderne, Munich; traveled to K21 Kunstsammlung Nordrhein-Westfalen, Düsseldorf (cat.)

2003
Nothing Ever Happens, Museum of Contemporary Art Cleveland, OH; traveled to Institute of Contemporary Art, Philadelphia; Contemporary Art Museum St. Louis; San Jose Museum of Art, CA; The Contemporary Museum, Honolulu (cat.)
S.M.L., graf media gm, Osaka, Japan (cat.)
Galerie Zink & Gegner, Munich
New Drawings, Tomio Koyama Gallery, Tokyo
The Good, the Bad, the Average...and Unique, Little More Gallery, Tokyo
Stephen Friedman Gallery, London

2002
Saucer Tales, Marianne Boesky Gallery, New York
Who Snatched the Babies?, Centre national de l'estampe et de l'arte imprimé, Chatou, France (cat.)
12 Etchings, Space Force, Tokyo

2001
In Those Days, Hakutosha, Nagoya, Japan
I DON'T MIND, IF YOU FORGET ME., Yokohama Museum of Art; traveled to Hiroshima City Museum of Contemporary Art; Ashiya City Museum of Art & History; Hokkaido Asahikawa Museum of Art; Aomori Museum of Art; Yoshii Brick Brew House, Hirosaki, Japan (cat.)
Drawing Days, Colette, Paris
Clear for Landing, Galerie Michael Zink, Munich
In the White Room: An Exhibition of Paintings and Drawings, Blum & Poe, Santa Monica, CA

2000
Stephen Friedman Gallery, London
In the Empty Fortress, Johnen + Schöttle, Cologne
Lullaby Supermarket, Santa Monica Museum of Art, CA
Walk On: Works by Yoshitomo Nara, Museum of Contemporary Art Chicago (cat.)

1999
done did, Parco Gallery, Nagoya, Japan
Happy Hour, Hakutosha, Nagoya, Japan
Somebody Whispers in Nuremberg, Institut für moderne Kunst in der SchmidtBank-Galerie, Nuremberg, Germany (cat.)
Fave Your Dreams, Marianne Boesky Gallery, New York
An Exhibition of Sculpture in Two Parts, Blum & Poe, Santa Monica, CA
Walking Alone, Ginza Art Space, Tokyo (cat.)
In the Floating World, NADiff Gallery, Tokyo
No, They Didn't, Tomio Koyama Gallery, Tokyo

1998
Institute of Visual Arts, University of Wisconsin, Milwaukee (cat.)

1997
Blum & Poe, Santa Monica, CA

Screen Memory, Tomio Koyama Gallery, Tokyo
Lonesome Puppy, Hakutosha, Nagoya, Japan
Drawing Days, Hakutosha, Nagoya, Japan
Sleepless Night, Galerie Michael Zink, Regensburg, Germany
Yumeooka Art Project, Wing Kamiooka Center Court, Yokohama, Japan

1996
Johnen + Schöttle, Cologne, Germany (collaboration with Karen Kilimnik)
Lonesome Puppy, Tomio Koyama Gallery, Tokyo
Hothouse Fresh, Hakutosha, Nagoya, Japan (cat.)
Empty Surprise, Mitsubishi-Jisho Artium, Fukuoka, Japan (cat.)
Cup Kids, Hakutosha, Nagoya, Japan

1995
Cup Kids, Museum of Contemporary Art, Nagoya, Japan
Pacific Babies, Blum & Poe, Santa Monica, CA
In the Deepest Puddle, SCAI THE BATHHOUSE, Tokyo
Nothing Gets Me Down, Galerie Humanité, Tokyo (cat.)
Oil on Canvas, Galerie Humanité, Nagoya, Japan (cat.)

1994
Lonesome Babies, Hakutosha, Nagoya, Japan (cat.)
Hula Hula Garden, Galerie d'Eendt, Amsterdam
Christmas for Sleeping Children, Itoki Crystal Hall, Osaka, Japan (cat.)

1993
Johnen + Schöttle, Cologne, Germany
Be Happy, Galerie Humanité, Nagoya and Tokyo (cat.)

1992
Loft Gallery, Deventer, Netherlands
Drawings, Galerie d'Eendt, Amsterdam

1991
Harmlos, Galerie im Kinderspielhaus, Düsseldorf
cogitationes cordium, Galerie Humanité, Nagoya, Japan
Galerie d'Eendt, Amsterdam

1990
Galerie d'Eendt, Amsterdam

1989
Irrlichttheater, Stuttgart, Germany

1988
Innocent Being, Galerie Humanité, Nagoya and Tokyo (cat.)
Goethe-Institut Düsseldorf

1985
Recent Works, Gallery Space to Space, Nagoya, Japan

1984
Wonder Room, Gallery Space to Space, Nagoya, Japan
It's a Little Wonderful House, Love Collection Gallery, Nagoya, Japan

Group Exhibitions

2020
STARS: Six Contemporary Artists from Japan to the World, Mori Art Museum, Tokyo (cat.)
Where We Now Stand—In Order to Map the Future [2], 21st Century Museum of Contemporary Art, Kanazawa, Japan

2019
Tobiu Art Festival, Tobiu Art Community, Shiraoi, Japan (as Yoshitomo Nara and Tobiu Kids)
Weavers of Worlds: A Century of Flux in Japanese Modern / Contemporary Art, Museum of Contemporary Art Tokyo
The Life of Animals in Japanese Art, National Gallery of Art, Washington, DC; traveled to Los Angeles County Museum of Art (cat.)
30th Anniversary of the Yokohama Museum of Art: Meet the Collection, Yokohama Museum of Art, Japan
Masterpieces of the National Museum of Art, Osaka: Clues for Art Appreciation, Toyohashi City Museum of Art and History, Japan
Our Collections!, Tottori Prefectural Museum, Japan
SYNCHRONICITY, Kasama Nichido Museum of Art, Japan
Grand Reopening Exhibition: Aichi Art Chronicle 1919–2019, Aichi Prefectural Museum of Art, Nagoya, Japan
Globe as a Palette: Contemporary Art from the Taguchi Art Collection, Hokkaido Obihiro Museum of Art; traveled to Kushiro Art Museum; Hakodate Museum of Art; Sapporo Art Museum, Japan
MURAKAMI vs MURAKAMI, Tai Kwun Contemporary, Hong Kong (cat.)
Takahata Isao: A Legend in Japanese Animation, National Museum of Modern Art, Tokyo (cat.)
Takahashi Collection, Tsuruoka Art Forum, Japan
ARTZUID Amsterdam Sculpture Biennial (cat.)
Bishōjo: Young Pretty Girls in Art History, Museum of National Taipei University of Education (cat.)
The Passion, Hall Art Foundation | Schloss Derneburg Museum, Derneburg, Germany
BLUE IS HOT AND RED IS COLD: Klasse A. R. Penck, Kunsthalle Düsseldorf

2018
My Favorites: Toshio Hara Selects from the Permanent Collection Part II, Hara Museum of Contemporary Art, Tokyo
My Favorites: Toshio Hara Selects from the Permanent Collection Part I, Hara Museum of Contemporary Art, Tokyo
WOW! The Heidi Horten Collection, Leopold Museum, Vienna
Bangkok Art Biennale
Taiwan Ceramics Biennale, Taipei (cat.)
Imagined Borders, 12th Gwangju Biennale, South Korea (curated by Yeon Shim Chung and Yeewan Koon) (cat.)
The Incongruous Body, American Museum of Ceramic Art, Pomona, CA
Constellation Malta, Malta (curated by Rosa Martínez)
Niko Pirosmani, Albertina Museum, Vienna; traveled to Fondation Vincent van Gogh, Arles, France (cat.)
Japanorama. A new vision on art since 1970, Centre Pompidou-Metz, France (curated by Yuko Hasegawa)
Treasure Box of Contemporary Art, Ōita Prefectural Art Museum, Japan
Bubblewrap, Contemporary Art Museum, Kumamoto, Japan (curated by Takashi Murakami)

2017
The Cosmos of the Takahashi Collection, Contemporary Art Museum, Kumamoto, Japan
Cool Japan: A Worldwide Fascination in Focus, Museum Volkenkunde, Leiden, Netherlands
Takashi Murakami's Superflat Consideration on Contemporary Ceramics, Towada Art Center, Japan
Seeds Sown in Shigaraki, Kaikai Kiki Gallery, Tokyo
Chewing Gum II, Pace Gallery, Hong Kong
Global New Art: The Essence of Taguchi Art Collection, Woodone Museum, Hiroshima, Japan
Contemporary Art, Now! From Yayoi Kusama to Hiraki Sawa (From Taguchi Collection), Onomichi City Museum of Art, Japan
The Art Show: Art of the New Millennium in Taguchi Art Collection, Museum of Modern Art, Gunma, Takasaki, Japan
The Riddle of Art: Takahashi Collection, Shizuoka Prefectural Museum of Art, Japan
Create Your Own Original Doraemon, Mori Arts Center Gallery, Tokyo (cat.)

2016
December (playback 2), Misako & Rosen, Tokyo
Takahashi Collection: Mindfulness! 2016, Museum of Art, Kōchi, Japan
Takashi Murakami's Superflat Collection: From Shōhaku and Rosanjin to Anselm Kiefer, Yokohama Museum of Art, Japan (cat.)
Hey! Ho! Let's Go: Ramones and the Birth of Punk, Queens Museum, New York; traveled to the Grammy Museum, Los Angeles (cat.)
How Western are Western-style Paintings Made in Japan?: From Takahashi Yuichi to Contemporary Painters, Aichi Prefectural Museum of Art, Nagoya, Japan
Revalue Nippon Project: Hidetoshi Nakata's Favorite Japanese Kogei, Panasonic Shiodome Museum, Tokyo
Turn the Page: The First Ten Years of Hi-Fructose, Virginia Museum of Contemporary Art, Virginia Beach (cat.)
Very Addictive: Re-extension of Aesthetics in Daily Life, Museum of Contemporary Art, Yinchuan, China
Mitsubishi-Jisho Artium, Fukuoka, Japan
The 100 Japanese Contemporary Artists: Season 4, Yamamoto Gendai Gallery, Tokyo (organized by DOMMUNE)
EARTH 2016: Roots and Routes, Aomori Museum of Art, Japan (cat.)
Masterworks on Loan, Jordan Schnitzer Museum of Art, University of Oregon, Eugene
Art Begins in the Forest: Aichi Prefectural University of Fine Arts and Music 50th Anniversary Exhibition, Aichi Prefectural University of Fine Arts and Music, Nagakute, Japan (cat.)
Horizon That Appears out of the Sleepy Woods, Stephen Friedman Gallery, London (cat.)

2015
COSMOS / INTIME La collection Takahashi, Maison de la culture du Japon à Paris (cat.)
Bow Wow Wonderful I Want to Meet That Dog, Migishi Kōtarō Museum of Art, Sapporo, Japan (cat.)

Messages, Towada Art Center, Japan
Summer Group Show, Pace Gallery, New York
Twentieth Anniversary Exhibition, Stephen Friedman Gallery, London
Takahashi Collection: Mirror Neuron, Tokyo Opera City Art Gallery
Forever Young, Asia University Museum of Modern Art, Taichung
Today Is the Day: Proposal to the Future, Art Gallery Miyauchi, Hatsukaichi, Japan (cat.)
Dual Nature: Selections from the Chaney Family Collection, Pearl Fincher Museum of Fine Arts, Spring, TX
Immortal Present: Art and East Asia, Berkshire Museum, Pittsfield, MA
The Wind Veers to the East: Contemporary Art Exhibition for the Boao Forum for Asia, Boao Forum for Asia, Hainan, China

2014
Everything Falls Faster than an Anvil, Pace Gallery, London (cat.)
Takahashi Collection 2014: Mindfulness!, Nagoya City Art Museum, Japan (cat.)
Exhibition of the Collection of the Yokohama Museum of Art (Part I), Yokohama Museum of Art, Japan
Carte Blanche, Pace Gallery, Chesa Büsin, Zuoz, Switzerland
Study from the Human Body, Stephen Friedman Gallery, London
MOMAT Collection, National Museum of Modern Art, Tokyo
Go-Betweens: The World Seen through Children, Mori Art Museum, Tokyo; traveled to Nagoya City Art Museum; Okinawa Prefectural Museum & Art Museum; Museum of Art, Kōchi, Japan (cat.)
Look at Me: Portraiture from Manet to the Present, Leila Heller Gallery, New York
Cinderella, Sky Art Museum, Seoul

2013
Damage Control: Art and Destruction since 1950, Hirshhorn Museum and Sculpture Garden, Washington, DC; traveled to Mudam Luxembourg; Kunsthaus Graz, Austria (cat.)
Awakening: Aichi Triennale 2013, Aichi Arts Center, Nagoya, Japan (as part of artist collective THE WE-LOWS) (cat.)
Flowers, Towada Art Center, Japan
Re: Quest—Japanese Contemporary Art since the 1970s, Museum of Art, Seoul National University (cat.)
Wonderful My Art, Kawaguchiko Museum of Art, Fujikawaguchiko, Japan
Takahashi Collection: Mindfulness!, Kirishima Open-Air Museum, Yūsui; traveled to Sapporo Art Park, Japan (cat.)
Why not live for Art? II, Tokyo Opera City Art Gallery
We Do What We Want, Zenkyo-an x FOIL, Kenninji Zenkyo-an Temple, Kyoto

2012
San Antonio Collects: Contemporary, San Antonio Museum of Modern Art, San Antonio, TX
Print/Out: Multiplied Art in the Information Era, 1990–2010, Museum of Modern Art, New York (cat.)
The Art of Cooking, Royal/T, Los Angeles
Double Vision: Contemporary Art from Japan, Moscow Museum of Modern Art; traveled to Tikotin Museum of Japanese Art and Haifa Museum of Art, Haifa, Israel (cat.)
Masahiko Kuwahara, Yoshitomo Nara, Hiroshi Sugito, Tomio Koyama Gallery, Singapore
A Curator's Message 2012, Hyōgo Prefectural Museum of Art, Kobe, Japan (cat.)
The Magic of Ceramics: Artistic Inspiration, Museum of Contemporary Ceramic Art and Shigaraki Ceramic Cultural Park, Kōka; traveled to Museum of Modern Ceramic Art, Gifu, Tajimi; Museum of Ceramic Art, Hyōgo, Sasayama, Japan (cat.)
WE LOVE KOKESHI!, Nishida Kinenkan, Fukushima, Japan
10th Anniversary Exhibition: To Wander a Garden, Vangi Sculpture Garden Museum, Shizuoka, Japan (cat.)
MOT Collection, New Acquisitions: Anish Kapoor, Yutaka Sone, Yoshimoto Nara, Nobuya Hitsuda, Mami Kosemura, Museum of Contemporary Art Tokyo
Collection, National Museum of Art, Osaka, Japan
Son et Lumière, et sagesse profonde, 21st Century Museum of Contemporary Art, Kanazawa, Japan (cat.)
The Contemporary Paintings through the Curator's Eye, Hyōgo Prefectural Museum of Art, Kobe, Japan (cat.)
When Art You Gonna Do, If Not Now?: Zenkyo-an x FOIL, Kenninji Zenkyo-an Temple, Kyoto

2011
Future Pass: From Asia to the World, 54th Venice Biennale
New Works in Ceramics, Japan 2011, Toyota Municipal Museum of Art, Japan
Bye Bye Kitty!!!: Between Heaven and Hell in Contemporary Japanese Art, Japan Society, New York (cat.)
CAFE in Mito 2011: Relationships in Color, Contemporary Art Gallery, Art Tower Mito, Japan
Collectors' Stage: Asian Contemporary Art from Private Collections, Singapore Art Museum
Collection, Part 3, Yokohama Museum of Art, Japan (cat.)
Creating the New Century: Contemporary Art from the Dicke Collection, Dayton Art Institute, OH (cat.)
The Most Requested Top 30: 10 Years of Takahashi Collection, Tabloid Gallery, Tokyo
The Most Requested Top 30: 10 Years of Takahashi Collection, Part 2, Tabloid Gallery, Tokyo
Taguchi Art Collection: Global New Art, Seiji Togo Memorial Sompo Japan Nipponkoa Museum of Art, Tokyo
Invisibleness is Visibleness, Museum of Contemporary Art, Taipei
Edo Pop: The Graphic Impact of Japanese Prints, Minneapolis Institute of Art
Paul Clay, Salon 94 Bowery, New York
Zenkyo-an x FOIL, Kenninji Zenkyo-an Temple, Kyoto
The 53 Stations of Tōkaidō: From Hiroshige to Artists of Our Days, Musée Bernard Buffet, Nagaizumi, Japan (cat.)
GOLDMINE: Contemporary Works from the Collection of Sirje and Michael Gold, University Art Museum, College of the Arts, California State University, Long Beach
Collection Exhibition: Floating Boat, Toyota Municipal Museum of Art, Japan
Tomorrow Never Knows, Zenkyo-an x FOIL, Kenninji Zenkyo-an Temple, Kyoto

2010
Trans-Cool TOKYO, Singapore Art Museum; traveled to Bangkok Art and Culture Centre
Best 100 Works from Museum Collection, Tokushima Modern Art Museum, Japan
Peko-chan World, Fujiya Ginza Building, Tokyo
12th International Cairo Biennale, El Bab Gallery, Museum of Contemporary Art, Cairo
Made in Popland, China and Japan, National Museum of Contemporary Art, Seoul (cat.)
Contemporary Magic: A Tarot Deck Art Project, National Arts Club, New York; traveled to Andy Warhol Museum, Pittsburgh; Virginia Museum of Contemporary Art, Virginia Beach (cat.)
Innocence – Art towards Life, Tochigi Prefectural Museum of Fine Arts, Utsunomiya, Japan
Garden of Painting: Japanese Art of the 00s, National Museum of Art, Osaka, Japan
Teruhisa Kitahara's Astounding Contemporary Art, Mori Arts Center Gallery, Tokyo
Daiwa Collection First Session, Okinawa Prefectural Museum and Art Museum, Naha, Japan
Yoshitomo Nara x Ei-Q: Departure of an Artist at Age 24, Toki-no-Wasuremono/Watanuki, Tokyo
Self Portrait: Watashi to iu tannin [Me as Others], Takahashi Collection, Hibiya, Japan
Aomori Museum of Art Collections: Shiko Munakata, Toru Nanita, Yoshitomo Nara: Idol3, Onomichi City Museum of Art, Japan
Collection 2010–2012 Memory/Memorial—for the Summer of the 65th Hiroshima Memorial Day, Hiroshima City Museum of Contemporary Art, Japan
Get Up, Even If by Yourself Alone: Zenkyo-an x FOIL, Kenninji Zenkyo-an Temple, Kyoto
Neoteny Japan Takahashi Collection, Museum of Art, Ehime, Matsuyama, Japan
Ateliers d'artistes, Musée Bernard Buffet, Nagaizumi, Japan
Figuratively Speaking: A Survey of the Human Form, Bellagio Gallery of Fine Art, Las Vegas
The Library of Babel / In and Out of Place, 176 Zabludowicz Collection, London
Facing East: Recent Works from China, India and Japan from the Frank Cohen Collection, Manchester Art Gallery, UK

2009
Walking in My Mind, Hayward Gallery, London (cat.)
Rites de Passage, Schunck Glaspaleis, Heerlen, Netherlands
6th Asia Pacific Triennial of Contemporary Art, Queensland Art Gallery, Gallery of Modern Art, Brisbane, Australia (cat.)
Weighing and Wanting: Selections from the Collection, Museum of Contemporary Art San Diego, CA
From Home to the Museum: Tanaka Tsuneko Collection, Museum of Modern Art, Wakayama, Japan
Stages: Lance Armstrong Foundation, Galerie Emmanuel Perrotin, Paris
15th Anniversary Inaugural Exhibition, Blum & Poe, Los Angeles
In the Little Playground: Hitsuda Nobuya and His Surrounding Students—Masako Ando, Mika Kato, Tamami Hitsuda, Yoshitomo Nara, Hiroshi Sugito, Aichi Prefectural Museum of Art and Nagoya City Art Museum, Nagoya, Japan (cat.)

Prospective Artium, Mitsubishi-Jisho Artium, Fukuoka, Japan

2008

The Masked Portrait, Marianne Boesky Gallery, New York

Selections from the Hara Museum's Permanent Collection, Hara Museum of Contemporary Art, Tokyo

A Perspective on Contemporary Art 6: Emotional Drawing, National Museum of Modern Art, Tokyo; traveled to the National Museum of Modern Art, Kyoto (cat.)

MOT Collection, Museum of Contemporary Art Tokyo

Mogi Kenichiro, Hana, Kakuta Mitsuyo, Araki Nobuyoshi: Four Views of the Collection of the Yokohama Museum of Art, Yokohama Museum of Art, Japan

Animals in Contemporary Art: Many Animals!! What? Art?, Towada Art Center, Japan

Order. Desire. Light. An Exhibition of Contemporary Drawings, Irish Museum of Modern Art, Dublin

Kankai Pavilion Opening Exhibition: Beyond Time, Beyond Space, Towada Art Center, Japan

Tomyam Pladib, Jim Thompson Art Center, Bangkok

KITA!!: Japanese Artists Meet Indonesia (Yoshitomo Nara + graf), Cemeti Art House, Yogyakarta, Indonesia (cat.)

Encounters, Pace Gallery, Beijing

Collection II: Shell—Shelter, 21st Century Museum of Contemporary Art, Kanazawa, Japan

Traces of Siamese Smile: Art + Faith + Politics + Love, Bangkok Art and Culture Centre

Happy Mother, Happy Children, Tokyo Fuji Art Museum, Hachiōji, Japan

Wonderland: Japanese Contemporary Art, Opera Gallery, Hong Kong

Shiko Munakata, Tohru Narita, Yoshitomo Nara: The Icons of the Time, Ōita City Art Museum, Japan

The Human Image in the Twentieth Century: Works from the Collection of Tokushima Modern Art Museum, Gunma Museum of Art, Tatebayashi; traveled to Yatsushiro Municipal Museum; Hekinan City Tatsukichi Fujii Museum of Contemporary Art, Japan

My Museum, Yokohama Museum of Art, Japan

Neoteny Japan: Contemporary Artists after 1990s from Takahashi Collection, Kirishima Open-Air Museum, Yūsui; traveled to Museum of Contemporary Art, Sapporo; Ueno Royal Museum, Tokyo; Niigata Prefectural Museum of Modern Art, Nagaoka; Akita Museum of Modern Art, Yokote; Yonago City Museum of Art, Japan (cat.)

20th Anniversary Memorial Collection + Hibikiau Oto, Iro, Katachi (Sympathize with Sound, Color and Shape), Takamatsu City Museum of Art, Japan

2007

Cult Fiction: Art and Comics, Hayward Gallery touring exhibition, New Art Gallery, Walsall; traveled to Castle Museum and Art Gallery, Nottingham; City Art Gallery, Leeds; Aberystwyth Arts Centre; Tullie House Museum and Art Gallery, Carlisle, UK

Pretty Baby, Modern Art Museum of Fort Worth, TX

The Door into Summer: The Age of Micropop, Art Tower Mito, Japan (cat.)

Disorder in the House, Vanhaerents Art Collection, Brussels

Musée Bernard Buffet, Nagaizumi, Japan

Silly Adult, Galleri Nicolai Wallner, Copenhagen

Portrait Session, NADiff, Tokyo; traveled to Hiroshima City Museum of Contemporary Art, Japan

Painting as Forest: Artist as Thinker, Okazaki Mindscape Museum, Japan

Sympathy for the Devil: Art and Rock and Roll since 1967, Museum of Contemporary Art, Chicago; traveled to Museum of Contemporary Art, North Miami, FL; Musée d'art contemporain de Montréal

The Zabludowicz Collection: When We Build, Let Us Think That We Build Forever, BALTIC Centre for Contemporary Art, Newcastle, UK

Don't Look: Contemporary Drawings from an Alumna's Collection (Martina Yamin, Class of 1958), Davis Museum and Cultural Center, Wellesley College, MA (cat.)

Selections from the Hara Museum's Permanent Collection Shinagawa, Hara Museum of Contemporary Art, Tokyo

Red Hot: Asian Art Today from the Chaney Family Collection, Museum of Fine Arts, Houston

Surrealism and Art, Utsunomiya Museum of Art; traveled to Toyota Municipal Museum of Art; Yokohama Museum of Art, Japan (cat.)

Show Me Thai, Museum of Contemporary Art Tokyo

Summer Show, Tomio Koyama Gallery, Tokyo

Mindscape Museum, Okazaki, Japan

Let's Go to the Museum! How to Enjoy Modern Art, Together with Dick Bruna, Musée Bernard Buffet, Nagaizumi, Japan

Hop, Stamp, Hanga! Child Print Art Museum, Musée Bernard Buffet, Nagaizumi, Japan

ShContemporary 2007 Shanghai in Art, Best of Artists Shanghai Exhibition Center

3L4D—3rd Life 4th Dimension, MetaPhysical Art Gallery, Taipei

2006

RADAR: Selections from the Collection of Vicki and Kent Logan, Denver Art Museum, CO

Museum of Contemporary Art, Sapporo, Japan

Temporary Art Museum Soi Sabai, Rajata Art House, Silpakorn University Art Gallery, Bangkok

Hiroshima City Museum of Contemporary Art Collection: Kono 20nen no 20 no art [Twenty Artworks from the Past Twenty Years], Sapporo Art Park, Japan (cat.)

Kazoku no jokei: Nihon no kazouku wo kangaeru [The Scene of Family: A Review of the Japanese Family], Museum of Modern Art, Ibaraki, Mito, Japan (cat.)

The Child, Toyota Municipal Museum of Art, Japan (cat.)

Long Live Sculpture!, Middelheim Open Air Sculpture Museum, Antwerp, Belgium

A Magical Art Life, Tokyo Wonder Site Shibuya

10th Anniversary, Tomio Koyama Gallery, Tokyo

Having New Eyes, Aspen Art Museum, CO

6th Shanghai Biennale, Shanghai Art Museum (cat.)

35° 40' N 139° 45' E, Archeus, London

Talking Pictures, Sammlung Goetz, Munich

Sapporo Art Park, Sapporo, Japan

2005

Yokohama International Triennial: Art Circus (Jumping from the Ordinary), Yokohama, Japan

Ten Year Anniversary Exhibition, Stephen Friedman Gallery, London

The Elegance of Silence: Contemporary Art from East Asia, Mori Art Museum, Tokyo

Little Boy: The Arts of Japan's Exploding Subculture, Japan Society, New York (cat.)

Rising Sun, Melting Moon: Contemporary Art in Japan, Israel Museum, Jerusalem

Kotaro Terada Collection, Kawagoe City Art Museum, Japan

Kiss Kiss, c/o – Atle Gerhardsen, Berlin

Well Done: The Art of Design World, Museum of Contemporary Art, Taipei

Unheimlich Jung: Kinder und Jugendliche in der zeitgenössischen Kunst, Städtische Galerie Waldkraiburg, Germany

Japan Pop: Manga and Japanese Contemporary Art, Helsinki City Art Museum

Portrait, Galerie Meyer Kainer, Vienna

Baby Shower, Galleri Nicolai Wallner, Copenhagen

Chairs and Japanese Design, Museum of Modern Art, Saitama, Japan (cat.)

New Acquisition, Hiroshima City Museum of Contemporary Art, Japan

2004

Fiction Love: Ultra New Vision in Contemporary Art, MOCA Taipei (cat.)

New Prints: Yoshitomo Nara, Tam Ochiai, Hiroshi Sugito, Space Force, Tokyo

Why Not Live for Art?, Tokyo Opera City Art Gallery

Time of My Life: Art with Youthful Spirit, Tokyo Opera City Art Gallery

Onkochishin, White Cube Gallery, Osaka, Japan

Unusual Combination, + Gallery, Nagoya, Japan

Dog Days of Summer, California Museum of Photography, University of California, Riverside

Non-sect Radical: Contemporary Photography III, Yokohama Museum of Art, Japan

Funny Cuts: Cartoons und Comics in der zeitgenössischen Kunst, Staatsgalerie Stuttgart, Germany (cat.)

Yoshitomo Nara, Tam Ochiai, Hiroshi Sugito: New Prints, Space Force, Tokyo

2003

Happiness: A Survival Guide for Art and Life, Mori Art Museum, Tokyo

Supernova: Art of the 1990s from the Logan Collection, San Francisco Museum of Modern Art (cat.)

Nichijou Seikatsu, Speak For, Tokyo

FOIL, Little More Gallery, Tokyo

Painting in Our Time, Niigata Bandaijima Art Museum, Japan

I bambini siamo noi, Galleria Civica d'Arte Moderna e Contemporanea, Turin, Italy

Trauer/GRIEF, Atelier Augarten Zentrum für zeitgenössische Kunst der Österreichischen Galerie Belvedere, Vienna

Girls Don't Cry, Parco Museum, Tokyo

Niños, Centro de Arte de Salamanca, Spain

Mars: Art and War, Neue Galerie Graz, Austria

Inaugural Group Show, Blum & Poe, Los Angeles

Splat, Boom, Pow! The Influence of Comics in Contemporary Art, Contemporary Arts Museum, Houston; traveled to Institute of Contemporary Art, Boston; Wexner Center for the Arts, Columbus, OH (cat.)

Hope: Do Hope for the Future, Laforet Museum, Tokyo

Comic Release: Negotiating Identity for a New Generation, Carnegie Mellon University, Pittsburgh;

traveled to Center for Contemporary Art, New Orleans; University of North Texas Gallery, Denton; Western Washington University, Bellingham (cat.)
Opening Exhibition, Tomio Koyama Gallery, Tokyo
My Room Somehow Somewhere, graf media gm, Osaka, Japan
Collection, Nagoya City Art Museum, Japan
Best Collection, Takamatsu City Museum of Art, Japan
Art de Zoo, Akita Museum of Modern Art, Yokote, Japan
Moving Energies #2: Aspekte der Sammlung Olbricht, Museum Folkwang, Essen, Germany
Ukiyo-e Avant-Garde, Tokyo Station Gallery
Room Air, It-Park, Taipei
Your Dog is Orange County, Orange County Museum of Art, Newport Beach, CA

2002
Weiche Brüche: Japan, Kunstraum Innsbruck, Germany
BABEL 2002, National Museum of Contemporary Art, Seoul
Fragile Figures, Palette School, Tokyo
The Doraemon, Suntory Museum, Osaka; traveled to Sogo Museum of Art, Yokohama; Hokkaido Asahikawa Museum of Art; Matsuzakaya Art Museum, Nagoya; Ōita Art Museum; Shimane Art Museum, Matsue; Akita Senshū Museum of Art; Takaoka Art Museum; Takamatsu City Museum of Art; Matsumoto City Museum of Art, Japan (cat.)
Bokura no Hero and Heroine, Otaru City Museum of Art, Japan
Backspace Drawing Days, Galerie Michael Zink, Munich
Drawing Now: Eight Propositions, MoMA QNS, Long Island City, NY
The Galleries Show 2002, Royal Academy of Arts, London
Pop! Pop! Pop!, Museum of Modern Art, Ibaraki, Mito, Japan
The 20th Century. Art Recognized Virtual Images: Between Monalisa and Mammon, Hiratsuka Museum of Art, Japan
Drawing Days, Galerie Michael Zink, Munich
Emotional Site, Sagacho Shokuryo Building, Tokyo
Traces, Imprints and Tales: Japanese Contemporary Art Draws from Tradition, Kerava Art Museum, Finland (cat.)
The Japanese Experience: Inevitable, Ursula Blickle Stiftung, Kraichtal, Germany; traveled to Museum der Moderne Salzburg, Austria (cat.)

2001
Neo Tokyo: Japanese Art Now, Museum of Contemporary Art, Sydney (cat.)
Jap in the Box: Mr., Tam Ochiai, Hiroshi Sugito, Yoshitomo Nara, Takashi Murakami, Masahiko Kuwahara, Stephen Friedman Gallery, London
Jam: Tokyo-London, Barbican Centre, London; traveled to Tokyo Opera City Art Gallery (cat.)
Public Offerings, Museum of Contemporary Art, Los Angeles (cat.)
My Reality: Contemporary Art and the Culture of Japanese Animation, Des Moines Art Center, IA; traveled to Brooklyn Museum of Art, NY; Contemporary Arts Center, Cincinnati, OH; Tampa Museum of Art, FL; Chicago Cultural Center; Akron Art Museum, OH; Norton Museum of Art, West Palm Beach, FL; Museum of Glass: International Center for Contemporary Art, Tacoma, WA; Huntsville Museum of Art, AL (cat.)
Superflat, Museum of Contemporary Art, Los Angeles; traveled to Walker Art Center, Minneapolis; Henry Art Gallery, University of Washington, Seattle (cat.)
Forms of Human Figures from the Terada Collection, Tokyo Opera City Art Gallery
Tsunami Raiders, Galerie Michael Zink, Munich
Camera Works: The Photographic Impulse in Modern Art, Marianne Boesky Gallery, New York
Dialogue with Nature: Graduation Works from the Collection of Aichi Prefectural University of Fine Arts and Music, Haruhi Art Museum, Kiyosu, Japan (cat.)
Senritsumirai: Future Perfect, Center for Contemporary Art Luigi Pecci, Prato, Italy (cat.)
Vertical Time: Past, Present, and Future of Sculpture, University Art Museum, Tokyo National University of Fine Arts and Music
Silence of the City, Gwangju Art Museum, South Korea
Pop Heart e Generazione MTV, Light Gallery, Faenza, Italy
Tokyo Pop, Kansas City Jewish Museum, Overland Park, KS
Galerie Emmanuel Perrotin, Paris
MURAKAMI/NARA NARA/MURAKAMI, Tomio Koyama Gallery, Tokyo

2000
The Darker Side of Playland: Childhood Imagery from the Logan Collection, San Francisco Museum of Modern Art (cat.)
Présumé innocents: L'art contemporain et l'enfance [Presumed Innocent: Contemporary Art and Childhood], CAPC musée d'art contemporain, Bordeaux, France
Trading Views: 4 x Japanische Kunst, Stadtgalerie Saarbrücken, Germany; traveled to Städtische Galerie Erlangen, Germany; Stedelijk Museum De Lakenhal, Leiden, Netherlands (cat.)
Kinder des 20. Jahrhunderts: Malerei, Skulptur, Fotografie, Galerie der Stadt Aschaffenburg; traveled to Mittelrhein-Museum, Koblenz, Germany (cat.)
00: Drawings 2000, Barbara Gladstone Gallery, New York
Dark Mirrors of Japan, de Appel Foundation, Amsterdam (cat.)
Gendai: Japanese Contemporary Art—Between the Body and Space, Ujazdowski Castle Centre for Contemporary Art, Warsaw
Drawn from Life, Marianne Boesky Gallery, New York
Super Flat, Parco Gallery, Tokyo; traveled to Parco Gallery, Nagoya, Japan (cat.)
Continental Shift, Ludwig Forum, Aachen, Germany
Viewing Path, Stadtgalerie Saarbrücken, Germany
Works from the Tokushima Modern Art Museum Collection 2000, Tokushima Modern Art Museum, Japan (cat.)
Works on Paper, Ota Fine Arts, Tokyo
Yoshitomo Nara and Hana Hashimoto: The Amazing Garden, Takayama Uichi Memorial Art Museum, Shichinohe, Japan
Kids World Aomori 2000, Aomori Prefectural Museum, Japan
Gosei Abe and His Influences, Namioka Town Hall Aomori, Japan
Cultural Ties, Westzone Gallery Space, London
Gallery Hakutosha, Nagoya, Japan
One Heart, One World: International Exhibition of the Heart, United Nations Public Lobby, New York (cat.)

1999
Spellbound, Karyn Lovegrove Gallery, Los Angeles
Vergiß den Ball und spiel' weiter: Das Bild des Kindes in zeitgenössischer Kunst und Wissenschaft, Kunsthalle Nürnberg, Nuremberg, Germany
New Modernism for a New Millennium, San Francisco Museum of Modern Art
Painting for Joy: New Japanese Painting in 1990s, Japan Information and Culture Center, Washington, DC; traveled to Japan Foundation Forum, Tokyo (cat.)
Art is Fun 10: Angelic, Devilish, or Both, Hara Museum ARC, Shibukawa, Japan
Almost Warm and Fuzzy: Childhood and Contemporary Art, Des Moines Art Center, IA; traveled to Tacoma Art Museum, WA; Scottsdale Museum of Contemporary Art, AZ; P.S. 1 Contemporary Art Center, Long Island City, NY; Fundació "La Caixa," Barcelona; Crocker Art Museum, Sacramento, CA; Art Gallery of Hamilton, Canada; Memphis Brooks Museum of Art; Museum of Contemporary Art Cleveland, OH (cat.)
Tendance, Abbaye Saint-André Centre d'art contemporain, Meymac, France
It's an Animal World, Hokkaido Museum of Modern Art, Sapporo, Japan
Yoshitomo Nara and Hiroshi Sugito, Gallery Hakutosha, Nagoya, Japan
ART/DOMESTIC: Temperature of the Time, Setagaya Museum of Art, Tokyo (cat.)
An Active Fault of Painting, Nagoya Citizens' Gallery Yada, Japan

1998
The Manga Age, Museum of Contemporary Art Tokyo; traveled to Hiroshima City Museum of Contemporary Art, Japan (cat.)
Innocent Minds, Space X and Forum Space at Aichi Arts Center, Nagoya, Japan (cat.)
Busan International Contemporary Art Festival 1998, Busan Metropolitan Art Museum, South Korea
Voor herhaling vatbaar: Henk Visch, Yoshitomo Nara, Peter Archer, Galerie d'Eendt, Amsterdam
Aomori Museum of Art Collection, Hachinohe City Museum of Art; traveled to Tokiwa Furusato Museum Asuka, Fujisaki; Aomori Prefectural Museum, Japan

1997
Dream of Existence: Exhibition of Young Japanese Artists, Kiscelli Museum, Budapest (cat.)
Japanese Contemporary Art Exhibition, National Museum of Contemporary Art, Seoul
Drawing Show, Galerie d'Eendt, Amsterdam (with Henk Visch)
Galería y Ediciones Ginkgo, Madrid
VOCA '97: Vision of Contemporary Art, Ueno Royal Museum, Tokyo (cat.)
Box: Its Cosmos, Galerie Humanité, Tokyo
React Presents, Gallery TAF, Kyoto

1996
Tokyo Pop, Hiratsuka Museum of Art, Japan (cat.)
Ironic Fantasy: Another World by Five Contemporary Artists, Miyagi Museum of Art, Sendai, Japan (cat.)
Kind of Blue, Hakutosha, Nagoya, Japan
Intangible Childhood, Mie Prefectural Art Museum, Tsu, Japan
Sunny Side Up, Gallery Nayuta, Yokohama, Japan

Drawings, Galerie d'Eendt, Amsterdam
Galerie d'Eendt, Amsterdam
L'Enfance retrouvé, Galerie d'Eendt, Amsterdam

1995
Galerie d'Eendt, Amsterdam
Drawing Chat, Shinanobashi Gallery, Osaka, Japan (with Katsuhige Nakahashi)
Endless Happiness, SCAI THE BATHHOUSE, Tokyo
Art x ∞ = @, SAM Museum, Osaka, Japan
That Figures, Galerie d'Eendt, Amsterdam
Book and Weight, Gallery Kuranuki, Osaka, Japan
POSITIV, Museum am Ostwall, Dortmund, Germany
Düsseldorf-andere Orte, Orangerie Schloß Brake, Lemgo, Germany
The Future of Paintings '95, Osaka Contemporary Art Center, Japan (cat.)
Takeoffs, Guggenheim Gallery, Chapman University, Orange, CA
Osaka Contemporary Art Center, Japan
Gunma Biennale for Young Artists '95, Gunma Prefectural Museum of Modern Art, Takasaki, Japan

1994
my room is your room, 7th Nagoya Contemporary Art Fair, Nagoya City Gallery, Japan
Harvest '94, Haus Bockdorf, Kempen, Germany
Harvest Kempen-Nagoya, Hakutosha, Nagoya, Japan (with Shiro Matsui)
Art Against AIDS, Art Cologne, Germany
Ironic Fantasy, Miyagi Museum of Art, Sendai, Japan

1993
Partners, Galerie d'Eendt, Amsterdam
Animals, Galerie Tanya Rumpff, Haarlem, Netherlands
Harvest '93, Haus Bockdorf, Kempen, Germany (with Shiro Matsui)
In Situ, Theater aan het Vrijthof, Maastricht, Belgium
Artomatic, Galerie d'Eendt, Amsterdam
Compositions, Galerie d'Eendt, Amsterdam

1992
Tijdelijk Asiel, Arti et Amicitiae, Amsterdam
Galerie d'Eendt, Amsterdam

1991
4th Nagoya Contemporary Art Fair, Electricity Museum Nagoya, Japan
Pack, SA-IN Gallery, Busan, South Korea

1990
Brille, Galerie Pentagon, Cologne, Germany
Acqua Strana, Galerie Ulla Sommers, Düsseldorf
Vivian Rowe, Yoshitomo Nara, Louis Darocha, Kees de Groot, Galerie d'Eendt, Amsterdam

1989
Mensch und Technik, Nixdorf AG, Düsseldorf

1988
Feeling House, Mie Prefectural Art Museum, Tsu, Japan

1987
New Artists in Nagoya, Westbeth Gallery, Nagoya, Japan

1986
Each Person's Expression of Space, Museum of Fine Arts, Gifu, Japan
Present '86, Gallery NAF, Nagoya, Japan

1985
Sense of Vision and Touch, Westbeth Gallery, Nagoya, Japan
Gonin Bayashi (Five Person's Musical Band), Love Collection Gallery, Nagoya, Japan

1984
Paranoia, Westbeth Gallery, Nagoya, Japan
Yoshitomo Nara, Kooji Miura, Gallery Denega, Hirosaki, Japan

Curatorial Projects

2017
Takeshi Motai the Dream Traveler, Chihiro Art Museum Azumino, Matsukawa, Japan; traveled to Chihiro Art Museum Tokyo

2016
Horizon That Appears Out of The Sleepy Woods, Stephen Friedman Gallery, London
MOMAT Collection by Yoshitomo Nara, National Museum of Modern Art, Tokyo

2015
PHASE 2015 COMPANY: SECRETS OF NORTHERN JAPAN, Aomori Museum of Art, Japan (cat.)

2014
PHASE 2014, Aomori Museum of Art, Japan (cat.)

2013
WE-LOW HOUSE, Aichi Triennale, Aichi Arts Center, Japan

2012
The Little Art Club in The Blue Woods, Towada Art Center, Japan

2001
morning glory, Tomio Koyama Gallery, Tokyo (cat.)

1997
World Peace Café, Hakutosha, Nagoya, Japan

Awards and Grants

Aichi Prefectural Art Encouragement Prize, Aichi Prefecture, Japan, 2019
Asia Arts Award, Asia Society, Hong Kong, 2016
To-ou Award, Tonippo, Aomori, Japan, 2014
The 63rd Annual Art Encouragement Prize of Fine Arts, Agency for Cultural Affairs, Japan, 2013
Award from the International Center, New York, 2010
Artist Award, Nagoya City, Japan, 1995

Public and Established Private Collections

21st Century Museum of Contemporary Art, Kanazawa
Aichi Prefectural Museum of Art, Nagoya, Japan
Aichi University of the Arts, Nagakute, Japan
Aomori Museum of Art, Japan
Art Institute of Chicago
Blenheim Art Foundation, London
British Museum, London
Centre national des arts plastiques, Paris
Centro de arte contemporáneo de Málaga, Spain
Clematis no Oka, Nagaizumi, Japan
Comico Art Museum Yufuin, Yufu, Japan
Cornell Fine Arts Museum, Rollins College, Winter Park, FL
Des Moines Art Center, IA
Flower Man Collection, Japan
Fondation Carmignac, Paris
Hall Collection, Derneburg, Germany, and Reading, VT
Hara Museum of Contemporary Art, Tokyo
Hirosaki Museum of Contemporary Art, Japan
Hiroshima City Museum of Contemporary Art, Japan
Iwate Prefecture Citizen's Cultural Exchange Center (Aiina), Morioka, Japan
Japan Foundation, Tokyo
Kadokawa Culture Promotion Foundation, Tokyo
Leeum, Samsung Museum of Art, Seoul
Long Museum, Shanghai
Los Angeles County Museum of Art
Marciano Art Foundation, Los Angeles
Maria Fareri Children's Hospital, Valhalla, NY
Minneapolis Institute of Art
Museum of Contemporary Art Chicago
Museum of Contemporary Art, Los Angeles
Museum of Contemporary Art San Diego, CA
Museum of Contemporary Art Tokyo
Museum of Fine Arts, Boston
Museum of Modern Art, New York
Museum of Modern Art, Wakayama, Japan
National Gallery of Art, Washington, DC
National Museum of Art, Osaka, Japan
Neues Museum Nürnberg, Nuremberg, Germany
New Century Art Foundation, Beijing
Ōita Prefectural Art Museum, Japan
Olbricht Collection, Berlin
Palm Springs Art Museum, CA
Patong Municipality, Phuket, Thailand
Peter Norton Family Foundation, Santa Monica, CA
Popov Foundation, Moscow
Queensland Art Gallery and Gallery of Modern Art, Brisbane, Australia
Rachofsky Collection, Dallas
Rubell Museum, Miami
San Francisco Museum of Modern Art
Shiseido Art House, Kakegawa, Japan
Taguchi Collection, Tokyo
Takahashi Collection, Tokyo
Takamatsu City Museum of Art, Japan
Tokushima Modern Art Museum, Japan
Tokyo Opera City Art Gallery
Tokyo Photographic Art Museum
Towada Art Center, Japan
Toyota Municipal Museum of Art, Japan
Yokohama Museum of Art, Japan
Yumeooka Kanri Kumiai (Yumeooka Art Project), Yokohama, Japan
Zabludowicz Collection, London

Monographs/Books

The World of Yoshitomo Nara. Special issue of *Eureka Poetry and Critique* 49–13, no. 706. Tokyo: Seidosha, August 2017.
Yoshitomo Nara: Self-Selected Works, Paintings. Kyoto: Seigensha Art Publishing, 2015.
Yoshitomo Nara: Self-Selected Works, Works on Paper. Kyoto: Seigensha Art Publishing, 2015.
Yoshitomo Nara: NO WAR! Tokyo: Bijutsu Shuppan-sha, 2014.
Yoshitomo Nara: The Complete BT Archives, 1991–2013. Tokyo: Bijutsu Shuppan-sha, 2013.
Yoshitomo Nara Photo Book 2003–2012. Tokyo: Kodansha, 2013.
NARA 48 GIRLS. Tokyo: Chikumashobo, 2012; Seoul: Sigongsa, 2012 (Korean edition); Beijing: Beijing Joint Publishing Company, 2012.
NARA LIFE: The Days of Yoshitomo Nara. Kyoto: FOIL, 2012.
Print Works. Tokyo: Mori Arts Center Museum Shop, 2011.
Yoshitomo Nara: The Complete Works, 1984–2010. Tokyo: Bijutsu Shuppan-sha, 2011; San Francisco: Chronicle Books, 2011 (US edition). Two volumes.
Ceramic Works. Tokyo: FOIL, 2010.
Drawing File. Tokyo: FOIL, 2005.
The Little Star Dweller. Tokyo: Rockin'on, 2004; Taipei: Locus Publishing, 2004; Seoul: Sigongsa, 2005 (Korean edition); Shanghai: Shanghai Motie Culture Development, 2010 (Chinese edition).
The Good, the Bad, the Average…and Unique. Tokyo: Little More, 2003.
Studio Portrait: A Document of Artist Yoshitomo Nara. Tokyo: Bijutsu Shuppan-sha, 2003. *Birth and Present: A Studio Portrait of Yoshitomo Nara*. Corte Madera, CA: Ginkgo Press, 2003 (US edition). Photographs by Mie Morimoto.
Lullaby Supermarket. Tokyo: Kadokawa Shoten, 2001; Nuremburg, Germany: Verlag für moderne Kunst Nürnberg, 2001 (German edition).
NARA NOTE. Tokyo: Chikumashobo, 2001; Seoul: Hongsi Communication, 2005 (Korean edition); Xinbei: Come Together Press, 2013; Changsha, China: Hunan People's Publishing House, 2017 (Chinese edition).
Nobody Knows. Tokyo: Little More, 2001; Tokyo: FOIL, 2005 (revised edition).
Yoshitomo Nara: Naive Wonderworld. Tokyo: KTC Chuoh Publishing, 2001. Edited by NHK Top Runner production crew.
The Lonesome Puppy. Tokyo: Magazine House, 1999; San Francisco: Chronicle Books, 2008 (US edition).
Ukiyo. Tokyo: Little More, 1999.
Slash with a Knife. Tokyo: Little More, 1998; Tokyo: FOIL, 2005 (revised edition).
In the Deepest Puddle. Tokyo: Kadokawa Shoten, 1997.

Solo Exhibition Catalogues

Yoshitomo Nara. Los Angeles: Los Angeles County Museum of Art; New York: DelMonico Books/Prestel, 2020. (artist book and special edition)
days 2014–2018: Sixteen springs and sixteen summers gone—Take your time, it won't be long now. Tokyo: Taka Ishii Gallery Photography/Film, 2018.
Yoshitomo Nara. New York: Pace Gallery, 2018.
Yoshitomo Nara: for better or worse: Works 1987–2017. Toyota, Japan: Toyota Municipal Museum of Art, 2017.
Yoshitomo Nara: Will the Circle Be Unbroken. Tokyo: Fine-Art Photography Association, 2017.
Once in Life: Encounters with Nara. Hong Kong: Asia Society Hong Kong Center, 2016.
Yoshitomo Nara: New Works. London: Stephen Friedman Gallery, 2016. (leaflet)
Shallow Puddles. Tokyo: Blum & Poe, 2015.
stars. Hong Kong: Pace Hong Kong, 2015.
Greetings from a Place in My Heart. London: Dairy Art Centre, 2014. (leaflet)
Yoshitomo Nara: Drawings: 1984–2013. Los Angeles: Blum & Poe, 2014.
Yoshitomo Nara. New York: Pace Gallery, 2013.
Yoshitomo Nara + YNG: Crated Rooms in Iceland. Reykjavík: Crymogea, 2013.
NARA Yoshitomo: a bit like you and me…. Kyoto: FOIL, 2012.
Yoshitomo Nara: Nobody's Fool. New York: Abrams, 2010.
Moonlight Serenade. Kanazawa, Japan: 21st Century Museum of Contemporary Art, Kanazawa, 2007.
Yoshitomo Nara + graf: Torre de Málaga. Málaga, Spain: Centro de arte contemporáneo de Málaga, 2007.
Yoshitomo Nara + graf: A to Z. Tokyo: FOIL, 2006.
From the Depth of My Drawer. Tokyo: FOIL, 2005.
From the Depth of My Drawer. Seoul: Rodin Gallery, 2005.
From the Depth of My Drawer: Yoshii Brick Brew House, Hirosaki. Hirosaki, Japan: Organizing Committee for the Yoshitomo Nara Exhibition, 2005. Photographs by Masako Nagano.
Yoshitomo Nara & Hiroshi Sugito: Over the Rainbow. Ostfildern, Germany: Hatje Cantz, 2005.
Nara Yoshitomo Hirosaki. Hirosaki: BPO Harappa, 2004. Photo documentation of *I DON'T MIND, IF YOU FORGET ME*. Photographs by Mikiya Takimoto.
This Is a Time of…S.M.L. Kyoto: Seigensha, 2004. Photographs by Masako Nagano.
Nothing Ever Happens. Santa Monica, CA: Perceval Press, 2003.
Who Snatched the Babies? Paris: Cneai, France, 2002.
I DON'T MIND, IF YOU FORGET ME. Kyoto: Tankosha, 2001. (with CD-ROM)
Somebody Whispers in Nuremberg. Nuremburg, Germany: Institut für Moderne Kunst in der SchmidtBank-Galerie, 1999. (leaflet)
Mitsubishi-Jisho Artium Exhibitions April 1995–March 1997 (vol. 4). Fukuoka, Japan: Mitsubishi-Jisho Artium, 1998.
Yoshitomo Nara. Milwaukee: Institute of Visual Arts at University of Wisconsin–Milwaukee, 1998. (leaflet with floppy disk)
Hothouse Fresh. Nagoya, Japan: Hakutosha, 1996 (pamphlet)
In the Deepest Puddle / Nothing Gets Me Down. Tokyo: SCAI THE BATHHOUSE and Galerie Humanite Tokyo, 1995. (leaflet)
Oil on Canvas. Nagoya, Japan: Galerie Humanité Nagoya, 1995. (pamphlet)
Lonesome Babies. Nagoya, Japan: Hakutosha, 1994. (pamphlet)
Nemureru kodomo no kurisumasu [Christmas for Sleeping Children]. Osaka, Japan: Itoki Crystal Hall, 1994. (pamphlet)
Be Happy. Nagoya and Tokyo: Galerie Humanité Nagoya and Tokyo, 1993. (pamphlet)
cogitationes cordium. Nagoya, Japan: Galerie Humanité Nagoya, 1991.
Innocent Being. Nagoya, Japan: Galerie Humanité Nagoya, 1988. (leaflet)

Original Art for Book Covers and Other Projects

Toyoda, Toshiaki. *Hanbun Ikita*. Tokyo: HeHe, 2019.
Asai, Kenichi, and Yoshitomo Nara. *Baby Revolution*. Tokyo: Crayonhouse, 2019.
Tanaka, Hiko. *Ohikkoshi*. Tokyo: Fukuinkan Shoten, 2013.
Prévert, Jacques. *Tori e no aisatsu* [Greetings to the bird]. Tokyo: Pia, 2006. Translated by Isao Takahata.
Yoshimoto, Banana. *Argentine Hag*. Tokyo: Rockin'on, 2002; Taipei: China Times, 2007; Shanghai: Shanghai Translation Publishing House, 2010 (Chinese edition); Seoul: Minumusa, 2010 (Korean edition).
Lotta Leaves Home (1993). Directed by Johanna Hald. Distributed by Eden Entertainment, 2000 (Japan release). (poster, pamphlet)
Visionaire No. 30: The Game – Japan. New York: Visionaire, 2000.
Yoshimoto, Banana. *Hinagiku no jinsei* [The life of Hinagiku]. Tokyo: Rockin'on, 2000; Gentosha, 2006 (paperback); Seoul: Minumusa, 2009 (Korean edition); Taipei: China Times, 2009.
Yoshimoto, Banana. *Hardboiled/Hard Luck*. Tokyo: Rockin'on, 1999; Gentosha, 2001 (paperback); *Dur, dur*. Paris: Rivages, 2001 (French edition); *H/H*. Milan: Feltrinelli, 2001 (Italian edition); *Hard-boiled Hard Luck: Zwei Erzaehlungen*. Zurich: Diogenes, 2004 (Swiss/German edition); London: Faber and Faber, 2005 (UK edition); New York: Grove Press, 2006 (US edition); St. Petersburg, Russia: Amphora, 2006 (Russian edition); Seoul: Minumusa, 2002 (Korean edition); Taipei: China Times, 2009.

Artwork Used on Book Covers

Tanaka, Hiko. *Sorry*. Tokyo: Fukuinkan Shoten, 2014.
Sakamoto, Ryuichi, et al. *NO NUKES 2012: A Guidebook for Our Future*. Tokyo: Shogakukan Square, 2012.
Itoi, Shigesato. *Sheep Thief*. Tokyo: Itoi Shigesato Jimusho, 2011.
Ko, Machida. *Gorannosupon*. Tokyo: Shinchosha, 2011.
Mado, Michio. *Uchu no me* [Eyes of the universe]. Tokyo: FOIL, 2010.
Read Real Japanese Fiction. Tokyo: Kodansha International, 2008. Edited by Janet Ashby.
Read Real Japanese Fiction. Tokyo: Kodansha International, 2008. Edited by Michael Emmeric.
The Constitution of Japan. Tokyo: FOIL, 2005.
Yamada, Switch. *Happiness Switch!* Tokyo: Pia, 2003.
Nakaba, Riichi. *Spin Kids*. Tokyo: Tokuma, 2001.
Kurihara, Akira, Yoichi Komori, Manabu Sato, and Shunya Yoshimi. *Knowledge That Crosses Borders*. Tokyo: University of Tokyo Press, 2000–2001. Six volumes.
Kurihara, Akira, Yoichi Komori, Manabu Sato, and Shunya Yoshimi. *Implosion of Knowledge: Reorganization of Body, Language, and Power*. Tokyo: Univerity of Tokyo Press, 2000.
Sendo, Naomi. *Moe no suzaku*. Tokyo: Gentosha, 1999.

Album Artwork

Kenzi Hatta. *Jidai ga fuzaketeru*. HARDNA POP, Japan, 2019.
Michinohi. *but to do*. SORACHI RECORDS, Japan, 2019.
noodles. *I'm not chic*. DELICIOUS LABEL, Japan, 2019.
Kenzi Hatta. *Ima ga arusa*. HARDNA POP, Japan, 2014.
Mitsutoshi Anbe. *Tohoku Love*. Crown Tokuma Music Distribution, Japan, 2014.
Various artists. *Yes, We Love butchers ~ Tribute to bloodthirsty butchers ~ Abandoned Puppy*. Nippon Crown, Japan, 2014.
Various artists. *Yes, We Love butchers ~ Tribute to bloodthirsty butchers ~ The Last Match*. Nippon Crown, Japan, 2014.
Various artists. *Yes, We Love butchers ~ Tribute to bloodthirsty butchers ~ Mumps*. Nippon Crown, Japan, 2014.
Various artists. *Yes, We Love butchers ~ Tribute to bloodthirsty butchers ~ Night Walking*. Nippon Crown, Japan, 2014.
Morio Agata. *Gusuperi yonenki*. QPORA PURPLE Hz, Japan, 2012.
Various artists. *Naninimo Makezu – songs for children from ARABAKI*. ARABAKI RECORDS, Japan, 2011.
Kimiko Itoh + Aki Takase. *Makkana ohirune*. Videoarts Music, Japan, 2010.
Jim Black/AlasNoAxis. *Houseplant*. Winter & Winter, Germany, and Bomba Records, Japan, 2009.
Momokomotion. *Punk in a Coma*. AWDR/LR2, Japan, 2009. Standard and special editions.
Absynthe Minded. *There Is Nothing*. Universal Music, Belgium, 2007.
Bloodthirsty Butchers. *Guitarist o korosanaide* [Don't kill the guitarist]. Columbia Music Entertainment, Japan, 2007.
Takako Tate. *Wasurenagusa*. Vap, Japan, 2007.
Day & Taxi. *Out*. Percaso Production, Switzerland, 2006.
Bloodthirsty Butchers. *Banging the Drum*. Columbia Music Entertainment, Japan, 2005.
Bloodthirsty Butchers. *bloodthirsty butchers VS +/- {PLUS / MINUS}*. Columbia Music Entertainment, Japan, 2005.
Fantômas. *Suspended Animation*. Ipecac Recordings, USA, 2005. Standard and limited editions.
Tiki Tiki Bamboooos. *cloudy, later fine*. O-chang BEAT, Japan, 2005.
Various artists. *Je suis comme Je suis: Les Chansons de Jacques Prévert*. Universal International, Japan, 2004.
Matthew Sweet. *Kimi Ga Suki*Raifu*. RCAM Records, USA, 2004.
Jim Black/AlasNoAxis. *Splay*. Winter & Winter, Germany, and Bomba Records, Japan, 2002.
Various artists. *Dengeki Bop! A Tribute to Ramones*. R&C, Japan, 2002.
Taisyo Kyunen. *Kyu-Box*. Vap, Japan, 2002.
Tiki Tiki Bamboooos. *Tiki Tiki Bamboooos*. Self-released, Germany, 2002.
The Busy Signals. *Pretend Hits*. Sugar Free Records, USA, 2001.
R.E.M. *I'll Take the Rain*. Warner Bros. Records, USA, 2001.
The Star Club. *Trigger*. Victor Entertainment, Japan, 2000.
The Star Club. *Kitty Missiles*. Victor Entertainment, Japan, 1999.
The Star Club. *Pyromaniac*. Victor Entertainment, Japan, 1999.
Shonen Knife. *Happy Hour*. Universal Victor, Japan, 1998.
The Birdy Num Nums. *Mannaka over the World*. King Size Records, Germany, 1991.

Picture Credits

All works by Nara © Yoshitomo Nara and provided courtesy of Yoshitomo Nara.

Courtesy of 21st Century Museum of Contemporary Art, Kanazawa, Japan: Figs. 166, 167; A.F. Archive/Alamy: Fig. 32; Courtesy of Aichi University of the Arts, Nagakute, Japan: Fig. 23; Courtesy of Aomori Museum of Art, Japan: Figs. 35, 44, 85, 92, 359a–b; © Nobuyoshi Araki. Courtesy of Taka Ishii Gallery, Tokyo: Fig. 286; *The Asahi Shimbun*/Getty Images: Figs. 100, 283; © Yusuke Asai: Fig. 353; Courtesy of Jim Black and Mariko Takahashi: Fig. 210; Courtesy of Blum & Poe, Los Angeles/New York/Tokyo: Figs. 75, 93, 121, 122, 183; Courtesy of Bohemian's Guild: Fig. 194; Bernie Boston/*The Washington Post*/Getty Images: Fig. 240; © Chaguin: Figs. 148–153; © 2019 Chihiro Art Museum. Courtesy of Chihiro Art Museum Tokyo: Figs. 18, 19; © Chim↑Pom. Courtesy of the artist, ANOMALY, and MUJIN-TO Production, Tokyo: Fig. 287; © Classic Film Preservation Society of Independent Film Production, Tokyo: Fig. 333; Courtesy of Georgian National Museum, Tbilisi: Figs. 337, 338; Courtesy of Hara Museum of Contemporary Art, Tokyo: Figs. 66, 96, 160, 161; Special thanks to Birgit Hoff: Fig. 55; Special thanks to Naoko Ichihashi and Reiko Kato: Fig. 164; Courtesy of Japan Platform: Fig. 278; © Keisuke Katano. Courtesy of Hamaya Hiroshi Estate: Figs. 216, 217; Courtesy of Rinko Kawauchi: Fig. 215; © Rinko Kawauchi. Special thanks to Nao Amino: Fig. 223; © Hiroyasu Kosukegawa and Kineta Kunimatsu: Figs. 355, 356; © Shiro Matsui: Fig. 59; The Metropolitan Museum of Art, New York. Fletcher Fund, 1929. JP1506: Fig. 70; The Metropolitan Museum of Art, New York. Harris Brisbane Dick Fund, 1946. JP3018: Fig. 120; The Metropolitan Museum of Art, New York. The Harry G. C. Packard Collection of Asian Art, Gift of Harry G. C. Packard, and Purchase, Fletcher, Rogers, Harris Brisbane Dick, and Louis V. Bell Funds, Joseph Pulitzer Bequest, and The Annenberg Fund Inc. Gift, 1975. 1975.268.191: Fig. 358; The Metropolitan Museum of Art, New York. Mary Griggs Burke Collection, Gift of the Mary and Jackson Burke Foundation, 2015. 2015.300.257a, b: Figs. 177, 178; Courtesy of Mie Prefectural Art Museum, Tsu, Japan: Fig. 16; MOMAT/DNPartcom. Courtesy of the National Museum of Modern Art, Tokyo: Fig. 15; MOMAT/DNPartcom. Courtesy of the National Museum of Modern Art, Tokyo, and Mayu Asō: Fig. 10; © 1998 Takashi Murakami/Kaikai Kiki Co., Ltd. All Rights Reserved: Figs. 117, 118; Courtesy of Takashi Murakami: Fig. 372; Courtesy of the Museum of Contemporary Art, Los Angeles, and groovisions: Fig. 115; Courtesy of the Museum of Modern Art, Kamakura & Hayama: Fig. 312; Courtesy of Masatako Nakano, gallery ART UNLIMITED, Tokyo, and Setagaya Art Museum, Tokyo: Fig. 102; Courtesy of Masataka Nakano, gallery ART UNLIMITED, Tokyo, Setagaya Art Museum, Tokyo, and Takashi Nemoto: Fig. 101; Courtesy of Ohara Museum of Art, Kurashiki, Japan: Fig. 31; Courtesy of Pace Gallery, New York: Figs. 291–293, 296–300, 302, 303; Courtesy of R.E.M./Athens LLC: Fig. 202; Sankei Archive/Getty Images: Fig. 7; Courtesy of SBI Art Auction, Tokyo: Fig. 51; Courtesy of SCAI THE BATHHOUSE, Tokyo: Fig. 90; © David Shrigley. All Rights Reserved, DACS/Artimage 2019. Image courtesy Stephen Friedman Gallery, London: Fig. 137; © Yoshitomo Nara and David Shrigley. All Rights Reserved, DACS/Artimage 2019: Figs. 135, 136, 139–143; Courtesy of Stephen Friedman Gallery, London: Figs. 162, 169; © Yoshitomo Nara and Hiroshi Sugito: Figs. 144–147; Courtesy of Toyota Municipal Museum of Art, Japan: Fig. 6; Courtesy of Watari-um: The Watari Museum of Contemporary Art, Tokyo: Fig. 247; Courtesy of THE WE-LOWS (Yoshitomo Nara + Shin Morikita + Kazumasa Aoki + Kazuhiro Koshiba + Yoko Fujita + Shiori Ishida + Yumeko Sakai): Fig. 351; Courtesy of Yokohama Museum of Art, Japan: Figs. 95, 107–111, 114, 305, 306.

Photographer Credits

Daichi Ano: Fig. 92; Olaf Bergmann: Fig. 59; Colin Davison: Figs. 158, 159, 173; Brian Forrest: Fig. 115; Kazuo Fukunaga: Fig. 67; Hako Hosokawa: Figs. 163, 165, 168, 172, 211; Ian Bavington Jones: Figs. 216, 217; Ester Keate: Fig. 169; Keizo Kioku: Figs. 6, 69, 72, 78, 127–132, 135, 171, 179–182, 184–191, 196, 304, 307–309, 313–315, 317–332, 334–336, 339–347, 351, 362–369, 371–373, 375–379; Yeewan Koon: Figs. 310, 311, 370; Kineta Kunimatsu: Fig. 356; Kerry Ryan McFate: Figs. 291–293, 296–300, 302, 303; Noriko Miyamura: Figs. 103, 349, 350; Mie Morimoto: Figs. 305, 306; Masako Nagano: Figs. 154–157; Atsushi Nakamichi/Nacása & Partners: Figs. 166, 167; Masataka Nakano: Figs. 101, 102; Yoshitomo Nara: Figs. 33, 62, 134, 192, 193, 288–290, 301, 316, 354, 360, 361; Nobuhiko Nukata: Fig. 34; Kei Okano: Figs. 233, 284, 285; Tadashi Okochi: Fig. 352; Alister Overbruck: Fig. 116; Oyamada Kuniya: Figs. 359a–b; Heather Rasmussen: Figs. 121, 122; Kai Takihara: Figs. 353, 355; Yoshitaka Uchida: Figs. 30, 68, 76, 84, 94, 95, 104–114, 119, 133, 170, 195, 197, 201, 205–209, 241–246; Norihiro Ueno: 61, 66, 71, 73, 77, 96, 98, 160, 161, 348; Ikuhiro Watanabe: Figs. 36–41, 50, 81, 125, 126, 228–232, 234–236; Joshua White: Figs. 75, 93.

Every reasonable effort has been made to acknowledge the ownership of copyright for images included in this volume. Any errors that may have occurred are inadvertent, and will be corrected in subsequent editions provided notification is sent in writing to the publisher.

Index

Page numbers in italics indicate illustrations

Phaidon Press Limited
2 Cooperage Yard
London E15 2QR

Phaidon Press Inc.
111 Broadway
New York, NY 10006

Phaidon SARL
55, rue Traversière
75012 Paris

phaidon.com

First published 2020
Reprinted 2021, 2022 (twice), 2023, 2024, 2025

ISBN 978 0 7148 7994 9

A CIP catalogue record for this book is available from the British Library and the Library of Congress.

Project Editor: Simon Hunegs
Designer: Anna Rieger
Production Controllers: Sue Medlicott, Nerissa Vales

Printed in China

Cover: *I WANT TO SEE THE BRIGHT LIGHTS TONIGHT*, 2017, Acrylic on canvas, 86 ⅝ × 76 ¾ in. (220 × 195 cm)

Author's Acknowledgments

As the first major monograph on Yoshitomo Nara covering over thirty years of art making, this project relied on the largesse of friends, colleagues, and supporters. First and foremost, my chorus of gratitude begins with Yoshitomo Nara, who over the past five years has shared his artworks and stories of his life with me. His generosity and trust gave me the freedom to open doors that are usually kept closed, a rare privilege, even if it was a little daunting at times. Satoko Hamada oversaw every step of this project and kept everyone on their toes with her elegant ease—she is the secret weapon behind the making of this book. Deborah Aaronson and her team at Phaidon directed the editing of this beautiful tome, in particular Simon Hunegs, who with his gentle but determined focus carried this project to its completion.

My research was made possible with the help of many. The Research Grants Council, Hong Kong, aided the initial stages of my research. Pace Gallery and Blum & Poe provided unstinting support. I would like to thank Arne Glimcher, Marc Glimcher, Joe Baptista, Hansi Liao, and Rose Broner of Pace Gallery, and Tim Blum, Jeff Poe, Sam Kahn, Ashley Rawlings, Marie Imai, Yusuke Nishimura, and Kana Miyazawa of Blum & Poe.

This project took me to different parts of the world. Among the most memorable were my trips to northern Japan. My visit to Aomori was much aided by Shigemi Takahashi. I would also like to thank Masaki Kakizaki for safely driving me to Hirosaki on a blizzardy day. In Tobiu, I owe my gratitude to Kineta Kunimatsu, who showed me around the school and the area of Shiraoi. Along my travels I also connected with Hiroshi Sugito, Jörg Johnen, Charles Worthen, and David Shrigley. My thanks to them for sharing their stories about Nara.

This book has almost four hundred images, and, as any art writer knows, getting all the pictures together is a mammoth task. To this end, I must thank Ippei Shinohara, Fumiko Uejima, Shin Morikita, Noriko Morikita, Naoko Ichihashi, Ariyoshi Kosugi, Hirotoshi Sudo, Nao Amino, Eriko Kimura, Noriko Miyamura, Reiko Kato, Takashi Murakami, Kaikai Kiki Gallery, Takahiro Okuwaki, Bohemian's Guild, and David Hubbard. Nagayuki Higuma, Hideto Yoshioka, and Misaki Funahashi at ABEISM CORPORATION helped to ensure the images were reproduced as accurately as possible. Anna Rieger brought all the images together with her thoughtful design.

I was also supported by fellow scholars, translators, and writers, including Chisato Uno, Yoshiko Nakano, Risa Ikeda, Yu Araki, Rei Kagitani, and Saka Matsushita, who helped me with translations and archival research. Regina de Luna's unbridled enthusiasm reminded me of the value of seeing through a fresh pair of eyes. Lastly, I would like to thank my constant friends and fellow writers Mei Chin and Chris Thomas, who listened to my endless rambles as I pieced together all the different strands of ideas and research to create a cohesive whole. If I have been too stubborn to heed some of the advice given along the way, it is entirely because I am.

Yeewan Koon
Associate Professor and Chair
Department of Art History
The University of Hong Kong

Publisher's Acknowledgments

This book would not have been possible without the unwavering support of Yoshitomo Nara; Satoko Hamada; Arne Glimcher, Joe Baptista, and Hansi Liao (Pace Gallery); Sam Kahn, Marie Imai, and Kana Miyazawa (Blum & Poe); and Nagayuki Higuma (ABEISM CORPORATION).

Special thanks to Nagi Araki (The Museum of Modern Art, Kamakura & Hamaya); Mayu Asō; Michiko Asō; Peter Bellars; Chris Bilheimer and Kevin O'Neil (R.E.M./Athens LLC); Victoria Clarke; Lisa Delgado; Heather Dubnick; Christoph Gallio; Julia Hasting; Yukiko Hiromatsu (Musée Motai); Birgit Hoff; Anne Hoffmann; David Hubbard and Báirbre O'Brien (Stephen Friedman Gallery); Reiko Ishiguro and Yumiko Nonaka (21st Century Museum of Contemporary Art, Kanazawa); Yasuko Kajita (Hara Museum of Contemporary Art); Akiyo Kaneko (Aichi University of the Arts); Aya Kato (Setagaya Art Museum); Eriko Kimura (Yokohama Museum of Art); Rob King, Mark Robson, and Andrea Chlad (Altaimage); Melissa Larner; Linda Lee; Patricia Liu (Blum & Poe); Takayuki Mashiyama (Taka Ishii Gallery); Lindsey McGuire and Davina Bhandari (Pace Gallery); Michida Miki (Mie Prefectural Art Museum); Hibiki Mizuno (Chim↑Pom Studio); João Mota; Yoko Nakahira (Chihiro Art Museum); Yoshimi Sanada (Kaikai Kiki); Toshi Shibata (SCAI THE BATHHOUSE); Cynthia Sternau (Japan Society); Toshiharu Suzuki (Toyota Municipal Museum of Art); Tsuguo Tada (Hamaya Hiroshi Estate); Shigemi Takahashi (Aomori Museum of Art); Yae Takahashi (Ohara Museum of Art); Miwako Takasuna (gallery ART UNLIMITED); Stefanie Weege (Hatje Cantz); Yoko Yamamoto (Dokuritsu Pro Meiga Hozonkai); and Mika Yoshitake.

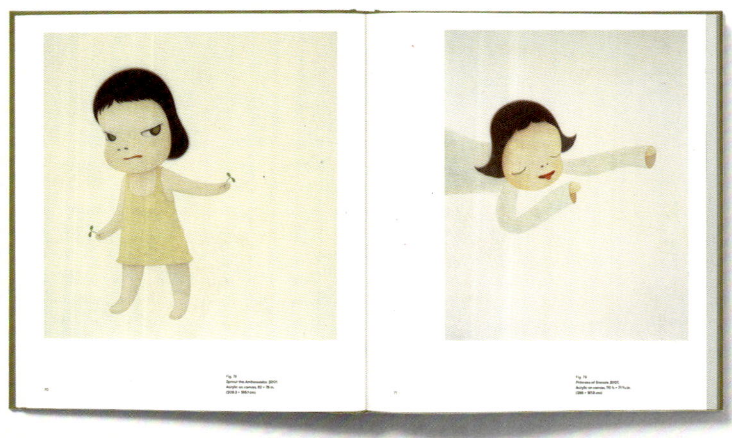

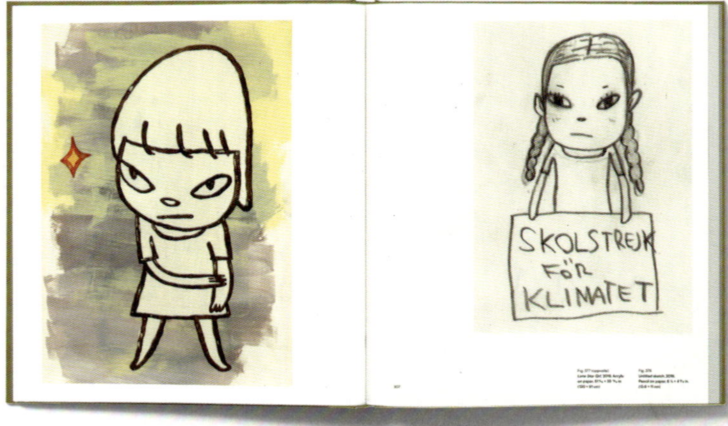

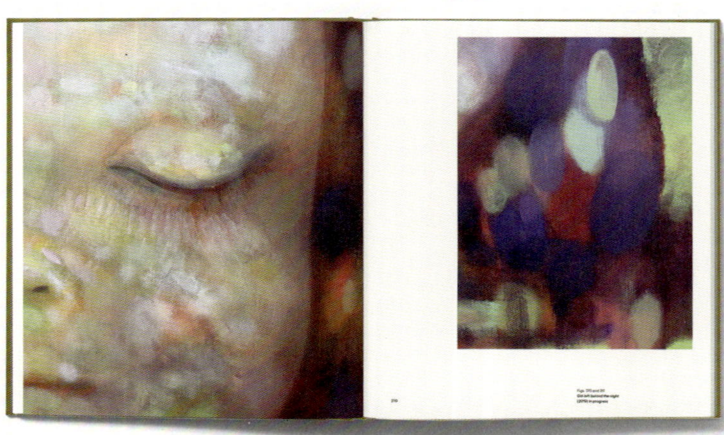

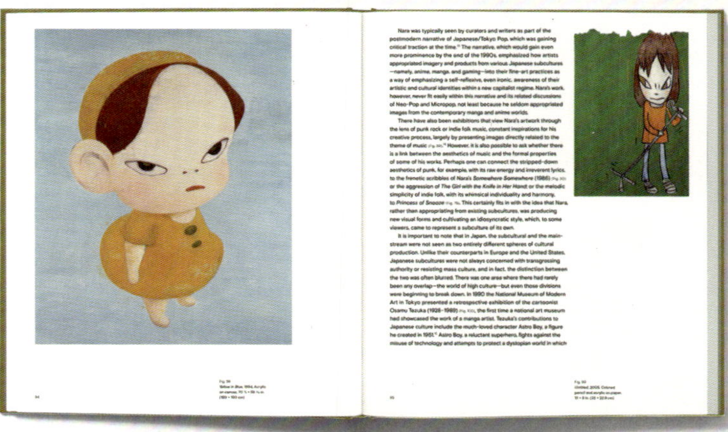

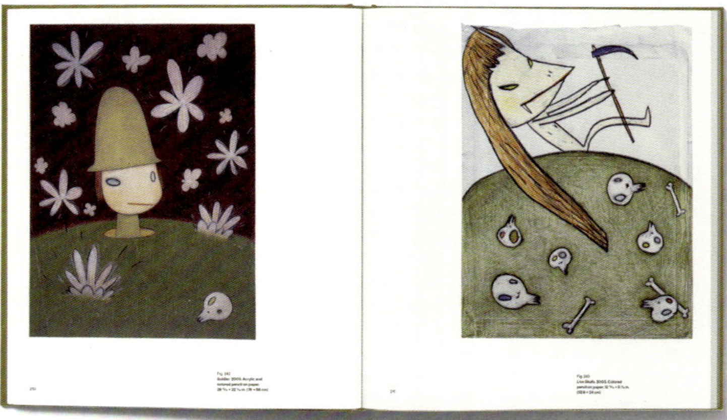

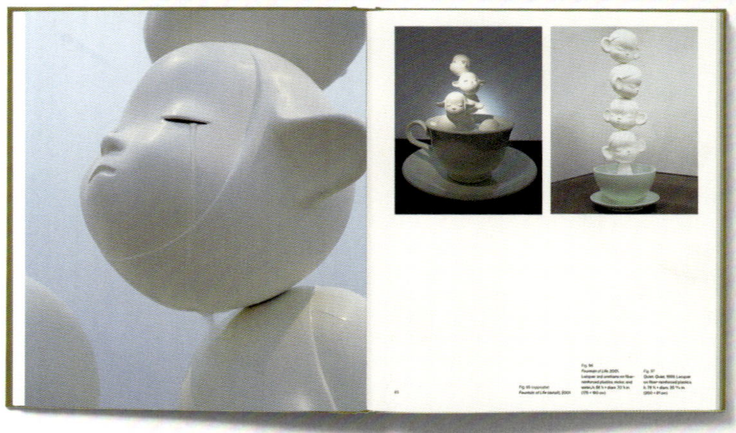

The definitive monograph on contemporary Japanese artist Yoshitomo Nara

"One of the most egalitarian visual artists since Keith Haring."
— Roberta Smith, *New York Times*

"Nara's work embodies a defiant spirit that comes with youthful optimism and belief that we can change the world."
— *Aesthetica*

Instantly recognizable and charmingly irreverent, Yoshitomo Nara's work is a powerful manifestation of his rich internal landscape. This book explores Nara's paintings, drawings, sculptures, ceramics, and photographs, charting his creative influences, which range from Japanese modernism to American counterculture interwoven with his own childhood memories. Stunningly illustrated with dozens of works never before published, the book is an unprecedented view into Nara's life and practice, and represents the first truly authoritative monograph on this beloved contemporary artist.

-

Yeewan Koon is associate professor of fine arts at the University of Hong Kong. In 2018 she was one of the selected curators for the 12th Gwangju Biennale, South Korea.

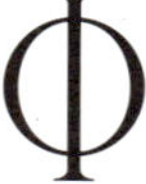